Recommended by Teachers
Trusted by Toppers

AF814354

All in One

Information Technology

Code-402

CBSE Class 10

Focused Theory | Practice Exercise | Sample Papers & Board Papers

Authors
Rashi Bansal,
Anurag Sharma

arihant
SUCCESS AND NOTHING LESS

arihant
SUCCESS AND NOTHING LESS

ARIHANT PRAKASHAN
(School Division Series)
All Rights Reserved

卐 © PUBLISHER

No part of this publication may be re-produced, stored in a retrieval system or by any means, electronic, mechanical, photocopying, recording, scanning, web or otherwise without the written permission of the publisher. Arihant has obtained all the information in this book from the sources believed to be reliable and true. However, Arihant or its editors or authors or illustrators don't take any responsibility for the absolute accuracy of any information published and the damage or loss suffered thereupon.

All disputes subject to Meerut (UP) jurisdiction only.
卐 ADMINISTRATIVE & PRODUCTION OFFICES

Regd. Office

'Ramchhaya' 4577/15, Agarwal Road, Darya Ganj, New Delhi -110002
Tele: 011- 47630600, 43518550; Fax: 011- 23280316

卐 *Head Office*

Kalindi, TP Nagar, Meerut (UP) - 250002, Tel: 0121-7156203, 7156204

卐 SALES & SUPPORT OFFICES

Agra, Ahmedabad, Bengaluru, Bareilly, Chennai, Delhi, Guwahati, Hyderabad, Jaipur, Jhansi, Kolkata, Lucknow, Nagpur & Pune.

PO No : TXT-XX-XXXXXXX-X-XX

Published By Arihant Publications (India) Ltd.

For further information about the books published by Arihant, log on to www.arihantbooks.com or e-mail at info@arihantbooks.com

Follow us on

卐 PRICE ₹375.00

PRODUCTION TEAM

Publishing Managers	*Cover Designer*	*Inner Designer*
Mahendra Singh Rawat & Keshav Mohan	Rakesh Rawat	Ankit Tyagi
Project Head	*Page Layouting*	*Proof Reader*
Shruti Aggarwal	Ravindra Kumar	Sumit

Index *cum* Study Planner

Latest Course Structure

	UNITS	No. of Hours for Theory and Practical		Max. Marks for Theory and Practical
Part A	**Employability Skills**			
	Unit 1: Communication Skills - II	10		2
	Unit 2: Self-Management Skills - II	10		3
	Unit 3: ICT Skills-II	10		1
	Unit 4: Entrepreneurial Skills-II	15		3
	Unit 5: Green Skills-II	05		1
	Total	**50**		**10**
Part B	**Subject Specific Skills**	**Theory**	**Practical**	**Marks**
	Unit 1: Digital Documentation (Advanced) using LibreOffice Writer	12	18	8
	Unit 2: Electronic Spreadsheet (Advanced) using LibreOffice Calc	15	23	10
	Unit 3: Database Management System using LibreOffice Base	18	27	12
	Unit 4: Maintain Healthy, Safe and Secure Working Environment	15	22	10
	Total	**60**	**90**	**40**
Part C	**PRACTICAL WORK**			
	Practical Examination			
	• Digital Documentation (Advanced) using LibreOffice Writer • Electronic Spreadsheet (Advanced) using LibreOffice Calc • Database Management System using LibreOffice Base	5 Marks 5 Marks 10 Marks		20
	• Viva Voce	10 Marks		10
	Total			**30**
Part D	**PROJECT WORK/FIELD VISIT** Any Interdisciplinary Real World Case Study to be taken. Summarised data reports of same can be presented in base. Input should be taken using forms and output should be done using reports using base. Documentation of the case study should be presented using writer.			10
	PORTFOLIO/ PRACTICAL FILE (Portfolio should contain printouts of the practical done using Writer, Calc and Base with minimum 5 problems of each).			10
	Total			**20**
	GRAND TOTAL	**200**		**100**

UNIT 1 : Digital Documentation (Advanced) Using LibreOffice Writer

SUB-UNIT	LEARNING OUTCOMES	THEORY	PRACTICAL
Chapter 1: Introduction To Styles	Learn to create, update, and apply various styles in LibreOffice Writer for effective and consistent document formatting.	• Styles/categories in Writer ◆ Page ◆ Paragraph ◆ Character ◆ Frame ◆ List ◆ Table • Styles and Formatting • Fill Format • Creating a new style ◆ From Selection method ◆ Drag and Drop method • Updating a new style • Load style from template or document. • Applying styles.	• **List Style Categories** Open the Styles and Formatting window, list available style categories and select one style from each. • **Use Fill Format** Apply a style to multiple areas of your document quickly using the Fill Format tool. • **Create and Update a New Style** Create a new style from selected text and update it by modifying its attributes. • **Load a Style from a Template or Document** Import and apply a style from a template or another document to your current work. • **Create a New Style Using Drag-and-Drop** Create a new style by dragging and dropping formatted text into the Styles and Formatting panel.
Chapter 2: Working with Images	Able to insert, modify, and position images and drawing objects in a document, using various methods and options for effective document layout and formatting.	• Inserting an Image in a Document ◆ Insert Image Option ◆ Drag and Drop option ◆ Copy and Paste method ◆ Inserting an image by linking • Options to modify image using image toolbar, resize, crop and delete an image. • Drawing Objects • Creating drawing objects • Setting or changing its properties. • Resizing and grouping drawing objects. • Positioning image in the text. • Arrangement • Anchoring • Alignment • Text Wrapping	• **Insert an Image** Insert an image into a document using options such as Insert Image, Drag and Drop, Copy and Paste, and linking. • **Modify an Image** Use the image toolbar to modify an image by resizing, cropping and deleting it. • **Create Drawing Objects** Create various drawing objects within your document. • **Set or Change Drawing Object Properties** Adjust the properties of drawing objects, including colour, line style and fill. • **Resize and Group Drawing Objects** Resize individual drawing objects and group multiple objects together for better document organisation. • **Position the Image in the Text** Adjust the image's position in the text using arrangement, anchoring, alignment and text wrapping options.

SUB-UNIT	LEARNING OUTCOMES	THEORY	PRACTICAL
Chapter 3: Advanced Features of Writer	Acquire skills in creating, customising, and managing a Table of Contents, using and editing templates, and tracking and reviewing changes in documents effectively	• Table of contents • Hierarchy of headings • Creating a Table of Content (ToC) • Customisation of Table of Contents(ToC) • Maintaining a Table of Contents(ToC) • Updating ToC • Deleting ToC • Using templates • Creating a Template • Using In-built/Saved Templates • Using Online Templates • Importing a Template • Editing a Template • Moving a Template • Exporting a Template • Applying Templates to a Blank Document • Track Changes Feature • Preparing a Document for Review • Recording Changes • Accepting and Rejecting Changes • Adding Comments • Deleting Comments • Comparing Documents	• **Create a Table of Contents (ToC)** Generate and customise a Table of Contents in a document. • **Maintain a Table of Contents** Update or delete the Table of Contents. • **Use Templates** Create, import, and apply templates to a blank document, using in-built, saved, or online templates. • **Edit a Template** Modify, move, and export an existing template. • **Track Changes** Prepare a document for review by recording, accepting, or rejecting changes, and manage comments by adding or deleting them. • **Compare Documents** Compare two versions of a document to identify and review differences.

UNIT 2 : Electronic Spreadsheet (Advanced) Using LibreOffice Calc

SUB-UNIT	LEARNING OUTCOMES	THEORY	PRACTICAL
Chapter 4: Analyse data using scenarios and goal seek	Learn skills in consolidating data, using groups and subtotals, performing what-if analysis and scenarios, and utilising the Goal Seek tool for decision-making.	• Consolidating Data • Groups and Subtotals • What-if Scenarios • What-if Analysis Tool • Goal Seek	• **Use Consolidating Data** Aggregate data from multiple sources into a single summary. • **Create Subtotals** Apply subtotals to data groups to summarise and analyse information. • **Use "What-If" Scenarios** Create and analyse different scenarios to forecast outcomes based on varying inputs. • **Use "What-If" Tools** Use tools like Scenario Manager for detailed what-if analyses. • **Use Goal Seek and Solver** Use Goal Seek to find specific input values needed to achieve a desired result and apply Solver for more complex problems.

SUB-UNIT	LEARNING OUTCOMES	THEORY	PRACTICAL
Chapter 5: Using Macros in Spreadsheet	Develop skills in recording, running, creating, and organising macros, and using them as functions for document automation.	• Recording a Macro • Running a Macro • Creating and Organising a Simple Macro • Macro as a Function	• **Demonstrate the Use of a Macro Recorder** Record a macro to automate repetitive tasks. • **Create a Simple Macro** Develop a basic macro to perform a specific function. • **Use a Macro** Execute an existing macro to automate tasks in a document. • **Pass Arguments to a Macro** Provide arguments to a macro to customise its behaviour. • **Pass the Arguments as Values** Supply values as arguments to a macro for dynamic operation. • **Write Macros as Built-in Functions** Create macros that function similarly to built-in functions for enhanced functionality. • **Access Cells Directly** Write macros to directly manipulate cell data in spreadsheets. • **Sort Columns Using a Macro** Develop and use a macro to sort columns in a spreadsheet.
Chapter 6: Linking Spreadsheet Data	Learn to set up multiple sheets, create references and hyperlinks within and across documents, and link to external and registered data sources.	• Setting up multiple sheets. • Creating reference to other sheets by using keyboard and mouse. • Creating reference to another document by using keyboard and mouse. • Hyperlinks to the Sheet • Relative and Absolute Hyperlinks • Creating Hyperlinks • Editing a Hyperlink • Linking to External Data • Linking to Registered Data Sources	• **Setup Multiple Sheets** Insert and organise new sheets within a workbook. • **Create References to Other Sheets** Use keyboard and mouse to create references between different sheets in a workbook. • **Create References to Other Documents** Use keyboard and mouse to link data from one document to another. • **Create, Edit and Remove Hyperlinks** Add, modify, and delete hyperlinks to sheets within a workbook. • **Link to External Data** Connect and import data from external sources into your document. • **Link to Registered Data Sources** Establish links to registered data sources for data integration.

SUB-UNIT	LEARNING OUTCOMES	THEORY	PRACTICAL
Chapter 7: Share and Review a Spreadsheet	Develop the ability to share, open, and save shared spreadsheets, track and review changes, and handle comments and merging for effective collaboration.	• Sharing Spreadsheet • Opening and saving a shared spreadsheet • Recording changes • Add, Edit and Format the comments • Reviewing Changes – View, Accept or Reject Changes • Merging and comparing	• **Set Up a Spreadsheet for Sharing** Configure a spreadsheet to enable sharing with others. • **Open and Save a Shared Spreadsheet** Access and save changes to a spreadsheet that has been shared with you. • **Record Changes** Track modifications made to the spreadsheet. • **Add, Edit, and Format Comments** Insert, modify and format comments within the spreadsheet. • **Review Changes** View, accept, or reject changes made by others in the shared spreadsheet. • **Merge and Compare Sheets** Combine and compare different sheets to integrate data effectively.

UNIT 3 : Database Management System using LibreOffice Base

SUB-UNIT	LEARNING OUTCOMES	THEORY	PRACTICAL
Chapter 8: Introduction to Database Management System	Understand data and information concepts, the advantages of databases, various data models and key terminology and objects of relational database systems.	• Data and Information • Databases and DBMS • Advantages of database • Data Models ◆ Hierarchical Data Model ◆ Network Data Model ◆ Relational Data Model • Relational database Model ◆ RDBS Terminology ◆ Objects of an RDBMS	• **Identify Data and Information** Distinguish between data and information within a database context. • **Identify Fields, Records and Tables** Recognise and describe fields, records and tables in a database. • **Prepare a Sample Table** Create a sample table with standard fields to illustrate database structure. • **Identify Different Types of Data Models** Identify and describe various data models such as hierarchical, network and relational. • **Different Types of Keys** Recognise and explain different types of keys used in databases, such as primary and foreign keys. • **Identify Different Objects of RDBMS** Identify and describe different objects in a relational database management system (RDBMS), including tables, queries and forms.

SUB-UNIT	LEARNING OUTCOMES	THEORY	PRACTICAL
Chapter 9: Starting with LibreOffice Base	Learn to navigate LibreOffice Base, manage data types, create and save tables using various methods, set primary keys, and perform data entry, editing, sorting and record deletion.	• Introduction to LibreOffice Base • Data types • Starting with LibreOffice • User Interface Of LibreOffice Base • Opening a Database • Creating a Table ◆ Using a Wizard ◆ Using design view, • Setting primary key • Saving a Table • Entering data into table • Navigating through the table • Editing Data • Deleting Records from Table • Sorting Data in the Table	• **Start LibreOffice Base and Observe the Main Window** Launch LibreOffice Base and familiarise yourself with the main window's components. • **Create a Sample Table Using Wizard** Use the wizard to create a sample table in any category. • **Create Different Tables from Available List** Practice creating various tables by selecting fields from the available options. • **Assign Data Types and Set Primary Key** Define data types for fields and set a primary key for the table. • **Edit the Table in Design View** Modify the table structure using the design view. • **Enter Data in the Fields** Input data into the fields of your table. • **Delete Records from Table** Remove records from the table as needed. • **Arrange Data in Ascending or Descending Order** Sort the table data in ascending or descending order.
Chapter 10: Working with Multiple Tables	Develop skills in editing and deleting tables, creating and managing table relationships and ensuring referential integrity.	• Editing and Deleting tables • Relationships between tables • Types of Relationships– one to one, one to many, many to many • Advantages of Relating Tables in a Database • Creating Relationships between Tables • Referential Integrity	• **Insert Data in the Table** Add new data entries to a table. • **Edit Records in the Table** Modify existing records within the table. • **Delete Records from Table** Remove specific records from the table. • **Sort Data in the Table** Arrange data in ascending or descending order within the table. • **Create and Edit Relationships** Establish and modify relationships between tables, including one-to-one, one-to- many, and many-to-many. • **Enter Various Field Properties** Set and adjust different properties for fields in the table.

SUB-UNIT	LEARNING OUTCOMES	THEORY	PRACTICAL
Chapter 11: Queries in Base	Acquire skills in creating and editing queries using both wizards and design view, and working with numerical data in queries.	• Queries • Query creation using wizard • Creation of query using design view • Editing a query • Working with Numerical Data	• **Prepare a Query for Given Criteria** Create a query based on specified criteria. • **Create a Query Using Wizard and Design View** Demonstrate how to generate a query using both the wizard and design view. • **Edit a Query** Modify an existing query to update its criteria or structure. • **Apply Various Criteria in a Query** Demonstrate applying different criteria in a query, including single field, multiple fields, and wildcard searches. • **Perform Calculations Using Query in Base** Execute calculations within a query in LibreOffice Base.
Chapter 12: Forms and Reports	Able to create and modify forms and reports in LibreOffice Base, use the Form Controls Toolbar, and insert additional controls, titles, headings and date/time elements in reports.	• Forms in BASE • Creating form using wizard • Modifying a Form • Form Controls Toolbar • Report in Base • Inserting other controls in report • Inserting Titles & Headings • Inserting Date & Time	• **Create a Form Using Form Wizard** Generate a form by following the steps in the Form Wizard. • **Enter or Remove Data from Forms** Input new data or delete existing data using forms. • **Modify Forms** Demonstrate how to adjust and customise forms. • **Change Label and Background** Modify the label text and background colour or design of a form. • **Search Records Using a Form** Use the form to find specific records based on search criteria. • **Insert and Delete Records Using Form View** Add new records or remove existing ones through the Form View. • **Create a Report Using Report Wizard** Illustrate the steps to generate a report using the Report Wizard. • **Demonstrate Various Report Examples** Provide examples of different types of reports created using the Report Wizard.

UNIT 4 : Maintain Healthy, Safe and Secure Working Environment

SUB-UNIT	LEARNING OUTCOMES	THEORY	PRACTICAL
Chapter 13. Health, Safety and Security at Workplace	Understand workplace health, safety, and security policies, identify various hazards, and learn how to manage risks and maintain a safe working environment.	• Introduction to Health, Safety and Security At Workplace • Policies and Procedures for Healthy, Safety and Security • Reasons for Health, Safety and Security Programmes or Policies in the Workplace • Workplace Safety Hazards • Physical Hazards • Falling Off Heights, Slipping and Tripping • Electrical Hazards • Fire Hazards • Health Hazards • Potential Sources of Hazards in an Organisation • Hazards using Computers • Handling Office Equipment • Handling Objects • Stress at Work • Working Environment • Hazard Control • Safety Guidelines Checklist	• **Practice Basic Safety Rules** Implement fire safety measures, prevent falls and slips, ensure electrical safety, and apply first aid procedures to protect workers and prevent accidents.
Chapter 14. Workplace Quality Measures	Learn about air and water quality monitoring, office ergonomics, health and safety guidelines for computer use, and methods to reduce risks associated with musculoskeletal problems and other work-related issues.	• Introduction • Air and Water Quality Monitoring Process • Guidelines for Clean Air and Clean Water • Importance of Cleanliness at Workplace • Office Ergonomics • Computer Health and Safety Tips • Musculoskeletal Problems: Occupational Overuse Syndrome, Strain in Legs and Feet, Eye Strain • To reduce the risks of visual problems: Headaches, Obesity, Stress Disorders, Injuries from Laptop Use, Sleeping Problems • Health and Safety Requirements for Computer Workplace • Cautions while Working on the Computer	• **Illustrate Handling Accidents at Workplace** Demonstrate the steps to manage and respond to accidents in the workplace. • **Demonstrate Following Evacuation Plan** Show how to effectively follow the evacuation plan and procedures during an emergency.

SUB-UNIT	LEARNING OUTCOMES	THEORY	PRACTICAL
Chapter 15. Prevent Accidents and Emergencies	Able to identify and handle accidents and emergencies, follow company policies, manage different types of accidents and emergencies, and apply fire safety and first aid procedures effectively.	• Accident and Emergencies ◆ Notice and Correctly Identify Accidents and Emergencies ◆ Get help Promptly and in the Most Suitable Way ◆ Follow Company Policies and Procedures for Preventing Further Injury While Waiting for Help to Arrive ◆ Act within the Limits of your Responsibility and Authority when Accidents and Emergencies Arise ◆ Promptly Follow Instructions given by Senior Staff and the Emergency Services • Types of Accidents ◆ Trip and Fall ◆ Slip and Fall ◆ Injuries caused due to Escalators or Elevators (or lifts) ◆ Accidents due to Falling of Goods ◆ Accidents due to Moving Objects • Handling Accidents ◆ Attend to the Injured Person Immediately ◆ Inform your Supervisor ◆ Assist your Supervisor • Types of Emergencies ◆ First Aid ◆ Electrical Safety ◆ Evacuation • General Evacuation Procedures • Fire Hazards in the Workplace • Fire Prevention • Identification of Material and Ignition Sources • First Aid for Electrical Emergencies • Electrical Rescue Techniques	• **Identify Hazards and Sources of Hazards** Recognise potential hazards and their sources in the workplace. • **Identify Problems at Workplace** Assess workplace issues that could lead to accidents. • **Practice General Evacuation Procedures** Execute evacuation procedures in simulated emergency situations.

PART A
Employability Skills

Unit 1

Communication Skills-II

In the present time, a thorough knowledge of language with communication skills is very important in any occupation or business. Communication skills are important to everyone to communicate effectively i.e. to give and receive information and convey our ideas and opinions to those around us.

Session 1 | Methods and Types of Communication

The exchanging of information by speaking, writing or using some other medium is called **communication**.

The word communication comes from the Latin word **communicare**, meaning **to share**.

Being able to communicate effectively is one of the most important life skills. Communication has three important parts:

- **Transmitting** The sender transmits the message through one medium to another.
- **Listening** The receiver listens or understands the message.
- **Feedback** The receiver conveys their understanding of the message to the sender in the form of feedback to complete the communication cycle.

1.1 Communication Process and Elements

The communication process is a systematic approach to how **information is exchanged between individuals or groups**. It involves several steps or stages that work together to ensure that a message is effectively conveyed and understood.

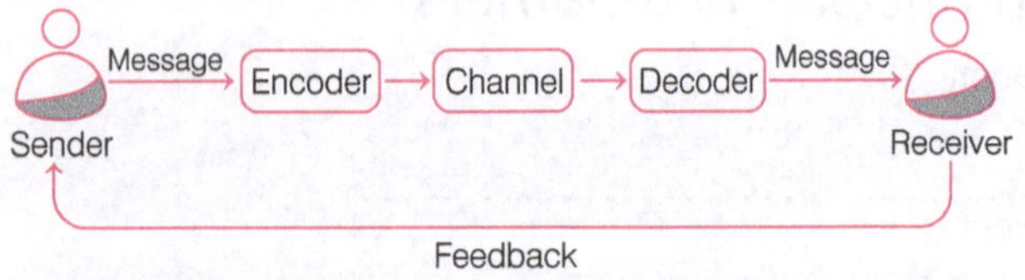

The main steps in a communication form are communication cycle. These steps are explained below:

- **Sender** The Communicator or Sender is the person or organization who creates and sends the message.
- **Message** The Message is the actual information that the sender wishes to convey to the receiver.
- **Encoding** This is the process of translating an idea or thought into a message. The factor which must be considered when encoding messages are language, cultural differences etc.
- **Communication channel** A Communication channel is a medium through which we can deliver or transfer the message. e.g., When we verbally communicate, air is the medium; When we messaging online, internet is the medium.
- **Decoder** It is the process of interpreting and understanding the message delivered by the sender.
- **Receiver** The receiver is the person or organization that receives and interprets the message.
- **Feedback** This is the reaction or response of the receiver to the message. Without feedback, the communication cycle remains incomplete.

Methods of Communication

- **Face to Face Informal Communication** Face-to Face communication helps the message to be understood clearly and quickly. Since we can see the body language in this case; it adds to the effectiveness of the communication.
- **E-mail** E-mail is a quick way of communicating with one or many individuals in various locations. It offers flexibility, convenience and low-cost.
- **Notice/Posters** When the same message has to go out to a large group of people this type of communication is very effective. It is generally used where email communication may not be effective.
- **Business Meetings** Communication during business meetings at an organization are generally addressed to a group of people. It can be related to business, management and organizational decision.
- **Print/Analog/Digital Media** This method includes conveying information using social media or through phone calls, newsletters, blogs, etc.

Note *Choosing the right method of communication depends on-target audience, costs, kind/type of information, urgency/priority.*

1.2 Types of Communication

Communication comes in various forms such as

- Verbal(sounds, language and tone of voice)
  - Oral(listening and hearing)
  - Written(journals, e-mails, blogs and text messages)
- Non-verbal(facial expressions, body language and posture)
- Visual(signs, symbols and pictures)

Verbal Communication

Verbal communication refer to the exchange of information through spoken or written words. It involves the use of words that form a language.

The effectiveness of the verbal communication depends on the tone of the speaker, clarity of speech, volume, speed, body language and the quality of words used in conversation.

Verbal communication are of two types. These are

1. **Oral Communication** It means communication through speaking (using the mouth) and listening (using the ears). Two individuals conversing with each other, either face-to-face or through the telephone is an example of oral communication.
2. **Written Communication** This is a medium of communication that entails the written word. Letters, e-mails, SMS, memorandums, reports, notices, manuals, quotations, newsletters, newspapers etc., are forms of written communication. It can be between two or more people.

   Methods of verbal communication can be classified into different categories
   - Intrapersonal communication
   - Interpersonal communication
   - Small group communication
   - Public communication
   - Mass communication

Intrapersonal Communication

Interpersonal Communication

Public Communication

Advantages of Verbal Communication

- It is quick in obtaining feedback once delivered.
- It saves time in communication.
- It is more reliable method of communication.
- It provides a complete understanding of the communication delivered and there is a chance to make it more clear in case of doubts in interpretation of words or ideas.

Disadvantages of Verbal Communication

- It has no legal validity and hence will lead to problems in certain situations. Emotions are visible and hence lead to trouble in certain cases.
- It has issues when communicating with distant people.
- It does not provide permanent record unless it is recorded with modern means of storage.

Non-Verbal Communication

Non-verbal communication occurs without using any spoken or written word. Instead, it relies on various non-verbal cues such as physical movements, colors, signs, symbols, body language etc., to express feelings, attitudes or information.

Facial Expression & Silence

Olfactics (smell)

Chronemics (time)

Vocal Intonations

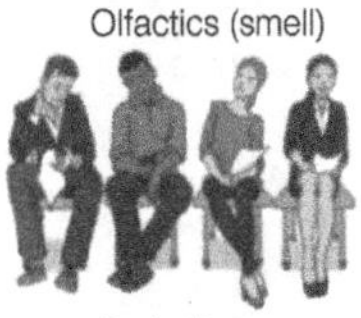
Body Gestures

Haptics (touch)

Various components or forms of non-verbal communication are

- Posture and body orientation
- Eye contact
- Gestures
- Space and Distance
- Humor
- Silence
- Symbol
- Facial expressions
- Body language
- Proximity
- Touch
- Personal appearance

Note *Prof. Albert Mehrabian in 1970s proved that in personal communication, non-verbal communication is very important as it conveys 93% while verbal communication conveys only 7%. The exact breakup percentage he came up with is:*

7% words } ***Verbal communication***

38% tone of voice
55% body language } ***Non – verbal communication***

Advantages of Non-Verbal Communication

- It conveys clear and precise meaning to the receiver.
- It can be presented through visuals, audio-visual and silent means.
- This type of communication serves as substitute for verbal communication.
- It is helpful in communicating with illiterate people.

Disadvantages of Non-Verbal Communication

- In the absence of language, this type of communication may not convey the actual meaning of the message, making it imprecise.
- It can be confusing as no clear message is conveyed.
- It can be costly as Neon signs, PowerPoint presentation and movies involve significant expenses.

Visual Communication

Visual communication conveys ideas and information in forms that can be seen. It is also known as **graphic communication.** It includes graphic design, illustration and animation, books, print, magazines, screen based media, interactive web design, motion graphics, short film, visual imagery for advertising and promotion, corporate identity and packaging design etc.

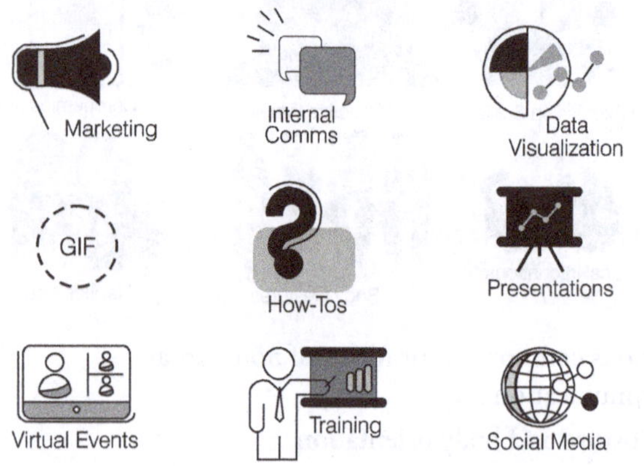

Advantages of Visual Communication

- Images and videos convey complex ideas quickly.
- We remembered visual information more effectively.
- It clears the language or qualification barrier.
- Visuals can simplify the complex concepts and makes it more easy to understand.

Disadvantages of Visual Communication

- Images can be misunderstood or misinterpreted.
- Visuals may have different meanings in various cultures.
- It is a very time consuming process.
- Visuals are not a form of communication; it requires some other forms of communication to ensure accurate interpretation.

Summary

The word 'communication' comes from the Latin word communicare, which means 'to share' your thoughts and ideas with some other person.

The communication process is a systematic approach to how information is exchanged between individuals or groups.

Its elements include the sender, message, encoding, channel, decoding, receiver and feedback which together complete the communication cycle.

Communication exists in multiple forms such as Verbal, Non-Verbal and Visual.

Verbal communication consists of oral and written communication whereas non-verbal communication includes postures, touch, eye contact, para language etc.

Visual communication is the process of conveying information and ideas through visual elements like images, symbols, graphs, charts, and videos, rather than relying solely on text or spoken words.

ACTIVITY Time

ACTIVITY 1

Group Practice Role play on communication and identify elements of the communication cycle

Material required

Paper and pencil

Procedure

- Form groups with four students in each group.
- The situation is that a student is Sales Executive at a toy store and he/she is supposed to communicate to customers about the various types of toys available with the store for different age group.
- The other students will reach the Sales Executive one by one and ask different types of questions related to toys.
- Develop a script for the role play and act on the same.
- Each student will draw a communication cycle.
- Discuss what you all learned from this activity and entire class will then discuss how each element affected communication.

ACTIVITY 2

Group-Practice Role Play of a Telephonic Conversation

Material required

Notebook, pen

Procedure

- Form groups with three students in each group.
- Write a phone conversation based on a given scenario of a student calling a university academic coordinator to know about study courses and admission procedure.
- One student acts as caller and the other as receiver.
- Read out the conversation by enacting the roles.
- The third student gives feedback based on the 7Cs of communication (clear, concise, concrete, correct, coherent, complete and courteous).

ACTIVITY 3

Group-Practice On Public Speaking

Material required

Notebook, pen

Procedure

- Form groups with three students in each group.
- Within the group, choose a topic for a short speech. For example, Importance of Punctuality, Healthy Food Habits, etc.
- Each person should make a speech to the others in the group; who then give feedback based on whether the person was able to communicate properly.
- One student from the group volunteers to give the same speech in front of the class.

ACTIVITY 4

Group-Practice Role-play on Non-verbal Communication

Material required

Notebook, pen

Procedure

- Form groups with three students in each group.
- Prepare the script for the role play, based on the given scenario. For example, a hearing impaired salesperson is attending a female customer at an apparel store.
- Act it out in front of your group.
- One group volunteers to act before your whole class.

  Discuss how students used non-verbal communication. Was this communication effective?

ACTIVITY 5

Group-Practice How to Avoid Body Language Mistakes

Material required

Notebook, pen

Procedure

- In the same group of three students as above, discuss what are the Dos and Don'ts of avoiding miscommunication because of body language.
- Each student should write down a list of these Dos and Don'ts. (Prepare the lists as homework, if there is less time left to complete the task in class).

ACTIVITY 6

Individual-Practice Comparing Methods of Communication

Material required

Notebook, pen

Procedure

- Discuss the three methods of communication (Verbal, Non-verbal and Visual).
- Ask each student to write a list of the advantages and disadvantages of each method.
- Practice: In all your conversations at home and school, pay attention to the non-verbal signs others are using. Practice using the non-verbal methods you learnt here in the right manner.

NCERT FOLDER

Complete Explanations of all NCERT's Questions

A. Multiple Choice Questions

Q.1 Which of the following is not an element of communication within the communication process cycle?

(a) Channel (b) Receiver
(c) Sender (d) Time

Q.2 You need to apply leave at work? Which method of communication will you use?

(a) E-mail (b) Poster
(c) Newsletter (d) Blog

Q.3 By which action can senders send their messages?

(a) Gestures (b) Speaking (c) Reading (d) Writing

Q.4 Which of the following is an example of oral communication?

(a) Newspapers (b) Letters
(c) Phone call (d) E-mail

Q.5 What are the types of words we should use for verbal communication?

(a) Acronyms (b) Simple (c) Technical (d) Jargons

Q.6 Why do we use e-mails?

(a) To communicate with many people at the same time.
(b) To share documents and files.
(c) To talk to each other in real-time.
(d) To keep a record of communication.

Q.7 Which of these is a positive (good) facial expression?

(a) Frowning while concentrating
(b) Maintaining eye contact
(c) Smiling continuously
(d) Rolling up your eyes

Q.8 What does an upright (straight) body posture convey or show?

(a) Pride
(b) Professionalism
(c) Confidence
(d) Humility

Q.9 Which of these is not an appropriate non-verbal communication at work?

(a) Keeping hands in pockets while talking
(b) Talking at moderate speed
(c) Sitting straight
(d) Tilting head a bit to listen

Q.10 Which of the following statement is true about communication?

(a) 50% of our communication is non-verbal
(b) 20% communication is done using body movements, face, arms, etc.
(c) 5% communication is done using voice, tone, pauses, etc.
(d) 7% communication is done using words

Answers

1. (d)	2. (a)	3. (d)	4. (c)	5. (b)
6. (a,b)	7. (b)	8. (c)	9. (a)	10. (d)

Q.11 Put a ✗ mark against the actions below which are examples of bad non-verbal communication.

- Laughing during formal communication
- Scratching head
- Smiling when speaking to a friend
- Nodding when you agree with something
- Standing straight
- Yawning while listening
- Sitting straight
- Maintaining eye contact while speaking
- Biting nails
- Firm Handshake
- Clenching jaws
- Looking away when someone is speaking to you
- Intense stare

Ans.

Laughing during formal communication	✗
Scratching head	✗
Smiling when speaking to a friend	✓
Nodding when you agree with something	✓
Standing straight	✓
Yawning while listening	✗
Sitting straight	✓
Maintaining eye contact while speaking	✓
Biting nails	✗
Firm Handshake	✓
Clenching jaws	✗
Looking away when someone is speaking to you	✗
Intense stare	✗

B. Subjective Questions

Q.1 List the different types of verbal communication. Include examples for each verbal communication type.

Ans. (i) **Face-to-Face Communication** Direct communication between individuals who are physically present in the same location.

Example Conversations between friends at a coffee shop.

(ii) **Telephone Communication** Communication conducted over the phone, allowing for real-time conversation between individuals who may be geographically distant.

Example Calling a family member to catch up on news.

(iii) **Video Communication** Communication using video technology, enabling individuals to see and hear each other in real-time.

Example Participating in a video conference call with colleagues from different offices.

Q.2 Draw any five common signs used for Visual Communication. Explain what each conveys and where did you see it?

Ans. The five common signs used for visual communication and their meanings:

Signs	What each conveys	Where did I see it
	It conveys a clear instruction to drivers and pedestrains : stop at the intersection or crossing.	I saw this sign at the traffic signal.
	It conveys that smoking is not allowed in that area.	I saw this sign in the hospital.
	It conveys that there is a potential hazard in the area.	I saw this sign at the construction sites.
	It conveys the location of the exit in a building or a room.	I saw this sign in my college.
	It conveys that parking is not allowed in that area.	I saw this sign at the fire lanes.

EXAM PATTERN EXERCISE

Including Competency Based Questions

Multiple Choice Questions

1 Oral communication is based on ________ .

(a) Facial expressions (b) Listening and Hearing
(c) Body language (d) Language and tone of voice

2 Visual communication among the people are dependent on ________ .

(a) Signs, symbols and pictures
(b) Text messages
(c) Posture
(d) Body language

3 ________ communication is the use of body language, gestures and facial expressions to convey information to others. CBSE SQP 2021-22 Term-I

(a) Verbal (b) Written
(c) Non-verbal (d) Visual

4 ________ is an instance of non-verbal communication.

(a) A speech (b) Proximity
(c) A notice (d) An e-mail

5 Which of the following is the process in which the receiver interprets and understands the message?

(a) Decoding (b) Encoding
(c) Feedback (d) None of these

6 Which of the following type of communication involves interchanging messages only through images or pictures? CBSE 2024

(a) Verbal (b) Gesture (c) Visual (d) Facial

7 The school is organizing a Career Counselling Workshop. Which of the following will be the most effective method of communication to inform all students of the school? CBSE 2025

(a) Face-to-face informal communication
(b) Notice/Poster
(c) Phone call (d) Meet everyone in person

8 Visual communication uses ______ and ______ to convey messages.

(a) sound , pictures (b) images, graphics
(c) letters, emails (d) None of these

9 **Which communication method would be least effective in ensuring that a message is understood in a multicultural team?** Competency Based Que.

(a) Email with clear and simple language
(b) Face-to-Face meeting
(c) Written communication using technical jargon
(d) Video conferencing with visual aids

10 **When explaining a technical concept to a non-expert, what is the most effective approach?** Competency Based Que.

(a) Break down the concept into simple terms and use analogies.
(b) Use technical jargon and assume familiarity.
(c) Speak quickly to cover all details.
(d) Avoid explaining and refer them to a specialist.

11 **Riya is the manager of a store and many workers are working under her. Which of the following method is effective to inform everyone about the change in duty hours?** Competency Based Que.

(a) E-mail (b) Notices and Posters
(c) Business Meetings (d) Face to Face

12 **Giya need to apply leave at work? Which method of communication will she use?** Competency Based Que.

(a) Newsletter (b) E-mail
(c) Poster (d) Blog

Answers

1. (d)	2. (a)	3. (c)	4. (b)	5. (a)
6. (c)	7. (b)	8. (b)	9. (c)	10. (a)
11. (b)	12. (b)			

Very Short Answer Type Questions

1 **Define verbal communication.**

Ans. Verbal communication means communication through spoken and written words. It implies use of words which make up a language. It is the ability to communicate by using words.

2 **Explain the process of decoding.**

Ans. Decoding is the process in which the receiver interprets and understands the message.

3 **Communication skills are very important for any business. Explain any two elements of a communication process.** CBSE SQP 2020-21

Ans Communication skills are crucial for business success. Two key elements of the communication process are:

1. **Sender** This is the person or source that initiates the communication by sending a message. For example, a manager sending an email to their team.
2. **Receiver** This is the person or target who receives the message and interprets it. In the above example, the employees who read the email are the receivers.

4 **What are the learning objectives of communication?** CBSE SQP 2023-24

Ans. The learning objectives of communication are to:

- Express ideas clearly
- Build relationships
- Critically analyze messages
- Respect diversity
- Receive feedback

5 **In a communication cycle, explain the term 'medium'.**

Ans. In a communication cycle, the term 'medium' refers to the channel through which the message is sent.

6 **Name the different methods of communication.**

Ans. Various methods of communication include:
(i) Business Meeting (ii) E-mail (iii) Notice/posters

7 **What do you understand by communication cycle?**

Ans. The communication cycle is a process that describes how messages are exchanged between a sender and a receiver.

8 **Consider a workplace scenario where team members are working on a project with tight deadlines. What type of communication would be most effective for quick updates and decision-making among the team, and why?** Competency Based Que.

Ans. In this scenario, verbal communication (e.g., face-to-face meetings, phone calls, or video conferences) would be the most effective. It allows for immediate feedback, clarification of ideas, and quick decision-making, which is crucial when working under tight deadlines. Verbal communication fosters collaboration and helps build a stronger team rapport.

9 **During a team meeting, Sarah is explaining a complex project idea to her colleagues. She speaks too quickly, uses jargon, and doesn't pause for questions.** CBSE SQP 2024-25

As a result, her team seems confused, and the project isn't fully understood.

What can Sarah do to improve her verbal communication skills?

Ans. **Think Before You Speak**

- Think about your topic.
- Think about the most effective ways to make your listeners understand the topic.
- Write or note down whatever you plan to say.

Concise and Clear

- Speak clearly, loudly and at moderate speed.
- Be sure the information you want to share is to the point.
- Do not repeat the same sentences.

Confidence and Body Language

- Be confident.
- Be friendly
- Maintain eye contact, stand straight and be attentive.

Session 2 | Feedback in Communication

Feedback in communication refers to the response or reaction that a receiver provides to a sender after receiving a message.

It is a crucial component of the communication process, as it enables the sender to assess whether the message was received and understood as intended.

Feedback can take various forms, including verbal, non-verbal, or written communication. It can also range from positive to negative, depending on how the receiver interprets the message.

Importance of Feedback

Feedback plays a vital role in the communication cycle for several reasons:

1. **Clarification** Feedback allows the sender to identify any misunderstandings. If the receiver struggles to comprehend the message, the sender can adjust their communication based on the feedback received.
2. **Improvement** Continuous feedback fosters improvement in communication skills, enabling senders to refine their messages for clarity and effectiveness.
3. **Engagement** Encouraging feedback creates a more interactive communication environment, enhancing engagement and collaboration.

Without feedback, communication can become ineffective and may lead to barriers, such as misunderstandings or confusion.

1.1 Characteristics of Feedback

Feedback in communication is most effective when it possesses certain characteristics. Here are some key characteristics of effective feedback:

- **Specific** Feedback should focus on particular behaviors, actions, or aspects of the communication rather than being general. Specific feedback provides clear guidance on what was done well or what needs to be improved.
- **Timely** Feedback is most useful when given immediately after the event or behavior in question. Timely feedback ensures that the information is relevant and fresh in the minds of both the sender and the receiver.
- **Clear** Effective feedback is clear and easy to understand and free of ambiguity. Clarity ensures that the receiver knows exactly what is being communicated.
- **Balanced** Feedback should include both positive and negative aspects, offering praise where due and constructive criticism where needed. Balanced feedback helps in maintain motivation while also encouraging improvement.
- **Objective** Feedback should be based on observable facts and behaviors rather than personal opinions or biases. Objectivity ensures fairness and increases the probability that the feedback will be well-received.
- **Constructive** Constructive feedback not only points out areas for improvement but also offers suggestions or solutions to help the receiver make positive changes.

1.2 Types of Feedback

There are some important feedback in communication cycle as follows:

1. Descriptive Feedback

A descriptive feedback, provides meaningful information in a detailed, comprehensive manner and it also includes some analysis or suggestions.

This form of feedback is most suited to teacher-student interactions when the students are attending a course taught by the teacher. In such a cases, it serves the specific purpose of helping students improve while they are still gaining knowledge and practising their skills in the subject.

2. Non-descriptive Feedback

A non descriptive feedback provides some specific information but does not give details descriptions.

e.g., "I like only second paragraph. Others needs improvement."

Each of the above discussed types of feedback can be either a positive feedback (i.e. it indicates that the sender can continue his communication in the same manner as before) or a negative feedback (i.e. it indicates a need for a change in the manner of communication).

3. Specific Feedback

The specific feedback talks about a thing or particularly without talking about a general overview.

e.g., I like the way you described your grandfather's character. It makes me feel like I know him too.

4. Non-Specific Feedback

The non-specific feedback, talks about the entire think while giving a general overview. It does not particularly pinpoint is specific think/feature.

e.g., I like your story. It is good.

5. Formal Feedback

A formal feedback follows a present format or structure using which the receiver sends feedback. Formal feedback covers many predefined points and has a specific blueprint. The receiver sends the feedback as per this blueprint. Formal feedback takes time to construct and hence, is not instant.

e.g., "Congratulation on scoring with A Grade in your final test performance. you are promoted to your next class."

"please accept my apologies."

6. Informal Feedback

Informal feedback, does not stick to a specific structure such as instant comments by the listener or audience. It does not take time to construct as it is initially conveyed.

e.g., "good job!   Congratulations !"   "sorry"

Summary

Feedback in communication refers to the response or reaction that a receiver gives to a sender after receiving a message.

Feedback plays a very important role in communication cycle. If no feedback is provided, it can lead to a communication barrier.

Characteristics of Feedback includes Specific, Timely, Clear, Balanced, Objective, Constructive.

There are some important feedbacks in communication cycle: Descriptive, Non-descriptive, Specific, Non-specific, Formal and Informal Feedback.

ACTIVITY Time

ACTIVITY 1

Role Play on Providing Feedback

Material required

Notebook, pen

Procedure

- Form groups with five students in each group.
- Two volunteers in the group should act out a role play of a hotel staff.
  For example, Volunteer A can act as a front desk executive and Volunteer B as a guest enquiring availability of rooms.
- After the role play, remaining members of group will give constructive feedback to both the volunteers.

ACTIVITY 2

Group-Practice on Constructive Feedback

Material required

Notebook, pen

Procedure

- Form groups with five students in each group.
- Each member in the group should write down three sentences showing how feedback should NOT be given.
- Then, each group forms a circle. One person in the circle starts by saying a sentence or feedback. The next person in the circle tries to make the feedback more constructive.
- Keep repeating until all written feedback have constructive alternatives.

NCERT FOLDER

Complete Explanations of all NCERT's Questions

A. Multiple Choice Questions

Q.1 Which of these are examples of positive feedback?

(a) Excellent, your work has improved.
(b) I noticed your dedication towards the project.
(c) You are always doing it the wrong way.
(d) All of the above

Q.2 Which of these are examples of negative feedback?

(a) I hate to tell you this but your drawing skills are poor.
(b) You can surely improve your drawing.
(c) This is a good drawing but you can do better.
(d) None of the above

Q.3 Which of the following are effective components of a good feedback?

(a) Detailed and time consuming
(b) Direct and honest
(c) Specific
(d) Opinion-based

Answers

1. (a) **2.** (a) **3.** (b, c)

B. Subjective Question

Q.1 What do you mean by feedback? Let's take a scenario.

Radha is your co-worker. Together you are making a report on how to manage the waste in your store. Since she has not finished her part of the report on time, the whole report has got delayed and the manager has given you both a warning. Write down the feedback you would like to give your co-worker on managing time. Try to keep the feedback specific and polite.

Ans. Feedback in communication refers to the response or reaction that a receiver gives to a sender after receiving a message.

It is an essential part of the communication process, as it allows the sender to know whether the message was received and understood as intended.

Here's the answer for the scenario that the question gave us:

"Hi Radha,

I appreciate your contributions on our report, the delay in receiving your part has impacted our overall deadline. To avoid similar situations in future, could we establish clearer timelines and check-in points for collaborative projects?

This will ensure we stay on track and deliver quality work on time."

EXAM PATTERN EXERCISE

Including Competency Based Questions

Multiple Choice Questions

1 __________feedback is specific information, in the form of written comments or verbal conversations that help the learner understand what she or he needs to do in order to improve. CBSE SQP 2021-22 Term I

(a) Descriptive (b) Specific (c) General (d) Sign

2 There are many reasons why interpersonal communications may fail. While communicating, the message may not be received exactly the way, the sender intended and therefore it is important that the communicator seeks .... to check that their message is clearly understood. CBSE 2021-22 Term I

(a) description (b) feedback (c) channel (d) sign

3 What is a common mistake to avoid when giving feedback?

(a) Making feedback personal and biased.
(b) Giving feedback with a neutral tone and focusing on the behavior.
(c) Giving feedback based on personal observations and evidence.
(d) Offering suggestions for improvement and additional support.

4 **Which of the following form of feedback is most suited to teacher-student interactions when students are attending a course taught by the teacher.**

(a) Descriptive Feedback (b)Non-Verbal Feedback
(c) Specific Feedback (d) Non-Specific Feedback

5 **Why feedback is so important in communication process?**

(a) It eliminates all the barriers to communication
(b) It is used for formal communication only
(c) It helps the sender ignore the receiver's response
(d) It allows the sender to correct or clarify the message

6 **Which of the following is a characteristic of a constructive feedback?**

(a) It is not as helpful as compare to other feedbacks
(b) It is critical and does not offer solutions
(c) It is specific and aimed at improving performance
(d) It avoids addressing the actual problems

7 **When giving feedback, why is it important to be specific rather than giving a general overview?**

(a) General feedback is less likely to upset the receiver.
(b) Specific feedback is easier to remember and act upon.
(c) Specific feedback takes less time to deliver.
(d) Specific feedback can be used to criticize the recipient more thoroughly.

8 **What approach should you take if you need to provide corrective feedback to a group member who is struggling?** **Competency Based Que.**

(a) Focus only on their deficiencies to emphasize the seriousness of the issue.
(b) Provide feedback in a manner that includes specific examples, suggestions for improvement, and encouragement.
(c) Offer feedback in a general way and hope they will improve on their own.
(d) Avoid providing feedback to prevent demoralizing the team member.

9 **When receiving feedback, you notice you become defensive. What ability should you develop to improve your response to feedback?** **Competency Based Que.**

(a) Assertiveness
(b) Emotional intelligence
(c) Communication skills
(d) Time management

10 **During a feedback session, you realize the person receiving feedback is not fully engaged. What skill could you employ to improve the interaction?** **Competency Based Que.**

(a) Continue speaking without interruption
(b) Ask open-ended questions to encourage dialogue
(c) Make the feedback more critical
(d) End the session early

Answers

1. (b)	2. (b)	3. (a)	4. (a)	5. (d)
6. (c)	7. (b)	8. (b)	9. (b)	10. (b)

Very Short Answer Type Questions

1 **What do you mean by specific feedback?**

Ans. Specific feedback is detailed information about what someone did well or what needs improvement. It focuses on particular actions or behaviors rather than general comments.

2 **In what ways can feedback improve performance?**

Ans. Feedback can improve performance by helping individuals make better decisions, focus on goals, motivate them to maintain or enhance their efforts, and ultimately develop improved products and services.

3 **Why is feedback considered a crucial component of the communication cycle?**

Ans. Feedback is crucial because it ensures the sender receives confirmation that the message has been understood, helping to improve performance and clarify communication.

4 **Describe the term descriptive feedback.**

Ans. Descriptive feedback provides specific, detailed information about a person's performance or behavior. It focuses on what was done well and what needs improvement.

5 **Explain the importance of feedback.**

Ans. Feedback is the receiver's response to the message, which enables the sender to evaluate the effectiveness of the message sent. Thus, feedback plays a very important role in communication cycle.

6 **How does feedback improve communication effectiveness?**

Ans. Feedback improves communication effectiveness by ensuring that the message is understood clearly and correctly interpreted. It allows the sender to adjust or clarify their message if there is any confusion.

7 **You see your colleague giving a presentation. After the presentation, your manager asks for feedback. If you were to give constructive feedback, how would you highlight areas of improvement without discouraging the presenter?** **Competency Based Que.**

Ans. I would start by acknowledging the colleague's strengths, such as their clear explanation and confident delivery. Then, I would suggest they could engage the audience more by asking questions or using visuals to make key points more memorable, ensuring that my feedback focuses on improving engagement rather than criticizing their performance.

Session 3 | Effective Communication (Principles and Barriers)

It is the process of exchanging ideas, thoughts, opinions, knowledge and data so that the message is received and understood with clarity and purpose. When we communicate effectively, both the sender and receiver feel satisfied.

1.1 Principles of an Effective Communication

Effective communication is built on several key principles. Here are the principles of effective communication in pointers:

- **Clarity** The delivered message should always be in easy understandable language, so that the communication is clear and concise which avoids confusion.
- **Attention** The receiver should be attentive in the process of communication.
- **Consistency** This maintains the continuity of planned objectives of the message in communication.
- **Active Listening** Listening attentively is the most crucial part in communication if you want to response thoughtfully to show engagement.
- **Timelines** The delivered message must be conveyed at exact time. Same goes with the feedback to retain its effectiveness.
- **Feedback** The feedback confirmation by the receiver is important to understand whether the receiver understood the message as the sender intended while delivering.
- **Economy** Always preferred less cost methods while communicating.

The key principle of effective communication is making sure that the message the sender wants to convey matches what the receiver understands. This alignment is the main goal of any communication, but it doesn't always happen. To improve communication, we should follow some guiding principles. One of the most well-known frameworks for these principles is called the 7 C's of Effective Communication.

The 7C's of Effective Communication

We communicate at home, at work, with our neighbors etc. We communicate in written or oral, audio or visual forms, so it is important that we follow the 7C's of effective communication.

These principles of effective communication are:

Completeness	The message must be complete, meaning that it should convey all the information required by the receiver. Nothing which may be required by the receiver should be left out of the message.
Conciseness	Remove any unnecessary words or information that do not add value to the message. This means conveying your message using the fewest possible words.
Coherent	It means logical communication ,i.e. all points are connected and relevant to the main topic, and the tone and flow of the text is consistent.
Concreteness	It implies being objective and clear, rather than vague, confused or obscure. A concrete message will have specific facts and figures.
Clarity	It implies emphasizing a specific message in a communication instead of trying to cover too many items. Complete clarity of thoughts and ideas enhances the meaning of the message.
Courtesy	It implies that the message should include words which show the sender's respect for the receiver. The sender of the message should be sincerely polite and well-mannered.
Correctness	It implies that there are no grammatical, spelling or punctuation errors in the communication.

1.2 Barriers to Effective Communication

Anything that prevents or disturbs the sending or receiving of a communication or message is considered as a barrier to communication. Such barriers can retard or distort the message or intention of the message being conveyed.

The types of barriers to effective communication include:

- **Physical Barriers** These are environmental factors which prevent or reduce the sending and receiving of communications. They include physical distance, distracting noises and similar interferences.
- **Interpersonal Barriers** They arise from the judgments, emotions and social values of people. They cause a

psychological distance between people similar to the physical distance. Thus, sometimes the message may not be understood at all. At other times, part of the communication is only understood.

- **Linguistic Barrier (Lingual Factors)** Language, whether spoken or written, is the most used method of communication. However, a major difficulty with language is that nearly every common word has several meanings, depending on the context in which it is used.
- **Organizational Barriers** Organizational barriers to effective communication are the barriers within a workplace that disturbs the smooth exchange of information. These barriers can arise from various aspects of an organization's structure and processes.
- **Cultural Barriers** Cultural barriers in effective communication arise from differences in cultural backgrounds, values, and practices that can affect how messages are interpreted.

1.3 Factors Causing Barriers

The factors causing barriers to communication include:

- **Poor Planning** Without adequate planning of the message to be sent, the result desired due to the communication may not be achieved.
- **Mistrust** If the sender and receiver of the communication do not trust each other, it may lead to disbelief of the message sent, causing a barrier.
- **Differences in Meaning/Ambiguity** Sometimes the receiver of the message does not correctly understand the meaning intended by the sender.
- **Distortion** Sometimes the message may be distorted by the receiver to suit his own convenience.
- **Noise** Noise is added in the channel or medium of communication. Noise can make the communication difficult to be understood.
- **Absence of Feedback** If feedback is absent, a misunderstanding may occur, thus causing a communication barrier.
- **Time and Distance** Time and distance act as barriers to the smooth flow of communication.

1.4 Measures to Overcome Barriers

To ensure that barriers to communication do not arise or can be overcome, we can take some steps related to the factors causing the barriers. The steps to be taken for overcoming some of these factors are:

- **Be Prepared before Communicating** Often we are not properly prepared for communicating a message because we do not have enough information or knowledge of what we want to communicate. At other times, we are not the behaviour expected of the receiver of the communication. Either of these creates a barrier between us and the receiver.
- **Give Sufficient Time** The message should not be communicated too fast; this is particularly true for oral messages.
- **Simplify the Language** Both the sender and receiver of the communication must have sufficient knowledge of the language in which they are communicating.
- **Don't Assume Anything** Without appropriate feedback, the sender of the message should not assume that his message has been understood. He should only rely on suitable feedback.
- **Avoid Overconfidence** Have a humble attitude when communicating a message.
- **Preconceived Notions/Expectations, Perceptions and Assumptions** When the receiver has a different perception from that of the sender, communication is affected. This can be overcome by thinking from the speaker's point of view.
- **Avoid Making Judgments** Communication can fail if the message communicated passes some judgment against the receiver. So, this kind of situation should be avoided.
- **Respect the Receiver** There should be mutual respect for each other by the sender and the receiver for a message to be successfully communicated.
- **Improve the Attitude** The receiver should not have apathy towards the sender and vice-versa, otherwise there will be a breakdown in communication.
- **Information Overload/ Attention Span** The sender must try to eliminate unnecessary information and stick to important information only.

Summary

The 7C's of Effective Communication: Completeness, Conciseness, Coherent, Concreteness, Clarity, Courtesy, Correctness.

Anything that prevents or disturbs the sending or receiving of a communication or message is considered as a barrier to communication.

The types of barriers include: Physical barriers, Interpersonal barriers, Linguistic barriers, Organizational barriers, Cultural barriers.

To ensure that barriers to communication do not arise or can be overcome, some steps follow related to factors causing the barriers-be prepared before communicating, give sufficient time ,etc.

ACTIVITY Time

ACTIVITY 1

Role Play on Barriers to Effective Communication.

Material Required

Notebook, pen

Procedure

- Form groups with five students in each group.
- Two volunteers from the group should act out a role play of a salesperson in a shopping mall.
- Enact the communication barriers or challenges the customer or salesperson may face while interacting with each other.

ACTIVITY 2

Group practice: Overcoming Barriers

Material Required

Notebook, pen

Procedure

- Form groups with five students in each group.
- Each member in a group should write down three ways to overcome barriers to effective communication. The group members will then stand in a circle. Each student should say aloud one point each; till all the ways have been discussed.

NCERT FOLDER

Complete Explanations of all NCERT's Questions

A. Multiple Choice Questions

Q.1 Which of these is not a common communication barrier?

(a) Linguistic barrier
(b) Interpersonal barrier
(c) Financial barrier
(d) Organizational barrier

Q.2 Which of these are ways to overcome communication barriers?

(a) Respecting each other's differences
(b) Using a translator
(c) Not communicating at all
(d) Using your own language for comfort

Answers

1. (c) 2. (a, b)

B. Subjective Question

Q.1 Write down the common communication barriers you may come across when you move to a new city or country.

Ans. (i) **Language Barrier** If the primary language spoken in the new city or country is different from your native language, you may encounter difficulties in understanding and expressing yourself effectively.

(ii) **Cultural Differences** Differences in cultural norms, customs, gestures, and communication styles can lead to misunderstandings and misinterpretations during interactions with locals.

(iii) **Accent and Dialect** Even if you speak the same language as the locals, differences in accent, dialect, slang, and pronunciation may pose challenges in understanding and being understood.

(iv) **Non-Verbal Communication** Non-verbal cues such as body language, facial expressions, gestures, and eye contact may vary across cultures, leading to misunderstandings of intentions and emotions.

(v) **Social Etiquette** Unfamiliarity with social norms, etiquettes, and taboos in the new environment can result in unintentional breaches of etiquette and social faux pas during interactions with others.

EXAM PATTERN EXERCISE

Including Competency Based Questions

Multiple Choice Questions

1 Which one of the following is not a barrier to effective communication? CBSE 2021-22 Term I

(a) Physical barrier (b) Linguistic barrier
(c) Interpersonal barrier (d) Subjective barrier

2 Speaking louder to drown out the noise is a ....barrier to communication.

(a) type of (b) factor causing a
(c) measure to overcome a (d) None of these

3 When it is difficult to communicate with someone who is not willing to talk or express their feelings and views it means there is a/an .... CBSE SQP 2023-24

(a) Culture Barrier (b) Interpersonal Barrier
(c) Physical Barrier (d) Language Barrier

4 Which of the following is an example of a physical barrier to communication?

(a) Language differences (b) Poor grammar
(c) Lack of feedback (d) Background noise

5 Which of the following communication barrier occurs when the message is too complex for the receiver to understand?

(a) Emotional barrier (b) Semantic barrier
(c) Physical barrier (d) Organizational barrier

6 When a receiver does not trust the sender, which of the following communication barrier occurs?

(a) Subjective barrier (b) Linguistic barrier
(c) Physical barrier (d) Psychological barrier

7 Rahul moved to Japan from India for work. However, he struggles to adapt because he is not familiar with Japanese customs and etiquette, which affects his interactions with coworkers. This is an example of: CBSE SQP 2024-25

(a) Interpersonal barrier (b) Cultural barrier
(c) Physical barrier (d) Linguistic barrier

8 A team leader frequently uses difficult technical terms while explaining the task to a team that also includes non-technical members. This is an example of which of the following communication barrier? Competency Based Question

(a) Physical barrier (b) Cultural barrier
(c) Semantic barrier (d) Linguistic barrier

9 A school has invited its old student Ajay, who has become a famous engineer, to the school to guide the students about science and engineering. However while guiding the students Ajay used complex terms and jargons and thus, students could not get what exactly he wanted to explain. What type of communication barrier is that? Competency Based Que.

(a) Physical barrier (b) Organizational barrier
(c) Cultural barrier (d) Linguistic barrier

Answers

1. (d)	2. (c)	3. (b)	4. (d)	5. (b)
6. (d)	7. (b)	8. (c)	9. (d)	

Very Short Answer Type Questions

1 How interpersonal barriers arise?

Ans. Interpersonal barriers arise from the judgments, emotions and social values of people. They cause a psychological distance between people similar to the physical distance.

2 How poor planning act as a barrier to communication?

Ans. Poor planning act as a barrier to communication as without adequate planning the result desired due to the communication may not be achieved. So, we need to properly plan what message we want to send before actually sending it.

3 Describe the principle of completeness of effective communication.

Ans. The principle of completeness implies that the message must be complete, means that it should convey all the information required by the receiver. Nothing which may be required by the receiver should be left out of the message.

4 How can cultural differences be a barrier to effective communication? CBSE 2024

Ans. Cultural differences can be a barrier to effective communication because people from different cultures may have different ways of speaking, interpreting body language, or understanding gestures and values. Misunderstandings can happen if people don't know or respect there differences, leading to confusion or offense.

5 How does active listening contribute to effective communication?

Ans. Active listening involves fully concentrating, understanding, and responding to the speaker. It improves communication by ensuring both sender and receiver are engaged and the message is interpreted correctly.

6 How does using the right medium to convey message improve communication effectiveness?

Ans. Choosing the right medium (i.e., face-to-face, email, phone) ensures that the message is conveyed in the most effective way. For example, urgent or sensitive topics may be best discussed in person rather than over text or email.

7 How can feedback help overcome communication barriers?

Ans. Feedback allows the sender to confirm if their message was understood correctly. It helps identify any communication barriers and provides an opportunity to clarify or improve the message if needed.

8 What are the factors that cause barriers to communication?

Ans. Factors which may cause barriers to communication includes:

(i) Poor Planning (ii) Distortion
(iii) Noise

9 You are conversing with your friend about something important in a newly open restaurant in a crowded market. Your friend has to rush to receive his mother from the station also.

What are the communication barriers in this scenario? How these could have been taken care of? **Competency Based Que.**

Ans. The physical barrier in this scenario is the crowded market. This makes it difficult to have a clear and uninterrupted conversation due to the noise and distractions.

To overcome this barrier, you and your friend could have:

- Found a quieter area within the restaurant or outside, away from the main crowd.
- Used non-verbal cues like nodding or making gestures to indicate understanding or agreement.
- Repeated key points to ensure that your friend has understood the conversation.

10 Simran have to make a presentation on her achievements in school to a global audience including students of other cities as well over video conferencing. Explain how will she take care of her effective communication? **Competency Based Que.**

Ans. Following points will ensure her effective communication during presentation:

1. She should prepare well and rehearse if possible.
2. Body language should be positive.
3. She should state the objectives of the presentation first.
4. The language of explanation should be simple and correct.
5. Explanation should cover right facts, clearly.
6. The voice, expressions and gestures should reflect confidence.

11 Raj is preparing for a presentation in class, but he often feels nervous and stumbles over his words, making it difficult for his classmates to understand him. Identify two communication barriers Raj is facing and suggest ways he can overcome them. **Competency Based Que.**

Ans. Raj is facing the following communication barriers:

(i) **Emotional Barrier (Nervousness)** Raj can practice relaxation techniques, such as deep breathing, to reduce anxiety before speaking.

(ii) **Language Barrier (Difficulty Articulating)** Raj can rehearse his presentation multiple times and use simpler language to express his ideas clearly. Additionally, practicing in front of friends or family can help boost his confidence.

12 Rahul is trying to explain a complex science concept to his younger sister, but she seems confused and frustrated. Despite Rahul's efforts to simplify his explanation, she doesn't grasp the idea. What communication barriers might be affecting their conversation, and how can Rahul overcome these barriers to ensure his sister understands? **Competency Based Que.**

Ans. The communication barriers could include age differences, language complexity, and Rahul's lack of patience. To overcome these barriers, Rahul can use simpler language, relate the concept to something his sister enjoys, and encourage her to ask questions for clarification.

13. Briefly explain the meaning of any 2 C's out of the 7 C's of effective communication. **CBSE 2025**

Ans. **Clarity** Ensuring the message is simple, clear, and easy to understand.

Conciseness Communicating information in a brief, yet complete, manner without unnecessary details.

Session 4 | Basic Writing Skills (Parts of Speech)

Writing skills are an important part of communication. Good writing skills allow you to communicate your message clearly and easily to a large audience. To ensure that we write correctly, we should understand some basic parts of a document such as kinds of sentences, phrases, parts of a sentence, parts of speech and construction of a paragraph.

1.1 Parts of Speech

According to their function in a sentence, words in the English language are classified as different parts of speech.

These are discussed below:

Parts of speech	Explanation	Examples	Example words
Noun	It is a word for a person, place or idea.	The young boy bought me a very long letter from the teacher.	Truth, India, January.
Pronoun	It is a word used in place of noun.	Jagdish was in hurry, so he wash the car himself.	He, She, I, You, They.
Verb	The verb express an action or the state of the subject.	He went to Rashid and told him the secret of his happiness.	Think, Run, Drink, Play.
Adjective	It is a word used to modify or describe a noun or a pronoun.	I have two large brown dogs in my spacious home.	Small, Large, Weak, Naughty.
Adverb	It describes or modifies a verb, an adjective, or another adverb.	Harish forgot to bring his lunch yesterday and again today.	Always, Before, Easily, Carefully.
Preposition	It is a word placed before a noun or pronoun to link it to another word in the sentence.	The mouse jumped off the table onto the floor of the room.	In, At, Of, To
Conjunction	It joins words, phrases, or clauses and indicates the relationship between them.	He not only plays the guitar but also the drums.	For, Nor, Yet
Interjection	It is a word used to express emotion.	Oh God! I don't know what to do about this mess.	Congratulations!
Articles	An article is a kind of adjective which is always used with a noun and gives some information about it.	I will reach home within an hour.	a,an,the

1.2 Capitalization and Punctuation

Capitalization and punctuation are essential aspects of writing that help to ensure clarity, meaning, and structure in written communication.

Here's a brief overview of capitalization and punctuation is given below:

Capitalization

Capitalization in writing skills refers to the practice of using uppercase letters at the beginning of sentences, proper nouns, and certain important words based on predefined grammatical rules. It helps convey the intended meaning, clarify relationships between elements in a sentence.

Proper use of capitalization rules enhances readability and gives your writing a professional appearance.

Capitalization Rules

Sentences The first word of every sentence should be capitalized.

Example The cat is sleeping on the couch.

Proper Nouns The names of specific people, places, organizations, countries and sometimes things should be capitalized.

Example Ajay went to Agra to visit the Taj Mahal.

Titles In titles of books, articles, and other works, the first and last words, as well as major words, should be capitalized.

Example To Kill a Mockingbird by Harper Lee.

Pronoun "I" The pronoun "I" should be capitalized always.

Example I am a doctor.

Punctuation

Punctuation is the set of symbols used in writing to clarify meaning, indicate pauses, separate ideas, and convey the structure of sentences. It helps the readers to understand the flow of the text, making written communication more effective.

Punctuation involves the marks (like periods, commas, question marks, etc.) to clarify the meaning of sentences and ensure proper sentence structure.

Punctuation Marks

Period(.) Used at the end of the sentences.

Example She went to the school.

Comma (,) Used to separate two or more items in a list, clauses, or to set off introductory elements.

Example I bought fresh apples, mangos, and bananas from the grocery store.

Question Mark(?) Used at the end of direct questions.

Example Where are you going?

Exclamation Mark (!) Used at the end of the word or sentence to express strong emotion or feeling.

Example What a beautiful day!

Quotation Marks (" ") Used to enclose direct speech or words spoken by a person.

Example Teacher said, "Do your best."

Apostrophe (') Used to show possession or in place of letters emitted in a contractions.

Example Mom's letter (possession) and isn't (contraction for "is not").

Colon (:) Used before a list, explanation, or after the salutation.

Example He had only one goal: to win the match.

Summary

Writing skills are an important part of communication. Good writing skills allows you to communicate your message clearly and easily to a large audience.

Parts of Speech: Noun, Pronoun, Verb, Adjective, Adverb, Preposition, Conjunction, Interjection and articles.

Capitalization and punctuation are essential aspects of writing the help to ensure clarity, meaning and structure in written communication.

ACTIVITY Time

ACTIVITY 1

Identifying Parts of Speech

Material required

Notebook, pen

Procedure

- Form groups with five students in each group.
- In the paragraph given below (taken from from 'La Bamba'—a short story; Gary Soto pp. 115), identify the different parts of speech and write them down accordingly. "Manuel walked on stage and the song started immediately glassy-eyed from the shock of being in front of so many people Manuel moved his lips and swayed in a made-up dance step he couldn't see his parents but he could see his brother Mario who was a year younger thumb-wrestling with a friend Mario was wearing Manuel's favorite shirt he would deal with Mario later. He saw some other kids get up and head for the drinking fountain and a baby sitting in the middle of an aisle sucking her thumb and watching him intently."
- This paragraph contains examples of the parts of speech you learnt about in this lesson.
- Identify as many of these parts of speech as you can and mark them. Discuss what was difficult in this activity.
- Write the paragraph with correct capitalization and punctuation. One of the groups will volunteer and present to the class what they have marked. They write out the paragraph on the board with proper punctuation. The other students will share if it is correct.

ACTIVITY 2

Pair Activity: Sentence Construction

Material required

Notebook, pen

Procedure

- Form pairs of students.
- List out nine parts of speech that you learnt in the lesson.

Select any three of them and create five simple sentences which use these parts of speech.

- For each part of speech, a volunteer reads out their sentences. The other students share if it is correct.

ACTIVITY 3

Group Practice: Identify Name, Place, Animal, Thing

Material required

Notepad and pens

Procedure

- Number yourselves from 1 to 5.
- One set of 1–5 is in one group and so on.
- Each member of a group has to say a word that is either a name, place, animal, thing or feeling; the fifth member has to perform any kind of action.
- Each group gets 30 seconds to think what they are going to say and do.

NCERT FOLDER

Complete Explanations of all NCERT's Questions

A. Multiple Choice Questions

Q.1 In which of the following, the underlined word is an adjective?

(a) Radha has a red dress.

(b) I can speak French.

(c) The Girl on the Train is a best-seller.

(d) Abdul can swim fast.

Q.2 Which of these sentences is capitalized correctly?

(a) Ravi and i are going to the movies.

(b) Salim is visiting India in july.

(c) The Tiger is a strong animal.

(d) She is arriving on Monday.

Q.3 Which of these sentences are punctuated correctly?

(a) When is the party.

(b) I had bread omelette and a Banana for breakfast.

(c) I am so excited about my first foreign trip!

(d) This is Abdul's notebook.

Q.4 In which of these sentences can you find an adverb?

(a) Divya drinks milk every day.

(b) Sanjay gifted me a new pen.

(c) I opened the door lock.

(d) Sita is 5-feet tall.

Answers

1. (a) 2. (d) 3. (c, d) 4. (a)

B. Subjective Question

Q.1 Identify the conjunctions and prepositions from the list below.

Over, Because, Under, And, Since, In, At, Although, Or, Up, On, Beside

Ans. **Conjunctions** And, Although, Or, Because, Since

Prepositions Over, Under, In, At, Up, On, Beside

C. Fill in the Blank

Q.1 Fill correct nouns and verbs from the given options to complete the sentence in table given below.

Nouns	Verbs
Boy, Ms Sen, Rahim, Children, Cat, Students	Swimming, Driving, Writing, Teaching, Eating, Playing

(a) The _____ is _____

(b) The _____ are _____

(c) The _____ are _____

(d) _____ is _____ the car.

(e) _____ is _____

(f) The _____ is _____

Ans. (a) The Rahim is swimming

(b) The children are playing

(c) The students are writing

(d) Boy is driving the car.

(e) Ms Sen is teaching

(f) The cat is eating.

EXAM PATTERN EXERCISE

Including Competency Based Questions

Multiple Choice Questions

1 It is a word used in place of noun that is............ .

(a) Adverb (b) Verb
(c) Pronoun (d) Preposition

2 A word used to express emotion and is often followed by an exclamation mark is called ....

(a) Preposition (b) Conjunction
(c) Interjection (d) Adverb

3 Which of the following parts of speech is used to name the person, thing or a place?

(a) Adjective (b) Noun
(c) Verb (d) Preposition

4 Identify the adverb in the following sentence: "He walks very fast".

(a) Very (b) Walks
(c) Fast (d) None of these

5 Identify the conjunction in the given sentence:
"He wanted to dance, but he was too tired."

(a) dance (b) wanted
(c) but (d) was

6 _____ is a word that expresses emotion.

(a) Noun (b)Pronoun
(c) Conjunction (d) Interjection

7 ....are a group of words that work together to communicate an element of speech.

(a) Phrases (b) Articles
(c) Adjectives (d) None of these

8 Which of the following is an example of a noun?

(a) Blue (b) Quickly
(c) Fastly (d) Run

9 Identify the noun(s): Ajay went to the park for a picnic. Competency Based Que.

(a) Ajay and picnic
(b) park and picnic
(c) Ajay and Park
(d) went

10 Identify the Pronoun(s):
Rashmi is a brave girl. She went to the forest at night alone. Competency Based Que.

(a) She (b) Rashmi
(c) brave (d) girl

11 Which of the following sentences is punctuated correctly?

(a) I need to buy milk, eggs and bread from the store.
(b) I need to buy milk eggs and bread, from the store.
(c) I need to buy: milk, eggs, and bread from the store.
(d) I need to buy milk, eggs, and bread from the store.

Answers

1. (c)	2. (c)	3. (b)	4. (a, c)	5. (c)
6. (d)	7. (a)	8. (a)	9. (c)	10. (a)
11. (d)				

Very Short Answer Type Questions

1 How writing skills are important part of communication?

Ans. Writing skills are an important part of communication because they enable you to convey your message clearly and effectively to a wide audience. Good writing helps avoid misunderstandings, ensures your ideas are presented in an organized manner, and allows readers to grasp complex information more easily.

2 What do you understand by punctuation?

Ans. Punctuation involves the use of marks (like periods, commas, question marks, etc.) to clarify the meaning of sentences and ensure proper sentence structure.

3 What is the purpose of using commas in a sentence?

Ans. Commas are used to separate items in a list, clauses in a compound sentence, and to set off non-essential information or introductory elements. Commas clarify meaning and enhance readability of the sentences and also prevent confusion or misreading.

4 What is the difference between a colon and a semicolon?

Ans. A colon is used to introduce lists, explanations, or to elaborate on a statement, while a semicolon connects two closely related independent clauses or separates complex list items.

5 How the knowledge of parts of speech can improve one's writing skills.

Ans. A good knowledge of parts of speech is essential for developing strong writing skills, as it allows the writer to make sentences that are clear and grammatically correct.

6 What is the role of a verb in a sentence?

Ans. A verb expresses an action, occurrence, or state of being in a sentence. For example, in "She sings," the verb "sings" describes an action.

7 Identify the pronouns in the sentence given below: "Rohan and Neha went to the park, and they played football."

Ans. The pronoun "they" replaces "Rohan and Neha," allowing us to avoid repeating their names. Pronouns simplify sentences by making them less repetitive, helping listeners and readers understand without extra efforts.

8 What part of speech expresses strong emotions or reactions? Give an example.

Ans. Interjection expresses the sudden or strong emotions like surprise, joy, or anger. For example, in the sentence "Oh no! I'm late for the movie," the interjection "Oh no!" conveys disappointment and surprise.

9 Correct the grammatical errors in the following sentence:

"She don't like the show because it was too boringly."

Ans. She doesn't like the show because it was too boring.

10 Construct a paragraph that effectively uses all parts of speech. Competency Based Que.

Ans. On a bright and sunny Sunday afternoon, an excited kid speedily ran across the grassy field, laughing cheerfully. His big dog bounded alongside him, swinging its tail energetically. They joyfully chased after butterflies, which danced elegantly in the gentle breeze. Every time they stopped, their faces beamed with pure delight, and the whole scene felt like a perfect moment of carefree bliss.

In this paragraph, we can see different parts of speech:

- **Nouns** afternoon, kid, dog, field, butterflies, breeze, faces, moment, bliss
- **Pronouns** his, they, their
- **Verbs** ran, laughing, joyfully, bounded, swinging, chased, danced, stopped, beamed
- **Adjectives** bright, sunny, excited, big, gentle, pure, perfect
- **Adverbs** speedily, cheerfully, energetically, happily, elegantly
- **Prepositions** on, across, after, in, with, like
- **Conjunctions** and, which, every

11 A junior team member frequently uses incorrect punctuation in emails, leading to misunderstandings. How would you help them improve their use of punctuation in professional communication? Competency Based Que.

Ans. I would explain the importance of correct punctuation in conveying the intended message and provide examples of common mistakes, such as misplacing commas or omitting periods. I'd guide them through proper use of punctuation marks, like commas for pauses, periods to end complete thoughts, and question marks for inquiries, while encouraging them to proofread emails before sending.

Session 5 | Basic Writing Skills (Sentences)

A sentence is a set of words that is complete in itself and which contains a subject and a predicate part.

It conveys a statement, question, exclamation or command. It consists of a main clause and sometimes one or more subordinate clauses.

Examples of sentences are:

- Lions roar.
- The house behind my home is the one where you have to go, isn't it?
- What a lovely shot that was!
- Go to the end of the road and turn right.

Kinds of Sentence

There are four types of English sentence, classified by their purpose:

form	function	example sentence (clause)	final punctuation
Declarative	**statement** It tells us something	John likes Mary.	.
Interrogative	**question** It asks us something	Does Mary like John?	?
Imperative	**command** It tells us to do something	Stop! Close the door.	! or .
Exclamative	**exclamation** It expresses surprise	What a funny story he told us!	!

Simple, Compound and Complex Sentences

- **Simple** It consists of an independent clause with no conjunction or dependent clause.

  For example, "My home has four rooms."
- **Complex** It contains one independent clause and at least one dependent clause.

  For example "Because it was chasing a rabbit, the dog jumped over the fence."
- **Compound** It contains two independent clauses joined by a conjunction.

  For example, "My home is very big and it has four rooms."
- **Compound-complex** It contains more than one independent clause and at least one dependent clause joined by conjunctions.

  For example, "The sun is shining now, so I think that we can go for swimming."

Phrases

Phrases are a group of words that work together in a sentence but does not contain a subject or a verb. Often phrases are used for descriptions of people, things or events.
Examples,
Filled with joy, the girl jumped up and down. The man **with the red jacket** is my father.

1.1 Parts of a Sentence

A sentence is composed of several parts, each serving a specific function to convey meaning. Here's a breakdown of the key parts of a sentence:

1. **Subject** The subject is the person, place, thing, or idea that the sentence is about or that performs the action.

   Example <u>The cat</u> chased the mouse.
2. **Predicate** The predicate tells what the subject does or is. It includes the verb and can also include objects, complements, and modifiers.

   Example The cat <u>chased</u> the mouse.
3. **Object** The object is the entity that is acted upon by the subject. It is typically affected by the action.

   Example The cat chased the <u>mouse</u>.

Types of Object

Objects can be categorized in two categories:

1. **Direct object** Direct Objects receives the action of the verb directly. For example "The Lion chased the mouse".
2. **Indirect object** Indirect Object receives the direct object or benefit from the action of the verb. For example "She gave him a flower".

1.2 Construction of a Paragraph

A paragraph is a group of sentences dealing with a particular topic. Paragraphs can be of any length and can vary from only one sentence to even more than ten sentences. However, for maintaining clarity, paragraphs should be as short as possible.

For example, the paragraph you are reading has only four sentences. The first sentence of a paragraph is usually the topic sentence, as it states the main point to be developed or explained in the paragraph. Each sentence following it should be relevant to that topic, giving the paragraph a look of unity.

Summary

A sentence is a set of words that is complete in itself and which contains a subject and a predicate part.

Types of sentences: Declarative, Interrogative, Imperative, Exclamative.

Phrases are a group of words that work together in a sentence but does not contain a subject or a verb.

A sentence is composed of several parts, each serving a specific function to convey meaning. Key parts of sentence: Subject, Predicate and Object.

A paragraph is a group of sentences dealing with a particular topic.

ACTIVITY Time

ACTIVITY 1

Pair-work: Making Sentences

Material required

Notebook, pen

Procedure

- Form pairs of students.
- First, write down five sentences that contain direct objects.
- Then, write down five other sentences that contain both direct and indirect objects.
- Use different colours to mark the different parts of each sentence. (Subject, Verb, Object). One volunteer shows their list to class, who correct them, if needed.

ACTIVITY 2

Individual Work: Types of Sentences

Material required

Notebook, pen

Procedure

- Each student will make a list of minimum 12 sentences.
- These should have at least three sentences of each type — declarative, interrogative, exclamatory and imperative.
- For each type of sentence, different volunteers read out their sentences to the class.
- The class gives feedback on the correctness of the sentences.

NCERT FOLDER

Complete Explanations of all NCERT's Questions

A. Multiple Choice Questions

Q.1 Identify the object, verb and subject in the sentence, 'The car crashed into a tree.'

(a) Object: a tree; Verb: crashed; Subject: the car
(b) Object: The car; Verb: crashed; Subject: a tree
(c) Object: crashed; Verb: the tree; Subject: the car
(d) Object: crashed; Verb: the car; Subject: the tree

Q.2 Identify the indirect object in the sentence, 'The band played music for the audience.'

(a) The band (b) played
(c) music (d) audience

Q.3 Which of these is an imperative sentence?

(a) Switch off the fan. (b) Sheila has gone to the market.
(c) Where are my pen colours? (d) Oh no! I missed my flight.

Answers

1. (a) 2. (d) 3. (d)

EXAM PATTERN EXERCISE

Including Competency Based Questions

Multiple Choice Questions

1 Which part of sentence contains two independent clauses joined by a conjunction?
(a) Compound Sentences
(b) Simple Sentences
(c) Complex Sentences
(d) Compound-Complex Sentences

2 The sentence "The Sun is shining now, so I think that we can go shopping" which of the following types of sentences is this?
(a) Simple (b) Complex
(c) Compound (d) Compound-Complex

3 Which of the following is sentences is a declarative sentence?
(a) "What do you do?"
(b) "Open the window!"
(c) "She loves to swim in the ocean."
(d) "What a lovely dress!"

4 Which of the following sentences contains a direct object?
(a) "They went to the pool."
(b) "He answered the phone."
(c) "She gave him a chocolate."
(d) "They speak very loud."

5 A sentence is a set of word that is completed in itself and which contains a subject and a .... part.
(a) predicate (b) noun
(c) paragraph (d) None of these

6 The first sentence of every paragraph is generally called the_______ sentence.
(a) predicate (b) independent
(c) topic (d) negative

7 Which of the following is a simple sentence?
(a) He went to the market, and he stayed home.
(b) Although it was raining, He went to the market.
(c) He went to the market.
(d) He went to the market because he needed groceries.

8. Which of the following sentences is the most concise?
(a) Since it was raining, we decided to stay inside.
(b) Because it was raining, we made the decision to stay inside.
(c) Due to the fact that it was raining, we decided to stay inside.
(d) It was raining, so we decided to stay inside.

9. Which of the following sentences is correctly structured?
(a) Not only is she talented but also hardworking.
(b) Not only she is talented but also hardworking.
(c) Not only is she talented but also she is so hardworking.
(d) Not only is she talented but also is she hardworking.

10. Which of the following is an example of a properly punctuated compound sentence?
(a) The sky was clear it was a perfect day for a picnic.
(b) The sky was clear, it was a perfect day for a picnic.
(c) The sky was clear; it was a perfect day for a picnic.
(d) The sky was clear because it was a perfect day for a picnic.

Answers

1. (a)	2. (d)	3. (b)	4. (b)	5. (a)
6. (c)	7. (c)	8. (d)	9. (a)	10. (c)

Very Short Answer Type Questions

1 What does a predicate in a sentence refer to?

Ans. The predicate part of a sentence includes the verb and the words that relate to it. It tells what the subject does with an action verb or describes the subject.

2 What is a compound-complex sentence?

Ans. A compound-complex sentence is one which contains more than one independent clause and at least one dependent clause joined by conjunctions.

3 How can you distinguish between a compound and a complex sentence?

Ans. A compound sentence has two or more independent clauses joined by a conjunction or semicolon, while a complex sentence contains one independent clause and at least one dependent clause.

4 How can you improve sentence variety in your writing?

Ans. You can improve sentence variety by using different sentence structures, such as using different sentences types simple, compound, and complex sentences, and combine short, impactful sentences with longer, more detailed ones. Improving sentence variety can make your writing more engaging and effective.

5 How does a complex sentence differ from a simple sentence?

Ans. A complex sentence contains one independent clause and at least one dependent clause, while a simple sentence has only one independent clause.

6 What is the importance of sentence variety in writing?

Ans. Variety in sentences keeps the writing engaging and dynamic by varying sentence structure and length. It helps in maintaining the reader's interest and prevents monotony in the text.

7 What is the role of a subject in a sentence?

Ans. The subject describe the person, place, thing, or idea that performs the action in a sentence. It tells us who or what the sentence is about. For example, in the sentence "The Lion chased the Deer," "The Lion" is the subject because it is performing the action.

8 Write two sentences of each type of sentence — statement, question, exclamatory and order.

Ans. Refer to text on page 24 (Kinds of Sentence).

9 You are helping a team member improve his writing. He often writes long, complex sentences that can be confusing to the readers. What advice would you give your team member to help him improve readability of his sentences? **Competency Based Que.**

Ans. I recommend him breaking down long sentences into shorter ones, focusing on the one main idea of the paragraph, each sentence should have a purpose.

Also try to use simple language or words, avoid using unnecessary jargons or technical terms and revise your work to eliminate redundancy.

10 You need to write an essay about your favourite leader. Which basic writing skills would you apply in doing so? **Competency Based Que.**

Ans. An essay includes more than one paragraph. We need to apply follow basic writing skills:

(i) Correct usage of grammar.

(ii) Give brief introduction about the leader, describe his qualities as a great leader, his achievements and failures too. How he learnt from his failures. How he influenced people positively and other important incidents of his life.

(iii) Keeping the sentences simple and short.

(iv) End the essay with a brief conclusion.

11 You are reviewing a report written by a colleague, and you notice that several sentences are too long and difficult to understand. How would you suggest improving the sentence structure to make the report clearer and easier to read? **Competency Based Que.**

Ans. I would recommend using appropriate punctuation like commas, periods, or semicolons to separate ideas and ensure each sentence expresses a single thought clearly. This will make the report more reader-friendly and less overwhelming.

SELF ASSESSMENT

Multiple Choice Questions

1 ……… is an instance of visual communication.
(a) An E-mail (b) A speech (c) Eye contact (d) Bar chart

2 Which of the following is not a factor causing a barrier in oral communication?
(a) Preconceived notions (b) Physical hearing problem
(c) Emotions (d) Semantics

3 "Suraj" is sending a message to "Raman". Who is receiver here?
(a) Suraj (b) Raman
(c) Both Suraj and Raman are receivers (d) None of these

4 _______ is the receiver's acknowledgement and response to the message.
(a) E-mail (b) Feedback (c) Information (d) None of these

5 Social media chats, reports, SMS is an example of ______?
(a) Small Group Communication (b) Written Communication
(c) Interpersonal Communication (d) Public Communication

6 What are the types of words we should use for verbal communication?
(a) Acronym (b) Technical (c) Simple (d) Complex

7 A group of words which does not make complete sense, is known as a _____.
(a) Sentence (b) Phrase (c) Paragraph (d) E-mail

Very Short Answer Type Questions

8 What is the semantic barrier to communication?

9 What is the function of an adjective in a sentence?

10 Explain the difference between specific feedback and non-specific feedback.

11 Name the types of barriers to effective communication in detail.

12 List the advantages of written communication.

13 How is a phrase different from a sentence?

Competency Based Questions

Multiple Choice Questions

14 What should you do when giving feedback to a classmate about their presentation?
(a) Focus only on what they did wrong
(b) Provide specific examples of strengths and areas for improvement
(c) Compare their presentation to others in a negative way
(d) Give no feedback at all

15 In a written communication, what is the importance of using proper grammar and punctuation?
(a) It makes the writing look more complex (b) It ensures the message is clear and professional
(c) It allows for more personal expression (d) It is not very important

Subjective Type Questions

16 You are assigned to give a presentation on a topic you are not very familiar with, and you have limited time to prepare.
How would you ensure your communication during the presentation is clear and effective, despite your time constraints?

17 In a cross-functional team, you notice that there is a misunderstanding between two departments due to unclear communication.
How would you facilitate communication between these departments to resolve the issue?

Unit 2

Self Management Skills-II

Self-management is our ability to regulate emotions and control actions and behaviours. Strong self-management skills prevent us from missing deadlines and help us navigate workplace conflicts. Simply put, self-management is about preparing for the future, not just acting in the present.

Session 1 | Stress Management

2.1 Stress

Stress is identified as a condition in which a person is tensed and worried. It can affect both our body and mind. People having large amount of stress can become tired, sick and unable to concentrate or think clearly. Sometimes they even suffer mental breakdown.

Stress is our body's way of responding to any kind of demand. Stress can cause symptoms such as cold hands or feet, increased sweating, a nervous stomach, a dry mouth etc.

These are all short term symptoms of stress. It can be caused by both good and bad experiences.

Note *The good stress is called* ***Eustress****, whereas the bad stress is termed as* ***Distress****.*

Types of Stress

There are three main kinds of stress: acute, episodic acute and chronic.

- **Acute stress** A short-term stress that can be positive or negative. It can occur when you're doing something new or exciting, or when you're in a dangerous situation.
- **Episodic acute stress** Episodic acute stress is when you experience acute stress on a regular basis. With this kind of stress, you don't ever get the time you need to return to a calm, relaxed state. Episodic stress frequently affects people working in certain professions, like healthcare providers.
- **Chronic stress** A long-term stress that can last for weeks or months. It can be caused by issues at work, money problems, or marriage troubles.

2.2 Stress Management

Stress management refers to focusing human efforts for maintaining a healthy body and mind capable of better with standing stressful situations.

Stress refers to a physical, mental or emotional strain or tension. Small amount of stress have a positive effect and they help us stretch ourselves to a new level.

Always keep in mind the ABC of stress management

A: Adversity or the stressful event
B: Beliefs or the way you respond to the event
C: Consequences or actions and outcomes of the event

Steps to Manage Stress are

Step 1 Be aware that you are stressed
Step 2 Identify what is causing you stress
Step 3 Apply stress management methods

Importance of Stress Management

Stress management is critical for dealing with challenges and setbacks. It helps people bounce back from failure and forge ahead.

- **For a better life** Learning stress management skills and applying them to everyday life helps a person take control of his or her life.
- **To improve health** Constantly being under stress affects your health. It makes you prone to various diseases and accelerates your aging process. Research shows that stressed individuals age faster than those who are stress free.
- **To enhance performance** Workplace stress may lead to low self-esteem or a feeling of worthlessness. It can also impact your career growth. Hence, believe in the importance of stress management and take necessary steps to reduce stress.
- **To improve communication** Once you start handling stress, everything falls in place. Your communication process improves. You open up more and try to express your feelings. Misunderstandings are cleared.

2.3 Stress Management Techniques

Stress management techniques help to guide and empower individuals to maintain equilibrium, stabilise their emotions, and live a productive life.

Let us take a look at some of these techniques

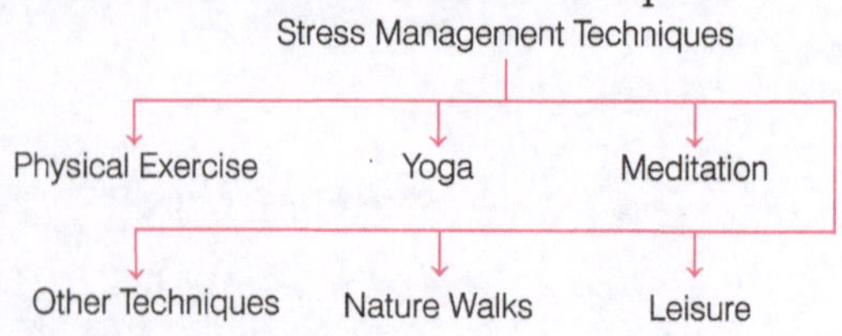

- **Physical Exercise** It is an activity done to achieve physical fitness and overall health. It improves blood circulation, lowers blood pressure, clears the mind of worrying thoughts, improves our self-image, makes us feel better about ourselves.
- **Yoga** Yoga is a mind-body practice that combines physical poses, controlled breathing and meditation or relaxation. It will help in stress management by relaxing the body and mind.
- **Meditation** In meditation, we change from our normal activities to silence. We go beyond the noisy thoughts in the mind and enter a state of restful alertness. During meditation, although we are in a state of deep rest, our mind is fully alert and awake.
- **Leisure** This means spending holidays with your family and friends, travelling to other areas in the country or outside and any other similar activities. Leisure gives you a 'break' from stress.
- **Nature Walks** It means walking in the local park or similar such activity. These walks may be done more than once a day for short periods of time during which we indulge in 'thought-stopping'.
- **Other Techniques** These include getting adequate sleep, which is a good stress reducer. When we wake refreshed after a night's sleep, we have adequate day time energy.

Ability to Work Independently

Ability to work independently means working without any support, interference or supervision. By working independently, work satisfaction increases because here the individual is responsible to tackle the duties and get credit for the success.

If you can become a calm and relaxed person, you will be able to work independently which means:

- ability to become self-aware, self-monitoring and self-correcting
- knowing what you need to do and setting priority of tasks
- taking initiatives yourself before being told what to do
- owning your tasks and recognising your mistakes
- having the ability and will to learn continuously

Emotional Intelligence

Emotional intelligence means the ability to identify and manage one's own emotions as well as the emotions of others.

It includes three skills are as follows:

- **Emotional awareness** It is the ability to identify and mention one's own emotions.
- **Harnessing emotions** It is the ability to harness and apply emotions to tasks like thinking and problem solving.
- **Managing emotions** It is the ability to regulate one's own emotions and also helping others to do the same.

Some steps to manage emotional intelligence are as follows:

- **Understand your emotions** Observe your behaviour pattern and list down the things you need to work on. You can then workout on the things that need improvement.
- **Rationalise** Do not take decisions abruptly but sort out problems and be rational in your thinking.
- **Practice** Do meditation, yoga, and exercise to keep yourself calm.

Summary

Stress is our body's way of responding to any kind of demand and can be caused by both good and bad experiences.

Stress may be classified into three different types : acute stress, episodic acute stress and chronic stress.

Stress can be managed by physical exercise, practices of yoga and meditation, leisure time, nature walks and other techniques.

We need to cultivate in us the ability of working independently by becoming a self-aware, self-motivated and self-regulating person.

ACTIVITY Time

ACTIVITY 1

Role Play on Avoiding Stressful Situation

Material required

Pen, notepad or sheets of paper

Procedure

- Form groups of three.
- Choose any one situation from below.
- Prepare a skit (role play) and perform within your groups.
- Two members will perform the skit and one member will observe and share feedback.

Situation 1

You have missed your school bus and you are getting late. What will you do? Will you panic or call for help or try to find a way?

Situation 2

You have to perform your best in the next cricket or badminton match so you get a chance to play for your school at the national level cricket or badminton tournament. You have been anxious (worried or stressed). Will you lose your sleep worrying about it or will you go to the field and practice?

ACTIVITY 2

Self-reflection

Material required

Pen or pencil

Procedure

- Complete the below table by listing the situation(s) that can cause stress and what will you do to avoid stress in such situations.
- Use the stress management techniques shared in the lesson to complete the exercise.

Stress Causing Situation(s)	Stress Management Techniques

ACTIVITY 3

Benefits of taking a holiday

Material required

Pen or pencil

Procedure

- Write an essay to describe the place and your experience during a holiday trip or summer camp.
- Highlight how the trip helped you de-stress.

NCERT FOLDER

Complete Explanations of all NCERT's Questions

A. Subjective Questions

Q.1 Describe stress and stress management in your own words.

Ans. Stress can be defined as our emotional, mental, physical and social reaction to any perceived demands or threats.

Stress management offers a range of ways to help you better deal with stress and difficulty, also called adversity, in your life.

Q.2 List your favorite stress management technique and elaborate why you find it the most effective.

Ans. Some of the most effective stress management techniques are:

- **Physical Exercise** releases endorphins, reducing stress hormones and boosting mood.
- **Yoga** combines physical postures, breathing exercise, and meditation, promoting relaxation and reducing anxiety.
- **Meditation** calms the mind, improves focus, and lowers stress levels.
- **Leisure** activities provide a welcome break, allowing for enjoyment and stress relief.
- **Nature Walks** connect with nature, reducing anxiety and promoting tranquility.

The listed techniques are effective for stress management due to their overall approach. These techniques, when practiced regularly, can significantly contribute to overall well-being and stress reduction.

EXAM PATTERN EXERCISE

Including Competency Based Questions

Multiple Choice Questions

1 Stress is identified as a condition in which a person is ________.

(a) tensed (b) worried
(c) relaxed (d) Both (a) and (b)

2 Physical exercise is used as a stress management technique because

(a) it improves blood circulation
(b) improves self-image
(c) makes us feel better
(d) All of the above

3 Managing stress is about making a plan to be able to cope effectively with daily pressures. Always keep in mind the ABC of stress management. The acronym ABC stands for **CBSE 2021-22 Term-I**

(a) Ability, Burden, Concise
(b) Adore, Belief, Cause
(c) Adversity, Beliefs, Consequences
(d) Adapt, Balance, Cooperate

4 Which of the following best describes self-management? **CBSE SQP 2024-25**

(a) The ability to ignore emotions and focus solely on tasks
(b) The ability to control one's emotions, thoughts, and behavior in various situations
(c) The ability to manage time efficiently without considering feelings
(d) The ability to rely on others for emotional support

5 We have the ability to work independently if we ________.

(a) need regular feedback to make progress in our work
(b) work best at our own pace
(c) need a structured environment to work efficiently
(d) need to be prodded to work faster

6 High expectations from self can leave one with chronic anxiety and stress, thus leading to ________ stress. **CBSE SQP 2021-22 Term I, CBSE SQP 2023-24**

(a) physical (b) emotional
(c) mental (d) financial

7 ________ means that we do not think about our day-to-day activities during a nature walk.

(a) Self-esteem
(b) Thought- Stopping
(c) Self-Independence
(d) Emotional intelligence

8 ________ refers to focusing human efforts for maintaining a healthy body and mind, capable of withstanding stressful situations. **CBSE 2023**

(a) Artificial Intelligence (b) Stress management
(c) Motivation (d) Emotional intelligence

9 Which of the following is not the benefit of stress management? **CBSE 2023**

(a) Boosts immunity (b) Reduces efficiency
(c) Improves mood (d) Prevents behavioral problems

10 ________ is a series of postures and breathing exercises practiced to achieve control of body and mind. **CBSE SQP 2022-23**

(a) Meditation (b) Nature Walk
(c) Yoga (d) Physical Exercise

11 How does regular physical exercise contribute to stress management? **Competency Based Que.**

(a) It can distracts you from stressful situations temporarily.
(b) It has no effect on stress management.
(c) It makes you more tired and increases stress.
(d) It help improve mood and reduce stress, by releasing endorphins.

12 Trisha is always tense during exam time. She is a sincere and studious student, but the thought of exams creates anxiety in her. Which stress management technique that you would suggest to help her? **SQP 2020-21, Competency Based Que.**

(a) Yoga (b) Exercise
(c) Vacation with Family (d) All of these

13 Which of the following is the most suitable term for the ability to regulate one's own emotions and help others also to do the same? **CBSE 2025**

(a) Managing emotions (b) Harnessing emotions
(c) Knowing emotions (d) Supressing emotions

Answers

1. (d)	2. (d)	3. (c)	4. (b)	5. (c)
6. (b)	7. (b)	8. (d)	9. (b)	10. (c)
11. (d)	12. (a)	13. (a)		

Very Short Answers Type Questions

1 What is Stress management? **CBSE 2025**

Ans. Stress management is the process of identifying stressors, coping with challenges, and using techniques like relaxation or time management to reduce stress levels.

2 What are the symptoms of stress?

Ans. Stress can cause symptoms such as cold hands or feet, tenseness, increased sweating, dry mouth etc. These are all short-term symptoms of stress.

3 How leisure activities benefits in stress management?

Ans. Leisure gives the benefits by enabling a person to indulge in his/her interests, hobbies, gives them a break and provides an outlet for relief.

4 How can a person manage stress?

Ans. With proper planning and use of the right techniques, stress can be reduced or managed to remain within tolerable limits.

5 How human body responds to a stressful situation?

Ans. The human body responds to a stressful situation by pumping adrenalin so that the muscles become tense and the heart rate increases.

6 What are the personal signs of stress?

Ans. We must understand our own personal signs of stress and some signs may be too much sweating, shivering, biting nails, lack of concentration, poor judgment, constant worrying etc.

7 How does the practice of yoga help in stress management?

Ans. The practice of yoga helps in stress management by relaxing the body and mind, developing a connection between the mind and the body, releasing emotional energy and helping to breathe more effectively.

8 What are the advantages of the ability to Work Independently? CBSE SQP 2022-23

Ans. The ability to work independently offers several advantages, such as greater flexibility, improve self-confidence, reduce dependence, increased productivity etc.

9 Name the stress casual agents? CBSE SQP 2022-23

Ans. Stress casual agents can be categorized into several categories:

- Mental stress
- Social stress
- Environmental stress
- Physical stress

10 You're feeling overwhelmed with schoolwork and extracurricular activities, leading to burnout. What strategies would you implement to manage your stress and regain balance? Competency Based Que.

Ans.
- I would assess my commitments and consider reducing non-essential activities.
- I would create a weekly schedule to allocate time for studying, relaxation, and hobbies.
- Incorporating regular breaks and self-care practices, such as exercise and meditation, would help me manage stress and maintain my well-being.

11 A team member frequently interrupts you while you are trying to work. How do you manage this situation while maintaining a positive relationship? Competency Based Que.

Ans.
- I would approach the team member politely and express my need for focused work time.
- I could suggest specific times to discuss ideas or questions. This approach helps set boundaries while fostering good communication and collaboration.

Session 2 | Self-Awareness

Self-awareness refers to our knowledge and understanding of ourselves. It includes our emotions, beliefs, assumptions, biases, knowledge base, abilities, motivations, interests etc.

So, we should make a conscious effort to learn about ourselves, i.e. our abilities, beliefs, likes and dislikes. The feeling of self-awareness enhances our self-confidence.

Types of Self-awareness

There are two types of self-awareness as follows

1. **Internal Self-awareness** Internal self-awareness is about focusing on your inner values. The emotions, values, goals, aspirations, everything which we possess in our inner feelings.

2. **External Self-awareness** External self-awareness deals with our feelings and behaviour with others. It is the ability to look at others.

This awareness helps you decide what others think about you.

2.1 Developing Self-Awareness

Developing self-awareness means understanding your thoughts, emotions, and behaviors to improve your relationships, decision-making, and overall personal growth. There are four areas of self-awareness that you should continuously develop

1. **About Your Strengths** To find out your strengths, find out what you like to do, what you are enthusiastic about doing and what work done by you is given good comments by others.
2. **About Your Weaknesses** If you know what you find difficult to do or cannot do, you can ask other people to help you in that task. Otherwise you can remove this weakness by learning that particular task.
3. **About Your Flaws** You should not hide your flaws but take other people's help in overcoming them.
4. **About Your Emotional Problems** A typical emotional problem is getting angry on small matters. Such emotional problems in your character should be kept under control when some incident triggers them.

2.2 Knowing Yourself

Knowing yourself, in self-management means understanding your strengths, weaknesses, values, and motivations. This self-awareness helps you set realistic goals, manage time effectively, and handle stress. It's the ultimate foundation for improving how you work and make decisions.

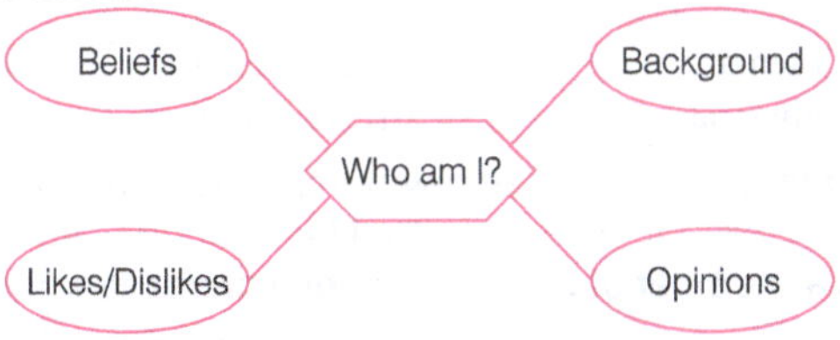

2.3 Strength and Weakness Analysis

Strength and weakness analysis is like making a list of what you find challenging and what you're really good at.

Your strengths are things you do well and feel confident about, while weaknesses are areas where you might need more practice or improvement.

Knowing both helps you focus on what you're good at and work on improving what you find hard.

To identify your strengths and weaknesses you can:

1. **Self-reflection** Consider your past experiences, successes, and challenges to find out areas where you excel or struggle.
2. **Feedback from Others** Ask for input from colleagues, friends, or mentors who know you well.
3. **Personality and Skills Assessments** Take online tests like the Type indicator or strengths finder to gain insights.
4. **Track performance** Analyze your performance in various tasks or roles over time.
5. **Set challenges** Push yourself in new situations and see where you encounter difficulties.

Difference between Interests and Abilities (Strength)

Interests	Abilities
Interests are activities, topics, or fields that an individual enjoys or like to do in free time.	Abilities are the skills or competencies an individual has developed, enabling them to performs specific tasks effectively.
e.g. Painting, drawing, sports, traveling etc.	**e.g.** Problem-solving, Writing, public speaking etc.

Summary

Self-awareness means our knowledge and understanding of our strengths, weaknesses, flaws and emotions.

Self-awareness can be categorized into two categories Internal and External self-awareness.

Knowing yourself, in self-management means understanding your strengths, weaknesses, values, and motivations.

Strength and weakness analysis is like making a list of what you find challenging and what you are really good at.

ACTIVITY Time

ACTIVITY 1

Pair Activity: Aim in Life

Material required

Pen, notepad or sheets of paper

Procedure

- Form pairs of students.
- Each student will make a list of things that they can do well based on the given format.
- Share your notes with your partner.
- One volunteer from the pair comes and reads, in front of the class.

Here is the format for you to fill in

I am
I can (abilities)
I will (plan)
My aim is

ACTIVITY 2

Individual Activity: Interests and Abilities Worksheet

Material required

Student textbooks, pen

Procedure

- Each student has to complete the given worksheet, containing a list of statements and questions.
- Each student has to be real and honest when filling the worksheet as it is for their own understanding of themselves.
- If they are not real and honest, they will get incorrect results about their own interests and abilities.

Worksheet - My Interests and Abilities

I am happiest when
My idea of a perfect day
Five things I really enjoy doing
Three things I like to do every day
I am most passionate about
Ideas or issues I care deeply about
If I had the talent or ability, I would
If I could choose any job, it would be
The three activities that I love to do?
How often do I do them?
What stops me from doing the activities more often?
What specific changes do. I need to make in order to engage in these activities more frequently?

EXAM PATTERN EXERCISE

Including Competency Based Questions

Multiple Choice Questions

1 Self-awareness refers to

(a) Our knowledge and understanding of ourselves
(b) Systematic efforts to direct thoughts and actions
(c) Ability to identify effective methods to move from thought to action.
(d) None of the above

2 Self-awareness about our .... problems means that we know the drawbacks in our character which should be kept under control when some incident triggers them. Competency Based Que.

(a) Mental (b) Emotional
(c) Physical (d) None of these

3 For improving our self-awareness, we may ask ourselves the question, "Do I like working with others as a member of a .... or do I prefer to work by ....?" Competency Based Que.

(a) member,team (b) team, me
(c) team, myself (d) myself, team

4 ...... is the ability to identify and manage one's own emotion as well as the emotions of others. CBSE 2024

(a) Self-Awareness (b) Emotional Intelligence
(c) Stress Management (d) Emotional Barrier

5 **Which of the following skills, self-awareness primarily involves?**
(a) Financial planning (b) Time management
(c) Emotional intelligence (d) None of these

6 **High self-awareness can help improve which of the following?**
(a) Interpersonal relationship
(b) Memory capacity
(c) Physical strength
(d) Mental ability

7 **A lack of self-awareness might result in which of the following?**
(a) Increased empathy for others
(b) Stronger relationships
(c) Improved decision making
(d) Frequent misunderstandings

8 **Which of the following practices can enhance self-awareness?**
(a) Avoiding challenges
(b) Focusing only on others
(c) Ignoring feedbacks
(d) Regular self-reflection

9. **What does "knowing yourself" primarily involve?**
(a) Learning new skills
(b) Understanding the behavior of others
(c) Recognize your own strengths
(d) Knowing every detail about everything

10 **How can self-awareness help in making better decisions?**
(a) By solely rely on on others' opinions
(b) By focusing only on logic and ignoring emotions
(c) By avoiding risks at all costs
(d) By understanding your values, which influences your choices

11 **When you are aware of your emotional triggers, you can:**
(a) Manage your reactions effectively
(b) Avoid all emotional situations
(c) Blame others for your reactions and behavior
(d) React impulsively without thinking

12 **Rahul did not like to lose any game or sports. This is his**
(a) positive feelings (b) weakness
(c) emotional intelligence (d) strength

13 **You are preparing for an exam and notice that you study better in the morning than at night. What does this indicate?** **Competency Based Que.**
(a) You need to study more often at night
(b) You are aware of your peak productivity time
(c) You should only study in the morning
(d) Time of day doesn't affect studying at all

Answers

1. (a)	**2.** (b)	**3.** (c)	**4.** (b)	**5.** (c)
6. (a)	**7.** (d)	**8.** (d)	**9.** (c)	**10.** (d)
11. (a)	**12.** (b)	**13.** (b)		

Very Short Answer Type questions

1 **How can we become self-aware about our strengths?**

Ans. We can become self-aware about our strengths by finding out what we like to do, what we are enthusiastic about doing and what work done by us is given good comments by others.

2 **What should we do when we become aware of our flaws?**

Ans. When we become aware of our flaws, we should not hide them, but take other people's help in overcoming them.

3 **What are the four areas of self-awareness that you should continuously develop?**

Ans. Four areas of self-awareness that you should continuously develop are:
- About Your Strengths
- About Your Weaknesses
- About Your Flaws
- About Your Emotional Problems

4 **What are the skills necessary for independent working?**

Ans. (i) Becoming self-aware, self-monitoring and self-correcting.
(ii) Knowing what we need to do.
(iii) Taking the initiative rather than waiting to be told what to do.
(vi) Learning to work at a pace that we can sustain for a long time.
(v) Taking ownership of our mistakes without looking for excuses.

5 **What is self-awareness? Also give any two benefits of self-awareness.** **CBSE 2023**

Ans. Self- awareness is the ability to recognize and understand your own emotions, thoughts and behavior. Two benefits of self- awareness are- improved decision making and better relationships.

6 **Give one example each of following stress causal agents for students :** **CBSE 2023**
(a) Mental (b) Social

Ans. (a) Mental- Constant worry
(b) Social- Conflict with friends or family

7 **Why is self-awareness is important in relationships?**

Ans. It helps individuals to understand how your actions and emotions affect others, leading to better communication and empathy.

8 **Name one method to increase self-awareness.**

Ans. Keeping a journal of your thoughts and emotions can help you to increase self-awareness.

9 **How does self-awareness is beneficial to personal growth?**

Ans. Self awareness helps in identifying areas where we need improvement, leading to more effective personal development.

10 **What role does self-awareness play in decision-making?**

Ans. It allows you to make choices that are aligned with your values and goals by understanding your motivations and biases.

11 **How do you regularly assess your own performance and development areas?** Competency Based Que.

Ans. I regularly assess my performance by setting clear goals and tracking progress, seeing how I do. I ask for feedback and then think what I did well and what didn't work.

12 **You often find yourself distracted by social media while trying to complete tasks. How do you manage this distraction to enhance your productivity?** Competency Based Que.

Ans. To minimize social media distractions, I use website blockers, schedule social media checks, and prioritize tasks. I work in focused intervals and replace social media with motivational content. This helps to enhance my productivity.

Session 3 | Self- Motivation

Self-motivation is the inner drive that pushes a person to take action towards a goal, even when they don't want to. It's the ability to start and succeed at a task without being forced to do so by others.

Here are some characteristics of self-motivated people:

- They are self-driven and have a strong desire to achieve their goals
- They maintain enthusiasm and stay committed to tasks, even when faced with challenges
- They are able to keep going even in the face of setbacks
- They are able to take up opportunities

Types of Motivation

1. **Internal Motivation** It arises from within the individual. It is driven by personal interest, enjoyment, or a sense of satisfaction. The activity itself is a reward.

2. **External Motivation** It arises from outside the individual. It is driven by external rewards or to avoid negative consequences. The motivation is tied to a specific outcome or reward.

2.1 Qualities of Self-Motivated People

Self motivated people have several key qualities that drive their success and enable them to achieve their goals.

1. **Goal Oriented** They set clear, achievable goals and are driven by a strong desire to accomplish them.
2. **Self-Disciplined** They have the ability to stay focused and manage their time effectively, avoiding distractions to meet their objectives.
3. **Positive Attitude** They maintain a positive attitude, which helps them stay motivated and overcome obstacles.
4. **Self-Confident** They believe in their abilities and trust their judgment, which fuels their motivation to pursue their goals.
5. **Accountability** They hold themselves accountable for their actions and outcomes, taking responsibility of their successes and failures.

2.2 Developing Self-Motivation

There are four steps for building self-motivation, which are as given below.

1. **Find out your strengths** Identify your strength is about your likes or dislikes and what makes you happy and sad.
2. **Set and focus on your goals** Define the goals that you want to achieve and focus all your energy to achieve your goal.
3. **Develop a plan to achieve your goals** Develop a plan and set timelines to achieve your goals and plan a list of activities that you will do to achieve each goal.
4. **Stay loyal to your goals** For achieving your goals stay loyal to work, even when you are facing difficult time.

Summary

Self-motivation is our ability to identify effective methods of making ourselves move, which turns thoughts into actions.

Self-motivation can be internal and external.

Qualities of self- motivated people includes: goal oriented, self-confident, positive attitude etc.

Building self-motivation involves finding your strengths and weaknesses, focus on your goals, develop a clear plan.

ACTIVITY Time

ACTIVITY 1

Staying Motivated (Group Discussion)

Material required

Pen, notepad or sheets of paper, chart paper

Procedure

- Form groups of three.
- Choose any one of the following situation and write down the steps you would take to motivate yourself.
- Your teacher gives you feedback on the essay you had written. There are a lot negative remarks. What will you do to motivate yourself to improve the essay?
- Your father has given you the responsibility of arranging for a birthday party for your little sister who is turning 3 years old. You do not want to do this task. How will you motivate yourself to do the work?

ACTIVITY 2

Self-Reflection

Material required

Pen or Pencil

Procedure

- Make a list of reasons that stop you from being motivated.
- Write down ways by which you will motivate yourself to overcome them.

Reasons for not being motivated	Ways to overcome
For example People make fun of the way I speak English.	**For example** I will learn to speak English correctly by attending classes after school.

NCERT FOLDER

Complete Explanations of all NCERT's Questions

A. Multiple Choice Questions

Q.1 What makes you complete work or studies without others cheering you?

(a) Self-confidence (b) Communication
(c) Self-motivation (d) Self-esteem

Q.2 Which of the following is a type of motivation?

(a) Internal (b) Intermediate
(c) External (d) Extensive

Q.3 Ravi works hard to get the best student award at the end of year. What type of motivation is this?

(a) Internal (b) External
(c) Both internal and external
(d) Not any specific type of motivation

Answers

1. (c) **2.** (a,c) **3.** (c)

EXAM PATTERN EXERCISE

Including Competency Based Questions

Multiple Choice Questions

1 Which of the following best describes the self-motivation?
(a) Having a strong desire to achieve goals
(b) Waiting for external rewards
(c) Avoiding challenging tasks
(d) Relying on others

2 .... is the driving force that pushes us to achieve our goal, feel happy and improve our quality of life. CBSE 2024
(a) Stress Management (b) Self-Awareness
(c) Self-Growth (d) Self-Motivation

3 _______________ ability of a person to do the things that need to be done without someone or something influencing us. CBSE SQP 2020-21
(a) Self-Motivation (c) Self Discipline
(b) Self Awareness (d) Self-Regulation

4 Establishing a .... plan can help keep you on track and focused on your objectives.
(a) developed (b) structured
(c) complex (d) different

5 Positive self-talk can help overcome feelings of...........and keep you motivated.
(a) motivation (b) depression
(c) self-doubt (d) Both (b) and (c)

6 Which of the following best describes a person with high self-motivation?
(a) They require external incentives to start working
(b) They need constant supervision
(c) They avoid setting goals
(d) They take initiatives and persists in tasks even when facing challenges

7 Which of the following is not a characteristic of self-motivation?
(a) goal-oriented behavior (b) persistent effort
(c) positive attitude (d) procrastination

8 Which of the following factors can decrease self-motivation?
(a) lack of interest in tasks (b) consistent goal-setting
(c) high self-discipline (d) None of these

9 Sonika gets up at 6 am and goes for her hobby classes. Then she comes back home and finishes her homework before going to school. She does all work by herself. No one tells her to do so. This is called _______. CBSE SQP 2021-22 Term I, Competency Based Que.
(a) Self-Awareness (b) Self-Motivation
(c) Self-Regulation (d) Discipline

10 Roshni studies in class X and is practising hard with a lot of sample papers to get good marks in her exams. She gets up early in the morning to study and completes her revision work. This is an example of .... CBSE 2025, Competency Based Que.
(a) self-awareness (b) self-motivation
(c) influential motivation (d) emotional intelligence

11 Amina studies diligently to improve her grades because she wants to feel proud of her achievements and also earn a scholarship. What type of motivation is this? CBSE SQP 2024-25, Competency Based Que.
(a) Internal
(b) External
(c) Both internal and external
(d) Not any specific type of motivation

Answers

1. (a)	2. (d)	3. (a)	4. (b)	5. (d)
6. (d)	7. (d)	8. (a)	9. (b)	10. (b)
11. (c)				

Very Short Answer Type Questions

1 What is self-motivation?

Ans. Self-motivation is the drive to take action and achieve goals based on internal desires and personal satisfaction, rather than external rewards or pressures. It involves setting your own goals, maintaining a positive mindset, and persisting through challenges to reach those goals.

2 How can self-motivation affect personal growth?

Ans. It encourages continuous learning and improvement, leading to personal development and achieving one's full potential.

3 What role does self-motivation play in overcoming obstacles?

Ans. Self-motivation plays a crucial role in overcoming obstacles by:
- Encouraging a positive mindset.
- Driving focus and determination.
- Building confidence and self-discipline.
- Enhancing problem-solving skills.

4 How can we self-motivate ourselves for completing a task which appears to be too large or too complex to be done by us?

Ans. For completing a task which appears to be too large or too complex to be done by us, we can break down the job into several smaller and easier tasks, each of which can be accomplished in a set time period.

5 What is the relationship between self-motivation and self-discipline?

Ans. Self-motivation drives the desire to achieve the goals, pushing you to take action. While self-discipline is the ability to stay focused and take consistent action.

6 Why is self-discipline crucial for maintaining self-motivation ?

Ans. Self-discipline helps people stay committed to their goals, even when motivation wanes. It make sure that actions are taken consistently, which is key to long term success.

7 Write down the three strategies to improve self-motivation in daily life?

Ans. Three strategies includes setting specific and realistic goals, rewarding yourself for small achievements, and creating a structured routine to maintain consistency.

8 Vimal works in the office because he has to repay his loan and look after his family he gets no satisfaction from his job. There is no chance of promotion either. What type of motivation does Vimal possess? **Competency Based Que.**

Ans. Vimal's motivation is primarily extrinsic motivation. This type of motivation arises from external factors such as obligations, rewards, or pressures rather than from personal satisfaction or enjoyment of the task itself.

9 Tarun is preparing a lecture for her students on self-motivation, which skills should she highlight to help the students become self-motivated and take charge of their learning? **Competency Based Que.**

Ans. Tarun should highlight several key skills to help students become self-motivated and take charge of their learning. These skills include:

- Teach students to set clear, achievable goals. Breaking large goals into smaller, manageable tasks helps provide a sense of direction and progress.
- Encourage students to regularly reflect on their progress, evaluate what works or needs improvement, and adjust their strategies accordingly.

10 Sneha wants to improve her physical fitness but finds it hard to stick to a routine. How can she motivate herself to maintain consistency in her workout plan? **Competency Based Que.**

Ans. To motivate herself to maintain consistency in her workout plan, Sneha can set specific fitness goals and create a regular schedule for her workouts. Tracking her progress in a journal or app will help her stay accountable.

Session 4 | Self-Regulation

Self-regulation focuses on your ability to influence personal and professional improvement based on your self-awareness and motivation.

Self-regulation involves being able to:

- control reactions to emotions like frustration or excitement
- calming down after something exciting or upsetting happens
- focus on a task
- refocus attention on a new task
- get along with everyone else

2.1 Goal Setting

It is all about finding and listing your goals and then planning on how to achieve them. Goals allow you to separate out what's important. It helps you to focus on the end result instead of less important work. This will make you successful in your career and personal life. We can use SMART method to set goals. SMART stands for:

- **Specific** Well defined, clear, and unambiguous
- **Measurable** With specific criteria that measure your progress toward the accomplishment of the goal
- **Achievable** Attainable and not impossible to achieve
- **Realistic** Within reach, realistic, and relevant to your life purpose
- **Timely** With a clearly defined timeline, including a starting date and a target date. The purpose is to create urgency.

2.2 Time Management

Time management is the ability to plan and control how you spend the hours of your day well and do all that you want to do.

Steps for Effective Time Management are

1. **Organize** Plan your day-to-day activities and make a timetable that you follow.
2. **Priorities** You make a to-do list that has all your activities and you rank them in the order of importance.

   It helps you to get the most important task done first and also to track what is pending.
3. **Control** You have a control over your activities and time.
4. **Track** You identify and note where you have spent your time. This will help you analyse if you have used your time effectively or not. It also helps you to identify time-wasting activities

Summary

Self-regulation is our ability to influence personal and professional improvement based on our self-awareness and motivation.

"SMART" methods are used for setting clear goals.

Acronym SMART refers to Specific, Measurable, Achievable, Realistic and Time-bound.

Time management is the process of complete planning and organizing how to use your time effectively to achieve specific goals.

ACTIVITY Time

ACTIVITY 1

SMART Goal or Not (Group Work)

Materials required

Pen, notepad or sheets of paper

Procedure

- Indicate whether the below mentioned goals are SMART or not. If they are SMART goals then tick mark against each aspect of SMART.

Goals	Specific (Yes or No)	Measurabl e (Yes or No)	Achievable (Yes or No)	Realistic (Yes or No)	Time bound (Yes or No)
I want to earn INR 1 crore in my first job.					
I want to become a teacher after my post-graduation.					
I want to travel to many places.					

ACTIVITY 2

Long-term Goals and Short-term Goals (Peer Feedback)

Material required

Pen, notepad or sheets of paper

Procedure

- Form groups of four. Work individually in your group and complete the below table. Once completed, share with your group and seek feedback on your goals. Share your feedback when other members of the groups are presenting their goals.

Short-term Goals (What are your goals in the next 6 months to 2 years?)	Long-term Goals (What are your goals in the next 5 years?)
1.	1.
2.	2.
3.	3.

ACTIVITY 3

Self Reflection

Material required

Pen or pencil

Procedure

- Complete the table below by writing how you will make sure that the goals you set for yourself are SMART. Use the tips shared in the lesson for doing this.

SMART Goals	How will make sure the goals are SMART
Specific	
Measurable	
Achievable	
Realistic	
Time-bound	

NCERT FOLDER

Complete Explanations of all NCERT's Questions

A. Subjective Questions

Q.1 What is Goal Setting?

Ans. Goal setting is all about finding and listing your goals and then planning on how to achieve them.

Q.2 In SMART goals, what does 'S' stand for? Explain.

Ans. In SMART goals, S refers for Specific, it refers to being as specific as possible with the desired goal.

Q.3 What is time management and how can you manage your time?

Ans. Time management is the ability to plan and control how you spend the hours of your day well and do all that you want to do.

You can manage your time simply by knowing the things that you are going to do from there you will know what time or what are your plans on doing it.

Q.4 How can tracking your time help you?

Ans. Time tracking helps you gain a better insight into how you spend your time, so you can prioritize better.

EXAM PATTERN EXERCISE

Including Competency Based Questions

Multiple Choice Questions

1 Which of the following best describes the self-regulation?

(a) The process of managing one's thoughts, emotions, and behaviours to achieve goals.
(b) The ability to set goals for others
(c) The process of achieving goals
(d) The ability to delegate tasks to others

2 What does the "A" in SMART goals stands for?

(a) Action
(b) Ambitious
(c) Achievable
(d) Accountable

3 How does self-regulation helps in overcoming challenges?

(a) By making you give up on your goal
(b) By enabling you to adapt your goals
(c) By ignoring the challenges
(d) By avoiding setting any goal

4 Which of the following is the primary purpose of setting goals?

(a) To provide direction and motivation
(b) To ensure failure
(c) To make life more compatible
(d) To avoid hard work

5 Which of the following is not a characteristic of a SMART goal?

(a) Measurable (b) Specific
(c) Achievable (d) Ambiguous

6 Which of the following is an example of a time-bound goal?

(a) I want to study 5 hours
(b) I want to study 5 hours every morning for the next month
(c) I want to be healthy
(d) I want to improve my health

7 Which of the following is the first step in goal-setting process?

(a) Identifying your values and priorities
(b) Reviewing past achievements
(c) Ignoring what you want to achieve
(d) None of the above

8 Which of the following best describes a long-term goal?

(a) A goal that is easy to accomplish
(b) A goal that can be achieved in a day
(c) A goal that has no timeline
(d) A goal that requires significant time and planning

9 When faced with a setback in achieving a goal, self-regulation involves: **Competency Based Que.**

(a) Ignoring the setbacks and continuing without change
(b) Giving up on the goal entirely

(c) Blaming external factors for the setbacks
(d) Reasoning the situations, adjusting the goal or approach and continuing

10 Rahul set a goal to improve his grades but finds himself distracted. What self-regulation strategy can help him stay focused? **Competency Based Que.**
(a) Blame others for his distractions
(b) Study only when he feels like it
(c) Create a study schedule and limit distractions
(d) Avoid studying altogether

11 Siya wants to save money for a new Phone. What is a good initial step in her goal-setting process? **Competency Based Que.**
(a) Spend all her money and hope to save later
(b) Set a specific savings target and timeline
(c) Ignore her current expenses
(d) Rely on others to contribute to her savings

12 To perform well at work and life in general, you must be able to manage and improve yourself in various skills. Which of the following skills helps you to prioritize the things you have to do remove waste and redundancy from work? **CBSE 2021-22 Term I, Competency Based Que.**
(a) Responsibility
(b) Time management
(c) Self-awareness
(d) Adaptability

13 What is the primary benefit of using to do list for time management?
(a) It helps in organizing and tracking tasks
(b) It creates unnecessary stress
(c) It distracts from the main objectives
(d) It increases the number of tasks to accomplish

14 Which of the following strategy is effective for managing time more effectively and avoiding procrastination?
(a) Complete the whole tasks without breaks
(b) Multitasking frequently
(c) Avoid using planners
(d) Setting deadlines for tasks

15 Which of the following actions best supports self-regulation in managing time effectively?
(a) Regular assessing and manage strategies
(b) Switching between tasks
(c) Avoiding task delegation
(d) Ignore progress reviews

16 You need to have set some............., to spend your time productively.
(a) boundaries (b) priorities
(c) ideas (d) goals

17 Time management is important to ....
(a) Everyone (b) Employees
(c) Students (d) All of these

18 Select the incorrect statement.
(a) Effective time management skills helps you accomplish more tasks
(b) Setting clear goals is essential for effective time management
(c) Procrastination is a time management strategy that can help improve productivity.
(d) Using a daily to do list can help in managing time effectively

19. Effective time management skills can reduce stress and improve ....
(a) work- life balance (b) Health
(c) Both (a) and (b) (d) None of these

20 Rashmi is constantly underestimating the time required for her tasks to be completed. What suggestion would you give Rashmi to overcome this problem? **Competency Based Que.**
(a) She should delegate them to others
(b) She should adjust her schedule by allocating more time to similar tasks in the future
(c) She should avoid those tasks altogether
(d) She should rush through them quickly

21 Siya gets up at 6 am and goes for her dance classes. Then she comes home and finishes her homework before going to school. This is an example of ____ **Competency Based Que.**
(a) Self-Awareness (b) Self-Motivation
(c) Self-Regulation (d) None of these

22 Megha has prepared a timetable to achieve her goal. This skill is known as
(a) Self-Awareness (b) Responsibility
(c) Time-Management (d) Adaptability

23 Karan has many extracurricular activities and schoolwork. How can he effectively manage his time to balance both? **Competency Based Que.**
(a) Focus on extracurriculars and neglect schoolwork
(b) Make a weekly schedule that allocates time for both activities
(c) Drop all extracurricular activities
(d) Work late into the night with a plan

Answers

1. (a)	2. (c)	3. (b)	4. (a)	5. (d)
6. (b)	7. (a)	8. (d)	9. (d)	10. (c)
11. (b)	12. (c)	13. (a)	14. (d)	15. (a)
16. (a)	17. (d)	18. (c)	19. (c)	20. (b)
21. (a)	22. (c)	23. (b)		

Very Short Answer Type Questions

1 Why self-regulation is important in life?

Ans. Self-regulation is important in life because it allows you to keep a tab on your own emotions. It helps in controlling negative impulses and reciprocates emotions for actualizing set goals.

2 How does self- regulation influences the process of setting and achieving goals?

Ans. Self-regulation influences goal setting by enabling people to set realistic goals, monitor their progress, and make necessary adjustments. It ensures that individuals remain committed and motivated throughout the process of achieving their goals.

3 What role does self-monitoring play in self-regulation and goal setting?

Ans. Self- monitoring is an essential component of self-regulation. It involves regular tracking of progress towards goals. It allows people to assess their performance and identifying areas of improvements.

4 Goal setting is a very essential factor in your personal life. List all the SMART methods to set the goals. Explain 'A' in brief. **CBSE SQP 2020-21**

Ans. **SMART methods of goal setting are**

Specific, Measurable, Achievable, Realistic, and Time-bound.

Achievable This step of SMART methods describes that your goal should be realistic and achievable. By breaking big goals into smaller parts we can make the goal achievable.

5 Imagine a young entrepreneur, Alex, who started a tech startup with the goal of revolutionizing online education. They initially focused on building a platform for video lectures and quizzes. However, after a few months, they realized that students were struggling with practical application. How would reviewing and adjusting their goals at this point help Alex and their team?

Ans. In Alex's case, reviewing and adjusting their goals would lead them to realize the need for interactive elements and hands-on projects on their platform. They might also decide to expand their target audience to include corporate training programs. By adapting to the changing needs of their users and the market, Alex can increase the chances of their startup's success.

6 What is the difference between short-term and long-term goals?

Ans. Short-term goals are achievable within a few weeks or months, while long-term goals require more time and efforts, typically spanning several months to years.

7 Setting personal boundaries is important for self-regulation explain why?

Ans. Setting personal boundaries is important because it helps individuals to protect their emotional well-being and maintain focus on their goals without any external distractions.

8 What strategies you can use to enhance self-regulation when working towards a complex goal?

Ans. Strategies includes setting specific, clear and achievable goals, using time management techniques, practicing mindfulness, regularly reviewing on progress and creating and managing a support system for accountability.

9 What do you understand by time management?

Ans. Time management is the process of planning and organizing how to divide your time between different tasks effectively to achieve goals. Effective time management skills allow an individual to complete more tasks in less time.

10 Briefly discuss the significance of time management skills in order to succeed in life. **CBSE 2024**

Ans. Time management skills are important for success because they help in prioritizing tasks, set clear goals, and allocate your time efficiently. Practicing these skills enhances productivity, reduces stress, and ensures you meet deadlines, leading to better performance in both personal and professional realms.

11 Riya, a Class X student, feels stressed with her exam preparation, extracurricular activities, and family commitments. How can tracking time help her? **CBSE SQP 2024-25**

Ans. Tracking time helps to

- Identify time-wasting activities and unproductive habits
- Improve time management for studies and tasks
- Balance academics with extracurriculars and personal time
- Allocate time for relaxation and self-care
- Achieve academic goals more efficiently and reduce stress before exams

12 It is important to evaluate how you spend your time daily, explain why?

Ans. Regularly evaluating how time is spent is crucial because it allows people to identify patterns and areas where they may be wasting time. By reflecting on daily activities, one can recognize time-consuming distractions or inefficiencies.

13 Rishi has a list of tasks to complete by the end of the month. To effectively manage his time and stay focused, how does creating a daily schedule help him with self-regulation?

Ans. Creating a daily schedule helps Rishi with self-regulation by providing a structured framework for managing his time and tasks.

By breaking down the month's tasks into smaller, manageable chunks, Rishi can prioritize, allocate specific time slots, and track his progress. This visual representation of his workload promotes self-awareness and helps him stay focused on the most important tasks.

SELF ASSESSMENT

Multiple Choice Questions

1. Which of the following skills are not required for developing an independent working style?
(a) Taking ownership of our mistakes. (b) Waiting to be told what to do.
(c) Knowing what we need to do. (d) Learning to work at a sustainable pace.

2. Stress can be identified as a condition in which a person is ________
(a) worried (b) tensed (c) Both (a) and (b) (d) relaxed

3. Which of the following plays a major role in reaction to stress?
(a) Personality (b) Emotions (c) Confidence (d) None of these

4. Physical exercise can be used as a stress management technique because
(a) improves self-motivation (b) It improves blood-circulation
(c) make us feel fress (d) All of these

5. Issues related to health of an individual can lead to low self-esteem and cause________stress.
(a) Emotional (b) Mental (c) Physical (d) None of these

6. _______ includes a series of postures and breathing exercises to control body and mind.
(a) Yoga (b) Meditation (c) Physical exercise (d) None of these

7. Which type of stress is termed as "fight or flight response"?
(a) Survival (b) Environmental (c) Internal (d) None of these

Very Short Answer Type Questions

8. What is the first step in getting self-motivated?

9. How is environmental stress different from internal stress? Explain two such differences.

10. How can we identify stress? Explain.

11. How can tracking your time help you?

12. Give any two examples where you find small amount of stress can be helpful.

13. Why is self-reflection is important for personal growth?

Competency Based Questions

Multiple Choice Questions

14. Ajay is always punctual at school. He has a regular schedule that he follows everyday. Sunny usually arrives late to work. He does not submit his assignments on time. He sometimes forget the main task. Who is better in Time Management Skill?
(a) Ajay (b) Sunny (c) Both Ajay and Sunny (d) None of these

15. Ritika performed in inter-school competitions and learn some new skills, such as dancing, painting etc. What type of motivation is this?
(a) Internal (b) External (c) Intermediate (d) None of these

16. Staying with the current situation with new updated plans and preparing yourself for new challenges is called ________
(a) Self-Motivation (b) Adaptability (c) Goal Setting (d) Self-awareness

Subjective Type Questions

17. You often find yourself losing track of your long-term goals. How do you ensure that you stay focused and make consistent progress towards them?

18. You notice that your colleague, Raman, often takes on too many responsibilities at work and seems stressed. How would you approach Raman to discuss their self-management skills?

Unit 3

ICT Skills-II

ICT skills help us to communicate, run our business and stay connected with our family and friends. Hence, every person needs to acquire ICT skills and build them to stay updated with the latest softwares and applications.

The basic ICT skills that you need are knowing how to

- operate computers.
- browse the Internet for collecting, storing and disseminating information.

Session 1 | Knowing About Operating System

3.1 Introduction to Operating System

Operating System (OS) is the system software that performs all the basic tasks of a computer system. It works like an interface between the user and the computer hardware resources. It actually controls the execution of all the tasks that are performed in a computer.

Some examples of operating systems are Unix, MS-DOS, Windows 98/2000/XP etc. It enables a user to utilise hardware resources very efficiently. So, operating system makes it easy for a user to use computer system.

"An operating system is a collection of programs that controls and coordinates all the tasks and functions in a computer system. It mediates between application programs and hardware components."

Types of Operating System

Types	Features
Time Sharing Operating System	• In this OS, a small amount of time is allocated for the processing simultaneously. • It provides scheduling to each process to be run on. e.g. Mac OS
Real-Time Operating System	• It was designed to respond to an event within a predetermined time. • It aims to execute real time applications such as auto pilot mechanism used in aircrafts. • It has very little user-interface capability and no end-user utilities. e.g. Windows CE, QNX, RTLINUX, Vx Works, Free RTOS, etc.
Single-User Operating System	• It is designed for one user to effectively use a computer at a time. e.g. Windows 95/NT/2000, DOS, etc.
Multi-User Operating System	• It allows many users to take advantage of the computer's resources simultaneously. • It ensures that problem with one user doesn't affect the entire community of users. e.g. Unix, VMS, Linux, Windows 2000, etc.
Single-Tasking Operating System	• It allows only a single program to run at a time. e.g. Palm OS, etc.
Multi-Programming Operating System	• It allows to run several programs at a time using time sharing. • This operating system keeps several jobs in memory at a time. e.g. Linux, Unix, etc.
Multi-Tasking Operating System	• This operating system is the logical extension of multi-programming operating system. • In this OS, more than one processes can be executed concurrently. • It reduces CPU idle time. e.g. Microsoft's Windows and Apple's Mac OS.
Distributed Operating System	• It uses multiple central processors to serve multiple real time applications. • It manages a group of independent computers and makes them appear to a single computer. • Data processing jobs are distributed among the processors according to their efficiency. e.g. LOCUS etc.
Batch-Processing Operating System	• Similar types of jobs are grouped under batch and these batches are executed without user's interruption. • Jobs are processed in the order of submission, i.e. on First Come First Serve (FCFS) basis. e.g. DOS, IBM OS/2, etc.
Multi-Processing Operating System	• Use of two or more CPUs within a single computer system. • Simultaneous processing of two or more programs by multiple processors. e.g. Linux, Unix, Windows 2000, etc.

Operating Systems for Desktop and Laptop

Some commonly used operating systems for desktop and laptop are as follows :

UNIX

It is an operating system which was first developed in the 1969s. UNIX systems have a Graphical User Interface (GUI) similar to different Microsoft Windows which provides an easy way to use platform.

It supports fully multi-tasking with protected memory which means multiple users can run multiple programs at the same time without interfering with each other or crashing the system.

UNIX was one of the first operating system to be written in a high level programming language, namely C. This meant that it could be installed on virtually any computer for which a C compiler existed.

Linux

It is an open source operating system designed primarily for the PCs and laptops. Linux was designed considering Unix compatibility.

Its functionality list is quite similar to that of Unix. One of the most valued advantage of Linux over the other platforms lies with the high security levels. It is a virus free operating system.

Mac OS (Apple Macintosh)

It is an operating system which was introduced on March 24, 2001 by Apple Inc and was initially named as system software, which was later renamed as Mac OS.
One drawback of this system is that it can only be run on Apple produced products.

MS-Windows

It is a series of Graphical User Interface (GUI) operating systems developed, marketed and sold by Microsoft. Microsoft introduced an operating environment named Windows on November 20, 1985 as an add-on to MS-DOS in response to the growing interest in Graphical User Interfaces. The most popular versions of Windows for personal computers, mobile devices and server computers are as follows :

(a) **Windows NT** (New Technology) The first version of Windows NT was Windows NT 3.1 released on July 27, 1993 by Microsoft. It is a processor independent, multi-processing and multi-user operating system.

(b) **Windows 95** It was developed in August, 1995 by Microsoft. It is an operating system based on consumer oriented application. Although, it can run older Windows and DOS applications. It has essentially removed DOS as a underlying platform.

(c) **Windows 98** It was released in 1998 by Microsoft. It was produced in two main versions, i.e. the first version was plagued with programming errors but the second edition (which came out later) was much better with many errors resolved.

(d) **Windows 2000** It was released in February, 2000 by Microsoft. A better version of the Windows NT OS, that works well both at home and as a workstation in a business.

(e) **Windows ME** (Millennium Edition) It was released in September, 2000 by Microsoft. An upgraded version of Windows 98 but it has been historically plagued with programming errors, which may be frustrating for home users. It includes Internet Explorer 5.5, Windows Media Player 7.

(f) **Windows XP** (eXPerience) It was released on October 25, 2001 by Microsoft. It is an OS produced for personal computers. Two versions of Windows XP are Windows XP Home Edition and Windows XP Professional Edition.

(g) **Windows Vista** It was released on January, 2007 by Microsoft. It offers an advancement in reliability , security, ease of deployment, performance and manageability over Windows XP.

(h) **Windows 7** It was released on July 22, 2009 by Microsoft. It is an upgrade of Windows XP and Vista. It does not include some standard applications like Windows Movie Maker, Windows Mail, etc. Now-a-days, it is the most commonly used operating system.

(i) **Windows 8** It was released on August 1, 2012 by Microsoft. It introduced major changes to the operating system's platform and user interface to improve its user experience on tablets, where Windows was now competing with Mobile OS, including Android and iOS.

(j) **Windows 10** It was released to manufacturing in July, 2015 by Microsoft. It is a personal computer operating system as a part of the Windows NT family of operating systems.

Solaris

It is a free operating system originally developed by Sun Microsystems in 1992. Oracle Solaris, as it is now known and owned by Oracle Corporation since Oracle's acquisitions of Sun in January 2010.

Solaris is known for its scalability, reduced cost, protected investments in applications. It is a standard operating system with excellent performance, system management and network functions.

MS-DOS (Microsoft-Disk Operating System)

It is an operating system that runs on PC and developed by IBM corporation in 1981. It was the most commonly used member of the DOS family of operating system.

Initially, MS-DOS was targeted at Intel 8086 processors running on computer hardware using floppy disks to store and access not only the operating system, but application software and user data as well.

Operating Systems for Mobile Phone and Tablets

It is an OS that operates on smartphones, tablets and digital mobile devices. A mobile OS controls a mobile device and its design supports wireless communication and different types of mobile applications. It has built-in support for mobile multimedia formats. The most common operating systems for mobile phone and tablets are as follows :

Android

It is the most popular Linux based open source software developed by Google in September, 2008. It is basically designed for touch screen mobile devices like tablets, smartphones, etc. Now-a-days, it is most common OS used in mobile phones.

iOS

It is the popular mobile operating system developed by Apple Incorporation. iOS was introduced on June 29, 2007 when the first iPhone was developed. This operating system is commonly used in Apple iPhone, iPod Touch, iPad, Second Generation Apple TV, etc.

BlackBerry

This is the most secure operating system used in leading smartphones developed by BlackBerry company. BlackBerry was introduced on January 19, 1999. It also supports WAP 1.2.

Symbian

Symbian is an open source mobile OS. It was developed on 5th June, 1997 and sold by Symbian Ltd. It is a mobile OS targeted at mobile phones that offer a high level of integration with communication and Personal Information Management (PIM) functionality. It has been used by many major handset manufacturers including Motorola, Nokia, Samsung, Sony, etc.

3.2 User Interface

The user interface is one of the most important parts of any operating system because it allows users to easily access the applications and the hardware. It is set of commands or menus. The user can interact with the computer by using mainly two kinds of interfaces:

1. **Character User Interface (CUI)** This is a mechanism of interacting with a computer system or software by typing commands to perform specific tasks. Programs with Character User Interface are generally easier to automate via scripting. CUI only uses text types one after another. It is also known as Command Line Interface (CLI).
2. **Graphical User Interface (GUI)** It is used as an interface between program and user. This is a computer program that enables a user to communicate with a computer through the use of symbols, visual metaphors and pointing devices. The first graphical user interface was designed by Xerox Corporation in 1970s. GUIs can be found in hand-held devices such as MP3 players, portable media players, gaming devices, etc.

3.3 Menu, Icons and Taskbar on the Desktop

Let's discuss about Windows 10 operating system.

Windows 10

Windows 10 is a personal computer operating system developed and released by Microsoft in 2015. It is easy to use social media sites like Facebook and Twitter. Windows 10 will also include a 'game DVR' mode to allow recordings of the last 30 seconds of play, all better for the social gaming. Windows 10 interface is adapted by hardware, it is running on.

Desktop

Desktop is the main screen of the Windows 10 operating system. The background image of desktop is called **wallpaper**. A small arrow or blinking symbol, moving on the desktop is called **cursor**. There are three components as Icons, taskbar and desktop background.

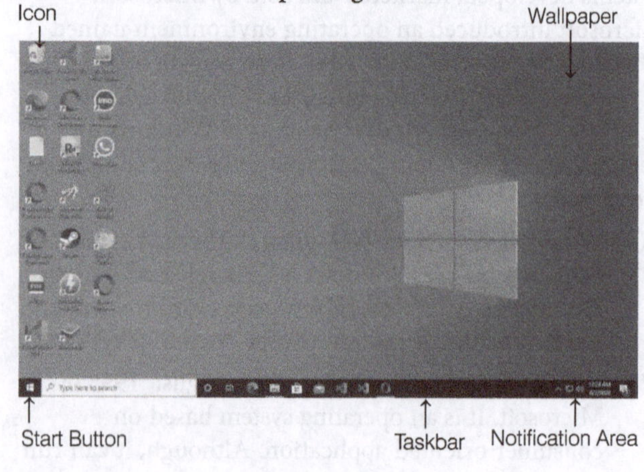

Icons An icon is a picture or graphic representation of an application or a file. If you want to open or access an icon, double click on it.

Taskbar It is present at the bottom of the screen. The parts or taskbar are :

1. Start menu 2. Opened program 3. Notification area

- **Start Menu** To search for an application, you can also open the Start menu. An alphabetical list of all the applications installed on the computer appears. To open the Start menu, click on Start button. The Windows 10 Start menu has two panes. The left pane displays a list of programs. A **program** is also called an application in Windows 10. The right pane features tiles. A **tile** is an application icon.
- **Notification Area** It is located at the right side of the taskbar. It shows different types of notifications for your computer such as, your Internet connection or the volume level. By default, the notification area shows only a few icons but you can click the upward arrow on its left side to see the other options.

Summary

ICT refers to the use of computers, telecommunications, software, and networks to store, retrieve, transmit, and manipulate digital information.

Operating system is the system software that performs all the basic tasks of a computer system.

MS-Windows is a series of Graphical User Interface (GUI) operating system developed, marketed and sold by Microsoft.

User interface is part of any operating system because it allows users to easily access the applications and the hardware.

Icon is a picture or graphic representation of an application.

ACTIVITY Time

ACTIVITY 1

Group Demo on Use of Computer

Material required

Pen, notebook, computer

Procedure

- Form groups depending on the number of computers available. One student starts the computer and logs in.
- Another student identifies the keys on the keyboard. A third student then performs all the functions of the mouse such as hover, click, double-click, etc.
- Discuss and note differences between hardware and software and also how they work together to perform a task on the computer.
- After you have performed all the activities, another student shuts down the computer.
- Other students watch and give feedback on what was done right and which tasks can be improved.

ACTIVITY 2

Group Practice: Using the Keyboard

Material required

Computer

Procedure

- Form groups depending on the number of computers available.
- Open a text editor in Ubuntu by typing 'editor' in the search bar and then selecting the Text Editor. You can also open Notepad in Windows by typing Notepad on the Windows Search bar and then selecting Notepad from the search result.
- One student positions his or her hands on the keyboard and types the following paragraph in the text editor.

  "People use computers at work, at school and at home every day. In factories computers are used to control the manufacturing process and in offices to make documents, such as reports.
- We also use computers for sending e-mails and playing games."
- Now, another student in the group will check the paragraph and correct the grammar and spelling mistakes.

NCERT FOLDER

Complete Explanations of all NCERT's Questions

A. Multiple Choice Questions

Q.1 Which of the following functions is not performed using a mouse?

(a) Turn on (b) Hover
(c) Right click (d) Drag and Drop

Q.2 What is the term used when you press and hold the left mouse key and move the mouse around?

(a) Highlighting (b) Dragging
(c) Selecting (d) Moving

Q.3 Here are the steps that take place when starting a computer. Rearrange the steps in the correct order.

(a) Desktop appears after login
(b) Login screen appears
(c) Power on Self-Test (POST) starts
(d) Operating system starts
(e) Welcome screen appears

Answers

1. (a) 2. (b) 3. (c → d → e → b → a)

B. Subjective Questions

Q.1 What is the function of the ENTER key?

Ans. The ENTER key is used to execute commands or actions in a program. It is also used to start a new line or paragraph when typing in text editors or word processors. In many situations, pressing ENTER confirms an input or selection, such as submitting a form or moving to the next step in a process.

Q.2 How will you prevent others from using your computer?

Ans. To prevent others from using your computer, you can:

- Set up a password-protected account or PIN for login.
- Enable a lock screen that activates after a period of inactivity.
- Use biometric authentication like fingerprint or face recognition if available.
- Log out or shut down the computer when you're done using it.
- Use security software like firewalls or antivirus programs to protect your data.

EXAM PATTERN EXERCISE

Including Competency Based Questions

Multiple Choice Questions

1 The primary purpose of the operating system is

(a) to make the most efficient use of the computer hardware
(b) to allow people to use the computer
(c) to keep systems programmer's employed
(d) to make computers easier to use

2 .... is responsible for creation and deletion of files and directories.

(a) Operating system
(b) Application software
(c) Programs
(d) Peripherals

3 It provides scheduling to each process to be run on.

(a) Time sharing OS (b) Distributed OS
(c) Real-time OS (d) Single-user OS

4 _______ operating system enables multiple users to work on the same computer at different times or simultaneously. CBSE SQP 2022-23

(a) multiprogramming
(b) multiprocessors
(c) multi-user
(d) multi-tasking

5 .... provides process and memory management services that allow two or more tasks, jobs or programs to run simultaneously.

(a) Multi-tasking (b) Multi-threading
(c) Multi-processing (d) Multi-computing

6 The simultaneous processing of two or more programs by multiple processors is

(a) multi-programming (b) multi-tasking
(c) time sharing (d) multi-processing

7 **Linux is which type of operating system?**
(a) Open-Source (b) Microsoft
(c) Windows (d) Mac

8 **A __________ operating system is a computing environment that reacts to input within a specific period of time.** CBSE SQP 2021-22 Term I
(a) Single User (b) Multi-User
(c) Real Time (d) Distribute

9 **GUI stands for**
(a) Graphical User Interface
(b) Graphical Used Interface
(c) Great User Interface
(d) None of the above

10 **GUI is used as an interface between**
(a) hardware and software (b) man and machine
(c) software and user (d) None of these

11 **It uses pictures (called icons) and menus displayed on the screen to send commands to the computer system.**
(a) Command-based user interface
(b) GUI
(c) System Utility
(d) API

12 **The 'desktop' of a computer refers to**
(a) the visible screen (b) the area around the monitor
(c) the top of the mouse pad (d) the inside of a folder

13 **A blinking indicator that shows you where your next action will happen, is**
(a) CPU (b) cursor (c) toolbar (d) boot

14 **A computer automatically runs a basic program called .... as soon as it is switched ON or the power button is pushed ON.** CBSE 2021-22 Term I
(a) BIOS (Basic Input/Output System)
(b) IOS (Input/Output System)
(c) BOSS (Basic On System Startup)
(d) POS (Power On System)

15 **Which software is a series of graphical user interface operating systems developed by Microsoft?**
(a) Mac OS (b) MS-Windows
(c) Linux (d) Solaris

16 **............ is a horizontal bar present at bottom of the window 7 desktop.** CBSE 2023
(a) Status bar (b) Menu bar
(c) Task bar (d) Recycle bin

17 **In a multi-user environment, why is it important to log out of a computer properly?** Competency Based Que.
(a) To prevent unauthorized access
(b) To avoid using up more disk space
(c) To speed up the startup process
(d) To improve internet connectivity

18 **You are working on a document, and the computer suddenly shuts down. What is the best strategy to prevent losing work in the future?** Competency Based Que.
(a) Increase the brightness of the monitor
(b) Turn off the computer's sleep mode
(c) Save the document frequently and enable auto-save
(d) Keep the document open at all times

19 **You are trying to shut down your computer, but a program isn't responding. What should you do?** Competency Based Que.
(a) Use Task Manager to end the unresponsive task before shutting down
(b) Unplug the computer
(c) Press the Power button until the computer turns off
(d) Close the laptop lid

20 **Indian distribution of GNU/Linux based on Debian is called**
(a) GNU/Linux (b) Indian Linux
(c) BOSS Linux (d) Indian GNU Linux

21 **An operating system in which commands can be entered by clicking/double clicking/right-clicking a mouse is** CBSE SQP 2021-22 Term I
(a) GUI-based (b) CUI-based
(c) TUI-based (d) AI-based

22 **Which one of the following is an example of Operating System?** CBSE SQP 2021-22 Term I
(a) Microsoft Word (b) Microsoft Windows
(c) Microsoft Excel (d) Microsoft Access

Answers

1. (a)	2. (b)	3. (a)	4. (c)	5. (a)
6. (d)	7. (a)	8. (c)	9. (a)	10. (c)
11. (b)	12. (a)	13. (b)	14. (a)	15. (b)
16. (c)	17. (a)	18. (c)	19. (a)	20. (c)
21. (a)	22. (b)			

Very Short Answer Type Questions

1 **Name any three operating systems.**
Ans. Linux, Windows, Unix.

2 **What is an operating system?**
Ans. Operating system is a system software that performs all the basic tasks of a computer system. It works like an interface between the user and the computer hardware resources.

3 **What is the difference between left and right click on a mouse?**
Ans. Left click is used to select items or open files, while right click is used to open a context menu with additional options related to the selected item.

4 What is the scroll wheel on the mouse used for?

Ans. Mouse scroll wheel is used to quickly move through pages or documents by scrolling up and down.

5 Why is it important to shut down a computer properly?

Ans. Proper shutdown insures that all files are saved, programs are closed correctly and the system hardware is protected from potential damage.

6 What is the difference between Shut Down and Restart on a computer?

Ans. "Shut Down" option turns off the computer completely while "Restart" option turns the computer off then automatically powers it back on.

7 What is the function of Esc (Escape) key?

Ans. The "Esc" key is used to close a current task or window.

8 What is a real-time operating system?

Ans. A real-time operating system is used to process data within a strict time limit, often used in missile launching systems and online exams.

9 What is the function of mobile operating system?

Ans. A mobile operating system is designed especially for mobile devices such as smartphones and tablets to manage hardware and software resources.

10 Name two common type of user interfaces?

Ans. 1. Graphical user interface (GUI)
2. Character user interface (CUI)

11 Explain the role of an operating system in a computer. How does it impact the computer's performance and usability? **Competency Based Que.**

Ans. The operating system (OS) is an important software that manages a computer's hardware and software resources. It works as an interface between the user and the computer hardware, which enables the users to interact with the system through a user-friendly environment. The operating system impacts the computer's performance by managing system resources effectively and enhances usability by providing a more user-friendly environment.

12 A beginner is more likely to prefer a GUI over a CUI. What do you think in this case? **Competency Based Que.**

Ans. A beginner prefers a GUI because it provides a more interactive and visual approach, which doesn't require memorizing commands, making it easier to learn and navigate.

13 You want to install new software on your computer. What role does the operating system play in this process? **Competency Based Que.**

Ans. The operating system controls the installation by allocating necessary resources, checking compatibility, and ensuring the software integrates correctly with existing hardware and other applications.

14 A team is developing a new software application. Why is it important for them to consider the different operating systems (e.g., Windows, Linux, macOS) that users may have? How does this affect the design and functionality of the application? **Competency Based Que.**

Ans. Considering different operating systems is important because each OS has unique features, file systems, and user interfaces. This affects design by requiring compatibility and potential modifications to the application's codebase.

Session 2 | Performing Basic File Operations

Storing information on your computer is similar to storing your dresses in a wardrobe in an organised manner.

3.1 Files and Folders

Everything you store on your computer is stored in the form of a **file**. File system is a way in which you give name to a file, store it and retrieve it. Files can be separately placed into groups, called **folders/directories**. Each folder can contain related files or sub-folders. This allows easy accessibility of files. Different types of files, store different data.

Each file given a file extension that identifies the file type.

File	Extension
Open Document Text	.odt
Open Document Database	.odb
Open Document Spreadsheet	.ods
Music	.mp3, .wav, etc.
Picture or Image	.png, .jpg, etc.
Open Document Presentation	.odp
Open Document Drawing	.odg
HTML Document	.html or .htm
XML Document	.xml
Portable Document Format	.pdf
Notepad	.txt

3.2 Creating and Managing Files and Folders

Creating a Folder

The steps to create a new folder are as follows

1. Double click on This PC.
2. Select the drive in which you want to create a new folder.
3. Window will open up showing files and folders in Local Disk.
4. Click New Folder on the toolbar.

Or Right click anywhere in the blank area.

A drop-down menu will appear. Select New → Folder.

5. A new folder is created with name New Folder highlighted.
6. Type a name for the folder.

Creating a File

To create a new file, steps are as follows:

1. Right-click anywhere in the blank area.
2. A drop down menu will appear. In the drop down menu, click New and select the type of the file you want to create.

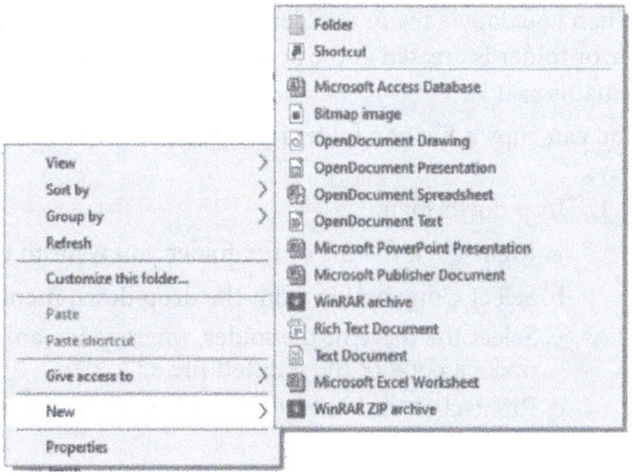

Renaming Folders and Files

To rename a file or a folder, the steps are as follows:

1. Right-click the file or the folder.
2. From the drop down menu, select Rename option.

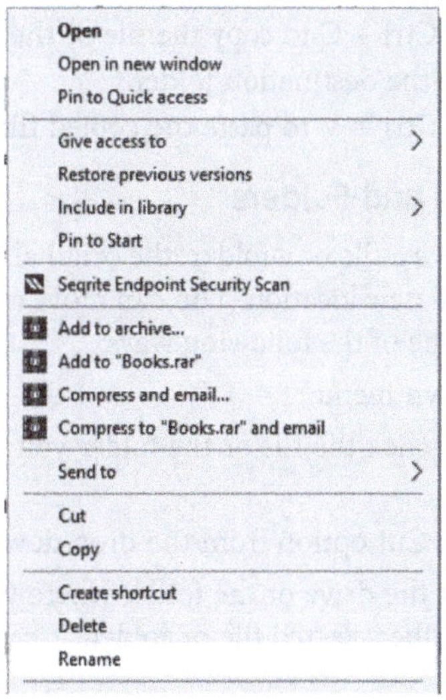

3. Type the new name or edit the existing name and press the Enter key.

Or

Just select the file/folder and press Function key F2.

Deleting Files or Folders

To delete a file or a folder, steps are as follows:

1. Click the file or the folder.
2. Press the Delete key.

Or

Right-click and select Delete option from the drop down menu.

Copying Files and Folders

When you copy a file or a folder, duplicate of the original file or folder is created at the new location, the original remains as it is.

You can copy a file or a folder in any one of the following ways:

1. Drop down menu:
   a. Right-click the file or the folder you want to copy.
   b. Select Copy option from the drop down menu.
   c. Select the drive or the folder, where you want to make a copy of the selected file or folder.
   d. Right-click and select Paste option from the drop down menu.
2. Drag and Drop method:
   To copy a file or a folder, hold down the Ctrl key while dragging it to the new location.
3. Using Keyboard:
   a. Select the file or the folder.
   b. Press Ctrl + C to copy the file or the folder.
   c. Open the destination folder.
   d. Press Ctrl + V to paste the copied file.

Moving Files and Folders

When you move a file or a folder, the original file or folder is moved to the new location. You can move a file or a folder in any one of the following ways:

1. Drop down menu:
   a. Right-click the file or the folder you want to move.
   b. Select Cut option from the drop down menu.
   c. Select the drive or the folder where you want to move the selected file or folder.
   d. Right-click and select Paste option from the drop down menu.
2. Drag and Drop method:
   To move a file or a folder, select the file and drag it to a new location.
3. Using Keyboard:
   a. Select the file or the folder.
   b. Press Ctrl + X to cut the file or the folder.
   c. Open the destination folder.
   d. Press Ctrl + V to paste the cutted file.

Permanently Delete Files

You can permanently delete the contents of the Recycle Bin in any one of the following ways:

Right-click the Recycle Bin icon and then click Empty Recycle Bin.

Or

1. Double-click the Recycle Bin icon.
2. The Recycle Bin window will appear.
3. Click Empty the Recycle Bin.

Restore Files/Folder from Recycle Bin Window

To recover a file from the Recycle Bin, right-click the file, and then click Restore.

Or

Select the file and click Restore this item option from the toolbar.

Summary

Everything you store on your computer is stored in the form of a file.

Folders are the organizational units used to group and manage related files.

File Extensions indicate the file type and determine which application can open it (e.g., .txt, .docx, .jpg).

Copying a file refers to creating a duplicate of a file or folder in a new location while keeping the original intact.

Moving a file means relocating a file or folder from one location to another.

Temporary files are created when you are running computer programs.

Permanently delete the contents of the recycle bin by clicking on the "Empty Recycle Bin."

ACTIVITY Time

ACTIVITY 1

Creating a folder

Material required

Pen, notebook, computer

Procedure

- Form groups depending on the number of computers available. Each member of the group creates a new folder. Others can watch and give feedback on what was done correctly and what can be improved.
- Open a text editor in Ubuntu or Notepad in Windows
- Create a 2 folders Demo1 and Test1
- Now delete the folder Test1

Each group can study the following shortcut commands together.

Ctrl+Z — Undo	Ctrl+C — Copy
Ctrl+Y — Redo	Ctrl+V — Paste
Ctrl+A — Select All	Ctrl+P — Print
Ctrl+X — Cut	Ctrl+S — Save

- The first group asks the other groups a question (e.g. what does Ctrl+Z do? (Answer is Undo) or what is the shortcut for Copy (Ctrl+C). Whichever group answers correctly gets one point otherwise the next group answers and so on. Whichever group gets most points, wins.

NCERT FOLDER

Complete Explanations of all NCERT's Questions

A. Multiple Choice Questions

Q.1 Which one of the following shortcut keys is used to paste a file?

(a) Ctrl + C
(b) Ctrl + P
(c) Ctrl + V
(d) Ctrl + X

Q.2 Which of the following is a valid file extension for Notepad file?

(a) .jpg
(b) .doc
(c) .text
(d) .txt

Q.3 What keys do you use to copy something?

(a) Ctrl+X
(b) Ctrl+C
(c) Ctrl+Z
(d) Ctrl+Y

Answers

1. (c) 2. (d) 3. (b)

B. Subjective Questions

Q.4 How is a computer file system similar to our physical file system in a school?

Ans. Both computer file systems and physical file systems in schools organize and store information:

Organization: They both use a hierarchical structure to organize files or documents into folders or categories.

Storage: Both systems allocate space to store data efficiently, whether it's on a computer's storage drive or in physical filing cabinets.

Access: Users can retrieve and modify files or documents stored in both systems as needed.

Navigation: They both allow users to navigate through the system to locate specific files or documents quickly.

Q.5 What are the steps you will perform to save a text file in ubuntu/windows?

Ans. To save a new file, steps are as follows:

1. Click on File → Save or Save As.
2. Choose a location to save the file.
3. Enter a file name then click on Save.

EXAM PATTERN EXERCISE

Including Competency Based Questions

Multiple Choice Questions

1 A .... is a collection of information saved as a unit.

(a) Folder (b) File
(c) Path (d) File extension

2 What is a file?

(a) A file is a section of main storage used to store data
(b) A file is a collection of information that has been given a name and have an extension
(c) A file is the part of a program that is used to describe what the program should do
(d) A file can be saved only in CDs.

3 Files are organized after storing in

(a) archives (b) folders
(c) indices (d) lists

4 A named area on a disk that is used to store related sub folders and files is called as a...........

(a) desktop (b) folder
(c) menu (d) window

5 A .... is a location where a group of files can be stored in the computer. CBSE 2025

(a) folder (b) SMPS
(c) CMOS (d) UPS

6 In a file name what is the purpose of a file extension?

(a) To indicate the file's creation date
(b) To display the file's contents
(c) To define the file's size
(d) To identify the file type and associated application

7 By which of the following operations you can delete a file permanently from the computer?

(a) By emptying the Recycle Bin
(b) By renaming the file
(c) By moving the file to the Recycle Bin
(d) By pressing "Delete" key on the file

8 Which of the following options allows you to create a new folder in Windows File Explorer?

(a) Select "Open" from the menu
(b) Press Ctrl + F
(c) Right-click and select "New Folder"
(d) Double-click on the desktop

9 It is a picture or graphic representation of an application or a file.

(a) Icon
(b) Taskbar
(c) Status bar
(d) Desktop

10 To search for an application, you can also open the

(a) title bar (b) file menu
(c) start menu (d) task bar

11 The filename and filename extension are separated by a .... CBSE 2024

(a) Dollar ($) (b) Dot (.)
(c) Underscore (_) (d) Hash (#)

12 To remove the files of temporary folder, we type ________ in Run dialog box after pressing "Windows button + R" on the keyboard. CBSE SQP 2022-23

(a) #temp# (b) %temp%
(c) $temp% (d) &temp&

13 What happens when you copy a file and paste it into another folder?

(a) The file is moved to the new folder and removed from the original location.
(b) A duplicate of the file is created in the new location.
(c) The file is compressed.
(d) The file is automatically deleted after 24 hours.

14 You have just completed a research report and need to save it on your computer. Where should you save your research report to ensure it is easy to find later? Competency Based Que.

(a) Save it with the default name provided by the computer.
(b) Save it in a generic folder called "Documents."
(c) Save it in a specifically named folder like "My-Reports" and use a descriptive file name like "History_Report_2024.docx."
(d) Save it on the desktop with a random name.

15 You have a folder named "myproject" and want to create a new folder inside it for your current assignment. Which of the following steps should you take to accomplish this? Competency Based Que.

(a) Right-click on the "myproject" folder and select "Delete."
(b) Double-click on the "myproject" folder and click "New Folder" from the ribbon.
(c) Open the "myproject" folder, press "Ctrl + C," and then press "Ctrl + V."
(d) Drag the "myproject" folder to the desktop.

16 You have several files with the same name in different folders. How can you differentiate them when saving a new file? Competency Based Que.

(a) Always overwrite the existing file.
(b) Use a different file extension.
(c) Include unique identifiers in the file name, such as dates or version numbers.
(d) Save all files in the same folder.

Answers

1. (b)	2. (b)	3. (b)	4. (b)	5. (a)
6. (d)	7. (a)	8. (c)	9. (a)	10. (c)
11. (b)	12. (b)	13. (b)	14. (c)	15. (b)
16. (c)				

Very Short Answer Type Questions

1 How can you delete a folder?

Ans. *Step 1.* Click on the folder

Step 2. Press the Delete Key

2 Name the set of commands to move a folder from one location to another.

Ans. Cut, Paste

3 What is the possible cause of slowing down of computer?

Ans. A large number of files are stored on the computer. These files can be disorganized and fragmented and may result in slowing down of the computer.

4 Why we create folders on a computer?

Ans. The purpose of creating folders on a computer is to organize and group related files together, making it easier to manage and locate them.

5 Differentiate between files and folders. CBSE 2023

Ans. A file is a single document or piece of data, such as a text document or image whereas a folder is a container used to organize multiple files and other folders.

6 What steps are involved in copying a file from one folder to another?

Ans. To copy a file, right-click on the file and select "Copy option," navigate to the destination folder, right-click inside the folder, and select "Paste option."

7 Explain how you can organize files within a folder for better management.

Ans. You can organize files within a folder by creating multiple subfolders, naming files descriptively, and sorting files by type, date, or size. You can also use tags or labels for easier identification.

8 State the difference between moving a file and copying a file?

Ans. Moving a file transfers it from one location to another, removing it from the original place.

Copying a file creates a duplicate in the new location while leaving the original file unchanged.

9 How would you create a new text document and ensure that the file is saved with a meaningful name? Explain why it is important to use clear naming conventions when saving files.

Ans. To create a new text document, you can right-click on the desktop or within a folder, select "New" from the context menu, and then choose "Text Document." You can name the file by typing a descriptive title that reflects its content. Using clear naming conventions is important because it helps you quickly identify and access the file later, prevents confusion, and promotes organization.

10 If you have a large number of files and folders on your desktop, and it's becoming hard to find what you need, what steps would you take to improve your organizational system?

Ans. I would start by categorizing files into broader folders, then create subfolders for specific subjects or projects. I would also consider renaming files for clarity and deleting anything unnecessary.

11 What is a shortcut menu? What is its significance?

Ans. A shortcut menu is a menu that shows the most frequently used commands for a selected item (file, folder or anything else). It is also called context-sensitive menu. without having to go here and there. The shortcut menu is useful in the sense that all related commands are available at one platform without having to go here and there. We can open shortcut menu by right-clicking at a selected item.

12 What is the significance of Recycle Bin ?

Ans. Recycle Bin is the place that holds the deleted files temporarily. If one wants to undelete a file, then it may be restored from recycle bin. However, if item are deleted from the recycle bin itself, then all of its items in it are permanently deleted and cannot be restored later.

13 What is the difference between copying and moving files and folders?

Ans. When a file or folder is copied, then it is duplicated at the target location. That is, the file or folder remains at the original location as well as it is copied at the target location. When a file or folder is moved, then it is removed from the original location and placed at the target location.

14 What happens when files and folders are deleted in Windows? Is it possible to retrieve deleted objects later ? If so, how?

Ans. When files and folders are deleted from a hard disk/Windows, they are moved into recycle bin. The files or folders removed from the pen drives are deleted permanently.

Yes, the deleted objects in recycle bin can be restored. To do so, firstly they are to be selected and then Restore command is clicked at the File menu of Recycle Bin.

15 What is the significance of Task bar ?

Ans. The taskbar is a bar that shows information about all the open windows. This can also be used to open programs (through start button available on it) and switch between open windows.

Session 3 | Computer Care and Maintenance

3.1 Importance and Need of Care and Maintenance of Computer

Computer systems require maintenance, so that the system works efficiently. Poor maintenance may lead to system failure. Regular care and maintenance may help you detect any issues at an early stage and keep it functioning well.

Since, a lot of important data is stored in the computer, it is necessary to have regular maintenance of the computer to be done. Computer virus, malware, and other harmful software can cause damage to the working of the computer.

A large number of files are stored on the computer. These files can be disorganised and fragmented and may result in slowing down of the computer.

Regular maintenance of the system includes installing updates, security, taking backups, scans, etc.

Both internal and external parts of the computer system should be taken care of

1. Keep the computer dust free.
2. Do not eat or drink while working on the computer.
3. To keep the keyboard clean, make sure your hands are clean before using it.
4. CDs and DVDs should be handled carefully, so that it does not get any scratches.
5. Keep keyboard covered when not in use.

3.2 Cleaning the Computer Components

Computer components need proper care to last longer. Preventive maintenance increases the life of the components.

For example, a cable is damaged, but still working. It should be replaced or repaired immediately to prevent any other damage.

General precautions to be taken while cleaning the computer components are:

- Always Power Off the computer system before cleaning.
- Never spray cleaning fluid directly on the components of the computer. First spray the liquid on the cloth and then wipe the component.
- Do not allow the cleaning liquid to drip near the circuit board.
- Preferably use anti-static wrist band which helps to prevent building up of static electricity near electronic device.

Let's discuss how to clean common peripheral devices of computer

Computer Monitor

To clean the computer monitor, you can use a soft lint-free cloth, like cotton and water or special cleaning liquid. You should not spray water or cleaning liquid directly on the computer monitor as it may run through the seams. Spray water or cleaning liquid on the cloth and gently wipe the computer monitor.

Keyboard

Dirt and dust can cause damage to the keyboard. Keys of the keyboard may not function properly, if dirt enters the keys. You should always clean the keyboard periodically by holding upside down and shaking it.

You can also clean it by blowing it with compressed air. After this, use a damp lint-free cloth to clean top of the keys. You should never spray any liquid cleaner or water directly on the keys of the keyboard.

Optical Mouse

You can clean the bottom of the optical mouse with a clean lint-free cloth. Lens area can be cleaned by blowing air or cotton swab.

Digital Camera

Never touch the lens of the camera. To remove the dust, you can use soft lens brush or wipe with a soft dry cloth. For stubborn dust, you can use special fluid for lens cleaning which should be first pot on the tissue and then wipe the lens. Never put the fluid directly on the lens.

CDs and DVDs

Keep CD/DVD in proper case to prevent damage. If there is some dirt on the CD or DVD, it may not work at all. Finger prints and dirt can be removed by lightly rubbing with a clean lint-free cotton cloth.

If the dirt is hard to remove, you can use special cleaning fluid. Put the drop of fluid on a swab of cotton and gently rub on the media.

3.3 Preparing a Maintenance Schedule

Some of the maintenance activities are:

- keep the components of the computer, like keyboard, mouse, monitor, etc. clean
- replace hardware that is not functioning properly
- keep food items away from the computer
- cables and chords should not be messed up
- removing unauthorized software from the computer
- take regular backups of the data
- ensure backups are working properly by periodically restoring or checking of data. You should use external hard drive for backup of data on your computer.
- update your operating system
- run anti-virus periodically
- keep anti-virus software up to date
- do not overcharge the batteries
- do not block the vents
- always shut down the computer properly
- A regular disk defragmentation should be done to remove all unnecessary information that slows down the computer. Disk defragmentation done at regular intervals helps the disc space to be used at an optimal level.

Take regular backup of the data on your computer. In case the data is lost due to any reason, system failure, virus attack, etc. , you can easily retrieve your data using backup files till your last update.

Summary

Computer systems require maintenance, so that the system works efficiently. Poor maintenance may lead to system failure.

System should be upgraded with new updates that were not there at the time of purchase, like, increasing RAM, to improve the performance.

Regularly back up important files and data to external drives or cloud storage to prevent data loss from hardware failure or other issues.

Computer's peripheral devices need proper care and maintenance to last longer.

NCERT FOLDER

Complete Explanations of all NCERT's Questions

A. Multiple Choice Questions

Q.1 What happens if you leave a device plugged in even after it is charged 100%?

(a) It can break.
(b) It can stop functioning.
(c) It can over-heat.
(d) Data can get corrupt.

Q.2 How can an anti-virus protect your device?

(a) It can protect it from over-heating.
(b) It can increase its performance.
(c) It can prevent data from getting corrupt.
(d) It can backup data.

Q.3 Which option is not required to keep a device cool?

(a) Keep the device unplugged when in use.
(b) Do not cover a laptop with a blanket.
(c) Make sure computer's CPU fan is working.
(d) Avoid leaving the device in the sun.

Q.4 Which of the following is essential for maintaining keyboard?

(a) Turn the keyboard upside down and shake it to remove foreign material.
(b) Blow dust and other particles with help of a blower.
(c) Use a very dilute combination of soap and water applied with a non-abrasive cloth to remove stains from the keycaps.
(d) All of the above.

Answers

1. (c) **2.** (c) **3.** (a) **4.** (d)

B. Subjective Questions

Q.1 Explain how to clean a computer on a daily basis.

Ans. (a) **Dust Removal:** Use a soft, dry microfiber cloth or compressed air to gently remove dust from the exterior surfaces.

(b) **Keyboard and Mouse**: Use compressed air to blow out dust and debris from between the keys and mouse crevices.

(c) **Monitor**: Clean the monitor screen with a lightly dampened microfiber cloth.

(d) **Cable Management**: Organize and untangle cables to prevent hazards and improve airflow.

(e) **Ventilation**: Ensure vents and air intake/exhaust ports are clear of dust using compressed air.

(f) **Desktop Organization**: Remove clutter from the desktop and organize files.

Q.2 How can you increase the performance of a computer?

Ans. Here are some ways to increase the performance of a computer in short:

(a) **Upgrade Hardware**: Increase RAM, upgrade to a solid-state drive (SSD), or install a faster processor.

(b) **Optimize Software**: Remove unnecessary startup programs, update drivers, and keep the operating system and software up to date.

(c) **Manage Storage**: Free up disk space by deleting unnecessary files and programs, and defragment the hard drive (if not using an SSD).

(d) **Adjust Power Settings**: Optimize power settings to balance performance and energy efficiency.

(e) **Cooling System**: Ensure proper ventilation and cooling to prevent overheating, which can degrade performance.

(f) **Use Antivirus Software**: Keep the system protected from malware and viruses that can slow down performance.

EXAM PATTERN EXERCISE

Including Competency Based Questions

Multiple Choice Questions

1 What is a recommended practice to protect your computer from dust?

(a) Use a soft cloth to clean the exterior and ensure the computer is placed in a clean, dust-free area.
(b) Use a vacuum cleaner directly on the computer's internal components.
(c) Always keep the computer covered up
(d) Open the computer case and leave it open.

2 What should you do to prevent your computer from overheating?

(a) Overclock the CPU to improve performance.
(b) Ensure that the computer's cooling fans are clean and functioning properly and keep vents unobstructed.
(c) Place the computer on a soft surface like a bed.
(d) Block all the ventilation openings with paper or tape.

3 Why is it important to use antivirus software on your computer?

(a) To increase the computer's processing speed.
(b) To make your computer look visually appealing.
(c) To add more storage space to your hard drive.
(d) To protect your computer from malware, viruses, and other security threats.

4 Which of the following should you avoid doing to prevent physical damage to your computer?

(a) Plugging and unplugging devices carefully.
(b) Using the protecting case for the computer.
(c) Dropping or jostling the computer frequently.
(d) Keeping drinks and food away from the computer.

5 What is the best way to manage your computer's storage space?

(a) Store all files on the desktop for easy access.
(b) Regularly delete unnecessary files and use disk cleanup tools to manage space.
(c) Keep all files in a single folder.
(d) Only use external storage for all files.

6 Which of the following is an effective method for maintaining a computer's performance over time?

(a) Regularly defragmenting the hard drive.
(b) Avoiding the use of antivirus software.
(c) Increasing the screen brightness for better performance.
(d) Keeping all programs running simultaneously to improve speed.

7 What is a good practice for maintaining your computer's battery health?

(a) Avoid deep discharges and over charges
(b) Keep it plugged in all the time
(c) Regularly clean the battery contacts with a dry cloth
(d) Use the computer while it's charging

8 **If your computer starts making unusual noises, what should you do?**
(a) Increase the fan speed (b) Ignore the noises
(c) Restart the computer
(d) Investigate the source of noises, and consult a technician if necessary

9 **What is the purpose of regularly performing a system backup?**
(a) To speed up the computer system
(b) To protect and restore data in case of hardware failure or data loss
(c) To make more storage space
(d) To update the operating system

10 **The cleaning of software installed in the computer cannot be achieved by ________.** CBSE SQP 2020-21
(a) Disk cleanup (b) backup
(c) Cleaning CPU cabinet
(d) Installing antivirus software

11 **During routine maintenance, you discover that a computer's hard drive is nearly full. What is the most effective action you can take to manage disk space?** Competency Based Que.
(a) Increase the size of the hard drive
(b) Remove unnecessary files and programs, and use disk cleanup tools
(c) Upgrade to a new operating system
(d) Change the computer's power settings

12 **Karan lives at a hostel in Shimla. He calls his mother who lives in Delhi, to get her approval for the robotics class which is going to start in his school next week onwards. However, due to disruption in the phone line, his mother could not understand and reply to him. He got very upset. Which another medium can he use to get immediate approval of his mother?** CBSE SQP 2020-21, Competency Based Que.
(a) E-mail (b) Letter
(c) Message through Friend (d) Fax

13 **Neha is receiving several mails from companies who are advertising a product or trying to attract her to their websites. Such type of mails are called ....** CBSE 2021-22 Term I, Competency Based Que.
(a) advertising mails (b) bulk mails
(c) spam mails (d) labelled mails

14 **Kartik's Computer was running very slow, hangs and often restarts. He is very confused and tensed as he was working on a very important assignment. Kartik's friend gave him the following suggestions. Identify who has given him a genuine suggestion.** CBSE SQP 2023-24, Competency Based Que.
(a) Radha : Restart your machine
(b) Ishan : Install reliable antivirus software and update
(c) Amar : Don't use Pendrive
(d) Sam : Install free antivirus from net

Answers

1. (a)	2. (b)	3. (d)	4. (c)	5. (b)
6. (a)	7. (c)	8. (d)	9. (b)	10. (c)
11. (b)	12. (a)	13. (c)	14. (b)	

Very Short Answer Type Questions

1 **What steps should you take if you accidentally spill liquid on your laptop?**
Ans. Turn OFF the laptop immediately, disconnect it from power, remove the battery if possible, and seek professional help.

2 **Why we use disk cleanup tools on a computer?**
Ans. We use disk cleanup tools to remove temporary files and free up disk space for improving overall performance.

3 **How can you protect your computer from viruses and malware?**
Ans. We can protect our computers from viruses and malware by using and updating antivirus software regularly, and avoid downloading suspicious files.

4 **How can regular software updates contribute to the maintenance of your computer?**
Ans. Regular software updates help fix security vulnerabilities, improve system stability, and enhance performance by providing bug fixes and new features.

5 **Explain the role of antivirus software in computer maintenance and why it is important for protecting your system.**
Ans. Antivirus software detects, prevents, and removes malware and viruses that can compromise your system's security and performance. It is important for protecting against cyber threats and ensuring that the system runs smoothly.

6 **How can you manage the storage space on your computer effectively?**
Ans. We can manage the storage space on our computer effectively by regularly deleting unused files, uninstall unused programs, use disk cleanup tools, and consider upgrading to a larger storage drive if needed.

7 **How can you ensure that your computer's peripheral devices such as printer, mouse, and keyboard are maintained properly?**
Ans. Keep them clean, update their drivers regularly, and check for any signs of damage.
Regularly perform maintenance tasks according to the manufacturer's instructions.

8 **Very often we hear about spam mails. Explain what are spam mails, and what should be done with such mails?** CBSE 2024
Ans. Spam mails are unsolicited emails, often used for advertising or scams. To handle them, mark as spam, avoid opening, and delete without clicking any links.

9 What do you mean by Disk Defragmentation? **CBSE SQP 2022-23**

Ans. Disk defragmentation refers to organizing scattered data on a hard drive. It store fragmented files in continuous blocks by rearranging them, improving the computer's speed and performance.

10 What are the measures to increase the performance of a computer system? **CBSE SQP 2020-21**

Ans. Measures to improve computer system's performance include updating software, increasing RAM, using disk cleanup tools, and limiting background programs.

11 If a user complains about frequent pop-up ads and potential malware on their computer, how would you address the situation and ensure that the computer is secure?

Ans. Run a full system scan with updated antivirus and anti-malware software to detect and remove any threats. Remove any suspicious or unwanted browser extensions and toolbars.

Clear browser caches and cookies. Review and adjust browser settings to block pop-ups. Educate the user on safe browsing habits and avoid downloading untrusted software.

12 What regular maintenance tasks should be performed to keep a computer running smoothly?

Ans. Regular maintenance tasks include updating software, running antivirus scans, clearing cache and temporary files, defragmenting the hard drive, and checking for system updates.

Session 4 | Computer Security and Privacy

3.1 Protecting Computer Against Viruses

A computer virus is a software program that attaches itself to other programs and alters their behavior. A virus may or may not be destructive. Some viruses erase data or corrupt programs on the computer. VIRUS is an acronym for **Vital Information Resources Under Seize.**

When a virus enters a computer system, it makes copies of itself and carries out the harmful tasks that it is programmed for. Some viruses get activated at a certain date and time. Viruses also attach to the files stored on the computer or the storage media and harm these files.

A computer virus can infect only the software and not the hardware, but computer may stop working.

A computer can get infected with virus in any of the following ways:

- infected files
- infected pen drives
- infected CD-ROMs/DVD-ROMs
- through infected file attachment of e-mails

A computer virus cannot do the following:

- it cannot infect files on CD or DVD, if they are closed for writing.
- it cannot infect computer hardware like, keyboard, mouse, etc.

Some of the common signs of a virus attack are:

- computer runs very slow
- there is change in the file size
- computer often stops responding
- there is an increase in number of files (unusual)
- unusual error message appears on the screen
- computer restarts on its own

Scanning and Cleaning Viruses and Removing Spam Files, Temporary Files and folders

The following points should be kept in mind to prevent virus infection:

- install and use anti-virus software
- keep anti-virus software updated
- scan all the files that you download from the Internet
- do not open e-mails of an unknown person/sender
- don't allow any untrustworthy person to use your system
- never use unknown pen drive/CD on your computer
- never click on the window that pop-up when you are surfing the Internet

3.2 Preparing Computer Against Virus

To prevent our computer from being infected with virus, we should install anti-virus software, run it periodically and keep it updated, so that it can scan and remove new viruses.

Anti-virus software is a program designed to detect and remove malicious programs from the computer.

Some examples of anti-virus software are McAfee Virus Scan, Norton Anti-virus, Microsoft Security Essentials, and Quick Heal.

For an anti-virus program to be effective:

- it needs to run in the background at all times.
- keep the anti-virus software updated, so that it can recognize new viruses.
- run full disk scans periodically.

3.3 Scanning and Cleaning Virus

Let us discuss how to use Quick Heal Total Security to scan the computer system.

1. Click Start → All Programs → Quick Heal → Total Security Quick Heal

   Or

   Double-click the Quick Heal Anti-virus icon on the desktop.
2. The main window of Quick heal Total Security will open up.

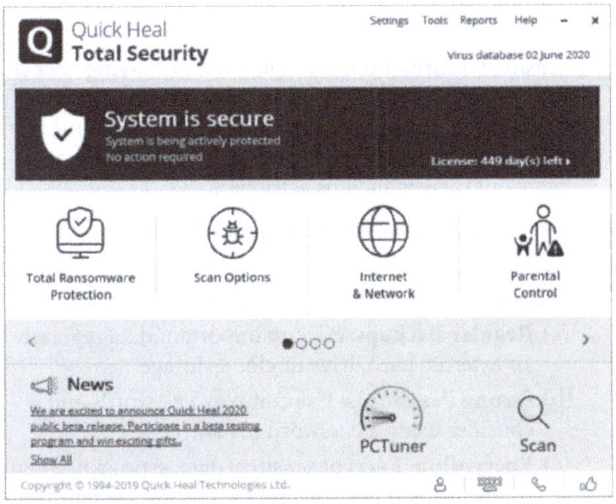

To perform full system scan,

1. Click Scan → Full System Scan.
2. The scan process will begin.
3. On completion of the scan, the scan statistics and reports are provided.
4. Click Close.

   Other anti-viruses, like, Norton Anti-virus, McAfee, etc. have almost the same method to scan full computer system for viruses and remove them.

3.4 Removing SPAM from your Computer

Spam emails are unwanted, unsolicited email messages sent in bulk. But they're not just annoying; spam emails can also contain dangerous links or lead to other malicious threats.

By following these steps, you can effectively remove spam from your computer

- **Enable Spam Filters** Activate built-in spam filters in your email settings.
- **Delete Unwanted Emails** Regularly delete suspicious emails or those from unknown senders.
- **Unsubscribe** Opt-out from unwanted mailing lists.
- **Block Senders** Block known spammers or persistent unwanted senders.
- **Use Security Software** Install and regularly update antivirus and anti-malware software.
- **Avoid Clicking Suspicious Links** Refrain from clicking on links in suspicious emails.
- **Clear Browser Data** Periodically clear browser cache and cookies to remove tracking data.

Removing Temporary Files

Temporary files are created when you are running computer programs. Microsoft Windows and Windows programs often create a .TMP file as a temporary file. Temporary files are also created by web browsers to store your web browser history. These temp files take up a large amount of disk space, so it should be removed to clear space.

The steps to remove temporary files are as follows:

1. Double-click This PC on the desktop.
2. This PC window will open.
3. Right-click Local Disk C: and select Properties option from the drop down menu.
4. The Properties window will appear. Click on Disk Cleanup.
5. The Disk Cleanup for C: window will appear.
6. Click the Check box next to Temporary Files, Temporary Internet files, etc. that you want to delete.
7. Click OK. A confirmation message will appear.

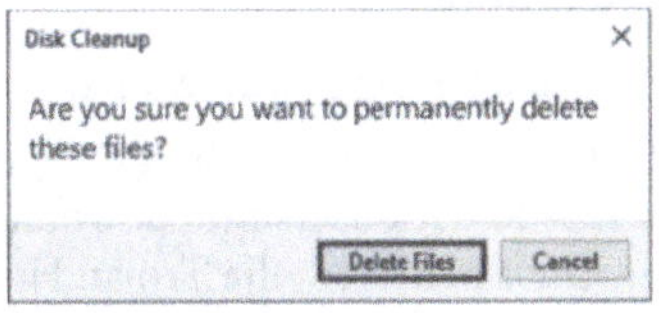

8. Click on Delete Files.
9. Windows will delete all the temporary files from the computer.

Removing Files of Temporary Folder

The steps to remove files of temporary folder are as follows:

1. Press Windows button + R on the keyboard.
2. The Run dialog box will appear.
3. Type %temp% and click on OK.
4. The Temp folder will open.
5. Click Ctrl + A to select all the files in the folder. Press Delete key.
6. A message box will appear. Click Yes to confirm.
7. All the files in the Temp folder will be deleted. Some files which are related to current open files may not get deleted. You can ignore those files and close the pop-up window.

Summary

A computer virus is a software program that attaches itself to other programs and alters their behaviour.

Computer security and privacy deals with the techniques used to prevent loss of data.

Temporary files created when you are running computer programs.

A computer firewall could be a programmable device or software that monitors and controls incoming and outgoing network traffic, based on user-defined security rules.

Key threats to computer system involves: hacking, phishing attacks, insider threats, data breaches etc.

NCERT FOLDER

Complete Explanations of all NCERT's Questions

A. Multiple Choice Questions

Q.1 What should you do to ensure secure online transactions?

(a) Lock your computer
(b) Give credit card or bank details only on safe websites
(c) Use anti-virus
(d) Do not use pirated software

Q.2 Which of the following trap small children into inappropriate relations?

(a) Online predators (b) Worms
(c) Trojan Horse (d) Anti-Virus

Q.3 What should a strong password consist of?

(a) Only letters
(b) Numbers and special characters
(c) Name of a person
(d) Letters, numbers and special characters

Answers

1. (b) 2. (a) 3. (d)

B. Subjective Questions

Q.1 Explain how Trojan Horse virus works.

Ans. A Trojan Horse virus disguises itself as legitimate software or files to trick users into downloading and executing it. Once activated, the Trojan Horse can perform various malicious actions, such as stealing sensitive information, damaging files, or giving hackers remote access to the infected computer. Unlike other types of malware, Trojans do not self-replicate but rely on social engineering tactics to infiltrate systems and carry out their malicious activities.

Q.2 List the various ways you can use to protect your data.

Ans. Here are various ways to protect your data in short:

(a) **Regular Backups**: Backup important data regularly to an external hard drive or cloud storage.
(b) **Strong Passwords**: Use complex passwords and consider using a password manager.
(c) **Encryption**: Encrypt sensitive data, especially when transmitting it over the internet or storing it on portable devices.
(d) **Update Software**: Keep your operating system, antivirus, and other software updated to patch security vulnerabilities.
(e) **Firewalls**: Use firewalls to monitor and control incoming and outgoing network traffic.
(f) **Secure Wi-Fi**: Secure your Wi-Fi network with a strong password and encryption to prevent unauthorized access.
(g) **Awareness Training**: Educate yourself and others about common cybersecurity threats and best practices.

EXAM PATTERN EXERCISE

Including Competency Based Questions

Multiple Choice Questions

1 __________ **are computer programs that can damage the data and software programs or steal the information stored on a computer.** CBSE 2023

(a) Spam (b) Viruses
(c) Junk mail (d) BIOS

2 Which of the following is the primary purpose of a firewall?

(a) To scan for malware (b) To block unauthorized access
(c) To encrypt data (d) To increase internet speed

3 Which of the following is not a strong password practice?

(a) Using a mix of upper and lower case letters
(b) Including special characters and numbers
(c) Using your name or date of birth
(d) Making the password at least 8 characters long

4 Which of the following is not a common type of malware?

(a) Worm (b) Firewall (c) Virus (d) Trojan

5 Computer privacy refers to____?

(a) Protecting computers from Malware and viruses
(b) Ensuring personal data and communications are secure and not accessible to unauthorized individuals
(c) Improving the performance of a computer system
(d) Preventing system from spam emails or other messages

6 Which of these actions can help protect your privacy online?

(a) Sharing your password with trusted friends
(b) Turning off automatic software updates
(c) Regularly clearing your browsing history and using strong passwords
(d) Posting personal details on social media

7 What do you understand by "ransomware"?

(a) A software used to harm computer
(b) A program that encrypts files and demands money for their release
(c) A method which provides secure communication
(d) A software used to monitor user activity

8 How can an anti-virus protect your device? CBSE SQP 2024-25

(a) It can protect it from over-heating
(b) It can increase its performance
(c) It can prevent data from getting corrupt
(d) It can backup data

9 Identify the measure to protect computer from threats and viruses: CBSE SQP 2021-22 Term I

(a) Sharing password with friends
(b) Allow anyone to use your device
(c) Use Antivirus
(d) Leave computer without logging out

10 Sakshi receives an email from an unknown source asking her to click on a link to claim a prize. The email looks official and is from a reputed company. What steps should Riya take to ensure her computer security and avoid falling victim to a potential cyber-attack? Competency Based Que.

(a) She should ignore the email and delete it.
(b) She should click the link to check if the prize is legitimate.
(c) She should respond to the email asking for more details.
(d) She should share the email with her friends to see if they've received the same.

11 Rajat often shares his vacation pictures on social media accounts with his friends. Which of the following actions can best protect his online privacy? Competency Based Que.

(a) Posting pictures with location tags enabled.
(b) Sharing his vacation details with everyone, including public followers.
(c) Making sure his privacy settings allow only friends to see his posts.
(d) Accepting all friend requests from unknown people to increase his follower count.

12 One of your coworker frequently uses the same password across multiple accounts. How would you address this security risk? Competency Based Que.

(a) Encourage them to keep using the same password for convenience
(b) Suggest they create unique passwords for different accounts and use a password manager
(c) Tell them that it doesn't really matter if they forget their passwords
(d) Recommend they write their passwords on a sticky note on their computer to remember them

13 Your friend is concerned about identity theft after losing their wallet. What immediate steps should they take? Competency Based Que.

(a) Ignore it; it's not a big deal
(b) Report the loss to their bank and credit card companies and monitor their accounts for unusual activity

(c) Wait a few weeks to see if anything happens
(d) Change all their passwords and do nothing else

Answers

1. (b)	2. (b)	3. (c)	4. (b)	5. (b)
6. (c)	7. (b)	8. (c)	9. (c)	10. (a)
11. (c)	12. (b)	13. (b)		

Very Short Answer Type Questions

1 Can computer virus infect hardware?

Ans. No, computer virus cannot infect hardware parts of computers.

2 How we can prevent computer against attack by viruses. CBSE SQP 2023-24

Ans. By installing anti-viruses and using firewalls we can prevent computer against attack by viruses.

3 What are the common signs of virus attack?

Ans. Some of the common signs of a virus attack are:

- computer runs very slow
- there is change in the file size
- computer often stops responding
- there is an increase in number of files

4 Name any two commonly used anti-virus software.

Ans. Two commonly used anti-virus software are McAfee and Norton.

5 What is cookie?

Ans. A cookie is a small text file stored on a user's computer by websites they visit. It helps websites remember user preferences, login details, or track browsing activity.

6 What is a firewall in computing?

Ans. A computer firewall could be a programmable device or a software that monitors and controls incoming and outgoing network traffic.

7 What is a computer virus, and how does it spread?

Ans. A computer virus is a malicious software program that can replicate itself and spread from one computer to another. It can damage files, steal information, or disrupt system operations.

8 List the various ways you can use to protect your data. CBSE SQP 2024-25

Ans. To safeguard your data from theft and viruses, consider the following measures:

1. **Use Strong Passwords** Create difficult-to-guess passwords using a mix of lowercase and uppercase letters, numbers, and special characters. This prevents unauthorized access to your computer.
2. **Install Anti-virus and Firewall** These tools monitor incoming and outgoing data, preventing viruses from entering and detecting any that may have already accessed your system.
3. **Encrypt Data** Important information can be encrypted using tools like BitLocker, requiring a decryption password to access the hard disk, thus blocking unauthorized usage.
4. **Secure Sites** Only share credit card or bank information on secure sites, indicated by "https://" and a lock symbol in the browser's address bar.

9 You receive an email claiming to be from your bank, asking you to verify your account details by clicking a link provided in the email. What steps should you take to ensure that the email is legitimate and protect your personal information? Competency Based Que.

Ans. To verify the legitimacy of the email, follow the given steps:

- **Do not click on the link** Instead, go directly to the bank's official website by typing the URL into your browser.
- **Check the email address** Verify that the sender's email address matches the official email domain of your bank.
- **Contact your bank directly** Use a known and trusted contact method such as a phone number from the bank's website to confirm if the request is legitimate.

10 One of your colleague is using their personal email account for work-related communications and is concerned about potential security risks. What advice would you give them to enhance their security while using personal email for work? Competency Based Que.

Ans. I would advise them to use a work email account for all work-related communications and to ensure their personal email has strong passwords and two-factor authentication enabled.

11 Give any four tips to keep the computer in perfect working condition. CBSE 2025

Ans. Four tips to keep a computer in perfect working condition:

(i) Regularly update software and security patches.
(ii) Clean hardware components to prevent dust buildup.
(iii) Backup important files frequently.
(iv) Use antivirus software to prevent malware.

12. You've recently heard about a friend's experience with online identity theft. What practical tips would you suggest to help them protect their personal data from online theft and viruses?

Ans. Few tips to protect our data from online theft and viruses are:

(a) Use passwords to login to your computer.
(b) Install Anti-virus and Firewall.
(c) Use Data Encryption.
(d) Give details of your credit card or bank account only on secure sites.

SELF ASSESSMENT

Multiple Choice Questions

1. The example(s) of operating system is/are
   (a) Windows (b) Linux (c) Unix (d) All of these
2. It is used as an interface between program and user.
   (a) GUI (b) CUI (c) CLI (d) None of these
3. The login screen on computer appears after
   (a) BIOS Screen (b) POST (c) Windows Start Screen (d) Welcome Screen
4. Which of the following is an example of interactive operating system.
   (a) DOS (b) Windows (c) Unix (d) All of these
5. Which of the following is the characteristic of the computer virus?
   (a) It may get activated at a certain date and time. (b) It makes copies of itself.
   (c) It makes the system slow. (d) All of these
6. What is the function of the task manager in an operating system?
   (a) To organize files and folders (b) To install new software
   (c) To manage hardware connections (d) To monitor and manage running applications

Very Short Answer Type Questions

7. Who developed the Android operating system?
8. Write two ways computer get infected with virus.
9. What is the use of operating system?
10. What is user interface?
11. Explain the function of the ENTER key?
12. List the various ways you can use to protect your data.

Competency Based Questions

Multiple Choice Questions

13. Rahul is working on Linux in his college lab. He created lot of scripts and other files and saved them in his home directory.
    Another new student Karan also worked on Linux with his own id and password after Rahul left. Karan was sitting on Rahul's seat. Karan also created many files and in the end deleted all his work. Rahul came and found out that Karan has deleted all files in home directory.
    Rahul is really angry with Karan thinking that Rahul's files are deleted. What would you tell Omar to do now?
    (a) Rahul needs to recreate all files in his home directory.
    (b) Rahul can undelete the deleted files.
    (c) Rahul should take Karan to the lab incharge and get him warned.
    (d) Karan deleted all the work from Karan's home directory. Rahul's home directory is intact and all his files are there.
14. Your classmate is worried about their computer overheating. What is the best preventive measure you could suggest?
    (a) Always use the laptop on a soft surface like a bed (b) Keep the laptop plugged in at all times
    (c) Regularly clean the vents and ensure proper airflow (d) Use the laptop in a warm environment

Subjective Type Question

15. You have been tasked with setting up a new computer. Describe the steps you would follow to install an operating system and explain how the operating system enables you to interact with the hardware and software.

Unit 4

Entrepreneurial Skills-II

Entrepreneurship is an individual's ability to turn ideas into action. It includes creativity, innovation and risk taking, as well as the ability to plan and manage projects in order to achieve objectives. Entrepreneurs are driven by a desire to make a difference and create something new. They are often resourceful and have a strong work ethic. In addition, successful entrepreneurs are adaptable and can pivot their businesses when needed.

Session 1 | Entrepreneurship and Society

The word 'entrepreneur' is derived from the French word 'entreprendre' which means "to do something" or "to undertake". An entrepreneur is an individual who creates a new business, bearing most of the risks and enjoying most of the rewards. According to **Howard W. Johnson**, "Entrepreneur is composite of these basic elements i.e. invention, innovation and adaptation".

The term **entrepreneurship** refers to the functions performed by an entrepreneur. It is the process involving various actions to be undertaken by the entrepreneur in establishing a new enterprise.

Advantages of Entrepreneurship

The main advantages of entrepreneurship are discussed below :

- **Independence** An entrepreneur is himself a boss or owner and he can take all the decisions independently.
- **Exciting** Entrepreneurship can be very exciting with many entrepreneurs considering their ventures highly enjoyable. Everyday will be filled with new opportunities to challenge your determination, skills and abilities.
- **Wealth Creation** The principal focus of entrepreneurship is wealth creation and improved livelihood by means of making available goods and services. Entrepreneurial venture generates new wealth, new and improved products, services or technology form entrepreneurs, enable new markets to be developed and new wealth to be created.
- **Flexibility** As an entrepreneur you can schedule your work hours around other commitments, including quality time you would spend with your family.
- **Status** Success in entrepreneurship beings a considerable fame and prestige within the society.
- **Ambition-fulfilment** Through entrepreneurship one can fulfil his ambitions into original products or services.

Disadvantages of Entrepreneurship

Some of the disadvantages of entrepreneurship are as follows :

- **Huge Amount of Time** You have to dedicate a huge amount of time to your own business. Entrepreneurship is not easy and for it to be successful, you have to take a level of time commitment.
- **Risk** An entrepreneurship involves high risk of loss. If the business fails then it will wipe away all the personal savings.
- **Hard Work** An entrepreneur has to work very hard to make the new business very successful.
- **Uncertain Income** There is no regular or fixed income available to an entrepreneur. So, there is uncertain kind of income received by an entrepreneur.
- **Incompetent Staff** A new entrepreneur may not be able to hire qualified and experienced staff so there are chances of incompetency by the staff due to lack of experience and knowledge.

4.1 Entrepreneurship and Society

While the concept of entrepreneurship has a wide meaning, it describes as starting a business using the resources available to a person.

Society is provided with goods and services. In turn, society provides market for products and services provided by the entrepreneur. Entrepreneurship has some positive impact on society such as

- Accentuates economic growth
- Fosters creativity
- Stimulates innovation and efficiency
- Creates jobs and employment opportunities
- Solves the problems of the society
- Encourages welfare of the society

Society plays a role in boosting entrepreneurship by

- Creates needs and demands
- Provides raw materials
- Enables financial support
- Creates a need for education
- Catalyses policy formation and reform
- Facilitates networking
- Supports infrastructure development

However, entrepreneurship also creates some adverse impact on society sometimes. This happens in the form of environmental degradation, trade imbalance, labour exploitation etc.

4.2 Types of Entrepreneurship Activities

Some common entrepreneurship activities related to society include:

1. Small-Scale Entrepreneurship

The small scale usually deals with a local or regional level with less than 50 employees. Here the main goal is to attain stability and sustain growth. This business often has its scope in its locality and it has a limited scale.

Examples Small restaurants, Local consultancies

2. Social Entrepreneurship

The social entrepreneur is all about dealing with social issues and problems beyond profit making. Here the entrepreneur will create and manage the ventures for the benefit of the positive environment. The main goal would be to tackle societal problems.

Examples Tata Industries, Ashoka Changemaker

3. Scalable Entrepreneurship

As the name indicates, scalable entrepreneurs will tend to stretch and extend their businesses. They will mostly concentrate on the services or products that can be easily stretched to larger markets. These entrepreneurs are highly conscious of their investments and innovative ideas because of their exponential growth. The main goal is to establish a business that can grow rapidly.

Examples Facebook, Uber

4. Large-Scale Entrepreneurship

Large-scale entrepreneurship is wide. It is at either national or international levels. The large-scale entrepreneurs have already achieved their market size and their market presence. It continues to maintain its growth level, focusing on expanding its business and staying as a competitor to its competitors. They have huge employees and will lead corporations.

Examples Automobile industries, Cement industries

Summary

Entrepreneurs are innovators who challenge the status quo by introducing new products and services, reshaping existing industries.

Entrepreneurship has a global scope, with international markets presenting both opportunities and challenges for growth and innovation.

Advantages of entrepreneurship include independence, excitement, wealth creation, flexibility, and ambition fulfillment.

Disadvantages of entrepreneurship involve significant time investment, high risk, hard work, uncertain income, and possibly incompetent staff.

Entrepreneurship positively impacts society by boosting economic growth, fostering creativity, driving innovation and efficiency, creating jobs, and solving societal problems.

Different types of entrepreneurship include small-scale, social, scalable, and large-scale entrepreneurship.

ACTIVITY Time

ACTIVITY 1

Entrepreneurs I know: Individual Practice

Procedure

- In this activity, we will think of the entrepreneurs we know.

Instructions

1. Think of 4 entrepreneurs whom you know or have seen.
2. Draw circles and in each circle write the name of that entrepreneur, what business they run, and one thing that you really like about their business.
3. After writing, share the details of the entrepreneurs with your class.

ACTIVITY 2

Field Work: Let's be an Entrepreneur

Procedure

- In this activity, students will find problems on their school campus that can be turned into business opportunities.

Instructions

1. Form groups of 3 each.
2. Take 30 minutes to go around your school.
3. Note down 2–3 problems you see on your school campus.
4. Write down some business ideas to solve these problems.
5. Also think about how your business ideas will help the school.

NCERT FOLDER

Complete Explanations of all NCERT's Questions

A. State Whether the Following Statements are True or False

Q.1 **Entrepreneurs can create jobs in the market.**

Q.2 **When many entrepreneurs sell mobile phones in a market, the prices of phones increase.**

Q.3 **Entrepreneurs identify a need in the market and build a product or service for it.**

Answers

1. True 2. False 3. True

B. Subjective Question

Q.4 **List the ways in which an entrepreneur affects a society.**

Ans. Here are various ways in which an entrepreneur affects society in short

(a) Job Creation
(b) Innovation
(c) Wealth Creation
(d) Social Impact
(e) Community Development
(f) Inspiration

EXAM PATTERN EXERCISE

Including Competency Based Questions

Multiple Choice Questions

1 **Which of the following roles is one of the primary roles of entrepreneurs in the society?**

(a) To decrease economic growth
(b) To create new businesses and job opportunities
(c) To help people living in poverty
(d) To decrease innovation

2 **Entrepreneurship contribute to social change by**

(a) maintaining the status
(b) promoting new social initiatives
(c) avoiding society involvement
(d) focusing only on personal profit

3 **What is social entrepreneurship primarily concerned with?**

(a) Increasing market share
(b) Addressing social issues and improving societal well-being
(c) Maximizing financial profits
(d) Expanding business operations

4 **A potential societal benefit of entrepreneurship is**

(a) Reduced environmental sustainability
(b) Widening wealth gap
(c) Decreased economic inequality
(d) Increased dependence on government subsidies

5 **Which of the following is the impact of entrepreneurship on local communities?**

(a) It often leads to the closure of local businesses
(b) It helps in developing local economies and improving community welfare
(c) It results in fewer local services
(d) It discourages community engagement

6 **A common challenge faced by many entrepreneurs is**

(a) No support from government
(b) Lack of funding resources
(c) Overabundance of market opportunities
(d) Limited competition in the market

7 **Which of the following is an entrepreneur's role in fostering community development?**

(a) Ignoring customer needs and focusing only on profit
(b) Establishing businesses that address local issues and create jobs
(c) Increasing the cost of goods and services
(d) Focusing only on personal growth

8 **What is one way entrepreneurship can help in reducing poverty?**

(a) By reducing the availability of financial resources
(b) By increasing the prices of essential goods
(c) By creating employment opportunities and stimulating local economies
(d) By concentrating wealth in a few hands

9 **Which of the following factor is important for an entrepreneur when identifying new business opportunities?**
(a) Focusing only on their personal growth
(b) Analyzing market needs and gaps
(c) Avoiding feedback from the society
(d) Following old business models

10 **Innovation of an entrepreneur includes**
(a) division of work
(b) opening new markets
(c) introducing new products
(d) Both (b) and (c)

11 **How can entrepreneur can get the work done from his/her team?**
(a) By creating a spirit of teamwork
(b) By motivation
(c) Using harsh words and actions
(d) Both (a) and (b)

12 **From the following statements, which one is not the positive impact of Entrepreneurship on society?** CBSE SQP 2022-23
(a) Stimulates Innovation and Efficiency
(b) Creates Jobs and Employment Opportunities
(c) Solves the problems of the society
(d) Discourages welfare of the society

13 **An entrepreneur wants to start a business that addresses local water scarcity issues. Which of the following approaches would be most effective for identifying community needs and developing a suitable solution?** Competency Based Que.
(a) Analysis market of existing water-related businesses
(b) Implementing a global solution
(c) Surveying local residents and analyzing their specific water needs
(d) Based on a successful international water company, creating a business plan.

14 **After doing a course on Tea farming, Megha has successfully started her business. She needs people to help her with her business so she decided to hire women of her village. How is Megha contributing to the society through her business?**
(a) It has created more jobs for people living in village
(b) Megha is now become a role model for other girls to be entrepreneurs
(c) It has raised standards for living of people employed
(d) All of the above

15 **Rajesh launches a new app, but it fails to attract users and he faces financial losses. He gathers his team to discuss the failure, takes accountability for the oversight, and assures them that he will conduct thorough market research before the next launch. He ________.** CBSE SQP 2024-25, Competency Based Que.
(a) takes responsibility for his mistakes
(b) thinks before making a decision
(c) does not give up
(d) is innovative

Answers

1. (b)	2. (b)	3. (b)	4. (c)	5. (b)
6. (b)	7. (b)	8. (c)	9. (b)	10. (d)
11. (d)	12. (d)	13. (c)	14. (d)	15. (a)

Very Short Answer Type Questions

1 **Why entrepreneurship is important?**

Ans. Entrepreneurship is important because it creates new jobs, boosts economic growth, and solves societal problems. It also helps in developing new products and services that improve people's lives.

2 **What are the key benefits of entrepreneurship to a community?**

Ans. Key benefits of entrepreneurship to a community include job creation, economic growth, innovation, and improved local services.

3 **What challenges entrepreneurs might face when starting a new business?**

Ans. Entrepreneurs may face challenges such as securing funding, managing cash flow, navigating regulatory requirements, dealing with market competition, and building a customer base.

4 **Why is it crucial for entrepreneurs to understand market needs?**

Ans. Understanding market needs is important because it allows entrepreneurs to develop products or services that fulfill customer demands, solve specific problems, and stand out in the market.

5 **Explain how entrepreneurial activities can affect economic growth.**

Ans. Entrepreneurship activities drive economic growth by creating new jobs, increasing competition, and generating wealth, which boosts overall productivity and development.

6 **What role does entrepreneurship play in improving quality of life?**

Ans. Entrepreneurship improves quality of life by offering new and improved products and services, enhancing access to essential goods, and creating solutions to everyday problems.

7 **A social enterprise aims to reduce plastic waste. What strategies could the enterprise implement to achieve its goal while maintaining profitability?** Competency Based Que.

Ans. The enterprise could develop and promote products made from recycled or biodegradable materials, partner with other organizations to increase awareness and create a circular economy, educate customers on the benefits of reducing plastic use and encourage sustainable practices.

8 Siya and Rahul both own garlands shop near a temple in their area. Rahul sits at his shop every day. When customers come, he sells to them. Siya walks around and gets customers to her shop. She also sells fresh flowers with her garlands. Who is Entrepreneur out of Siya and Rahul and why?

Competency Based Que.

Ans. Siya is entrepreneur as she is working to grow her business. She has also added a different idea to her business.

9 Explain how entrepreneurship can drive economic development in a region. Provide specific example.

Competency Based Que.

Ans. Entrepreneurship stimulates economic growth by creating jobs, increasing competition, and fostering innovation.

For example, a new tech startup can attract investments and boost local employment, enhancing the overall economic landscape of the region.

Session 2 | Qualities and Functions of an Entrepreneur

4.1 Qualities of Entrepreneur

For the successful enterprise, it is important to understand the characteristics/qualities of successful entrepreneurs and it is described below:

Risk Taking
An entrepreneur with rational planning and firm decisions bear the risks. They have differentiated approach towards risks.Good entrepreneurs are always ready to invest their time and money but they always have a back up for every risk they take.

Goal Oriented
Goal-oriented entrepreneurs achieve the maximum results from their efforts in business due to the fact they work towards clear and measurable targets.

Highly Optimistic
A successful entrepreneur is always optimistic and the present problems does not matter to them. He is always hopeful that the situation will became favourable for business in future.

Self-Confident
An entrepreneur should have confidence to achieve his goals otherwise he won't be able to convince his team to achieve his goals.

Industry Experience
Industry experience is the understanding of a specific market or sector that comes from working or studying in that field.

Trust in Self
An entrepreneur believes on their own decisions and actions as he has trust in his perseverance and creations. He does not believe in luck.

Leadership
An entrepreneur must possess the characteristics of leadership and must lead a team for achievement of goals. The leader is able to clearly articulate their ideas and has a clear vision.

Innovativeness
With the changing needs and requirements of customers production should meet requirements with the help of innovative ideas.

Decision Maker
An entrepreneur has to take many decisions to put his business idea into reality. He chooses the best suitable and profitable alternative.

Motivator
An entrepreneur has to create a spirit of team work and motivate them. So that he gets full cooperation from the employees.

Action-Oriented
An entrepreneur should have an action oriented vision and ideology to plan things well.

High Achiever
Entrepreneurs are high achievers as they have a strong urge to achieve. The most important characteristic is his achievement motivation.

4.2 Functions of an Entrepreneur

The various functions of an entrepreneur are as follows :

- **Innovation** It includes introducing new products, opening new markets, new sources of raw material and new organisation structure.
- **Decision-Making** It includes stabilising organisation's aims and objectives and changing them according to changing conditions, taking decisions on effective techniques, utilisation of financial resources etc.
- **Organisation and Management** An entrepreneur organise and manage various economic and human factors through planning, coordination, control, supervision and direction.
- **Size and Scale of Business Unit** An entrepreneur has to decide about the size of business unit as he wants to establish one production unit or more dependent upon the demand of the product. Similarly, he has to decide about scale of production i.e. small scale, middle scale or large scale.
- **Appointment of Managerial and Other Work Force** It is the entrepreneur who appoints the management staff as well as other work force as per the requirement and needs of the enterprise.
- **Factors of Production** The factors of production i.e. land, labour, capital etc., should be in appropriate proportion and to maximise output of these factors is the responsibility of the entrepreneur.
- **Finding Suitable Market** A proper research must be done to find a suitable market for selling the products. Other functions like advertisement and publicity, appointment of selling agents, providing incentives to various selling intermediaries to promote sales should be given priority.
- **New Inventions and Innovations** New inventions and innovations must be encouraged and introduced in production, sales, marketing, advertisement etc.
- **Establishing Relations with Government** An entrepreneur must establish good relations with government and its functionaries. His functions are to obtain licences, payment of taxes, selling the product to government, provision for export-import etc.
- **Establishing Contacts with Competitors** An entrepreneur must form contacts with the competitors to analyse the market. He must be in a position to make opportunities out of the given situation.

Role and Significance of Entrepreneurs

The role and significance of entrepreneurs are as follows :

- **Organiser of Society's Productive Resources** An entrepreneur is the organiser of society's productive resources. He is the person who assembles the unused natural, physical and human resources of the society, combines them as properly, establishes effective coordination between them and makes the economic activities dynamic.
- **Helpful in Capital Formation** An entrepreneur is helpful in capital formation as we know that increase in the rate of capital formation is quite essential for the economic development of any country. Those nations which are not able to increase the rate of capital formation or does it nominally remain backward from industrial development's point of view.
- **Increase in Employment Opportunities** An entrepreneur creates maximum employment opportunities in the society by way of establishing new industries, developing and expanding the existing industries and by undertaking innovative activities.
- **Development of New Production Techniques** An entrepreneur does not feel contended only with the existing techniques of production. Hence, he carries out various experiments for saving time, labour and capital in the production, as also to improve the variety and quality of the product and service.
- **Visionary Leader** An entrepreneur has a good vision towards the achievement of his goals. He is able to recognise profitable opportunities and conceptualise strategies.
- **Contribution of the Execution of Government Policies** An entrepreneur provides an important contribution in implementing government policies and achieving the national goals. An entrepreneur cooperate with the government for implementations of development plans of the country.
- **Higher Productivity** Entrepreneurs have the ability to produce more goods and services with less inputs. They play an important role in raising productivity.
- **Initiator** An entrepreneur is the one who initiates the process of creating an enterprise by coming up with the idea for the business and planning out how to turn that idea into reality.

Summary

Successful entrepreneurs are imbibed with characteristics such as leadership, innovativeness, decision-maker, risk-taker etc.

An entrepreneur performs important functions which includes decision-making, risk taking, organization, management, appointment of work force, control, direction etc.

Entrepreneurs possess strong leadership qualities and are skilled at managing teams, resources, and operations.

ACTIVITY Time

ACTIVITY 1

My Entrepreneurial Qualities: Self-assessment

Procedure

- In this activity, the students will rate themselves on the entrepreneurial qualities mentioned below.

Qualities of an Entrepreneur

	Y/N
I believe in myself and what I can do. I am confident.	
Problems take time to get solved. I am patient about solving them.	
I take responsibility for my actions and mistakes.	
I work hard on every task.	
I keep trying new ideas.	
I think of different ways to solve a problem. I am creative.	
I think before I make a decision.	
I do not give up when I face a problem.	

Instructions

1. Listed in above figure, are all the qualities of successful entrepreneurs.
2. Think about yourself. Mark yes or no against each quality.
3. Give yourself a point for every 'yes' answer.

ACTIVITY 2

Let us Solve a Problem!

Procedure

- In this activity, students will try and solve a problem in their vicinity.

Instructions

1. Select a problem in the area near your home. This could be a problem that really bothers you.
2. Make a 5-step plan for how you will solve the problem.
3. Implement step 1 of your solution!
4. After that, try implementing all the steps. Try your solution for a week.
5. At the end of the week, rate yourself again on the entrepreneurial qualities.

ACTIVITY 3

Interview an entrepreneur

Procedure

- In this activity, students will observe entrepreneurs at work, and speak to them and their employees about their work.

Instructions

1. Identify an entrepreneur in your area that you like or know.
2. On a weekend, spend some time in their shop and note everything that they do.
3. After that, speak to the entrepreneur and ask them in detail what activities they do in a day.
4. Also speak to somebody who works for them. Ask them what activities they see the entrepreneur do in a day. Write all your notes in below figure.

ENTREPRENEUR INTERVIEW

Name of the Entrepreneur

What business do they run?

Spend 30 minutes at their shop. Write down what you see them do.

Speak to the entrepreneur. Ask them what work they do in a day.

Speak to someone working there. Ask them what work they see the entrepreneur doing.

Write any other things you see here.

5. After you are back in class, make a list of all the actions you listed with your teacher. Compare your list with the list of your friends. Notice how many actions get repeated.

NCERT FOLDER

Complete Explanations of all NCERT's Questions

A. Here are some stories of some entrepreneurs. Tick the option for the quality they are showing.

Q.1 Ravi's customer comes to his store and starts shouting at him. He does not get angry. He listens to what his customer is saying. He is ___________.

(a) hardworking
(b) confident
(c) patient
(d) trying new ideas

Q.2 Susheela decides to sell her company tyres in Sri Lanka. It does not sell and she has a loss. She apologizes to the people who work for her. She says she will plan better next time. She ___________.

(a) takes responsibility for your mistakes
(b) thinks before making a decision
(c) does not give up
(d) is creative

Answers

1. (c) 2. (a)

B. Tick the correct option for the function that the entrepreneur is doing.

Q.1 Ali has a diamond factory. He pays his employees on the 1st of every month.

(a) Creates a new product (b) Manages the business
(c) Takes risk

Q.2 Mary buys bulbs for her business from Noida. She learns that bulbs are cheaper in Faridabad. So, she decides to start buying bulbs from there.

(a) Makes decisions (b) Divides income
(c) Takes risk

Q.3 Rehnuma has two people who work for her. Every day, she spends one hour with them to learn about what they've done that day.

(a) Creates a new product (b) Divides income
(c) Manages the business

Answers

1. (b) 2. (a) 3. (c)

C. Subjective Question

Q.1 What do you think is the most important function of an entrepreneur? Write your answer giving suitable examples.

Ans. The most important function of an entrepreneur is innovation—creating new products or improving existing ones to solve real-world problems. For example, Steve Jobs revolutionized the tech industry by introducing the iPhone, which redefined mobile communication and computing. Similarly, Elon Musk's Tesla pushed the boundaries of electric vehicles, making sustainable transportation more accessible. Through innovation, entrepreneurs create value, open new markets, and drive economic growth.

EXAM PATTERN EXERCISE

Including Competency Based Questions

Multiple Choice Questions

1 Which of the following is a key quality of a successful entrepreneur?

(a) Creativity
(b) Risk-aversion
(c) Dependence on others
(d) Inflexibility

2 Which of the following functions is performed by an entrepreneur?

(a) Avoiding risks at all costs
(b) Hiring only friends and family
(c) Developing business strategies
(d) Monitoring the stock market

3 To find a suitable market an entrepreneur performs the functions of

(a) advertisement and publicity
(b) appointment of selling agents
(c) new organisation structure
(d) Both (a) and (b)

4 **Which of the following is not a function of an entrepreneur?**
(a) Risk-taking
(b) Market research
(c) Managing production
(d) Providing loans to customers

5 **An entrepreneur's ability to identify business opportunities is known as**
(a) Vision (b) Risk management
(c) Opportunity recognition (d) Leadership

6 **What role does an entrepreneur play in managing resources?**
(a) Hoarding resources
(b) Delegating all resource decisions
(c) Ignoring resource allocation
(d) Efficiently utilizing and allocating resources

7 **Which quality is essential for an entrepreneur to adapt to changing market conditions?**
(a) Innovative (b) Flexibility
(c) Time management (d) Self-confidence

8 **Which of the following is a key function of an entrepreneur in a startup?**
(a) Maintaining a static business model
(b) Avoiding market research
(c) Creating a vision and setting goals
(d) Overseeing daily operations without innovation

9 **Which of the following is not an essential quality to become successful entrepreneur?** CBSE 2024
(a) Confidence (b) Creativity
(c) Patience (d) Wealthy

10 **Entrepreneurship has a crucial role in the ______ of the society.** CBSE SQP 2020-21
(a) Evolution (b) Planning
(c) Functioning (d) None of these

11 **To ensure their business remains competitive, an entrepreneur needs to stay informed about industry trends. Which competency does this involve?**
(a) Risk Assessment
(b) Industry Analysis
(c) Leadership
(d) Negotiation

12 **One day Anil's customer comes to his shop and starts shouting at him. Except of getting angry , he listens to what his customer is saying. He is ______.**
(a) Patient (b) Confident
(c) Hardworking (d) Good listner

13 **An entrepreneur realizes that their current business strategy is no longer effective. They decide to pivot and implement a new approach. Which quality is crucial for this decision?**
(a) Decision Making (b) Adaptability
(c) Fearlessness (d) Confidence

14 **Samiksha is planning to launch a new fitness app. She conducts surveys to understand user preferences and market trends before finalizing the app's features. Which function is she demonstrating?**
(a) Innovation
(b) Resource allocation
(c) Market research
(d) Risk management

Answers

1. (a)	2. (c)	3. (d)	4. (d)	5. (c)
6. (d)	7. (b)	8. (c)	9. (d)	10. (a)
11. (b)	12. (a)	13. (b)	14. (c)	

Very Short Answer Type Questions

1 **Give any one quality of a successful entrepreneur.** CBSE SQP 2021-22 Term I

Ans. Leadership is one quality of an entrepreneur. An entrepreneur is essentially a leader. Entrepreneurs are people who exhibit qualities of leadership in solving problems. They have to lead a team for achievement of goals.

2 **How decision-making is an important function of an entrepreneur?**

Ans. Decision-making is an important function because it includes stabilizing organization's aims and objectives and changes them according to the changing conditions.

3 **What quality helps an entrepreneur to effectively handle business risks?**

Ans. Risk tolerance is crucial as it allows entrepreneurs to take calculated risks and navigate uncertainties without being deterred by potential failures.

4 **How does creativity benefit an entrepreneur?**

Ans. Creativity benefits entrepreneurs by enabling them to develop unique products or services that stand out in the market.

It also helps in solving problems in innovative ways and adapting to changing conditions.

5 **Name one way an entrepreneur can foster innovation in their business.**

Ans. One way an entrepreneur can foster innovation is by encouraging a culture of creativity within the team. This involves supporting experimentation, open idea sharing, and continuous improvement.

6 **What is the role of market research for an entrepreneur?**

Ans. Market research helps entrepreneurs understand customer needs, preferences, and market trends. It provides valuable insights that inform product development, marketing strategies, and competitive positioning.

7 Why is adaptability a vital quality for an entrepreneur?

Ans. Adaptability is vital because it allows entrepreneurs to respond effectively to changes in the market, industry trends, or unexpected challenges. It helps them pivot strategies and maintain business resilience.

8 What is the function of an entrepreneur in market analysis?

Ans. Entrepreneurs conduct market analysis to understand market trends, customer needs, and competition. This helps them make informed decisions about product development, pricing, and positioning.

9 Write any four roles of Entrepreneurs. CBSE SQP 2022-23

Ans Four roles of entrepreneurs are:
(i) Innovator
(ii) Risk-taker
(iii) Leader
(iv) Job creator

10 Why do we say that an entrepreneur should be open-minded? CBSE SQP 2023-24

Ans. An entrepreneur should be open-minded to embrace new ideas, adapt to changes, and identify opportunities for business growth and innovation.

11 Give any two promotional functions of an entrepreneur. CBSE 2023

Or **Explain any two functions of an entrepreneur.** CBSE SQP 2021-22 Term I

Or **What are the functions of entrepreneurs?** CBSE SQP 2024-25

Or **Mention any four main functions of an entrepreneur.** CBSE 2025

Ans. Refer to text on page 79 (Functions of an entrepreneur).

12 List any four characteristics of entrepreneurship.

Ans. Four characteristics of entrepreneurship are:
(i) Innovation (ii) Risk-taking
(iii) Leadership (iv) Goal-oriented

13 How would you ensure that your products or services meet customer needs and expectations? What approaches and competencies are important for achieving this?

Ans. To meet customer needs, you would gather and analyze customer feedback, conduct market research, and continuously improve your offerings based on insights. Essential competencies include customer focus, market analysis, and product development.

14 Manisha has successfully grown her small business over the last two years. However, she is now facing increased competition. What qualities should Manisha exhibit to adapt her business strategy and continue to thrive in this competitive environment?

Ans. Manisha should exhibit qualities such as adaptability, creativity, and strategic thinking. She can analyze her competitors' strengths and weaknesses and identify her unique selling points.

By being open to change, she can adjust her marketing strategies or diversify her product offerings, ensuring that her business remains relevant and appealing to customers in a competitive market.

Session 3 Myths about Entrepreneurship and Entrepreneurship as a Career Option

4.1 Myths about Entrepreneurship

Entrepreneurship is a set of activities performed by the entrepreneur. It is the process of identifying opportunities in the market place.

It is the attempt to create value. Many entrepreneurs believe a set of myths about entrepreneurship and the most common are as follows:

- **Starting a Business is Easy** In reality, it is a very difficult and challenging process to start a successful business. The rate of failure of new ventures is very high but small entrepreneurships are comparatively easier to start.
- **Entrepreneurs Are Born, Not Made** People often believe that entrepreneurs have a natural talent to succeed in business. While entrepreneurship is largely about learning, adapting, and developing skills over time.
- **Lot of Money to Finance New Business** Successful entrepreneurs design their business with little cash also.
- **Start up's cannot be Financed** Under the schemes like MUDRA, entrepreneurs can raise loans from banks.

- **Talent is More Important than Industry** This is not true as the nature of industry an entrepreneur chooses greatly effects the success and growth of the business.
- **Most Start up's are Successful** Mostly in the developing countries start up's fail as they could not manage to earn high profits.
- **Only young entrepreneurs succeed** Age is not a barrier to entrepreneurship, in fact, older entrepreneurs often have better knowledge and industry expertise.
- **Failure means the end** Failure is often part of entrepreneurship. Many successful entrepreneurs have faced multiple failures before achieving success in life. Failure can provide valuable lessons that lead to future success.

4.2 Entrepreneurship as a Career Option

There is nothing wrong with working for any organisation, it is basic for youngsters to be educated that they have two options-they can be job creators or job seekers. Once the awareness of the two career choices comes in, it is important to understand how taking the route of entrepreneurship benefits an individual.

There are various example of entrepreneurship around us

1. Nurtures Development of Entrepreneurial Skills and Capabilities

Entrepreneurship cultivates unique skills and encourages outside the box thinking. It instils confidence, creates opportunity, offers solutions and stimulates the economy. Entrepreneurship education provides with the skills and knowledge to come up with business ideas and develop ventures. It is broadly about learning to practice core business areas such as marketing, sales, finance, accounting, management etc., and developing skills such as effective communication, creative problem solving, etc.

2. Enables Application of an Entrepreneurial Mindset

Entrepreneurial mindset and skills are not necessarily only relevant to becoming an entrepreneur, but also in any field. Even the top employability skills of today are basically entrepreneurial skills. In fact, having an entrepreneurial mindset and wide range of business-relevant skills acquired through studying entrepreneurship would make one an ideal candidate in most fields.

3. Develops Ability to Handle Failure and Ambiguity

In the Indian culture, since childhood failure is looked upon as something intolerably bad. However, a critical part of learning in the entrepreneurial process is to learn from failure. Hence, going through this process helps to learn from mistakes, take failure positively and stay motivated to work towards achieving the goal. Similarly, just like life is uncertain, business is full of ambiguity. While actually finding solutions to deal with ambiguity, one develops certain traits such as risk management, perseverance and persistence.

4. Enhances Critical Thinking and Problem-Solving Ability

The ability to think critically and solve problems is essential to succeed in the world of business. The focus of learning is not on these aspects during our school years. Learning entrepreneurship exposes one to numerous opportunities that force one to think critically, analyze all alternatives and consider possible solutions.

5. Provides Early Exposure to the Real World

Ultimately, working professionally in the real world requires one to collaborate, think creatively and demonstrate proficiency. In most cases, real life exposure during educational years remains limited.

Entrepreneurship practice at an early stage in one's career encourages activities such as going out and interacting with customers, creating tangible concepts and ideas, preparing detailed documents, working with investors etc., which gives great exposure and knowledge about the trends and needs of the real world.

6. Leads to Creating Difference in Society

Entrepreneurs not only economically impact society but they also work on identifying the real needs and problems of people and solving them. Learning entrepreneurship encourages one to find problems that need to be solved, invent a solution for them, and ultimately, make the world a better place.

Summary

Common myths include beliefs that starting a business is easy, entrepreneurs are born with natural talents, a lot of money is needed, and only young people succeed. In reality, entrepreneurship requires learning, adaptation, and persistence.

Entrepreneurship offers individuals the opportunity to be job creators rather than job seekers, providing both personal and economic benefits.

Entrepreneurs learn to handle uncertainty and view failure as a learning opportunity, developing resilience and risk management skills.

Entrepreneurs play a crucial role in solving societal problems by identifying needs and offering innovative solutions, making a positive difference in communities.

ACTIVITY Time

ACTIVITY 1

Identifying Everyday Heroes

Procedure

- In this activity, the teacher will make chits about different professions and the students will act them out. There will be a discussion after that. The professions are
  1. a vegetable seller not using plastic bags
  2. a business woman running a delivery system
  3. a chai wala selling fruit flavoured tea
  4. a gold seller selling gold teeth

Instructions

1. There will be professions of different people written on each chit of paper. The student reads the profession and acts it out for the class.
2. Identify what each person is doing differently in their business.

ACTIVITY 2

Talking to Entrepreneurs: Interview

Procedure

- In this activity, students speak to entrepreneurs and learn about the money needed to start a business and how to raise money needed for the business. Students should find out how the entrepreneur raised the money for their business.

Instructions

1. Identify three different types of successful entrepreneurs in your area.
2. Ask them how much money they started their businesses with.
3. What are the sources?
4. How did they raise the money?
5. Caution — not everyone likes talking about money. Please ask your questions with respect. If someone does not want to answer, let it be!
6. Fill the table after the conversation.

Entrepreneur Name	E.g. Kailash			
Type of business	Lightbulb shop			
Capital	50,000-1,00,000			
Year of starting	2001			
How does one raise money or business? What are the sources?	Borrow money from your family, use your own money, etc.			
How did you do it?	I borrowed money from my family.			

ACTIVITY 3

Make and sell

Procedure

- In this activity, students make an item in class and step out to sell it to someone.

Instructions

1. Form groups of 5 people each. The group should have a mix of boys and girls.
2. Look into your bags and desks and find any three items. Put them on your desk.
3. With the materials you've collected, make an object. Take 15 minutes to do this.
4. Now, take 30 minutes to sell it for money, to someone in school.

ACTIVITY 4

Talking about entrepreneurship as a life option

Procedure

- In this activity, you will compare entrepreneurship and wage employment.

Instructions

1. Get into pairs.
2. Imagine five years in the future — one person in the pair is wage employed and the other person is an entrepreneur. Discuss how your lives are similar and different from each other.
3. Have a debate with your class and your teacher.

ACTIVITY 5

Presenting about the Power of Entrepreneurship

Procedure

- In this activity, students shall prepare and present why they think entrepreneurship is a good life option for a person and for the society

Instructions

1. Get into groups of 5 each.
2. Imagine you believe that people should become entrepreneurs.

   You are speaking at your school assembly. You have to talk to the audience about the power of entrepreneurship. Prepare a presentation for the same.
3. You can use any way to present - talk, draw, act, sing, or dance.
4. You have 15 minutes to prepare. You will have 5 minutes to present.

NCERT FOLDER

Complete Explanations of all NCERT's Questions

A. Subjective questions

Q.1 What is the difference between a misconception and reality? Give an example.

Ans. A misconception is a belief or idea that is incorrect or based on false information, while reality refers to the actual state of things as they exist.

For example: Misconception "Cracking your knuckles causes arthritis."

Reality Scientific research has shown that cracking knuckles does not increase the risk of arthritis.

Q.2 Match each story below with the misconception about entrepreneurship.

Story	Misconception
Ramu owns a large clothes shop. Shamu has a small store selling handmade sarees. Shamu does not call himself an entrepreneur.	Every business idea needs to be unique or special.
Anna has a great idea for a website. She has `5,000. She is waiting for `20,000 more, so that she can start it.	Entrepreneurs are born, not made.
In a city of thousands of tailoring shops, Gauri is a tailor who stitches good quality clothes and has a very successful business.	A person needs to have a big business to be called an entrepreneur.

Ans. Match each story below with the misconception about entrepreneurship.

Story	Misconception
Ramu owns a large clothes shop. Shamu has a small store selling handmade sarees. Shamu does not call himself an entrepreneur.	A person needs to have a big business to be called an entrepreneur.
Anna has a great idea for a website. She has `5,000. She is waiting for `20,000 more, so that she can start it.	Every business idea needs to be unique or special.
In a city of thousands of tailoring shops, Gauri is a tailor who stitches good quality clothes and has a very successful business.	Entrepreneurs are born, not made.

B. Multiple Choice Questions

Q.1 Write against the option, if the business idea is of self-employment or wage employment.

(a) Cooking in a restaurant

(b) Owning a clothing business

(c) Having a dosa selling stall

Q.2 Match the columns

1.	Surabhi opens 5 painting stores across India.	a.	Enter
2.	There are many coaching classes in Mumbai. Jacob owns one of them. He is starting morning batches to attract more students to his classes.	b.	Survive
3.	Salma has started her clothing line on the Internet.	c.	Grow

Answers

1. (a) Wage employment, (b) Self-employment, (c) Self-employment
2. (1) → (c), (2) → (b), (3) → (a)

EXAM PATTERN EXERCISE

Including Competency Based Questions

Multiple Choice Questions

1 Which of the following is a myth about entrepreneurs? CBSE 2025

(a) An entrepreneur should be confident and should be able to take decisions.
(b) Every business idea must be unique or special.
(c) An entrepreneur should keep trying new ideas.
(d) An entrepreneur should be creative and should have different solutions to the problem.

2 Which myth about entrepreneurship concerns the nature of business ideas?

(a) Any idea can be turned into a successful business
(b) Only revolutionary ideas can succeed
(c) All ideas must be new and innovative
(d) Small improvements to existing ideas can be successful

3 Which of the following is/are a myth about Entrepreneurship? CBSE SQP 2023-24

(a) Need a lot of Money
(b) Must have a great Idea
(c) Should know everything about business
(d) All of the above

4 Which of the following statements is a misconception about entrepreneurial failure?

(a) Many successful entrepreneurs have faced multiple failures
(b) Entrepreneurs who fail once will never succeed
(c) Entrepreneurs learn from their failures and adapt
(d) Failure is part of the entrepreneurial journey

5 Which is a myth about the work-life balance of entrepreneurs?

(a) Many entrepreneurs work long hours, especially in the beginning
(b) Entrepreneurship requires discipline to balance work and personal life
(c) Entrepreneurs can easily take long vacations whenever they want
(d) Entrepreneurs have the flexibility to manage their own schedules

6 What is a common misconception about the age at which entrepreneurs can start a business?

(a) Entrepreneurs can start a business at any age
(b) Experience and expertise often contribute to entrepreneurial success
(c) Many entrepreneurs start their businesses later in life
(d) Only young people can become successful entrepreneurs

7 What does a study from the Centre for Entrepreneurial Studies reveal about the myth "entrepreneurs are motivated only by money"? Competency Based Que.

(a) Non-monetary motivations such as passion and purpose play a significant role
(b) Entrepreneurs are primarily driven by financial growth
(c) Entrepreneurs avoid public goals to focus only on their financial success
(d) Money is the main motivation for most entrepreneurs

8 It is commonly assumed that entrepreneurs must have extensive industry experience before starting a business. What does the truth say about starting a business? Competency Based Que.

(a) Starting a business without industry experience is always a recipe for failure.
(b) While experience can be helpful, many successful entrepreneurs start without it and learn as they go.
(c) Only those with years of experience can succeed in entrepreneurship.
(d) Extensive industry experience is necessary for all entrepreneurs.

9 A common motivation for choosing entrepreneurship as a career option is______.

(a) The desire for unlimited income resources
(b) The benefit to be one's own boss
(c) Guaranteed financial success
(d) Less responsibilities

10 Entrepreneurship can be a suitable career option for individuals who_____.

(a) Are not interested in working for others
(b) Enjoy solving problems and taking initiative
(c) Are risk-averse
(d) Prefer working for a reputed organization

11 Entrepreneurship offers the opportunity to _______as a career.

(a) Directly contribute job creation and economic growth
(b) Work for someone else's vision
(c) Follow a strict hierarchy
(d) Avoid taking any financial risks

12 One of the challenges of entrepreneurship as a career option is:

(a) Limited autonomy
(b) Inflexible working conditions
(c) Uncertainty and financial risk
(d) Lack of opportunities for growth

13 **Entrepreneurship is considered as a rewarding career choice because it______?**

(a) requires minimal time and effort
(b) gives you opportunity to innovate and bring new ideas to life
(c) gives you Long-term job security
(d) Guaranteed instant success

14 **When evaluating entrepreneurship as a career, which critical thinking skill is most relevant?**

(a) Accepting all ideas without questioning them
(b) For business growth avoiding detailed planning
(c) Following instinct without gathering any data or information
(d) Study market trends, customer needs, and competitive landscapes to make informed decisions

15 **As a new entrepreneur, you face a sudden drop in sales. What is your first step to manage the situation?** **Competency Based Que.**

(a) Reduce product prices immediately
(b) Blame the team for poor performance
(c) Close the business before losses increase
(d) Analyze the reasons for the drop and identify potential solutions

16 **A competitor releases a similar product to yours. How would you react on that situation?** **Competency Based Que.**

(a) Lower your prices drastically to outcompete them
(b) Identify what makes your product unique and market that differentiation
(c) Copy their features to stay competitive
(d) Give up on the product to avoid the competition

Answers

1. (b)	2. (b)	3. (d)	4. (b)	5. (c)
6. (a)	7. (a)	8. (b)	9. (b)	10. (b)
11. (a)	12. (c)	13. (b)	14. (d)	15. (d)
16. (b)				

Very Short Answer Type Questions

1 **Explain any two misconceptions about entrepreneurship.** **CBSE 2024, CBSE SQP 2020-21**

Or **Explain any two Myths about Entrepreneurship.** **CBSE SQP 2022-23**

Ans. Two misconceptions about entrepreneurship are that entrepreneurs are born with special skills and that they always take big risks. Both skills and risk management can be learned.

2 **Name the term used for a false belief or opinion about something.**

Ans. Myth is the term used for a false belief or opinion about something. There are many myths about entrepreneurship. It is a myth that 'it is easy to start a business', 'Startups cannot borrow from bank and many more'.

3 **Explain the myth that "entrepreneurs are born, not made." Why this belief is not accurate?**

Ans. This is a false myth because entrepreneurial skills can developed over time through education, experience, and perseverance, not just inborn traits.

4 **Why is the belief that "entrepreneurs always work alone" considered as a myth? How does collaboration play a role in entrepreneurship?** **Competency Based Que.**

Ans. Entrepreneurs often collaborate with partners, employees, and mentors. Teamwork and good relationship with co- workers are essential to scaling a business and bringing in diverse expertise.

5 **Disprove the myth that "entrepreneurs become rich overnight." What factors contribute in the financial success of entrepreneurs?** **Competency Based Que.**

Ans. Financial success often takes years of hard work, persistence, and continuous investment. Entrepreneurs face many risks, failures, and challenges before finally achieving success.

6 **How does the misbelief that "entrepreneurs don't need formal education" differ from the reality of skills development in entrepreneurship?** **Competency Based Que.**

Ans. While formal education is not always required, skills like financial management, leadership, and strategic planning often come from learning and experience, making education valuable.

7 **Why is the myth "entrepreneurs must create something complete new" is misleading? What role does innovation play in improving existing products or services?** **Competency Based Que.**

Ans. Many successful entrepreneurs improve existing products or services rather than creating something new. By incrementing innovations, like better services or business models, often lead to success.

8 **Why the belief that "entrepreneurs don't need a business plan" is a myth. Explain the importance of proper planning in entrepreneurship?** **Competency Based Que.**

Ans. A proper business plan is important for guiding the company's direction, securing funding, and assessing risks. Entrepreneurs refine their plans as they grow, but planning remains key.

9 **Why is the myth that "entrepreneurs must have lot of money to start a business" dishonest? What are some other ways by which entrepreneurs can fund their ventures?** **Competency Based Que.**

Ans. Entrepreneurs can start small and use various funding sources like personal savings, loans, crowd funding, or investors to grow their business.

10 **Why is entrepreneurship considered a viable career option?**

Ans. Entrepreneurship considered as a viable career option because it offers independence, flexibility, the opportunity to innovate, and the potential for financial rewards.

11 What are the various challenges all the entrepreneurs face when choosing entrepreneurship as a career?

Ans. Entrepreneurs often face challenges such as financial risk, uncertainty, intense competition, and the need for continuous adaptation and learning.

12 What are the essential skills for success in entrepreneurship as a career?

Ans. Some essential skills for entrepreneurship include creativity, risk management, problem-solving, decision-making, and good communication skills.

13 Define the importance of flexibility in entrepreneurship as a career option?

Ans. Flexibility allows entrepreneurs to set their schedules, adapt to different changes, and explore more creative solutions, which makes it a desirable career path for those seeking work-life balance and independence.

14 What are the potential financial benefits of entrepreneurship as a career?

Ans. Entrepreneurs have the potential for unlimited financial growth based on the success of their ventures, unlike fixed salaries in traditional jobs.

15 Write two disadvantages of Entrepreneurship as a career option.

Ans. Two disadvantages of Entrepreneurship as a career option are:

1. Problem of generating finance in the beginning of career.
2. No fixed income resources

16 How would you make sure that your business remains focused on customer needs and preferences? Give an example of how you might gather and incorporate customer feedback into your business strategy. Competency Based Que.

Ans. To keep the business focused on customer needs, I would regularly gather feedback through surveys, interviews, and social media engagement. For example, if customer feedback indicates dissatisfaction with a product feature, I would analyze the feedback, prioritize necessary changes, and update the product according to the customer's needs. By continuously monitoring customer opinions and adapting based on their input, I ensure that the business remains aligned with their preferences and needs.

17 You want to expand your business into a new region, but you are unfamiliar with the local market. What steps would you take to ensure a successful expansion? Competency Based Que.

Ans. I would start by researching the local market, including customer preferences, competitors, and regulatory requirements. I would also test the market by launching a project to gather feedback and refine the business model. Local partnerships or hiring experts from the region could also help in navigating the market effectively.

SELF ASSESSMENT

Multiple Choice Questions

1. Decision-making function of entrepreneur includes
   (a) Hard work (b) Risk bearing
   (c) Utilisation of financial resources (d) All of these
2. Which system is being promoted by Entrepreneurs indirectly?
   (a) Capitalist (b) Socialist (c) Both (a) and (b) (d) None of these
3. Entrepreneur is a ______ of growing society.
   (a) citizen (b) builder (c) destroyer (d) None of these
4. Which of the following social problems are tackled by social entrepreneurs?
   (a) Child labor (b) Low reach of quality education
   (c) Unemployment (d) All of these
5. Which of the following is the primary goal of marketing for an entrepreneur?
   (a) To attract and retain customers (b) To create products no one wants
   (c) To sell at a loss (d) To confuse potential buyers
6. Which of the following is a benefit of having a mentor in entrepreneurship?
   (a) Receiving constant criticism (b) Gaining insights and guidance from experience
   (c) Reducing networking opportunities (d) None of these

Very Short Answer Type Questions

7. Describe the risk taking factor of an entrepreneur.
8. Do you think an entrepreneur is innovative by nature? Explain?
9. Explain the wealth creation factor of entrepreneurship.
10. What is the risk taking quality of an entrepreneur?
11. List four positive impact of Entrepreneurship on society.
12. What is the purpose of advertising for a business?

Competency Based Questions

Multiple Choice Questions

13. Dr. Rashmi has his own clinic so she is a ______ person.
    (a) wage employed (b) self-employed
    (c) Both a and b (d) None of these
14. Megha, a tech entrepreneur, notices a decline in user engagement on her platform. She decides to redesign the user interface based on customer feedback. Which entrepreneurial function is she applying?
    (a) Innovation (b) Financial management
    (c) Market research (d) Decision making

Subjective Type Questions

15. You've developed a great product, but sales are lower than you expected. How would you adapt your marketing strategy to boost sales of your product?
16. You are launching a new business in a competitive market. How would you ensure that your business stands out and attracts customers?

Unit 5

Green Skills-II

Green skills are the knowledge, abilities, values and attitudes needed to live in, develop and support a sustainable and resource-efficient society. These skills are becoming increasingly important as the world transitions towards a more sustainable future.

Session 1 | Sustainable Development

5.1 Introduction

Sustainable development is the development that satisfies the needs of the present without compromising the capacity of future generations, guaranteeing the balance between economic growth, care for the environment and social well-being.

The concept of sustainable development was popularised in 1987 by the United Nations World Commission on Environment and Development. In its **Our Common Future Report** or **Brundtland Report** it defined the idea as "Development that meets the needs of the present, without compromising the ability of future generations to meet their needs."

In our daily life, we can contribute to creating a Sustainable Society by following 4Rs' and 1U of Sustainability. These are:

Names	Definitions
Refuse	Not to use products that may harm the environment.
Reduce	To minimize the use of the products that may cause harm to the environment.
Reuse	To reuse products as far as possible, in order to reduce the waste generation.
Recycle	After reusing the product, we must try to recycle it as far as possible.
Upcycle	Any product that is not usable can be upcycled with creativity and innovation. It gives a new look to the old product and makes it look desirable.

Importance of Sustainable Development

Sustainable development is necessary for the maintenance of the environment. The importance of sustainable development are as follows:

- **Proper Use of Means and Resources** Sustainable development teaches people to make use of means and resources for the maximum benefit without wastage. It helps to conserve and promote the environment.
- **Development of Positive Attitude** Sustainable development brings about changes in people's knowledge, attitude and skills. It awares the people about the responsibility to use and preserve natural resources. It creates the feeling that natural resources are the common property of all and nobody can use the property according to his personal will. It helps to conserve natural and social environment.
- **Development Based on People's Participation** People's participation is to be given priority in development work in order to achieve the aim of sustainable development. It creates the interest of local people in development work and environment conservation with the feeling of ownership.
- **Limitation of Development** Limited but effective use of means and resources are enough for the people to satisfy their basic needs. Limited and non-renewable means and resources go on decreasing in globally due to over-use. Development works should be conducted as per carrying capacity.
- **Long Lasting Development** Sustainable development aims at achieving the goal of economic and social development without destroying the Earth's means and resources. It attempts to create the concept of maintaining the present work for the future and conserving the natural resources for future generation.

So, due to the realisation of importance of sustainable development, now there is a transcending concern for survival of the people and planet. We need to take a holistic view of the very basis of our existence. It is important to reconcile ambitious economic development and preserving the natural resources and ecosystem.

5.2 Problems Related to Sustainable Development

- Poor management of natural resources combined with growing economic activities will continue to pose serious challenges to environment.
- The most significant environmental problems are associated with resources that are renewable such as air and water. They have finite capacity to assimilate emissions and wastes but if pollution exceeds this capacity ecosystem can deteriorate rapidly.

- To assess the regenerative capacity of natural resources is difficult to determine. In the cases of soil erosion, atmospheric pollution etc., there is substantial uncertainity about the extent and outcomes of environmental degradation.
- The overall effects of economic activities on the environment are continuously changing.
- Due to rise in income, the demands for improvement in environmental quality will increase as well as the resources available for investment but it is not mandatory in some cases as problems are observed to get worse as income rise.
- Rise in population is another problem that would further lead to severe environmental degradation in the future.
- Another challenge is rise in demand for energy as it is estimated that the total manufacturing outputs in developing countries will increase to about six times the current levels by 2030.
- An environment friendly way for production of power is using solar energy from the sun which is unlimited. One major example of large scale production of solar power is seen in Charanka-Gujarat Solar Park. This has reduced the dependence on non-renewable fossil fuels in Gujarat.
- Another challenge is rise in demand of food crops with the growth of population. To protect fragile soils and natural habitats, this will have to be achieved by raising yields on existing crop land.

5.3 Solutions for Sustainable Development

- Inspite of difficult circumstances sustainable development is achievable however, it would require a lots of concentrated and coordinated effort. The achievement of sustainable development requires the integration of economic, environmental and social components at all levels.
- The main principles of sustainable development are:
    - Respect and care for all forms of life.
    - People should learn to conserve the natural resoures in order to protect the living beings.
    - Conserving the Earth's vitality and diversity.
    - Improving the quality of human life.
    - Changing personal attitude and practices towards the environment.

Short-Term Solutions

- Illegal deforestation and smuggling of forest resources should be stopped.
- Proper balance ought to be maintained between deforestation and afforestation.
- Planning and building of industrial zones to manage and process are types of wastes.
- Proper treatment system, recycling of waste and their proper disposal should be undertaken.
- Adoption of Rainwater Harvesting Techniques, drip/Sprinkler irrigation and use of alternative sources of energy. Less chemical fertilizers should be used along with environment-friendly pesticides and weedicides.
- Polluting industries should be relocated outside the cities, far away from the populated areas.

Long-Term Solutions

- Government should make policies against illegal activities.
- Awareness campaigns should be launched for farmers and industrialists.
- Ecology must be protected through imposition of taxes and fines.
- Practice of sustainable agriculture must be promoted such as permaculture, agroforestry, mixed farming, multiple cropping and crop rotation.

Summary

Sustainable development means using our resources wisely so that we can meet our needs today while also protecting these resources for future generations. It's about finding a balance between economic growth and environmental health.

Sustainable development helps us make the best use of our resources, encourages a positive attitude towards our environment, involves everyone in the development process, and ensures that development can last over time.

There are several problems that affect sustainable development, such as poor resource management, increasing population, and a growing demand for energy. These issues make it harder to achieve sustainability.

To reach the goal of sustainable development, we can implement both short-term and long-term solutions. This requires careful planning and teamwork from individuals, communities, and governments.

ACTIVITY Time

ACTIVITY 1

Create a Garden in School or Plant Trees

Material Required

Seeds, garden waste, sprinkler, gardening tools

Procedure

- Form groups depending on the number of students available. Ask teacher to allot a piece of land in the school premises.
- Assign different tasks to different groups of students.
- The tasks can be ploughing, sowing seeds, making manure using vermicomposting and setting up a sprinkler system to water the plants.

ACTIVITY 2

Discussion on How to Prevent Wastage.

Procedure

- Form groups depending on the number of students available.
- Every student in the group will name way in which wasting of water and food can be stopped or prevented.
- Make a list and share it with the rest of the class.

NCERT FOLDER

Complete Explanations of all NCERT's Questions

A. Multiple Choice Questions

Q.1 How many sustainable development goals are given by the United Nations?

(a) 18
(b) 17
(c) 15
(d) 20

Q.2 Choose the option which defines sustainable development.

(a) Taking care of future generations
(b) Taking care of only ourselves
(c) Taking care of ourselves and the future generations
(d) Well-being of all

Q.3 Which organization has made the Sustainable Development Goals. CBSE SQP 2023-24

(a) United Nations
(b) League of Nations
(c) UNICEF
(d) World Health Organization

Answers

1. (b) 2. (c) 3. (a)

B. Subjective Questions

Q.1 What is the meaning of sustainable development?

Ans. Sustainable development refers to a mode of development that meets the needs of the present generation without compromising the ability of future generations to meet their own needs.

It involves achieving economic growth, social inclusion, and environmental protection in a balanced and integrated manner.

Q.2 Why do you think the United Nations has made the 17 Sustainable Development Goals?

Ans. The United Nations has made the 17 Sustainable Development Goals (SDGs) to provide a comprehensive framework for addressing the world's most pressing economic, social, and environmental challenges in a coordinated and integrated manner. These goals aim to guide global efforts towards achieving sustainable development by 2030 by addressing issues such as poverty, inequality, climate change, environmental degradation, and social injustice. In short, the SDGs serve as a roadmap for international cooperation and action to build a more sustainable and equitable future for all.

EXAM PATTERN EXERCISE

Including Competency Based Questions

Multiple Choice Questions

1 Which of the following is a foundation of sustainable development?
(a) Reducing biodiversity
(b) Maximizing economic growth
(c) Promoting the use of non-renewable resources
(d) Meeting the needs of present and future generations

2 Sustainable development requires the judicious use of
(a) natural resources (b) human resources
(c) Both (a) and (b) (d) None of these

3 Sustainable development is necessary because
(a) It helps to promote and conserve the environment
(b) It aware the people for effective use of natural resources
(c) It aims at achieving the goal of economic and social development
(d) All of the above

4 In total, how many SDGs were adopted by the United Nations 2015 as a universal call to action to end poverty, protect the planet and ensure that by 2030 all people enjoy peace and prosperity? CBSE 2024
(a) 13 (b) 11 (c) 17 (d) 19

5 Energy demand in developing countries will increase to______ times the current levels by 2030.
(a) four (b) five
(c) six (d) eight

6 The biggest problem related to sustainable development is
(a) to safeguard forests (b) to safeguard fisheries
(c) to safeguard croplands (d) All of these

7 According to the concept of sustainable development, the environment and development are _________issues. CBSE SQP 2020-21
(a) Inseparable (b) Separate
(c) Independent (d) None of these

8 A city council wants to encourage recycling among residents. What competency would be most valuable for the project coordinator responsible for this campaign?
(a) Experience in social media marketing
(b) Knowledge of software coding
(c) Understanding of waste management and recycling processes
(d) Skills in graphic design

9 A local government has launched a sustainable public transportation initiative. Which competency is crucial for the project manager overseeing this initiative? Competency Based Que.
(a) Skills in software development
(b) Understanding of international trade laws
(c) Knowledge of traditional marketing techniques
(d) Expertise in urban planning and transportation systems

10 An urban farmer is promoting sustainable agriculture practices within the city. What is one key skill they should possess to educate the community effectively? Competency Based Que.
(a) Experience in corporate finance
(b) Proficiency in data analysis
(c) Knowledge of local flora and fauna
(d) Expertise in mechanical engineering

Answers

1. (d)	2. (c)	3. (d)	4. (c)	5. (a)
6. (d)	7. (a)	8. (c)	9. (d)	10. (c)

Very Short Answer Type Questions

1 Write any two challenges to sustainable development.

Ans. The two challenges to sustainable development are:
(i) Rise in population level would lead to severe environmental degradation in the future.
(ii) Poor management of natural resources combined with growing economic activities will continue to pose serious challenges to environment.

2 Why has United Nations has made the 17 Sustainable Development Goals? CBSE SQP 2024-25

Ans. The 17 SDGs have been made with the aim of taking care of important issues facing businesses, governments and society. Some of these issues are poverty, gender equality, water use, energy, climate change and biodiversity. Countries are now making policies and regulations that will promote sustainable systems needed in all economic sectors to provide a secure, affordable and sustainable economy.

3 Explain any two problems related to sustainable development. CBSE 2025

Ans. Two problems related to sustainable development.
(i) Resource depletion due to overconsumption.
(ii) Environmental pollution from industrial activities.

4 **Give one short-term solution related to sustainable development.**

Ans. The practice of illegal deforestation and smuggling of forest resources should be stopped.

5 **"Green economy promotes sustainable development". Justify the statement.** **CBSE SQP 2023-24**

Ans. A green economy promotes sustainable development by integrating economic growth with environmental protection and social equity.

6 **List any four factors causing ecological imbalance.**

Ans. (i) Deforestation (ii) Pollution (iii) Overfishing (iv) Climate Change

7 **Mention any two ways to get clean and affordable energy.** **CBSE 2024**

Ans. (i) Solar Power (ii) Biomass Energy

8 **Give any one practice / sustainable process that is being used to help preserve the environment.** **CBSE SQP 2021-22 Term I**

Ans. Recycling: Collecting and processing materials like paper, plastic, and glass to create new products, and reducing waste.

9 **Give an example of large scale production of solar power in India.** **CBSE SQP 2021-22 Term I**

Ans. An example of large-scale production of solar power in India is the "Bhadla Solar Park" in Rajasthan. It is one of the largest solar parks in the world.

10 **What are three simple steps you can take in your daily life to contribute to sustainable development?**

Ans.
1. **Reduce, Reuse, Recycle** Minimize waste by reducing consumption, reusing items, and recycling materials.
2. **Conserve Energy** Turn off lights and appliances when not in use, opt for energy-efficient devices, and use renewable energy sources.
3. **Plant Trees** Trees absorb carbon dioxide and release oxygen, helping to improve air quality and combat climate change.

11 **You are given a task to designing a school project on sustainable living. What key areas would you focus on to encourage students to adopt sustainable habits in their daily lives?** **Competency Based Que.**

Ans. For a school project on sustainable living, focus on the following key areas to encourage students to adopt sustainable habits:
1. **Waste Management** Teach students about recycling, composting, and reducing waste. Encourage them to create a waste segregation plan for their homes.
2. **Energy Conservation** Discuss ways to save energy, like turning off lights, using energy-efficient appliances, and promoting the use of renewable energy sources such as solar power.
3. **Water Conservation** Highlight the importance of saving water. Suggest practical tips like fixing leaks, using water-efficient fixtures, and collecting rainwater.
4. **Sustainable Transportation** Encourage walking, biking, carpooling, or using public transportation to reduce carbon footprints.

Session 2 | Our Role in Sustainable Development

Sustainable development is all about making sure our world can thrive today and in the future.

The United Nations 17 Sustainable Development Goals (SDGs) help us do this. United Nations in 2015 adopted 17 SDGs as a universal call to action to end poverty, protect the planet and ensure that all people enjoy peace and prosperity by 2030.

These SDGs are :

1. No Poverty

Help others by donating to charities, supporting job creation, and promoting education to lift people out of poverty.

2. Zero Hunger

Reduce food waste, support local farmers, and donate food to those in need to ensure everyone has enough to eat.

3. Good Health and Well-being

Eat healthy food, do exercise, and support health programs. Help others access healthcare and mental well-being support.

4. Quality Education

Encourage learning, volunteer to teach others, and support efforts that ensure everyone, especially children, has access to education.

5. Gender Equality

Treat everyone equally, speak up against discrimination, and support opportunities for women and girls in education and the workplace.

6. Clean Water and Sanitation

Use water wisely, avoid pollution, and support efforts to bring clean water and sanitation to areas in need.

7. Affordable and Clean Energy

Use energy-efficient appliances, save electricity, and support clean energy sources like solar or wind power.

8. Decent Work and Economic Growth

Promote fair working conditions, support local businesses, and encourage entrepreneurship that creates jobs for others.

9. Industry, Innovation, and Infrastructure

Support new technologies and sustainable industries, and encourage investments in infrastructure like clean transport and eco-friendly buildings.

10. Reduced Inequalities

Stand up against inequality. Support policies that ensure fair treatment for all, regardless of race, gender, or income level.

11. Sustainable Cities and Communities

Use public transport, support eco-friendly housing, and get involved in making our communities safe and resilient to environmental challenges.

12. Responsible Consumption and Production

Buy only what you need, avoid waste, recycle, and support companies that follow ethical and sustainable production practices.

13. Climate Action

Reduce your carbon footprint by using less energy, planting trees, and supporting actions that fight climate change.

14. Life Below Water

Avoid plastic pollution, support ocean-friendly products, and join efforts to protect marine life and clean up beaches.

15. Life on Land

Protect forests, plant trees, and help in conservation efforts to preserve wildlife and natural habitats.

16. Peace, Justice, and Strong Institutions

Promote peace and fairness, report corruption, and support efforts that strengthen justice and human rights.

17. Partnerships for the Goals

Work together with others communities, governments, and organizations to achieve these goals for a better world.

Summary

United Nations has formed 17 Sustainable Development Goals (SDGs) so that countries and nations can work towards finding a solution to the growing problems in the world.

These goals have been made so that all the nations take action to protect our air, water and land from pollution and provide clean water, air and energy to all people.

Educating others about sustainability and leading by example helps build a culture of responsibility towards the environment.

ACTIVITY Time

ACTIVITY 1

Group Discussion

Procedure

- Form groups depending on the number of students available.
- Every student will describe one way in which they can work to conserve and protect the environment.
- Make a list and share it with the rest of the class.

ACTIVITY 2

Make art project using waste

Procedure

- Form groups depending on the number of children available. Make a list of waste material that is thrown away.
- Now think of creative ideas in which you can use the waste material to make something useful.

NCERT FOLDER

Complete Explanations of all NCERT's Questions

A. Multiple Choice Questions

Q.1 Which of the following sources of energy is from a renewable source?

(a) Solar energy (b) Wood
(c) Coals (d) Petrol

Q.2 Choose the option which is not a sustainable development goal according to United Nations.

(a) Clean Water and Sanitation (b) Gender Equality
(c) Population (d) Reduced Inequalities

Answers

1. (a) 2. (c)

B. Subjective Questions

Q.3 List some ways in which we can use resources sensibly.

Ans. Here are some ways to use resources sensibly

- Reduce, reuse, recycle
- Conserve energy and water
- Opt for sustainable transportation
- Support sustainable agriculture
- Protect natural habitats
- Practice mindful consumption
- Raise awareness through education

Q.4 Explain the importance of education towards sustainable development.

Ans. Education plays a crucial role in advancing sustainable development by raising awareness, fostering critical thinking, and empowering individuals and communities to take action towards a more sustainable future. In short, education promotes understanding of sustainability issues, equips people with the knowledge and skills to address them, and inspires collective action to achieve environmental, social, and economic goals in a balanced manner.

EXAM PATTERN EXERCISE

Including Competency Based Questions

Multiple Choice Questions

1 Which one of the following is the most important factor for sustainable development and helps us become aware of our role as a responsible citizen? CBSE 2025

(a) Sports (b) Education
(c) Business (d) Illiteracy

2 Which of the following practices supports sustainable development?

(a) Urban development
(b) Overfishing the oceans
(c) Using various renewable energy sources like solar and wind
(d) Using only the non-recyclable products

3 Which of the following daily activities can significantly reduce water consumption?

(a) Washing cars with a hose
(b) Letting the faucet drip
(c) Running the tap while brushing teeth
(d) Taking shorter showers

4 What can you do to reduce plastic waste in your daily life?

(a) Buy more single-use plastic items
(b) Use reusable water bottles and bags
(c) Increase plastic packaging use
(d) Burn the plastic waste

5 The life underwater is majorly threatened by our ________ habit.

(a) Using Plastic
(b) Using excessive fuel
(c) Eating meat
(d) None of the above

6 What would you do to reduce waste?

(a) Reuse whatever possible
(b) Reduce the usage
(c) Recycle whatever possible
(d) All of the above

7 Why is protecting natural habitats is necessary for sustainability?

(a) It increases pollution
(b) It decreases biodiversity
(c) It leads to deforestation
(d) It preserves ecosystems and supports wildlife

8 Which of the following is the environmental benefit of buying locally-produced products?

(a) It increases transportation emission
(b) Support for local economies and reduced environmental impact
(c) Higher packaging waste
(d) None of the above

9 A community initiates a tree-planting campaign to restore local forests, aiming to enhance biodiversity, prevent soil erosion, and provide habitats for wildlife. This initiative also includes educating residents about sustainable land use practices to protect their natural environment.

Which SDG can you relate this initiative to?

(a) Clean Water and Sanitation
(b) Life on Land
(c) Affordable and Clean Energy
(d) Climate Action

10 A local community in your area is planning to build a park. They have two options: using natural grass or synthetic turf.

Which of the following option would be more sustainable for the park's development? **Competency Based Que.**

(a) Natural grass, as it improves air quality and supports local biodiversity
(b) Synthetic turf, as it more eco-friendly
(c) Both options are sustainable
(d) None, as both options have negative effects on the environment

11 In your role as a student leader, how can you encourage your school to adopt more sustainable practices? **Competency Based Que.**

(a) Collaborate with teachers to integrate sustainability into the curriculum.
(b) Start an awareness campaign about environmental issues.
(c) Propose a "green" committee to oversee sustainability initiatives.
(d) All of the above

12 As a consumer, what practice can you adopt to contribute to sustainable development? **Competency Based Que.**

(a) Choose second-hand or up cycled items whenever possible.
(b) Buy only new products to support the economy.
(c) Ignore labels and choose based on brand popularity.
(d) Purchase fast fashion items frequently.

13 Climate change is creating unstable and extreme weather patterns that can have a harmful impact on health. Every year, extremely high or low temperatures affect the health of many people, particularly older people, and people who work outdoors. Extreme Heat or Cold can trigger exhaustion or heat stroke and can make existing conditions such as respiratory, cardiovascular, kidney or mental diseases worse.

Which of the following Sustainable Development Goal does this scenario relate to? **Competency Based Que.**

(a) Climate Action
(b) Sustainable cities and communities
(c) Life on Land
(d) Life below Water

Answers

1. (b)	**2.** (c)	**3.** (d)	**4.** (b)	**5.** (a)
6. (d)	**7.** (d)	**8.** (b)	**9.** (b)	**10.** (a)
11. (d)	**12.** (a)	**13.** (a)		

Very Short Answer Type Questions

1 Why is clean water and sanitation important for sustainable development?

Ans. Clean water and sanitation are crucial for health, reducing poverty, and improving living standards. Access to these resources ensures a healthy population, which is necessary for sustainable social and economic development.

2 How can an individual contribute to Sustainable Development Goals? **CBSE SQP 2020-21**

Ans. An individual can contribute to Sustainable Development Goals by reducing waste, conserving energy and water, and supporting sustainable practices.

3 List some ways by which we can use the resources sensibly.

Ans. (i) Conserve Water
(ii) Save Energy
(iii) Support Renewable Energy
(iv) Use Sustainable Products

4 How can reducing single-use plastics contribute to sustainability?

Ans. Reducing single-use plastics can help in decreasing environmental pollution and waste, as well as the strain on recycling systems.

5 How can we help the environment by using public transportation?

Ans. Public transportation decreases the number of individual vehicles on the road, leading to reduced greenhouse gas emissions and less traffic congestion.

6 What role does quality education play in promoting sustainability?

Ans. Education raises awareness about environmental issues, teaches sustainable practices, and empowers individuals to make choices that contribute to the environmental protection.

7 Explain three steps you would take to make your home more energy-efficient and also explain their benefits. **Competency Based Que.**

Ans. **Install LED Light Bulbs** Replace your old bulbs with LED bulbs to save up to 75% on energy and reduce waste.

Use a Programmable Thermostat Set it to adjust temperatures automatically based on your schedule, cutting energy use and costs.

Seal Windows and Doors Fix drafts with weather stripping to improve insulation and prevent heat loss, lowering heating and cooling bills.

8 Analyze the importance of innovation in achieving sustainable development goals. How can you contribute creatively to sustainability efforts in your community? **Competency Based Que.**

Ans. Innovation is crucial for developing new solutions to sustainability challenges, such as renewable energy technologies or waste reduction strategies. I can contribute creatively by organizing programs that encourage participants to develop apps promoting sustainable practices or by proposing community workshops that brainstorm innovative approaches to local environmental issues.

9 'Reduced Inequalities' is one of the Sustainable development goals set by the UN. Give any two ways to reduce inequalities. **CBSE SQP 2021-22 Term I**

Ans. Two ways to reduce inequalities are:

(i) Provide equal access to education and healthcare.

(ii) Be helpful to one another.

10 Give some measures to support SDG 3 (Good Health and Well-being) in your community. Explain what actions would you take to improve health, and how would you monitor the success of these measures? **Competency Based Que.**

Ans. **Organize Health Workshops** By educating people on nutrition and exercise we can improve awareness and healthier lifestyle choices.

Offer Free Health Check-ups By providing regular health check-ups to detect issues early we can promote better health management.

Improve Water and Sanitation By enhancing local water quality and sanitation facilities we can reduced waterborne diseases and improve overall health.

For monitoring success of these measures we can use health statistics, participant feedback, and health records to evaluate effectiveness.

SELF ASSESSMENT

Multiple Choice Questions

1. The concept of sustainable development was popularized in
   (a) 1985 (b) 1986 (c) 1987 (d) 1988
2. Sustainable development requires proper use of
   (a) natural resources (b) man-made resources (c) human resources (d) Both (a) and (b)
3. What is the role of education in fostering green skills?
   (a) It has no significant impact on sustainable development.
   (b) It raises awareness about environmental issues and promotes critical thinking.
   (c) It focuses only on technical knowledge without practical applications.
   (d) It primarily prepares individuals for jobs in traditional industries.
4. Which of the following best defines "sustainable agriculture"?
   (a) Agriculture that relies solely on synthetic fertilizers
   (b) Agricultural practices that maintain soil health, conserve water, and reduce pollution
   (c) Farming methods that focus exclusively on profit maximization
   (d) Any form of agriculture that produces high yields
5. What of the following is an example of a sustainable practice in waste management?
   (a) Incinerating all waste materials (b) Landfilling biodegradable waste without processing
   (c) Composting organic waste to enrich soil (d) Using single-use plastics for convenience

Very Short Answer Type Questions

6. When did the idea of sustainable development become popular?
7. Mention any one serious problem relating to sustainable development.
8. What are the main principle of sustainable development?
9. Explain any 2 sustainable development goals.
10. Discuss two major problems associated with sustainable development.
11. How can businesses encourage employees to develop green skills?

Competency Based Questions

Multiple Choice Questions

12. As a community member, how can you influence local leaders to prioritize sustainable development initiatives?
    (a) Attend public meetings and voice your concerns about sustainability.
    (b) Provide evidence-based suggestions for sustainable policies.
    (c) Collaborate with local organizations to amplify your message.
    (d) All of the above.
13. While volunteering for an environmental NGO, you notice a lack of engagement from the community. What could be your approach to increase participation?
    (a) Develop a strategy for outreach and community involvement.
    (b) Criticize the community for not participating.
    (c) Assume that people are not interested in sustainability.
    (d) Limit communication to only the core team.

Subjective Type Questions

14. Many people believe that sustainable development is only a concern for governments and large corporations. How would you explain the role of individuals in achieving sustainability?
15. In your opinion, how can businesses integrate green skills into their operations? What impact could this have on sustainability?

PART B
SUBJECT SPECIFIC SKILLS

Unit 1

Digital Documentation (Advanced) Using LibreOffice Writer

In this unit you will explore the advanced features of LibreOffice Writer, enabling you to create professional and visually appealing documents. You'll learn to format text using styles, insert and modify images, and utilize features like Table of Contents and Track Changes. These skills will help you produce documents that are easy to read, understand, and edit.

CHAPTER 01

Introduction to Styles

Styles are the predefined sets of formatting options that helps to create consistent and professional-looking documents. By applying styles, you can quickly format text, paragraphs, and other elements to match your desired appearance. This eliminates the need for manual formatting and saves your time.

A style is a combination of font effects, colors and background that you can apply the selected pages, text and other elements in your document to quickly change their appearance.

Styles are used to apply a whole group of formats simultaneously to a document. The styles can be saved and applied whenever needed into the Writer document. Apart from in-built styles, you may create and save your own style and apply it in a document.

Using style allows to:

- create a consistent document.
- format a document with minimal effort.
- quickly change the appearance of the entire document.
- create a table of content.
- create an outline view of document.

1.1 Styles Categories in Writer

Styles help to maintain consistency in the document. They also make major formatting changes easy.

Writer is style-based software and provides six style categories:

- **Paragraph styles** can contain formatting information for the entire paragraph such as text body, heading, header & footer, caption, etc. It is also used for compiling a table of content.
- **Character styles** are used for formatting a block of text inside a paragraph such as text colour, text size, highlight, emphasize, etc. It is used to provide exception(s) to Paragraph style(s).
- **Frame styles** are used to organize a document in sections. Frame style allows to format frames and images, by specifying its size, position, border, placement of text and pictures, etc. in the document.

Note *A graphical object is always inserted in an invisible frame.*

- **Page styles** are used to store formatting information for a page, such as its layout, size, margins, placement of header & footer, borders, background, etc.
- **List styles** are used to store formatting information for numbered or bulleted list(s), such as indentation, numbering style, punctuation after number, etc. Using this style text font, borders, text flow cannot be changed. List style can also be used for creating outlines.
- **Table styles** are used to store formatting information for table(s) of data, such as aligning text inside table, text or border colour, etc.

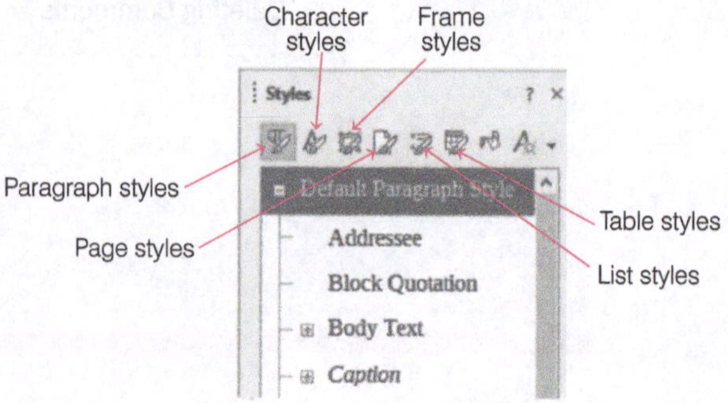

1.2 Styles and Formatting

Writer provides many options and tools to create and apply style(s) to format a document, using sidebar and Styles tab.

All style management options (apply styles, create and modify styles) are available through **Styles deck** on the sidebar along with all Style categories.

There are many predefined Styles in Writer, which can be accessed by using the following methods:

Method 1 Click on the **Styles** menu.

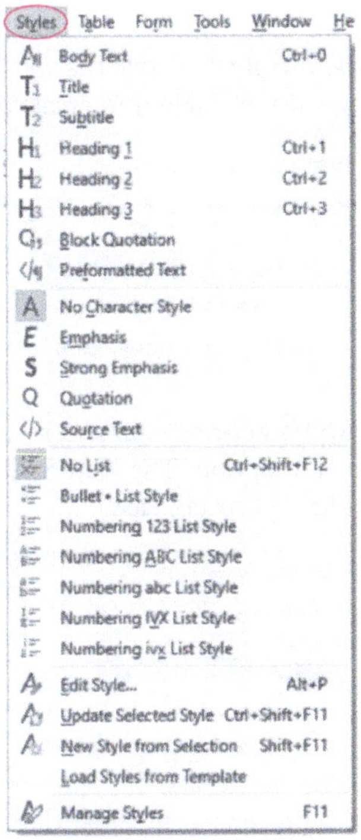

Method 2 Click on the **Styles** option from menu bar using style drop down list box from the toolbar. The current paragraph style is displayed in the textbox.

If the Toolbar is not visible then, click on **View →** **Toolbars**, and enable **Formatting/Formatting (Styles)**.

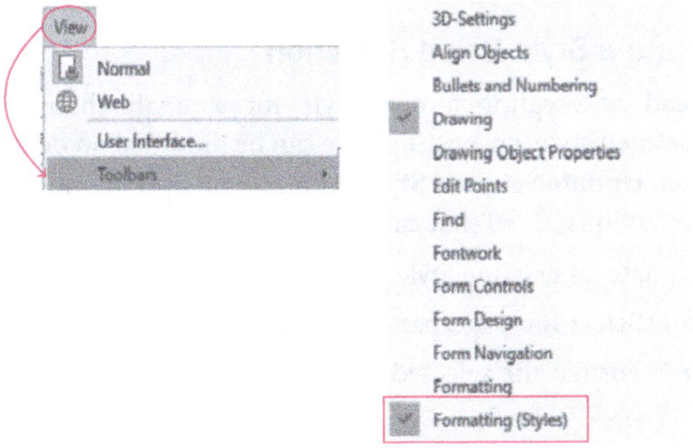

Method 3 Click on Styles icon from Sidebar. The Style sub-menu appears.

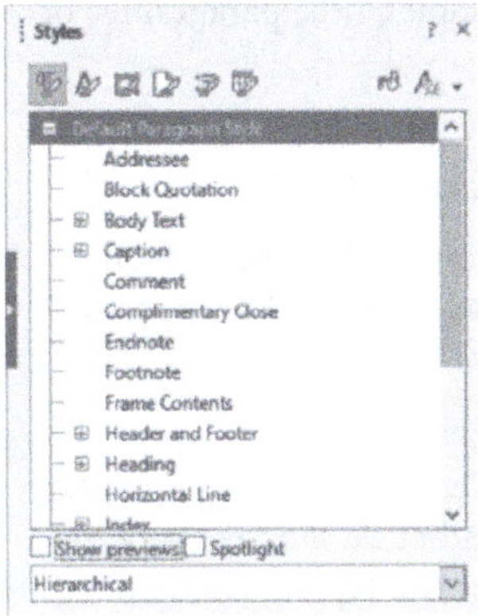

Fig. (a)

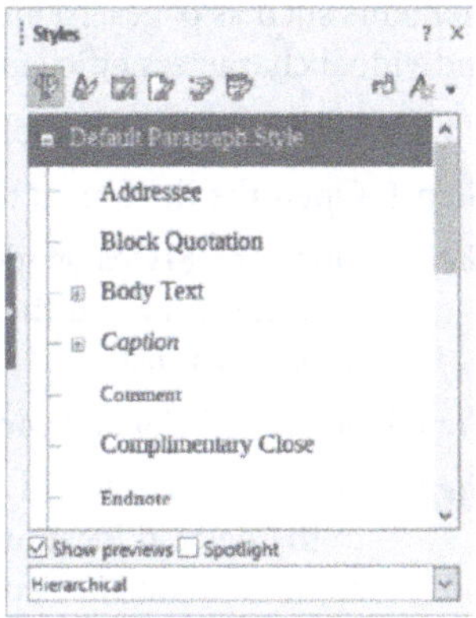

Fig. (b)

Click on any one of these buttons to display a list of existing styles in that category. From the bottom of the window selecting **Show Preview** option displays its style along with the name in the list.

Figure (a) shows the list when preview is not selected and Figure (b) shows when the preview is selected.

At the bottom of this menu, there is a Drop Down list, to select the filter for the style list to be displayed above. By default, this filter is set to Hierarchical as shown at the bottom.

Method 4 Using the keyboard shortcut F11 key.

1.3 Applying Styles

To apply styles, follow the given steps

Step 1 Select the text to be formatted. The selected text may be a collection of characters, words, lines, paragraph, page, frame or table.

Step 2 To format the selected text, choose appropriate style by clicking the button from the top of the Styles bar.

Step 3 A list of styles for that category appears. Double click on the desired style to apply to the selected text.

1.4 Using Fill Format Mode

To apply a style to words located in different parts of a document, you would typically need to go to each word individually and apply the style. However, Writer offers a more convenient method with the **Fill Format** option, which is the second icon from the right in the Styles menu. This feature is especially helpful when you need to apply the same style to multiple scattered elements throughout the document. Fill Format can be used to style various elements such as pages, frames, tables, lists, paragraphs, or individual characters efficiently.

To use Fill Format option, follow given steps

Step 1 Open the document to be styled.

Step 2 Open the **Styles** window and select the desired style category and then select desired style from drop-down list.

Step 3 Select **Fill Format Mode(**) button.

Step 4 To apply the selected style, take the mouse pointer to the desired location and click. Do take care to apply style on the appropriate type of content.

Step 5 Repeat step 4 until all the changes have been made for that style in the entire document.

Step 6 To quit **Fill Format** mode, click the **Fill Format Mode** button again or press the **Esc** key.

Note *When fill format mode is active, a right-click anywhere in the document undoes the last fill format action. Be careful, not to accidentally right click and thus undo actions you want to keep.*

Try These 1.1

1. **Which style in LibreOffice Writer is used to format an entire paragraph, including the text body, heading, and caption?**
   (a) Character Style (b) Paragraph Style
   (c) Frame Style (d) List Style
2. **What does the Page Style in LibreOffice Writer store information about?**
   (a) List formatting
   (b) Table alignment
   (c) Page layout, size, margins, and header & footer placement
   (d) Frame positioning and size
3. **Which style allows you to format frames and images by specifying their size, position, and border?**
4. **How many types of styles are there in LibreOffice Writer?**
5. **How is fill format useful for applying styles?**

1.5 Creating and Updating Styles

Sometimes, you used only predefined styles to format a document. However, if the existing styles in Writer don't meet your needs, you can create a custom style. There are several methods to do this, and two of them—"New Style From Selection" and "Drag and Drop" are explained here

New Style from Selection

Styles actions( ) option in the **Styles** menu is used to create a new style or modify an existing style.

It can also be used to load a style defined in a document or template, in the list. Let us learn how to create a new style; which is the first function in the drop-down list of action buttons.

Once a portion of the document is formatted, as per the requirement, then a new style may be created and saved for formatting other documents.

To create a new style from selection, use following steps:

Step 1 Select a portion of the document using which a new style is to be created.

Step 2 Click on the Styles option on Sidebar, to open it.

Step 3 Choose the category of style (paragraph, character, frame, page, list and table) to create a new one.

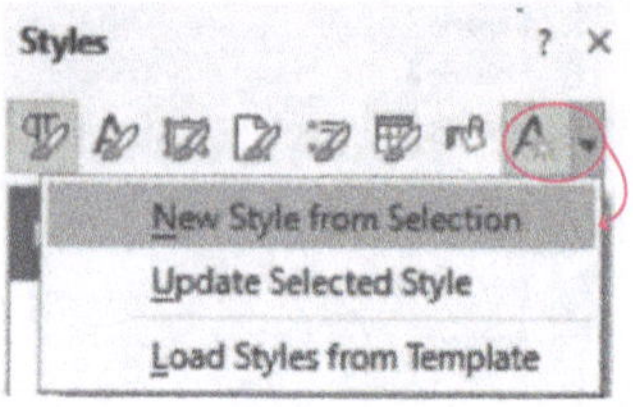

Step 4 Click on **Styles actions** icon and select New Style from Selection option. The New Style from Selection dialog box appears.

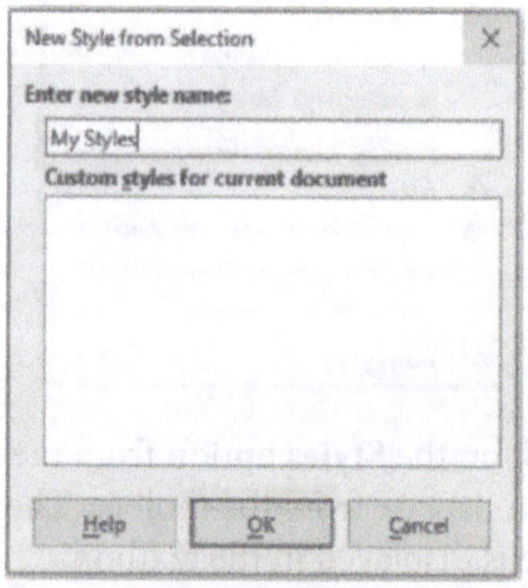

Step 5 Type the name of new style.

Step 6 Click **OK** to save changes.

Update a Style Using Selection

Instead of creating a new style for a small change in predefined style, an existing style can be modified on desired aspect. **Update Selected Style** is the second option under the Styles actions( ) that can be used for doing so.

To update an existing style, follow the given steps:

Step 1 Select the page/paragraph to be modified.

Step 2 Format the selected portion as per the requirement.

Step 3 Click on the **Styles** option on sidebar.

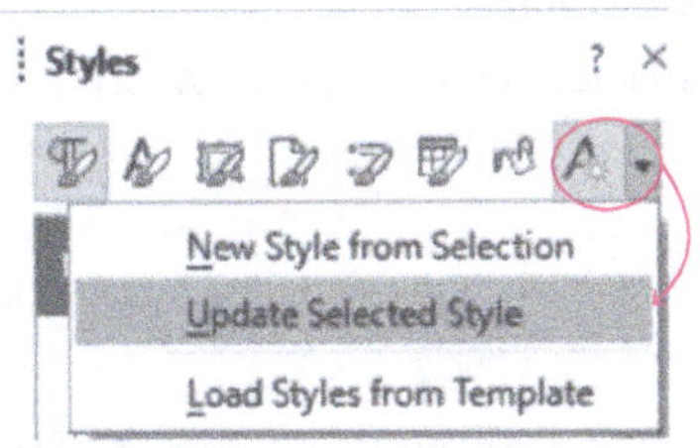

Step 4 Using **Styles actions** button, click on **Updated Selected Style.**

Note *Ensure that the modified aspect remains consistent throughout the selection. For example, when changing the font face or size in a paragraph, it should stay the same across the entire paragraph.*

Using Drag and Drop

Another way of creating a new style is using **Drag and Drop** method. It is very easy and convenient to use. To create a new Style using Drag and Drop method, follow the given steps:

Step 1 Select the text from the document and change its formatting as desired.

Step 2 Apply the desired style on the text.

Step 3 Click on the desired style under which, the new style is to be created.

Step 4 From the document, drag the selected portion of text to the Style menu. The New Style from Selection dialog window appears.

Note *While dragging the text, check the cursor shape, as it changes to indicate whether the desired operation is possible or not.*

Step 5 Type the name of new style.

Step 6 Click on the OK button to save the name of new style.

Note *Drag and Drop cannot be used to create a Page Style.*

1.6 Load Styles from Template or Document

Load Styles From Template

This is the third option listed in Styles actions drop-down list. This option enables a document to be formatted by copying Style by loading it from a template.

Template allows you to copy all styles or a group of styles at one time.

To copy Styles from a template, follow the given steps:

Step 1 Open the document to be formatted by copying styles.

Step 2 Click on the Styles option on Sidebar and click on Styles actions icon.

Step 3 Click on Load Styles from Template option. The Load Styles from Template dialog box appears.

Step 4 Choose the Categories and then select the template, to copy a style from.

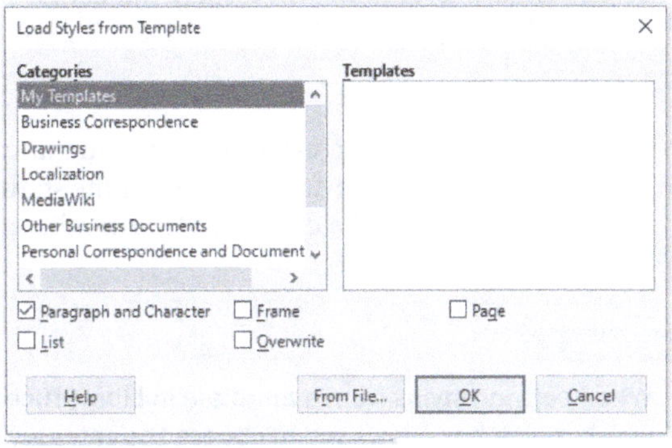

Step 5 Select the options for the type of styles to be copied – Paragraph and Character (for text style), Frame, Pages, List (for numbering style).

Step 6 Click **OK** to copy the style.

Note *By selecting overwrite, the styles being copied will replace any existing styles with the same name.*

Load Style from Another Document

A document can also be formatted using styles, from another document using Load Style of Template dialog box. Use following steps to copy Styles from another document:

Step 1 Open the document where you want to copy the styles.

Step 2 Click on the Styles option on Sidebar (or press F11) and then click on Styles actions icon.

Step 3 Click on Load Styles from Templates option, a dialog box appears.

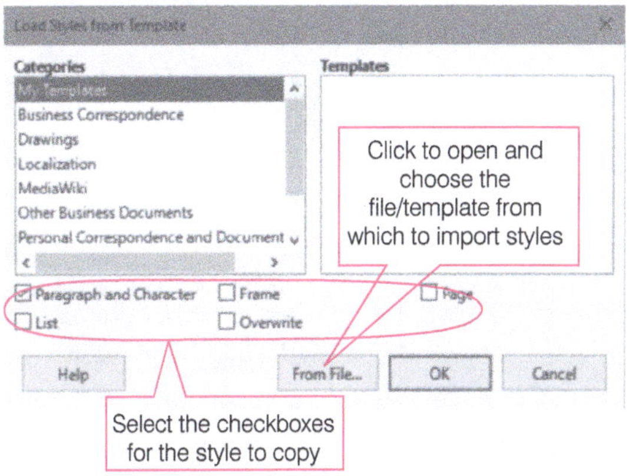

Step 4 Select the checkboxes for the style categories you want to copy.

Step 5 To replace the existing styles with the copied ones, select 'Overwrite' and click 'OK' to duplicate the styles into the target document.

Step 6 The screen won't update, but the Styles and Formatting window will display the names of the newly imported styles.

Applying Default Style

When a new document is created, Writer automatically applies default style, which are displayed in the status bar. You can choose to keep the default style or modify it as needed.

Try These 1.2

1. **When copying styles from a template in LibreOffice Writer, which dialog box allows you to choose the category and select the template?**
   (a) Create New Style from Selection dialog box
   (b) Load Styles from Template dialog box
   (c) Update Selected Style dialog box
   (d) Fill Format mode dialog box
2. **To update an existing style using a selection, which option is selected from the Styles actions icon drop-down list?**
3. **What is the first step to create a new style from a selection in LibreOffice Writer?**
4. **The keyboard shortcut to create a new style is ______ .**

Summary

A Style is a set of formatting aspects, applied to text, tables, list, etc.

Writer is style-based software and provides six style categories – Paragraph, Character, Page, Frame, List and Table.

Paragraph styles are the most frequently used styles for formatting a document.

Formatting options which can be applied on a document, using Formatting toolbar, can also be applied using Styles.

There are many ways of working with Styles, but all style management options (apply styles, create and modify styles) are available through Styles deck on the Sidebar.

Fill Format mode allows to apply a style to many areas, without having to go back to Styles deck.

Writer allows to create custom Styles by creating new styles or modifying existing ones.

Selection, Drag & Drop, Template and other documents can be used to create new Styles.

ACTIVITY Time

ACTIVITY 1

Apply an existing Heading style, from Paragraph Styles.

Step 1 Create a new document named 'noise.odt' with the text as shown in figure.

Step 2 Add a title, 'Noise Pollution' on top.

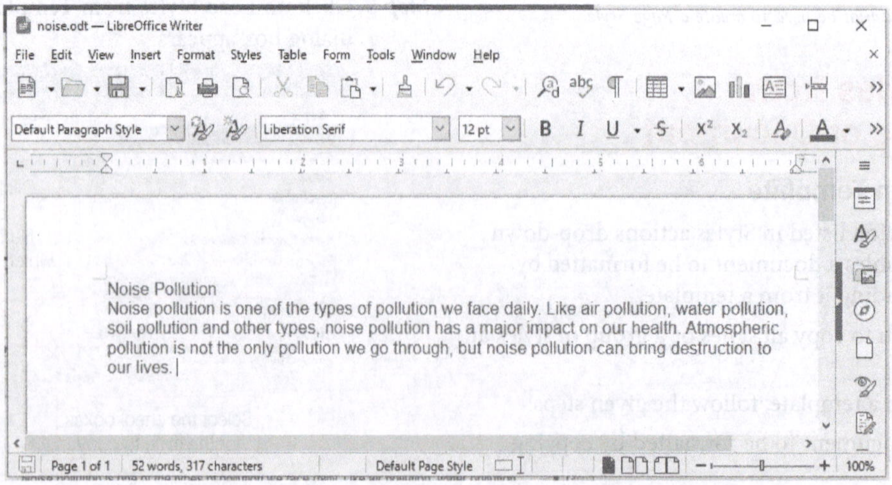

Step 3 Select the Title – Noise Pollution

Step 4 Open **Styles** menu using Sidebar and go to Headings option.

Step 5 Double click on Heading 4 to apply. Observe that the below figure shows the Heading 4 style is applied to the heading 'Noise Pollution'.

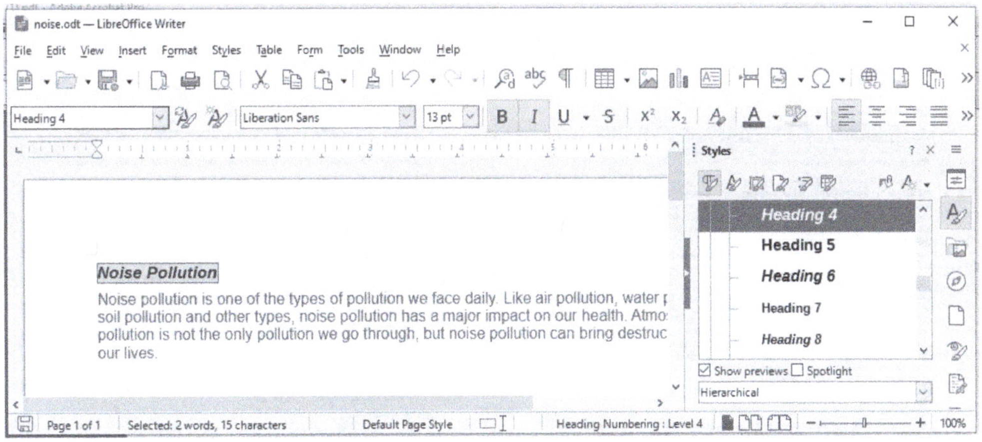

Using predefined heading style, allow you to use them as a bookmark for browsing the document.

ACTIVITY 2

Apply an existing page style on 'noise.odt'

Step 1 Open file 'noise.odt' created in Activity 1.

Step 2 Insert a blank page in the beginning by selecting Insert → Page Break from main menu bar.

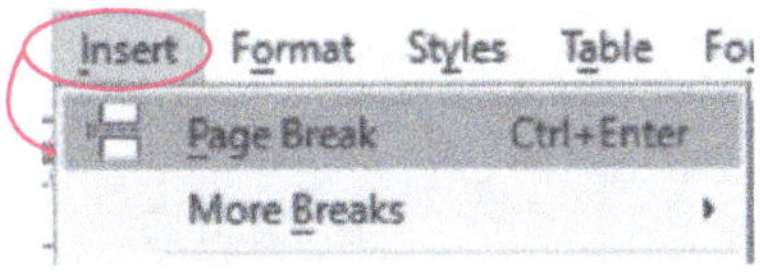

Step 3 Inserting a page break will shift the matter to the second page. Now, place the cursor at the beginning of page 2, where the matter appears.

Step 4 Open **Styles** menu from sidebar and select the **Page Styles** option as shown in figure.

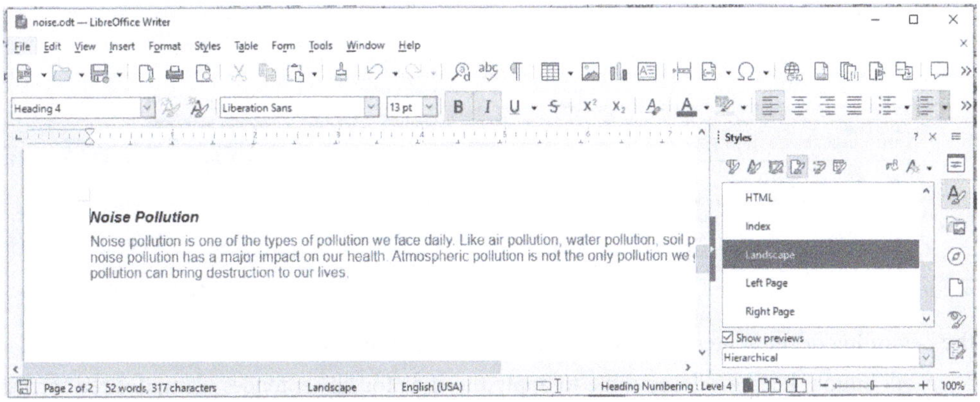

Step 5 Double click on Landscape to change page orientation to Landscape. After applying Page Styles, you can observe that the document pages orientation is changed to Landscape from Portrait.

Note *Applying page style on a page may affect the entire document.*

ACTIVITY 3

Use Fill Format to change appearance of paragraphs at different places in the document using paragraph formatting. A file 'documentation.odt' with at least 2 pages of text is used for the activity.

Step 1 Open a file 'documentation.odt' having 2 pages of text.Observe the indented sentences in second page.

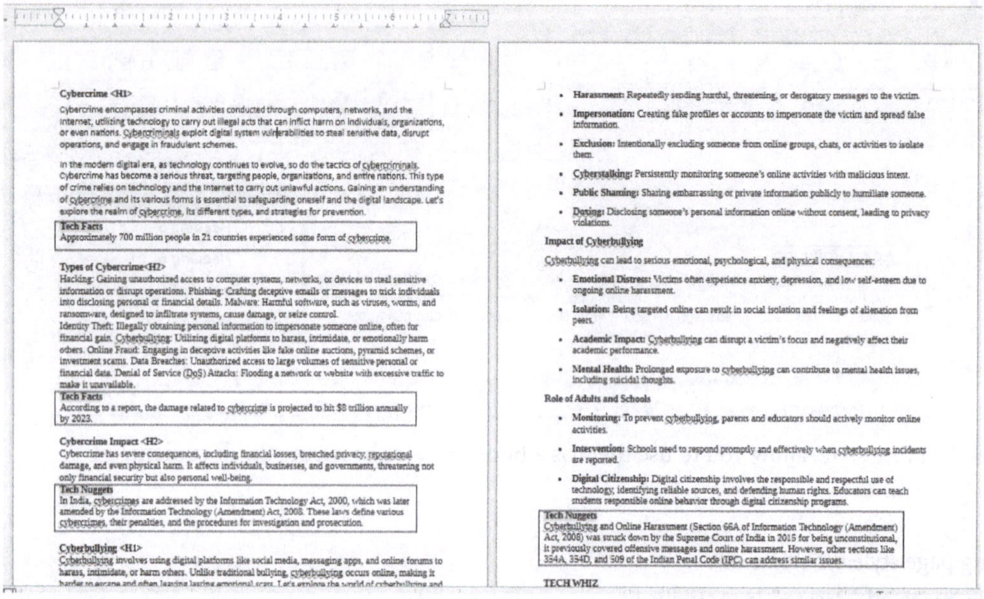

Step 2 Go to Styles menu from sidebar and click on Paragraph category, and select List Paragraph from the drop down list as shown in figure.

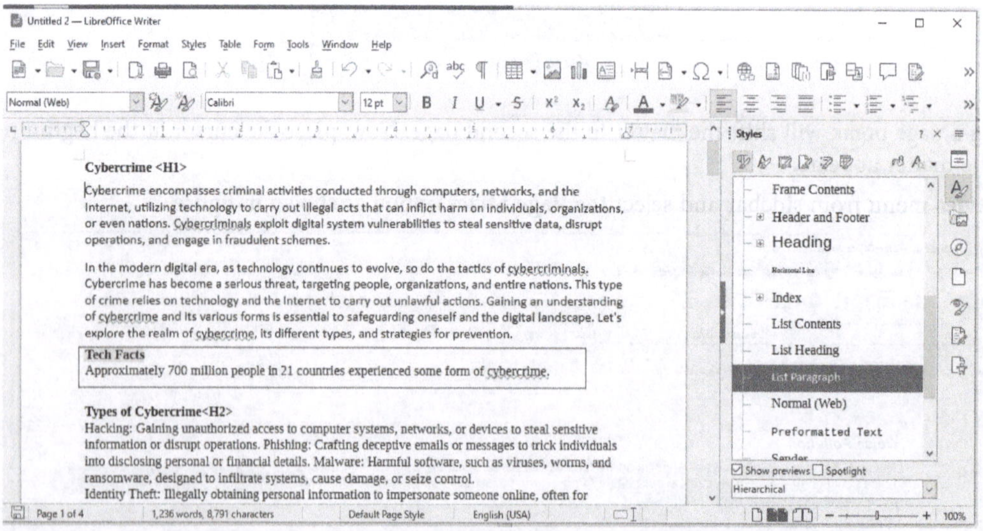

Step 3 Click at the beginning of the sentence to be styled using List Paragraph.

Step 4 Now click on Fill button, keep on doing same to apply the style for all sentences using desired format.

Refer to below figure to view the effect of fill format on indented list.

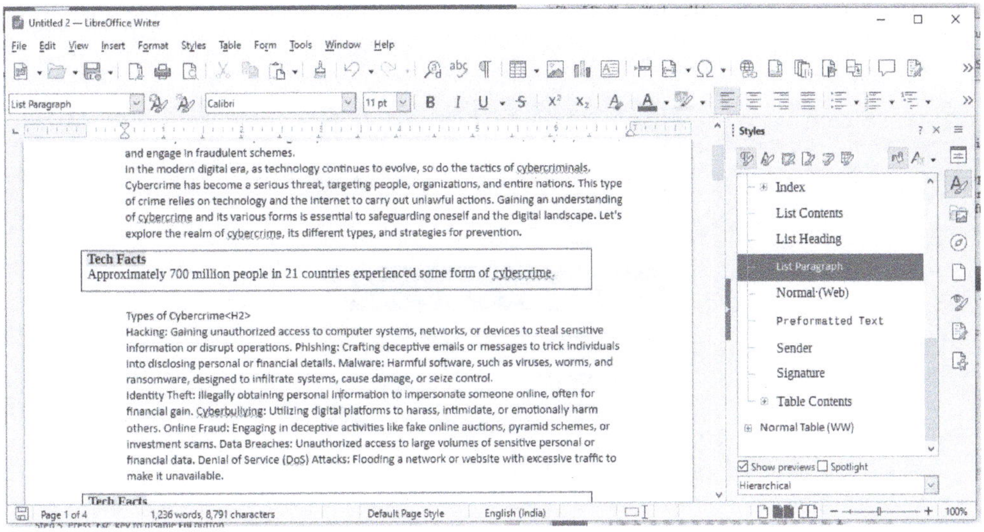

Note *Press* ***Esc*** *key to disable fill button.*

ACTIVITY 4

To create a custom paragraph style 'My New Style', using file 'noise.odt' created in Activity 1.

Step 1 Open file 'noise.odt' created in Activity 1.

Step 2 Format the content of the paragraph with Font face –Adobe Caslon Pro Bold, Font size 18.

Step 3 Select paragraph button from Styles menu of sidebar.

Step 4 Select Style actions button as shown in figure.

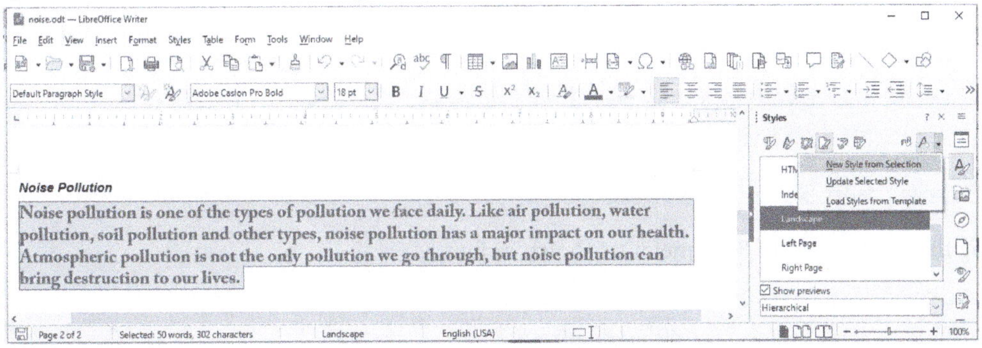

Step 5 Click on New Style from Selection. A New Style from Selection dialog box will appear as shown in figure.

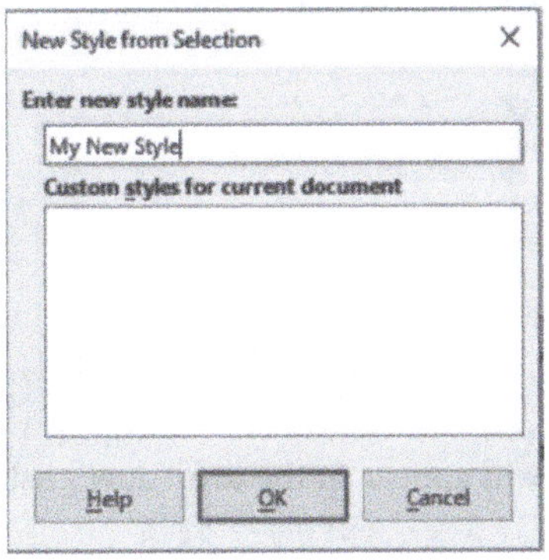

Step 6 Type 'My New Style' as style name in the box and click OK.The Style Name (My New Style) will appear in the drop down list under Paragraph category.

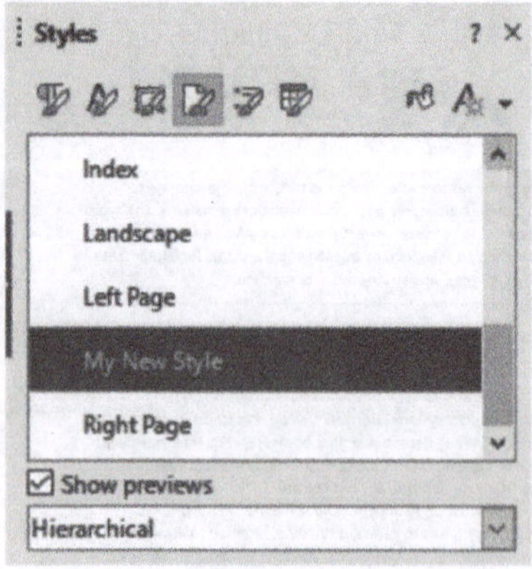

ACTIVITY 5

Create a new style 'myStyle1' using drag and drop, by changing line spacing to 1 and font size to 12.

Step 1 Open file 'noise.odt' created in Activity 1.

Step 2 Format the content of the paragraph with Font size 12 and line spacing 1.

Step 3 Select Paragraph button from Styles menu of sidebar.

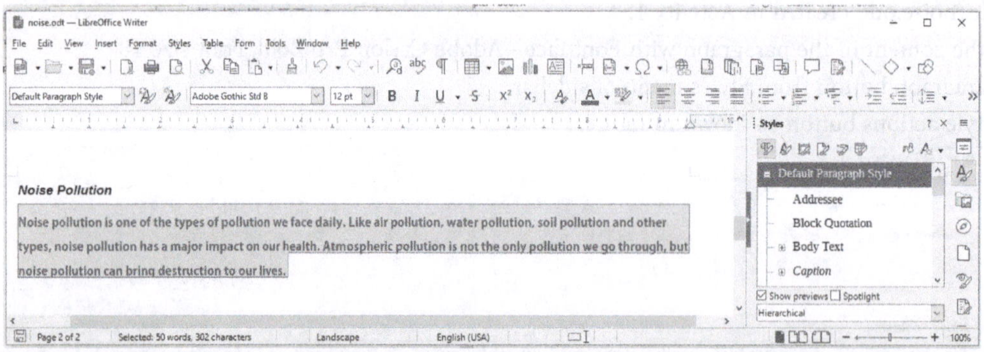

Step 4 Now drag the selected text to Style menu, as shown in figure.

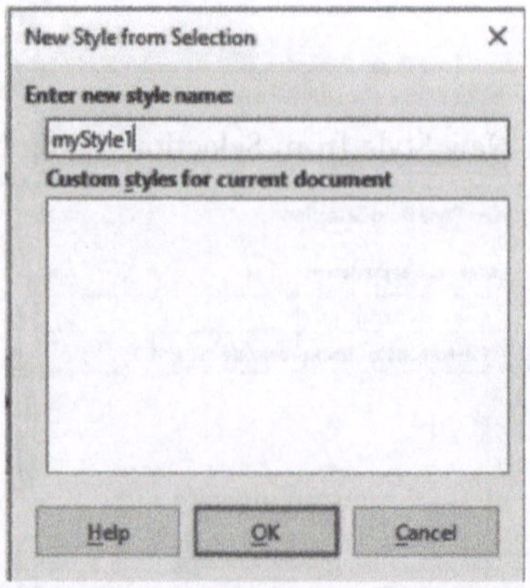

Step 5 Press OK. The style name (myStyle1) will appear in the drop down list under Paragraph category.

NCERT FOLDER

Complete Explanations of all NCERT's Questions

A. Multiple Choice Questions

Q.1 **Which of the following features in LibreOffice Writer is/are used to create the given document?**

(a) Page borders (b) Envelope
(c) Picture from File (d) Indexes and Tables

Q.2 **Styles menu (from sidebar) in Writer provide options to work on**
(a) Paragraph Styles (b) Frame Styles
(c) Page Styles (d) All of these

Q.3 **What is style template in LibreOffice Writer?**
(a) Pre-determined form and mode of document file
(b) One kind of model style
(c) One type of document
(d) Cluster of documents in Writer

Q.4 **Which of the following gives the status of your document like page numbers, number of pages?**
(a) Status bar (b) Standard toolbar
(c) Formatting (d) Title bar

Q.5 **Which of the following can be used to access a style menu?**
(a) F11 function key (b) Sidebar Menu
(c) Formatting toolbar (d) All of these

Answers

1. (b) **2.** (d) **3.** (b) **4.** (a) **5.** (d)

B. Fill in the Blanks

Q.1 **A ______ is a collection of different formats.**

Q.2 **Styles are especially handy in ______.**

Q.3 **Proper use of styles improves ______ in a document.**

Q.4 **The first five buttons at the top of the Styles window select the category of ______.**

Q.5 **Using predefined ______ creates Bookmark in the document.**

Q.6 **On opening a new file ______ Style is used for formatting the document.**

Q.7 **In page layout documents, you can arrange ______ like text boxes and graphics.**

Q.8 **Character styles are often integrated in ______ Style.**

Q.9 **______ allows to apply style at different places in the document.**

Q.10 **Predefined Style ______ be updated by Drag and Drop method.**

Answers

1. Style **2.** LibreOffice
3. Consistency **4.** Styles
5. Heading Style **6.** Default
7. Objects **8.** Paragraph
9. Fill Format **10.** cannot

C. Short Answer Questions

Q.1 **What do you understand by styles in LibreOffice Writer document?**

Ans. A style is a collection of all formatting information, which you want to save and then apply on the document.

Q.2 **Write advantages of using Style over manual formatting, for designing a document?**

Ans. It helps us to apply consistent formatting to the documents, easily change the existing format, and makes major formatting changes simple.

Q.3 **What are the different categories of style in LibreOffice Writer document?**

Ans. It provides six Style categories – Page, Paragraph, Character, Frame, List and Table.

Q.4 **Write down the steps to update a style?**

Ans. Refer to text on page no. 108 and 109 (Update a Style Using Selection).

Q.5 What do you understand by custom styles in LibreOffice Writer?

Ans. Custom style means creating a new style as per the user requirement.

There are two ways to create a custom style:

- From selection
- By using drag and drop

Q.6 In a document Introduction paragraph is to be designed extensively by setting its font (face, size, weight, colour), space above it and giving number to heading. Given below are the steps used to do so.

(i) Select the Introduction (paragraph)
(ii) Open Font list from Toolbar
(iii) Select the font
(iv) Open Font size from Toolbar
(v) Select the desired font size
(vi) Select Font weight (Bold) from the toolbar
(vii) Open Font color from Toolbar
(viii) Select desired color
(ix) Using Format menu option, select Spacing → Paragraph → Indent and Spacing
(x) Edit space above paragraph
(xi) Add number by Selecting Numbered list from Toolbar.

Ans. To design the Introduction paragraph extensively in LibreOffice Writer by setting its font (face, size, weight, color), space above it, and adding numbering to the heading, follow these steps:

(i) **Select the Introduction paragraph** Click and drag to highlight the text of the Introduction paragraph.

(ii) **Open Font list from Toolbar** In the toolbar at the top, locate the font dropdown. Click on it to view available fonts.

(iii) **Select the font** From the font dropdown, select the desired font (e.g., Arial, Times New Roman, etc.).

(iv) **Open Font size from Toolbar** Next to the font list, find the font size dropdown.

(v) **Select the desired font size** Choose an appropriate font size (e.g., 12 pt, 14 pt) from the dropdown.

(vi) **Select Font weight (Bold) from the toolbar** In the toolbar, find the bold icon (typically represented by a "B"). Click it to make the text bold.

(vii) **Open Font color from Toolbar** Locate the font color icon in the toolbar (it usually shows a letter "A" with a color bar beneath it).

(viii) **Select desired color** Click on the font color icon and select the color you want from the color palette.

(ix) **Using Format menu option, select Spacing → Paragraph → Indent and Spacing** From the menu at the top of the screen, click on Format → Paragraph. This opens the Paragraph settings window.

(x) **Edit space above paragraph** In the Paragraph window, go to the Indents & Spacing tab. Under Spacing, find the Above paragraph field, and set the desired space (e.g., 6 pt, 12 pt) to adjust the space above the paragraph.

(xi) **Add number by Selecting Numbered list from Toolbar** Finally, to add a number to the heading, click on the Numbering icon in the toolbar (it looks like a numbered list). This will add numbering to your Introduction heading.

Q.7 Give two examples, where instead of Style, using manual formatting will be beneficial.

Ans. Manual formatting beneficial in writing out text and applying formatting rules manually, such as underlining or bolding specific text, adding margins, spacing, etc.

Q.8 Give one situation, in which you will prefer to use Fill Format for styling your document.

Ans. This method is useful when a same style is to be applied at many places scattered in the document.

Fill Format can be used to style scattered – pages, frames, tables, lists, paragraphs or characters.

Q.9 Write steps to load style(s) from a template.

Ans. To load Styles from a template, follow the given steps:

Step 1 Open the document to be formatted by copying styles.

Step 2 Click on the Styles option on Sidebar and click on Styles actions icon.

Step 3 Click on Load Styles from Template option. The Load Styles from Template dialog box appears.

Step 4 Choose the Categories and then select the template, to copy a style from.

Step 5 Select the options for the type of styles to be copied – Paragraph and Character (for text style), Frame, Pages, List (for numbering style).

Step 6 Click **OK** to copy the style.

EXAM PATTERN EXERCISE

Including Competency Based Questions

Multiple Choice Questions

1 Which feature in Writer allows you to apply the same style to multiple words scattered throughout the document? CBSE SQP 2024-25

(a) Format Painter (b) Fill Format option
(c) Style Inspector (d) Font Adjustment Tool

2 .... include fonts, alignment, borders, background, number formats (for example, currency, date, number), and cell protection in document. CBSE SQP 2021-2022 Term I

(a) Cell Style (b) Numbering Style
(c) Paragraph Style (d) Character Style

3 Which of the following features allows one to apply a group of formats at the same time? CBSE 2024

(a) Fill (b) Styles
(c) Images (d) Drag and Drop

4 When you apply a ________, you apply a group of formatting effects together in one single step. CBSE SQP 2021-2022 Term I

(a) Effect (b) Style
(c) Template (d) Format

5 ________ styles in a text document affect selected text within a paragraph, such as the font and size of text, or bold and italic formats. CBSE SQP 2021-2022 Term I

(a) Cell (b) Paragraph
(c) Formatting (d) Character

6 ________Styles help to improve consistency in a document. Identify the style that is used to format graphic and text frames, including wrapping type, borders, backgrounds and columns. CBSE 2021-2022 Term I

(a) Numbering (b) Character
(c) Graphics (d) Frame

7 In a document, _______ is used to apply a style to many different areas quickly without having to go back to the Styles and Formatting window and double click every time. CBSE 2021-2022 Term I

(a) Fill format mode
(b) Formatting window
(c) Painter mode
(d) Text wrapping

8 Tanu explained her class that to apply an existing style, except for _______ , position the insertion point in the paragraph, frame or page and then double-click on the name of the style in one of these lists. CBSE 2021-2022 Term I

(a) Window style (b) Character style
(c) Paragraph style (d) Cell style

9 ________ controls all aspects of a paragraph's appearance, such as text alignment, tab stops, line spacing, and borders, and can include character formatting. CBSE 2023

(a) Page Style
(b) Character Style
(c) Cell Style
(d) Paragraph Style

10 In Writer, styles and formatting option is available under ________ menu. CBSE 2024

(a) Insert (b) Tools
(c) Format (d) Window

11 Which of the toolbars can't be used to style a document?

(a) Styles (b) Formatting (Styles)
(c) Format (d) Styles deck

12 How many style categories are available in Writer?

(a) Six (b) Seven (c) Five (d) Many

13 Which of the following will not open Styles Deck from Sidebar?

(a) Styles icon on Sidebar
(b) More Styles on Formatting toolbar
(c) Styles tab on Menu bar
(d) Format tab on Menu bar

14 Which of the following Styles are recommended to be used with List?

(a) Paragraph (b) List
(c) Table (d) All of these

15 Ravi has to prepare a project report. He wants to save certain formatting features and then apply them on the project report. He can use the .... feature of OpenOffice Writer. CBSE 2025

(a) Styles (b) Image
(c) Mail Merge (d) Preview

16 What is the primary benefit of using styles in LibreOffice Writer?

(a) They increase the document file size.
(b) They allow for consistent formatting across the document.
(c) They only apply formatting to text in tables.
(d) They automatically create backups of the document.

17 You have created a new style called "Quote" in LibreOffice Writer. You want to apply this style to multiple quotes scattered throughout your document. What is the most efficient method to do this? Competency Based Que.

(a) Manually format each quote individually.
(b) Use the Fill Format mode to apply the "Quote" style to each quote.
(c) Copy and paste the formatted quote.
(d) Create a new document and reformat the quotes.

18 Shanta is creating a project report in Writer and wants to apply the same style on headings / titles in the entire document as she has done at the beginning of the document. She can use the .... feature of Writer to apply the same format on each line / word, wherever needed. CBSE 2025

(a) Fill Style (b) Fill Format
(c) Apply Feature (d) Apply Character

Answers

1. (b)	2. (a)	3. (b)	4. (b)	5. (d)
6. (d)	7. (a)	8. (a)	9. (d)	10. (c)
11. (c)	12. (a)	13. (d)	14. (b)	15. (a)
16. (b)	17. (b)	18. (b)		

Very Short Answer Type Questions

1 What is a style in LibreOffice Writer?

Ans. A style is a combination of font effects, colors, and backgrounds that can be applied to selected pages, text, and other elements in a document to change their appearance quickly.

2 Name the six style categories available in LibreOffice Writer.

Ans. The six style categories are Paragraph Styles, Character Styles, Page Styles, Frame Styles, List Styles, and Table Styles.

3 Out of various style categories provided by Writer, briefly explain Frame style category in brief. CBSE 2025

Ans. The Frame style category in Writer refers to text and graphic containers, like text boxes or images, which can be positioned, resized, and formatted independently within the document.

4 How can you open the Styles deck in LibreOffice Writer?

Ans. The Styles deck can be opened by going to Styles → Manage Styles on the Menu bar. or Clicking on the Styles icon from the Sidebar, or selecting More Styles from the Formatting toolbar.

5 What is Fill Format mode used for?

Ans. Fill Format mode is used to apply a style quickly to multiple areas in a document without having to make multiple selections.

6 What are the steps to create a new style from selection?

Ans. Select the desired portion of the document, open the Styles Deck, choose the style category then click the Styles Actions icon, and select "New Style from Selection."

7 What does the Page Style in LibreOffice Writer store?

Ans. The Page Style stores formatting information for a page, including layout, size, margins, header & footer placement, borders, and background.

8 What is the significance of character styles?

Ans. Character styles are used to format specific blocks of text within a paragraph, such as text color, size, and emphasis, providing exceptions to paragraph styles.

9 How can styles from a template be loaded into a document?

Ans. Click on the Styles actions icon in the Styles deck and select "Load Styles from Template," then choose the desired template and style options.

10 Why is it important to use styles in a document?

Ans. Using styles ensures consistency in formatting, allows for minimal effort in formatting changes, enables quick adjustments across the document, and aids in creating a table of contents and outline views.

Short Answer Type Questions

1 Explain the benefits of using styles in LibreOffice Writer.

Ans. Styles provide several benefits in LibreOffice Writer:

- **Consistency** They help maintain a uniform look throughout the document, ensuring that all headings, paragraphs, and other elements adhere to the same formatting.
- **Efficiency** Styles allow users to apply a group of formatting options with a single click, reducing the time spent on manual formatting.
- **Flexibility** Users can quickly change the appearance of the entire document by modifying or updating styles, which is far more efficient than adjusting individual elements.
- **Document Organization** Styles facilitate the creation of tables of contents and outlines, enhancing the organization of longer documents.

2 Discuss the procedure to create a new style from a selection and its advantages.

Ans. To create a new style from a selection, follow these steps:

- Select the portion of the document that is formatted as desired.
- Open the Styles deck on the Sidebar.

- Choose the category of the style you want to create (paragraph, character, etc.).
- Click on the Styles actions icon and select "New Style from Selection."
- In the dialog box, enter a name for the new style and click OK to save it.

Advantages of this method are:

- **Time-Saving** Users do not need to remember the formatting settings as the formatting is applied directly from the selection.
- **Visual Confirmation** The effect of formatting is visible on the screen, making it easier to ensure the style looks as intended.

3 Explain how to load styles from another document in LibreOffice Writer.

Ans. Refer to text on page no. 109 and 110. (Load Style from Another Document)

4 Aamna is a book editor. She wants to change the indentation of all paragraphs and change the font of all titles in the book. Which feature should she use to do it easily? **Competency Based Que.**

Ans. Aamna should use Styles because they allow her to apply consistent formatting changes across multiple paragraphs and titles simultaneously.

By updating the Paragraph Style for all body text, she can change the indentation of all paragraphs at once. Similarly, she can modify the Heading Style for titles to change the font throughout the book easily.

5 You are formatting a research paper in LibreOffice Writer, and you need to apply consistent formatting to all the headings, subheadings, and body text. **Competency Based Que.**

(a) Which styles should you apply to the main title, section headings, and subheadings to ensure a hierarchical structure?

(b) What steps would you take to modify an existing style if you decide to change the font size of the section headings?

Ans. (a) Use a Paragraph Style for the main title, a different Paragraph Style for section headings, and another one for subheadings to maintain a clear hierarchical structure.

(b) Select a formatted section heading, open the Styles deck, select the style for section headings, click the Styles actions icon, choose "Update Selected Style," make the necessary font size changes, and click OK to save.

6 You are working on a document that includes several tables, and you want to maintain a consistent appearance across all of them. **Competency Based Que.**

(a) What style should you apply to the tables for consistent formatting, and what elements can you control with this style?

(b) If you need to make a slight adjustment to the borders of one table without affecting others, how would you do this?

Ans. (a) Apply a Table Style to ensure consistent formatting across all tables. This style can control elements such as text alignment, border color, background color, and padding within the table cells.

(b) Select the specific table, then manually adjust the border settings using the formatting options available in the Properties sidebar or the toolbar, instead of changing the Table Style.

7 What is the importance of styles and formatting window?

Ans. The Styles and formatting window in LibreOffice is crucial for efficient document formatting and management. Its importance lies in:

- **Centralized formatting control** Manage all styles (paragraph, character, frame, page, and list) in one place.
- **Time-saving** Quickly modify and update styles, rather than manually formatting individual elements save a lot more time.
- **Organization** View and manage all styles, including custom and imported ones to ensure clarity, consistency, and easy maintenance.
- **Efficiency** Streamline formatting tasks with easy access to styles, reduce repetitive work, and increase productivity through effective use of styles and formatting tools.

PRACTICAL ASSIGNMENT

1 Mr R K Sharma is planning to change his job. He approaches a company (www.naukri.in) for helping him in finding new job. Mr Sharma is asked to submit his CV/Resume in the company. He has downloaded a sample CV from "template.com". Help him in creating his CV in the same format. Also save the format as "CV1" on the computer, for future reference.

2 Raghav receives a non-styled text document as shown in Fig. (a), from his teacher to convert it into desired appearance as shown in Fig. (b). He has to save it as "reportStyle" for future reference. Write the process that he should follow.

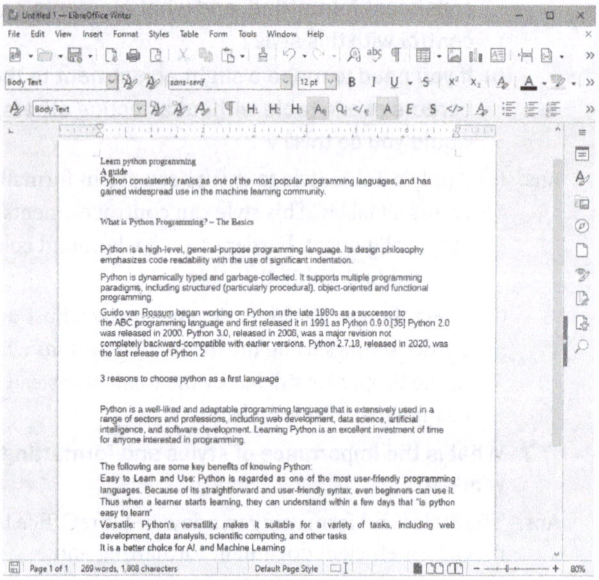

Fig (a)

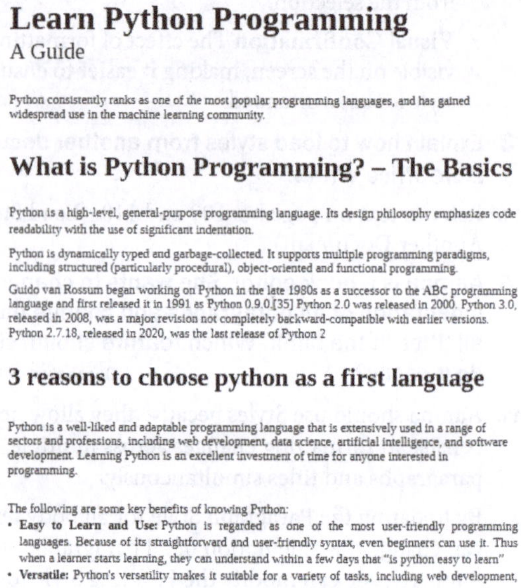

Learn Python Programming

A Guide

Python consistently ranks as one of the most popular programming languages, and has gained widespread use in the machine learning community.

What is Python Programming? – The Basics

Python is a high-level, general-purpose programming language. Its design philosophy emphasizes code readability with the use of significant indentation.

Python is dynamically typed and garbage-collected. It supports multiple programming paradigms, including structured (particularly procedural), object-oriented and functional programming.

Guido van Rossum began working on Python in the late 1980s as a successor to the ABC programming language and first released it in 1991 as Python 0.9.0.[35] Python 2.0 was released in 2000. Python 3.0, released in 2008, was a major revision not completely backward-compatible with earlier versions. Python 2.7.18, released in 2020, was the last release of Python 2

3 reasons to choose python as a first language

Python is a well-liked and adaptable programming language that is extensively used in a range of sectors and professions, including web development, data science, artificial intelligence, and software development. Learning Python is an excellent investment of time for anyone interested in programming.

The following are some key benefits of knowing Python:
- **Easy to Learn and Use:** Python is regarded as one of the most user-friendly programming languages. Because of its straightforward and user-friendly syntax, even beginners can use it. Thus when a learner starts learning, they can understand within a few days that "is python easy to learn"
- **Versatile:** Python's versatility makes it suitable for a variety of tasks, including web development,

Fig (b)

3 Kendriya Vidyala No. 3, is planning to publish a monthly digital newsletter for their school. Ravish Pandey of class 12, heads the group responsible to design it on computer. Size of news letter finalised is 5 inch (length) by 8 inch (height). It was also decided that:
- The newsletter will have two pages with 4 leaves.
- The first leaf will provide brief information about school.
- The second leaf will have a table, displaying the school's last year's Board exam results.
- On the third leaf School achievements (at least 4) for the current session will be given.
- The last leaf will have articles or poems (at least 2) written by students.

You being part of the team are required to perform the following using Style Menu from the Sidebar:

(a) Suggest appropriate style category (page, frame, and table) to be used to design the newsletter.
(b) Create digital copy of it.
(c) Apply Left Page and Right Page format on appropriate leaves.
(d) Also set the same margins on all leaves, having same border on all.
(e) Add page number on each leaf. The page number should appear in Footer as "Page – number". Right align these numbers on each leaf.
(f) For heading(s) and sub heading(s) use Heading 2 and Heading 4, in the newsletter.
(g) On the first leaf, while displaying information about school, use character styling of your choice to make it attractive.
(h) Use table to style Board Results, using grid rows and columns.
(i) Each row of the table should have a number – in Roman, prefixed to content.
(j) Organise school achievements in frames, where individual frame is to be styled using Frames of Paragraph category.
(k) Using selection method, save the style in respective category, so that the same can be used to publish future newsletters to maintain consistency.

CHAPTER 02

Working with Images

Word processing applications offer rich features that allow the creation of interactive documents. Including pictures in a document makes it more engaging and easier to comprehend than plain text.

These pictures can be drawings, charts, photos, logos, graphs, or even a single video frame. In digital documents, pictures are represented as graphics or digital images.

LibreOffice Writer offers various tools for working with images. A picture is essentially a digital image, represented by a finite set of digital values (0 or 1), known as **pixels**. These images are stored in different types of graphic files with extensions such as GIF, JPG, JPEG, PNG, BMP, and others.

2.1 Inserting an Image File

When the image file stored on the computer, you can insert it into a LibreOffice document using any one of the following methods

Method I Insert Image Option

To insert an image using Insert Image dialog box, follow the given steps:

Step 1 Position the cursor where you want to insert an image.

Step 2 Click on the Insert menu.

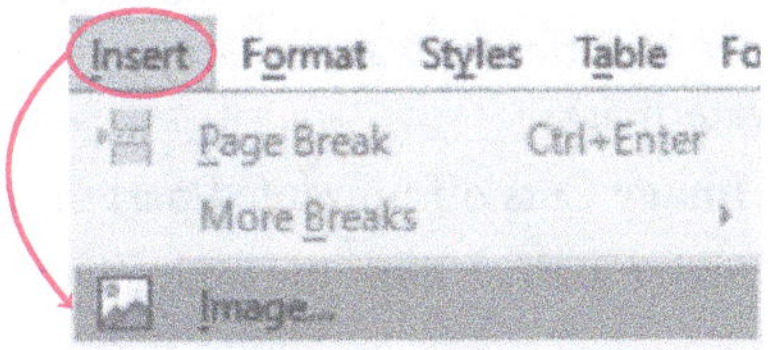

Step 3 Click on the Image option. The Insert Image dialog box appears.

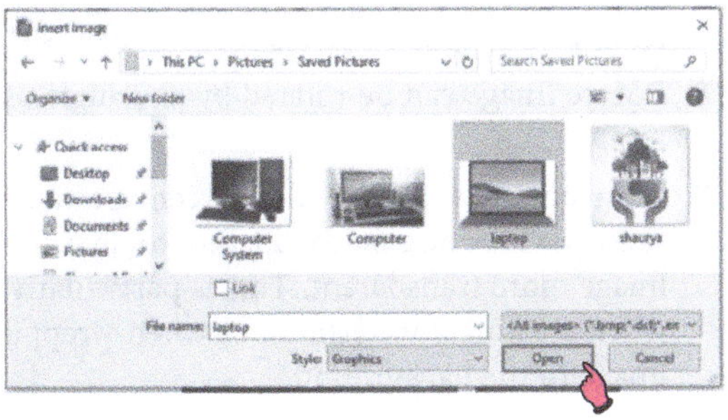

Step 4 Select the file image.

Step 5 Click on the Open button to add it to your document.

Method II Inserting an Image using Drag and Drop

Drag and drop refers to selecting an image from a particular location and dragging and dropping it in the document where required.

To do so, follow the given steps:

Step 1 Open the document and move the cursor to the location where you want to insert the image.

Step 2 Now, locate the image on your computer using the File Explorer window (in Windows 10).

Step 3 Select the image and drag it in your document. The image will be inserted in the document.

Method III Inserting an Image using Copy and Paste

Sometimes, you may want to insert an image in your document from any other previously created document. In order to do this, follow the given steps:

Step 1 Open the document in which the image already exists.

Step 2 Click on the image and press Ctrl+C to copy it. The image gets copied to the clipboard.

Step 3 Now, open the other document and place the cursor where you want to paste the image.

Step 4 Press Ctrl+V. The copied image is pasted in the document.

Method IV Insert an image by linking

If the same image needs to be inserted multiple times in a document, it is more efficient to save the image link rather than embedding the image repeatedly. By inserting a link, only a reference to the image is stored instead of the image itself, which helps reduce the document's size. The actual image is saved separately as a file along with the document. When the document is opened, the linked image is automatically merged and displayed at the referenced locations on the screen.

In order to do this, follow the given steps:

Step 1 Click on the document where you want the image to be appear.

Step 2 Choose Insert → Image on the Menu bar or click the Insert Image icon on the standard toolbar.

Step 3 Navigate and select the image.

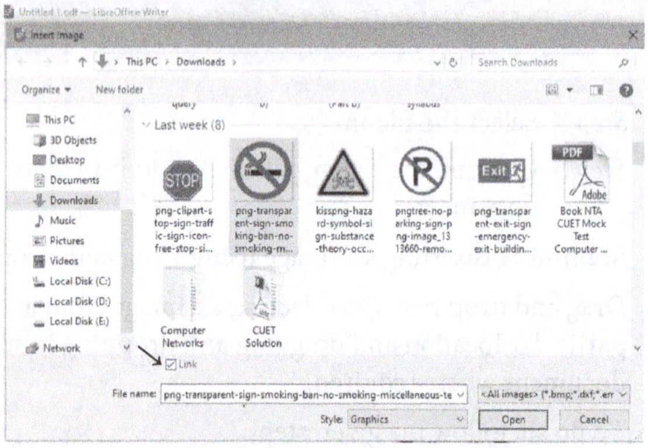

Step 4 At the bottom of the dialog a Link option is mentioned. Click this for the use of Link.

Step 5 Click Open.

Note *If you choose the Link option, a message box will appear asking if you want to embed it instead. You can choose "Keep Link" to maintain the link or "Embed Graphic" to embed the image directly. To prevent this message from appearing again, uncheck the "Ask when linking a graphic" option at the bottom of the message box.*

2.2 Modifying an Image

When you insert a new image, an Image toolbar appears. There are various options to resize, crop, delete and rotate an image in the Image toolbar.

Using the Image Toolbar

The Image toolbar automatically appears whenever you insert or select an image in your document.

If you want to keep it always on screen, you can do by clicking on View → Toolbars → Image in the menu bar. Once activated, the Image toolbar will be displayed as illustrated in the given figure.

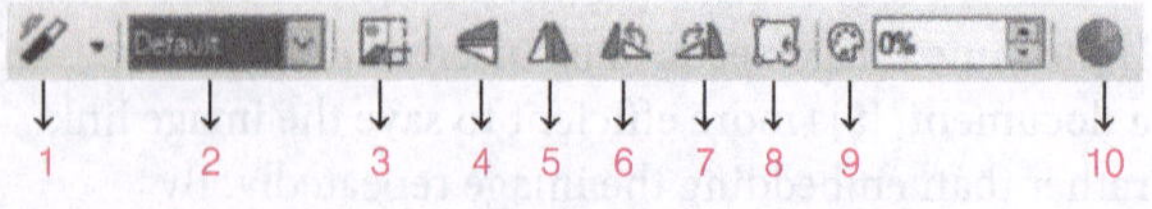

1. **Filter** There are various filters available to enhance the appearance of an image. These filters are

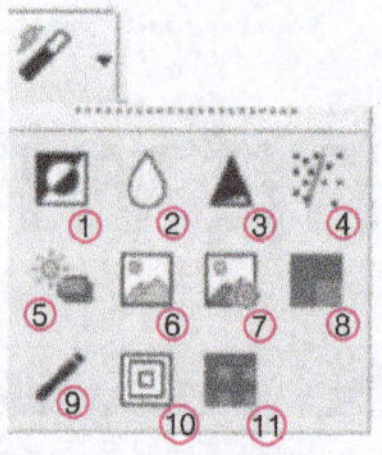

Filters and their Effects

S.No.	Tool	Effect on Images
1.	Invert	Inverts the colour values of coloured image. In case image is gray-scale then its brightness is inverted.
2.	Smooth	Softens the contrast of image. Another dialog box appears to adjust parameter
3.	Sharpen	Increases the contrast of image
4.	Remove Noise	Removes single pixels from the image
5.	Solarisation	Used in Photographs to reverse the tone. Dark appears light and light appears dark.
6.	Aging	Simulates the effect of time on picture.
7.	Posterise	Makes a picture appear like painting by reducing colours in the image
8.	Pop Art	Applies a visual style reminiscent of the Pop Art movement
9.	Charcoal Sketch	Changes image as charcoal sketch
10.	Relief	Adjusts light source to create shadow
11.	Mosaic	Joins group of pixels into a single area of one colour.

2. **Image Mode** By this, you can change the appearance of image in different ways as Grayscale, black/white and watermark.
3. **Crop Image** Cuts off unwanted part of the image.
4. **Flip Horizontally** Flips the image Horizontally by 180°.
5. **Flip Vertically** Flips the image Vertically by 180°.
6. **Rotate 90° Left** Rotates the image by 90° left.
7. **Rotate 90° Right** Rotates the image by 90° right.
8. **Rotate** Image can be rotated by any angle using this tool.
9. **Transparency** Modify the percentage value in the Transparency box on the Picture toolbar to make the image more transparent. This is particularly useful when creating a watermark or when wrapping the image in the background.

10. **Color** Use this toolbar to modify the individual RGB color components of the image (red, green, blue) as well as the brightness, contrast, and gamma of the image. If the result is not satisfactory, you can press Ctrl+Z to restore the default values.

Changing Colour of Image

To change the colour of an image, follow the given steps:

Step 1 Select the image.

Step 2 Click on the Color( ) option. A colour palette appears.

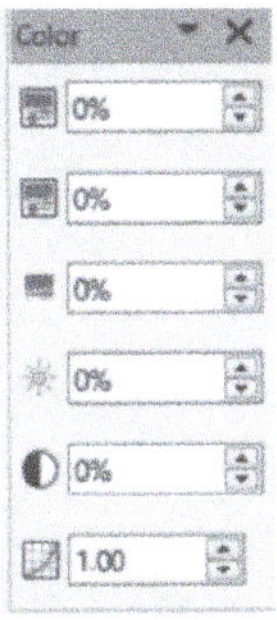

- **Red** To increase or decrease the percentage of Red.
- **Green** To increase or decrease the percentage of Green.
- **Blue** To increase or decrease the percentage of Blue.
- **Brightness** To change the percentage of brightness.
- **Contrast** To change the percentage of contrast.
- **Gamma** Gamma refers to a tool that adjusts the gamma correction of an image. Gamma correction is a method used to adjust the brightness and contrast of an image by changing the midtones without significantly affecting the highlights and shadows.

Try These 2.1

1. **What happens when you link an image instead of embedding it in a LibreOffice document?**
   (a) The image file is duplicated in the document
   (b) The document size increases
   (c) The actual image is saved separately, reducing document size
   (d) The image cannot be displayed when the document is opened
2. **When you want to insert multiple copies of the same image in a document without increasing file size, you should use _______.**
3. **_______ tool in the Image toolbar allows you to adjust the brightness and contrast of an image.**
4. **What is the purpose of the Image toolbar in LibreOffice?**
5. **What does the Gamma correction do to an image?**

2.3 Cropping Image

When you are only interested in a section of the image for the purpose of your document, you may wish to crop (cut off) parts of it.

Method I Using the Crop tool

To use the Crop tool, follow the given steps:

Step 1 Right-click on the image. A context menu appears.

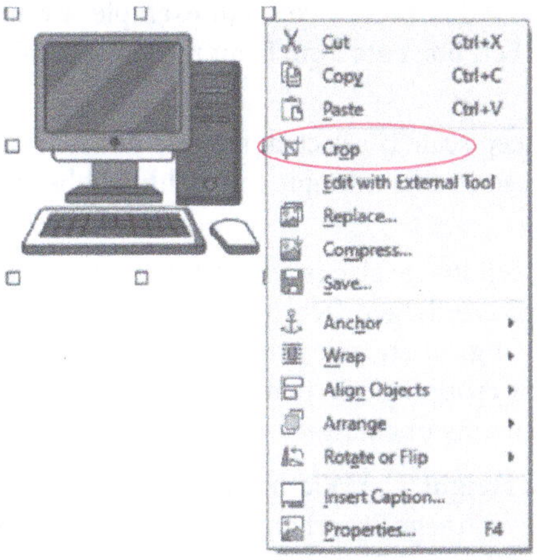

Step 2 Select the Crop option. Cropping handles appear at the corners and mid-points of the sides of the image.

Step 3 Drag a handle to cut off part of the image.

Step 4 Click outside the image to turn OFF cropping mode.

Method II Using Image dialog box

To use the Image dialog box, follow the given steps:

Step 1 Right click on it.

Step 2 Select the properties option from the pop-up menu. Image dialog box will appear.

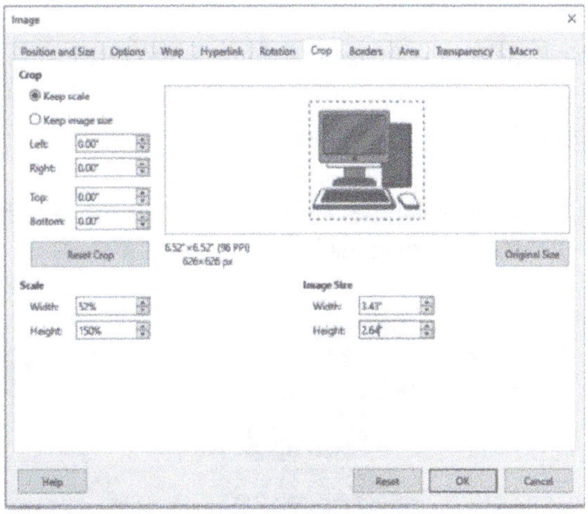

Step 3 In the Image dialog box, select Crop tab.

In the Crop page, you can control the following parameters

Keep Scale/Keep Image size When Keep scale is selected (default), cropping the image does not change the scale of the picture. When **Keep image size** is selected, cropping produces enlargement (for positive cropping values), shrinking (for negative cropping values), or distortion of the image, so that the image size remains constant.

Left, Right, Top and Bottom The image is cropped by the amount entered in these boxes. For example, a value of 3cm in the Left box cuts 3 cm from the left side of the picture.

- When Keep scale is selected, the size of the image also changes, so in this example the width will be reduced by 3 cm.
- When Keep image size is selected, the remaining part of the image is enlarged (when you enter positive values for cropping) or shrunk (when you enter negative values for cropping), so that the width and height of the image remains unchanged.

Width and Height The Width and Height fields under either Scale or Image Size change as you enter values in the Left, Right, Top, and Bottom fields. Use the thumbnail next to these fields to determine the correct amount by which to crop.

Note *If you crop an image in Writer, the image itself is not changed. Writer hides, not cuts off, part of the image.*

Resizing an Image

Resizing is the process of altering the image size without cutting any part of the image. When resizing an image, we change the dimension of the image so that it fits in the desired area.

Method I To quickly resize an image ,follow the given steps:

Step 1 Select the image that you want to resize. You will notice four corner handles and four side handles.

Step 2 Drag any Side handle in or out to shrink or stretch it in a direction.

Corner handles enable you to increase and decrease the size, diagonally.

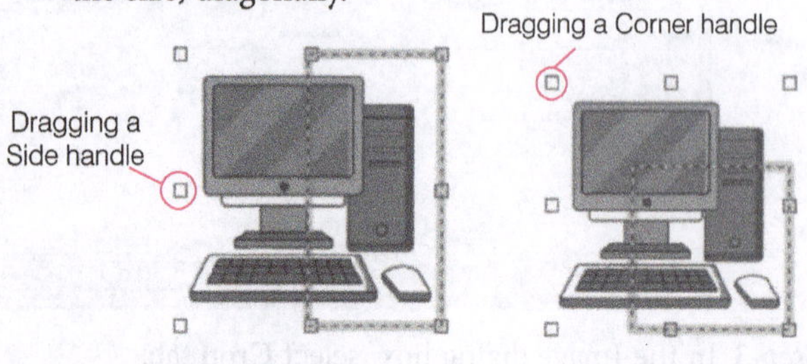

Method II Using Image Dialog Box

Step 1 Select the image.

Step 2 Click on the 'Format' menu and then select the 'Image' option. Click on Properties from context menu.

Step 3 'Image' window appears on the screen. Click on the 'Position and Size' tab.

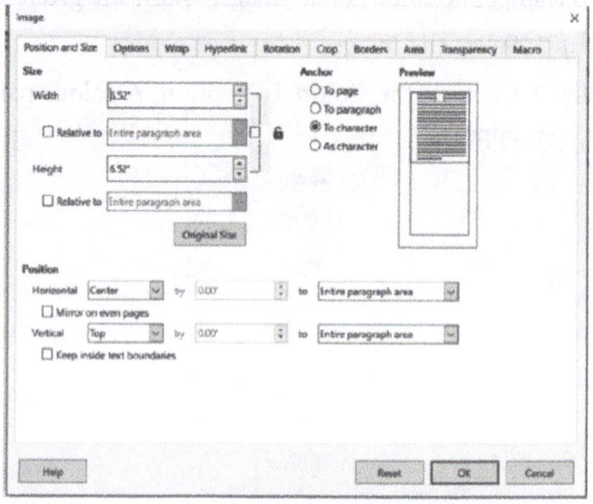

Step 4 Set the 'Width' and the 'Height' of the image.

Step 5 Click on the 'Keep ratio' checkbox to proportionately increase or decrease the size of image.

Step 6 Click on 'OK' button.

Deleting an Image

To delete an image

Step 1 Select the image to be deleted

Step 2 Press Delete key from the keyboard. The image will be deleted from workspace of Writer.

Try These 2.2

1 **How can you quickly resize an image in LibreOffice?**

2 **_______ allows you to crop an image by dragging handles at the corners and sides.**

3 **To change the mode of an image, click on the _______ option on the Image toolbar.**

4 **To resize an image using the Image dialog box, you need to change the units of _________ and _________.**

2.4 Drawing Objects

You can use Writer's drawing tools to create graphics such as simple diagrams using rectangles, circles, lines, text and other pre-defined shapes. You can place the drawing objects directly on a page in your document, or you can insert them into a frame.

Using Drawing Tools

To begin using the drawing tools, display the Drawing toolbar

Step 1 Choose View tab.

Step 2 Select Toolbars that will open sub menu.

Step 3 Select Drawing.

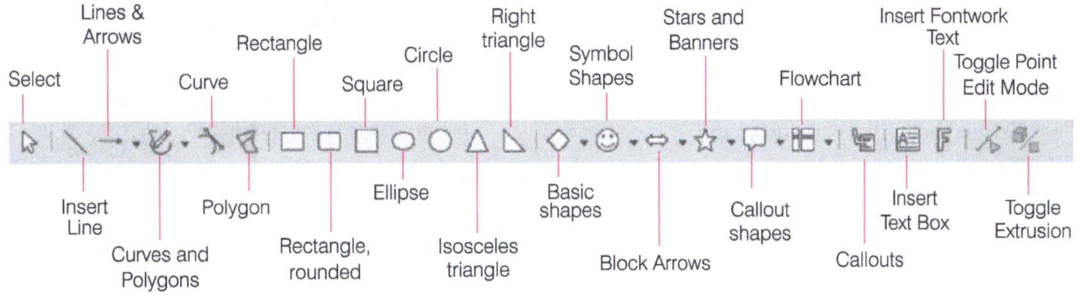

To use a drawing tool:

1. Click in the document where you want the drawing to be anchored. You can change the anchor later, if necessary.
2. Select the tool from the Drawing toolbar. The mouse pointer changes to pointer.
3. Move the pointer to the place in the document where you want the graphic to appear and then click-and-drag to create the drawing object. Release the mouse button. The selected drawing function remains active, so you can draw another object of the same type.
4. To cancel the selected drawing function, press the Esc key or click on the Select icon (the arrow) on the Drawing toolbar.
5. You can now change the properties (fill color, line type and weight, anchoring, and others) of the drawing object using either the Drawing Object Properties toolbar or the choices and dialog boxes reached by right-clicking on the drawing object.

2.5 Set or Change Properties for Drawing Objects

To set the properties for a drawing object before you draw it:

1. On the Drawing toolbar, select the object you want to draw.
2. On the Drawing Object Properties toolbar, click on the icon for each property and select the value that you want.
3. For more control, or to define new attributes, you can click on the Area or Line icons on the toolbar to display detailed dialog boxes.

You can also specify the position and size, rotation, and slant and corner radius properties of the drawing object:

1. Right-click on the drawing object and then click Position and Size from the pop-up menu that appear. The Position and Size dialog box will appear.
2. Select the appropriate tab and do the changes as required.

Resizing a Drawing Object

Resizing a drawing object is done same as image resizing. To resize a drawing object, follow the below steps

Step 1 Click the object to show the gray resizing handles.

Step 2 Position the pointer over one of the gray resizing handles. The pointer changes shape giving a graphical representation of the direction of the resizing.

Step 3 Click and drag to resize the object.

Step 4 Release the mouse button when satisfied with the new size.

Grouping Drawing Objects

To group drawing objects, follow the below steps:

Step 1 Select an object, then hold down the Shift key and select the others you want to include in the group. The bounding box expands to include all the selected objects.

Step 2 With the objects selected, hover the mouse pointer over one of the objects and follow below steps :

- Choose Format tab.
- Select Group that will open sub menu.
- Select Group option.

To ungroup the objects,

Step 1 Select the object first →Select Format→ Group → Ungroup.

Step 2 You cannot include an embedded or a linked graphic in a group with drawing objects.

Positioning Images in the Text

When you add a graphic to a text document, you need to choose how to position it with respect to the text and other graphics.

Positioning of a graphic is controlled by four settings:

1. Arrangement
2. Anchoring
3. Alignment
4. Text Wrapping

These settings can be accessed using three ways:

- Using Format menu.
- Using context menu after right clicking on the object.
- Using Drawing Object Properties Toolbar.

Arrangement

In the case of overlapping objects, the arrangement setting defines the position of the current drawing in relation to other drawings or text. The Drawing Object Properties toolbar includes tools specifically for managing this arrangement.

The following table gives the description of different Image Arrangement tools:

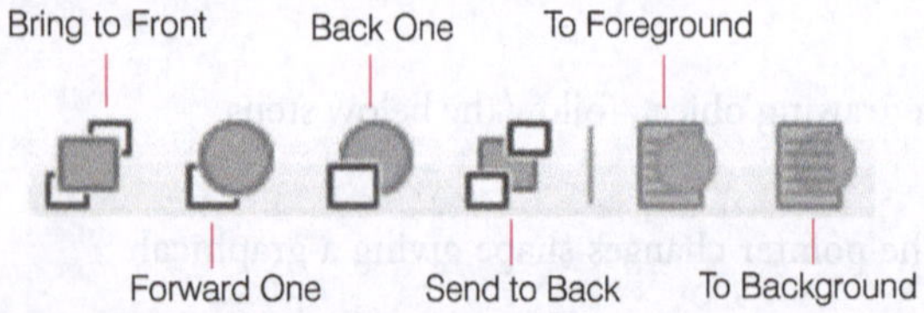

- **Bring to Front** Place image on top of all objects / images
- **Forward One** Bring image one level up, when there are overlapping images
- **Back One** Sends image one level down in overlapping images
- **Send to Back** Place image at the bottom of all objects/images
- **To Foreground** Moves the drawing object in front of the text
- **To Background** Moves the drawing object behind the text

Note *First four settings can be applied on an image or drawing, but last two are available for drawings only.*

Anchoring

Anchoring refers to the reference point for the images. This point could be the page, or frame where the object is, a paragraph, or even a character. An image always has an anchor point.

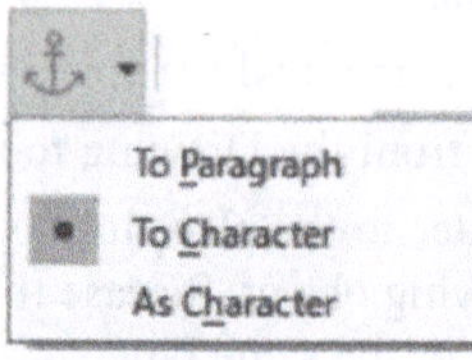

(i) **To Paragraph** Graphics move with associated paragraphs, the most frequently used method.

(ii) **To Character** Graphics are linked to specific characters, moving in sync.

(iii) **As Character** Graphics integrate as text characters, influencing line height and moving with paragraphs as text is added/removed before them, ideal for inline icons in a sentence.

Aligning

It allows the vertical or horizontal placement of the image with respect to its anchor.

The image can be aligned by using the Align ( ) option of the drawing toolbar.

The various options under Align are:

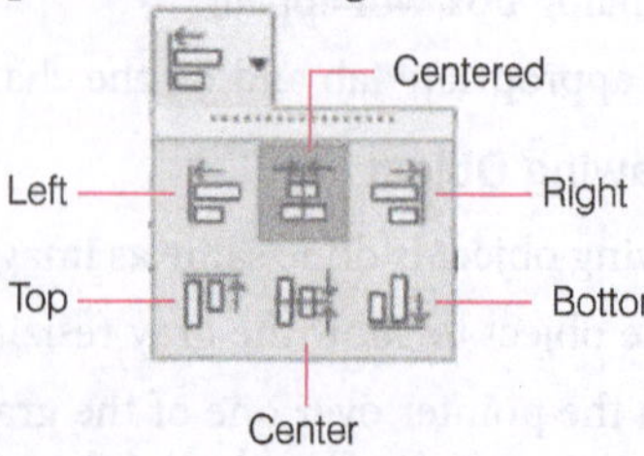

- **Left** The image gets left aligned.
- **Centered** The image gets centered aligned.
- **Right** The image gets right aligned.
- **Top** The image gets on top of the anchor.

- **Center** The image gets on the middle of the anchor.
- **Bottom** The image gets on the bottom of the anchor.

Text Wrapping

It allows the placement of image in relation to text. Use the following options of the Image toolbar to wrap the text.

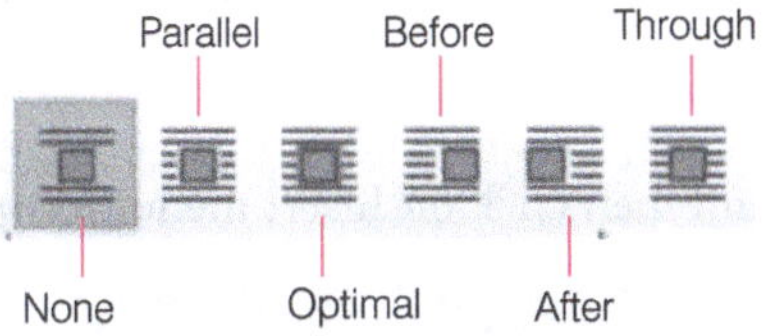

- **None** The image appears either on the top or at the bottom of the text.
- **Parallel** The text on both sides of the image.
- **Optimal** The text appears either to the left or to the right of the image.
- **Before** The text appears to the left of the image.
- **After** The text appears to the right of the image.
- **Through** The text appears behind the image.

Try These 2.3

1. **What is the purpose of grouping drawing objects in LibreOffice Writer?**
   (a) To ungroup the objects
   (b) To move and edit all objects at once
   (c) To create separate files for each object
   (d) To delete the objects
2. **To edit an individual object within a group without ungrouping it, you should select the group and choose the __________ option.**
3. **The four key settings for positioning images in the text are Arrangement, Anchoring, __________, and Text Wrapping.**
4. **What is anchoring in the context of positioning images?**
5. **How can you reposition grouped objects in LibreOffice Writer?**

Summary

In a digital document, a graphic or image is referred to as a digital image.

A digital image is composed of pixels.

You can insert predefined images using methods such as Drag-and-Drop, Copy-Paste, or through the Insert Image dialog box.

When you insert an image, a copy of the image is embedded in the document.

Images can also be linked to a document using the Insert Image dialog box.

Linking an image saves only its reference rather than embedding the actual image, which helps conserve space, especially when multiple copies of the same image are needed.

The Image Toolbar provides tools for modifying images, including options for filtering, resizing, cropping, deleting, and rotating.

You can use Writer's drawing tools to create graphics such as simple diagrams using rectangles, circles, lines, text and other pre-defined shapes.

The properties of an object can be customized through actions like resizing, rotating, moving, or editing.

Positioning of graphic is controlled by four settings: Arrangement, Anchoring, Alignment and Text Wrapping

In case of overlapping objects, the arrangement setting defines the position of the current drawing in relation to other drawings or text.

Anchoring refers to the reference point for the images.

Aligning allows the vertical or horizontal placement of the image with respect to its anchor.

ACTIVITY Time

ACTIVITY 1

Insert an image using Insert Image dialog box in the file "noise.odt" created in previous chapter.

Step 1 Ensure that you have an image file on your computer hard disk. Otherwise download a relevant image from Internet.

Step 2 Open "noise.odt" file created in Activity 1 of Chapter 1.

Step 3 Place the cursor to the next line of the text to insert the image file, and then click on Insert menu from the menu bar.

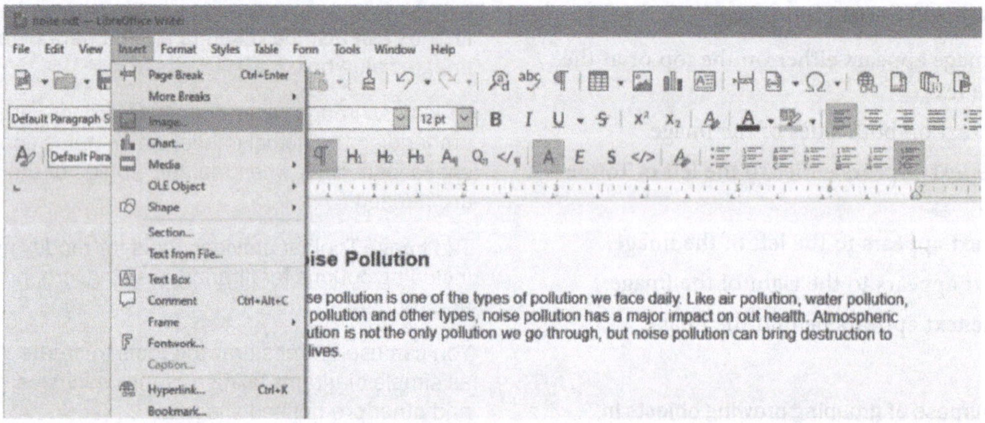

Step 4 Click on Image option, opens Insert Image browsing window to select an image. Select desired image.

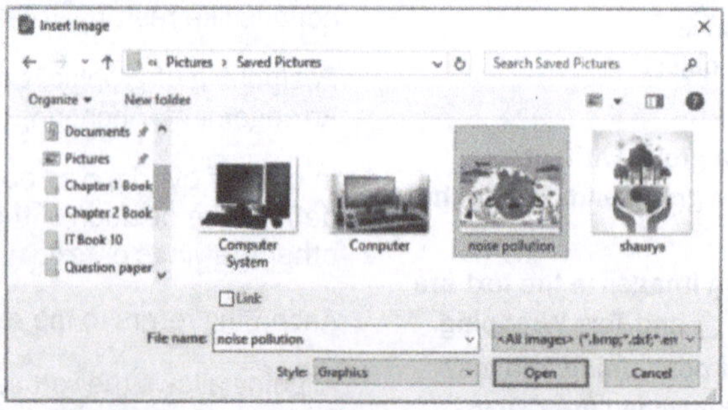

Step 5 Click Open button. The image appears at desired place.

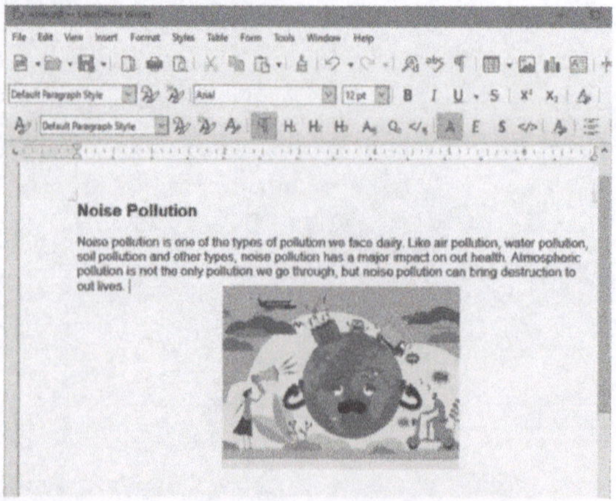

ACTIVITY 2

Insert an image from one document (source) to another document (target) using Clipboard. Source file is "typewriter.odt" having different images of typewriter, and target file is "documentation.odt" created in Chapter 1.

Step 1 Open source file "typewriter.odt" and target file "documentation.odt".

Step 2 In the source document, select the image to be copied.

Step 3 Move the mouse pointer over the selected image and copy the image by using keyboard shortcut Ctrl+C or right-click and select Copy option from the context menu to copy the image to the clipboard.

Step 4 Switch to the target file, "documentation.odt".

Step 5 Place the cursor on the location where you want to insert the image.

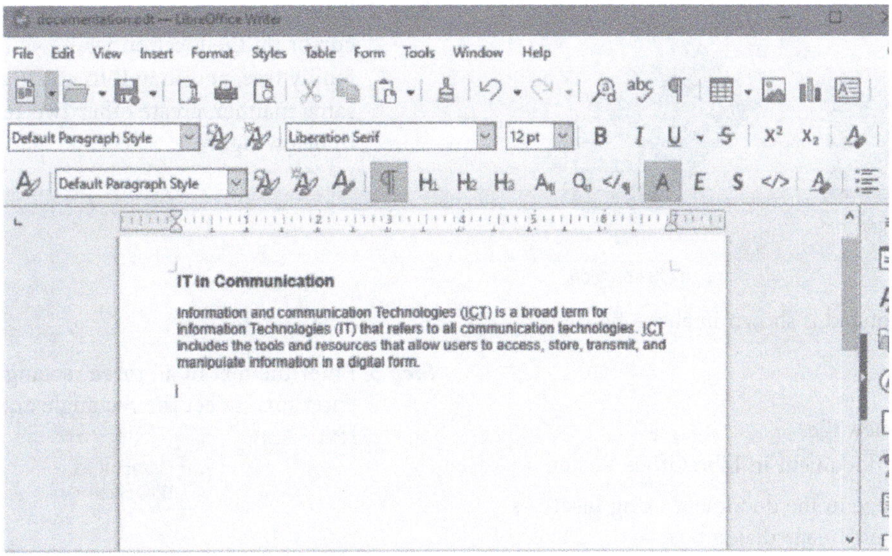

Step 6 Paste the image by using the keyboard shortcut Ctrl+V or right click and select Paste option from the context menu to paste the image as shown in figure.

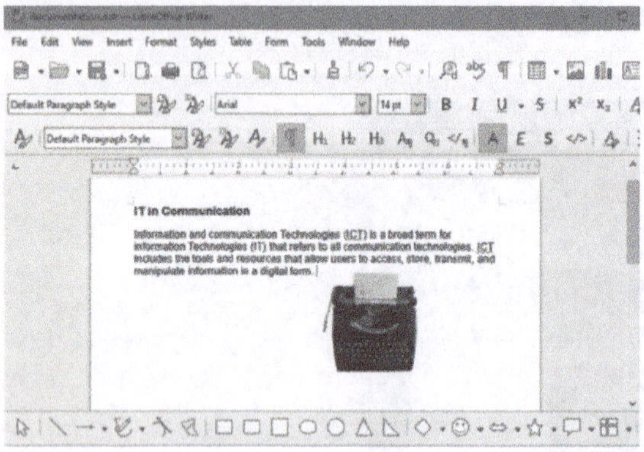

ACTIVITY 3

Insert an image in a document and rotate the image.

Step 1 Open a new document in LibreOffice Writer.

Step 2 Go to Insert menu and select Image option.

Step 3 Insert an image from Library.

Step 4 Select image and then click on rotate tool. Observe that four dots known as handles, appeared on four corners of the image.

Step 5 Move the mouse on any corner and observe that the 'rotate' symbol is activated.

Step 6 Click on rotate symbol on the top right corner of the image and drag it to downward direction.

Image before rotation

Image after rotation

Step 7 The image rotated is shown in above figure.

ACTIVITY 4

Crop an image in a new file.

Step 1 Open a new document in LibreOffice Writer.

Step 2 Insert an image in the document using Insert → Image → Insert Image dialog box.

Step 3 Select the image by clicking on the image. Observe that the selected image is surrounded by eight small squares.

Step 4 Click on crop tool from Image toolbar. Now observe that the eight small squares surrounding the image will be changed into the blue coloured handles. These are the handles used to crop the image.

Step 5 Click any of these edges of the image and drag the cursor towards the center of image. Observe that the image is being cropped up to the dotted lines.

It is possible to crop the image by clicking on dragging any of the edge as per the requirement.

Step 6 Click anywhere on the page or press Esc key to leave the crop tool and observe the cropped image.

ACTIVITY 5

Draw a family tree with 3 family members, Mr B. K. Sharma (Grandfather), Mr Rajan Sharma (Father), Mrs Sunita Sharma (Mother).

Step 1 Open a new document in LibreOffice Writer. Enable the Drawing toolbar and ensure that it is displayed on the bottom of the document.

Step 2 Select Rectangle tool from the toolbar. Place the cursor on the location where you want to draw the family tree, and drag it to create a rectangle. In the same manner, create other two rectangles as shown in below figure.

Step 3 Enter the text in all three rectangular boxes . To enter text, select the rectangle and then type the text.

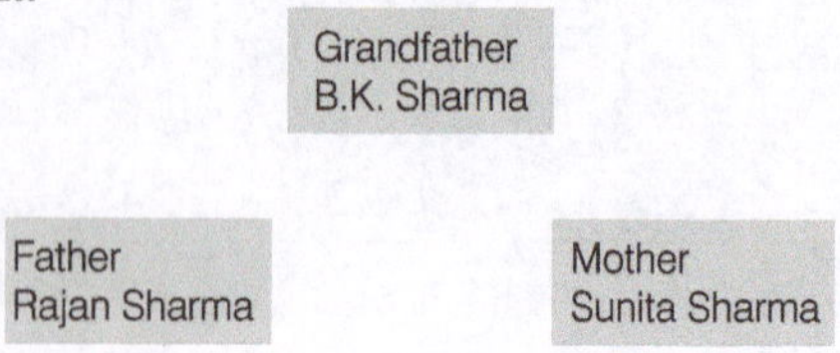

Step 4 Select the type of line (simple line and line with arrow) from Line tool to draw lines showing hierarchical relation.

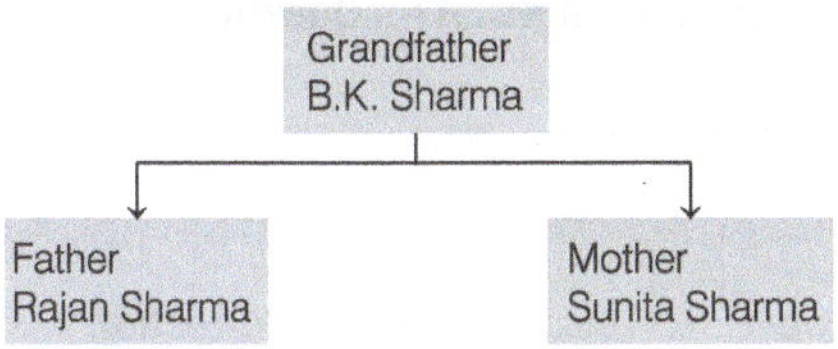

Step 5 Save the diagram in file "family.odt".

ACTIVITY 6

In the file "family.odt" created in Activity 5, add two more members, a son Master Rohit Sharma and a daughter Baby Deepika Sharma. Make a copy of the file. Then, change the properties of Rectangle and Line used in Family Tree.

Step 1 Open file "family.odt" in LibreOffice Writer.

Step 2 Add two rectangles and add text in them to reflect two more members in the diagram.

Step 3 Save a copy as "family1.odt". Keep on working in "family.odt"

Step 4 Select a rectangle using selection tool.

Step 5 Click on Fill Color tool in Drawing Object Properties toolbar, and change the color selected rectangle.

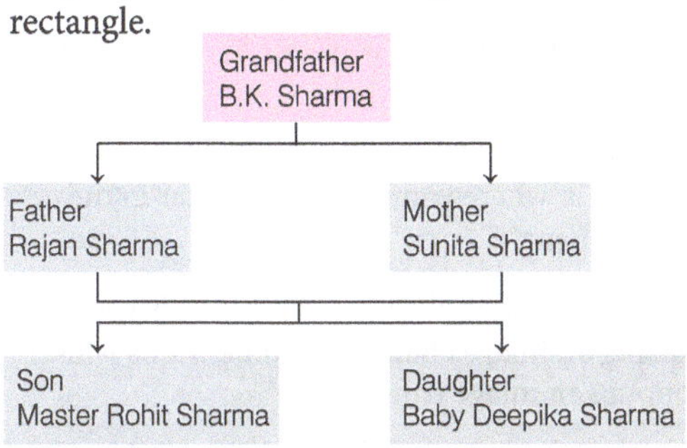

Step 6 In the same way change color of all the rectangles.

Step 7 Select a line in the drawing. Click on Line Color tool and select Pink color to change the line color from Black to Pink. In the same way, change the color of all the lines to Pink.

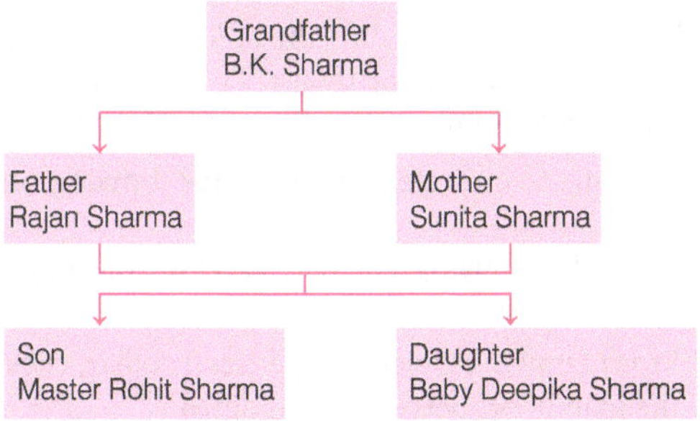

Step 8 You can also change the border color of rectangle using Line color tool and width of the border by specifying the value in line width option.

Step 9 Alternately you can change the line color and width by right clicking on the object and then selecting the "Line" option from the context menu.

Step 10 To change the line color and width of all the rectangles, select all the rectangles by holding shift key and clicking on each rectangle.

This will open the Line dialog window. Change the line color to "Pink" and specify the line width as "0.08" and click on the OK button.

Observe in figure ,the line color and width changed as specified.

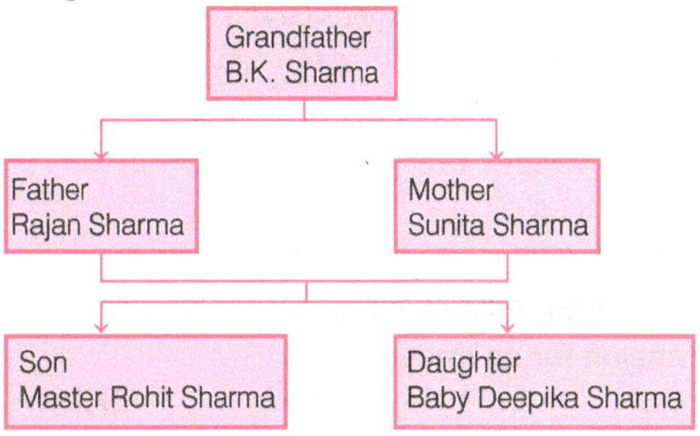

ACTIVITY 7

Group all items of Family tree created in Activity 5 and 6, in the file "family1.odt".

Using the group, change the properties of Rectangle and Line used in Family Tree.

Step 1 Open the document "family.odt" created earlier in Writer.

Step 2 Select all the lines. For this, click on the first line, hold the Shift key and keep on selecting other lines to group them.

Step 3 Click on Group tool in Drawing Object Properties toolbar. Observe that all the lines are grouped together as shown in above figure.

Now change the color of all lines grouped together to Pink.

Step 4 Similarly select all the rectangles, group them and change its fill color to lime yellow, border line to pink color and border width to 0.08, as done in previous activity.

Observe that the color of all the rectangles changed to pink colour.

NCERT FOLDER

Complete Explanations of all NCERT's Questions

A. Multiple Choice Questions

Q.1 The text or image which appears faintly in the background of a page is called ______.

(a) Water mark (b) Trade mark
(c) Copyright (d) Embossing

Q.2 JPG or JPEG in image format stands for ______.

(a) Joint Photographic Experts Group
(b) Joint Picture Experts Group
(c) Joint Photographic Experts Graph
(d) Joint Photographic Experts General

Q.3 In Drawing Object Properties toolbar, Grouping options provided are ______.

(a) Exit Group (b) Ungroup
(c) Enter Group (d) All of these

Q.4 Which of the following is not the correct file extension for an image file?

(a) GIF (b) JPEG (c) Odt (d) PNG

Q.5 Image toolbar does not provide a tool for ______.

(a) filtering (b) cropping
(c) copying (d) flipping

Answers

1. (a) 2. (a) 3. (d) 4. (c) 5. (c)

B. Fill in the Blanks

Q.1 ______ tool cuts off non-desirable part of the image.

Q.2 To change both brightness and contrast of the image______ tool can be used.

Q.3 To simulate the effect of time on picture ______ tool is used.

Q.4 ______ place image at the bottom of all objects.

Q.5 An image can be deleted by ______ it and pressing DELETE key.

Q.6 In drawing tools, basic shapes list provide ______ shapes.

Q.7 Anchor act as ______ point for a drawing.

Q.8 There are ______ options for aligning an image horizontally.

Q.9 The ______ handles of image are used for rotating it.

Q.10 Changing properties of an object ______ creation, retain them throughout the session.

Answers

1. Crop 2. Gamma Correction
3. Ageing 4. Send back
5. Selecting 6. 25
7. Reference 8. Three
9. Corner 10. Before its

C. Short Answer Type Questions

Q.1 What is a digital image? How can you create one?

Ans. A digital image is a visual representation of an object or scene stored in a digital format, made up of pixels arranged in a grid. You can create a digital image using a digital camera, scanner, or graphic design software like Photoshop, GIMP, or MS Paint.

Q.2 Write steps to insert an image from the gallery using Drag and Drop method?

Ans. A general procedure to insert an image using drag and drop option, is as follows.

Step 1 Open the document to insert an image in LibreOffice Writer.

Step 2 Open a file browser window (Win+E) and select the image file to be inserted.

Step 3 Drag the image into the document

Step 4 Drop it, where you want it to appear in the document.

Q.3 How is resizing of image different from cropping it?

Ans. Resizing an image changes its dimensions while cropping an image trims it.

Q.4 What are the tools available in drawing toolbar?

Ans. Select, insert line, line & arrow, curve, rectangle, ellipse, isosceles triangle, arrow, callout, points, font, flowchart, list etc.

Q.5 How is linking of an image different from embedding?

Ans. Linking an image saves only the link of the image instead of embedding the image. This saves space in case multiple copies of the same image are required.

Q.6 Write steps to change properties for drawing objects?

Ans.

Step 1 From the Drawing Toolbar, select the object you want to draw.

Step 2 From Drawing Object Properties Toolbar, click on the icon of property to be modified.

Step 3 Change the value of parameter.

Step 4 Repeat steps 2 and 3 to change all desired properties.

Q.7 What are the benefits and drawbacks of grouping drawing objects?

Ans. **Benefits** Grouping enhances faster and easier way of moving objects than moving one by one.

Drawback The alignment of the object will not change when you move the objects.

Q.8 Describe any two tools from Drawing Object Properties toolbar?

Ans.
- **Select** select an object.
- **Insert line** Insert a line.

Q.9 Write steps to insert an image in a basic drawing shape.

Ans. A general procedure to insert an image using Insert Image dialog box, is as follows.

Step 1 Open the document to insert an image in LibreOffice Writer.

Step 2 Place the cursor where you want to insert an image.

Step 3 Select and click on Insert → Image from menu bar.

Step 4 An Insert Image dialog box will open which will allow to choose the picture file to be inserted.

Step 5 Select the file and click on Open button to insert an image in document.

Q.10 Write factors controlling positioning of an image in a document.

Ans. Positioning of an image is controlled by four settings.

(i) Arrangement (ii) Anchoring
(iii) Alignment (iv) Text Wrapping

EXAM PATTERN EXERCISE

Including Competency Based Questions

Multiple Choice Questions

1 **In a document, _______ refers to the vertical or horizontal placement of a graphic in relation to the chosen anchor point.** CBSE SQP 2021-22 Term I

(a) Arrangement (b) Anchoring
(c) Alignment (d) Text Wrapping

2 **______ controls how graphics are stacked upon each other or relative to the text.** CBSE SQP 2021-22 Term I

(a) Arrangement (b) Alignment
(c) Anchoring (d) Wrapping

3 **It is a reference point for the graphics which is created while positioning any image. This point could be the page, or frame where the object is either a paragraph, or even a character in a word processor.** CBSE SQP 2022-23

(a) Wrap Text (b) Alignment
(c) Anchoring (d)BookMark

4 **In Writer, ... refers to the reference point for the graphics. This point could be the page or frame where the object is, a paragraph or even a character.** CBSE 2021-22 Term I

(a) Arrangement
(b) Anchoring
(c) Framing
(d) Text wrapping

5 **Which of the following Graphic filter is used to increase the contrast of an image in a document?** CBSE 2023

(a) Smooth (b) Sharpen
(c) Remove Noise (d) Invert

6 **Resizing a .... may badly affect the resolution of an image.** CBSE 2024

(a) Vector image (b) Raster image
(c) CAD image (d) Coloured image

7 **During a recent excursion, Roshni has taken some pictures for making a report in Writer. She wants to increase the contrast of the images. Which one of the following image filters should she use in Writer?** CBSE 2025

(a) Aging (b) Mosaic (c) Sharpen (d) Smooth

8 **Which one of the following image arrangement options in Writer sends the drawing object behind the text?** CBSE 2025

(a) To background (b) To foreground
(c) Behind the text (d) Back one

9 **What does the Crop tool do in a document?**

(a) Changes the color of the image
(b) Cuts off unwanted parts of the image
(c) Resizes the image
(d) Adds a border to the image

10 To link an image instead of embedding it, which option must be selected in the Insert Image dialog box?

(a) Copy (b) Paste (c) Link (d) Open

11 Which option allows for the modification of brightness and contrast of an image?

(a) Image Filter (b) Drawing Tools
(c) Border Color (d) Image Mode

12 What happens when you group drawing objects?

(a) They cannot be moved
(b) They function as a single unit
(c) They lose their relative position
(d) They can only be resized individually

13 What does the 'Send to Back' tool do?

(a) Moves the image to the foreground
(b) Places the image behind all objects
(c) Brings the image one level up
(d) Flips the image horizontally

14 How can you resize an image using the Image dialog box?

(a) By dragging the corner handles
(b) By adjusting the Height and Width values
(c) By selecting the Crop tool
(d) By using the Color option

15 Which of the following options allows text to wrap around an image?

(a) None (b) Parallel
(c) Optimal (d) All of these

16 What does the 'Invert' filter do to an image?

(a) Increases brightness (b) Reverses the color values
(c) Changes the color mode (d) Crops the image

17 Krishna wants to make a flowchart for his programs in a Word document. Which option should he use to accomplish this task efficiently? **CBSE SQP 2020-21, Competency Based Que.**

(a) Drawing/Shapes (b) Symbols
(c) Pictures (d) All of these

18 Fatima has inserted a picture in a document. But she wants to cut off a part of the picture. Which option she should use to accomplish the task? **CBSE SQP 2020-21, Competency Based Que.**

(a) Cut (b) Copy (c) Crop (d) Layout

19 Vineeta has to prepare a report on her research work in which she needs to include images with text. Which feature helps to balance the relation of graphics to the surrounding text, which may wrap around the graphic on one side or both sides, be overprinted behind or in front of the graphic or treat the graphic as a separate paragraph or character? **CBSE 2021-22 Term I, Competency Based Que.**

(a) Arrangement (b) Alignment
(c) Table of content (d) Text wrapping

20 Jagriti has inserted an image in a document. She wants to resize the image. Which option of the word processor image format should be selected to let the two dimensions (height and width) change so that the proportion is maintained, allowing for a scaled resizing? **CBSE 2021-22 Term I, Competency Based Que.**

(a) Keep ratio (b) Keep aspect
(c) Crop (d) Contrast

21 Reema has created a pamphlet on 'Tour toWest India'. She has inserted many images to make it more presentable but the size of images is occupying a lot of space.Her friend has suggested her to reduce the size of images.Which of the following options will help her in doing the task without losing any content of the image? **CBSE 2023, Competency Based Que.**

(a) Recolor (b) Docking
(c) Resize (d) Rotate

22 Rama has inserted an image in a document. He wants to remove the unwanted area of the image. Which option should he use to complete the task? **Competency Based Que.**

(a) Clipart (b) Cut
(c) Crop (d) Consolidate

23 While working on a document in LibreOffice Writer, you need to resize an image without distorting its proportions. Which of the following actions will help you achieve this? **Competency Based Que.**

(a) Dragging a side handle of the image
(b) Dragging a corner handle of the image
(c) Using the Crop tool
(d) Resizing from the center handle of the image

24 You are creating a diagram using the Drawing toolbar in LibreOffice Writer. To maintain the alignment and size of multiple shapes, you decide to group them. Which sequence of actions should you follow? **Competency Based Que.**

(a) Select objects → Right-click → Select Properties → Group
(b) Select objects → Right-click → Select Group
(c) Select objects → Click on Format → Group
(d) Select objects → Right-click → Enter Group

25 You need to insert an image into your document and keep the file size minimal. What method would you use? **Competency Based Que.**

(a) Insert Image
(b) Drag and Drop
(c) Copy and Paste
(d) Link the Image

26 If you want to modify an image's brightness and contrast, which option from the Image toolbar would you select? **Competency Based Que.**

(a) Crop (b) Color
(c) Image Filter (d) Resize

27 **Gaurav is creating a report in Writer. The image gets embedded in his document whenever he drags and drops the image and the document size increases. Suggest a way to link the image file instead of embedding it.** CBSE 2024, Competency Based Que.

(a) Drag and drop the image.
(b) Hold down the Ctrl key while dragging.
(c) Hold down the Shift key while dragging the image.
(d) Hold down the Ctrl and Shift key while dragging and dropping the image.

28 **Gaurav has inserted an image in a document. He wants to remove the unwanted area of the image. Which option of the word processor he will use to complete the task?** CBSE SQP 2021-22 Term I, Competency Based Que.

(a) Clip art (b) Cut
(c) Crop (d) Contrast

29 **It allows the placement of image in relation to text** CBSE SQP 2024-25

(a) Water mark
(b) Trade mark
(c) Copyright
(d) Text Wrapping

30 **Saurabh has made an advertisement in Digital Document. He is facing difficulty in positioning the images within the text. Suggest him how he can adjust the image?** CBSE SQP 2023-24, Competency Based Que.

(a) Wrap text (b) Crop
(c) Alignment (d) Layout

31 **To increases the contrast of an image, ____________ option is used in a document.** CBSE SQP 2023-24

(a) Smooth
(b) Sharpen
(c) Aging
(d) mosaic

Answers

1. (b)	2. (a)	3. (c)	4. (b)	5. (b)
6. (a)	7. (c)	8. (a)	9. (b)	10. (c)
11. (a)	12. (b)	13. (b)	14. (b)	15. (d)
16. (b)	17. (a)	18. (c)	19. (d)	20. (b)
21. (c)	22. (c)	23. (b)	24. (b)	25. (d)
26. (c)	27. (d)	28. (c)	29. (d)	30. (a)
31. (b)				

Very Short Answer Type Questions

1 **What is the purpose of inserting an image in a document?**

Ans. Images enhance communication by visually conveying concepts, capturing attention, and reinforcing the accompanying text.

2 **Describe two methods for inserting an image into a LibreOffice document.**

Ans. You can insert an image using the Insert Image dialog box or by using the Drag-and-Drop method.

3 **List three features available in the Image toolbar.**

Ans. The Image toolbar allows you to resize, crop, and rotate an image.

4 **What is the role of drawing tools in LibreOffice Writer?**

Ans. Drawing tools allow users to create graphics such as diagrams, shapes, and annotations in documents.

5 **Explain the function of the 'Flip Horizontally' option.**

Ans. It flips the image along the vertical axis and creating a mirror effect.

6 **How can you change the transparency of an image?**

Ans. You can adjust the transparency using the Transparency tool on the Image toolbar by setting a percentage value.

7 **What does the Crop tool provide?**

Ans. The Crop tool allows users to cut off unwanted parts of an image, focusing on the desired section.

8 **How can images be grouped in LibreOffice Writer?**

Ans. Images can be grouped by selecting them, holding the Shift key, and right-clicking to choose the Group option.

9 **What do you mean by Anchoring in Word Processor?** CBSE SQP 2023-24

Ans. Anchoring determines the reference point of an image in relation to the text, paragraph, or page, affecting how the image is positioned.

10 **What is the utility of text wrapping in a document?** CBSE SQP 2020-21

Ans. Text wrapping refers to the relation of graphics to the surrounding text, which may wrap around the graphic on one or both sides, be overprinted behind or infront of the graphic, or treat the graphic as a separate paragraph or character.

11 **Write the main steps to group drawing objects in Writer.** CBSE 2024

Ans. The main steps to group drawing objects in Writer are:
1. Select the drawing objects you want to group.
2. Right-click on any of the selected objects.
3. Choose "Group" from the menu that appears.
4. Now, you can move and resize them together.

12 **Differentiate between Keep scale and Keep image size options while cropping an image in a document.** CBSE 2023

Ans. When keep scale is selected (default), cropping the image does not change the scale of the picture. While when keep image size is selected, cropping produces enlargement, shrinking or distortion of the image so that the image size remains constant.

Short Answer Type Questions

1 Explain the following terms with respect to positioning the graphics in a document: **CBSE 2023**

(a) Arrangement (b) Text Wrapping

Ans. (a) **Arrangement** refers to the placement of a graphic on an imaginary vertical axis. It controls how graphics are stacked upon each other or relative to the text.

(b) **Text wrapping** refers to the relation of graphics to surrounding text which may wrap around the graphic on one or both sides, be overprinted behind or in front of the graphic.

2 Explain the different methods available for inserting images into a LibreOffice document. Provide a detailed description of at least two methods.

Ans. Images can be inserted into a LibreOffice document using several methods, including:

- **Insert Image Dialog Box** This method involves clicking the Insert menu, selecting the Image option, and navigating to choose the desired image file. Once the image is selected, clicking the Open button inserts it into the document.
- **Drag and Drop** This method allows users to resize the Writer window and simply drag the image from its file location into the document, dropping it at the desired location. This embeds a copy of the image directly into the document.

3 (a) What is the benefit of grouping drawing objects in Writer?

(b) Differentiate between text wrapping and image alignment feature in Writer. **CBSE 2025**

Ans. (a) Grouping drawing objects in Writer allows for easier management, alignment, and positioning of multiple objects as a single unit. This improves the efficiency of layout adjustment and prevents objects from moving independently, ensuring a more organized document.

(b) Text wrapping in Writer allows text to flow around an image or object, making the layout more dynamic. Image alignment, on the other hand simply positions the image in relation to the surrounding text without affecting text flow. Text wrapping directly interacts with text, whereas image alignment affects the position of the image.

4 Describe the steps to crop an image using both the Crop tool and the Image dialog box in LibreOffice Writer.

Ans. Using the Crop Tool

- Right-click on the image and select the Crop option. This displays cropping handles around the image. Drag these handles to remove unwanted sections and click outside the image to exit cropping mode.

Using the Image Dialog Box

- Right-click on the image and select Properties. Navigate to the Crop tab in the Image dialog box, adjust the measurement units, set desired crop values, and click OK to apply the changes.

5 You have a presentation that requires multiple copies of the same image, and you want to keep the document size down. **Competency Based Que.**

(a) Describe the steps to link an image in the document.

(b) Why is linking the image preferable in this case?

Ans. (a) Open the Insert Image dialog box, select the desired image, and ensure the Link option is checked before clicking Open.

(b) Linking saves space in the document since only the reference is stored, and the actual image is saved separately.

6 You want to create a visually appealing diagram that combines text and images in a LibreOffice document. **Competency Based Que.**

(a) What tools would you use to create the diagram?

(b) How can you ensure the text wraps around the diagram effectively?

(c) What is the advantage of grouping the drawing objects in the diagram?

Ans. (a) You would use the Drawing Tools to create the diagram.

(b) Adjust the text wrapping settings using the Image toolbar to allow text to flow around the diagram.

(c) Grouping allows for easier movement and editing of the entire diagram as a single entity while maintaining the relative positions of individual elements.

7 You have inserted an image into your document and want to apply a border to it. **Competency Based Que.**

(a) Which tool would you use to add a border to the image?

(b) Describe the process of adding a border to the image.

(c) Why would you choose to add a border to the image?

Ans. (a) You would use the Image dialog box to add a border.

(b) Right-click the image, select Properties, navigate to the Borders tab, choose the desired style and color, and apply the changes.

(c) Adding a border enhances the visual separation of the image from surrounding text, making the document more visually appealing.

PRACTICAL ASSIGNMENT

1. Master Udit is helping his drawing teacher to create digital drawings. His teacher asks him to write down the steps to create the following two drawings. In the first drawing, objects are grouped and second drawing was created by resizing objects of first drawing. How would you help him to do so using drawing tools of Writer?

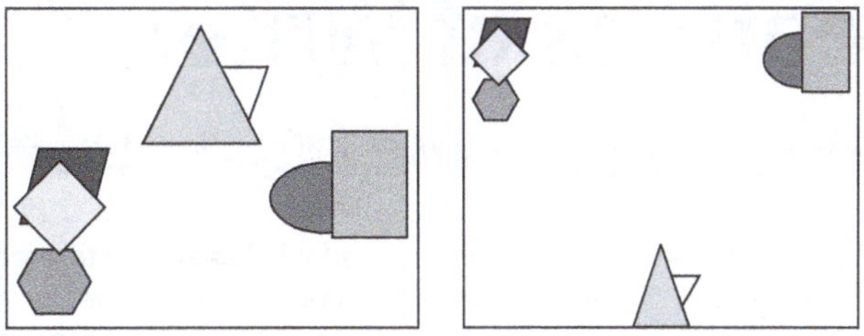

2. Miss Roshni has downloaded a flowchart to be included in her report. She asks for your help, in creating an editable copy of the flowchart. Write steps to draw it using Drawing tools of Writer.

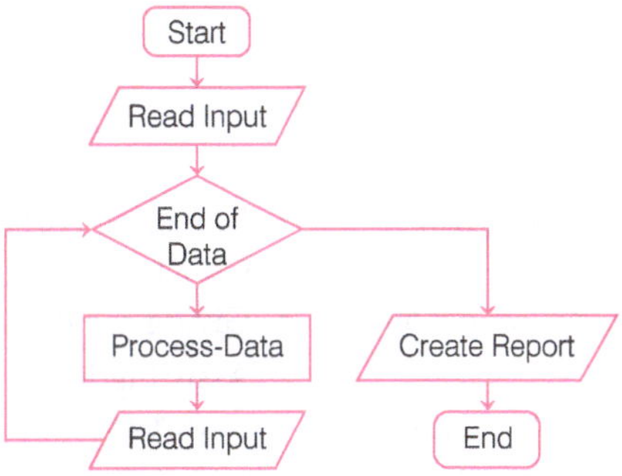

3. Perform the following lab activity.
- Draw four drawing objects on the document.
- Group the objects.
- Change the different properties of the grouped objects.
- Enter the grouped objects and enlarge one of the objects.
- Insert an image in between the text in the Writer document.
- Use the different wrapping and alignment options and notice the change.

4. Create the following in Writer:

Immersive learning enabled by technology.

Technology can transform a school's functioning, by making the teaching-learning process as well as administration more efficient. We have adopted blended learning and technology in all aspects of our operations - by digitalising all processes, creating digital resources, and setting up a continuous teacher upskilling programme. Also, our schools have integrated cutting-edge technologies like Robotics, Mobile Apps, Augmented Reality, and Virtual Reality in their curriculum.

CHAPTER 03

Advanced Features of Writer

The advanced features of Writer, enhance the documents. You will learn how to create a Table of Contents (ToC) that automatically updates as you make changes to your document, use pre-designed templates to quickly create professional-looking documents, and track changes made to your document to facilitate collaboration and review. These features will significantly enhance your document creation and editing efficiency.

LibreOffice Writer is a word processor that offers a wide range of features. The Table of Contents feature allows you to list the contents of a document based on various heading styles.

Additionally, LibreOffice Writer provides templates to help create polished and professional documents. When multiple users collaborate on a single document, the Track Changes feature can be utilized to monitor and manage the edits made by each user.

3.1 Table of Contents

A Table of Contents (ToC) is a list of chapters and sections typically found at the beginning of a book, also known as the **index**.

It provides readers with an overview of the book's structure, detailing what they can expect, the number of chapters and sections, and their locations within the book. Essentially, it serves as a map of the book, offering a navigation tool for the reader's convenience.

In a digital document, a Table of Contents (ToC) is a list that includes chapter titles and major sections (headings) in the order they appear in the document. The ToC is generated using the headings within the document.

A well-organized ToC enhances the presentation of the content within a document. With a ToC, readers can quickly navigate to specific sections of the document. Additional benefits of a ToC include:

- Providing readers with a high-level overview of the content
- Giving the document a professional appearance
- Assisting in the creation of a structured outline for the document

3.2 Hierarchy of Headings

The Table of Contents (ToC) is automatically generated using the predefined heading styles in Writer. To ensure a properly organized ToC, it's important to use heading styles consistently throughout the document. By default, the ToC includes headings from levels 1, 2, and 3.

Headings are used to structure the document or sections within it. Writer offers ten different heading levels (H1 to H10) to help organize the information in the document. For example:

- **Heading 1** Represents the title of the document
- **Heading 2** Denotes the main sections of the document
- **Heading 3** Indicates higher-level subsections within the document
- **Heading 4** Refers to subsections under Heading 3 .... and so on.

To apply these headings in a document, follow the given steps:

Step 1 Create a new document with different text headings.

Step 2 Click on the Styles button from the sidebar.

Step 3 Click on the Paragraph Styles and then Heading option. The different headings get displayed.

Step 4 Select the text from the document.

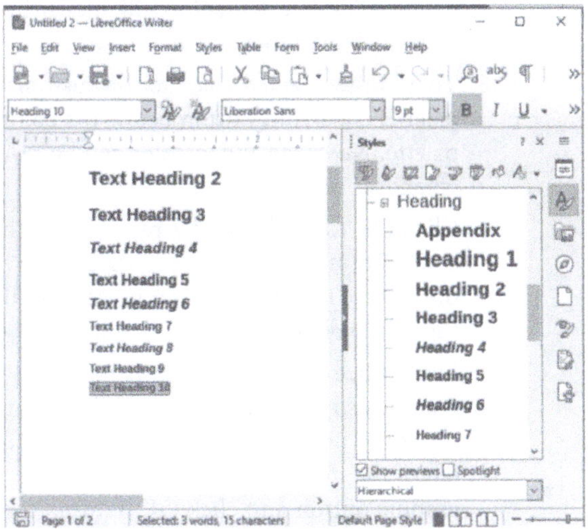

Step 5 Double-click on the heading style. The selected heading style get applied onto the text.

3.3 Creating a Table of Contents

Before creating the Table of Contents (ToC) in a document, make sure that appropriate heading styles, such as Heading 1, Heading 2, Heading 3, and so on, are applied throughout the document.

To create a table of contents, follow the given steps:

Step 1 Create a document that contains different heading styles such as Heading 1, Heading 2, Heading 3, as given below.

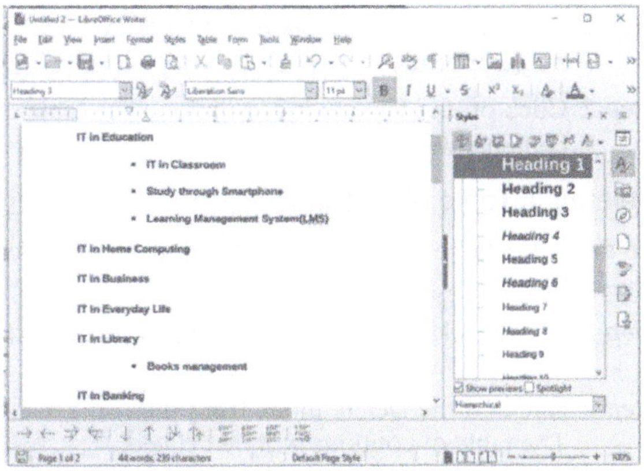

Step 2 Keep the cursor on the top of all the text in the document.

Step 3 From main menu Select Insert → Table of Contents and Index → Table of Contents, Index or Bibliography option.

The Table of Contents, Index or Bibliography dialog box appears.

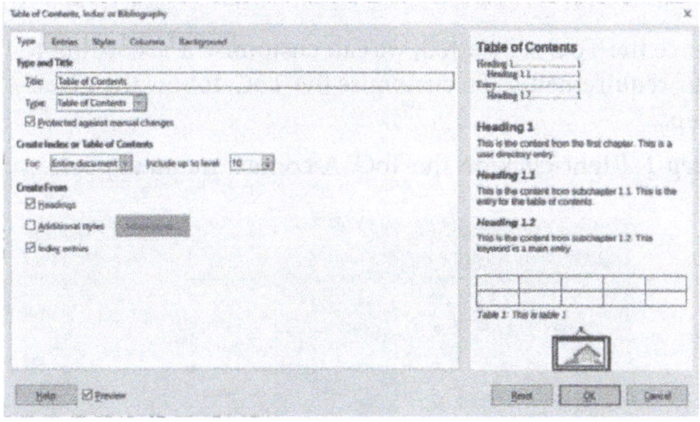

Step 4 Change the required setting and click on the OK button. The table of contents of that particular document appears.

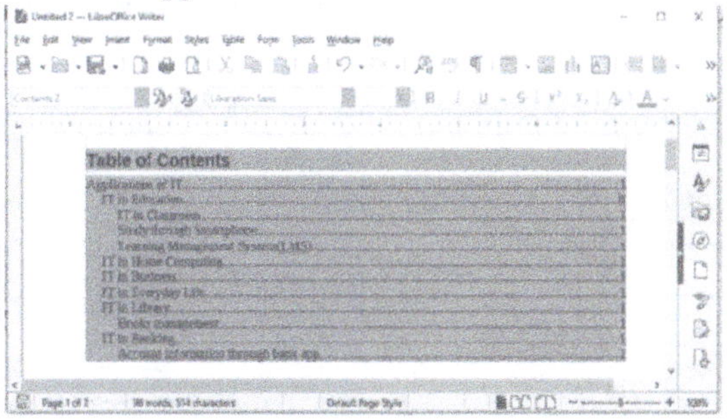

Note *By default, the checkbox for Protected against manual changes option is selected. This protects the ToC from any accidental change. If this box is unchecked, then the contents of ToC can be changed directly on the document page, just like any other text on the document.*

Try These 3.1

1 **Which tab in the Table of Contents, Index, or Bibliography dialog box allows you to set styles for various entries in the ToC?**

(a) Type Tab (b) Entries Tab
(c) Styles Tab (d) Background Tab

2 **What is the default level of headings included in a Table of Contents (ToC) in LibreOffice Writer?**

(a) Levels 1, 2, and 3
(b) Levels 1, 2, and 4
(c) Levels 2, 3, and 4
(d) Levels 1, 3, and 4

3 **A well-organized ________enhances the presentation of the content within a document, allowing readers to navigate easily to specific sections.**

4 **In LibreOffice Writer, the _______ option in the Table of Contents, Index or Bibliography dialog box protects the ToC from accidental changes.**

5 **What is the purpose of using heading styles in a document?**

3.4 Customisation of Table of Contents

Once the ToC is inserted, we can customise it according to our requirements. To customise the ToC, follow the given steps:

Step 1 Right-click on the ToC. A context menu appears.

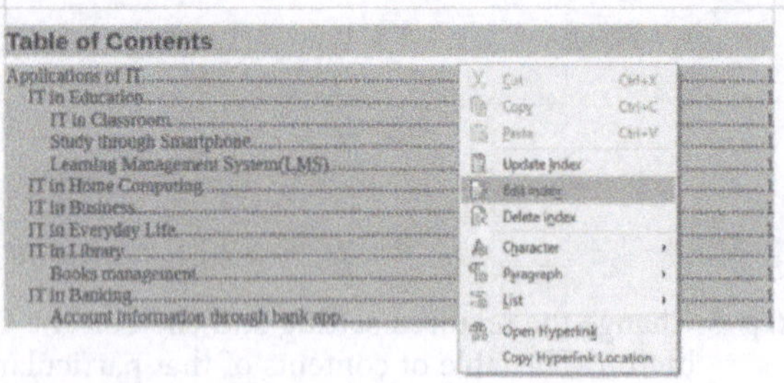

Step 2 Select Edit index option. The Table of Contents, Index or Bibliography dialog box opens.

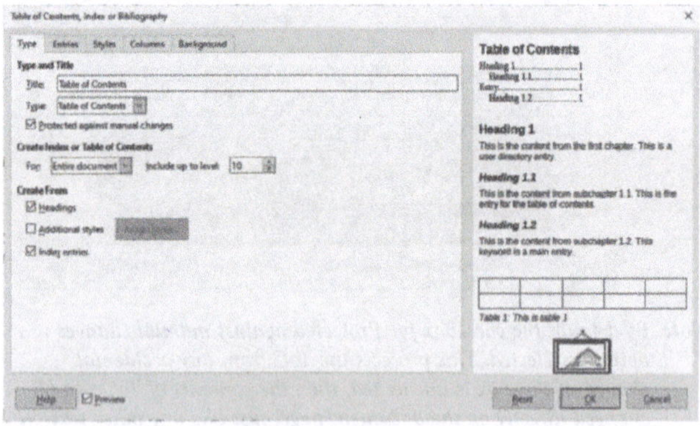

Step 3 Perform the required changes by clicking on the different tabs as given below:

- **Type Tab** is active by default after opening the Table of Contents, Index or Bibliography dialog box to insert the ToC.
- **Entries Tab** contains options to set styles for various entries in the ToC.
- **Styles Tab** contains options to apply the desired styles to the text of each level in the table of contents.
- **Columns Tab** contains options to set the number of columns that we want to have in our ToC.
- **Background Tab** contains options to change the background of the ToC. Just click on this tab and choose the required colour to apply to the background of the index.

  To change the background color follow the following steps

  1. Click the Color button on the top of the dialog box.
  2. Select the desired color from the Colors palette. The selected color will appear in the New color window.
  3. To add the selected color to the custom palette, click Add Button below the color palette. Now, the added color can be re-used whenever required.
  4. Click OK to apply the desired color to the ToC . To remove the background color from the ToC, click None button present on the top of the dialog box.

  LibreOffice Writer also allows to add a graphic as a background of the ToC. For this, select the Bitmap button in the Background tab of the dialog box. Select the desired graphic option and click OK button.

Step 4 Click on the OK button to apply the changes to the ToC.

3.5 Maintaining a Table of Contents

Maintaining a table of contents consists

- update a table of contents
- delete a table of contents

Updating a Table of Contents

Writer does not update the TOC automatically, so after any changes to the headings, you need to update it manually.

To update table of contents, follow the given steps:

Step 1 Right-click on the table of contents. A context menu appears.

Step 2 Click on the Update index option. The table of contents will be ready to update.

Deleting a Table of Contents

To delete the table of contents from a document, follow the given steps:

Step 1 Right-click on the table of contents. A context menu appears.

Step 2 Click on the Delete index from the context menu. The table of contents will be deleted.

3.6 Introduction to Templates

A template is a preset layout for creating professional or formal documents easily. Previously, we learned to style document objects using templates.

Now, we'll learn to create templates, which allow copying specific content—like logos, taglines, or legal notices—across multiple documents without reformatting. Templates can be used for resumes, reports, or chapters and can include text, graphics, styles, headers, footers, and more.

New documents created from templates maintain the same structure and formatting. In Writer, all documents are based on templates; if none is specified, a blank default template is used.

Checking the Template of the Document

To view the template associated with a document, select Properties from the File menu. The Properties dialog box will appear. If the document uses the default template, no template will be listed.

To create a document using a template, follow these steps:

Step 1 Go to File → New → Templates... to create a new document.

Step 2 In the template selection window, choose a template (e.g., 'Modern business letter') shown in given figure.

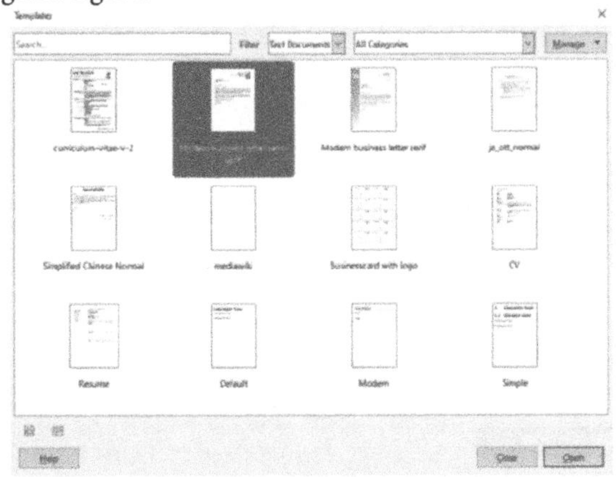

Step 3 Click Open to load the document with the selected template.

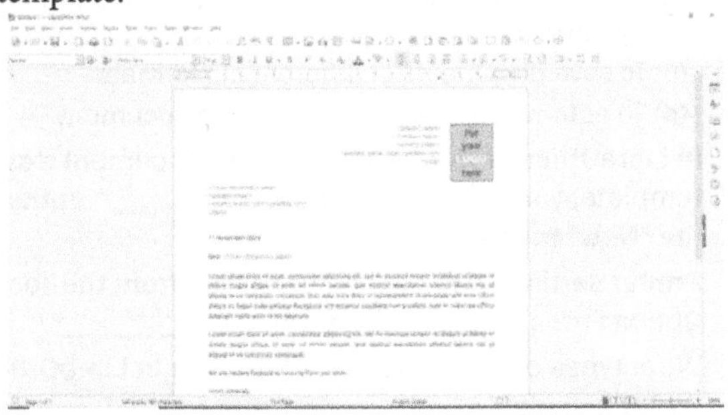

Step 4 To verify the template, go to File → Properties—the template name will be shown under Template in the Properties dialog as shown in given below figure.

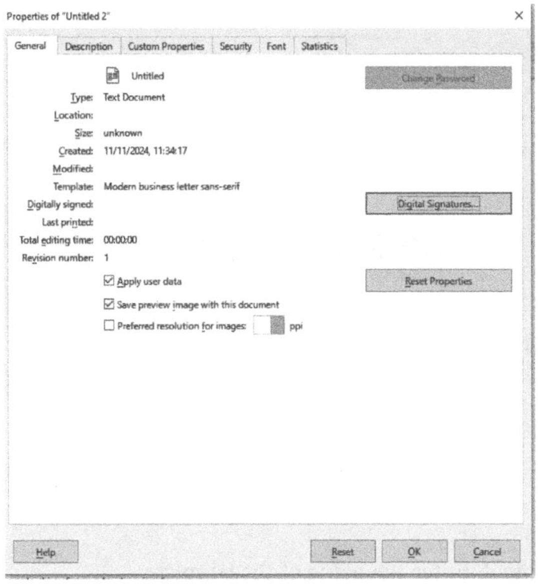

Creating a Template

You have learned how to use a document with a predefined template. You can also create your own template to save the styles and appearance of a document for future use.

To create a new template, follow the given steps:

Step 1 Open a document and enter data in it. Format the data according to your needs.

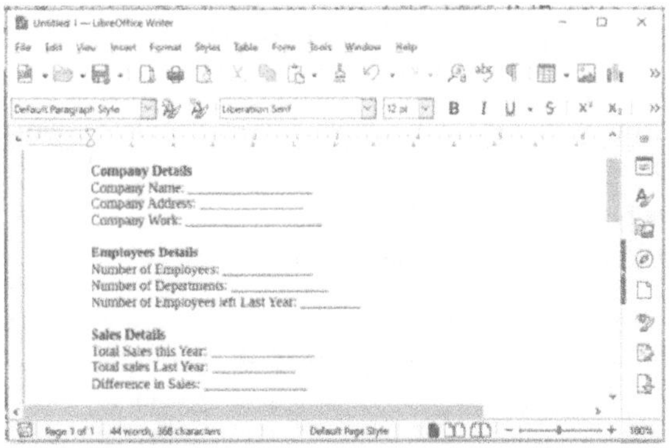

Step 2 Click on the File → Templates option.

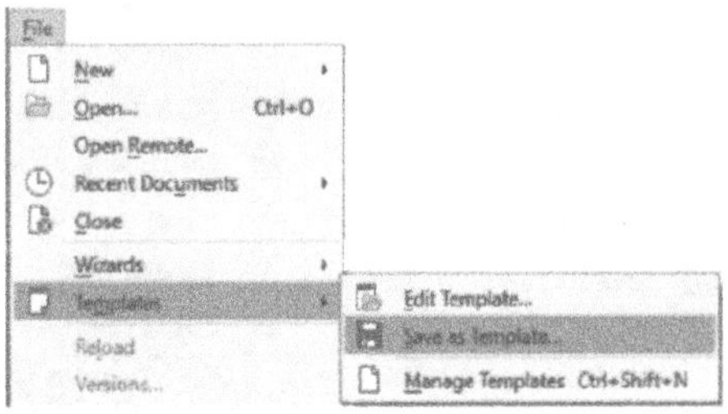

Step 3 Click on the Save As Template option. The Save As Template dialog box appears.

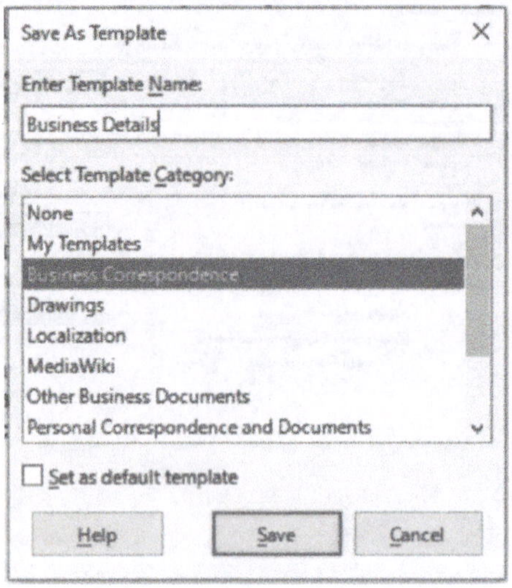

Step 4 Enter the name of the template.

Step 5 Choose the category in which this template will appear.

Step 6 Click on the Save button. The template will be saved in the selected category. (To ensure whether the template is created or not, click on the File → New→ Templates option. Choose the category as Business Invoice and the template created under it will be displayed).

Using Inbuilt/Predefined Template

LibreOffice provides various templates to enhance document styling. To use a predefined template, follow the given steps:

Step 1 Click on the File menu.

Step 2 Click on the New option.

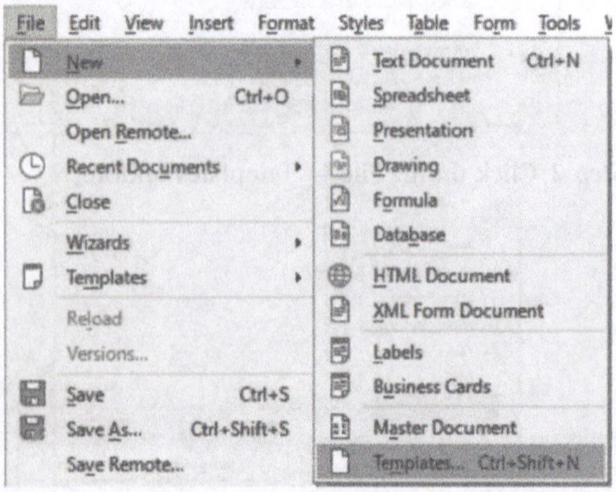

Step 3 Click on the Templates option. The Templates dialog box appears.

Step 4 Select the required template.

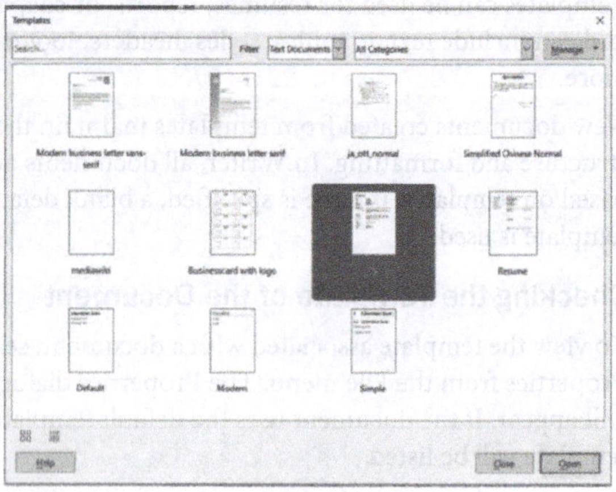

Step 5 Click on the Open button. The template gets opened.

Step 6 Make changes in the document according to your requirement and save it.

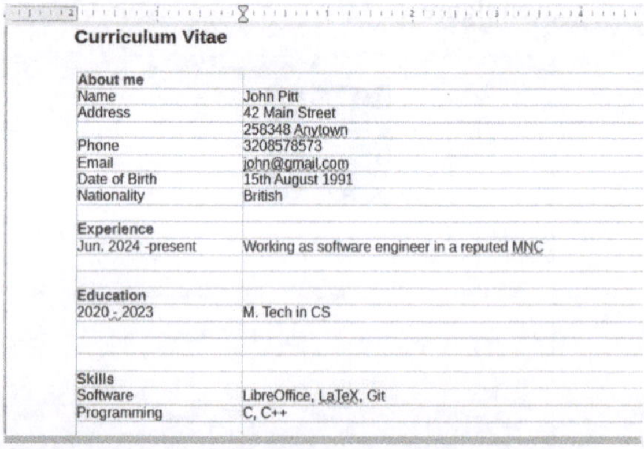

Try These 3.2

1 What is the purpose of a template in LibreOffice Writer?
 (a) To manually format individual elements in a document
 (b) To simplify the creation of professional and formal documents
 (c) To save documents in different file formats
 (d) To automatically insert images in a document

2 In LibreOffice Writer, to create a new document from a template, you need to select the "__________" option under the "New" menu.

3 Printer settings and general behaviors from the Tools → Options menu can be saved within a __________.

4 What types of elements can a template in LibreOffice Writer include?

5 How can you check the properties of a template in LibreOffice Writer?

3.7 Using Online Template

LibreOffice offers a variety of online templates that can be downloaded from the internet. LibreOffice refers to sources of templates as repositories. A repository can be local (a directory on your computer to which you have downloaded templates) or remote (a URL from which you can download templates). To get to the official LibreOffice template repository, type https://extensions.libreoffice.org/ in your web browser's address bar or click the Get more extensions online... link in the Extension Manager. This opens the Extensions web page.

To use online templates in LibreOffice, follow these steps:

Step 1 Start LibreOffice and go to the Templates dialog by clicking on the File menu, then selecting Templates → Manage Templates.

Step 2 In the Templates dialog, locate the Manage button in the upper-right corner and click it to open the submenu.

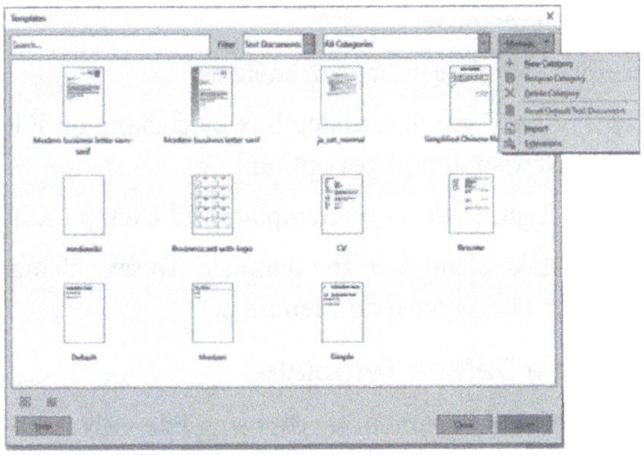

Step 3 From the submenu, choose Extensions. This opens the Extensions: Templates dialog.

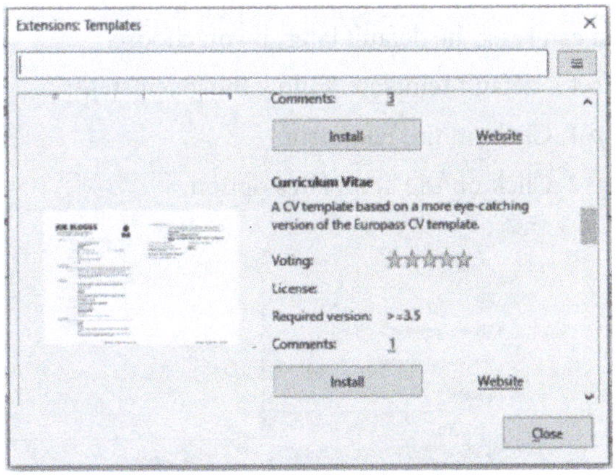

Step 4 In the Extensions dialog, you can scroll through a list of available templates and extensions.

Note *LibreOffice doesn't currently offer a filter option, so you may need to manually search.*

Step 5 For easier browsing, you can go directly to the official LibreOffice Extensions and Templates website (https://extensions.libreoffice.org).

Step 6 Once you find a template you'd like to use, download it from the website and save it to a directory on your computer.

Step 7 Select the given category of the template or create a new category for storing the downloaded template.

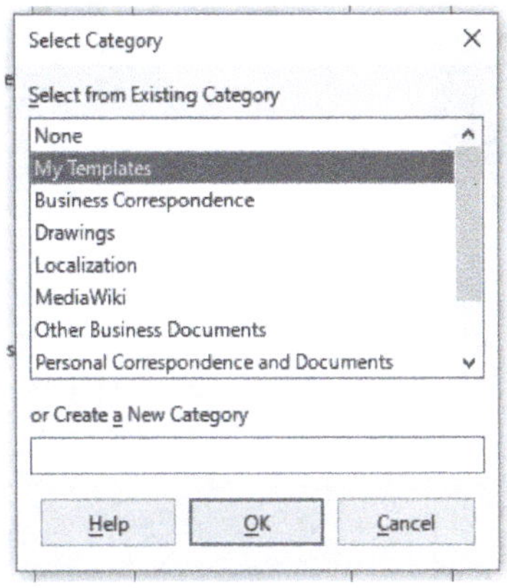

Step 8 In the Templates dialog, you can navigate to your local directory where the template is saved and add it for future use.

Step 9 After adding it, the template will be available in your Templates dialog, and you can open it directly from there to start a new document with the chosen template.

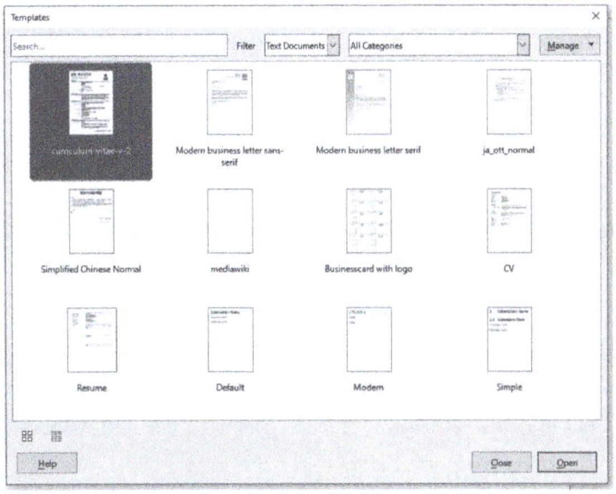

Importing a Template

Importing a template in LibreOffice allows you to bring a pre-existing template from another source into your own template library. This is useful for incorporating professionally designed templates or templates shared by others into your workflow. By importing a template, you can quickly apply consistent styles, formatting, and settings across your documents without having to create these elements from scratch. It also helps in maintaining uniformity in documents when working within a team or across different projects. To import a template or a downloaded template accessible in the Templates dialog box, follow these steps:

Step 1 Click on the File → Templates → Manage Template option. The Templates dialog box appears.

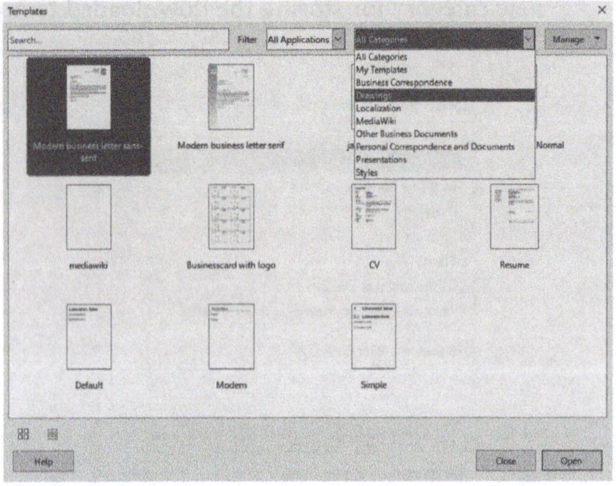

Step 2 Choose a Category: Select an existing category from the list or create a new category by clicking on Manage → select "New Category", New Category dialog box will appear. Write down the category's name (e.g., "CVs") and press Enter.

Step 3 After selecting the category Click on Manage → Import. The Open dialog box appears.

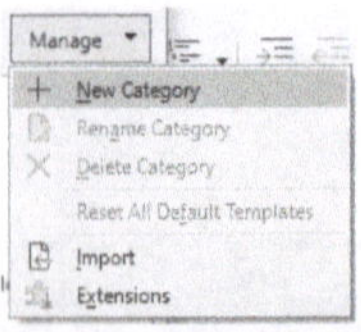

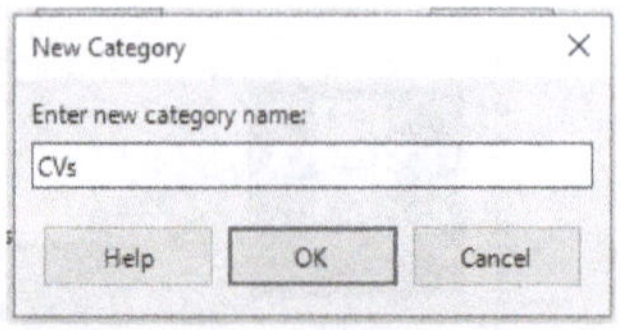

Step 4 Navigate to the location where the template file (e.g., "New_CV") is saved. Select the required template and click on Open button. The selected template gets imported.

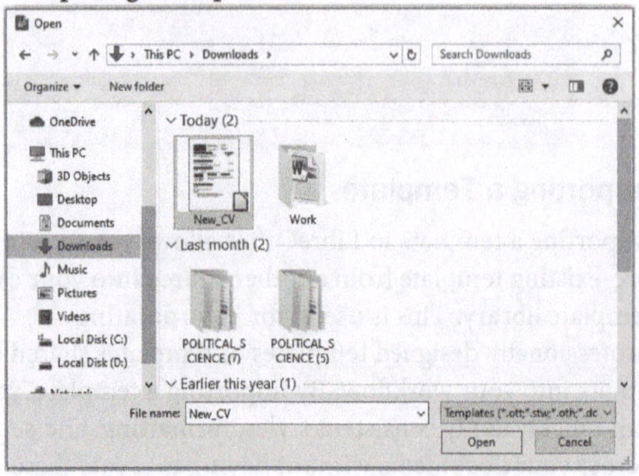

Step 5 The chosen file will now appear in the list of templates.

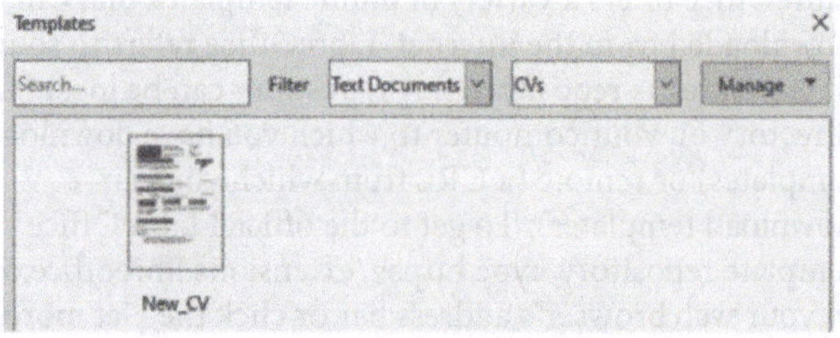

Editing Template

Predefined templates installed with LibreOffice can't be edited. So only templates which were imported or created by user can be edited.

Style as well as content of the template can be edited and can be re-applied style to the documents which were created using that template. Modified content of a template can't be re-applied on the document(s) created earlier using that template.

To edit a template, follow given steps:

Step 1 Open Template dialog box by clicking on File → New → Templates option.

Step 2 Right click on the template and click on Edit.

Step 3 Make changes in the template. To save changes, Go to File → Save on Menu bar.

Setting a Default Template

If you create a document by choosing File → New → Text Document from the menu bar, Writer creates the document from the default template for text documents. You can, however, set a custom template to be the default. You can reset the default later, if you choose.

To set a default template, follow the given steps:

Step 1 Click on the File menu.

Step 2 Click on the Templates option.

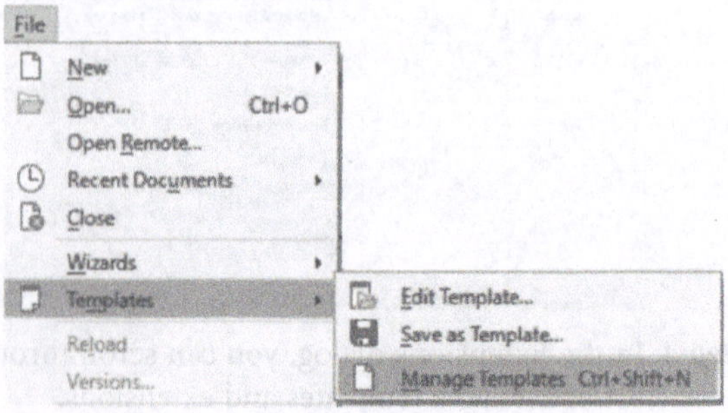

Step 3 Click on the Manage Templates option. The Templates dialog box appears.

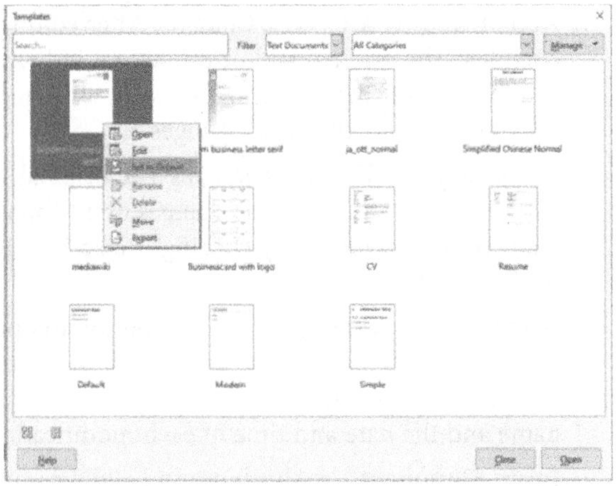

Step 4 Click and then right-click on the desired template.

Step 5 Click on the Set as Default option. The next time that you create a document of that type by choosing File → New, the document will be created from this template.

Moving a Template

When you place a mouse pointer on any of the templates in the Templates dialog box, a tool tip appears displaying the name of the template and its respective category.

To move a template to a different category in the Templates dialog box, follow these steps:

Step 1 Open the Templates dialog box by clicking on File → New → Templates option.

Step 2 Choose the category of template.

Step 3 Select the template which you want to move.

Step 4 Right-click and select Move option. The Select Category dialog box appears.

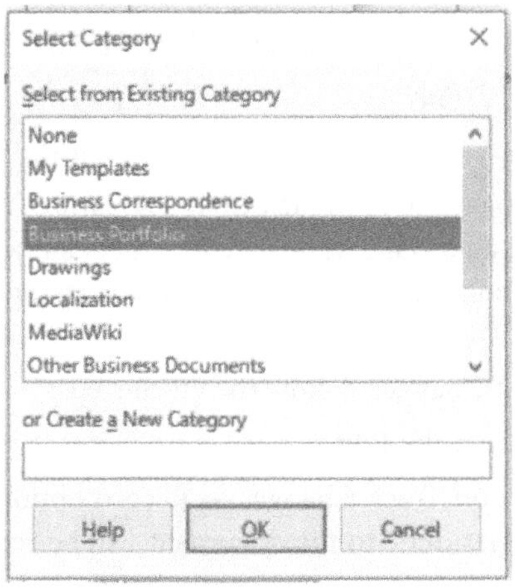

Step 5 Select the required category and click on the OK button. The template gets moved to the selected template category.

Exporting a Template

Exporting a template in LibreOffice allows you to save the template as a separate file, which can then be shared with others or used on different devices.

This is especially useful for maintaining consistency across multiple projects or teams, as it ensures that the same styles, formatting, and settings are used no matter where or by whom the document is created.

Additionally, exporting a template makes it easy to back up your templates or transfer them to another computer.

To export a template, follow the given steps:

Step 1 Click on the File → Templates → Manage Templates option. The Templates dialog box appears.

Step 2 Right-click on the template to be exported.

Step 3 Select Export option. The Select Folder dialog box appears.

Step 4 Select the folder.

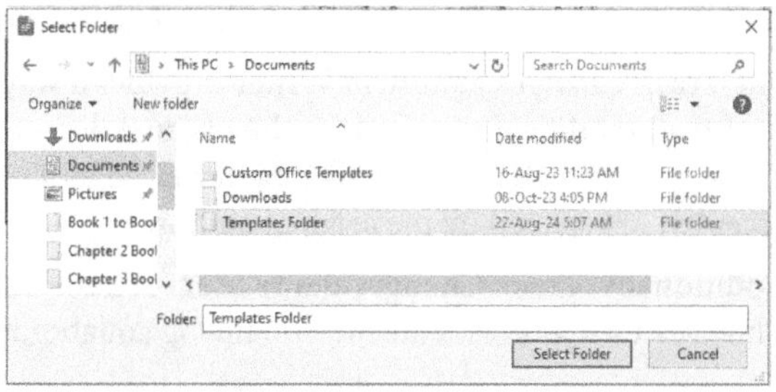

Step 5 Click on the Select Folder button. The selected template gets exported and save as a file.

Applying Templates to a Blank Document

You can apply a template from the available list to any blank document. Follow these steps to apply a template:

Step 1 Open a new document in LibreOffice Writer by selecting File → New → Text Document.

Step 2 Go to File → New → Templates to display the Templates dialog box.

Step 3 Choose the desired template and click on Open button. The template will open in a new window.

Step 4 Press Ctrl+A to select all content in the template, then Ctrl+C to copy it.

Step 5 Return to the blank document and press Ctrl+V to paste the copied template content.

Step 6 Modify the content as needed, then save the document as a text file.

Try These 3.3

1. In LibreOffice, templates can be used for
   (a) creating new documents with a predefined structure
   (b) only formatting existing documents
   (c) saving files automatically
   (d) running macros automatically
2. Which option should you select to export a template in LibreOffice?
   (a) Delete (b) Save As
   (c) Export (d) Move
3. When exporting a template, after selecting the template and choosing the Export option, you must click on the ______ button to finalize the export process.
4. How can you create a new template category in LibreOffice Writer?

3.8 Track Changes

Track Changes is a powerful tool that simplifies the process of commenting, editing, and reviewing a document among multiple users. When a document created by one user needs to be reviewed and edited by others, making changes directly could risk losing the original content.

The Track Changes feature in Writer provides a way to record all modifications made to the original document. These recorded changes can then be reviewed and either accepted or rejected by the original author.

Additionally, Track Changes allows users to add comments while reviewing the document, enhancing collaboration.

To make Track Changes toolbar visible, click on View menu → Toolbars → Track Changes option. The Track Changes toolbar appears to the bottom side of the window.

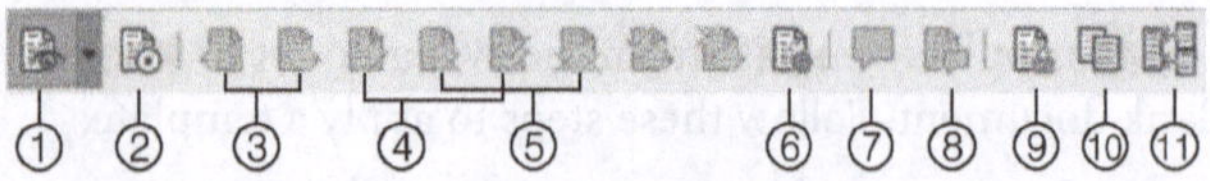

The various buttons on the Track Changes toolbar is given below:

1. **Show track changes** Click this button to display all changes made in the document by various users.
2. **Record track changes** Click this button to enable the Track Changes feature. Once activated, any edits will be tracked: added text will appear in a different color, and deleted text will be shown with a strikethrough.
3. **Previous/Next Track Change** Use these buttons to navigate through the changes made in the document.
4. **Accept/Accept All Track Changes** After editing is complete, the original author can accept individual changes by clicking "Accept," or accept all changes by clicking "Accept All Track Changes."
5. **Reject/Reject All Track Changes** The original author can reject individual changes or all changes made to the document by clicking "Reject" or "Reject All Track Changes."
6. **Manage Track Changes** Click this button to open the Manage Changes dialog box, which provides a detailed list of all changes, including the author's name and the date and time of each modification.
7. **Insert Comment** Use this button to add a comment to the document.
8. **Insert Track Change Comment** It allows users to add comments or notes to specific parts of the document while tracking changes.
9. **Protect Track Changes** It is used to safeguard the integrity of tracked changes and comments in a document. When this feature is enabled, it prevents unauthorized users from accepting, rejecting, or modifying tracked changes and comments, ensuring that the document's review process remains controlled and secure.
10. **Compare Non-Track Changed Document** It is used to compare two versions of a document, even if the Track Changes feature was not used in either version.
11. **Merge Track Changed Document** It is used to combine changes from multiple versions of a document that have been edited independently by different users.

3.9 Preparing a Document for Review

Before sharing a document for review or editing, it is important to enable the Track Changes feature. This ensures that all modifications are recorded, allowing the original author to later accept or reject the changes made by others.

To use Track Changes, follow the given steps:

Step 1 Click on the Edit menu.

Step 2 Click on Track Changes → Record option. The changes done to the document will be recorded.

Password Protecting Track Changes

To make sure that no user is able to disable the track changes option, we can protect the document with password. To perform the same, follow the given steps:

Step 1 Create a new document in LibreOffice writer.

Step 2 From the main menu, click on Edit menu → Track Changes → Protect option. The Enter Password dialog box will appear.

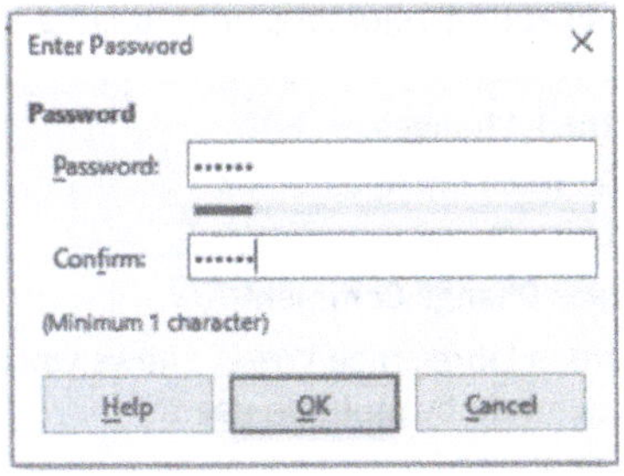

Step 3 Enter the password and click on OK button. After protecting the document with a password, if any user tries to disable the Track Changes feature, Writer will prompt to enter the password.

Record Changes

Once the Track Changes features is ON, the reviewers can begin recording the changes in the document. For that, click Edit → Track Changes → Record option. Alternatively select Record button from the toolbar.

Once the Record option is selected, the Track Changes feature is ON. Now, any character being deleted will be shown as strike through text and any character added will be shown in different colour.

Also when you place the mouse pointer over any of the changes, a tool tip is displayed giving details of the author, change made, date and time of change done as shown in figure.

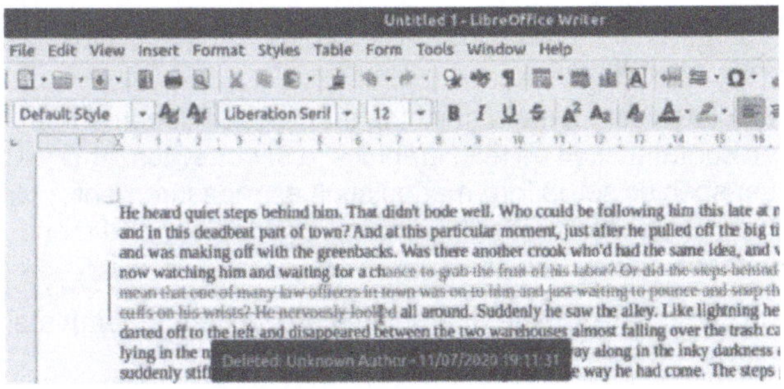

To stop recording, deselect the record option by selecting Edit → Track Changes → Record or click the Record button on the toolbar.

Accepting and Rejecting Changes

After all reviewers have made their changes, the original author can choose to accept or reject them.

To accept or reject changes, follow the given steps:

Step 1 Click on the change and then select Accept Track Change or Reject Track Change button.

Step 2 To navigate between the changes made to the document click on Previous Track Changes and Next Track Changes buttons.

Step 3 To accept or reject all the changes made, select Accept All Tracked Changes / Reject All Tracked Changes button respectively.

Step 4 On clicking Manage Track Changes button. The Manage Changes dialog box appears. It contains the details of all the changes made in the document. The dialog box contains buttons to accept and reject changes as well.

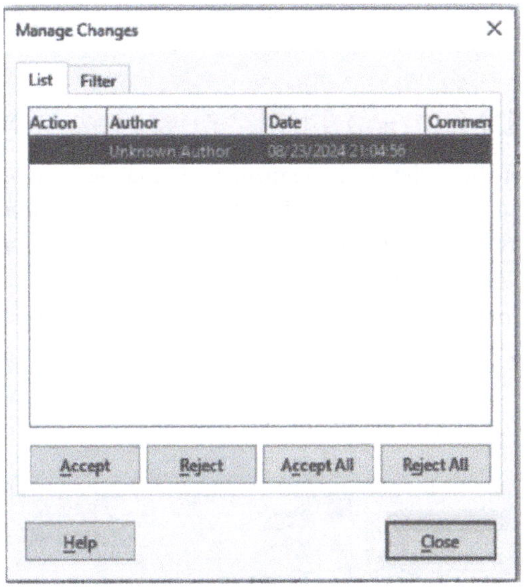

3.10 Adding Comments

To add comments during the review process, you can use the Track Changes toolbar.

Simply click at the place in the document where you want to place the comment.

To add comments, follow the given steps:

Step 1 Click on the Insert Comment button on the Track Changes toolbar. A comment box will be inserted on the right side of the window. (In comment box the name of the author or reviewer and date and time of the comment will be shown)

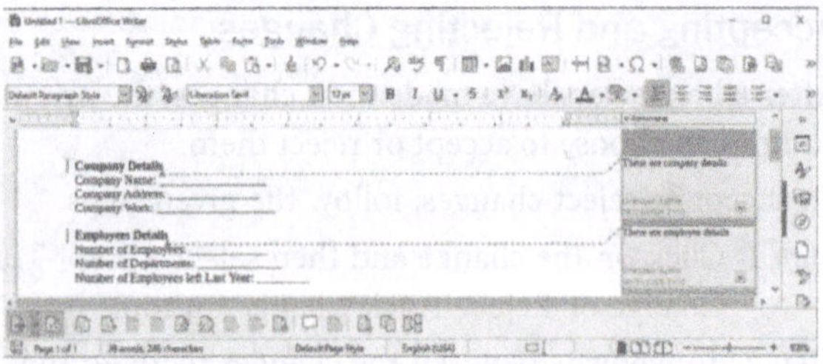

Step 2 Type the comment.

Step 3 Click anywhere to activate the comment.

Note *If more than one or two users add comments then the comments by different users will be shown in different coloured comment boxes.*

3.11 Deleting Comments

To delete a comment, follow the given steps:

Step 1 Right-click on the comment. A context menu appears.

Step 2 Click on Delete Comment option. That particular comment get deleted.

3.12 Comparing Documents

After the reviewers have made their changes and provided comments, the original document can be compared with the reviewed version in Writer, allowing the author to select the options that best fit their needs.

To compare the documents, follow the given steps:

Step 1 Click on Edit → Track Changes → Compare Document option. The Compare To Original Document dialog box will appear.

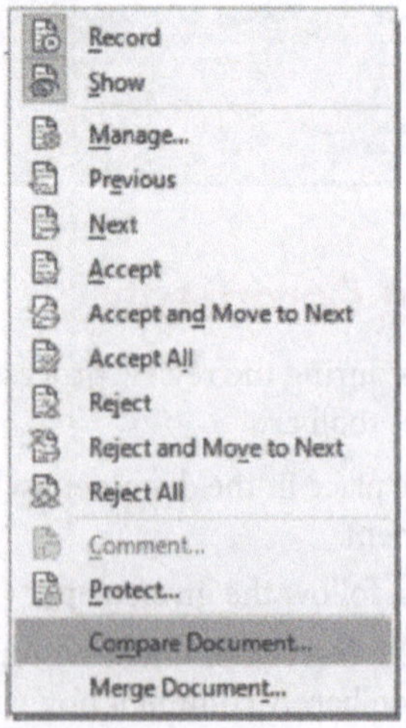

Step 2 Select the document with which the current document is to be compared. Click on Open button. The Manage Changes dialog box appears.

Step 3 Accept or reject the desired changes.

Step 4 Close the dialog box when done. Save the edited file.

Try These 3.4

1. **Which feature in LibreOffice Writer prevents unauthorized users from accepting, rejecting, or modifying tracked changes?**
   - (a) Record Track Changes
   - (b) Accept All Track Changes
   - (c) Protect Track Changes
   - (d) Insert Track Change Comment
2. **Which feature in LibreOffice Writer allows you to track and manage edits made by multiple users?**
   - (a) Table of Contents
   - (b) Templates
   - (c) Track Changes
   - (d) Styles
3. **To stop recording changes in LibreOffice Writer, you can deselect the ________option in the Track Changes menu.**
4. **The ________button in the Track Changes toolbar allows the original author to combine changes from multiple versions of a document that have been edited independently by different users.**

Summary

Writer's table of contents feature lets you build an automated ToC from the headings in a document.

Writer does not update the ToC automatically, so after any changes to the headings, you need to update it manually.

To delete the ToC from a document, right-click anywhere in the ToC and choose Delete Index from the context menu.

A template is a document model that you use to create other documents.

Templates can contain anything that regular documents can contain, such as text, graphics, a set of styles, and user-specific setup information such as measurement units, language, the default printer, and toolbar and menu customization.

You can create/delete a template category and a template in it.

ACTIVITY Time

ACTIVITY 1

Rimjhim has created a report on Environmental Pollution in LibreOffice Writer. She has applied proper heading styles to all section headings of the document. Now, to add table of contents to the document with the heading as Rimjhim's Table of Contents, follow the steps given below.

Step 1 Open the document in LibreOffice Writer.

Step 2 Select Insert → Table of Contents and Index → Table of Contents, Index or Bibliography. The Table of Contents, Index and Bibliography dialog box will be displayed.

Step 3 In the Type, in the Title text box, type Rimjhim's Table of Contents.

Step 4 Click OK. The Table of Contents will be inserted in Rimjhim's document.

ACTIVITY 2

Some more sections are added in the document, accordingly the ToC needs to be changed. To update a ToC manually, follow the steps given below.

Step 1 Right-click anywhere in the ToC.

Step 2 From the pop-up menu, select Update Index option. Writer updates the ToC so as to reflect any changes made in the document. The reflected changes in ToC.

ACTIVITY 3

Rimjhim has edited her document after the ToC was inserted. Now she wants to update the ToC and also wants a pink coloured background. Write the steps that Rimjhim should follow.

Step 1 To update the ToC, right-click anywhere in the ToC. From the pop-up menu, select Update Index option.

Step 2 To apply a coloured background, right click anywhere on the ToC and select Edit Index option from the popup menu.

Step 3 From the Table of Contents, Index or Bibliography dialog box, select the Background tab. The current background color will be displayed in the Active Color window.

Step 4 Click the Color button on the top of the dialog box.

Step 5 Select the desired color from the Colors palette. The selected color will appear in the New color window.

Step 6 Click OK to apply the desired color to the ToC.

ACTIVITY 4

Niaz works in a garment factory. He has to give the report of each garment being designed and stitched in his factory. His manager wants the same type of report for each garment. Instead of typing every time, he has been suggested to use the template feature of Writer. He wants to create his own default template and then use it to create multiple reports with same format and style. Give the solution to complete this task.

Procedure

Follow the below steps to create and save a template in Writer:

Step 1 Create or open the document whose template is to be created.

Step 2 From main menu bar, select File → Templates → Save as Template. The Save As Template dialog box appears.

Step 3 Type the name of the new template (Niaz_template) in the Template Name text box.

Step 4 Select the category of the template (Business Correspondence).

Step 5 Click and select Set as default template check box.

Step 6 Click Save button to save the template with an extension.ott.

Now follow the steps given below to use the template:

Step 1 Select File → Templates → Manage Templates.

Step 2 Select the desired template, (Niaz_template) from the Templates dialog box.

Step 3 Click on Open button. The new document with name as Untitled, will be opened with the same content, appearance and formatting effects as the saved template.

Step 4 Make the desired changes and save the file.

ACTIVITY 5

Niaz wants to store the template created by him and another one that was imported by Balwinder in a folder named Company_Templates on the desktop.

Follow the steps given below to complete this task.

Step 1 Create a new document in LibreOffice Writer and press Ctrl+Shift+N to open the Templates dialog box.

Step 2 Select the template (Niaz_template) to be exported.

Step 3 Right-click on that template and choose Export option from pop-up menu. Select folder dialog box appears.

Step 4 Click Select Folder button to export the selected template.

Step 5 Repeat the steps 1 to 4 to import the template Employee ID Badge in the Company_Templates folder.

ACTIVITY 6

Pradeep has created a document on 'Humans and Nature'. He wants his friends to review the document and give their comments wherever required. The following process will demonstrate how his friends add comments in the document.

Step 1 Open the document created by Pradeep to review.

Step 2 Click on Insert Comment button on the toolbar.

Step 3 Type the comment in the comment box.

Step 4 Once done click anywhere on the document to activate it.

Step 5 Repeat the steps given above to add more comments in the document.

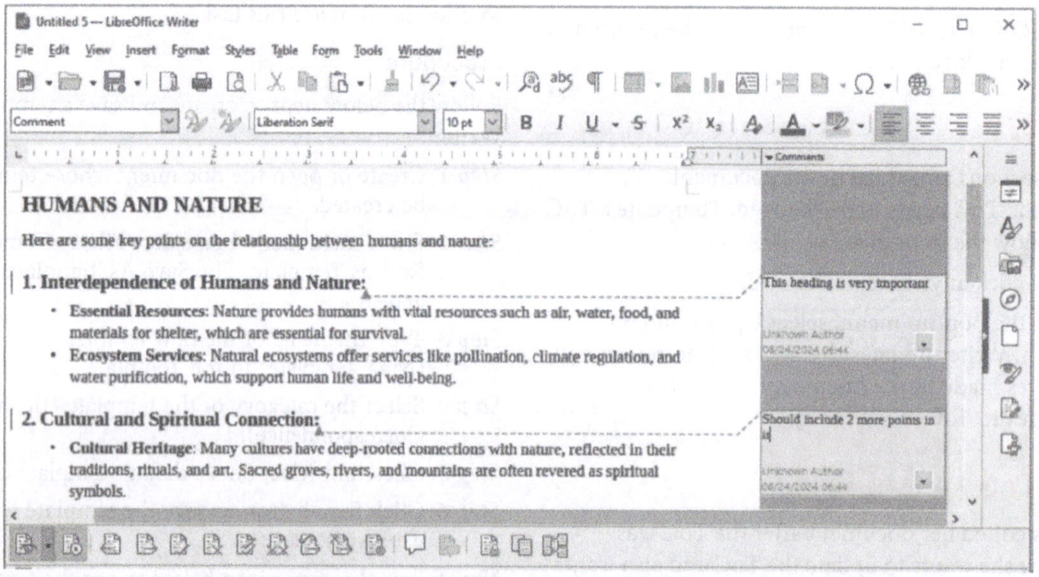

ACTIVITY 7

After incorporating the reviews, Pradeep mailed the document to his editor with the Track Changes ON. He made certain changes in the document. Pradeep wants to compare his original document with the reviewed document. The following process will demonstrate how Pradeep will compare the edited document with the original document.

Step 1 Open the edited document.

Step 2 Select Edit → Track Changes → Compare Document option.

Step 3 The Compare To Original Documents dialog box will appear. Browse and select the original file to be compared.

Step 4 The Manage Changes dialog box is displayed.

Step 5 Accept or reject the desired changes.

Step 6 Close the dialog box when done.

Step 7 Save the edited file.

NCERT FOLDER

Complete Explanations of all NCERT's Questions

A. Multiple Choice Questions

Q.1 Which of the following is not true about Table of Contents, Index or Bibliography dialog box?

(a) It has four tabs
(b) On the Type tab, by default, the checkbox for Protected against Manual Changes option will be selected.
(c) The Styles tab contains options to change the background colour.
(d) None of the above

Q.2 Which of the following tabs is by default active when the Table of Contents, Entries or Bibliography dialog box is opened?

(a) Entries (b) Background (c) Styles (d) Type

Q.3 Which of the following tabs contains options to set styles for various entries in the ToC?

(a) Entries (b) Background (c) Styles (d) Type

Q.4 Which of the following can be added in the background of Table of Contents in LibreOffice Writer?

(a) Color (b) Graphic
(c) Both (a) and (b) (d) Neither (a) nor (b)

Q.5 Which of the following is true about Track Changes feature of Writer?

(a) You cannot record a change made in the document.
(b) A comment of a particular author only can be deleted
(c) Any change made to the document is permanent.
(d) None of the above

Q.6 Which of the following menus contains the Track Changes option?

(a) File (b) Edit (c) View (d) Insert

Q.7 Which of the following is the shortcut key to start recording the changes being made in the document?

(a) Ctrl+Shift+C (b) Alt+Shift+C
(c) Ctrl+Alt+C (d) Shift+C+F2

Q.8 Which of the following is not true about templates?

(a) The styles and formatting features can be reused
(b) LibreOffice provides online templates
(c) We cannot create our own templates
(d) None of the above

Q.9 Which of the following is the shortcut key to open the Templates dialog box?

(a) Ctrl+Alt+N (b) Shift+Ctrl+N
(c) Ctrl+Alt+T (d) Shift+Alt+T

Q.10 Which of the following buttons, in the Templates dialog box, will be clicked to save a template displayed in the list of templates?

(a) Export (b) Import (c) Move (d) None of these

Q.11 Which of the following is the shortcut key to select the entire document?

(a) Ctrl+S (b) Ctrl+A (c) Ctrl+D (d) Ctrl+B

Q.12 Which of the following is the correct sequence of options to open the Templates dialog box?

(a) File → Manage Templates → Templates
(b) File → Templates → Manage Templates
(c) Insert → Templates → Manage Templates
(d) Insert → Manage Templates → Templates

Answers

1. (a)	2. (d)	3. (c)	4. (c)	5. (d)	6. (b)
7. (a)	8. (c)	9. (b)	10. (b)	11. (b)	12. (b)

B. Fill in the Blanks

Q.1 To navigate to the topic from the ToC, press _______ key while clicking the mouse button on that topic.

Q.2 To remove the applied paragraph styling in the ToC, select the outline level in the Levels list box, and then click the _______ button.

Q.3 If the checkbox for _________ option is selected, the ToC is protected from any accidental change.

Q.4 To update the ToC manually, right click and select _______ option from the pop up menu.

Q.5 The _______ tab contains options to set the number of columns that we want to have in our ToC.

Q.6 The _______ feature of Writer offers us an alternative method to keep a record of all the changes made in the original document.

Q.7 The shortcut key to start recording the changes is__.

Q.8 After the Track Changes feature is ON, the added characters are shown as _______ text.

Q.9 A ________ is a preset layout that helps us to create professional and formal documents easily.

Q.10 The default template in Writer is ________.

Q.11 To find the template that is being used in the current document, select ______ option from the File menu.

Q.12 The _________ button is clicked in Templates dialog box to view online templates.

Answers

1. Ctrl 2. Default 3. Protected against manual changes
4. Update index 5. Columns 6. Track Changes
7. Ctrl + Shift + C 8. Coloured 9. Template
10. Blank document template 11. Properties
12. Browse online template

C. State Whether the given Statements are True or False

Q.1 **The topics in Table of Contents are hyperlinked.**

Q.2 **The Table of Contents in LibreOffice Writer can be updated automatically.**

Q.3 **Table of Contents can be inserted even if the section headings are not styled.**

Q.4 **Once a ToC is created, it cannot be edited.**

Q.5 **We cannot add a graphic as a background of ToC.**

Q.6 **The changes recorded have to be accepted by the original author.**

Q.7 **We can delete the comments added in a document by the user.**

Q.8 **A single template can be used for multiple documents.**

Q.9 **A template cannot contain graphics.**

Q.10 **All documents in Writer are based upon templates.**

Q.11 **The online templates cannot be added to the list of templates in the templates dialog box.**

Q.12 **A template once created can be edited again and again.**

Answers

1. True 2. False 3. False 4. False 5. False
6. False 7. True 8. True 9. False 10. True
11. False 12. True

D. Answer the Following Questions

Q.1 **What is the need of table of contents?**

Ans. Table of Contents allows to insert an automated table of contents in a document. The entries or contents of this table are automatically taken from the headings and sub headings of the document.

Q.2 **What will happen if the 'Protected Against Manual Changes' option is not selected in the Type tab of Table of Contents, Index or Bibliography dialog box?**

Ans. This option protects the ToC from any accidental change. If this box is unchecked, then the contents of ToC can be changed directly on the document page, just like any other text on the document.

Q.3 **Name the five tabs present in the Table of Contents, Index or Bibliography dialog box.**

Ans. Five Tabs – Type, Entries, Styles, Columns and Background.

Q.4 **What do you mean by customization of ToC?**

Ans. When ToC is inserted, we can customize it according to our requirements. To do so, right click anywhere on the ToC and select Edit Index option.

Q.5 **How headings and sub-headings of a document differentiated in ToC?**

Ans. Headings and subheadings in the Table of Contents (ToC) are differentiated by hierarchy levels, with main headings appearing in bold or larger fonts and subheadings indented beneath them. The structure follows the applied heading styles (e.g., Heading 1, Heading 2, Heading 3) to create a nested format in the ToC.

Q.6 **Define a template.**

Ans. A template is a layout that helps to create professional and/or formal documents easily.

Q.7 **Give any one advantage of using a template for your document.**

Ans. Templates can be used to create a resume, chapter or project report. A template can contain all the features or objects that a regular document can contain – text, graphics, and styles and can even use any language.

Q.8 **What is the difference between importing and exporting a template?**

Ans. In LibreOffice Writer, importing a template means bringing a template file from an external source into your template library for use in documents, while exporting a template saves an existing template from your library as a standalone file, which can be shared or used in other installations.

Q.9 **Name any two categories of templates.**

Ans. Category- My Template and Business Correspondence

Q.10 **When is exporting of templates useful? Give any one reason.**

Ans. Exporting templates is useful when you want to share a custom template with others or backup your templates for use on another device.

Q.11 **What is the difference between Accept Track Change and Accept All Tracked Changes buttons?**

Ans. Accept Track Change button approves a single selected change in the document, keeping the rest unchanged. Accept All Tracked Changes button approves all tracked reviewing each change individually.

Q.12 **How do we prepare a document for review?**

Ans. Before the document is sent for review, the original author should prepare the document for review and start recording the changes being made. For that, select Edit → Track Changes → Record option. Alternatively, select the Record button from the Track Changes toolbar.

EXAM PATTERN EXERCISE

Including Competency Based Questions

Multiple Choice Questions

1 **How many levels of headings does LibreOffice Writer support?** CBSE SQP 2024-25

(a) 5 (b) 8
(c) 10 (d) 12

2 **Which of the following is NOT true about templates?** CBSE SQP 2024-25

(a) The styles and formatting features can be reused.
(b) Libre Office provides online templates
(c) Templates can have headings, text formats, styles, page numbers, headers and footers
(d) We cannot create our own templates

3 **After incorporating the reviews, Krishna mailed the document to his editor with the Track Changes ON. He made certain changes in the document. Pradeep wants to compare his original document with the reviewed document.**

What is the first step Krishna should take to compare his edited document with the original document? CBSE SQP 2024-25, Competency Based Que.

(a) Open the Manage Changes dialog box.
(b) Select Edit → Track Changes → Compare Documents option.
(c) Save the edited file.
(d) Accept or reject the desired changes.

4 **How can you prevent unauthorized users from disabling the Track Changes feature in a document?**

(a) Use the "Show track changes" button
(b) Protect the document with a password
(c) Disable the Track Changes toolbar
(d) Lock the document's content

5 **Which one is not the tab of the insert/index Table window of Writer Document?** CBSE SQP 2023-24

(a) Entries (b) Background
(c) Style (d) Row

6 **Writer's table of contents feature lets you build an automated table of contents from the.........in your document.** CBSE 2021-22 Term I

(a) Template (b) Style
(c) Headings (d) Tables

7 **A ____ is a model that you use to create other documents.** CBSE SQP 2020-21, CBSE SQP 2021-22 Term I

(a) Styles (b) Template
(c) Wizard (d) Sample

8 **When you apply a ____________, you apply a group of formatting effects together in one single step.** CBSE SQP 2021-22 Term I

(a) Effect (b) Style
(c) Template (d) Format

9 **In Writer, you can create your own template in .... way(s).** CBSE 2024

(a) One (b) Two (c) Three (d) Four

10 **Which feature in LibreOffice Writer is used to automatically generate a list of chapters and sections in a document?**

(a) Styles
(b) Track Changes
(c) Table of Contents (ToC)
(d) Index

11 **............... feature of Writer is based on different types of heading styles and is used to give the listing of the contents of the document.** CBSE 2025

(a) Table of Heading (b) Index
(c) Label of Contents (d) Table of Contents

12 **What is the purpose of the Track Changes feature in LibreOffice Writer?**

(a) To format text automatically.
(b) To insert images and tables.
(c) To monitor and manage edits made by multiple users.
(d) To create a Table of Contents.

13 **In the hierarchy of headings in LibreOffice Writer, which heading level typically represents the title of the document?**

(a) Heading 1 (b) Heading 2
(c) Heading 3 (d) Heading 4

14 **To apply a character style to an element in the Table of Contents, which tab in the "Table of Contents, Index or Bibliography" dialog box should you use?**

(a) Type Tab (b) Entries Tab
(c) Styles Tab (d) Columns Tab

15 **Which menu is used to insert table of contents?**

(a) Insert menu (b) Format menu
(c) Tools menu (d) File menu

16 **Which option is used to update the table of contents?**

(a) Index Update (b) Update Index
(c) Update (d) Change Index

17 **Which option is used to delete the table of contents?**

(a) Delete index (b) Index Delete
(c) Modify index (d) None of these

18 Which tab in the "Table of Contents, Index or Bibliography" dialog box allows you to change the number of columns in a ToC?
(a) Type Tab (b) Entries Tab
(c) Styles Tab (d) Columns Tab

19 What is the first step to customize a Table of Contents (ToC) in LibreOffice Writer?
(a) Click on the Insert menu
(b) Right-click on the ToC
(c) Select the text in the document
(d) Click on the Styles button

20 What must you do after making changes to headings in a document to update the Table of Contents (ToC)?
(a) Delete the ToC
(b) Right-click on the ToC and select Update index
(c) Reinsert the ToC
(d) Click on the Styles button

21 Which button in the Track Changes toolbar is used to start recording changes made to a document?
(a) Show track changes
(b) Record track changes
(c) Accept/Reject Track Changes
(d) Insert Comment

22 Using which of the following Templates dialog box gets opened?
(a) File → New → New Template
(b) File → New → Manage Template
(c) File → New → Templates
(d) File → Templates → Manage

23 .... is the default template for the files being created in Writer. CBSE 2025
(a) Resume template (b) Project Report
(c) Blank document (d) Chapter

24 Which of the following is not true about templates in Writer?
(a) LibreOffice provides online templates
(b) Templates are used to copy styles and content in the document
(c) Writer does not allow to create customized template
(d) All of the above

25 What is a template?
(a) A type of font
(b) A document model for creating other documents
(c) A computer program
(d) A picture

26 Which menu do you start with to use a template?
(a) Edit (b) View
(c) File (d) Help

27 What can you save in a template besides text?
(a) Printer settings (b) Video files
(c) Music files (d) Web links

28 How do you set a template as the default?
(a) Double-click it
(b) Right-click and choose "Set as Default"
(c) Drag it to the desktop
(d) Rename it

29 What should you do first to apply a different template to a document?
(a) Copy the text (b) Delete the text
(c) Change the font (d) Print the document

30 How do you create a new template category?
(a) Click "New Category" in the Templates dialog
(b) Click "Open File"
(c) Choose "Rename"
(d) Select "Print"

31 Can predefined templates be edited?
(a) Yes, always
(b) No, only user-created templates can be edited
(c) Yes, but only once
(d) No, they are locked

32 Why would you import a template?
(a) To use a template from another source
(b) To delete it
(c) To rename it
(d) To print it

33 John has written a book consisting of fifteen chapters. He wanted to make the index of the book. Suggest him the option used to create the index automatically in a word processor. CBSE SQP 2022-23, Competency Based Que.
(a) Tables (b) Mail Merge
(c) Columns (d) Table of Content

34 Maria is preparing a research paper and needs to track the changes made by her collaborators. Which feature in a word processor should she enable to monitor edits made to the document? Competency Based Que.
(a) Spell Check (b) Track Changes
(c) AutoCorrect (d) Commenting

35 Sarah has written a lengthy report and wants to create a clear overview of its structure, including all main sections and subsections. Which feature in her word processor can she use to automatically generate this overview based on her document's headings? Competency Based Que.
(a) Outline View (b) Table of Contents
(c) Index (d) Header and Footer

36 Monty is collaborating with his team on a project document. He wants to provide feedback on specific sections without altering the original text. Which feature should he use to add his observations? Competency Based Que.
(a) Track Changes (b) Footnotes
(c) Insert Comment (d) Annotations

37 **You have created a new invoice template for your company and want to use it for every new invoice you create. Which steps should you follow to set this template as default?** Competency Based Que.

(a) File → Templates → Import → Set as Default
(b) File →Templates → Manage Templates → Right-click on the template → Set as Default
(c) File → New → Templates → Set as Default
(d) File → Templates → New Category → Set as Default

38 **You have received a template file from a colleague and want to organize it in a specific category in your LibreOffice Writer. How can you achieve this?** Competency Based Que.

(a) File → Templates → Import → Select Category → Save
(b) File → Templates → New Category → Select Category → Save
(c) File → Templates → Import → Select the file → Choose Category → Open
(d) File → New → Templates → Move to Category → Save

Answers

1. (c)	2. (d)	3. (b)	4. (b)	5. (d)
6. (c)	7. (b)	8. (b)	9. (d)	10. (c)
11. (d)	12. (c)	13. (a)	14. (c)	15. (a)
16. (b)	17. (a)	18. (d)	19. (b)	20. (b)
21. (b)	22. (c)	23. (c)	24. (c)	25. (b)
26. (c)	27. (a)	28. (b)	29. (a)	30. (a)
31. (b)	32. (a)	33. (d)	34. (b)	35. (b)
36. (c)	37. (b)	38. (c)		

Very Short Answer Type Questions

1 **How do you update the Table of Contents (ToC) after making changes to the headings in a document?**

Ans. To update the Table of Contents, right-click on the ToC and select Update Index. This will refresh the ToC to reflect any changes made to the document's headings.

2 **Which toolbar option in LibreOffice Writer allows you to track the changes made by multiple users?**

Ans. The Track Changes toolbar option in LibreOffice Writer allows you to monitor and manage edits made by multiple users, showing who made each change and when.

3 **What is the function of the 'Protect Track Changes' feature in LibreOffice Writer?**

Ans. The Protect Track Changes feature prevents unauthorized users from accepting, rejecting, or modifying the tracked changes in a document. This feature can be protected with a password, ensuring only authorized individuals can modify tracked edits.

4 **How can you apply a specific character style to an element in the Table of Contents (ToC)?**

Ans. To apply a character style to an element in the ToC:

- Right-click on the ToC and select Edit Index.
- Go to the Entries tab, click on the specific part (e.g., chapter number, page number), and assign a character style from the dropdown list next to the element you want to style.

5 **State any two purposes of using Templates.** CBSE SQP 2022-23

Ans. Two purposes of using Templates :

- **Consistency** Templates help maintain uniform formatting and structure across multiple documents, such as resumes, reports, and business letters, ensuring a professional appearance.
- **Time-saving** By using templates, users can avoid repetitive formatting tasks, as predefined settings like font styles, headers, and footers are already applied.

6 **Give any two characteristics of a template in LibreOffice Writer.** CBSE 2023

Ans. Two characteristics of a template in LibreOffice Writer:

- **Predefined formatting** A template in LibreOffice Writer comes with predefined text formatting, layouts, and styles that can be reused across multiple documents.
- **Customizability** Users can create, edit, or update their own templates based on their specific needs, which can then be used as default for future documents.

7 **How can you quickly open the Template dialog box using a shortcut?**

Ans. You can quickly open the Template dialog box in LibreOffice Writer by pressing Ctrl + Shift + N. This shortcut opens the Templates dialog where you can select, manage, or create templates for your documents.

8 **What are the properties that creating a template using document allows to save?**

Ans. Creating a template using a document allows saving various properties, such as text formatting (font type, size, style), page layout (margins, orientation), styles (headings, paragraphs), and additional elements like headers, footers, page numbers, and graphics. It also saves general settings like printer configurations and predefined content.

9 **How do you set a custom template as the default in LibreOffice Writer?**

Ans. To set a custom template as the default, follow these steps:

- Click on the File menu and choose Templates.
- Click on Manage Templates.
- Right-click on the desired template and select Set as Default.

10 **What steps should you follow to apply a different template to an existing document in LibreOffice Writer?**

Ans. Steps to apply a different template to an existing document:

- Open the document and select all text by pressing Ctrl+A.
- Copy the selected text by pressing Ctrl+C.
- Go to File → New → Templates and select the desired template.
- Delete the content in the new template and paste the copied text with Ctrl+V.

11 How can you create a new template category in LibreOffice Writer?

Ans. To create a new template category:

- Click on the File menu and select New, then choose Templates.
- Click on Manage and select New Category.
- Enter the name of the category and click OK.

12 Can predefined templates in LibreOffice Writer be edited?

Ans. No, predefined templates installed with LibreOffice cannot be edited. Only user-created or imported templates can be edited, including modifying styles and content.

13 How can you move a template from one category to another in LibreOffice Writer?

Ans. To move a template to a different category:

- Open the Templates dialog by clicking on File → New → Templates.
- Choose the category of the template.
- Select the template you want to move.
- Right-click on the template and select Move.
- In the Select Category dialog, choose the desired category and click OK.

14 How would you update and delete the table of contents?

Ans. **To Update** Right-click on the ToC and select Update Index to refresh it after making changes to headings.

To Delete Right-click on the ToC and choose Delete Index to remove it.

15 Write the steps to enable Track Changes.

Ans. To enable track changes:

- Go to the Edit menu.
- Select Track Changes.
- Click Record to enable tracking.

Optionally, you can enable Show to view the changes while editing.

Short Answer Type Questions

1 A team of writers is collaborating on a report using a word processing software with a Track Changes feature. One writer creates the initial draft, which then needs to be reviewed and edited by the rest of the team.

(a) Why is the Track Changes feature essential for collaborative document editing?

(b) Which menu option can be used to access this feature?

(c) Can reviewers add comments?

(d) Once the changes are made by all the reviewers, who can accept or reject them? **CBSE SQP 2024-25, Competency Based Que.**

Ans. (a) Track Changes is a powerful tool that makes the process of commenting, editing and reviewing a document easy between multiple users.

A document created by one user needs to be reviewed and edited by self or other users. If any modifications are made in the document directly, the original document might get lost.

Instead, the Track Changes feature of Writer offers an alternative method to keep a record of all the changes made in the original document. All the changes that are recorded can be either accepted or rejected by the original author.

(b) View → Toolbars → Track Changes.

(c) Yes

(d) Original Author

2 What do you understand by the term Table of Contents? List the characteristics of a good 'Table of content' in a word processor. **CBSE SQP 2023-24**

Ans. A Table of Contents (ToC) is an organized list of the headings and subheadings in a document, usually placed at the beginning, providing a roadmap for the reader to navigate through the document easily.

A good ToC should

- Include all major sections and headings.
- Be automatically updated when changes are made to the document.
- Be well-structured with hierarchical indentation for subsections.

3 Write the steps to create a template.

Ans. Steps to Create a Template:

- Open a document and enter the required data.
- Format the document as needed.
- Click on the File menu.
- Select the Templates option.
- Click on Save as Template. The Save As Template dialog box appears.
- Enter a name for the template.
- Choose the category in which to save the template.
- Click Save.

4 How do you export a template?

Ans. Steps to Export a Template:

- Open the Templates dialog by clicking on File → Templates → Manage Templates.
- Select the template you want to export.
- Right-click on the template and select Export.
- Choose the location where you want to save the template.
- Click Select Folder to finalize the export.

5 Write the steps to import a template.

Ans. Steps to Import a Template:

- Click on the File menu.
- Select Templates and choose Manage Templates.
- In the Templates dialog box, click Import.
- Browse and select the template file you want to import.
- Choose the category to place the template in.
- Click Open to complete the import process.

6 Write the steps to insert table of contents in the document.

Ans. To insert a Table of Contents in LibreOffice Writer:

- Position the cursor where you want the ToC.
- Go to Insert → Table of Contents and Index → Table of Contents, Index or Bibliography.
- In the dialog box, customize the settings as needed.
- Click OK to insert the ToC.

7 Discuss the importance of using a well-organized Table of Contents (ToC) in professional documents.

Ans. A well-organized Table of Contents (ToC) is crucial in professional documents as it enhances readability and navigation.

It helps readers quickly locate sections, provides a logical structure, and reflects the document's hierarchy, making it easier to understand the content flow. It also gives a polished and professional appearance, essential for formal reports, manuals, and academic papers.

8 You are tasked with creating a standardized letter template that all employees can use for official communication. **Competency Based Que.**

(a) Describe the steps to create this template.

(b) How can you ensure that the template is the default option when employees create a new letter?

(c) If you need to move this template to a different category later, how would you do it?

Ans. (a) Steps to create a template:

- Open a document, enter data, and format it accordingly.
- Click on File → Templates → Save as Template.
- Name the template and choose a category.
- Click Save.

(b) To set the template as default:

- Click on File → Templates → Manage Templates.
- Right-click on the letter template and select Set as Default.

(c) To move the template to a different category:

- Open File → Templates → Manage Templates.
- Right-click on the template, select Move, and choose the desired category.

9 You've been asked to update a template with new company branding and distribute it to the team. **Competency Based Que.**

(a) How do you edit the existing template?

(b) Once edited, what steps should you follow to export the updated template and share it with others?

(c) How can team members import this template into their own LibreOffice?

Ans. (a) To edit an existing template:

- Go to File → Templates → Manage Templates.
- Right-click on the template and select Edit.
- Make changes and save the template.

(b) To export the updated template:

- Right-click on the template in Manage Templates and select Export.
- Choose a location and save the template.

(c) For team members to import the template:

- Open File → Templates → Manage Templates.
- Click on Import, select the file, and choose a category to save it.

10 You frequently create both business reports and draft documents. To organize your templates, you want to create separate categories. **Competency Based Que.**

(a) How do you create a new template category in LibreOffice Writer?

(b) How can you move a template between categories after creation?

Ans. (a) To create a new category:

- Go to File → Templates → Manage.
- Click New Category, name the category, and click OK.

(b) To move a template:

- Go to File → Templates → Manage Templates.
- Right-click the template, select Move, and choose the new category.

PRACTICAL ASSIGNMENT

1. Rajnikant has created a detailed report on Education in India using the LibreOffice Writer tool. He has styled the document well by inserting proper paragraph and section headings. His colleague Murugan advised him to insert a Table of Contents that will give a complete glimpse of his report. Help Rajnikant to insert a ToC with a green background.
2. After the ToC was inserted, Rajnikant made some changes in the report but the changes were not reflected in the ToC. Will he have to again insert a new ToC? Suggest him a better way to update the ToC.
3. Rukhsat has just downloaded a template from libreoffice.org. Now she wants to import it in My templates category of the Templates folder. How can she complete her task?
4. Rimit loves to create cards on his computer. This time he decided to make his own Christmas cards and send them to his friends. He wants to do the task using the templates feature of Writer. He has already saved and imported the desired template(card.ott). Help him to create cards for atleast five of his friends.
5. Teena is a member of the editorial team of her school. She wants to set the newspaper template as her default template. Write the steps to help Teena complete the task.
6. Venkat has created a document on India's Trade Review. He wants two of his friends, Rinky and Sujoy to review his document and if required, add comments to it. But none of them know how to use the Track Changes feature of Writer. Help them to complete the task.
7. Venkat has received the reviewed file with modifications and comments. What steps will he follow now to accept or reject the changes done by his friends.
8. Write steps to compare the original document created by Venkat and the edited document sent by Rinky and Sujoy.
9. Identify and label "Browse Online Templates button, Export button, Import button" in the following Templates dialog box.

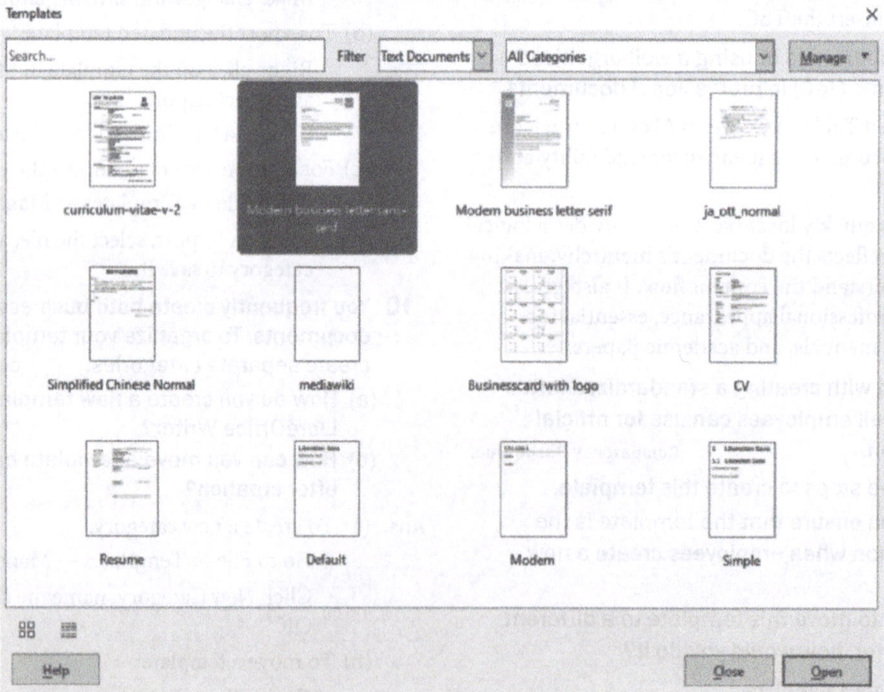

SELF ASSESSMENT

Multiple Choice Questions

1. What is the primary benefit of using styles in LibreOffice Writer?
   (a) Increased file size (b) Maintaining consistency across the document
   (c) Limiting the formatting options (d) Applying only manual formatting
2. Which of the following styles is used to format paragraphs in LibreOffice Writer?
   (a) Page Style (b) Frame Style (c) Paragraph Style (d) Table Style
3. What is the keyboard shortcut to open the Styles window in LibreOffice Writer?
   (a) F10 (b) Ctrl + S (c) F11 (d) Alt + Enter
4. Which of the following file formats is NOT used for images in LibreOffice Writer?
   (a) JPG (b) PNG (c) DOCX (d) GIF
5. What is the primary function of the "Crop" tool in LibreOffice Writer?
   (a) Resize the image proportionally (b) Cut off unwanted parts of the image
   (c) Change the color of the image (d) Rotate the image
6. Which of the following is a mode option in the Image toolbar?
   (a) Posterize (b) Grayscale (c) Sharpen (d) Pop Art
7. What is a key benefit of using templates in document creation?
   (a) They reduce document size.
   (b) They help reuse specific content across multiple documents.
   (c) They eliminate the need for text formatting.
   (d) They automatically translate the document.
8. To set a default template, which option should you choose from the File menu?
   (a) Open (b) Properties
   (c) Templates (d) Save As
9. What happens when you delete a template category in LibreOffice?
   (a) All templates in the category are deleted.
   (b) The category remains, but no new templates can be added.
   (c) Templates are moved to a new category automatically.
   (d) The templates are backed up before deletion.
10. What is the purpose of a Table of Contents (ToC) in a document?
    (a) To include a summary of each chapter
    (b) To provide navigation and an overview of the document's structure
    (c) To add images to the document
    (d) To list references for the document
11. You need to apply the same character style to several non-consecutive words in your document. Which feature would you use? **Competency Based Que.**
    (a) New Style from Selection (b) Drag and Drop
    (c) Fill Format Mode (d) Load Styles from Template
12. You have formatted a portion of text and want to create a new style based on this format. Which method is the most efficient? **Competency Based Que.**
    (a) Update Selected Style (b) New Style from Selection
    (c) Load Styles from Template (d) Apply Manual Formatting
13. You want to place an image behind the text in your LibreOffice Writer document. Which of the following options should you choose from the Drawing Object Properties Toolbar? **Competency Based Que.**
    (a) Send to Back (b) Bring to Front
    (c) Forward One (d) Flip Horizontally

14. You are working on a project report and need to reuse the same header and footer across multiple documents. Which feature will help you achieve this efficiently? **Competency Based Que.**

(a) Styles (b) Templates
(c) Formatting toolbar (d) Manual input

15. You've inserted a ToC but made additional changes to the document's headings. How can you ensure the ToC reflects these changes? **Competency Based Que.**

(a) Delete the ToC and recreate it
(b) Right-click the ToC and select 'Update index'
(c) Modify the ToC manually
(d) Save and close the document

Very Short Answer Type Questions

16. Explain how the 'Load Styles from Template' option can be beneficial in formatting a document.
17. Explain the difference between anchoring an image to a paragraph and anchoring it as a character in LibreOffice Writer.
18. What are the steps to create a new template in LibreOffice from an existing document?
19. What are the steps to delete an existing Table of Contents in LibreOffice Writer?
20. How does the Track Changes feature improve collaboration in document review?

Short Answer Type Questions

21. What are the advantages of using styles in LibreOffice Writer compared to manual formatting?
22. Explain how to modify and position an image in LibreOffice Writer.
23. Explain the process of creating, editing, and managing templates in LibreOffice Writer.
24. Explain the process of creating and customizing a Table of Contents (ToC) in LibreOffice Writer. Why is it important to use heading styles, and how can you update and maintain a ToC?
25. Describe the Track Changes feature in LibreOffice Writer. How can it be used for collaborative editing, and what are the key functionalities offered for managing edits?

Answers

1. (b)	**2.** (c)	**3.** (c)	**4.** (d)	**5.** (b)	**6.** (a)	**7.** (b)	**8.** (c)	**9.** (a)	**10.** (b)
11. (a)	**12.** (a)	**13.** (a)	**14.** (b)	**15.** (b)					

Unit 2

Electronic Spreadsheet (Advanced) Using LibreOffice Calc

This chapter will explore the advanced features of LibreOffice Calc, a powerful spreadsheet software. You'll learn to analyze data to make informed decisions, automate repetitive tasks using macros, create and link multiple sheets for efficient data management, and collaborate with others by sharing spreadsheets. These skills will empower you to work with numbers and data more effectively and efficiently.

Analyze Data Using Scenarios and Goal Seek

CHAPTER 04

Analyzing data means finding useful information to help make good decisions. Spreadsheets are great tools for this. They let you collect, organize, explore, and visualize data to spot patterns, trends, and connections. LibreOffice Calc, a spreadsheet program, has many features to help you analyze data. You can use it to manipulate data and understand the results. In this chapter, you'll learn how to analyze data using LibreOffice Calc.

Analyzing data involves extracting valuable information to make informed decisions. Spreadsheets are among the most effective tools for data analysis, allowing users to retrieve, correlate, explore, and visualize data to uncover patterns, trends, and relationships.

The spreadsheet component of LibreOffice known as **Calc**, provides various tools for data manipulation. In this chapter, you will learn how to use LibreOffice Calc to analyze data and interpret the results.

4.1 Consolidating Data

Data Consolidation allows you to gather data from separate worksheets into a single master worksheet.

In other words, the Data Consolidation function takes data from a series of worksheets or workbooks and summaries it into a single worksheet that you can update easily.

You need to check the following before consolidating data.

- Open each sheet in the spreadsheet and check that the data types must match which you want to consolidate.
- Match the labels from all the sheets which are used for consolidating.
- Enter the first column as the primary column on the basis of which the data is to be consolidated.

Steps to consolidate the data are as follows:

Step 1 Open the worksheet that contains the cell ranges to be consolidated.

Step 2 Choose the Consolidate option under the Data menu. The Consolidate dialog box will appear.

Step 3 If the list of source data ranges includes named ranges, you can choose a specific cell range to consolidate with other areas. However, if the source range doesn't have a name, click in the field to the right and either:

- **Type** Enter the reference for the first source data range.
- **Select** Use the mouse to directly choose the range on the sheet.

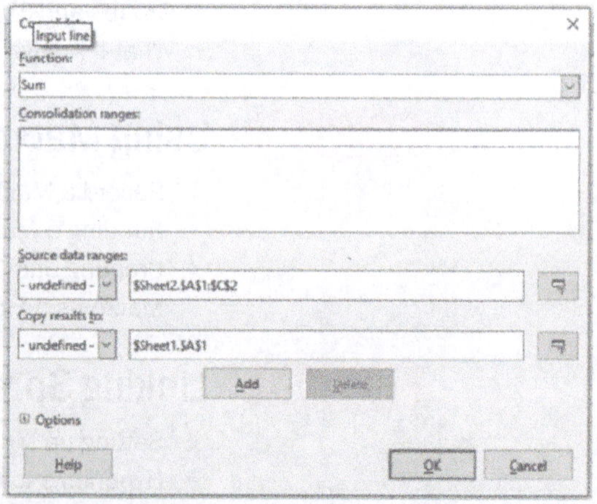

Step 4 Click Add. The selected range now appears on the Consolidation ranges list.

Step 5 Select additional ranges and click Add after each selection.

Step 6 Specify where you want to display the result by selecting a target range from the Copy results to box. If the target range is not named, click in the field next to "Copy results to" and enter the reference of the target range or select the range using the mouse or position the cursor in the top left cell of the target range.

Step 7 Select a function from the Function list. The function specifies how the values of the consolidation ranges are linked. The Sum function is the default setting. Most of the available functions are statistical (such as AVERAGE, MIN, MAX, STDEV), and the tool is most useful when you are working with the same data over and over.

Step 8 Optionally click Options in the Consolidate dialog box to display additional settings.

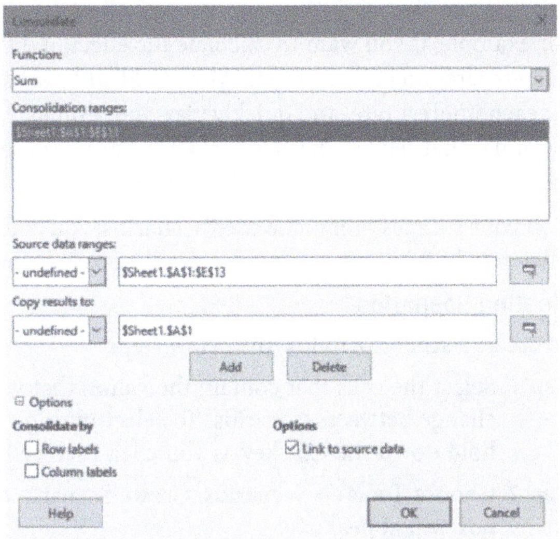

- Select Link to source data to insert the formulas. This generates the results in the target range instead of the actual results. If you link the data, any values modified in the source range are automatically updated in the target range.

  The corresponding cell references in the target range are inserted in consecutive rows, which are automatically ordered and then hidden from view. Only the final result, based on the selected function, is displayed.

- Under Consolidate by setting, select either Row labels or Column labels, if the cells of the source data range are not to be consolidated corresponding to the identical position of the cell in the range, but instead according to a matching row label or column label.

  To consolidate by row labels or column labels, the label must be contained in the selected source ranges. The text in the labels must be identical, so that rows or columns can be accurately matched. If the row or column label does not match any that exist in the target range, it will be appended as a new row or column.

Step 9 Click OK to consolidate the ranges.

Step 10 If you are continually working with the same range, then you probably want to use Data → Define Range to give it a name. The data from the consolidation ranges and target range are saved when you save the worksheet. If you later open a worksheet in which consolidation has been defined, this data will again be available.

4.2 Groups and Subtotals

In Calc, the Group and Outline feature allows you to create an outline of selected data by grouping rows or columns together. This enables you to collapse (hide) or expand (reveal) the grouped sections with a single click. To use this feature, select the data you want to group, then go to Data → Group and Outline. Choose Group.

SUBTOTAL Tool

The Subtotal tool in Calc automatically creates groups and applies common functions such as sum and average to the grouped data. It allows you to use various summary functions for each column according to your data analysis needs. Additionally, it can group subtotals by category and sort them in ascending or descending order, eliminating the need for filters. SUBTOTAL is listed under the Mathematical category when you use the Function Wizard (Insert → Function or press Ctrl+F2). This function is a relatively limited method for generating a subtotal.

Follow the below steps to insert subtotal values into a sheet

Step 1 Ensure that the columns have labels.

Step 2 Select the range of cells that you want to calculate subtotals for, and then choose Data → Subtotals. Subtotals dialog box will appear.

Step 3 In the Subtotals dialog box, in the Group by box, select the column that you want to add the subtotals to. If the contents of the selected column change, the subtotals are automatically recalculated.

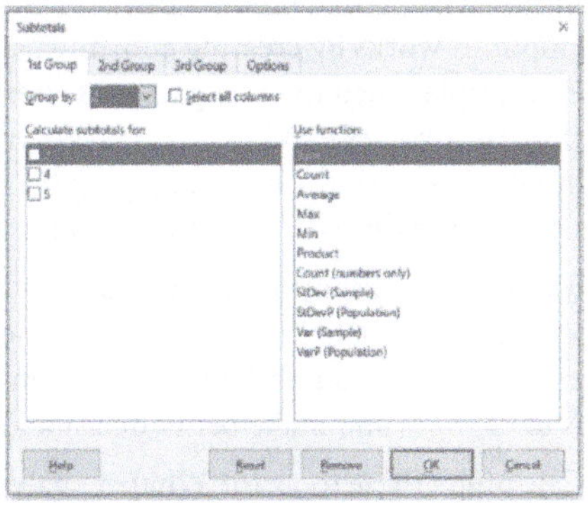

Step 4 In the Calculate subtotals for, select the columns containing the values that you want to subtotal.

Step 5 In the Use function, select the function that you want to use to calculate the subtotals.

Step 6 You can use the 2nd Group and 3rd Group tabs to group the data in further levels.

Step 7 Click on OK button.

Observe that outline to the left of the row numbers which is inserted after performing the subtotal tool.

This outline shows the hierarchical structure. If you want to remove the outline feature, click on Data → Group and Outline → Remove Outline.

Try These 4.1

1. **What is the purpose of the Consolidate function in LibreOffice Calc?**
   - **(a) To delete unnecessary data**
   - **(b) To combine data from multiple sheets into a single location**
   - **(c) To format cells**
   - **(d) To create charts**
2. **Which of the following is not a requirement for data consolidation in LibreOffice Calc?**
   - **(a) Matching labels from all sheets**
   - **(b) Data types must match**
   - **(c) Data must be sorted in ascending order**
   - **(d) Designating the first column as the primary column**
3. **The Consolidate function allows users to merge data from __________ into a new range.**
4. **To apply a function like Sum or Average during data consolidation, you need to select a __________ from the function list in the Consolidate dialog box.**
5. **How can you display the results of the consolidated data in LibreOffice Calc?**

4.3 What-if Analysis Tools

The What-if tool, accessed via Data → Multiple Operations, is a powerful planning tool for exploring different scenarios. Unlike direct cell outputs, this tool utilizes a drop-down list to dynamically display results based on the input. It works by creating a formula array that calculates multiple outcomes using a set of alternative values. This process involves two key cell arrays—one holding the input values and the other applying the formula to generate and display the results seamlessly.

What-if analysis is a spreadsheet tool that lets you experiment with different data inputs to see how they change the results. It helps you understand how sensitive your model is to changes and make better decisions.

LibreOffice Calc offers these tools for What-if analysis:

(i) Scenarios (ii) Goal Seek (iii) Solver

Let's talk about them and learn how to use.

Using "what if" Scenarios

Scenarios are a tool to test "what-if" questions. Each scenario is named, and can be edited and formatted separately. When you print the spreadsheet, only the content of the currently active scenario is printed.

A scenario is essentially a saved set of cell values for your calculations. You can easily switch between these sets using the Navigator or a drop-down list which can be shown beside the changing cells.

For example, if you want to calculate the effect of different interest rates on an investment, you could add a scenario for each interest rate, and quickly view the results. Formulas that rely on the values changed by your scenario are updated when the scenario is opened.

If all your sources of income used scenarios, you could efficiently build a complex model of your possible income.

Creating Scenarios

To create a scenario, follow the below steps

Step 1 Select the cells that contain the values that will change between scenarios. To select multiple cells, hold down the Ctrl key as you click each cell.

Step 2 Choose Tools → Scenarios. Create Scenario dialog box will appear.

Step 3 On the Create Scenario dialog box, enter a name for the new scenario. This name is displayed in the Navigator and on the title bar of the scenario on the sheet itself.

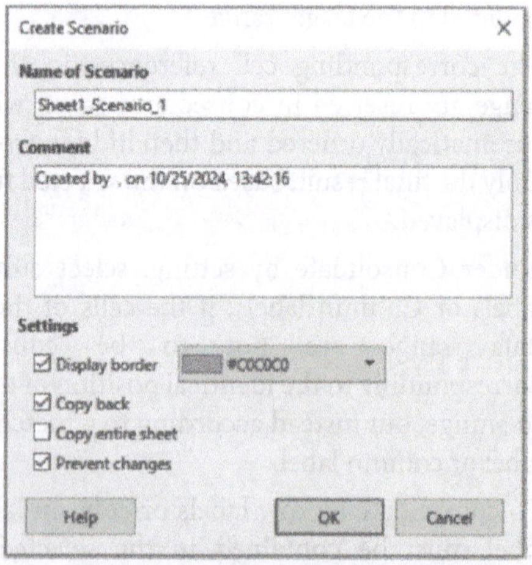

The lower section of the Create Scenario dialog box includes several options. The default settings are generally suitable for most situations.

- **Display border** This option places a border around the range of cells affected by your scenario. You can select the border color using the field next to this option. The border includes a title bar that shows the name of the active scenario. Clicking the arrow button next to the scenario name opens a drop-down list of all scenarios defined for the cells within the border. You can switch between these scenarios at any time.

- **Copy back** This option allows any changes you make to the values in the scenario cells to be saved back into the active scenario. If this option is not selected, the saved scenario values remain unchanged when you make modifications. The actual function of the Copy back setting is influenced by cell protection, sheet protection, and the Prevent changes setting.

Know More

If you are viewing a scenario which has Copy back enabled and then create a new scenario by changing the values and selecting Tools → Scenarios, you also inadvertently overwrite the values in the first scenario.

This is easily avoided if you leave the current values alone, create a new scenario with Copy back enabled, and then change the values only when you are viewing the new scenario.

- **Copy entire sheet** This option adds a new sheet to your document that permanently displays the new scenario in its entirely. This is in addition to creating the scenario and making it selectable on the original sheet as usual.
- **Prevent changes** When enabled, this option prevents changes to a scenario with the Copy back feature, even if the cells are unprotected but the sheet is protected. It also blocks modifications to the settings described in this section while the sheet is protected.

Step 4 Optionally add some information to the Comment box. The example shows the default comment. This information is displayed in the Navigator when you click the Scenarios icon and select the desired scenario.

Step 5 Optionally select or deselect the options in the Settings section.

Step 6 Click OK. The new scenario is automatically activated. You can create several scenarios for any given range of cells.

Using Goal Seek

Goal seeking is the process of finding the correct input value when only the output is known. The function of goal seeking can be built into different kinds of computer software programs like OpenOffice Calc, LibreOffice Calc etc. Usually, you run a formula to calculate a result based upon existing values. By contrast, using Goal Seek option under Tools menu, you can discover what values will produce the result that you want.

Following is the procedure for using Goal Seek once your spreadsheet is prepared.

Step 1 Select the cell containing the formula that will result in your desired goal.

Step 2 Choose Tools → Goal Seek. Goal Seek dialog box will appear.

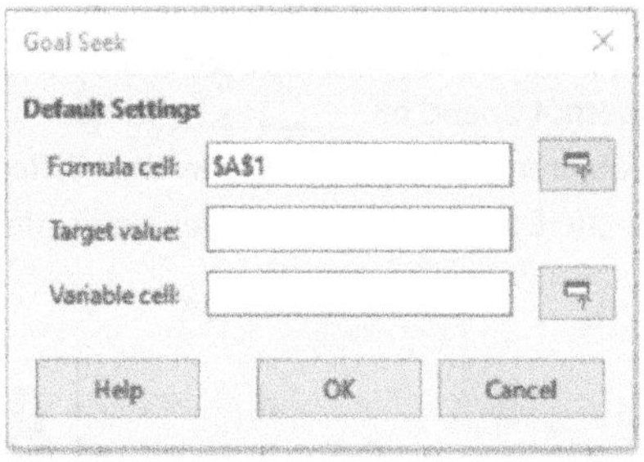

Step 3 On the Goal Seek dialog box, the correct cell is already entered in the Formula cell field.

Step 4 Place the cursor in the Variable cell field. In the sheet, click in the cell that contains the value to be changed.

Step 5 Enter the desired result of the formula in the Target value field.

Step 6 Click OK. A dialog appears informing you that the Goal Seek was successful. Click Yes to enter the result in the cell with the variable value.

Using the Solver

Solver is a more descriptive form of Goal Seek. Solver can deal with multiple variables as the Goal Seek is used to manipulate one variable cell. It is specifically designed to minimize or maximize the result according to a set of rules that you define.

Each of these rules sets up whether an argument in the formula should be greater than, lesser than, or equal to the value you enter. If you want the argument to remain unchanged, you enter a rule that the cell that contains it should be equal to its current entry.

For arguments that you would like to change, you need to add two rules to define a range of possible values: the limiting conditions. You can also define the constraint that one or more variables must be integers (values without decimals), or binary values (where only 0 and 1 are allowed).

Once you have finished setting up the rules, you can adjust the argument and the results by clicking the Solver button.

Try These 4.2

1. **What is the primary purpose of a What-if scenario in LibreOffice Calc?**
   (a) To perform statistical analysis
   (b) To explore and compare different alternatives based on changing conditions
   (c) To format data in charts
   (d) To protect the document
2. **Which tool in LibreOffice Calc allows you to determine the specific input needed to reach a particular output?**
   (a) Consolidate (b) What-if Analysis Tool
   (c) Goal Seek (d) Data Validation
3. **The What-if Analysis Tool in Calc uses a drop-down list to show the output based on __________ values.**
4. **How can you create a new scenario in LibreOffice Calc?**
5. **What does the Goal Seek tool help you determine?**

Summary

Analyzing the data involves extracting valuable information to make informed decisions.

Data Consolidation allows you to gather data from separate worksheets into a single master worksheet.

The subtotal tool in Calc automatically creates groups and applies common functions such as sum and average to the grouped data.

LibreOffice Calc provides tools for What-If analysis: Scenarios, Goal Seek, Solver.

Goal seeking is the process of finding the correct input value when only the output is known.

Solver is a more descriptive form of Goal Seek.

ACTIVITY Time

ACTIVITY 1

Let us take an example that we have two branches of our shop namely ABC and XYZ. We have the Sales records for the month of January and February of both the branches in two different sheets named ABC_Branch and XYZ_Branch. Now we have to consolidate these two sheets to get the sum of both the sheets monthly to get the insight about the sale as per product and branch.

Now let us create the following sheets in a spreadsheet sales.

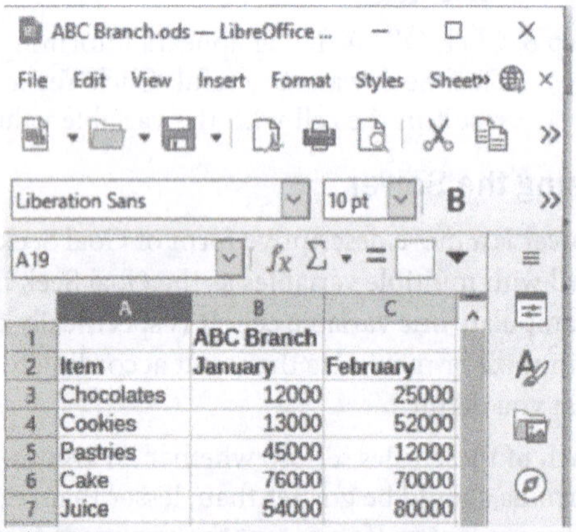

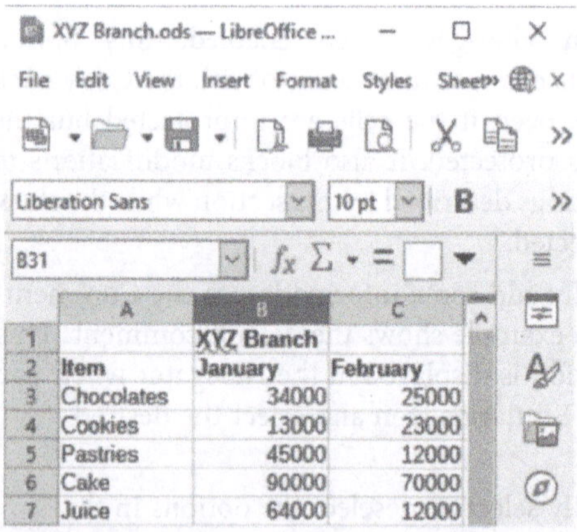

Now let us use the two sheets 'ABC_Branch' and 'XYZ_Branch' of a spreadsheet sales.ods which will be consolidated using the following steps:

Step 1 Add a new sheet and rename it as Consolidate.

Step 2 Click on Data → Consolidate or use the keyboard shortcut key ALT+D, the Consolidate dialog window will open.

Step 3 In the Function box, choose Sum function from the drop down as we want to add the data from all the sheets.

Step 4 Click in the Source data ranges box and then click on the worksheet ABC_Branch and select the area to be consolidated and then click on the Add button will add the copy reference in the consolidation ranges.

Step 5 Click on the sheet XYZ_Branch and select the area to be consolidated and then click on Add will add the next consolidation range.

Step 6 Click on the '+' sign next to Options in the Consolidate dialog window to change the settings.

'Consolidate by' has two options Row labels and Column labels. Check row label or column label or both if you want to consolidate it by matching the label. If Link to source data is checked, then it will keep on updating the data of the Consolidate sheet automatically if there is any change made in the selected ranges.

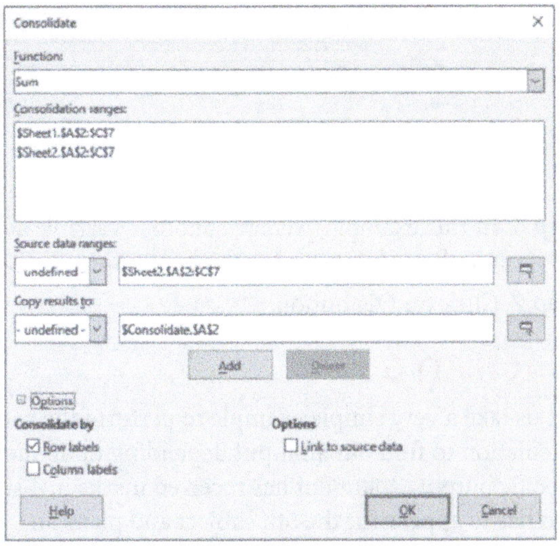

Step 7 Click on 'Copy results to' and then click on any of the cell in the Consolidate sheet where you want to copy the final result after consolidation.

Step 8 Click on OK button. The given Consolidate sheet with data after consolidation.

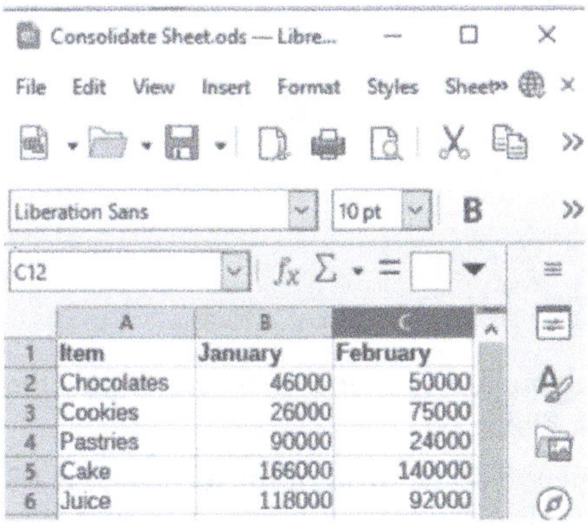

	A	B	C
1	Item	January	February
2	Chocolates	46000	50000
3	Cookies	26000	75000
4	Pastries	90000	24000
5	Cake	166000	140000
6	Juice	118000	92000

The consolidated sheet will have all the consolidated data along with the original data.

ACTIVITY 2

Let us take an example to store marks in various subjects by students of Class X as shown in the table given. To take out the average of the subjects scored in each class, use the subtotal tool which automatically group the data on a particular column and perform the selected function on any of the column.

To solve this, perform the following steps:

Step 1 Create a sheet as shown below, to take the marks for students in a term for a class.

	A	B	C	D	E	F	G
1	Roll No	Class	Name	English	Maths	Science	Social Science
2	1	X-A	Aadhya	56	78	78	90
3	2	X-B	Armaan	71	82	88	78
4	3	X-A	Aarav	55	23	34	67
5	4	X-C	Aariv	55	77	27	90
6	5	X-A	Aasma	63	55	64	78
7	6	X-C	Aashna	78	89	90	81

Step 2 Now, to calculate the average marks scored by the students of each class in each subject, i.e. class-wise and subject analysis.

Step 3 To do so, click on Data → Subtotals, the Subtotals dialog box appears.

Step 4 Choose the column i.e. Class under Group by in the 1st Group on which we need to group the whole data. Also, select the subjects i.e.

English, Maths, Science and Social Science under Calculate subtotals for.

For each subject click on the Average under Use function individually otherwise Sum function will be used by default.

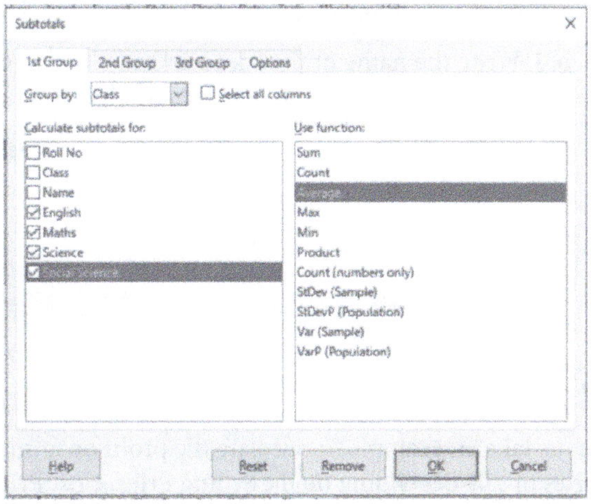

Step 5 Click OK. The data subtotaled by class appears.

	A	B	C	D	E	F	G
1	Roll No	Class	Name	English	Maths	Science	Social Science
2	1	X-A	Aadhya	56	78	78	90
3	3	X-A	Aarav	55	23	34	67
4	5	X-A	Aasma	63	55	64	78
5		X-A Result		58	52	58.66666667	78.3333333333
6	2	X-B	Armaan	71	82	88	78
7		X-B Result		71	82	88	78
8	4	X-C	Aariv	55	77	27	90
9	6	X-C	Aashna	78	89	90	81
10		X-C Result		66.5	83	58.5	85.5
11		Grand Average		63	67.3333333	63.5	80.6666666667
12							

ACTIVITY 3

Let us take an example to get the insight of the Simple Interest, Principal, Rate of Interest and Number of years. So,now we want to see what will be the Simple Interest and how much is the total interest paid for different loan amount and time period.

To do so, let us use the Scenario tool by using the following steps:

Step 1 Create the following sheet and remember to put the formula to calculate simple interest in the cell : B6(Principal*Rate of Interest*Number of years)/100

D10 | f_x Σ ▾ =

	A	B
1	Simple Interest	
2	Principal	100000
3	Rate of Interest	5.00%
4	Number of years	10
5		
6	Simple Interest	500

Step 2 Select the cells B2 and E1 using Ctrl + Click on these cells as these two are the variables in this situation.

Step 3 Choose Tools → Scenarios will display the Create Scenario dialog window.

Step 4 Write the name of the Scenario and click on OK button will add this in the scenario list.

	A	B	C	D	E
1	Simple Interest				
2	Principal	10000			
3	Rate of Interest	5.00%			
4	Number of years	10			
5					
6	Simple Interest	50			
7	Sheet1_Scenario_2				
8					

ACTIVITY 4

Let us take an example to calculate the profit on annual series of sale depending on the Selling Price, Cost Price and Fixed Cost expenses.

Step 1 Create the sheet as given below.

B4 | f_x Σ ▾ = | =B3*(B1-B2)

	A	B	C	D
1	Selling Price	450		
2	Cost Price	300		
3	Items sold	100		
4	Profit	15000		
5				

Step 2 In Cell B4 enter the formula = B3 * (B1 – B2)

Step 3 Select the cell range from D2:E11.

Step 4 Click on Data → Multiple Operations will display the Multiple Operations dialog window.

Step 5 We have formula in cell B4, as we want to use the same cell address to be copied therefore, we have used absolute cell referencing and written it as B4.

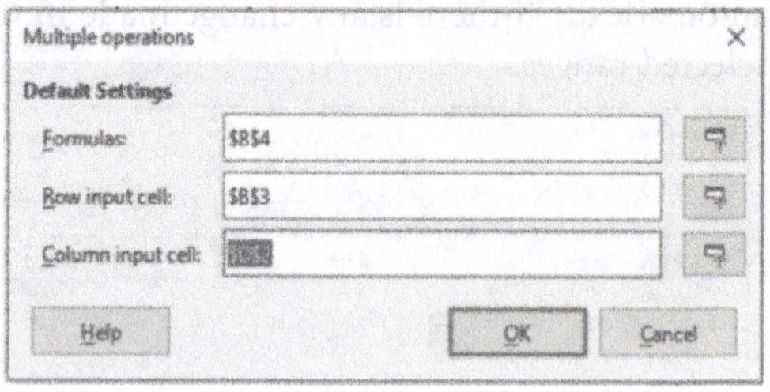

Step 6 In this example, we have another variable as number of items sold which is in the cell B3.

Step 7 Click on OK button.

ACTIVITY 5

Let us take a very simple example to perform the backward calculation to find out an input depending upon the specific output. A student has received marks in 4 subjects and has to appear for the 5th subject and plans an aggregate as 70. So, he can use goal seek tool to check how many marks he has to score in the 5th subject to get the required percentage. Follow the below steps to perform this task:

Step 1 Create the marksheet as shown below. Enter the average function in cell B7 as =Average(B2:B6)

B7 | f_x Σ ▾ = | =AVERAGE(B2:B6)

	A	B	C
1	SUBJECT	Marks	
2	English	56	
3	Maths	67	
4	Science	45	
5	Social Science	78	
6	Hindi	32	
7	Average	55.6	

Step 2 Click on Tools → Goal Seek will display the Goal Seek dialog box.

Step 3 Write the cell address of the formula, i.e. B7 in the Formula cell box.

Step 4 Write the cell address of the cell which is to be generated by the system in the Variable cell box. In this example, it is cell B6 which we want to be filled as per the average marks needed.

Step 5 Enter the result in the Target value box. As per our question, we have to get minimum 70 aggregate so we will write 70 in the target value.

Step 6 Clicking on OK will display an error as LibreOffice Calc will not accept the Variable cell to be empty. So, this error dialog window will prompt to add 0 value in the variable cell.

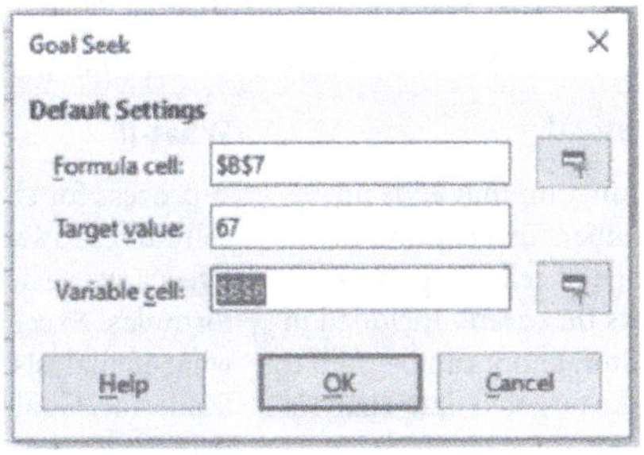

Step 7 Click on Yes and then repeat the step 2 will display the dialog window and prompts whether to change the cell with the calculated value.

Step 8 Click on Yes will change the value with the calculated one in the sheet.

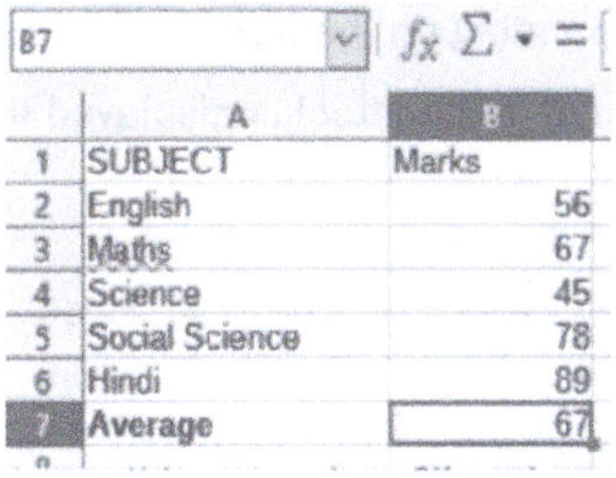

NCERT FOLDER

Complete Explanations of all NCERT's Questions

A. Multiple Choice Questions

Q.1 Which of the following feature is not used for data analysis in spreadsheet?

(a) Consolidating data (b) Goal Seek
(c) Subtotal (d) Page layout

Q.2 Which of the following office tool is known for data analysis?

(a) Writer (b) Calc
(c) Impress (d) Draw

Q.3 Which of the following operations cannot be performed using Libre Office Calc?

(a) Store and manipulate data
(b) Create graphical representation of data
(c) Analysis of data
(d) Mail merge

Q.4 What is the extension of spreadsheet file in Calc?

(a) .odb (b) .odt
(c) .odg (d) .ods

Q.5 The default function while using Consolidate is____________.

(a) Average (b) Sum
(c) Max (d) Count

Q.6 Group by is used in ____________ tool to apply summary functions on columns.

(a) Consolidate function (b) Group and Outline
(c) What-if scenario (d) Subtotal tool

Q.7 Which tool is used to predict the output while changing the input?

(a) Consolidate function (b) What-if scenario
(c) Goal seek (d) Find and Replace

Q.8 Which of the following is an example for absolute cell referencing?

(a) C5 (b) C5
(c) $C (d) #C

Q.9 ____________ analysis tool works in reverse order, finding input based on the output.

(a) Consolidate function (b) Goal seek
(c) What-if analysis (d) Scenario

Answers

1. (d)	2. (b)	3. (d)	4. (d)	5. (b)
6. (d)	7. (b)	8. (b)	9. (b)	

B. State Whether the Following Statements are True or False

Q.1 Consolidate function is used to combine information from two or more sheets into one.

Q.2 Consolidate function cannot be used to view and compare data.

Q.3 Link to source data is checked updates the target sheet if any changes made in the source data.

Q.4 Using subtotal in Calc needs to use filter data for sorting.

Q.5 Subtotal tool can use only one type of summary function for all columns.

Q.6 Only one scenario can be created for one sheet.

Q.7 What-if analysis tool uses one array of cells.

Q.8 Goal seek analysis tool is used while calculating the output depending on the input.

Q.9 The output of What-if tool is displayed in the same cell.

Answers

1. True 2. False 3. True 4. False 5. False
6. False 7. False 8. False 9. False

C. Fill in the Blanks

Q.1 Consolidate function is used to combine information from multiple sheets to _______ the information.

Q.2 Data can be viewed and compared in a single sheet for identifying trends and relationships using ________function.

Q.3 ________ under Data menu can be used to combine information from multiple sheets into one sheet to compare data.

Q.4 The ________ tool in Calc creates the group automatically and applies functions on the grouped data.

Q.5 ________ scenario is used to explore and compare various alternatives depending on changing conditions.

Q.6 _______ is a planning tool for what-if questions.

Q.7 What-if analysis tool uses _______ array of cells, one array contains input values and the second uses the_______.

Q.8 _______ helps in finding out the input for the specific output.

Answers

1. Summarize 2. Consolidate 3. Sub Total
4. Sub Total 5. What if 6. What if tool
7. Two, formula and display output
8. Goal seek

D. Answer the Following Questions

Q.1 Define the terms

(a) Consolidate function (b) What-if analysis

(c) Goal seek

Ans. (a) **Consolidate function** is used to combine information from multiple sheets of the spreadsheet into one place to summarize the information.

(b) **What-if analysis** is a process of changing input values to observe how they affect the outcome of formulas in a spreadsheet.

(c) **Goal Seek** is in general we fill in the values in the cells and then create formula on these values to get the required result.

Q.2 Give one point of difference between (a) Subtotal and What-if (b) What-if scenario and What-if tool

Ans. (a) Difference between Subtotal and What-if:

Subtotal	What-if
A function that adds up numbers in a column or range of cells. It ignores rows that aren't included in a filter, and it can be used to make targeted data analysis easier.	A process for changing cell values to see how they affect a worksheet's formulas. Excel has three what-if analysis tools: Scenarios, Goal Seek, and Solver.

(b) Difference between What-if scenario and What-if tool

What-if scenario	What-if tool
A what-if scenario is a way to anticipate and prepare for potential situations, usually during the scheduling phase of a project. It's a tool for exploring and comparing different plans and schedules in response to changing conditions.	A what-if tool is a visualization tool that helps analyze models and datasets. It can help users test performance in hypothetical situations, compare models, and understand how specific inputs change the output.

Q.3 Give any two advantages of data analysis tools.

Ans. Data analysis tools can help businesses in many ways, including:

- **Informed decision-making** Data analytics helps businesses make decisions based on evidence and trends.
- **Improved customer experience** Data analytics can help businesses understand customer behavior, preferences, and buying patterns. This information can be used to create personalized experiences for customers.

Q.4 Name any two tools for data analysis.

Ans. Scenarios and Goal Seek

Q.5 What are the criteria for consolidating sheets?

Ans. The consolidated sheet will have all the consolidated data along with the original data. You can view the original data of both the sheets and by clicking on the '+' sign in front of the consolidated row.

Q.6 Which tool is used to create an outline for the selected data?

Ans. Sub-Total.

EXAM PATTERN EXERCISE

Including Competency Based Questions

Multiple Choice Questions

1 Radha is planning a school event and wants to decide how much money to allocate for different activities, like games, food, and decorations. She creates several different budget plans to see how changing the amount for each category affects the total expenses.

How can Radha efficiently compare the different budget plans for her school event in the same spreadsheet? **CBSE SQP 2024-25, Competency Based Que.**

(a) By writing down each budget on paper
(b) By using the What-if scenario feature in the spreadsheet to create and analyze different budget options
(c) By asking her friends to guess the costs
(d) By using the Filter function to look at one category at a time

2 What is the primary function of the Subtotal tool in Calc? **CBSE SQP 2024-25**

(a) It creates a chart for the data.
(b) It automatically groups data and applies common functions like sum and average.
(c) It highlights cells with conditional formatting.
(d) It removes duplicate data from the spreadsheet.

3 Sahil and his partners have created a list of their company employees in one of the spreadsheets in the office. Now the rest of the task they want to complete from home. Which option they should use to access the same Spreadsheet from home? **CBSE SQP 2023-24, Competency Based Que.**

(a) Consolidate Worksheet (b) Link Worksheet
(c) Merge Worksheet (d) Lock Worksheet

4 ____________ can help to clarify the relation between cells while using "Multiple Operations". **CBSE SQP 2023-24**

(a) Detective (b) Solver
(c) Navigation (d) Hyperlink

5 ________ function takes data from a series of Worksheets or Workbooks and summaries it into a single Worksheet that you can update easily. **CBSE SQP 2022-23, CBSE 2021-22 Term I**

(a) Data Combination (b) Data Merging
(c) Data Consolidation (d) Data Concatenation

6 Which function cannot be performed through Subtotal in a Spreadsheet? **CBSE SQP 2021-22 Term I**

(a) Sum (b) Product
(c) Average (d) Percentage

7 In Calc, using the Subtotals dialog, you can select arrays and then choose a statistical function to apply to them. For efficiency, you can choose up to .... groups of array to which to apply a function. **CBSE 2021-22 Term I, Competency Based Que.**

(a) two (b) three (c) four (d) five

8 __________ is specifically designed to minimize or maximize the result according to a set of rules that you define in a spreadsheet. **CBSE SQP 2020-21**

(a) Goal Seek (b) Scenario
(c) Solver (d) Subtotal

9 ___________ is a tool to test "what-if" questions. **CBSE SQP 2020-21**

(a) Scenario (b) Solver (c) Macro (d) Average

10 Scenarios are a tool to test questions. **CBSE SQP 2021-22 Term I**

(a) Auto (b) Goal Seek
(c) What-if (d) Drop Down

11 Which of the following is more elaborate form of Goal Seek? **CBSE SQP 2021-22 Term I**

(a) Subtotal (b) Scenario
(c) Solver (d) Consolidate

12 ___________ is specifically designed to minimize the results according to a set rules that we define in a spreadsheet. **CBSE SQP 2023-24**

(a) Goal Seek (b) Scenario
(c) Solver (d) Subtotal

13 Solve option under Tools menu amounts to a more elaborate form of .... The difference is that the Solver deals with equations with multiple .... **CBSE 2021-22 Term I**

(a) Unknown variables, Goals Seek
(b) Variables, Equation
(c) Goal Seek, Unknown variables
(d) Subtotal, Goal Seek

14 Usually, you run a formula to calculate a result based upon existing values. By contrast, using ...., you can discover what values will produce the result that you want. **CBSE 2021-22 Term I**

(a) Subtotal (b) Scenario
(c) Sort Lists (d) Goal Seek

15 _________ feature adds data arranged in a group of cells in Calc, with labels for columns and/or rows. **CBSE 2023**

(a) Average (b) Subtotal
(c) Goal seek (d) Solver

16 __________ **feature of Calc is used to test 'what-if ' questions.** CBSE 2023

(a) Solver (b) Goal seek
(c) Scenario (d) Styles

17 While consolidating data, a cell range can be named using .... option. CBSE 2024

(a) Name range (b) Define range
(c) Consolidate name (d) Define name

18 .... is a more elaborate form of Goal Seek. CBSE 2024

(a) Database (b) Hyperlink
(c) Report (d) Solver

19 Which menu is used to use the Consolidate option?

(a) Tools menu (b) Data menu
(c) Insert menu (d) None of these

20 .... is a set of values that can be used within the calculations in the spreadsheet to explore and compare various alternatives depending on changing conditions. CBSE 2025

(a) Sort (b) Filter
(c) What-if Scenarios (d) Comments

21 This tool in Calc allows you to create a group of cells automatically and apply common functions like sum, average on the grouped data. It is known as .... CBSE 2025

(a) Sum tool (b) Subtotal tool
(c) Function tool (d) Common tool

22 Rohit scored 25 out of 30 in English, 22 out of 30 in Maths. He wants to calculate the score in IT he needs to achieve 85 percent in aggregate. Suggest him the suitable option out of the following to do so. CBSE SQP 2020-21, Competency Based Que.

(a)Macro (b) Solver
(c) Goal Seek (d) Sub Total

23 Statement I The data from the consolidation ranges and target range are saved when you save the worksheet.

Statement II If you later open a worksheet in which consolidation has been defined, this data will not be available again. CBSE 2021-22 Term I, Competency Based Que.

Consider above two statements, identify the correct one.

(a) Statement I is wrong.
(b) Statement II is wrong.
(c) Both the statements I and II are wrong.
(d) Both the statements I and II are correct.

24 In Spreadsheet,

Statement I To consolidate by row labels or column labels, the label must be contained in the selected source ranges.

Statement II The text in the labels must be identical, so that rows or columns can be accurately matched.

Statement III If the row or column label does not match any that exist in the target range, it will be appended as a new row or column. CBSE 2021-22 Term I, Competency Based Que.

Consider the above three statements, identify the correct one.

(a) Only statements I and II are correct.
(b) Only statements II and III are correct.
(c) Only statement II is correct.
(d) All the statements are correct.

25 Rohan has ₹ 50,000 that he wants to invest in two mutual funds for one year. Fund A is a low risk fund with 18%interest rate and Fund B is a higher risk fund with 21% interest rate.Which feature of Spreadsheet (Calc) will help him to decide? CBSE 2021-22 Term I, Competency Based Que.

(a) Solver (b) Subtotal
(c) Linking sheets (d) Macros

Answers

1. (b)	2. (b)	3. (b)	4. (b)	5. (c)
6. (d)	7. (b)	8. (c)	9. (a)	10. (c)
11. (c)	12. (c)	13. (c)	14. (d)	15. (b)
16. (c)	17. (d)	18. (d)	19. (b)	20. (c)
21. (b)	22. (c)	23. (b)	24. (d)	25. (a)

Very Short Answer Type Questions

1 Define the following: CBSE SQP 2020-21

(a) Subtotals
(b) Consolidating Data

Ans. (a) Subtotals in a spreadsheet are used to summarize data in a specific range by applying a specified function (such as SUM, AVERAGE, COUNT, etc.) to a set of grouped data.

(b) Consolidating data refers to the process of combining data from multiple ranges or sheets into a single location to summarize or analyze the information collectively. This process allows for better comparison and identification of trends across different data sets.

2 How is Goal Seek different from Solver in a Spreadsheet? CBSE SQP 2023-24

Ans. Goal Seek different from Solver in a Spreadsheet are as follows:

Goal Seek	Solver
Determines the value you need to enter in a single input cell to produce a desired result.	Determines the values you need to enter in multiple input cells to produce a desired result.

3 What is the purpose of consolidating data in spreadsheets? Discuss briefly. CBSE 2024

Ans. The purpose of consolidating data in spreadsheets is to bring together information from various sources or sheets into a single, coherent summary. This helps in analyzing data trends, making comparisons, and facilitating decision-making processes.

By consolidating data, users can quickly visualize overall performance, identify patterns, and derive insights that might not be apparent when viewing individual datasets.

4 How do you access Solver from Calc?

Ans. To access Solver in LibreOffice Calc, follow these steps:

- Click on the Tools menu.
- Select Solver from the dropdown list. If Solver is not visible, you may need to install the Solver add-in or enable it in the settings.

5 What is the main purpose of Goal Seek in Calc? Give an example to support your answer. CBSE 2025

Ans. Goal Seek in Calc helps determine the necessary input value to achieve a specific result. For example, it can find the interest rate needed to reach a specific investment goal.

6 How do you delete an entry in the Consolidation ranges list?

Ans. To delete an entry in the Consolidation ranges list in LibreOffice Calc:

- Open the Consolidate dialog box.
- Select the range you want to remove from the Consolidation ranges list.
- Click the Remove button (or the equivalent option) to delete the selected range from the list.

Short Answer Type Questions

1 Explain the term 'Scenarios' in relation to the Spreadsheets with example. CBSE SQP 2023-24

Ans. In spreadsheets, scenarios refer to different sets of input values that can be used to analyze various outcomes based on changing conditions. Each scenario allows users to create hypothetical situations to test potential results without altering the actual data.

For example, in a financial model, you might create three scenarios for sales forecasts: a best case (high sales), worst case (low sales), and most likely case (average sales). By switching between these scenarios, users can see how different sales figures impact total revenue and make more informed decisions based on the analysis.

2 What are the fields that occur in the Goal Seek dialog box? Explain.

Ans. The Goal Seek dialog box contains several key fields:

- **Formula cell** This is the cell containing the formula whose result you want to achieve.
- **Target value** Here, you specify the target value you want the set cell to reach.
- **Variable cell** This field identifies the variable cell whose value will be changed to reach the target result in the set cell. These fields work together to allow users to determine what input value is necessary to achieve a desired output.

3 How do you create scenarios for a spreadsheet?

Ans. To create scenarios in LibreOffice Calc, follow these steps:

- Select the cells containing values that need to change.
- Go to the Tools menu and select Scenarios to open the Scenario dialog box.
- Enter a name for the new scenario and define the desired input values.
- Click OK to save the scenario. The new scenario can now be activated and compared with others, allowing users to see how changes in input affect outcomes.

4 What are the following terms:
(a) What-if analysis (b) Scenarios

Ans. (a) **What-if analysis** This is a technique used in spreadsheets to evaluate the potential effects of changing specific input values on the output. It helps users explore different scenarios and make informed decisions based on hypothetical situations.

(b) **Scenarios** In spreadsheets, scenarios represent sets of input values that allow users to analyze various outcomes based on changing conditions. Each scenario can be saved and compared with others, facilitating effective decision-making.

5 You are working on a financial analysis project and need to forecast the potential profit for a product based on different sales volumes. You have entered the sales volume data in one column and the corresponding profit formula in another cell.

How would you use the Multiple Operations tool in LibreOffice Calc to determine the potential profits for various sales volumes? Describe the steps you would follow to set up and execute this analysis.

Competency Based Que.

Ans.
- **Enter Data** First, create a column with different sales volume values and another column with the corresponding profit formula (e.g., Profit = Sales Volume × Price - Costs).
- **Select Arrays** Highlight the range containing the sales volumes (input array) and the range containing the profit formula (output array).
- **Open Multiple Operations Tool** Navigate to the Data menu and select Multiple Operations.
- **Input Formula** In the Multiple Operations dialog, enter the cell reference of the profit formula in the Formulas box.

- **Define Input Cell** Specify the sales volume cell that varies in the Column Input Cell box.
- **Execute** Click OK to generate a range of potential profit outputs based on the different sales volumes provided.

6 You are tasked with determining how many units of a product need to be produced to achieve a target revenue. You have a formula in a cell that calculates revenue based on the number of units produced, but you need to find the exact number of units required to meet a specific revenue goal.

How would you use the Goal Seek tool in LibreOffice Calc to find out the number of units that need to be produced to achieve the target revenue? Outline the steps to use Goal Seek for this purpose. Competency Based Que.

Ans.
- **Input Values** Enter the relevant data into the worksheet, including the formula that calculates revenue based on units produced (e.g., Revenue = Units × Price).
- **Select Formula Cell** Click on the cell where the revenue formula is calculated.
- **Open Goal Seek** Go to the Tools menu and select Goal Seek.
- **Set Cell** The Set Cell box should already contain the cell with the revenue formula.
- **Target Value** Enter the desired revenue goal in the To Value box.
- **Variable Cell** Click on the By Changing Cell box and select the cell representing the number of units produced.
- **Execute** Click OK. The Goal Seek tool will calculate and provide the exact number of units that need to be produced to meet the specified revenue target.

7 Anshita is preparing spreadsheet notes for her term exam. Help her to write short note on the following: CBSE SQP 2022-23

(i) Scenarios
(ii) Goal Seek
(iii) Solver
(iv) Subtotal

Ans. (i) **Scenarios** Scenarios are a tool to test "What-if" questions. Each scenario is named and can be edited and formatted separately.

It is essentially a saved set of values for calculations. We can easily switch between these sets using the Navigator or a Drop-down list which can be shown beside the changing cells.

(ii) **Goal Seek** It is used to calculate a result based upon existing values. Using Goal Seek option under tools menu, we can discover what values will produces the result that we want.

(iii) **Solver** It is an elaborated form of Goal seek. The difference is that the solver deals with equations with multiple unknown variables. It is specifically designed to minimize or maximize the result according to a set of rules defined by us.

(iv) **Subtotal** It is a function listed under the Mathematical category when we use the Function Wizard (Insert > Function). Because of its utility, the function has a graphical interface.

SUBTOTAL, gets the total/adds the data arranged in array-that is, a group of cells with labels for columns and/or rows. For increasing the efficiency, we can choose up to three groups of arrays to which the function can be applied.

8 What is the purpose of consolidating data in spreadsheets? Discuss briefly. CBSE 2024

Ans. The purpose of consolidating data in spreadsheets is to combine information from multiple sources or worksheets into a single, organized dataset.

Consolidating data allows users to analyze, summarize, and report on large volumes of information more effectively. Here are some key reasons for consolidating data:

- **Centralized Analysis** Consolidating data brings together related information from different sources or worksheets into one central location. This allows users to perform analysis and make informed decisions without having to switch between multiple files or tabs.
- **Data Summarization** By consolidating data, users can summarize large datasets into manageable reports or summaries.
- **Comparative Analysis** Consolidated data facilitates comparative analysis by allowing users to compare information across different categories, time periods, or regions. This enables users to identify similarities, differences, and trends more easily.
- **Elimination of Duplicate Data** Consolidating data helps in identifying and eliminating duplicate or redundant information. This ensures data accuracy and integrity, reducing the risk of errors in analysis and reporting.
- **Streamlined Reporting** Consolidated data provides a unified view of information, making it easier to generate reports and share insights with stakeholders. This streamlines the reporting process and improves communication of findings to decision-makers.
- **Efficient Data Management** Consolidating data streamlines data management by reducing the need to maintain and update multiple datasets separately. This saves time and effort, especially when dealing with large volumes of data or complex datasets.

PRACTICAL ASSIGNMENT

1. Create two sheets Marks_Term1 and Marks_Term2 to store the marks in Term1 and Term2 for a set of students taking the following columns:
   1. Name
   2. Marks in English
   3. Marks in Hindi
   4. Marks in Maths
   5. Marks in Science
   6. Marks in Social Science
   7. Total marks (using function Sum)
   8. Percentage (using function Average)

   Now, use the consolidate function to merge these two sheets.

2. Create a sheet as shown below and then calculate the average of marks subject wise on the basis of class and stream. Also, try out another function Count to calculate the number of students in each subject.

E10

	A	B	C	D	E	F	G
1	Roll No	Class	Name	English	Maths	Science	Social Science
2	1	X-A	Aadhya	56	78	78	90
3	2	X-B	Armaan	71	82	88	78
4	3	X-A	Aarav	55	23	34	67
5	4	X-C	Aariv	55	77	27	90
6	5	X-A	Aasma	63	55	64	78
7	6	X-C	Aashna	78	89	90	81
8							

3. Calculate the income tax by entering the salary using different scenarios for two variables income tax slab and tax rate. The different scenarios to be taken as given below:

Income Slab	**Tax rate**
7.5 to 10 lakhs	15%
10 to 12.5 lakhs	20%
12.5 to 15 lakhs	25%
>15 lakhs	30%

4. Create a sheet to calculate the profit and then decide how many books are to be published based on the profit.

5. Create the following spreadsheet to find out the quantity to be sold for the item Talc so as to get the total amount of 50000.

E8

	A	B	C	D
1	Item	Unit Price	Quantity Sold	Amount
2	Soap	67	156	10452
3	Shampoo	89	123	10947
4	Talc	100	188	
5	Total Amount			34000

6. Mr Gurdeep has to take a loan of Rs. 10 lakhs to buy a house. After assessing his situation, he has realized that he can pay the loan in 15 years by paying out an EMI of 20,000.
   (a) Use Goal seek to find out the interest rate at which he can borrow the loan.
   (b) Use What If Scenario to depict payment of loan in 25 years by paying out an EMI of 10,000.
   (c) Use Scenario manager to find the best case.

7. Power Motors has 3 branches all over Bhopal. Each branch maintains monthly sales of different models of electric scooter and at the end of month mails it to the State Head. Prepare a consolidated sheet that shows total and average sales made for each model of the electric scooter with respect to the spreadsheet sent by the branches to the head office. You are required to identify the column headings for the various branches, enter data in three different spreadsheets indicating different branches and consolidate data to find total sales and average sales for each model.

CHAPTER 05

Using Macros in Spreadsheet

Macros in LibreOffice Spreadsheets are a powerful tool that help automate repetitive tasks, saving time and reducing errors. By recording a sequence of actions or writing simple code, users can perform tasks like formatting cells, calculating values, or organizing data with a single click. In LibreOffice, macros are created using a programming language called LibreOffice Basic, which is easy to understand for beginners.

Macros are the set of stored functions that can be used to automate processes that are repeated often. A macro is a saved sequence of commands or keystrokes that are stored for later use. In other words, a macro is a single command that executes a set of instructions. This series can consist of multiple commands or keystrokes, which can be reused as needed. Actions like keystrokes and mouse clicks can be recorded and replayed whenever required.

Enabling Macro Recorder

By default, the macro recorder is disabled. To use macro recorder, it should firstly be enabled.

To enable the macro recorder, follow the given steps:

Step 1 Click on the Tools menu.

Step 2 Click on the Options option. The Options-LibreOffice-Advanced dialog box appears.

Step 3 Click on the Advanced option.

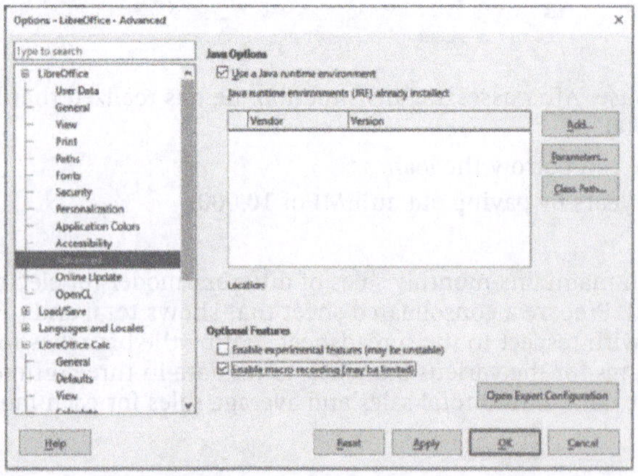

Step 4 Check the checkbox adjacent to Enable macro recording.

Step 5 Click on the Apply button.

Step 6 Click on the OK button. The macro recorder gets enabled.

Note *Click on the Record Macro option found under Tools → Macros is visible now.*

5.1 Record a Macro

To record a macro, follow the given steps:

Step 1 Click on Tools → Macros and then click on the Record Macro option.

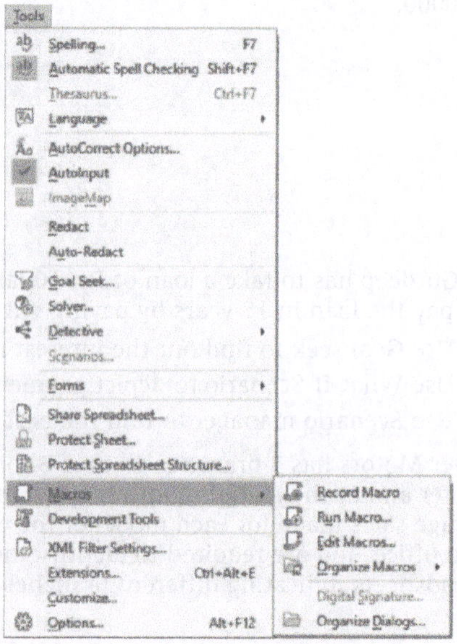

Step 2 Now start taking actions that will be recorded.

Step 3 Once you click on Record Macro option, recording of actions starts and a small alert will be displayed.

Clicking on "Stop Recording" button will stop the recording of actions. The BASIC Macros dialog window appears.

Step 4 To save the macro, first select the object where you want the macro to be saved in the Save Macro to list box.

Step 5 The name of the macro by default is Main and is saved in the Standard Library in Module1. Enter the name of the macro.

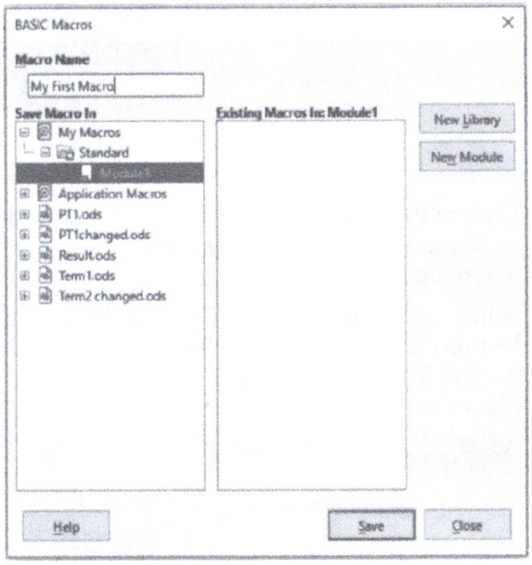

Step 6 Click on Save button.

Note *A Library is a collection of modules which in turn is a collection of macros.*

Rules for naming a Macro, Module or a Library:

While naming a Macro, Module or a Library the name should :

- Begin with a letter
- Not contain spaces
- Not contain special characters except for _ (underscore)

The Macro Recorder has some limitation, so the following actions cannot be recorded:

- Opening of windows
- Actions carried out in another window
- Window switching
- Actions that are not related to the document contents, for example, changes made in the Options dialog box, macro organizer, and so on
- Selections are recorded only if they are done by using the keyboard but not when the mouse is used.

Try These 5.1

1 **What is the primary purpose of using macros in a spreadsheet?**
   (a) To change the color of cells
   (b) To automate repetitive tasks
   (c) To create graphs
   (d) To save files in different formats

2 **Which of the following actions is not recorded by the Macro Recorder in LibreOffice Calc?**
   (a) Keyboard actions
   (b) Mouse clicks within the spreadsheet
   (c) Window switching
   (d) Formula input

3 **A macro is a sequence of ________ or keystrokes that are saved for later use.**

4 **The macro recorder is functional only in _____ and Writer.**

5 **What must be done before you can start recording a macro in LibreOffice Calc?**

6 **Where can you save a recorded macro in LibreOffice Calc?**

5.2 Running a Macro

To run or apply the existing macro, follow the given steps:

Step 1 Type the data.

Step 2 Use Tools → Macros → Run Macro option. Macro Selector dialog box appears.

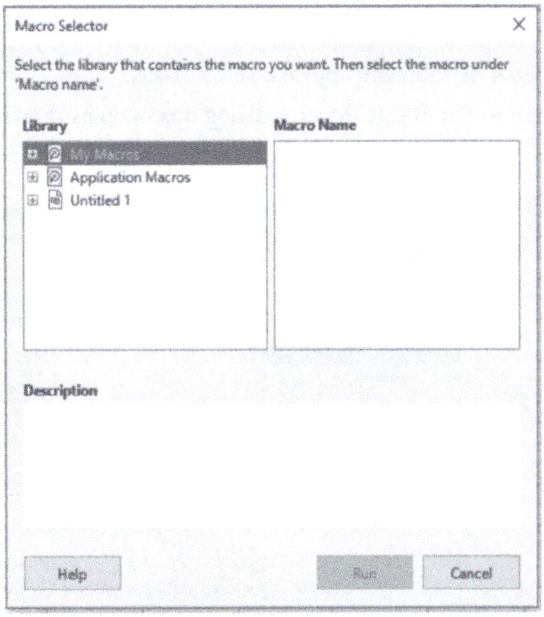

The Macro Selector dialog box appears with three names in the library as:

- Application Macros is provided by LibreOffice and contains modules with pre-recorded macros and should not be changed.

- **My Macros** contain macros that we write or add to LibreOffice.
- **Untitled1** is the name of the worksheet we are working on. Since at this time we have not saved the worksheet with another name it is showing Untitled1. You will see further that Untitled1 will be replaced with the name of the spreadsheet.

Step 3 Select the library and module in the Library list.

Step 4 Select the macro in the Macro Name list.

Step 5 Click Run to run the macro.

5.3 Creating and Organising a Simple Macro

LibreOffice macros are usually written in a language called LibreOffice Basic.

A text editor is included with LibreOffice that allows you to create and edit macros. Let us create a macro to display a message 'The sum of 20 and 40 is : 60' by following these steps:

Step 1 Create a new Calc document named Macro.ods.

Step 2 Select the Tools menu on the menu bar.

Step 3 Choose Macros → Organize Macros.

Step 4 A submenu appears. Select Basic.

Step 5 The BASIC Macros dialog box open as shown in the figure. It shows the macros that you have added or created in the My Macros library.

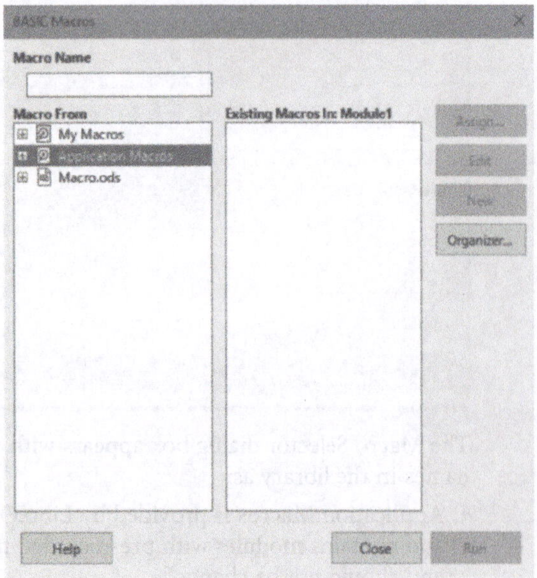

Step 6 Click on the Organizer button. The Basic Macro Organizer dialog box open as shown in the figure.

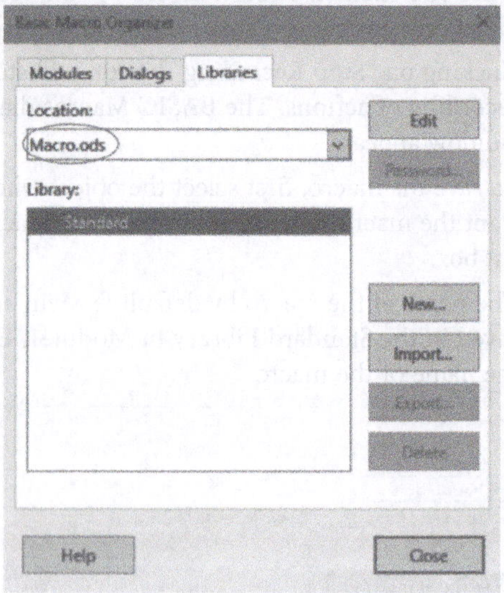

Step 7 Choose the Libraries tab and select the spreadsheet to contain the macro. For example, select Macro.ods.

Step 8 Click on the New button. The New Library dialog box opens. Enter the name for the library and click on OK. The new library name is shown in the library list.

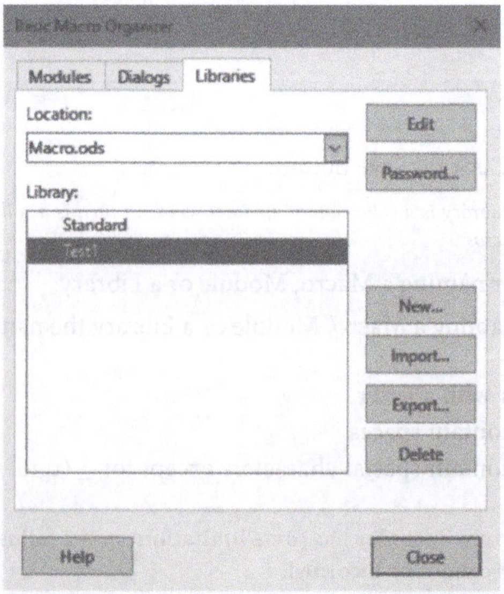

Step 9 Select the library name Test1 and click on the Edit button.

Step 10 The LibreOffice Basic Text Editor opens as shown in the figure.

Note *Calc automatically creates a module named Module1 and a macro named Main.*

Step 11 Enter the code for Module1 as shown in the figure.

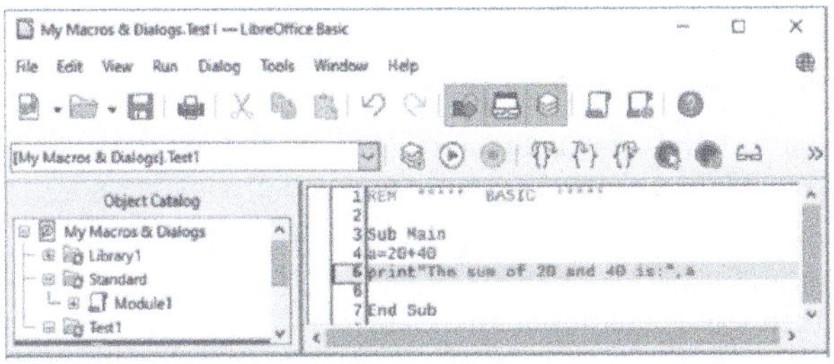

Step 12 Save the modified Module1 by clicking on the Save button.

Step 13 Now, run the macro by Run icon. You will get the result in the pop-up window.

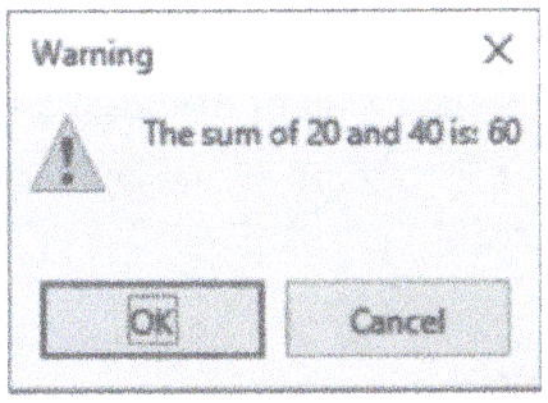

5.4 Macro as a Function

A function is a line of code that executes when you call it.When you invoke a function ,it returns a value.

To define a macro as function ,use the keyword Function. Each function has a name and may have parameters whose values you pass when you invoke the function.

The following is the syntax to define a simple function without parameters:

```
Function Function_Name ()
Body of Function
Function_Name=Result
End Function
```

Example

```
Function Total ()
Total=10+20
End Function
```

To create a macro as a function, follow these steps:

Step 1 Till now we created a library name Test1 moving forward and now select that Test1 library and click on the Edit button.

Step 2 The LibreOffice Basic Text Editor opens as shown in the figure.

Note *Calc automatically creates a module named Module1 and macro named Main.*

Step 3 Enter the code for Module1 as shown in the figure.

- Replace Sub with Function.
- Add Function Name (Argument1, Argument2, ...) at the beginning.
- Use the arguments in your calculations.
- Use the Function Name = statement to assign the result.
- Add End Function at the end.

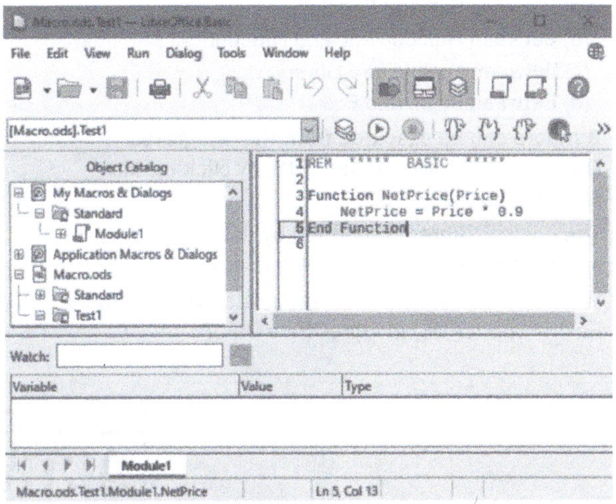

Step 4 In your spreadsheet, type =FunctionName (Argument1, Argument2, ...) in a cell.

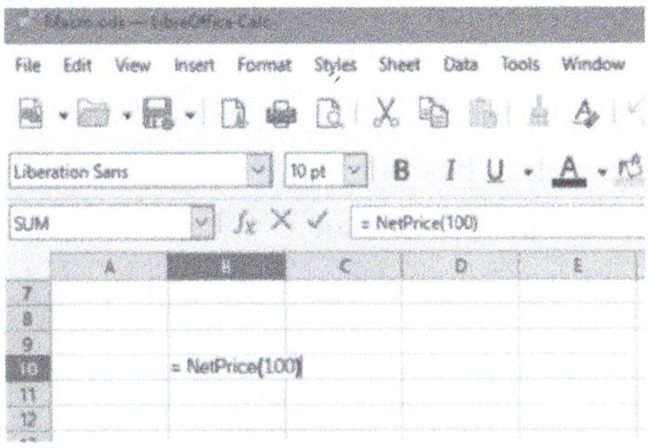

Step 5 After Pressing Enter, you get (you can use that function in any cell of the spreadsheet)

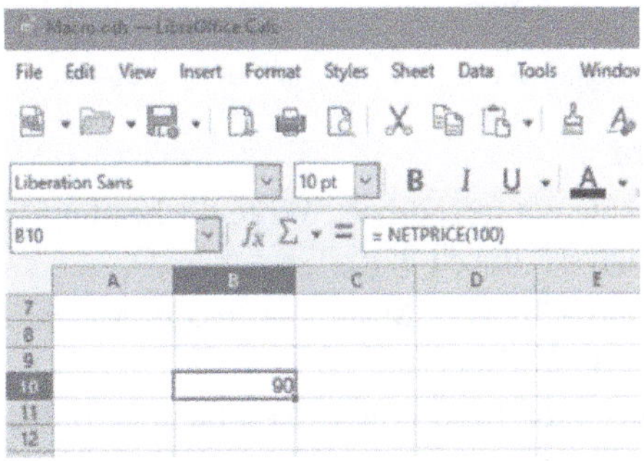

Step 6 Save the modified Module1 by clicking on the Save button.

Try These 5.2

1. What is the purpose of the Macro Selector dialog box in LibreOffice Calc?
   (a) To save macros
   (b) To edit macros
   (c) To run macros
   (d) To delete macros
2. When creating a macro as a function, where should the instructions be placed?
   (a) Between Sub and End Sub
   (b) Between Function and End Function
   (c) Between Module and Library
   (d) Between Begin and End
3. A macro can be executed from the Integrated Development Environment (IDE) by clicking the _______ button or pressing F5.
4. The _______ library is created by default when a spreadsheet is saved and macros are stored within it.
5. What is the function of the Integrated Development Environment (IDE) in LibreOffice Calc?

Summary

A macro is a recorded sequence of commands or keystrokes that automates repetitive tasks within Calc, enhancing efficiency.

Macros can be invoked directly in Calc as functions, allowing for seamless integration into spreadsheets.

When a new document is created and saved, it automatically includes a default library called Standard, which stores user-defined macros.

If a macro is complex or if multiple macros are created, a placeholder (or "stub") with the specified name is stored in the Standard library, allowing for easier management and organization.

Calc automatically generates a module named Module1 and a default macro named Main when a new macro is created.

Users can edit, delete, or create new macros in the Macro Organizer, providing flexibility in managing automated tasks.

ACTIVITY Time

ACTIVITY 1

Record a macro to apply the following style to the Heading "Data Analysis" in the cell A1.

The font style should be "Times New Roman"

The font size should be "14"

The font colour should be "Blue"

Cells from A1 to C1 should be merged and centred

	A	B	C
1		ABC Branch	
2		Sales Analysis	
3	Item	January	February
4	Chocolates	12000	25000
5	Cookies	13000	52000
6	Pastries	45000	12000
7	Cake	76000	70000
8	Juice	54000	80000

Procedure

Step 1 Create the spreadsheet. Write the heading "Sales Analysis" in cell B2.

Step 2 Choose Tools → Macros → Record Macro. Perform above function.

Step 3 Click Stop Recording to stop the Macro Recorder.

Step 4 The Basic Macro dialog appears,in which you can save and run the macro.

Step 5 A Standard library is present by default when a spreadsheet is created and saved.

Step 6 To save the macro, first select the object where you want to save the macro in the Save macro in list box.

The Main macro is saved by default in the Standard Library in Module1. You can change the name of the macro. Here, we have named the macro as Format_Heading.

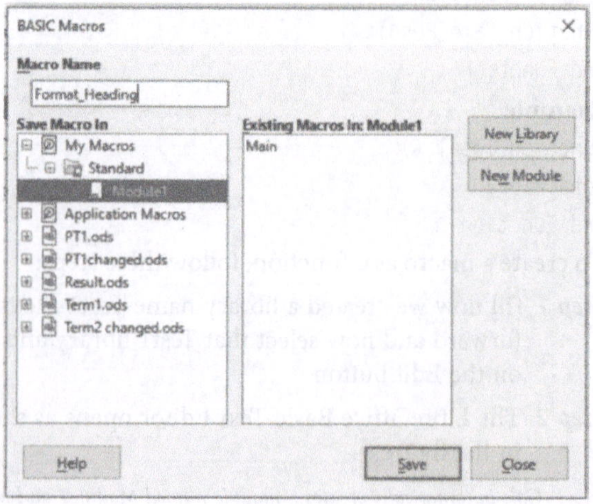

Step 7 Click on Save button. The macro will be saved.

Spreadsheet after applying changes

	A	B	C	D	E
1		ABC Branch			
2		Sales Analysis			
3	Item	January	February		
4	Chocolates	12000	25000		
5	Cookies	13000	52000		
6	Pastries	45000	12000		
7	Cake	76000	70000		
8	Juice	54000	80000		

Note *If all the macros will be given the same name then they will overwrite the previous Macro created by that name.*

ACTIVITY 2

Run the previously created Macro Format_heading.

	A	B	C
1		XYZ Branch	
2		Sales Analysis	
3	Item	January	February
4	Chocolates	12000	25000
5	Cookies	13000	52000
6	Pastries	45000	12000
7	Cake	76000	70000
8	Juice	54000	80000

Step 1 Type the heading in cell B2.

Step 2 Open the Macro selector dialog box by clicking Tools → Macros → Run Macro.

Step 3 Click on MyMacros → Standard → Module1. Then select Format_Heading from the Macro Name box and click Run.

	A	B	C	D	E
1		XYZ Branch			
2		Sales Analysis			
3	Item	January	February		
4	Chocolates	12000	25000		
5	Cookies	13000	52000		
6	Pastries	45000	12000		
7	Cake	76000	70000		
8	Juice	54000	80000		

You'll notice that the heading in Cell B2 is formatted. The actions recorded by a macro is recorded as instructions in a programming language called BASIC.

It's also possible to view and edit the macro's code, but it's recommended to do so only if you're familiar with the language, which is BASIC in the case of CALC.

To view the code generated for macros, navigate to Tools → Macros → Edit Macros. Select the macro name from the Object Catalog, and the corresponding code will be displayed.

Note *The code of a macro begins with Sub followed by the name of the macro and ends with End Sub.*

ACTIVITY 3

Create a simple Macro using BASIC programming instructions that will display Hello in a dialog box stored in the Standard module.

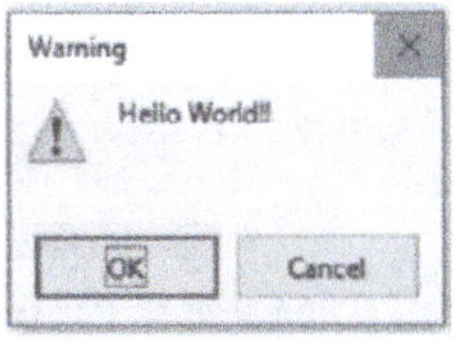

Step 1 Open the LibreOffice Basic Macro dialog box using Tools → Macros → Organize Macros → Basic.

Step 2 From the Basic Macros dialog box select Organizer.

Step 3 From Modules tab, select My Macros folder and click on New button.

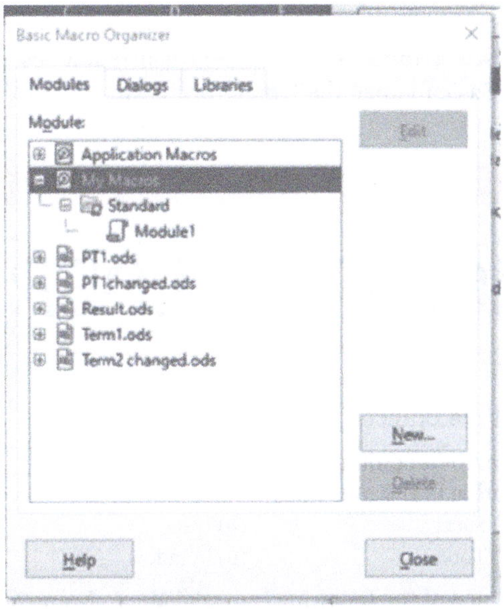

Step 4 Give a name to the New Module say 'Hello'.

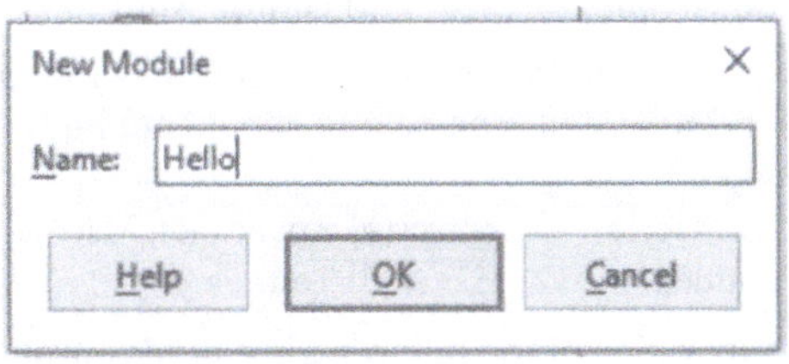

Step 5 Click OK. You will see Hello under Standard Library in My Macros Library.

Step 6 Select Hello and click Edit to open the Integrated Development Environment (IDE). It is a text editor that allows you to create and edit macros. Type Print "Hello" between Sub Main and End Sub.

Step 7 Now run the macro, you will get the result in the pop-up window.

ACTIVITY 4

Calculate the number of tiles required for flooring of a room using macro as a function.

The length and width of the room and the length and width of a tile is entered in the sheet.

	A	B	C	D	E
1	Length of the room(in feet)	Width of the room(in feet)	Length of a tile(in feet)	Width of a tile(in feet)	Number of tiles required for the room
2	10	10	2	2	
3	18	24	4	4	
4	12	14	3	2	
5	30	40	5	5	

Step 1 Enter data in a sheet and save it with the name as Calculate_tiles.ods

Step 2 Select Tools → Macros → Organize Macros → Basic to open the LibreOffice Basic Macros dialog.

Step 3 Choose Calculate_tiles.ods. Click on New and type a name.

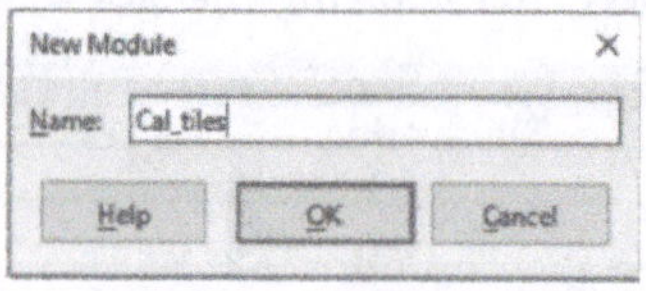

Step 4 We have named it as Cal_tiles and press OK.

Step 5 Write a function to calculate the number of tiles. A function starts with Function followed by the name of the function and then the statements to calculate area of the floor, tiles and number of tiles and store the final result in the name of the function. Press the Save button on the toolbar or press Ctrl+S.

Note *The text in grey is preceded by ' (single quote) indicating it is a comment. A comment is written to write descriptive text to support the code.*

Step 6 Use the function in the sheet by calling the function as =Calculate_Tiles_Re(A2,B2,C2,D2)

NCERT FOLDER

Complete Explanations of all NCERT's Questions

A. Multiple Choice Questions

Q.1 Macro Recordings can be enabled from the ________ option in the menu bar.

(a) Sheet (b) Data
(c) Tools (d) Window

Q.2 Which of the following is a valid Macro Name?

(a) 1formatword (b) format word
(c) format*word (d) Format_word

Q.3 Which of the following Libraries contains modules with prerecorded macros and should not be changed?

(a) My Macros (b) Application Macros
(c) Untitled1 (d) Test.

Q.4 Identify which of the following is a programming Language?

(a) Calc (b) BASIC (c) Writer (d) Macro

Q.5 The Module can be executed from the IDE by pressing ______.

(a) F3 (b) F4 (c) F5 (d) F6

Q.6 Which of the following is the default name of the Macro?

(a) Default (b) Main
(c) Macro1 (d) Main_Macro

Answers

1. (c) 2. (d) 3. (b) 4. (b) 5. (c)
6. (b)

B. Fill in the Blanks

Q.1 ______ library is automatically loaded when the document is opened.

Q.2 IDE stands for ______.

Q.3 Macro as a function is capable of accepting ______ and returning a ______.

Q.4 Macro ______ allows us to add, delete a module.

Q.5 The code of macro begins with ______ followed by the name of the macro and ends with ______. **CBSE SQP 2024-25**

Q.6 By default a macro is saved in the ______.

Answers

1. Standard
2. Integrated Development Environment
3. Augment, Result
4. Organizer
5. Sub, End Sub
6. Standard Library

C. State Whether the Following Statements are True or False

Q.1 Macro is a group of instructions executing a single instruction.

Q.2 Once created, Macro can be used any number of times.

Q.3 By default, the Macro recording feature is turned ON.

Q.4 It is not possible to stop recording of a Macro.

Q.5 Every Macro should be given a unique name.

Q.6 A macro once created can be edited later.

Answers

1. False 2. True 3. False 4. False
5. True 6. True

D. Answer the Following Questions

Q.1 What is a Macro?

Ans. A macro is a single instruction that executes a set of instructions. These set of instructions can be a sequence of commands or keystrokes that can be used for any number of times later. A sequence of actions such as keystrokes and clicks can be recorded and then run as per the requirement.

Q.2 List the actions that are not recorded by a macro?

Ans. The Macro Recorder has some limitation, so the following actions cannot be recorded:

- Opening of windows
- Actions carried out in another window
- Window switching
- Actions that are not related to the document contents, for example, changes made in the Options dialog box, macro organizer, and so on
- Selections are recorded only if they are done by using the keyboard but not when the mouse is used.

Q.3 How is Libre Office Macros Library different from my Macros?

Ans. LibreOffice Macros library is provided by library office and contains modules with pre recorded macros and should not be changed whereas My Macros contain macros that we write or add to LibreOffice.

Q.4 Differentiate between predefined function in Calc and Macros as a function?

Ans. Differentiate between predefined function in Calc and Macros as a function are as follows

Predefined Functions	Macros
Already available in the program, like SUM, AVERAGE, COUNT, etc.	Record or write a series of commands to automate tasks.
Automatically execute a particular calculation or operation.	Perform complex operations, interact with user inputs, and adapt to specific needs.
Simply enter the function name and required arguments.	Create and edit macros to suit specific requirements.
Cannot be modified or customized.	Can be modified, edited, or deleted as needed.

Q.5 List the rules that should be kept in mind while naming a macro?

Ans. Rules for naming a Macro, Module or a Library: notes while naming a Macro, Module or a Library the name should:

- Begin with a letter
- Not contain spaces
- Not contain special characters except for _(underscore).

Q.6 Give any one advantage of macros?

Ans. Macros perform repeated tasks such as typing school name, address, contact numbers with a specific formatting or apply the same formula at a particular cell for different sheets in a workbook.

EXAM PATTERN EXERCISE

Including Competency Based Questions

Multiple Choice Questions

1 Macros are especially useful to __________ the same way over and over again. **CBSE 2023**

(a) repeat a task
(b) reject a task
(c) report a task
(d) comment a task

2 The recorded macros are actually stored as .... **CBSE 2025**

(a) a set of instructions in a programming language.
(b) a sequence of data cells
(c) a document
(d) a list of values

3 **Which menu option should you use to start recording a macro?**
(a) File → New
(b) Tools → Macros → Record Macro
(c) Edit → Macros → Start Recording
(d) View → Macros → Record

4 **What action is not recorded by the macro recorder?**
(a) Typing text
(b) Mouse clicks
(c) Opening a new window
(d) Formatting cells

5 **Where is the recorded macro saved by default?**
(a) My Documents
(b) Custom Library
(c) Standard Library in Module1
(d) System folder

6 **What should a name for a macro, module, or library not contain?**
(a) Letters (b) Spaces
(c) Underscores (d) Numbers

7 **What action is performed when you click on "Run" in the Macro Selector dialog box?**
(a) Creates a new macro
(b) Executes the selected macro
(c) Saves the macro
(d) Deletes the macro

8 **Which menu option allows you to enable the macro recorder in LibreOffice Calc?**
(a) File (b) Tools (c) Edit (d) View

9 **Which dialog box is used to organize and edit macros?**
(a) LibreOffice Options (b) Macro Selector
(c) Basic Macros (d) Format Cells

10 **What is the default library where a newly recorded macro is saved?**
(a) My Macros
(b) LibreOffice Macros
(c) Standard
(d) Untitled1

11 **Which command is used to stop recording a macro?**
(a) Stop Recording
(b) End Recording
(c) Pause Recording
(d) Save Recording

12 **In which tab can you create a new module to store a macro?**
(a) Libraries (b) Modules
(c) Macros (d) Options

13 **What type of instructions are written between Function and End Function?**
(a) Commands (b) Macros
(c) Formulas (d) Functions

14 **How can you access the Basic Macros dialog box to organize macros?**
(a) Tools → Macros → Organize Macros → Basic
(b) Edit → Macros → Manage Macros
(c) Tools → Macros → Edit Macros
(d) File → Macros → basic

15 **You need to apply a specific formatting style to the heading "Annual Report" in a spreadsheet. This formatting includes changing the font to Arial, setting the font size to 16, and centering the text across cells A1 to D1. What would be the most efficient way to automate this task using LibreOffice Calc?** Competency Based Que.
(a) Manually format the heading each time you create a new report.
(b) Write a function in BASIC to format the heading.
(c) Record a macro to perform the formatting and save it for future use.
(d) Use a pre-built template for the report.

16 **Imagine you need to apply the same complex formula to calculate total expenses across multiple sheets in a workbook, and this formula is not available as a predefined function. What is the best approach to efficiently apply this formula to all sheets without manually typing it each time?** Competency Based Que.
(a) Manually enter the formula in each sheet.
(b) Use the copy-paste function to duplicate the formula across sheets.
(c) Create a macro function that applies the formula to each sheet and save it.
(d) Create a new predefined function in LibreOffice.

17 **In Calc, Arguments passed to a macro from Calc are always ____________.** CBSE SQP 2022-23
(a) Cell Reference
(b) Value
(c) Both (a) and (b)
(d) Sheet Reference

Answers

1. (a)	2. (a)	3. (b)	4. (c)	5. (c)
6. (b)	7. (b)	8. (b)	9. (c)	10. (c)
11. (a)	12. (b)	13. (d)	14. (a)	15. (c)
16. (c)	17. (b)			

Very Short Answer Type Questions

1 **What is the use of Macros in a Spreadsheet?** CBSE SQP 2020-21

Ans. Macros help in saving time in cases when the same set of tasks are to be done repeatedly like formatting or applying a similar formula in a similar range of data. It can be used to name and record a set of actions or set of actions.

2 Mention any two operations that can be performed using Macros in a spreadsheet. CBSE SQP 2022-23

Ans. Here are two operations that can be performed using macros in a spreadsheet:

- **Data manipulation** Macros can sort, filter, and merge data from multiple cells or sheets.
- **Formatting** Macros can format cells and ranges of cells by changing the font, color, or size of text, or applying cell borders and shading.

3 What are the steps to enable the macro recorder in LibreOffice Calc?

Ans.
- Click on Tools → Options → LibreOffice → Advanced, check the box for "Enable macro recording,".
- Click Apply, and then OK.

4 What does the Basic Macros dialog window allow you to do after recording a macro?

Ans. It allows you to save the recorded macro by selecting the desired library and module, entering a name for the macro, and clicking Save.

5 What is the significance of the comment text in a macro?

Ans. Comment text (preceded by a single quote) is used to write descriptive notes in the code to explain what the code does.

6 Describe how to create a new library for storing macros.

Ans.
- Click on Tools → Macros → Organize Macros → Basic.
- Click on Library → New to create a new library.

7 What is the role of the Integrated Development Environment (IDE) in macro creation?

Ans. The IDE is a text editor that allows users to create and edit macros by writing and modifying code.

8 How can you use a macro as a function in LibreOffice Calc?

Ans. Write the macro code between Function and End Function to create a function that accepts arguments, performs operations, and returns a result.

Short Answer Type Questions

1 Explain the process of recording, saving, and running a macro in LibreOffice Calc. Include details about the dialog boxes involved and any important considerations.

Ans. To record a macro in LibreOffice Calc, follow these steps:

1. Click on Tools → Macros → Record Macro.
2. Perform the actions you want to record (e.g., formatting cells or applying formulas).
3. Click on Stop Recording to finish the session. The Basic Macros dialog box will appear.
4. In this dialog box, select the library and module where you want to save the macro. Enter a name for the macro and click Save.

To run the macro, navigate to Tools > Macros > Run Macro, then select the appropriate library, module, and macro from the Macro Selector dialog box, and click Run.

Important considerations Ensure that the macro recorder is enabled before starting. Note that actions such as switching windows or modifying elements outside the spreadsheet will not be recorded.

2 What is the significance of enabling the macro recorder before recording a macro in LibreOffice Calc? What issues might arise if it is not enabled?

Ans. Enabling the macro recorder before recording is crucial because it allows LibreOffice Calc to capture the user's actions and convert them into a macro. If the macro recorder is not enabled, any actions performed will not be recorded, rendering the effort pointless. Consequently, users may find themselves repeating tasks manually instead of automating them, leading to inefficiencies and increased chances of errors in repetitive processes.

3 A Class X student is participating in a school competition where they need to analyse the performance of different sports teams based on match scores and statistics. The student has collected data over several matches and needs to calculate averages, determine rankings, and generate charts for a presentation. CBSE SQP 2024-25, Competency Based Que.

(a) How are Macros in Calc helpful to him?
(b) How to enable Macro in Calc?
(c) Is solution*word a valid macro name? Justify.
(d) Mention any one operation which cannot be recorded by macro.

Ans. (a) Repetitive tasks like calculating average scores, ranking teams based on performance, and generating graphs could be done with macros. It will save time and effort.

(b) Tools → Options → LibreOffice → Advanced. Observe the Optional Features. Two options are not check marked. Put the checkmark on the option "Enable macro recording"

(c) No, solution*word is not a valid macro name. Macro names cannot include special characters such as asterisks (*) or spaces. Valid characters typically include letters, numbers, and underscores.

(d) Opening or switching of windows

PRACTICAL ASSIGNMENT

1. Record a Macro that performs Bold, Underline on the Heading in Cell A1. Give macro the name BoldunderlineA1 and save it in a New Module named Basic Formatting which is created in a New Library named DocumenHeadingA1.

2. Record a Macro that creates a bar chart for data stored in cells A2 – A9 and K2 to K9.

3. Run the macro recorded in (1) and display a barchart for the following data showing Minimum and Maximum temperature from 2010-2017.

	A	B	C	D	E	F	G	H	I	J	K
1	Year	Annual -Min	Annual -Max	Jan-Feb - Min	Jan-Feb -Max	Mar-May-Min	Mar-May-Max	Jun-Sep-Min	Jun-Sep-Max	Oct-Dec-Min	Oct-Dec-Max
2	2010	20.15	30.13	14.51	25.96	22.09	33.47	23.57	31.43	17.42	27.78
3	2011	19.58	29.82	13.84	25.33	20.68	32.07	23.56	31.55	17.16	28.23
4	2012	19.54	29.81	13.68	25.03	20.78	32.33	23.68	31.77	16.8	27.88
5	2013	19.83	29.81	14.38	25.58	21.14	32.58	23.61	31.33	16.82	27.83
6	2014	19.77	29.72	14.26	24.9	20.66	31.82	23.8	32	17.2	27.81
7	2015	19.96	29.9	14.53	25.74	20.91	31.68	23.62	31.87	17.75	28.27
8	2016	21.28	31.63	16.17	28.33	23.15	34.57	24.61	32.28	18.37	30.03
9	2017	21.17	31.42	15.72	27.95	22.68	34.13	24.58	32.41	18.73	29.69

Collect information about the population of the South Asian countries from the Internet and store it in a Calc sheet. Run the Macro created in (1) to display a chart for the data stored. Create Macro as a function to calculate Amount to be paid after a 5% discount. A sample sheet for the same is given below

	A	B	C	D	E
1	Sn	Item name	Price per unit	No. of units	Total amount after 5% discount
2	1	Toothpaste	35	150	
3	2	Tooth brush	15	120	
4	3	Mouthwash	120	80	
5	4	Sanitizer	50	150	

4. Anuja has to create a Marks list for every term. The format is as follows :

	A	B	C	D	E	F	G	H	I	J	K	L	M	N	O	P	Q
1	Mark List																
2	Roll No.	Student Name	English			Hindi			Maths			Science			Social Science		
3			50	100	150	50	100	150	50	100	150	50	100	150	50	100	150
4																	
5																	
6																	
7																	
8																	
9																	
10																	
11																	

(a) Record two macros to create the format given above.

(b) To enter names of students in the list so that she doesn't need to retype or copy the names.

Run the above created macros for a new sheet.

5. Use Macro as a function to calculate Mileage of a vehicle. Mileage (in km/L) is calculated as Distance Travelled (in km)/ Fuel filled (in Litre). Create a sheet with three columns Distance Travelled (in Km), Fuel filled (in L) and Mileage (in km/L).

CHAPTER 06

Linking Spreadsheet Data

When working with spreadsheets, one of the most powerful techniques for managing and analyzing data is linking data across multiple sheets or even different workbooks. This allows you to create dynamic relationships between sets of data, making it easier to manage large datasets, perform complex calculations, and maintain consistency across related information.

Linking spreadsheet data enables you to keep the information up-to-date without editing multiple locations every time the data changes. The ability to create links eliminates the need to have identical data, entered and updated in multiple sheets. This saves time, reduces errors, and improves data integrity. In this chapter, you will learn about the various ways to link the spreadsheet data.

6.1 Setting up Multiple Sheets

When you launch Calc on your computer, it opens one worksheet,by default named Term1. You can add as many worksheets as you want.The following are the different ways to insert a new worksheet

Method-1 To add a new sheet, just click on the (+) sign located in the left bottom of the spreadsheet.

Method-2 Follow the given steps:

Step 1 Right-click on the sheet tab. A context menu appears.

Step 2 Click on the Insert Sheet option. The Insert Sheet dialog box appears.

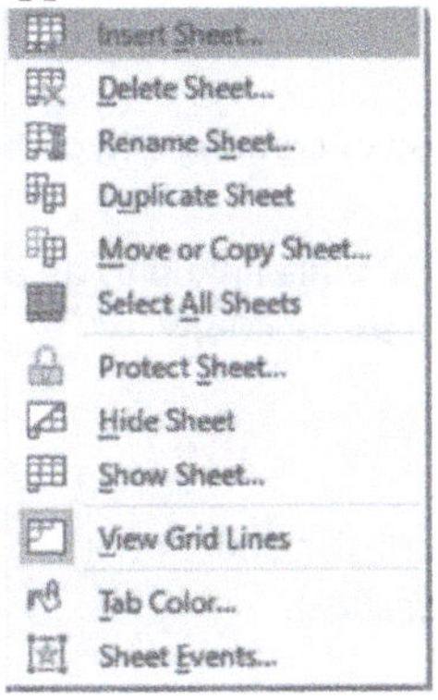

Step 3 Click on the required criteria. A new sheet will get inserted.

Inserting Sheets from a Different Spreadsheet

You can also add a sheet from a different spreadsheet file (for example, another Calc or Excel spreadsheet).

To add a sheet from file, follow the given steps:

Step 1 Right-click on the sheet tab and click on the Insert Sheet option. The Insert Sheet dialog box appears.

Step 2 Click on the From file radio button.

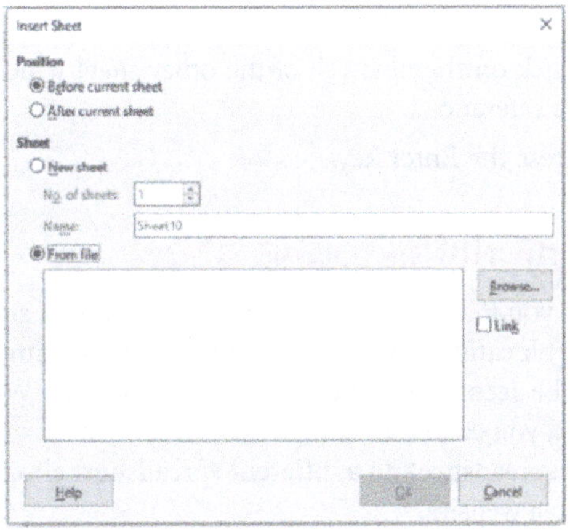

Step 3 Click on the Browse button. The Insert dialog box appears.

Step 4 Select the file.

Step 5 Click on the Open button. The file appears in the Insert Sheet dialog box.

Step 6 Click on the OK button. The file gets opened.

Creating Reference to Other Sheets by Using Keyboard and Mouse

To create the reference with the mouse, follow the given steps:

Step 1 Both spreadsheets need to be open.

Step 2 Select the cell in which formula is to be entered.

Step 3 Press the equal to(=) from the keyboard.

Step 4 Switch to the other spreadsheet (the process to do this will vary depending on which operating system you are using).

Step 5 Select the sheet and then the reference cell (C2).

Step 6 Switch back to the original spreadsheet.

Step 7 Click on the green check mark on the input line.

Note *Any change made to the referenced sheet is reflected or shown in the final sheet.*

Creating Reference to Other Documents by Using Keyboard and Mouse

Steps to perform the same are given below:

Step 1 Open both the spreadsheets which are to be referenced.

Step 2 Click on the cell of the sheet where the result of the reference will appear.

Step 3 Type equal to(=) and the formula like SUM(), MAX(), MIN(), etc.

Step 4 In the formula, click on the cell of the other sheet which is to be referenced.

Step 5 Insert a comma(,).

Step 6 Click on the next cell of the other sheet which is to be referenced.

Step 7 Press the Enter key.

6.2 Hyperlinks to the Sheet

At times, you may need to navigate to a document stored in a different location from within your current document. This can be accomplished by creating a hyperlink. With a hyperlink, you can easily jump to a different sheet within the same spreadsheet, to a different spreadsheet altogether, or even to a website.

A hyperlink, commonly referred to as a link, is an embedded command that enables you to jump (transfer control) to another document or a different section within the same document.

This command can be embedded in text, an image, an icon, or a graphic. In simple terms, a link is a clickable pointer to a resource.

In Calc, you can use hyperlinks to navigate to a resource located elsewhere from within the current sheet. This location can be:

- Within the same sheet or worksheet.
- In another worksheet.
- A different type of resource on your local computer or network.
- A webpage on the Internet.

Absolute Hyperlink and Relative Hyperlink

An **absolute hyperlink** stores the full path to the file's location, so if the file is moved or removed from that location, the hyperlink will no longer work.

For example, C:\Users\ADMIN\Downloads\try.ods is an absolute link because it specifies the complete file path.

A **relative hyperlink** stores the file location relative to the current location.

For example, Admin\Downloads\try.ods is a relative hyperlink, as it depends on the current location of the active spreadsheet. The folder "Admin" is searched in relation to where the spreadsheet is saved. If the entire folder containing the active spreadsheet is moved, the relative link will still work, as it remains linked to the source folder where the spreadsheet is stored.

Try These 6.1

1. **What is the first step to insert a new sheet in LibreOffice Calc?**
   (a) Click on the green check mark on the input line
   (b) Click on the (+) sign at the bottom left of the spreadsheet
   (c) Press the Enter key
   (d) Type the formula SUM() in the cell
2. **Which of the following is an example of an absolute hyperlink?**
   (a) Admin\Downloads\try.ods
   (b) C:\Users\ADMIN\Downloads\try.ods
   (c) Downloads\try.ods
   (d) Admin\try.ods
3. **To insert a sheet from a different spreadsheet file, you must first click on the ____________ button in the Insert Sheet dialog box.**
4. **What is the purpose of creating a hyperlink in a spreadsheet?**
5. **What happens when a file linked by an absolute hyperlink is moved to a different location?**

6.3 Creating Hyperlink

It is possible to hyperlink a sheet of other spreadsheet document in a spreadsheet.

To create a hyperlink, follow the given steps:

Step 1 Open the spreadsheet where the link is to be created.

Step 2 From the main menu, click on Insert → Hyperlink. The Hyperlink dialog box will appear.

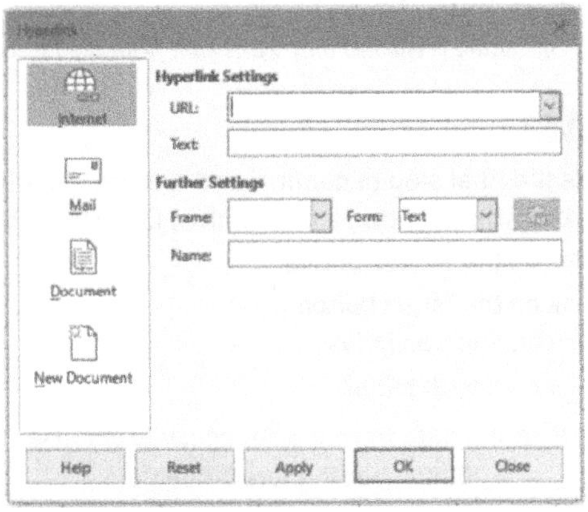

Step 3 To insert the spreadsheet document, click on the Document on the left pan of dialog box, then to select the spreadsheet document, click on the button located after the Path.

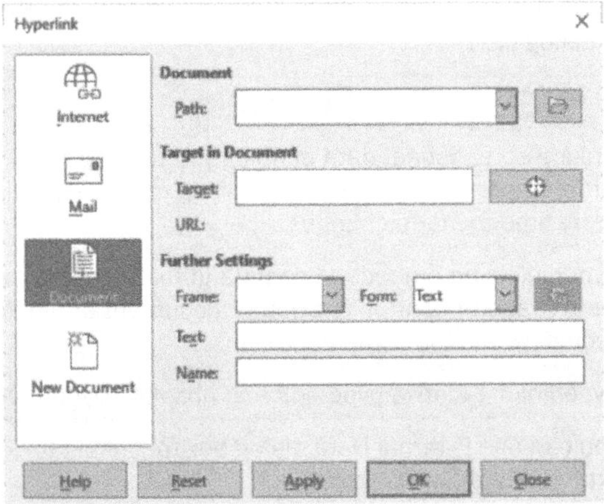

Step 4 Select the required document.

Step 5 Then click on the Target button to choose the sheet which is to be hyperlinked.

Target in Document helps to specifically choose a target in the document such as sheet, tables, frames, images, headings and so on.

Step 6 Click on Apply and Close button to exit the Target Document window.

Step 7 Enter the text in the Text box to assign the hyperlink to that text.

Step 8 Click on Apply and Close button to confirm the changes and exit the Hyperlink dialog box.

Step 9 Observe the assigned hyperlink.

Step 10 To open the hyperlinked sheet, press the Ctrl key and click on the hyperlinked word.

Editing a Hyperlink

To edit an existing link, follow the given steps:

Step 1 Place the cursor anywhere in the link and right-click the hyperlink. A context menu will be displayed.

Step 2 Click on Edit Hyperlink.... The Hyperlink dialog box will be displayed, where you can make changes to the hyperlink.

Deleting the Hyperlink

On clicking to the Remove Hyperlink option, the link will be removed from the text and thus it will not point to any other location.

Linking to External Data

The Internet is a vast source of information, organized in the form of web pages. These pages are typically written as HTML documents, and the data within them can often be found in tables. One of the strengths of a spreadsheet like Calc is its ability to import tables from HTML documents. To do this, you can use the External Data dialog box. The steps to insert tables from an HTML document are outlined below.

Step 1 Open the spreadsheet where external data is to be inserted.

Step 2 Select the cell to store the first cell of the table in the external data.

Step 3 Select Sheet → External Links.... External Data dialog box is displayed.

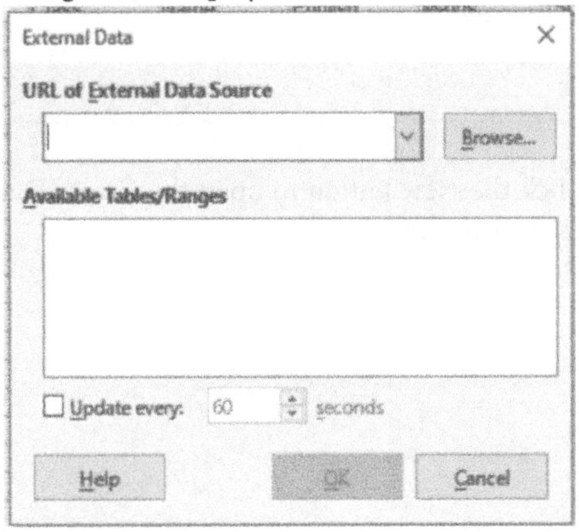

Step 4 Type the URL of the source document or select it from the drop-down list if it is listed and click on OK button.

Step 5 A dialog box is displayed to select the language for import. Selecting Automatic shows data in the same language as in the webpage.

Linking to Registered Data Sources

LibreOffice Calc enables you to link spreadsheet documents with databases and other data sources. To do this, the data source must first be registered with LibreOffice, which involves specifying the type of data source and the file's location.

In this discussion, we'll focus on LibreOffice Base, which has a file extension of .odb. You'll learn more about LibreOffice Base in detail in Unit 3. By linking Calc documents to a variety of databases and other data sources, you can enhance your data management and analysis capabilities.

To register a data source that is in *.odb format, follow the steps given below.

Step 1 Select Tools → Options → LibreOffice Base → Databases.

The Options – LibreOffice Base-Databases dialog box appears.

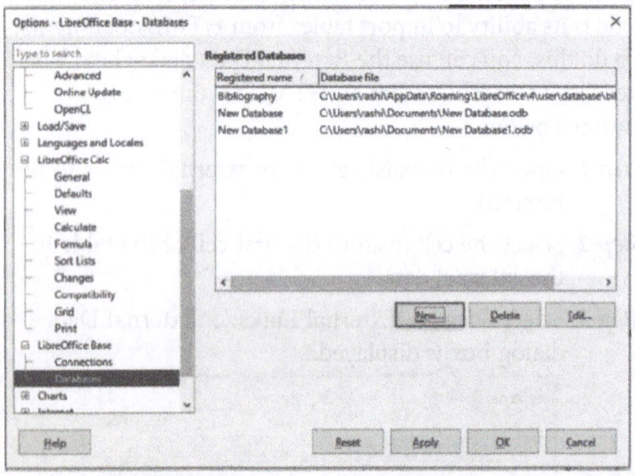

Step 2 Click the New button to open the Create Database Link dialog box.

Step 3 Enter the location of the database file, or click Browse to open a file browser and select the database file.

Step 4 Type a name to use as the registered name for the database and click OK. The database is added to the list of registered databases.

Note *The OK button is enabled only when both fields are filled in.*

Try These 6.2

1. **What is the final step to confirm and exit the Hyperlink dialog box after creating a hyperlink in LibreOffice Calc?**
   (a) Click on the Browse button
   (b) Click on the Target button
   (c) Click on Apply and Close
   (d) Click on the OK button
2. **To link external data from a webpage, you can use the ____________ dialog box in LibreOffice Calc.**
3. **When registering a data source in LibreOffice Calc, the data source must first be registered with LibreOffice by specifying the ____________ and the file's location.**
4. **How can you edit an existing hyperlink in LibreOffice Calc?**
5. **What is the function of the "Target" button in the Hyperlink dialog box?**

Summary

Linking spreadsheet data enables you to keep the information up-to-date without editing multiple locations every time the data changes.

Hyperlink is an embedded command that enables you to jump (transfer control) to another document or a different section within the same document.

Hyperlinks: Relative hyperlink and Absolute hyperlink.

You can use External Data dialog box for linking to external data (like Web pages).

LibreOffice Calc enables you to link spreadsheet documents with databases and other data sources.

ACTIVITY Time

ACTIVITY 1

Add a new sheet to store data for Term2 in the spreadsheet by using the Insert Sheet Dialog box.

Step 1 Open the Insert Sheet dialog box and add a sheet after the current sheet by selecting After current sheet option. The current sheet is our active sheet which in this case is Term1.

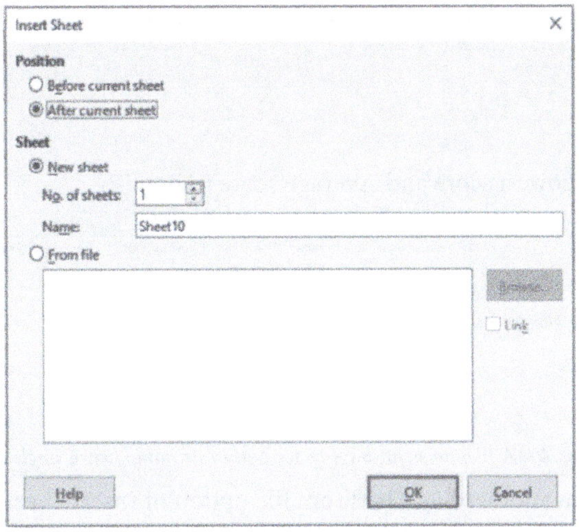

Step 2 Name the Sheet as Term2.

Step 3 Enter the marks obtained by the students in second term in Term2 sheet as shown in below figure.

	A	B	C	D	E	F	G
1			Term 2 Marks				
2	Roll No	Class	Name	English	Maths	Science	Social Science
3	1	X-A	Aadhya	67	88	33	87
4	2	X-B	Armaan	71	82	33	33
5	3	X-A	Aarav	55	55	34	67
6	4	X-C	Aariv	46	76	27	90
7	5	X-A	Aasma	63	55	22	78
8	6	X-C	Aashna	90	89	44	81

Step 4 Insert a new sheet and name it as "Result".

ACTIVITY 2

Create Summary of result in a spreadsheet document named Result Analysis of class X-A and class X-B

C10

	A	B	C	D
1			Result Analysis	
2	SUBJECT	Highest Score	Lowest Score	Average Score
3	English			
4	Maths			
5	Science			
6	Social Science			

Since the marks of both the classes are stored in separate spreadsheet file and Result Analysis itself is a separate spreadsheet, therefore we need to create reference to other spreadsheets.

Step 1 Open the spreadsheets namely Result-X-A, Result-X-B and Result Analysis.

Step 2 Click on cell B3 of Result Analysis spreadsheet and type =MAX().

Step 3 Click between the brackets of MAX() and then click on the cell range containing marks of English in Result-X-A spreadsheet.

Step 4 Type (,) comma and click on the cell containing marks of English in the Result-X-B spreadsheet.

Step 5 Press Enter, Maximum of the marks will be displayed in cell B3 as shown in below figure.

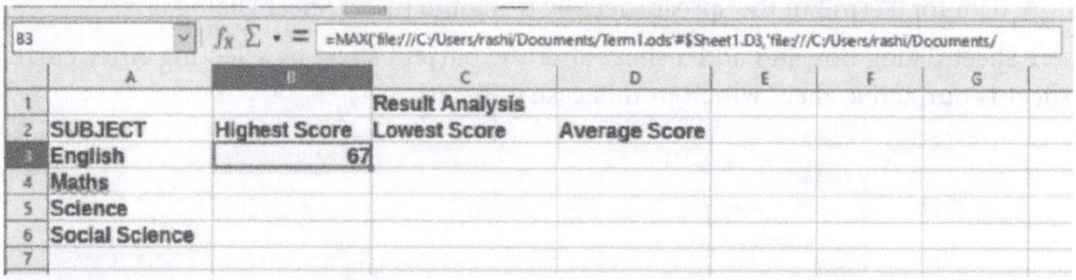

Sheet after finding the highest score, Lowest score and Average score in English.

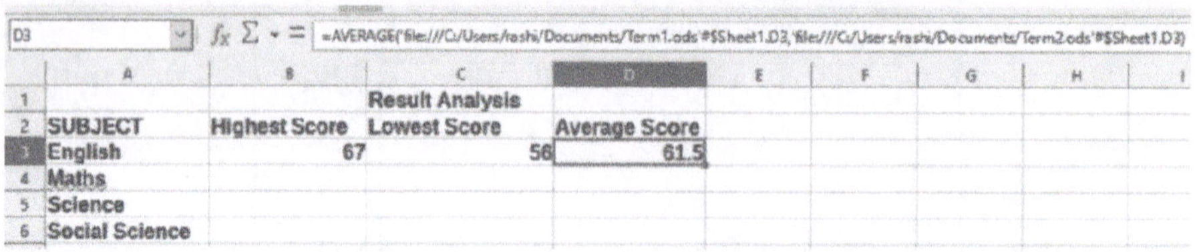

Note *The path of a file has three forward slash ///. A filename can have space within its name hence single quotes (' ') are used.*

It is also possible to insert a sheet from another file. The From file option of Insert Sheet dialog box allows us to insert sheet from another file as well.

ACTIVITY 3

Step 1 To insert the sheet "Result" from Result Analysis spreadsheet, open the Result Analysis spreadsheet.

Step 2 Select Sheet → Insert Sheet → From File.

Step 3 Click on Browse button, which will open Insert Sheet dialog box.

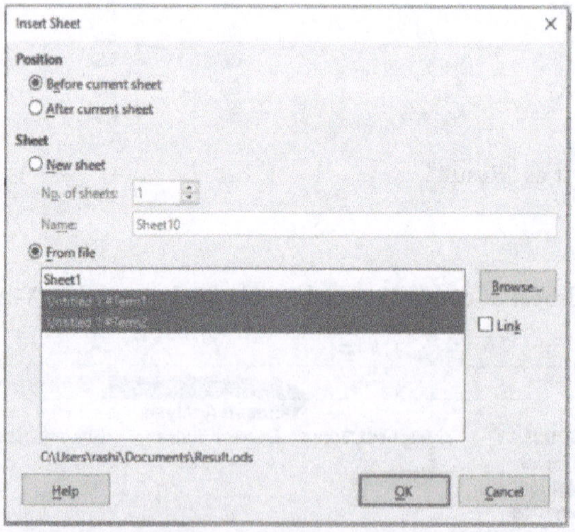

Step 4 Select the file from which you want to import the sheets.

After selecting the file, the sheets contained in it are displayed in the list box. The file path is displayed below this box. Select the sheet to be inserted from the list box.

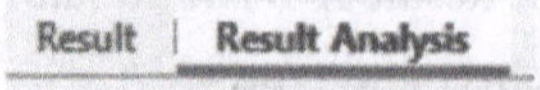

Instead of simply copying and pasting data, linking a sheet keeps the information dynamic and up-to-date. This means you will always have access to real-time data that mirrors any changes made in the original file, ensuring accuracy and consistency effortlessly.

The links can be updated by selecting Tools → Options → LibreOffice Calc → General , whenever the file is opened to ensure that you have access to the updated data always.

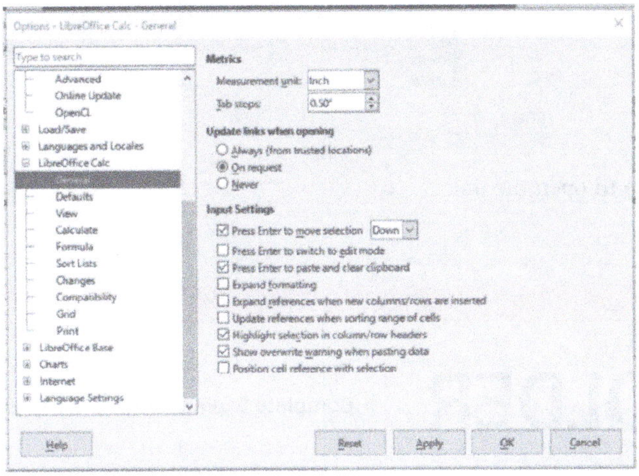

ACTIVITY 4

Create a hyperlink of "Term1" sheet in "Term2" sheet in LibreOffice Calc.

To perform the same, follow the given steps:

Step 1 Open the Term2 spreadsheet document.

Step 2 Click on Insert → Hyperlink.A Hyperlink dialog box will appear.

Step 3 To insert the spreadsheet document, click on the Document on the left pan of dialog box, then to select the spreadsheet document, click on the button located after the Path. Select the spreadsheet document "Term1".

Step 4 Then, click on the Target button to choose the sheet which is to be hyperlinked. We will select the sheet Result.

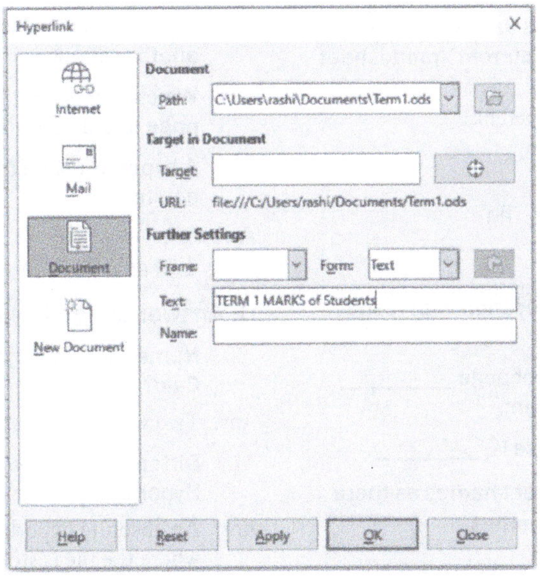

Step 5 Click on Apply and Close button to exit the Target Document window.

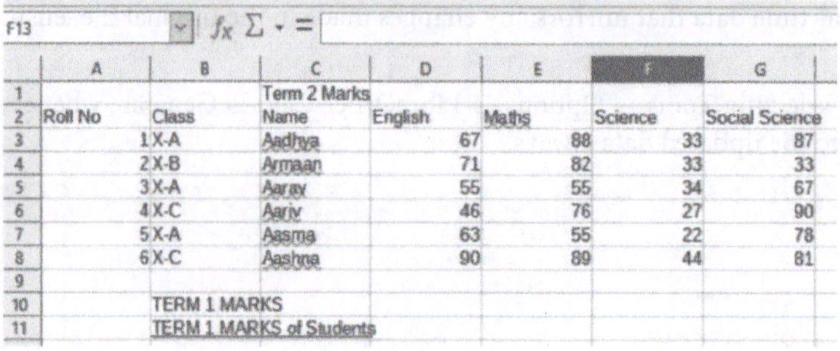

	A	B	C	D	E	F	G
1			Term 2 Marks				
2	Roll No	Class	Name	English	Maths	Science	Social Science
3	1	X-A	Aadhya	67	88	33	87
4	2	X-B	Armaan	71	82	33	33
5	3	X-A	Aarav	55	55	34	67
6	4	X-C	Aariv	46	76	27	90
7	5	X-A	Aasma	63	55	22	78
8	6	X-C	Aashna	90	89	44	81
9							
10		TERM 1 MARKS					
11		TERM 1 MARKS of Students					

Step 6 Just Ctrl+Click the mouse to open the link.

NCERT FOLDER

Complete Explanations of all NCERT's Questions

A. Multiple Choice Questions

Q.1 Insert Sheet dialog can be invoked from ________.

(a) sheet (b) insert
(c) tools (d) Windows

Q.2 ________ refers to cell G5 of sheet named MySheet.

(a) $My Sheet.'G5' (b) $My Sheet_'G5'
(c) $ 'MySheet'.G5 (d) $ 'MySheet'_G5

Q.3 The path of a file has ________ forward slashes.

(a) four (b) three (c) two (d) one

Q.4 Which of the following feature is used to jump to a different spreadsheet from the current spreadsheet in LibreOffice Calc?

(a) Macro (b) Hyperlink
(c) connect (d) Copy

Answers

1. (a) 2. (c) 3. (b) 4. (b)

B. Fill in the Blanks

Q.1 A relative hyperlink stores the location with respect to the________ location.

Q.2 While inserting tables from a webpage ________ selects the entire HTML document.

Q.3 The extension of LibreOffice base is ________.

Q.4 ______ are used to enclose sheet names as there might be a space within sheet names.

Q.5 The From file option of ________ dialog box allows to insert sheet from another file.

Answers

1. Current 2. HTML_all 3. .odb
4. Single Quote (' ') 5. Insert Sheet

C. State Whether the Following Statements are True or False

Q.1 A sheet can only be added before the current sheet.

Q.2 If 'sales' sheet has a reference to 'cost' sheet then any changes made to 'cost' sheet will be reflected in the sales sheet as well.

Q.3 It is not possible to link a sheet as a reference in another sheet.

Q.4 We can insert data from a table created on a web page into a spreadsheet.

Q.5 A hyperlink once created on a sheet cannot be deleted.

Answers

1. False 2. True 3. False 4. True 5. False

D. Answer the Following Questions

Q.1 Name the two ways to link the sheets in a LibreOffice Calc?

Ans. Two ways are: create a reference and Link external data.

Q.2 Differentiate between Relative and Absolute Hyperlink.

Ans. An absolute hyperlink stores the complete location where the file is stored whereas a relative hyperlink stores the location with respect to the current location.

Q.3 Write steps to extract a table from a web page in a spreadsheet?

Ans. To insert the tables from a HTML document, we can use the External Data dialog box. The steps are given below.

Step 1 Open the spreadsheet where external data is to be inserted.

Step 2 Select the cell to store the first cell of the table in the external data.

Step 3 Select Sheet → External Links.

Q.4 Write steps to register a data source that is in *.odb format?

Ans. Refer to text on page no. 190 (Linking to registered data sources).

Q.5 State advantages of extracting data from a web page into spreadsheet.

Ans. Advantages of extracting data from a web page into spreadsheet are:

1. **Accuracy** Extracting data directly from a webpage, ensure that the information is up-to-date and accurate.
2. **Efficiency** Extracting data automates the process of gathering data from a webpage.
3. **Collaboration** It also facilitates organization and collaboration of data.

EXAM PATTERN EXERCISE

Including Competency Based Questions

Multiple Choice Questions

1 **________can be used in a spreadsheet software to jump to a different location from within a spreadsheet and can lead to other parts of the current file, to different files or even to web sites.** CBSE SQP 2020-21

(a) Illustrations (b) Hyperlinks
(c) Links (d) Filter

2 **A ______ hyperlink contains the full address of the destination file or web page.** CBSE SQP 2021-22 Term I

(a) Relative (b) Absolute
(c) Mixed (d) Address

3 **Which feature allows you to jump to a different document, spreadsheet, or website from within a document?** CBSE SQP 2024-25

(a) Bookmark (b) Page Break
(c) Hyperlink (d) Format Painter

4 **An __________ link will stop working only if the target is moved while a__________ link will stop working only if the start and target locations change relative to each other.** CBSE SQP 2021-22 Term I

(a) absolute, fixed (b) Relative, Absolute
(c) absolute, relative (d) permanent, absolute

5 **How can you add a new sheet in LibreOffice Calc?**

(a) Click on the green check mark
(b) Right-click on the sheet tab and select Insert Sheet
(c) Press the Enter key
(d) Click on the "Save As" option

6 **Which option should you select to insert a sheet from another spreadsheet file?**

(a) From file
(b) From template
(c) New sheet
(d) Duplicate sheet

7 **What is the purpose of the "Target" button in the Hyperlink dialog box?**

(a) To browse for a file
(b) To select a specific sheet or section in the document
(c) To close the dialog box
(d) To edit the hyperlink text

8 **Which key do you press while clicking a hyperlink to open it in Calc?**

(a) Shift (b) Alt
(c) Ctrl (d) Enter

9 **What must be done first when linking a Calc document to an external database?**

(a) Create a new database
(b) Register the data source with LibreOffice
(c) Save the spreadsheet
(d) Insert a new sheet

10 **Which of the following hyperlinks is an absolute hyperlink?**

(a) Admin\Documents\report.ods
(b) C:\Users\Admin\Documents\report.ods
(c) Documents\report.ods
(d) Admin\report.ods

11 How do you start the process of importing tables from an HTML document into Calc?

(a) File → Import
(b) Sheet → External Links
(c) Insert → Link
(d) Data → External Data

12 In the External Data dialog box, what do you enter to specify the data source?

(a) File path (b) Sheet name
(c) URL (d) File type

13 What is the purpose of registering a data source in LibreOffice Calc?

(a) To enable editing of the data source
(b) To inform LibreOffice about the type and location of the data source
(c) To create a backup of the data source
(d) To convert the data source into a spreadsheet

14 Which file extension is associated with LibreOffice Base?

(a) .xls (b) .ods
(c) .odb (d) .csv

15 You need to generate a report that consolidates data from multiple sheets within a single LibreOffice Calc document. Which feature would you use to accomplish this efficiently?

(a) Hyperlinks
(b) External Data Dialog Box
(c) Cell References
(d) Import Wizard

16 If you want to create a summary sheet that aggregates data from several different spreadsheets, how would you incorporate data from another spreadsheet into your current sheet?

(a) By creating a hyperlink to the external spreadsheet
(b) By copying and pasting the data directly
(c) By using the "Insert Sheet" option and selecting "From file"
(d) By importing the data through the "External Data" dialog box

17 You are working on a spreadsheet that needs to pull updated data from a web-based HTML table. What is the most efficient way to include this data in your spreadsheet?

(a) Manually copy the table data from the website and paste it into your spreadsheet
(b) Use the "Insert Sheet" option to add the HTML file directly
(c) Use the "External Data" dialog box to import the HTML table
(d) Create a hyperlink to the HTML table and access the data online

18 A colleague needs to navigate between different sheets and documents quickly using hyperlinks. What steps would you recommend to create a hyperlink that points to a specific sheet in another spreadsheet?

(a) Use the "Insert" menu to create a link to the entire document
(b) Open the Hyperlink dialog, select "Document," choose the target file, and then select the specific sheet
(c) Copy the URL of the sheet and paste it as a link
(d) Insert a hyperlink to the file location and instruct your colleague to manually find the sheet

19 Which creating a hyperlink in Calc, if the complete path along with filename is given then it is an example of .... CBSE 2025

(a) Relative hyperlink
(b) Mixed hyperlink
(c) Absolute hyperlink
(d) Folder hyperlink

20 A _______ hyperlink stores the location with respect to the current location in LibreOffice Calc. CBSE SQP 2024-25

(a) Absolute (b) Relative
(c) Mixed (d) Reference

21 _______ is a text editor that allows you to create and edit macros. CBSE SQP 2024-25

(a) IDE (b) Notepad
(c) Open Office Writer (d) MS Word

Answers

1. (b)	2. (b)	3. (c)	4. (c)	5. (b)
6. (a)	7. (b)	8. (c)	9. (b)	10. (b)
11. (d)	12. (c)	13. (b)	14. (c)	15. (c)
16. (d)	17. (c)	18. (b)	19. (c)	20. (b)
21. (a)				

Very Short Answer Type Questions

1 Differentiate between Relative and Absolute Hyperlinks with the help of an example. CBSE SQP 2020-21

Ans. Relative Hyperlink stores the file location relative to the current location. Example, Admin\Downloads\try.ods.

Absolute Hyperlink stores the full path to the file's location. Example, C:\Users\ADMIN\Downloads\try.ods.

2 What are the two parts of a cell reference while referencing data on other sheets? Explain with an example. CBSE 2024

Ans. A cell reference consists of two parts:

Sheet Name The name of the sheet where the cell is located.

Cell Address The specific location of the cell within the sheet, represented by its column letter and row number (e.g. A1,B2).

Example

If you want to reference cell A1 on a sheet named "Sheet2" from your current sheet, you would use the reference: Sheet2!A1.

3 What is the first step to insert a sheet from a different spreadsheet file in LibreOffice Calc?

Ans. Right-click on the sheet tab and select the "Insert Sheet" option.

4 How do you create a reference to a cell in another spreadsheet using the keyboard and mouse?

Ans. Open both spreadsheets, select the cell in which the formula is to be entered, press "=", switch to the other spreadsheet, select the reference cell, and press Enter.

5 What is an absolute hyperlink, and why might it stop working?

Ans. An absolute hyperlink stores the full path to a file's location. It might stop working if the file is moved or deleted from that location.

6 How can you edit an existing hyperlink in LibreOffice Calc?

Ans. Right-click the hyperlink, select "Edit Hyperlink," and make the necessary changes in the dialog box.

7 What is the purpose of the "From file" radio button in the Insert Sheet dialog box?

Ans. It allows you to insert a sheet from another spreadsheet file.

8 What steps are involved in linking a Calc document to an external database?

Ans. First, the data source must be registered with LibreOffice. Then, you can link the document to the registered data source.

9 How do you apply and confirm changes when creating a hyperlink in Calc?

Ans. Click on the "Apply" and "Close" buttons in the Hyperlink dialog box.

10 What does the External Data dialog box in Calc allow you to do?

Ans. It allows you to insert tables from HTML documents or link to external data sources.

11 What are the steps to delete a hyperlink in LibreOffice Calc?

Ans. Right-click the hyperlink and select "Remove Hyperlink" from the context menu.

Short Answer Type Questions

1 Distinguish between the following with respect to spreadsheets: CBSE 2023

(a) Relative and Absolute hyperlink.

(b) Internet hyperlink and Document hyperlink.

Ans. (a) Relative and Absolute Hyperlink

- **Relative Hyperlink** The target location is specified relative to the current location. If you move the source file or the target file, the hyperlink will break.
- **Absolute Hyperlink** The target location is specified with an absolute path, so it remains valid even if the files are moved.

(b) Internet Hyperlink and Document Hyperlink

- **Internet Hyperlink** It means pointing the resource on the internet, such as a website or a web page.
- **Document Hyperlink** It means pointing the resource within the same document or another document on the local drive.

2 Explain four types of hyperlinks that can be applied in spreadsheets. CBSE 2024

Ans. Here are four types of hyperlinks commonly used in spreadsheets:

(i) **Cell Hyperlink** Links to a specific cell within the same spreadsheet or another spreadsheet.

(ii) **Document Hyperlink** Links to another document, such as a word processor document or a PDF file.

(iii) **Internet Hyperlink** Links to a webpage on the internet.

(iv) **Email Hyperlink** Links to an email address.

3 Describe the steps to create a hyperlink in LibreOffice Calc that links to a specific sheet in another spreadsheet document.

Ans. Here are the steps to create hyperlink in LibreOffice Calc

Step 1 Open the spreadsheet where the hyperlink will be created.

Step 2 Select "Insert" from the main menu and click on "Hyperlink."

Step 3 In the Hyperlink dialog box, click on "Document" in the left pane.

Step 4 Click the button after the "Path" field to browse and select the spreadsheet document.

Step 5 After selecting the document, click on the "Target" button to choose the specific sheet you want to hyperlink to.

Step 6 Enter the hyperlink text in the "Text" box.

Step 7 Click on "Apply" and then "Close" to confirm the hyperlink. To open the hyperlinked sheet, press the Ctrl key and click on the hyperlink.

4 Explain the process of importing tables from an HTML document into LibreOffice Calc. Include all necessary steps.

Ans. Here are the steps to import a table from an HTML document into LibreOffice Calc

Step 1 Open the spreadsheet where the external data is to be inserted.

Step 2 Select the cell where you want to store the first cell of the imported table.

Step 3 Go to "Sheet" in the main menu and select "External Links."

Step 4 In the External Data dialog box, type the URL of the source document or select it from the drop-down list if it is listed.

Step 5 Press Enter. A dialog box will appear prompting you to select the language for import.

Step 6 Selecting "Automatic" will display the data in the same language as on the webpage. The data from the HTML document will be imported into Calc.

5 Mr. Amit, Sales Manager of ABC Sales Corporation has created a spreadsheet in LibreOffice Calc that lists Sales for different years in different regions in different worksheets. He wants to summarise and make certain decisions based on it.

Competency Based Que. CBSE 2025

Help him by answering the following questions:

(a) Which tool in Calc can be used to combine the sales data from multiple sheets into a single summary sheet?

(b) Name the Menu Option and Sub-Menu Option that can be used to generate combined summary of all the worksheets.

(c) Name the function that can be used to display total of all sales.

(d) He wants to open a summary document stored at a different location from within the sheet by clicking on a text stored in a cell. How can it be done?

Ans. (a) To combine the sales data from multiple sheets into a single summary sheet, Mr. Amit can use the consolidate tool in Calc.

(b) The Menu option is Data, and the sub-menu option is consolidate to generate combined summary of all the worksheets.

(c) The SUM function can be used to display the total of all sales.

(d) To open a summary document stored at a different location, Mr. Amit can insert a hyperlink in the cell by using Insert → Hyperlink option. He can link the text to the file path of the summary document.

PRACTICAL ASSIGNMENT

1. Organize and manage data across multiple sheets in LibreOffice Calc, and create references between these sheets.Name the sheets as "Sales", "Expenses", and "Summary".

- On the "Sales" sheet, input sample sales data including columns for "Product", "Quantity Sold", and "Revenue".
- On the "Expenses" sheet, input sample expense data including columns for "Expense Type", "Amount", and "Date".
- On the "Summary" sheet, create a reference that calculates the total revenue from the "Sales" sheet using a formula.
- On the same sheet, create a reference that calculates the total expenses from the "Expenses" sheet.

Save your work.

2. Create hyperlinks to navigate between sheets and documents, and integrate external data into a LibreOffice Calc spreadsheet.

- Open LibreOffice Calc and create a new spreadsheet.
- Add two sheets to the spreadsheet. Name them "Project_Details" and "Team_Members".
- On the "Project_Details" sheet, create a table with project names and descriptions.
- On the "Team_Members" sheet, create a table with team member names and their roles.
- Create a hyperlink in the "Project_Details" sheet that links to the "Team_Members" sheet.
- Also, create a hyperlink in the "Team_Members" sheet that links back to the "Project_Details" sheet.
- Save your work.

3. Create three sheets named Jan, Feb and March. In each sheet store the attendance of employees for a month.
Apply count function to count the number of days the employees were present by counting P.

4. Add another sheet named 'Consolidated Attendance' that stores total attendance of three months and calculates the percentage.

5. Create a spreadsheet containing the list of Prime ministers of India with their tenure from the website https://knowindia.gov.in/general-information/prime-ministersof-india.php. Perform steps to extract the table from the website into a Calc Sheet and display the count of Prime Ministers of India till date.

6. Create a hyperlink to a specific cell or a range of cells on another sheet within the same spreadsheet?

Share and Review a Spreadsheet

CHAPTER 07

Sharing and reviewing a spreadsheet is a helpful way to work with others on the same document, without having to pass around multiple copies. Whether you're working on a project, creating a report, or handling data, sharing a spreadsheet allows everyone to see and edit the same file in real-time.

In LibreOffice Calc, a spreadsheet can be shared, allowing multiple users to access and edit it simultaneously. This eliminates the need to manage multiple versions of the same file, as all users work on the same document. Sharing a spreadsheet facilitates collaboration, enabling everyone to contribute, make changes, and view updates in real time.

This chapter covers how one can share spreadsheets, edit and review the shared spreadsheets and merge and compare them.

7.1 Sharing Spreadsheet

Sharing a spreadsheet is similar to teamwork, enabling collaboration with other users. To share the spreadsheet, follow the given steps:

Step 1 Create a new spreadsheet and save it with some name or open an existing one.

Step 2 Select and click on Tools → Share Spreadsheet option. The Share Document dialog window appears.

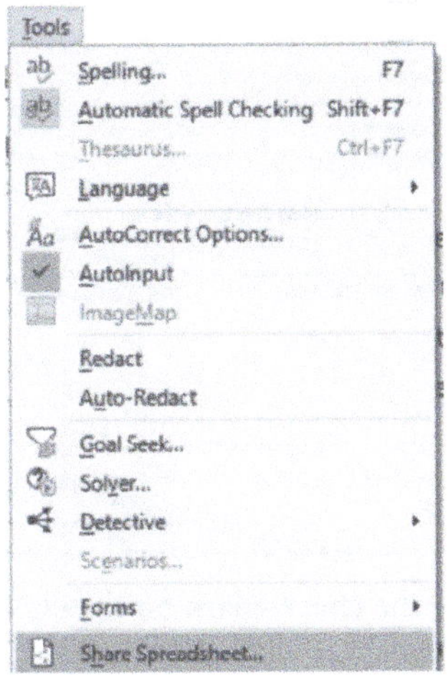

Step 3 Click on the checkbox "Share this spreadsheet with other users" to share the spreadsheet.

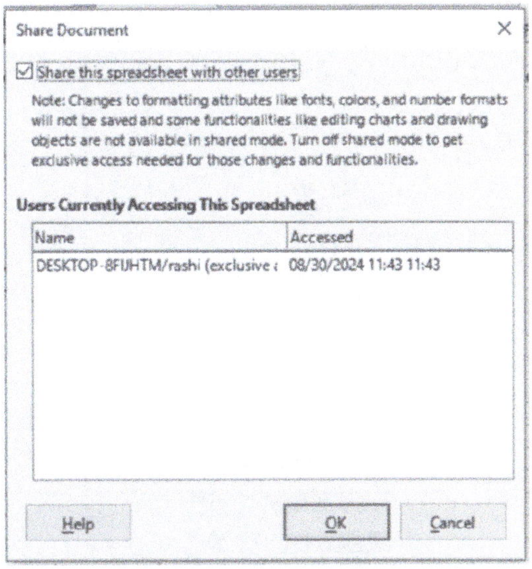

Step 4 Click on OK button. This will open the confirmation dialog window to save the spreadsheet to activate the shared mode.

Step 5 Click on Yes to continue.

Once the spreadsheet is saved, the name of the spreadsheet in the title bar will display (shared) along with the name of the spreadsheet.

7.2 Opening a Shared Spreadsheet

To open a shared spreadsheet, follow the given steps:

Step 1 While opening a spreadsheet which is a shared spreadsheet, a message will appear that the spreadsheet is in shared mode and some of the features are not available to use in this spreadsheet.

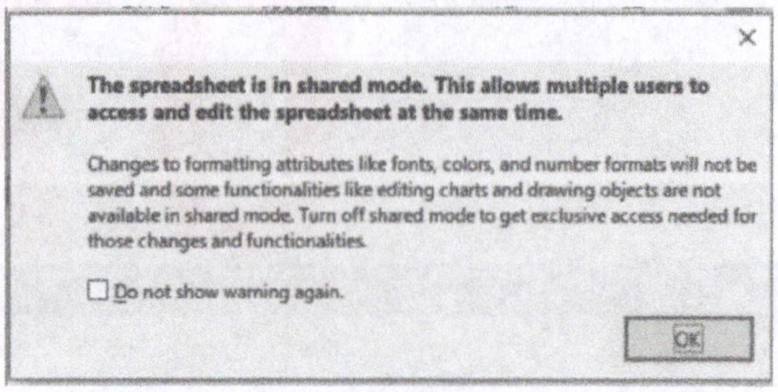

Step 2 Click on OK button to open the spreadsheet in shared mode.

Step 3 If you don't want this warning option to be displayed again, then check the mark in the checkbox 'Do not show warning again'.

Step 4 Once the spreadsheet is saved in shared mode, some of the features will become unavailable for used.

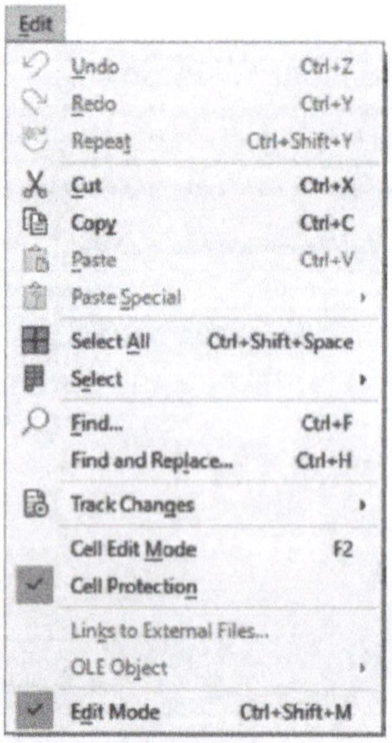

Step 5 Observe the Edit menu on the main menu bar, that shows Undo,Redo, Repeat, Paste, Links to External files, OLE Object are not available for use.

Try These 7.1

1. **What happens when you share a spreadsheet in LibreOffice Calc?**
   (a) The spreadsheet becomes read-only for all users.
   (b) Multiple users can access and edit the same document simultaneously.
   (c) The spreadsheet is automatically deleted from the system.
   (d) Only the owner can edit the spreadsheet while others can view it.
2. **Which of the following options is NOT available when working with a shared spreadsheet in LibreOffice Calc?**
   (a) Undo (b) Redo (c) Paste (d) Share Document
3. **To activate the shared mode for a spreadsheet, you need to click on the checkbox labeled "__________" in the Share Document dialog window.**
4. **When a shared spreadsheet is opened, a message will appear indicating that some features are not available, such as Undo, Redo, and __________.**

7.3 Saving a Shared Spreadsheet

Follow the steps given below to save a shared spreadsheet:

Step 1 After making changes to the shared spreadsheet, be sure to save your work before closing the file.

Step 2 If multiple users are working simultaneously and there are no conflicting changes, a message will indicate that the spreadsheet has been updated with changes saved by others.

Step 3 If there are conflicting changes, a "Resolve Conflict" dialog box will appear.

Step 4 While you are resolving conflicts, no other user can save the shared spreadsheet.

Step 5 If another user attempts to save the document and resolve conflicts, you will receive a notification that the file is locked, and you will be unable to save it.

Disabling the Shared Mode

To disable the share mode of a spreadsheet, follow the given steps:

Step 1 Open the spreadsheet in shared mode.

Step 2 Click on Tools → Share Spreadsheet from main menu bar. The Share Document dialog window appears.

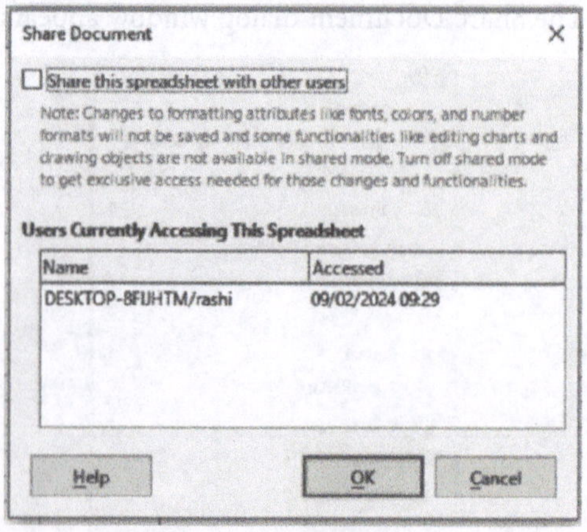

Step 3 Remove the check-mark on the check box, "Share this spreadsheet with other users".

Step 4 Click on OK button. It will display the Confirmation dialog window to disable the sharing mode. It will give warning to disable the shared mode of a spreadsheet.

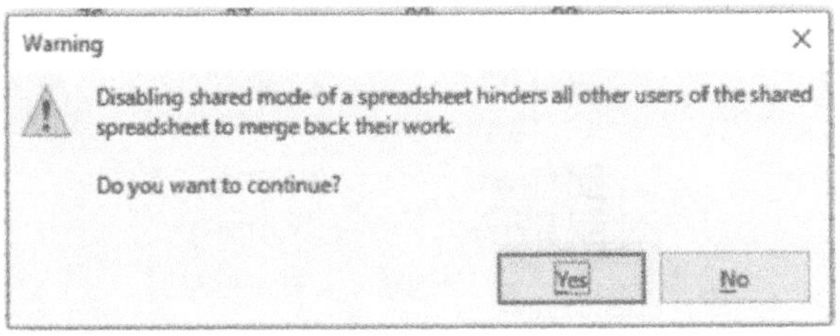

Step 5 Click on Yes to continue.

Step 6 Observe that (shared) word from the name of the spreadsheet has disappeared from the title bar of the spreadsheet.

Recording Changes

This feature in LibreOffice Calc offers various ways to track the changes made by different users in the spreadsheet.

When changes are being recorded, the sharing feature of the spreadsheet will be temporarily disabled.

To record the changes, follow the given steps:

Step 1 Open the spreadsheet or create a new one which is not in the shared mode.

Step 2 Click on Edit → Track Changes → Record option.

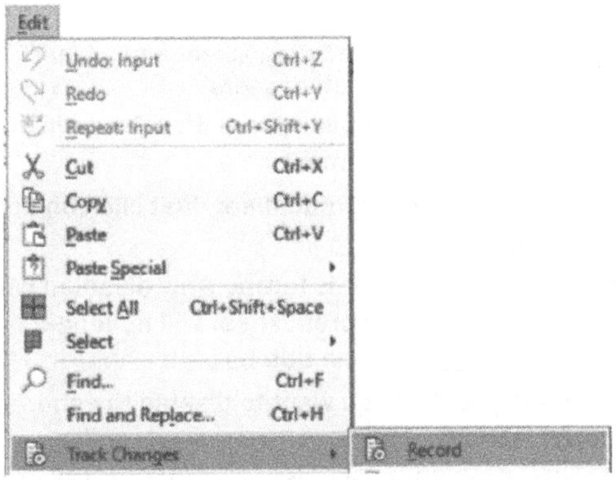

Step 3 Now change the content and observe the change. The changed content appears in red border.

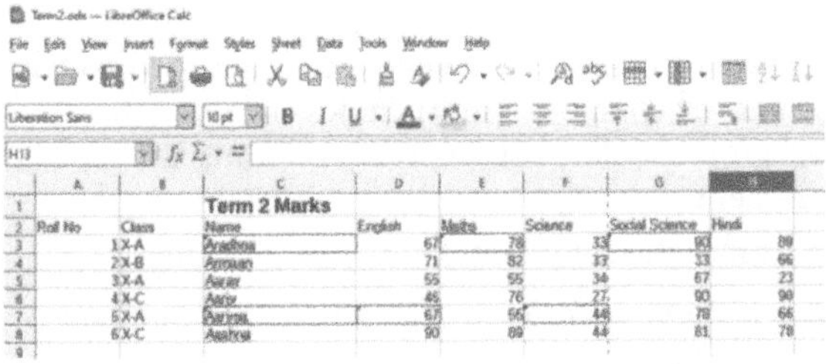

This allows other users to easily see what changes were made in the spreadsheet and who made them.

Add, Edit and Format the Comments

In Calc, comments are added automatically. Additionally, the author or reviewer can add their own comments.

Method I To add your comments, follow the given steps:

Step 1 Select the cell on which the user had changed the content.

Step 2 Click on Edit → Track Changes → Comment option. A window appears.

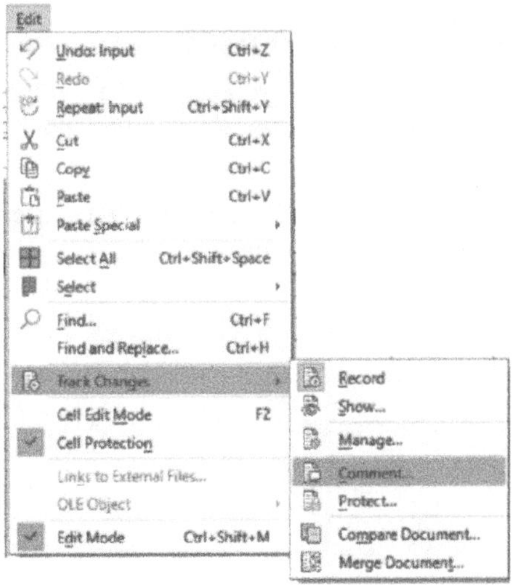

Step 3 Enter your comments.

Step 4 Click on OK button.

Step 5 Now to view the entered comment, click on the respective cell(In this case it is cell E3). It shows the complete description of the comments entered.

Method II You can also insert a comment by following the given steps:

Step 1 Click on the cell where you want to insert comments.

Step 2 Click on Insert → Comment option.

Note *This type of comments is known as notes or suggestions in the spreadsheet.*

Step 3 The box will appear to write the comment. Once this text is typed in the text box, you can observe a coloured dot in the upper-hand corner of the cell where the comment is added.

Edit and Delete a Comment

Once the comment is added, you can display, edit or delete it. To perform these operations, follow the given steps:

Step 1 Right-click on the cell where you have inserted the comments. A popup menu.

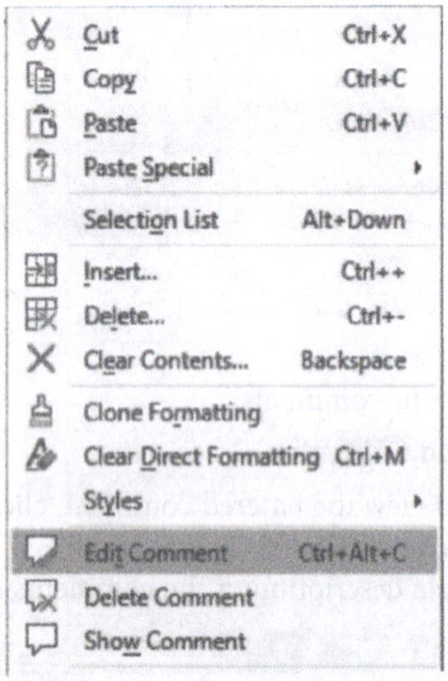

Step 2 Select the:

- "Edit Comment" option to edit the comments. The comment textbox appears to make any changes.
- "Delete Comment" option to delete the comment.
- "Show Comment" to view the comment. By selecting this option, the comments will be displayed.

Step 3 When you right-click on the cell again, you'll notice that the "Hide Comment" option is now available instead of "Show Comment." This is because, when comments are being displayed, they are already in view mode and need to be hidden.

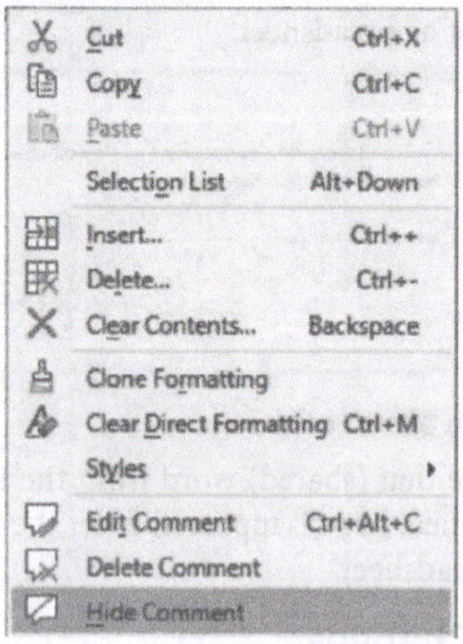

Try These 7.2

1 **What happens when you attempt to save a shared spreadsheet with conflicting changes?**
  (a) The spreadsheet will save the conflicting changes automatically.
  (b) A "Resolve Conflict" dialog box will appear.
  (c) The spreadsheet will be locked for all users.
  (d) The changes will be ignored.

2 **How do you disable the shared mode of a spreadsheet in LibreOffice Calc?**
  (a) Click on File → Save As
  (b) Click on Tools → Share Spreadsheet and uncheck "Share this spreadsheet with other users"
  (c) Click on Edit → Track Changes → Stop Recording
  (d) Click on Insert → Comment

3 **To record changes in a spreadsheet, first click on Edit → Track Changes → ________.**

4 **When the sharing feature is temporarily disabled while recording changes, the spreadsheet will no longer display the word ________ in the title bar.**

5 **What should you do if you want to disable the shared mode of a spreadsheet?**

6 **What indication will you see if a comment is added to a cell in LibreOffice Calc?**

7.4 Formatting Comment

You can format the comment box similarly to how you format cell contents. This includes changing the background color, border style, and transparency of the comment.

To format the comment, follow the give steps:

Step 1 Right-click on the cell where the comment is added.

Step 2 Click on the "Format Cells" option. The Format Cells dialog box appears.

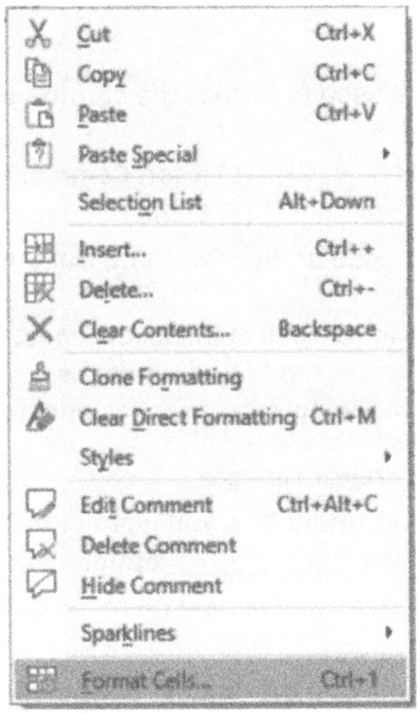

Step 3 You can apply various formatting options from the relevant tabs, such as Font, Font Effects, Alignment, Borders, Background, and Cell Protection. Adjust the font, text color, fill color, and line color for the comment box as desired.

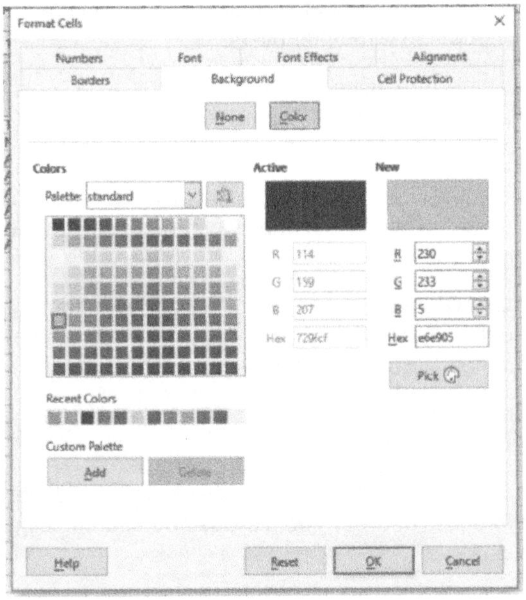

Step 4 Click on the OK button to apply the changes. The selected formatting features applied to the comment box.

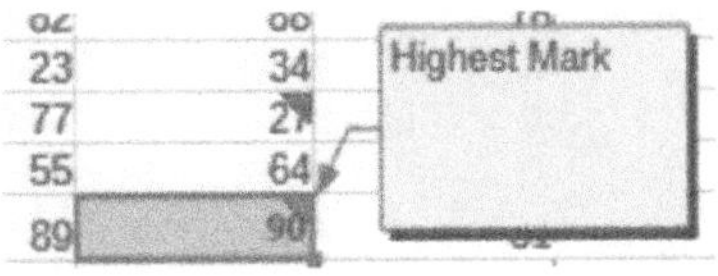

Reviewing Changes–View, Accept or Reject Changes

After editing the spreadsheet, it's time for the final review before submission. At this stage, you'll review all the changes made by the team members and decide whether to accept or reject them to finalize the spreadsheet.

Reviewing Changes

To review changes, follow the given steps:

Step 1 Click on Edit → Track Changes option.

Step 2 Click on the Show option. The Show Changes dialog box appears.

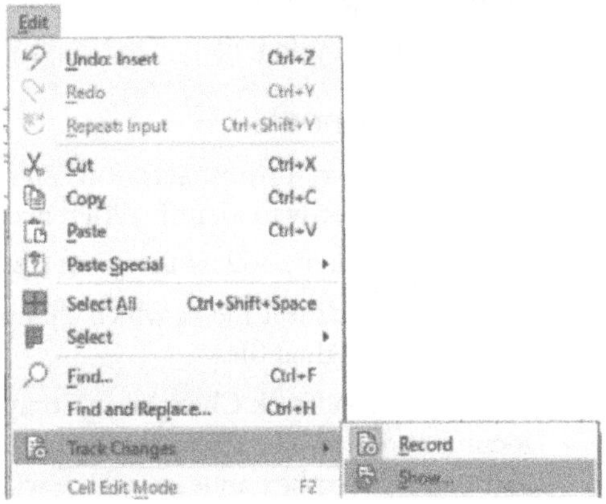

This is used to plan what all changes are to be displayed while reviewing the spreadsheet.

Managing Changes

To manage changes done using Track Changes, follow the given steps:

Step 1 Click on Edit → Track Changes → Manage. The Manage Changes dialog box appears.

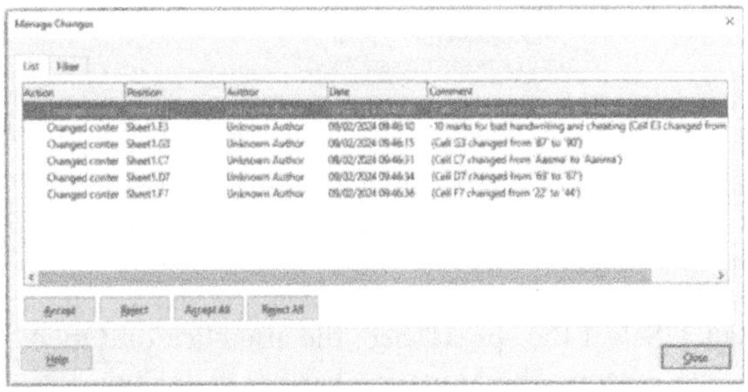

Step 2 Click on the change shown in the dialog box.

Step 3 Click on Accept or Reject or Accept All or Reject All button to review the changes.

Step 4 Click on Close button once the review is done.

Merging and Comparing

If the same spreadsheet is reviewed by different team members, you might end up with two different versions of the file.

To merge the document, follow the given steps:

Step 1 Open both the files(file before changes done and after the changes done)

Step 2 Click on Edit → Track Changes → Merge Document option. The Merge with dialog box appears.

Step 3 Select the file to be merged with.

Step 4 Click on Open button. The Manage Changes dialog box appears.

Step 5 Click on Accept All to accept all the changes. The two files will get merged.

Step 6 Click on Close button.

Comparing Documents

Rather than merging two spreadsheets, you can compare the two documents directly to identify differences.

To compare the documents, follow the given steps:

Step 1 Open the spreadsheet file in which changes are not done,i.e. the original file.

Step 2 Click on Edit → Track Changes → Compare Document option.The Compare to Original Document dialog box appears, which will allow to open the spreadsheet to be compared.

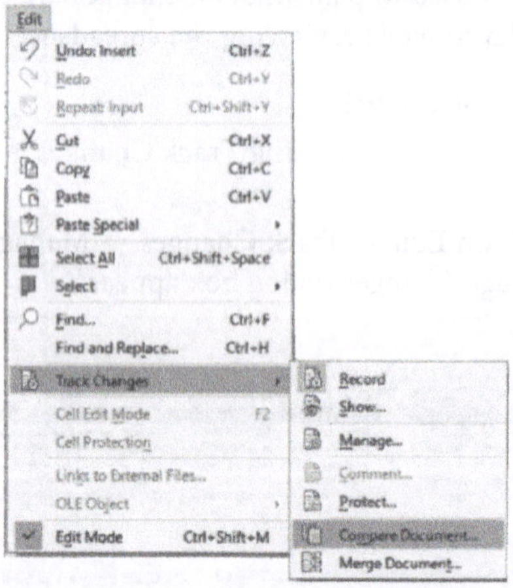

Step 3 Select the spreadsheet file and click on Open button. The Manage Changes dialog window appears to accept/reject the changes. Click on Accept button.

Step 4 Finally click on Close button to close the Manage Changes dialog box.

Try These 7.3

1. **Which option is used to format the comment box in LibreOffice Calc?**
   (a) Format Cell (b) Insert Comment
   (c) Track Changes (d) Share Document
2. **What is the purpose of the "Compare Document" feature in LibreOffice Calc?**
   (a) To merge two versions of the spreadsheet
   (b) To track changes made by different users
   (c) To identify differences between the original and changed spreadsheets
   (d) To accept or reject changes
3. **To format the comment box, you need to right-click on the cell and select the "__________" option.**
4. **To manage changes and review them, go to Edit → Track Changes → __________.**
5. **What does clicking on the "Show" option under Edit → Track Changes do?**
6. **How do you merge two versions of a spreadsheet in LibreOffice Calc?**

Summary

Sharing a spreadsheet is similar to teamwork, enabling collaboration with other users.

To share spreadsheet, Create file → Click on Tools → Share Spreadsheet → Click on Checkbox → Click OK then Yes.

Recording changes is a feature which offers various ways to track the changes made by different users in the spreadsheet.

In LibreOffice Calc, comments are added automatically. Additionally, the author or reviewer can add their own comments (Select the cell → Press "Ctrl + Alt + C").

You can format the comment box similarly to how you format cell contents.

To join multiple files into one, use Merge. To identify the differences between two files, use Compare in LibreOffice Calc.

ACTIVITY Time

ACTIVITY 1

Step 1 Open the spreadsheet and enter the data.

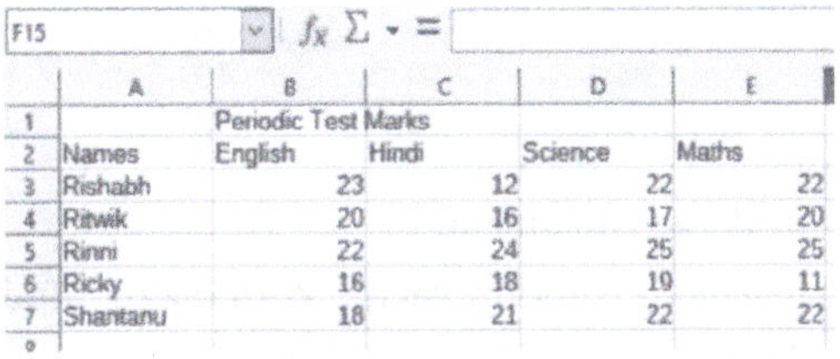

	A	B	C	D	E
1		Periodic Test Marks			
2	Names	English	Hindi	Science	Maths
3	Rishabh	23	12	22	22
4	Ritwik	20	16	17	20
5	Rinni	22	24	25	25
6	Ricky	16	18	19	11
7	Shantanu	18	21	22	22

Step 2 Select and click on Tools → Share Spreadsheet from main menu bar. This will open the Share Document dialog window. Put the checkmark on the check box, "Share this spreadsheet with other users".

Step 3 Click on OK button. It will display the Confirmation dialog window to activate the sharing mode. Click Yes to continue.

Step 4 Observe that shared is added with the name of the document in the title bar.

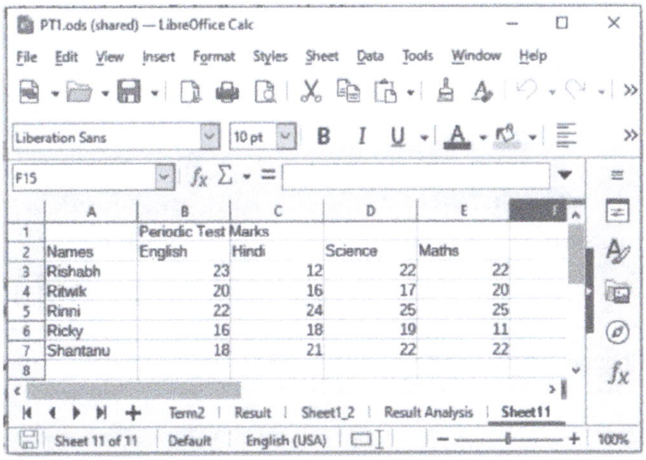

	A	B	C	D	E
1		Periodic Test Marks			
2	Names	English	Hindi	Science	Maths
3	Rishabh	23	12	22	22
4	Ritwik	20	16	17	20
5	Rinni	22	24	25	25
6	Ricky	16	18	19	11
7	Shantanu	18	21	22	22

ACTIVITY 2

Merge two files

To work on our earlier created spreadsheet PT1.ods, save the file PT1.ods with another name say PT1changed.ods and make some changes in the spreadsheet PT1changed.ods. Now, we have two files that are to be merged.

Step 1 Open the spreadsheet file PT1.ods. Also note the contents of spreadsheet PT1changed.ods before merging in another image.

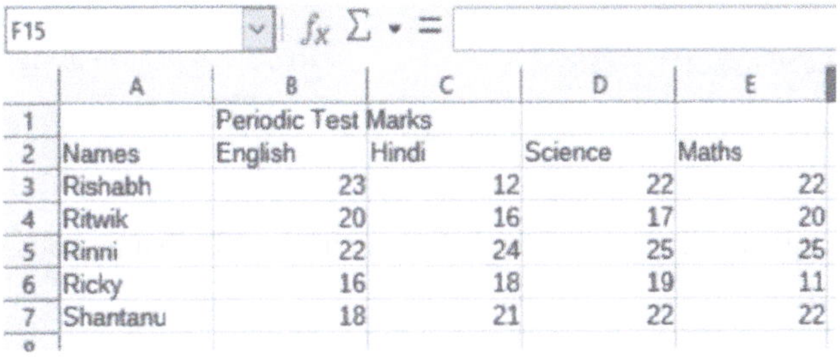

	A	B	C	D	E
1		Periodic Test Marks			
2	Names	English	Hindi	Science	Maths
3	Rishabh	23	12	22	22
4	Ritwik	20	16	17	20
5	Rinni	22	24	25	25
6	Ricky	16	18	19	11
7	Shantanu	18	21	22	22

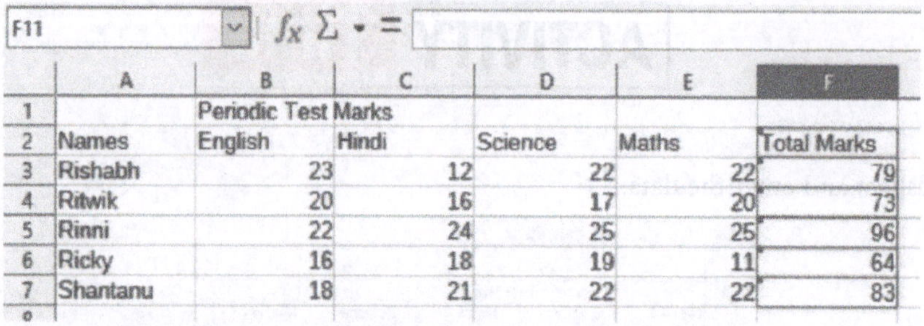

Step 2 Click on Edit → Track Changes → Merge Document.

Step 3 Select the spreadsheet file PT1changed.ods from the Merge With dialog window to open the spreadsheet PT1changed.ods to merge with PT1.ods and Click on Open button.

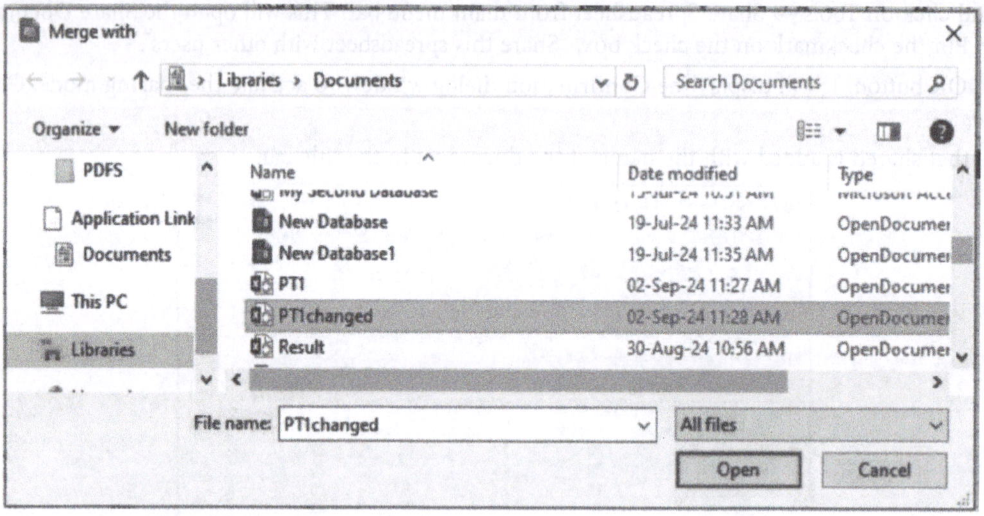

Step 4 This will open Manage Changes dialog window.

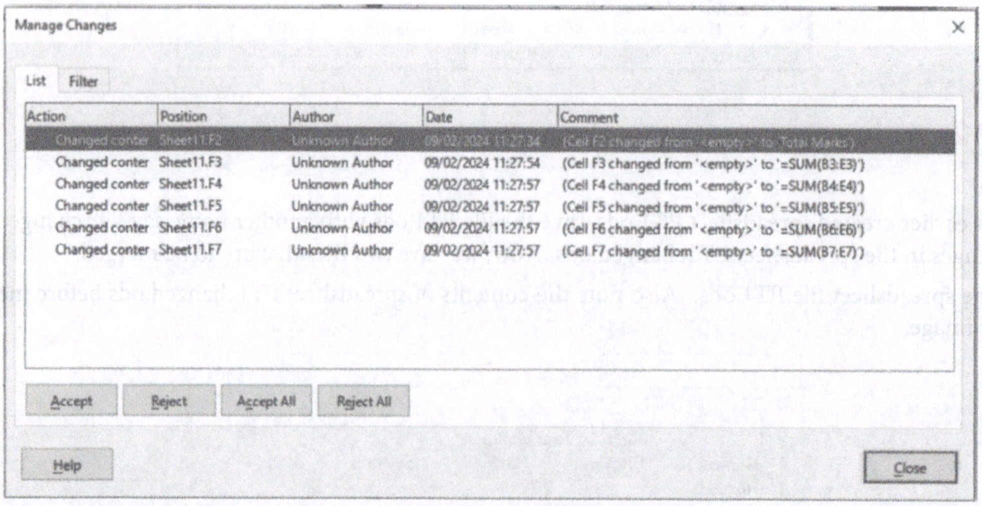

Step 5 Click on Accept All to accept all the changes which is done in the PT1changed.ods spreadsheet to the PT1.ods.

Step 6 Now open the first spreadsheet PT1.ods after merging and observe its contents.

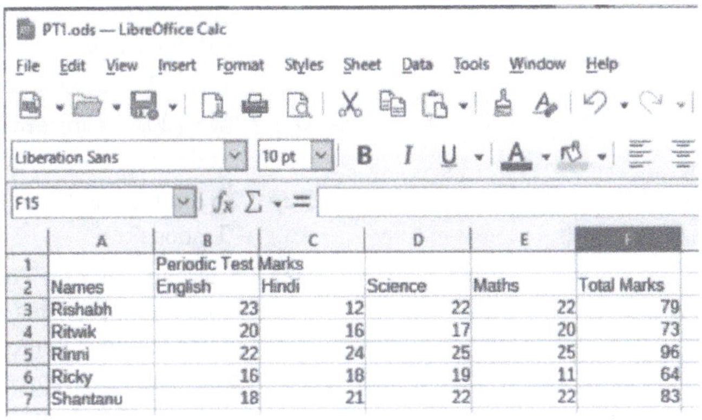

	A	B	C	D	E	F
1		Periodic Test Marks				
2	Names	English	Hindi	Science	Maths	Total Marks
3	Rishabh	23	12	22	22	79
4	Ritwik	20	16	17	20	73
5	Rinni	22	24	25	25	96
6	Ricky	16	18	19	11	64
7	Shantanu	18	21	22	22	83

NCERT FOLDER

Complete Explanations of all NCERT's Questions

A. Multiple Choice Questions

Q.1 Sharing allows to edit the spreadsheet by

(a) single user (b) different users simultaneously
(c) one by one users (d) one after other users

Q.2 Sharing spreadsheet feature allows to save the changes in

(a) multiple sheets (b) user's sheet
(c) in a same sheet (d) in different sheet

Q.3 The Recording Changes feature of LibreOffice Calc provides different ways to record the changes made by ____________in the spreadsheet.

(a) one user (b) other user
(c) the user (d) one or other users

Q.4 In Calc, the comments are added

(a) automatically (b) by author
(c) by reviewer (d) All of these

Q.5 The changes by team members in the spreadsheet can be accepted or rejected by

(a) the team members (b) any of the user
(c) owner (d) other users

Answers

1. (b) 2. (a) 3. (d) 4. (d) 5. (c)

B. State Whether the Following Statements are True or False

Q.1 Spreadsheet cannot be shared to work with more than one user.

Q.2 Some of the features becomes unavailable when the spreadsheet is in shared mode.

Q.3 You can record changes in the spreadsheet when the spreadsheet is opened in shared mode.

Q.4 File menu is used to Record changes for the spreadsheet.

Q.5 You can add a note or suggestion in the spreadsheet using Insert Comment.

Q.6 Formatting comment can be used to change the font colour of the comment.

Answers

1. False 2. True 3. False 4. False 5. True 6. True

C. Fill in the Blanks

Q.1 The title bar of the document shows ___________ along with the filename for the shared mode of the spreadsheet.

Q.2 The shared mode spreadsheet allows ______ users to access and edit the spreadsheet at the same time.

Q.3 Recording changes automatically ________ the shared mode of a spreadsheet.

Q.4 Click on Edit menu, Track Changes and then select _________ to record the changes in the spreadsheet.

Q.5 The border color of the changed cell will be _______.

Q.6 ________ is used to add notes or suggestions to a celling a spreadsheet.

Q.7 The comment box can be formatted just like formatting the _______

Answers

1. Shared	2. Many
3. Turn off	4. Record
5. Red	6. Comment
7. Cell contents	

D. Answer the Following Questions

Q.1 Define the terms (a) Sharing Spreadsheet (b) Record changes

Ans. (a) Sharing a spreadsheet is just like a teamwork to work in collaboration with other users.

(b) Record Changes provides different ways to record the changes made by one or other users in the spreadsheet. While recording the changes, the spreadsheet will turn off its shared feature.

Q.2 Write the steps to perform (a) Sharing Spreadsheet (b) Record changes

Ans. (a) The following are the steps to share the spreadsheet.

Step 1 Open a new spreadsheet and save it with some name.

Step 2 Select and click on Tools → Share Spreadsheet from main menu bar. This will open the Share Document which can be used to enable or disable sharing option.

Step 3 Click on the checkbox "Share this spreadsheet with other users" to share the spreadsheet and click on OK button.

Step 4 Click on Yes to continue.

Step 5 Once the spreadsheet is saved, the name of the spreadsheet in the title bar will display (shared) along with the name of the spreadsheet.

(b) Follow the below steps for recording changes:

Step 1 To enable the Record changes, first disable the shared mode of spreadsheet.

Step 2 To disable the shared mode, open the spreadsheet "Test.ods".

Step 3 Select and click on Tools → Share Spreadsheet from main menu bar. This will open the Share Document dialog window. Remove the check-mark on the check box, "Share this spreadsheet with other users", and click on OK button.

Q.3 Which menu is used to perform the functions (a) Track Changes (b) Saving Spreadsheet?

Ans. (a) Edit menu (b) File menu

Q.4 What do you understand by reviewing the changes in the spreadsheet?

Ans. Reviewing changes in a spreadsheet means tracking, accepting, or rejecting edits made by users. In LibreOffice Calc, this is done using Edit → Track Changes → Manage Changes to view modifications.

Q.5 Differentiate between Merging and Comparing Spreadsheet.

Ans. Merging a spreadsheet in LibreOffice Calc combines data from multiple shared copies into one, integrating changes.

Comparing a spreadsheet highlights differences between two versions, showing modifications, additions, or deletions.

EXAM PATTERN EXERCISE

Including Competency Based Questions

Multiple Choice Questions

1 A colored border, with ________, appears around a cell where changes are made in a shared worksheet. **CBSE 2023**

(a) a dot in the upper left-hand corner
(b) a dot in the lower left-hand corner
(c) a cross in the upper left-hand corner
(d) a cross in the upper right-hand corner

2 ________ feature adds data arranged in a group of cells in Calc, with labels for columns and/or rows. **CBSE 2023**

(a) Average (b) Subtotal (c) Goal seek (d) Solver

3 Reviewers and authors can add their ________ to explain their changes in the cell of Spreadsheet. **CBSE SQP 2022-23**

(a) Comments (b) Hyperlink
(c) Worksheet (d) Macros

4 Spreadsheet software can find the changes by ________ sheets. **CBSE SQP 2023-24**

(a) Changing
(b) Comparing
(c) Renaming
(d) Editing

5 __________ feature of Calc helps to track what data was changed, when the change was made, who made the change and in which cell the change has occurred. **CBSE 2023**

(a) Record Changes (b) Edit record
(c) Change record (d)Macro

6 What does sharing a spreadsheet in LibreOffice Calc allow you to do?

(a) Only view the spreadsheet
(b) Edit and access the spreadsheet simultaneously with multiple users
(c) Delete the spreadsheet
(d) Encrypt the spreadsheet

7 Which option in LibreOffice Calc is used to disable the shared mode of a spreadsheet?

(a) Edit → Track Changes (b) Tools → Share Spreadsheet
(c) File → Save As (d) Insert → Comment

8 What will happen if you save a shared spreadsheet with conflicting changes?

(a) The changes will be automatically merged.
(b) A "Resolve Conflict" dialog box will appear.
(c) The spreadsheet will be locked for all users.
(d) The changes will be discarded.

9 Which of the following features is not available in a shared spreadsheet?

(a) Undo (b) Redo
(c) Share Document (d) Paste

10 How do you format a comment box in LibreOffice Calc?

(a) Click on Insert → Comment
(b) Right-click on the cell and select "Format Cells"
(c) Use the "Track Changes" menu
(d) Use the "Merge Document" option

11 To view all changes made in a spreadsheet, which option should you select?

(a) Edit → Track Changes → Manage
(b) Edit → Track Changes → Record
(c) Edit →Track Changes → Show
(d) Edit → Track Changes → Compare Document

12 What happens to the spreadsheet's title bar when you enable shared mode?

(a) It shows "locked."
(b) It displays "(shared)" alongside the spreadsheet name.
(c) It displays "Read-Only."
(d) It displays "(encrypted)."

13 Which dialog box allows you to manage and review changes made by different users?

(a) Compare to Original Document
(b) Manage Changes
(c) Share Document
(d) Show Changes

14 What does the "Compare Document" feature do?

(a) Merges two versions of the spreadsheet
(b) Compares the original and changed spreadsheets to identify differences
(c) Encrypts the document
(d) Formats comments

15 To add your own comments in Calc, select .... → Track changes → Comment. **CBSE 2025**

(a) File (b) Edit
(c) Insert (d) Data

16 Which option is used to accept or reject changes in LibreOffice Calc?

(a) Edit → Track Changes → Show
(b) Edit → Track Changes → Manage
(c) Edit → Track Changes → Record
(d) Edit → Track Changes → Compare Document

17 To add a new sheet in the spreadsheet, click on the .... sign located at the left bottom of the spreadsheet. **CBSE 2025**

(a) * (b) /
(c) % (d) +

18 How can you disable the shared mode in LibreOffice Calc?

(a) Click on File → Save As
(b) Click on Tools → Share Spreadsheet and uncheck the share option
(c) Click on Edit → Track Changes → Record
(d) Click on Insert → Comment

19 Which feature temporarily disables sharing while changes are being recorded?

(a) Track Changes (b) Compare Documents
(c) Merge Documents (d) Share Document

20 What does the "Show Comment" option do?

(a) Hides the comment (b) Displays the comment
(c) Edits the comment (d) Deletes the comment

21 Krish and Kritika have done a survey of age wise literacy rates of their locality as a school project, which they have created in a Spreadsheet. They both want to work simultaneously to complete it on time. Which option they should use to access the same Spreadsheet to speed up their work. **CBSE SQP 2020-21, Competency Based Que.**

(a) Consolidate Worksheet (b) Shared Worksheet
(c) Link Worksheet (d) Lock Worksheet

22 Raj has created a worksheet where he has added all the information of his employees. He wants every employee to go through the worksheet and update their address and phone number, if required. He also would like to know the changes done by his employees. Which feature of spreadsheet he should enable to see the changes made by his employees? **CBSE SQP 2021-22 Term I, Competency Based Que.**

(a) Macro (b) Link Workbook
(c) Change Worksheet (d) Track Changes

23 **Sunita is making a project in spreadsheets. Her friend has told her how to rename a spreadsheet as it will help her identify the worksheet data easily. She was very excited and told the same to her brother. Her brother told her that in spreadsheets, a worksheet can be renamed using _______ ways.**

CBSE SQP 2021-22 Term I, Competency Based Que.

(a) 2 (b) 3 (c) 4 (d) 1

24 **Sahil and his partners have created a list of their company employees in one of the spreadsheets in the office. Now the rest of the task they want to complete from home. Which option they should use to access the same Spreadsheet from home?**

CBSE SQP 2023-24, Competency Based Que.

(a) Consolidate Worksheet (b) Link Worksheet
(c) Merge Worksheet (d) Lock Worksheet

25 **Rama and two of her friends are doing survey of genderwise employment rates of their locality as a school project using Spreadsheet. They all want to work simultaneously to complete it on time. What option they should use to access the same Spreadsheet to speed up their work.**

CBSE 2021-22 Term I, Competency Based Que.

(a) Consolidate Worksheet (b) Shared Worksheet
(c) Link Worksheet (d) Lock Worksheet

26 **Kawal and his friends are working on a Spreadsheet for entering data and updating records. They wish to keep a track of changes.Which of the following options will help in knowing whomade the changes and what done in the spreadsheet?** **CBSE 2024, Competency Based Que.**

(a) View changes (b) Record changes
(c) Store changes (d) Track changes

Answers

1. (c)	2. (b)	3. (a)	4. (b)	5. (a)
6. (b)	7. (b)	8. (b)	9. (d)	10. (b)
11. (c)	12. (b)	13. (b)	14. (b)	15. (b)
16. (b)	17. (d)	18. (b)	19. (a)	20. (b)
21. (b)	22. (d)	23. (b)	24. (b)	25. (b)
26. (b)				

Very Short Answer Type Questions

1 **Why do we need to merge worksheets?** **CBSE 2023**

Ans. We merge worksheets to consolidate data from multiple sources into one place, making it easier to analyze, compare, and work efficiently. This reduces errors, simplifies calculations, and ensures accurate, up-to-date information for decision-making.

2 **What should you do if you don't want to see the shared mode warning message again?**

Ans. Check the box labeled 'Do not show warning again'.

3 **How can you format the background color of a comment box?**

Ans. Right-click on the cell, select "Format Cells," and adjust the Background color in the Format Cells dialog box.

4 **What does the "Record" option under Track Changes do?**

Ans. It starts recording the changes made to the spreadsheet.

5 **How do you view the comments entered in a cell?**

Ans. Click on the cell where the comment is added to view the comment.

6 **What does clicking "Accept All" do in the Manage Changes dialog box?**

Ans. It accepts all changes made to the spreadsheet.

7 **Which menu option allows you to manage changes done by multiple users?**

Ans. Edit → Track Changes → Manage

8 **What feature is used to compare two different versions of a spreadsheet?**

Ans. Compare Document

9 **How can you delete a comment from a cell?**

Ans. Right-click on the cell, select "Delete Comment" from the popup menu.

10 **What will happen if you try to save a shared spreadsheet with conflicting changes?**

Ans. A "Resolve Conflict" dialog box will appear.

11 **How can you format the text color of a comment box?**

Ans. Right-click on the cell, choose "Format Cells," and adjust the text color in the Format Cells dialog box.

Short Answer Type Questions

1 **What are the benefits of sharing a spreadsheet?**

CBSE SQP 2024-25

Ans. A shared spreadsheet is a same sheet that can be accessed by more than one user and can allow them to make changes simultaneously on it.

It saves the trouble of keeping track of multiple copies of the same spreadsheet. Sharing allows working in collaboration so that everyone can contribute, make changes and view it.

2 **Describe the process of sharing a spreadsheet in LibreOffice Calc.**

Ans. To share a spreadsheet, follow the given steps:

Step 1 First create a new spreadsheet or open an existing one.

Step 2 Click on Tools → Share Spreadsheet to open the Share Document dialog window.

Step 3 Check the box "Share this spreadsheet with other users" and click OK.

Step 4 Confirm the action by clicking on Yes. The spreadsheet title bar will then display "(shared)" to indicate it is in shared mode.

3 Explain how to open and work with a shared spreadsheet in LibreOffice Calc.

Ans. To open and work with a shared spreadsheet in LibreOffice Calc, follow the given steps:

Step 1 When opening a shared spreadsheet, a message will appear indicating that the spreadsheet is in shared mode and some features may be unavailable.

Step 2 Click OK to proceed. To prevent seeing this warning again, you can check the box 'Do not show warning again'. Note that some features like Undo, Redo, and Paste will not be available in shared mode.

4 How do you manage changes made to a spreadsheet using Track Changes?

Ans. To manage changes made to the spreadsheet, follow the given steps:

Step 1 Click on Edit → Track Changes → Manage. The Manage Changes dialog box will appear showing all changes.

Step 2 Click on a change to select it, then choose Accept, Accept All, or Reject, Reject All to process the changes as needed.

Step 3 Finally, click on Close to exit the dialog box.

5 What steps are involved in disabling the shared mode of a spreadsheet?

Ans. To disable shared mode, follow the given steps:

Step 1 Open the spreadsheet in shared mode.

Step 2 Click on Tools → Share Spreadsheet.

Step 3 In the Share Document dialog window, uncheck the box "Share this spreadsheet with other users."

Step 4 Click on OK to open the confirmation dialog and click Yes to proceed. The "(shared)" label will be removed from the title bar of the spreadsheet.

6 Describe the process for comparing two versions of a spreadsheet using LibreOffice Calc.

Ans. The process for comparing two versions of a spreadsheet using LibreOffice Calc is as follows:

Step 1 Open the original (unmodified) spreadsheet file.

Step 2 Click on Edit → Track Changes → Compare Document.

Step 3 In the Compare to Original Document dialog box, select the file to compare with and click Open. The Manage Changes dialog window will appear, allowing you to accept or reject the identified changes.

Step 4 Click on Accept to incorporate the changes and Close to finish.

7 You and a colleague are working on the same spreadsheet. How can you handle conflicts if both of you make changes to the same cell?

Competency Based Que.

Ans. If you and your colleague make conflicting changes to the same cell, a "Resolve Conflict" dialog box will appear when saving the spreadsheet. Use this dialog to review and resolve the conflicting changes.

While resolving conflicts, no other user can save the spreadsheet, and you will be notified if another user tries to save or resolve conflicts while you are working.

8 You want to track and review changes made to a spreadsheet by multiple users and finalize the document. How would you proceed?

Competency Based Que.

Ans. First, ensure that Track Changes is enabled by clicking Edit → Track Changes → Record.

After all changes are made, review them by clicking Edit → Track Changes → Show to display the changes. Use Edit → Track Changes → Manage to accept.

PRACTICAL ASSIGNMENT

1. Assume that you are captain of your school cricket team. Prepare the budget in the spreadsheet for the current academic year. Turn ON the feature Track Changes → Record and ask other team members to make necessary changes in the spreadsheet.
2. Create a spreadsheet that contains personal details of 10 of your friends. Save the spreadsheet with some other name. Keep the worksheet in shared mode. Start Track Chnages. Tell your friends to add their details in it. View the changed sheet and accept the changes done to the spreadsheet. Save it.
3. Anushka and Niyaz have been made the class representative. Anushka has been asked to collect the class assignments for the various subjects. Create a spreadsheet to store the roll number,name of the students and subject names. Perform the following operations so that Niyaz can access the file:

   (a) Enable Track changes

   (b) Add comment to show the date on which the assignment has been submitted.

   (c) Share the document with the class teacher.
4. Carry out the same exercise as the previous one but this time, do not use the Record Changes mode. Rather let the four student make changes in individual documents and then compare them with previous year's worksheet.

   Paste the four worksheets of students and the final worksheet after accepting/rejecting the changes.

SELF ASSESSMENT

Multiple Choice Questions

1. Which feature of LibreOffice Calc allows you to automate repetitive tasks?
   (a) Goal Seek (b) Macros (c) Solver (d) Subtotal
2. In LibreOffice Calc, which function is used to merge data from multiple sheets into a single summary?
   (a) Goal Seek (b) Scenarios (c) Solver (d) Consolidate
3. Which feature of Calc helps in determining the specific input needed to achieve a desired output by adjusting one variable?
   (a) Solver (b) Goal Seek (c) Subtotals (d) Data Consolidation
4. What is the purpose of referencing data from other sheets in Calc?
   (a) To manually re-enter data for accuracy (b) To reduce time and errors by linking data directly
   (c) To avoid any changes in the original data (d) To increase the number of sheets
5. What does a relative hyperlink depend on?
   (a) The full path of the file's location (b) The location of the currently active spreadsheet
   (c) The name of the document being referenced (d) The size of the spreadsheet
6. What is the main advantage of sharing a spreadsheet in LibreOffice Calc?
   (a) Reduces the number of versions of the document
   (b) Prevents any changes to the document
   (c) Automatically deletes old versions
   (d) Enables the Undo function for all users
7. When tracking changes in LibreOffice Calc, what happens to the shared mode?
   (a) It remains active (b) It is temporarily disabled
   (c) It locks the file for editing (d) It highlights all comments
8. Which of the following actions cannot be captured when recording a macro in LibreOffice Calc?
   (a) Typing data into a cell (b) Selecting cells using the keyboard
   (c) Opening windows (d) Applying a formula to a range of cells
9. What is the default name of the macro when you save it in LibreOffice Calc?
   (a) Main (b) Macro1
   (c) DefaultMacro (d) StandardModule1
10. Where are user-created macros stored by default in LibreOffice Calc?
    (a) LibreOffice Macros Library (b) My Macros
    (c) Standard Macros (d) Calc Macros Library
11. Rohan wants to invest 50,000 across two mutual funds with different interest rates. To determine the best investment distribution to maximize his return, which Calc tool should he use? **Competency Based Que.**
    (a) Solver (b) Macros (c) Goal Seek (d) Subtotals
12. You need to predict how many units of a product need to be produced to meet a specific revenue target. Which tool in Calc will help you adjust the number of units to achieve this goal? **Competency Based Que.**
    (a) Goal Seek (b) Solver (c) Subtotals (d) Scenarios
13. If you want to reference data from another sheet using the mouse and keyboard, what is the first step? **Competency Based Que.**
    (a) Press the equals sign (=) on your keyboard
    (b) Switch to the referenced spreadsheet first
    (c) Select the target cell in the current spreadsheet
    (d) Click the formula icon on the toolbar

14. You are working with a team on a shared spreadsheet in LibreOffice Calc. After making some edits, you attempt to save the document, but a notification appears stating that another user has already saved changes. What will likely happen next? **Competency Based Que.**

(a) Your changes will overwrite the other user's edits
(b) A "Resolve Conflict" dialog box will appear, allowing you to manage the conflicting changes
(c) The file will lock automatically, and no one can save it
(d) Your changes will be saved without any issues

15. You have created a macro that automatically formats a table in your spreadsheet. Which of the following methods will you use to apply this macro to a new sheet in the same workbook? **Competency Based Que.**

(a) Open the new sheet, and the macro will apply automatically
(b) Use Tools → Macros → Run Macro, select the macro, and click Run
(c) Use File → Save As and save the macro
(d) Macros cannot be applied to different sheets

Very Short Answer Type Questions

16. What is the purpose of the Goal Seek tool in LibreOffice Calc?
17. How does the SUBTOTAL function differ from the Subtotal tool in Calc?
18. Explain the difference between an absolute hyperlink and a relative hyperlink.
19. Explain how you can review changes made by other users in a shared spreadsheet in LibreOffice Calc.
20. What is the difference between Goal Seek and Consolidate data?

Short Answer Type Questions

21. Explain how you would use the Solver tool in LibreOffice Calc to optimize a financial investment based on multiple constraints. Describe the process, including the key parameters you need to set.
22. Describe the steps to insert a sheet from a different spreadsheet into your current spreadsheet.
23. Describe the steps to disable the shared mode of a spreadsheet in LibreOffice Calc.
24. Explain the process of recording, saving, and running a macro in LibreOffice Calc. What are some actions that cannot be recorded by the macro recorder, and how can you organize macros in different libraries or modules?
25. Imagine you are a project manager organizing a team for a construction project. You have a spreadsheet in LibreOffice Calc that tracks the materials ordered from different suppliers. Each supplier has delivered materials multiple times, and you need to summarize the total amount of materials delivered by each supplier.

(a) Which tool in Calc can be used to organize the data and summarize the deliveries?
(b) Which functions can you apply to this summarized data to calculate totals or averages?
(c) Which menu option would you use to access and apply this tool?
(d) What is the purpose of the (-) or (+) signs that appear when summarizing data in this way?

Answers

1. (b)	**2.** (d)	**3.** (a)	**4.** (b)	**5.** (b)	**6.** (a)	**7.** (b)	**8.** (c)	**9.** (b)	**10.** (b)
11. (a)	**12.** (a)	**13.** (a)	**14.** (b)	**15.** (b)					

Unit 3

Database Management System Using LibreOffice Base

This chapter will introduce you to database management using LibreOffice Base, an open-source database tool. You'll learn about fundamental database concepts, how to create and manage databases, and how to retrieve and present data effectively. By the end of this chapter, you'll be able to efficiently manage data and generate insightful reports.

Introduction to Database Management System

CHAPTER 08

A database is a collection of related information, and a database system is a software-based tool for organizing, maintaining, and accessing that information. We interact with them in almost all spheres of life, from searching for a word in a dictionary to withdrawing money from an ATM.

8.1 Data and Information

Data consists of raw facts, which can relate to people, places, activities, or things. These facts may be stored in various forms, such as text, graphics, audio, or video.

e.g. Student marks, weights, prices, costs, quantities of items sold, employee names, product names, addresses, tax codes, and registration numbers.

Information is the processed or organized form of data. If the data is incorrect or inaccurate, the resulting information may also be flawed.

e.g. The marks obtained by students and their roll numbers are data, whereas the report card is the information.

8.2 Database Concept

A database is a collection of logically related information/data, which is available for one or more users organised in a way, so that it can be easily accessed, managed and updated. It is actually a place, where related piece of information is stored and various operations can be performed on it by the user.

A database is basically a computer based record/data/information keeping system. Data is raw, unorganised facts and entities relevant to the user need to be processed such as a digital representation of text, numbers, graphical images or sound. The data are stored in such a way that they are independent of the programs used by the people for accessing the data.

8.3 Database Management System (DBMS)

A Database Management System is a set of programs that enables users to define, create and maintain the database and provides controlled access to this database.

The primary goal of a DBMS is to provide a way to store and retrieve database information that is both convenient and efficient. Data in a database can be added, deleted, changed, sorted, searched, etc., using a DBMS. e.g. MySQL, Ingres, MS-Access, Oracle, etc., are the most popular DBMS softwares. The purpose of a DBMS is to bridge the gap between the information and data. The data stored in memory or on a disk must be converted to usable information.

Advantages of DBMS

Various advantages of DBMS are as follows

(i) **Reduced Data Redundancy** Duplication of data is known as data redundancy. In the database approach, ideally each data item is stored only at one place in the database, thus reducing redundancy.

(ii) **Elimination of Inconsistency** Various copies of the same data may no longer be same. It causes mis-matching of data and this mis-matching known as data inconsistency.

The main advantage of avoiding duplication is the elimination of inconsistencies that tend to be present in redundant data files. Any redundancy that exist in the DBMS is controlled and the system ensures that these multiple copies are consistent.

(iii) **Data Sharing** The data stored in the database can be shared among multiple users or application programs.

(iv) **Data Integrity** It means that the data contained in the database is accurate and consistent. Enforcing data integrity is much easier because data is stored at single location. Integrity constraints or consistency rules can be applied to database so that the correct data values can be entered into the database.

(v) **Data Security** Data is very important to an organisation and may also be confidential. Such confidential data must not be accessed by unauthorised persons. In database, different levels of security could be implemented for various types of data and operations.

(vi) **Backup and Recovery** The DBMS provides the most vital feature known as backup and recovery. It is responsible for backup and recover the data from any hardware and software failures.

(vii) **Concurrency Control** A DBMS schedules concurrent access of data in such a way that multiple users can access the data at the same time and no one is aware about the presence of the other.

(viii) **Ease of Application Development** The application programmer needs to develop the application programs according to the user's needs. The other issues like concurrent access, security, data integrity, etc., are handled by the database itself. This makes the application development an easier task.

Disadvantages of a Database/DBMS

There are many advantages of database, but database also have some minor disadvantages. These disadvantages are as follows:

(i) **Cost of Hardware and Software** Through the use of a database system, new costs are generated due to additional hardware and software requirements.

(ii) **Complexity** A database system creates additional complexity and requirements.

(iii) **Database Failures** If database is corrupted due to power failure or it is corrupted on the storage media, then our valuable data may be lost or the system will stop working.

(iv) **Lower Efficiency** A database system is a multi-user software, which is less efficient.

Note • ***Multiple mismatching copies of the same data is known as data inconsistency.*** *If a field value is stored in two places in the database, then storage space is wasted and changing the data in one place will not cause data inconsistency.*

• *Data redundancy leads to data inconsistency.*

Try These 8.1

1 Which of the following is not an example of data?
(a) Report Card
(b) Pay Slip
(c) Student Grades
(d) Bar Chart

2 A _______ is an organized collection of logically related data items that can be added, modified, deleted, or retrieved based on user needs.

3 A DBMS helps reduce ______ by ensuring that data changes are automatically reflected across all related tables.

4 What is the advantage of data consistency in a DBMS?

8.4 Data Models

Data model can be defined as an integrated collection of concepts for describing and manipulating data, relationship between data and constraints on the data in an organisation. A data model provides a way to describe the design of a database at the internal, conceptual and external level. The three data models, that are used for database management system:

Hierarchical Data Model

In this data model, data is organised in a tree-like structure. There is a hierarchy of parent and child data segments.

It comprises a set of records connected to one another through links. The link is an association between two or more records. To create links between these records, the hierarchical model uses parent child relationship. In a hierarchical database, the parent child relationship is One-to-Many.

This restricts a child segment to having only one parent segment but a parent segment can have one or more child segments. Top of the structure consists of a single segment and known as root segment. The operations that can be performed on hierarchical model are retrieval, insertion, deletion and modification of records.

The following figure represents a hierarchical structure:

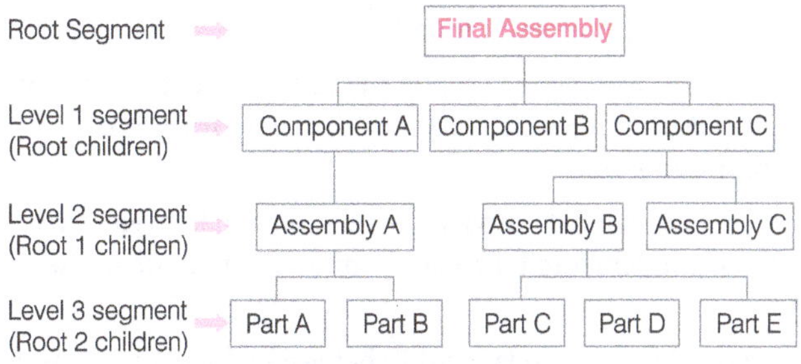

Hierarchical data model

Network Data Model

In network data model, the data is represented by collection of records and relationships among data by links like hierarchical data model.

The only difference is that in the network data model, records are organised as arbitrary graphs rather than trees. In this model, the parent child relationship is Many-to-Many, i.e. one child segment can have multiple parent segments.

e.g. a supplier S1 supplies three items I4, I5 and I7 in the quantities 20, 20 and 10 respectives. Now, this relationship has been shown in the following figure

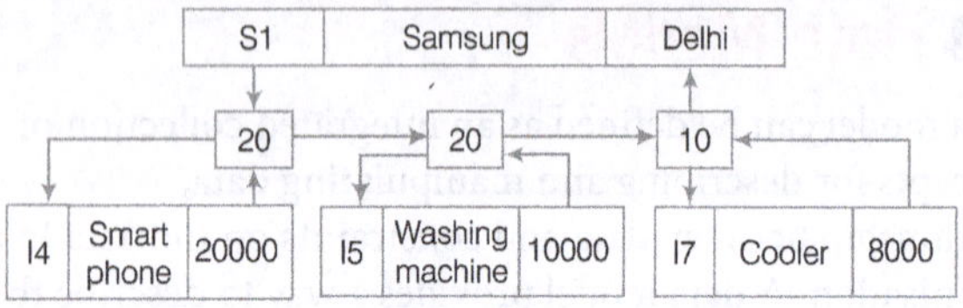

Network data model

The operations that can be performed on a network model include find, insert, delete, modify, etc. The inserting or removing records involve connect, disconnect and reconnect operations.

Relational Data Model

The relational data model uses a collection of tables to represent both data and the relationship among data. A table is a collection of records and each record in a table contains the same fields.

Each record (rows) in the table represents an entity and a field (columns) represents an attribute of entity. The tables are referred to as relations in a relational data model.

Properties of relational data model

(i) Values are atomic.

(ii) Each row is unique.

(iii) Column values are of the same kind.

(iv) The sequence of columns and rows is insignificant.

(v) Each column has a unique name.

e.g. The following figure shows the relational data model of book-publication, which contains the tables for Book, Author and Publisher.

In the relational data model, the relationship between two tables is implemented through a common attribute in the tables.

In below figure, the relationship between tables Author and Book is implemented by the common attribute Author_id and the relation between tables Publisher and Book is implemented by common attribute Pub_id.

Table : Author

Author_id	Name	Dob
A001	Henry Korth	6/7/55
A002	Ivan Byross	23/6/65
A003	R.J. Patel	10/10/75

Table : Publisher

Pub_id	Name	City
P001	TTM	Delhi
P002	BPB	Mumbai
P003	Atul	Ahmedabad

Book_id	Author_id	Pub_id	Book_title
B001	A001	P001	DBMS
B002	A002	P002	SQL,PL/SQL
B003	A003	P003	Programming in C

Table : Book

Relational data model

8.5 Relational Database Model

Relational database model is the most common type of database model proposed in **1970** by **E.F. Codd.** It organizes data into tables with rows and columns, establishing relationships between tables through shared fields.

That's why this model is termed as relational database model.

Relational Database Terminology

Let's familiarize with key terminology used in Relational Database Management System (RDBMS).

- **Entity** An entity is a real-world object about which information is to be stored in a database. The details associated with an entity, such as admission number, name, and DOB etc., are called **attributes.** These attributes are represented as columns in a database table.
- **Table** A table is basically a collection of logically related records. It is organized as a set of columns, and can have any number of rows.
- **Field/Columns/Attributes** A field is the smallest entity in the database. A collection of fields makes a record, a collection of records makes a table and a collection of tables make a database.
- **Data Values** Data values are the raw data represented in numeric, character or alphanumeric form.
- **Record or Row** The data values for all the fields related to a person or an object is called a record. It is represented as rows within a table.

- **Relational Database** In a relational database, data is stored in different tables with relationships to each other. These tables communicate and share information, which facilitates data search ability, organization and reporting.

Fields

Purchase table

TransactionID	CustomerID	ProductID	PurchaseDate
1112	24221	8977	03-22-2010
1113	24222	8978	03-22-2010
1114	24223	8979	03-22-2010

Records

CustomerID	Customer	Address
24221	Bob	123 East street
24222	Alice	223 Main street
24223	Martha	465 North street

Customer table

ProductID	Name	Price
8977	Banana	.79
8978	TV	400
8979	Watch	50

Product table

8.6 Keys

The key is defined as the column or attribute or a combination of attributes that is used to identify records of the database table.

Sometimes we might have to retrieve data from more than one table, in those cases we require to join tables with the help of keys. It also controls and maintains the integrity of information stored in the database.

Candidate Keys | Alternate Key | Relationship (Foreign Key) | Primary Key

studentId	firstname	lastname	courseId
L0002345	Jim	Black	C002
L0001254	James	Harradine	A004
L0002349	Amanda	Holland	C002
L0001198	Simon	McCloud	S042
L0023487	Peter	Murray	P301
L0018453	Anne	Norris	S042

Primary Key

Student table

courseId	courseName
A004	Accounts
C002	Computing
P301	History
S042	Short Course

Course table

There are various types of keys, which are as follows:

Primary Key

The primary key of a relational table uniquely identifies each record in the table. In some tables, combination of more than one attributes is declared as primary key. In that case, primary key is known as **composite key**. The value of primary key should be unique and not null. Every relation does have a primary key.

e.g. in above Student table, studentId works as a primary key because it contains Id's, which are unique for each student.

Candidate Key

The set of all attributes, which can uniquely identify each tuple of a relation are known as candidate keys. Each table may have one or more candidate keys and one of them will become the primary key. e.g. columns studentId and the combination of firstname and lastname work as the candidate keys for the given Student table.

Alternate Key

From the set of candidate keys after selecting one of the keys as primary key, all other remaining keys are known as alternate keys. These keys are also unique but they allow nulls. e.g. from the candidate keys (studentId, firstname and lastname), studentId chosen as a primary key then the firstname and lastname column work as a alternate key.

Foreign Key

A foreign key is a non-key attribute, whose value is derived from the primary key of another table. The relationship between two tables is established with the help of foreign key. A table may have multiple foreign keys and each foreign key can have different referenced table.

Foreign key play an essential role in database design, when tables are broken apart then foreign keys make it possible for them to be reconstructed.

e.g. courseId column of Student table work as a foreign key for Student table, as well as a primary key for Course table (referenced table).

8.7 Objects of an RDBMS

An object in a database is a structure or a feature that is used to store, represent or retrieve data. In fact, a database is a collection of these objects that work on multiple sets of data related to each other.

Various objects in a database are as discussed below:

- **Table** A table is the basic unit of any DBMS. The data is first stored in tables in row and column format.
- **Forms** A form is a feature of a database using which we can enter data in a table in an easy and user friendly manner. The data entered through the forms is stored in tables.
- **Queries** A query is used to retrieve the desired information from the database.
- **Reports** The output of a query may be displayed in the form of reports. The usual result of the query is in the form of rows and columns.

Try These 8.2

1. In the Relational Database Model, what is the primary purpose of a primary key?
   (a) To establish relationships between tables
   (b) To uniquely identify each row in a table
   (c) To store data values in fields
   (d) To reduce data redundancy
2. In a relational database, a ______ key is used to uniquely identify each record in a table and ensure that no two rows have the same value for this key.
3. What is data values? Give a suitable example.
4. Consider the following table and answer the questions that follow. NCERT

ItemNo	Name	Price	Quantity	Discount (in%)
A001	Pen	20	12	0
A003	Pencil	15	5	1
A010	Notebook	50	25	5

   (a) From the above table, identify the primary key. Justify your choice.
   (b) How many fields and how many records does the table have?

Summary

A database is a collection of logically related information/data, which is available for one or more users organized in a way, so that it can be easily accessed.

Data model is a conceptual representation of data organization, structure, and relationships.

There are different data models such as hierarchical, network, and relational data model.

Relational database model organizes data into tables with rows and columns, establishing relationships between tables through shared fields.

The key is defined as the column or attribute or a combination of attributes that is used to identify records of the database table.

An object in a database is a structure or a feature that is used to store, represent or retrieve data.

NCERT FOLDER

Complete Explanations of all NCERT's Questions

A. Multiple Choice Questions

Q.1 Which of the following cannot be considered as an example of a database?
(a) Dictionary (b) Telephone directory
(c) Marks Register (d) Newspaper

Q.2 Which of the following is not a DBMS?
(a) MS Access (b) Open Office Base
(c) MS Excel (d) MySQL

Q.3 DBMS stands for ______.
(a) Data and Books Management System
(b) Database Management System
(c) Duplicate Books Management System
(d) Data Management Multi System

Q.4 Which of the following data models sets a relation between the two or more tables?
(a) Relational Data Model (b) Network Data Model
(c) Hierarchical Data Model (d) Connection Data Model

Q.5 The details associated with an entity are called ____.
(a) Table (b) Attributes
(c) Records (d) Primary key

Q.6 A ______ is represented as rows in a table.
(a) field (b) attribute
(c) record (d) candidate key

Q.7 In which of the following forms can a data value be represented?
(a) Numeric (b) Character
(c) Alphanumeric (d) All of these

Q.8 Which of the following uniquely identifies a row in a table?
(a) Primary key (b) Alternate key
(c) Foreign key (d) Candidate key

Q.9 A ______ is a feature of a database using which we can enter data in a table in an easy and user friendly manner.
(a) query (b) report (c) form (d) field

Q.10 A ______ is a question asked from a database.
(a) query (b) report (c) form (d) field

Answers

1. (d) 2. (c) 3. (b) 4. (a) 5. (b)
6. (c) 7. (d) 8. (a) 9. (c) 10. (a)

B. State Whether the Following Statements are True or False

Q.1 A database cannot be organised.

Q.2 Data is the collection of raw facts.

Q.3 A table can be created without a primary key.

Q.4 Two tables can be related in a network data model.

Q.5 MS Access is an example of a database.

Answers

1. False 2. True 3. False 4. True 5. True

C. Fill in the Blanks

Q.1 The raw facts constitutes ________.

Q.2 An ________ is a real world object about which information is to be stored in a database.

Q.3 The output of a query may be displayed in the form of________.

Q.4 The data values for all the fields related to a person or object is called a ________.

Q.5 All the field values that are eligible to be the primary key are the ________ keys for that table.

Answers

1. Data 2. Entity 3. Report 4. Record 5. Candidate

D. Answer the Following Questions

Q.1 **Define the terms (a) Database (b) Data redundancy (c) Report**

Ans. (a) Refer to text on page no. 216 (Database concept).

(b) Duplication of data is known as data redundancy.

(c) Refer to text on page no. 219 (Reports).

Q.2 **Give one point of difference between (a) Data and Information, (b) Form and Query, (c) Network and hierarchical data model**

Ans. (a) Data and Information

Data	Information
The raw, unprocessed facts and figures that have lack of context and meaning. It is the input for information processing.	The processed and organized data that is meaningful and useful. It provides context and helps in decision-making.

(b) Form and Query

Form	Query
A user-friendly interface that allows users to input and edit data in a structured way. It provides a visual representation of data and simplifies data entry.	A request or command used to retrieve specific information from a database. It allows users to filter, sort, and analyze data based on their needs.

(c) Network Data Model and Hierarchical Data Model

Network Data Model	Hierarchical Data Model
A complex data model that allows records to have multiple parents, representing a many-to-many relationship. It is more flexible than a hierarchical model but can be more difficult to manage.	A data model that organizes data in a tree-like structure, with each record having only one parent. It is simpler than network model but less flexible in representing complex relationships.

Q.3 **Give any four advantages of a DBMS.**

Ans. Refer to text on page no 216-217 (Advantages of DBMS).

Q.4 **Consider the table given below and answer the questions that follow**

Table: Library

Book_Id	Book Name	Author Name	Price	Publisher
F001	Pride and Prejudice	Jane Austen	550	ABC
S004	Amazing Astronomy	E. Shane	1050	ABC
C005	IT and Mankind	MHA Diwaan	2500	HYM

(a) Name the fields in the given table.

(b) Which field should be made the primary key?

(c) Is there any alternate key in the table?

(d) How is primary key different from foreign key? Explain with example.

Ans. (a) Book_Id ,Book Name ,Author Name ,Price, Publisher

(b) Book_Id

(c) Since, none of the other fields uniquely identify a book ,there is no alternate key in this table.

(d)

Primary Key	Foreign Key
A primary key is a unique identifier for each record in a table.	A foreign key establishes a relationship between tables by referencing the primary key of another table.

e.g. Students Table

StudentID	Name	Age
101	Bob	22
102	Alice	20

e.g. Enrollments Table

EnrollmentID	StudentID	Course
1	101	English
2	102	Science

In the Students table, StudentID is the Primary Key, meaning each student has a unique ID.	In the Enrollments table, StudentID is a Foreign Key, linking it to the StudentID in the Students table.

EXAM PATTERN EXERCISE

Including Competency Based Questions

Multiple Choice Questions

1 Which of the following statements are true about primary key in a database? CBSE SQP 2024-25
(a) It is a field that can have duplicate values.
(b) It uniquely identifies each record in a table.
(c) It can have null values
(d) It is an optional field in a database table.

2 Which of the following best defines "information"? CBSE SQP 2024-25
(a) Unprocessed raw facts such as names, marks, and addresses.
(b) Organized and processed data that provides meaningful insights.
(c) Audio, video, and graphics stored without any processing.
(d) A collection of unrelated raw facts.

3 Which of the following data models sets a relation between the two or more tables? CBSE SQP 2024-25
(a) Relational Data Model (b) Network Data Model
(c) Hierarchical Data Model (d) Connection Data Model

4 A table can have only ____ primary key in a database.
(a) 1 (b) 2 (c) 3 (d) Many

5 .... is the database software that is used to create, manipulate and manage data. CBSE 2025
(a) Ingress (b) Writer
(c) Paint (d) Windows

6 A table is a set of data elements that is organized using a model of vertical ______ and horizontal ______. CBSE SQP 2021-22 Term I
(a) Rows, Tables (b) Columns, Rows
(c) Rows, Columns (d) Forms, Reports

7 Akshat wants to store a huge amount information about his firm in a database.
Which type of table organization would be most suitable for this purpose? CBSE SQP 2021-22 Term I
(a) Relational (b) Flat File
(c) Either (a) or (b) (d) Hierarchical

8 Which one of the following is an example of RDBMS ? CBSE SQP 2021-22 Term I
(a) MongoDB (b) Windows registry
(c) Publisher (d) Oracle

9 Malini wants to store a huge amount of information about her zone in a database. Should not be repeated in her file. Her friend Gargi explained her various benefits or storing data in RDBMS. It helps in preventing/controlling duplication of data.Which of the following terms is used to refer to duplication data? CBSE SQP 2021-22 Term I, Competency Based Que.
(a) Data sharing (b) Data privacy
(c) Data redundancy (d) Data integrity

10 Which one of the following is not an example of DBMS ? CBSE 2023
(a) PostgresSQL (b) SQLite
(c) FoxPro (d) Impress

11 Which data model organizes data in a tree-like structure?
(a) Network Data Model (b) Relational Data Model
(c) Hierarchical Data Model
(d) Object-Oriented Data Model

12 What is the main advantage of a DBMS regarding data redundancy?
(a) It increases data redundancy.
(b) It ensures all data is stored in a single table.
(c) It helps minimize data redundancy.
(d) It eliminates data redundancy completely.

13 Which field in the Orders table serves as the foreign key?
(a) Order_id (b) Product Ordered
(c) Customer_id (d) Order Amount

14 What does the primary key of a table do?
(a) It establishes relationships between tables.
(b) It uniquely identifies each record in a table.
(c) It stores data values in a field.
(d) It reduces the size of the database.

15 Which of the following is not a common feature of a DBMS?
(a) Data Analysis (b) Data Sharing
(c) Data Inconsistency (d) Organized Storage

16 What is a composite key?
(a) A key that consists of only one field.
(b) A primary key made up of two or more fields.
(c) A key used to link two different databases.
(d) A unique identifier for a table.

17 In a relational database, what is a table composed of?
(a) Rows and Columns (b) Records and Fields
(c) Entities and Attributes (d) All of these

18 Which data model connects multiple records to a single master file?
(a) Relational Data Model (b) Hierarchical Data Model
(c) Network Data Model
(d) Object-Oriented Data Model

19 **Which of the following is used to store data in a user-friendly manner?**
(a) Table (b) Form (c) Query (d) Report

20 **What is the purpose of a query in a DBMS?**
(a) To create new tables
(b) To retrieve specific information from the database
(c) To enter data into a table
(d) To generate reports

21 **Which of the following is not an example of data?**
(a) A report card (b) Pay slip
(c) Student grades (d) Bar chart

22 **What does a DBMS ensure about the data consistency?**
(a) Inconsistencies are increased
(b) Data is only stored in one format
(c) Data is consistently updated across related tables
(d) Duplicate data entries

23 **Which model is most widely used and organizes data into tables?**
(a) Network Data Model
(b) Hierarchical Data Model
(c) Relational Data Model
(d) Object-Oriented Data Model

24 **What does a field or column in a database represent?**
(a) A record
(b) A data value
(c) An attribute of a record
(d) A complete set of information

25 **In the context of data models, what is a real-world object referred to as?**
(a) Attribute (b) Record (c) Table (d) Entity

Answers

1. (b)	2. (b)	3. (a)	4. (a)	5. (a)
6. (b)	7. (a)	8. (d)	9. (c)	10. (d)
11. (c)	12. (c)	13. (c)	14. (b)	15. (c)
16. (b)	17. (d)	18. (b)	19. (b)	20. (b)
21. (d)	22. (c)	23. (c)	24. (c)	25. (d)

Very Short Answer Type Questions

1 **Differentiate between Primary key and Foreign key.**
CBSE SQP 2020-21, CBSE SQP 2023-24

Ans. Differentiate between Primary key and Foreign key are as follows

Primary key	Foreign key
Primary key is a unique identifier for a record in a table.	Foreign key is a field in one table that refers to the primary key of another table.
It cannot contain null values and must be unique for each record.	It establishes a relationship between two tables.

2 **What is DBMS? Explain any two advantages of DBMS.**
CBSE SQP 2020-21

Ans. A DBMS (Database Management System) is a software application that interacts with user, applications, and database itself to capture and analyze data.

Advantages

(i) Data Integrity means that the data contained in the database is accurate and consistent.
(ii) Data Security is very important to an organization and may also be confidential. It protects data from unauthorized access and manipulation.

3 **What is a Primary Key? How is it different from foreign key ?** CBSE 2023

Ans. A primary key uniquely identifies a record in a table, while a Foreign key establishes a link between two tables based on their primary keys.

4 **What is the primary purpose of a database management system (DBMS)?**

Ans. The primary purpose of a DBMS is to create, update, and retrieve data, making it easier for users to manage and maintain databases efficiently.

5 **Define 'foreign key' in a relational database.**

Ans. A foreign key is a field or a combination of fields in one table that uniquely identifies records in another table, establishing a relationship between the two tables.

6 **What is meant by 'data redundancy' and how does a DBMS address it?**

Ans. Data redundancy refers to the unnecessary repetition of data within a database. A DBMS addresses it by organizing data efficiently and ensuring that each piece of data is stored only once, reducing duplication.

7 **Explain candidate key.**

Ans. A candidate key is a field or combination of fields in a table that can uniquely identify each record. It must have unique values and cannot be null.

8 **What is the difference between a primary key and an alternate key?**

Ans. A primary key is the field chosen to uniquely identify records in a table, whereas an alternate key is any candidate key not selected as the primary key but still has unique values.

9 **How does a 'form' facilitate data entry in a database?**

Ans. A form provides a user-friendly interface for entering data into a database. It includes elements like text boxes, labels, and checkboxes, which simplify and streamline the data entry process.

10 **What role does a 'query' play in a DBMS?**

Ans. A query is used to retrieve specific information from the database based on given criteria. It helps in searching and filtering data to get relevant results.

11 Describe what is meant by 'data consistency'.

Ans. Data consistency ensures that data is accurate and remains the same across the database. When data is updated in one part of the database, it should be consistently updated in all related parts.

12 Give an example of data and an example of information.

Ans. **Example of Data** '45' (numeric value).

Example of Information A summary report showing average scores from a dataset.

13 What is the function of a 'report' in a DBMS?

Ans. A report presents the results of queries in a structured and formal layout, often used for printing or sharing data in a professional format.

Short Answer Type Questions

1 Your cousin runs a small bookstore and wants to maintain an inventory of books. He needs to record information such as book titles, authors, ISBNs, publication dates, prices, and stock levels. However, he is not familiar with database management systems. Explain the following concepts to help him understand DBMS: **CBSE SQP 2024-25**

(a) What is DBMS?

(b) What are the advantages of using DBMS?

(c) Name any two database programs that can be used to create a table and store the data according to his requirements.

(d) Which field can be set as a Primary Key?

Ans. (a) A Database Management System (DBMS) is software that helps users create, manage, and manipulate databases. It allows for efficient data storage, retrieval, and organization.

(b) Advantages of using DBMS

- **Data Integrity** Ensures accuracy and consistency of data.
- **Data Security** Provides access controls to protect sensitive information.
- **Reduced Data Redundancy** Minimizes duplication of data across the database.
- **Data Management** Simplifies data handling through structured query language (SQL).

(c) Two database programs:

- MySQL
- Open Office Base

(d) The ISBN (International Standard Book Number) can be set as a primary key, as it uniquely identifies each book in the inventory.

2 Explain the advantages of using a database management system (DBMS) over a manual system.

Ans. A DBMS offers several advantages over manual systems:

- **Organized Storage** Data is stored in a structured manner, facilitating fast and accurate retrieval.
- **Data Analysis** DBMS allows for complex data analysis, including calculations and comparisons.
- **Data Sharing** Data can be shared across multiple applications, reducing redundancy and effort.
- **Minimal Data Redundancy** DBMS tools help to minimize data duplication.
- **Data Consistency** Updates in one part of the database are automatically reflected elsewhere, maintaining consistency.
- **Increased Efficiency** Operations like saving, retrieving, and searching data are more efficient.
- **Improved Accuracy** By reducing redundancy and errors, DBMS ensures accurate data.
- **Enhanced Validity** Validation rules can be set to ensure data quality.
- **Security** Access can be controlled and data encrypted to prevent unauthorized access.

3 Describe how a foreign key is used to establish relationships between tables in a relational database.

Ans. A foreign key is a field in one table that links to the primary key of another table. This relationship allows for the integration of related data across multiple tables. For example, in a database with a Customers table and an Orders table, the Customer_id in the Orders table acts as a foreign key linking it to the primary key of the Customers table. This setup ensures that each order is associated with a valid customer and maintains data integrity across the database.

4 Consider the following table: **Competency Based Que. CBSE 2025**

Table: Student

Student_ID	Name	Age	Phone_Number
S001	Amit	15	9876543210
S002	Priya	16	8765432109
S003	Priya	15	7654321098

Answer the following questions:

(a) You are given the task to design the student database for your school in LibreOffice Base. Based on the given table structure, suggest the data type of student_id and age field that would be suitable to store student's-id and age respectively.

(b) As a database administrator, you need to ensure each student has a unique identifier. Which field in the table would you choose as the primary key and why?

(c) Identify the field that can serve as an alternate key. Justify your answer.

(d) How many attributes and records are present in the above shown table?

Ans. (a) Suggested datatype for Student_ID and Age fields:

Student_ID The datatype for Student_ID should be Text because student IDs typically consist of alphanumeric characters (e.g., "S001", "S002"). The text datatype in LibreOffice Base allows storing these mixed characters without restriction.

Age The datatype for Age should be Integer, as age is represented by whole numbers, and Integer is used to store numeric values without decimals.

(b) Primary key selection

The Student_ID field should be the primary key since it uniquely identifies each student.

(c) Alternate key identification

The phone number field could serve as an alternate key, assuming it's unique to each student. While phone numbers may sometimes repeat, they are generally unique to each individual in a school database, making it a good candidate for this role.

(d) The table has 4 attributes (Student_ID, Name, Age, Phone Number) and 3 records (Amit, Priya, Priya).

5 Your friend owns a chemist shop, he needs to keep records of the medicines with their id's, date of purchase, expiry date, price, etc. in a database program. But he does not have any knowledge about the database. Explain to him the following to get a better understanding of the DBMS concepts.

(a) What is DBMS? Explain in brief. CBSE SQP 2022-23

(b) Name any two database programs which can be used to create a table and store the data as per the requirement.

(c) Which field can be set as a Primary Key?

(d) Is it possible to make more than one field as a primary key in your table? (Yes/No). Justify your answer.

Ans. (a) A Database Management System (DBMS) is a software application that interacts with user, applications, and database itself to capture and analyze data. It helps in organizing, storing, retrieving, and managing data efficiently.

(b) Microsoft Access and MySQL

(c) The "MedicineID" field can be set as the primary key as it uniquely identifies each medicine in the database.

(d) No, it's not possible to make more than one field as the primary key in a table. A primary key must be unique, and having multiple primary keys would violate this principle. A single field or a combination of fields should be designated as the primary key to ensure data integrity and efficient database operations.

6 A company wants to track its employees' project assignments and hours worked. They decide to create a database with two tables: Employees and Projects. The Employees table has fields for Employee_ID, Name, and Department, while the Projects table has fields for Project_ID, Project_Name, Employee_ID, and Hours_Worked.

How would the Employee_ID field in the Projects table function in this database?

Ans. The Employee_ID field in the Projects table would act as a foreign key that links to the Employee_ID field in the Employees table.

This foreign key establishes a relationship between the two tables, allowing for tracking which employee is assigned to which project and how many hours they have worked on it.

7 You are tasked with updating the contact information for a customer who has recently moved to a new address. The customer's details are stored in a Customers table, and their orders are recorded in an Orders table.

How does a DBMS help ensure that the customer's new address is consistently updated in both tables?

Ans. A DBMS helps ensure consistency by using relationships between tables. If the Customers table and Orders table are linked through a foreign key relationship, updating the customer's address in the Customers table will automatically update or reflect the change in related records in the Orders table, maintaining data consistency across the database.

8 You need to generate a report showing the average amount spent by customers on their orders. The data is stored in two tables: Customers and Orders. How would you use a DBMS to create this report?

Ans. To generate the report, you would use a query to join the Customers and Orders tables based on the customer's ID, then calculate the average amount spent by aggregating the Order Amount field from the Orders table. The DBMS will retrieve and process the data from both tables, and the result can be formatted into a report for presentation.

Starting with LibreOffice Base

CHAPTER 09

LibreOffice Base is a powerful, user-friendly, free and open-source DBMS available for both Linux and Windows. This software allows us to organize and store data efficiently. LibreOffice Base provides a comprehensive set of tools to create, manage, and query databases, making it an ideal choice for individuals and organizations alike.

LibreOffice Base is a free and open-source Database Management System (DBMS) that is part of the LibreOffice. Base provides tools to create, manage, and manipulate databases. It is similar in functionality to Microsoft Access, offering features for beginners and advanced users. It can be downloaded from www.libreoffice.org and is available for both Linux and Windows operating systems.

Uses of LibreOffice Base

1. **Creating Databases** You can create and manage different types of databases, including relational databases that use tables and relationships between them.
2. **Database Connectivity** Base supports popular database engines like MySQL, PostgreSQL, and Microsoft Access databases. It also allows you to connect to external databases or use internal ones like HSQLDB (the default embedded database).
3. **Forms and Reports** You can design forms to input or view data and create reports to summarize or present the data in a meaningful way.
4. **Queries** You can use SQL (Structured Query Language) to query databases, retrieve specific information, and filter records based on certain conditions.
5. **Macros and Scripting** For advanced users, Base supports automation through macros, allowing you to perform repetitive tasks or customize workflows.
6. **Data Storage** It can be used for personal, small business, or educational purposes to store and manage data, such as contact lists, inventory, or financial records.

9.1 Data Types

The type of data entered into various fields can vary based on the nature of the information.

For example, names are stored as text, age is stored as numbers, tuition fees may be stored as decimal values, and birthdates are stored in a date format. A data type defines the kind of data that will be stored in a specific field, and the memory size allocated to that field depends on its data type.

Here are some commonly used data types:

Text Data Type Text data consists of a mix of letters, numbers, or special characters. Arithmetic operations cannot be performed on text data.

Examples of text data types include Address, or Grade.

Name	Data type	Description
Memo	LONGVARCHAR	Stores up to the maximum length indicated by user. It is used to store some descriptive data having more than 255 characters. Memo data type allows to store text data up to 64,000 characters.
Text (fix)	CHAR	Stores exactly the length specified by user. Character data type is used to enter fixed number of characters. It can be used for license number, passport number as they have fixed number of characters.
Text	VARCHAR	Stores upto the specified length. The number of bytes allocated depends on the number of characters entered by the user. For example, the address is defined as varchar (50), and if the address entered by the user is of 20 characters then only 20 bytes will be occupied in the database.

Numeric Data Type

Numeric data types consist of numbers that can be either integers or real (decimal) numbers, allowing various arithmetic operations to be performed on them. Examples of numeric data include values like 10, -34.8, 90.6789, and -86, all of which are numeric data types. The table below lists different numeric data types, the memory they consume in bits or bytes, and their respective ranges.

Name	Data type	Signed	Range
Tiny Integer	TINYINT	No	0-255
Small Integer	SMALLINT	Yes	-32768 to 32768
Integer	INTEGER	Yes	-2.14×10^{9} to 2.14×10^{9}
BigInt	BIGINT	Yes	-2.3×10^{18} to 2.3×10^{18}
Number	NUMERIC	Yes	Unlimited
Decimal	DECIMAL	Yes	Unlimited
Float	FLOAT	Yes	
Real	REAL	Yes	5×10^{-324} to 1.79×10^{308}
Double	DOUBLE	Yes	

Currency Data Type

The currency data type is used to represent monetary values and can store amounts in different currencies. For example, $100, £500, or Rs. 25.50.

Date Data Type

This data type is used to store dates and times. Examples include 12/25/2019 or 08:45 AM. Dates and times can be stored in various formats, offering flexibility in how the information is displayed.

The table below lists different formats of the date data type

Name	Description
Date	Stores the year, month and day as it is stored in the system.
Time	Stores the time of the day as hour, minute and second.
Timestamp	Stores date and time information at once.

Boolean Data Type

The Boolean data type can only have two possible values: True or False. These values can also be represented in other formats, such as Yes/No, True/False, or On/Off.

Binary Data Type

The Binary data type is used to store digitized images, audio, and other media, represented as long sequences of zeros and ones.

For example, you can store product images, employee photos, or audio clips, such as voice messages, within a Base database.

Try These 9.1

1. **Which data type in LibreOffice Base is used to store text data up to 64,000 characters?**
   (a) CHAR (b) VARCHAR
   (c) LONGVARCHAR (d) TEXT
2. **What is the range of the Tiny Integer numeric data type?**
   (a) – 32768 to 32768 (b) 0 to 255
   (c) -2.3×10^{18} to 2.3×10^{18} (d) -2.14×10^{9} to 2.14×10^{9}
3. **The ______ data type is used to represent monetary values and can store amounts in various currencies.**
4. **The Boolean data type can only have two possible values: ______ or ______.**
5. **What type of data does the VARCHAR data type store?**
6. **Which data type is used to store both date and time information in LibreOffice Base?**

9.2 Starting with LibreOffice Base

Before starting the LibreOffice Base, the user must decide the fields of the table. Once the table with its fields has been decided, it's time to create the database.

To create the database, follow the given steps:

Step 1 Click on Start → LibreOffice 24.2(or any other version).

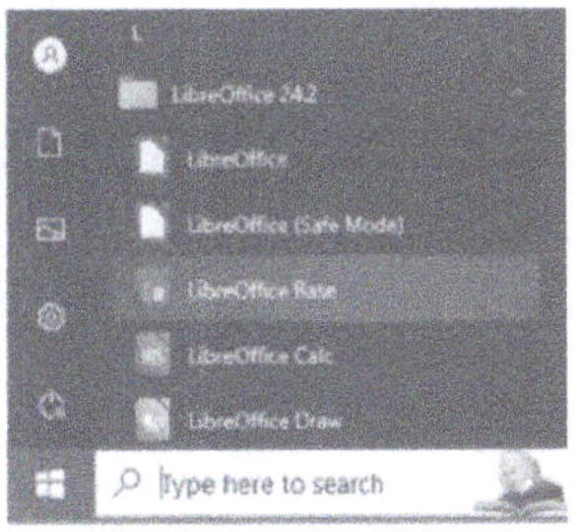

Step 2 Click on the LibreOffice Base option. The Database Wizard window appears.

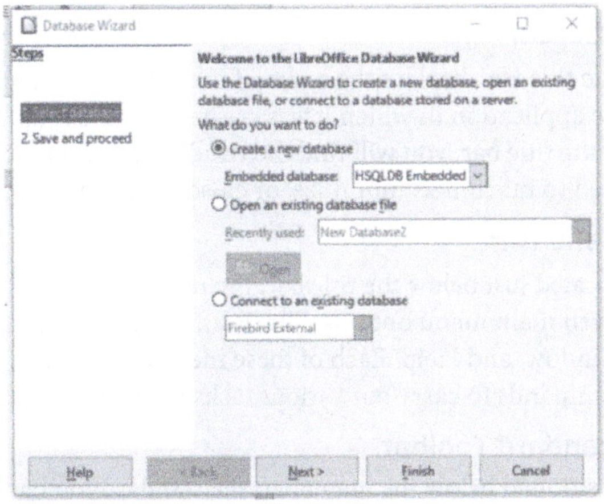

Step 3 The option "Create a new database" is selected by default. Click on the Next button.

Step 4 On the next window that appears, click on Finish button. The Save As dialog box appears.

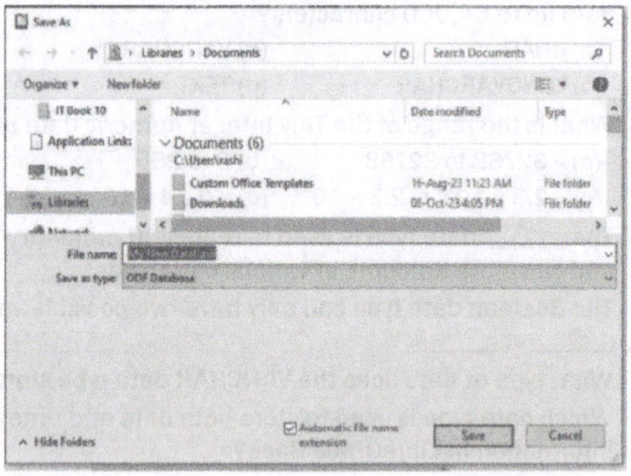

Step 5 Write the name of the database and click on Save button. The LibreOffice window of the created database appears.

9.3 User Interface of LibreOffice Base

The various components of the LibreOffice Base User Interface are discussed below:

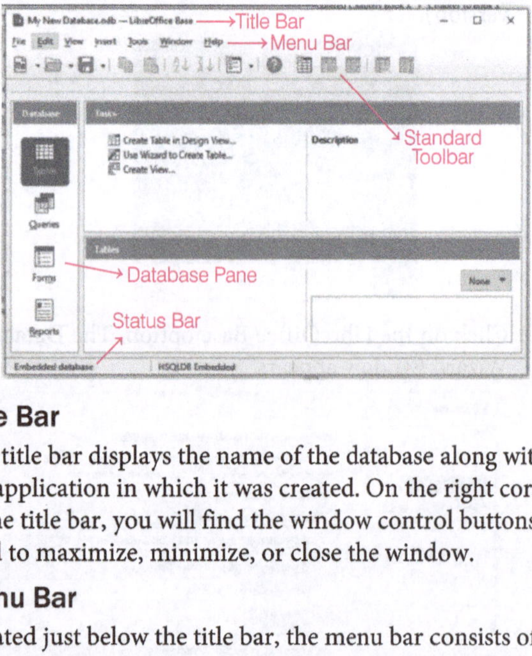

Title Bar

The title bar displays the name of the database along with the application in which it was created. On the right corner of the title bar, you will find the window control buttons used to maximize, minimize, or close the window.

Menu Bar

Located just below the title bar, the menu bar consists of seven main menu options: File, Edit, View, Insert, Tools, Window, and Help. Each of these menus contains commands to carry out various tasks on the database.

Standard Toolbar

Positioned below the menu bar, the standard toolbar provides quick access to commonly used tools and functions.

Status Bar

At the bottom of the interface window, the status bar displays information about the current view of the object in the database.

Database Pane

The database pane is found on the left side of the window. In LibreOffice Base, it holds related data objects such as Tables, Forms, Queries, and Reports. Based on the selected object, the corresponding Task Pane and Object Area, which shows the created objects, will be displayed.

Try These 9.2

1. **What does the Title Bar of LibreOffice Base display?**
   (a) The current object in use
   (b) The name of the database and the application
   (c) The status of the database
   (d) The menu options available
2. **Which component of the LibreOffice Base User Interface provides quick access to commonly used tools and functions?**
   (a) Menu Bar
   (b) Status Bar
   (c) Standard Toolbar
   (d) Database Pane
3. **To create a new database in LibreOffice Base, after selecting "_______," you need to click on the Next button.**
4. **The ______ pane, located on the left side of the LibreOffice Base window, displays related data objects such as Tables, Forms, Queries, and Reports.**
5. **Where is the Status Bar located in the LibreOffice Base interface?**

9.4 Opening a Database

To open an already created database, follow the given steps:

Step 1 Click File → Open. The Open dialog box appears.

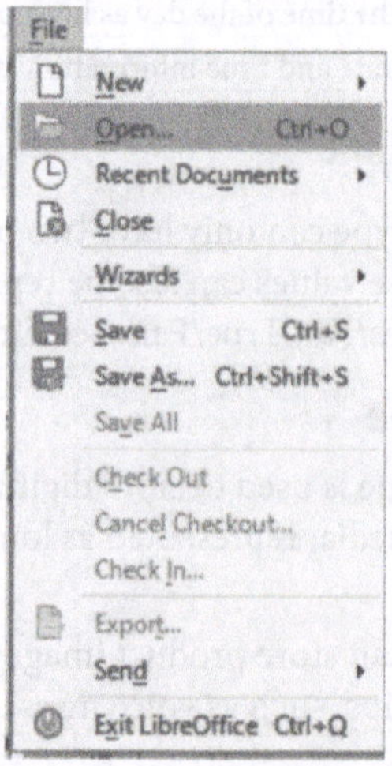

Step 2 Browse for the folder where the database to be opened is stored.

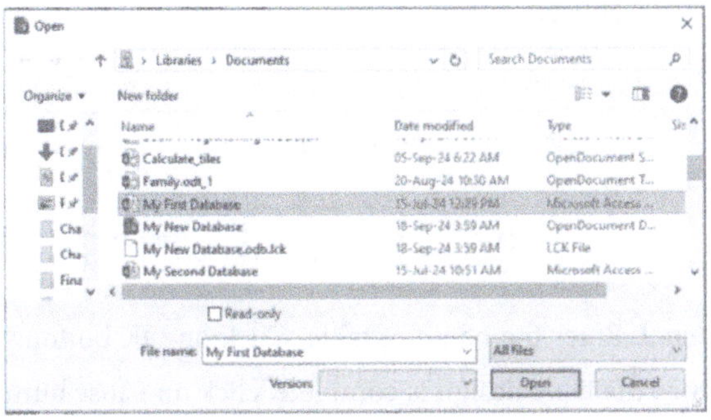

Step 3 Select the desired database and click on Open button.

Note *Use the keyboard shortcut key Ctrl+O to open an already existing database.*

9.5 Creating a Table

After creating the database, you can begin working with its objects. The first essential step is creating a table and then entering data into it. In LibreOffice Base, tables can be created either by using a wizard or by utilizing the Design view.

Using Wizard

A table can be created at the time of creating a database or after creating a database.

To create a table using wizard, follow the given steps:

Step 1 In the database window, click on the Use Wizard to Create Table option. The Table Wizard window appears.

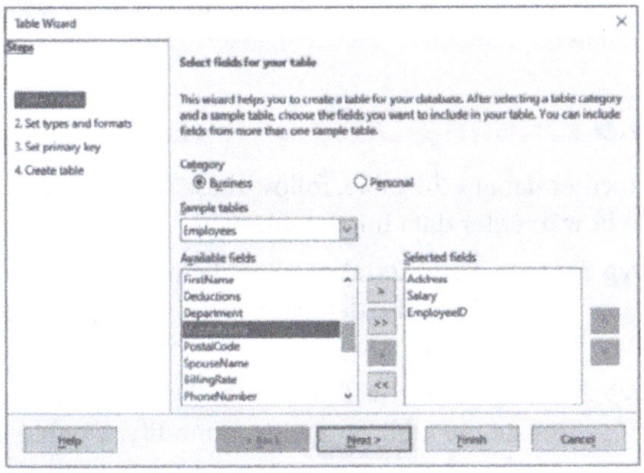

Step 2 Select the category as "Business" or "Personal" and sample table.

Step 3 Select the desired field and click on [>] and click on Next button. The next window of the wizard appears.

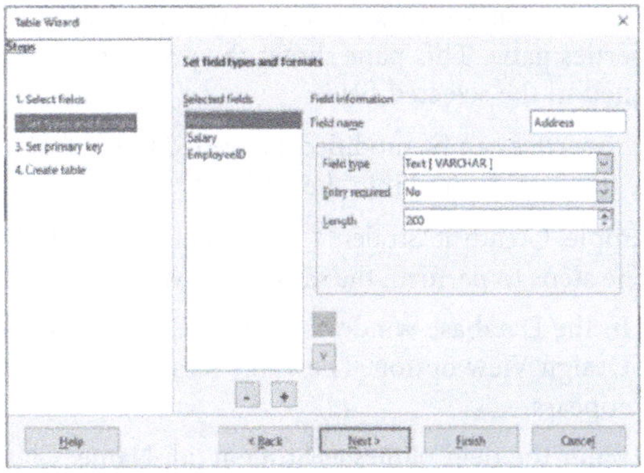

Step 4 Select the data type for each field of the table.

Step 5 After finishing the task, click on Next button.

Step 6 Set Field as the primary key of the table and click on Next button.

Step 7 Give a name to the table and click on Finish button. The Table Data view of the table appears to enter records into it.

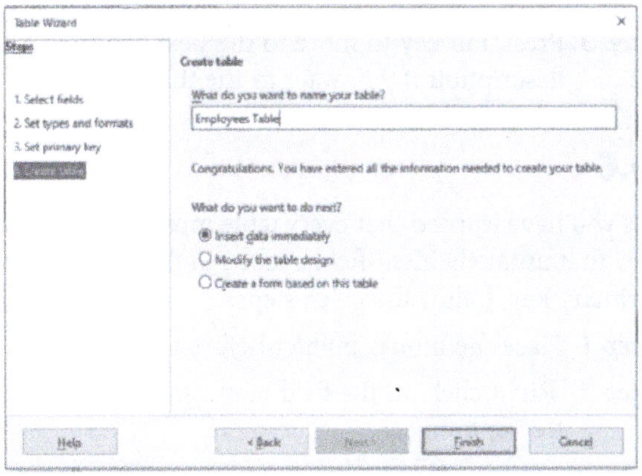

Using Design View

To create a table in Design View, navigate to the main Database window, and select the option Create Table in Design View from the Tasks Pane. This will open the Table Design window.

The window is divided into two main sections:

- The upper half section contains a grid with three columns: Field Name, Field Type, and Description.
  - **Field Name** The name assigned to the field when creating the table.
  - **Field Type** Allows you to specify the data type for each field.
  - **Description** A brief explanation of the field's purpose. This is optional and is meant for user reference; it does not appear in the actual database table.

- The bottom half of the screen displays the Field Properties pane. This pane shows the properties assigned to the selected field.

These properties can be modified as needed to control and validate the data entered into the table.

For example, Create a "Students_Info" table using Design view. The steps to perform the same are given below:

Step 1 In the Database window, click on Create table in Design View option. The Table Design view appears.

Step 2 Enter the field names as Student_id, Name, Class, Sec.

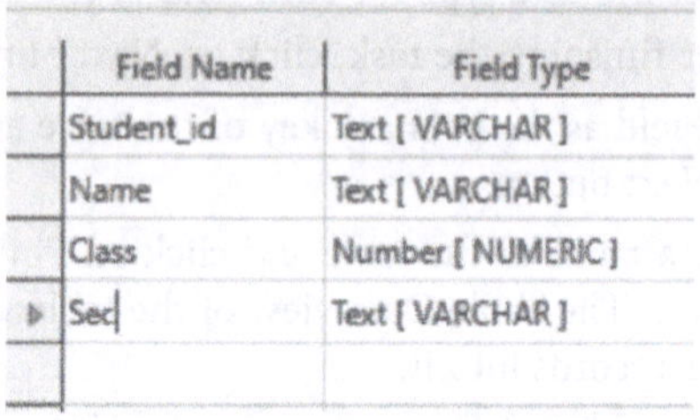

Field Name	Field Type
Student_id	Text [VARCHAR]
Name	Text [VARCHAR]
Class	Number [NUMERIC]
Sec	Text [VARCHAR]

Step 3 Press Tab key to move to the next column. Add any description if you want in the third column.

9.6 Setting the Primary Key

As you have learned that every table must have a primary key that uniquely identifies a record in the table. To set a primary key, follow the given steps:

Step 1 Place the mouse pointer before the field name.

Step 2 Right click on the field name and click on Primary Key option.

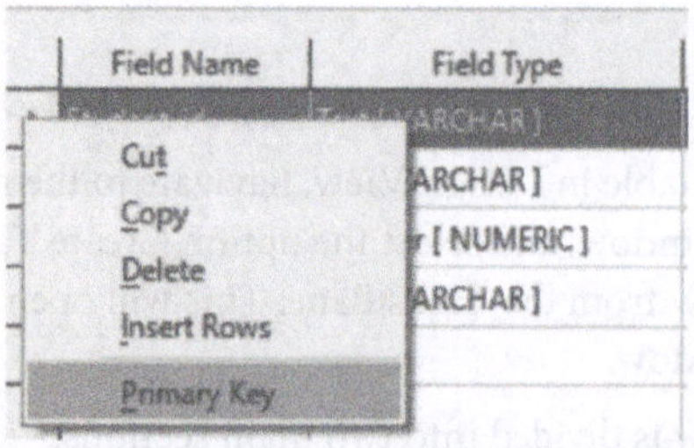

The primary key will be set on that field.

Note *To set a composite key, i.e. a primary key consisting of two fields, keep the Ctrl key pressed and then click on multiple fields to select them. Thereafter right click on selected fields and choose primary key option from the pop-up menu.*

9.7 Saving the Table

After creating the table you need to save it on the disk. To save the table, follow the given steps:

Step 1 Click on the Save button on the Standard toolbar or click on File → Save As. A Save As dialog box appears.

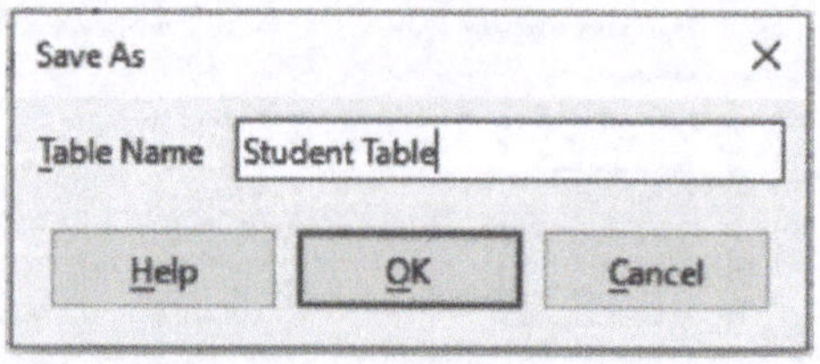

Step 2 Enter the name of table. Click on OK button.

Once the table design is complete, click on Close button on the toolbar to return to the Database screen. The name of the table will appear in the Tables Object Area.

Try These 9.3

1. **Which of the following steps is not part of creating a table using the wizard in LibreOffice Base?**
   (a) Select the category as "Business" or "Personal"
   (b) Set a field as the primary key
   (c) Choose the data type for each field
   (d) Enter data directly into the table
2. **What is the purpose of the "Create Table in Design View" option in LibreOffice Base?**
   (a) To open an existing table
   (b) To design a table with custom fields and properties
   (c) To use predefined table templates
   (d) To save changes to a table
3. **In the Design View, the bottom half of the Table Design window shows the ________ pane, which displays and allows modification of field properties.**
4. **What should you click on after selecting the desired fields in the Table Wizard to proceed with creating the table?**
5. **How do you set a field as the primary key in the Design View?**

9.8 Entering Data in a Table

To enter data in the table, follow these step-by-step guide on how to enter data into a table.

Step 1 **Open Your Database** First launch LibreOffice Base, Open the database containing the table you want to edit.

Step 2 **Navigate to the Table** In the Database Navigator, locate the table you wish to modify. Double-click on the table name to open it in data view.

Step 3 **Enter Data into Cells** Click on the desired cell where you want to input the data. Once selected type the information directly into the cell. Use Tab key to move to the next cell or the arrow keys to navigate within the table.

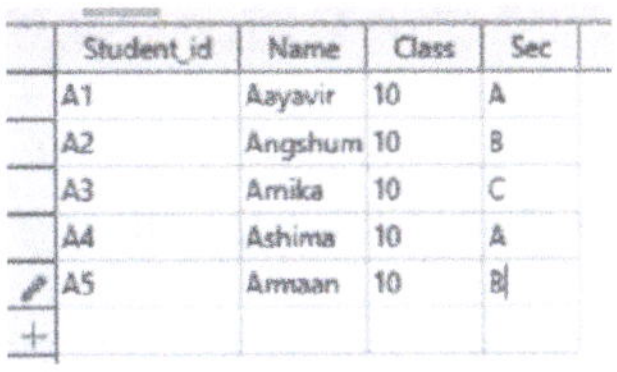

Student_id	Name	Class	Sec
A1	Aayavir	10	A
A2	Angshum	10	B
A3	Amika	10	C
A4	Ashima	10	A
A5	Armaan	10	B

Step 4 **Save Your Changes** Once you've finished entering data, save your changes. You can either use the File → Save menu or the shortcut key Ctrl+S.

9.9 Navigating through the Table

The black pointing arrow just before the field name is the record pointer. To navigate through various records of the table, we use the navigation box present at the bottom of the datasheet window. It indicates a current record of the table at any given time.

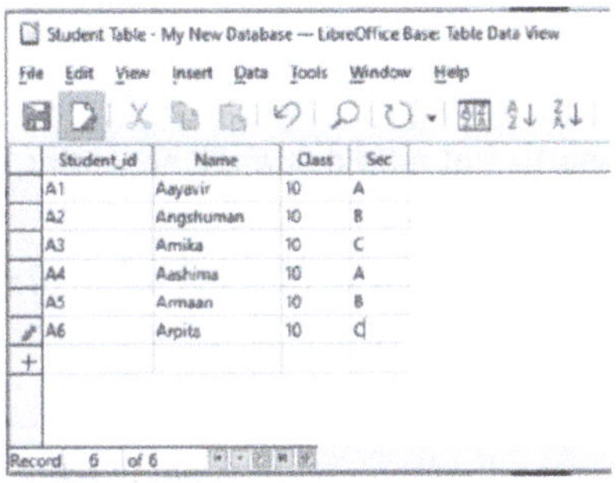

Student_id	Name	Class	Sec
A1	Aayavir	10	A
A2	Angshuman	10	B
A3	Amika	10	C
A4	Aashima	10	A
A5	Armaan	10	B
A6	Arpita	10	C

The various components of Navigation Box are as follows:

- **Record Selector Box** This is the text box where the currently active record number is displayed. We may enter the record number that we want to see in this text box.
- **Navigation Buttons** These are used to scroll vertically in the table.

  Press ◀ to move to the first record

  Press ▶ and ◀ to move to the next and previous records respectively.

  Press ▶| to move to the last record.

  Above figure shows the datasheet view after entering six records in the table. Note that the record pointer is on six record, the Navigation Bar shows the "Record 6 to 6".

9.10 Editing Data

To edit or modify existing data, simply place the cursor on the field you wish to change and enter the new value. While editing, an Edit icon will appear next to the record being modified. This icon remains visible until the table is saved with the updated changes. To undo any changes and revert to the original data, press the Esc key.

9.11 Deleting Records from Table

To delete a record, open the table and select the record you want to remove. You can delete it by pressing the Del key on your keyboard or by choosing the Delete Record option from the Edit menu. Alternatively, right-click on the record and select Delete Rows from the pop-up menu.

When attempting to delete a record, a confirmation box will appear. Clicking Yes will permanently delete the record, while clicking No will cancel the action.

9.12 Sorting Data in the Table

Data in a table can be arranged in ascending or descending order. This process of arranging the records in particular order on any field is called as sorting.

To sort the table, follow the given steps:

Step 1 Open the Student table in datasheet view and select the field on which you want to sort. It shows that the field "Points" is selected to sort the records in ascending order.

Step 2 From the tool bar click Sort Ascending icon if the table has to be sorted in ascending order of selected field. Alternatively select Sort Descending icon if the table has to be sorted in descending order of selected field.

Step 3 The table will be sorted in selected order. Here, the Student table is sorted based on the Name field in ascending order.

Closing LibreOffice Base

To close the application window of LibreOffice Base, click on the File → Close or click on the cross ☒ button of the LibreOffice Base window.

Summary

LibreOffice Base is a free and open-source database component of the LibreOffice suite. You can download it from www.libreoffice.org.

A data type specifies the kind of data that will be stored in a particular field. In Base, data types are categorized into Text, Numeric, Currency, and Date.

LibreOffice Base comprises a collection of related data objects, including Tables, Forms, Queries, Reports, and application modules.

The user interface displays different Task Panes and Object Areas depending on the selected object.

Tables in LibreOffice Base can be created either using a wizard or through Design View.

NCERT FOLDER

Complete Explanations of all NCERT's Questions

A. Multiple Choice Questions

Q.1 Which of the following is not a type of text data type?

(a) Memo (b) Varchar
(c) Float (d) Char

Q.2 A currency data type can only store monetary data that is in dollars.

(a) True (b) False
(c) Neither a nor b (d) Both (a) and (b)

Q.3 Which of the following data can a date data type store?

(a) Date (b) Time
(c) Both date and time (d) Neither date nor time

Q.4 Which of the following is true about LibreOffice Base?

(a) It is a spreadsheet software
(b) It is free and open source software
(c) It can store only character data
(d) It is a licensed software.

Q.5 Which of the following methods can be used to create a table in Base?

(a) Using a table wizard (b) Design View
(c) Both (a) and (b) (d) Neither (a) nor (b)

Q.6 The related objects of a database can be seen in ____________ pane of the Base Database window.

(a) Database (b) Task (c) Title Bar (d) Menu Bar

Q.7 Which is the shortcut key to open an existing database?

(a) Ctrl+ D (b) Ctrl+O (c) Ctrl+E (d) Ctrl+F

Q.8 The Design view of Table Creation window in LibreOffice Base is divided into ______ sections or panes.

(a) 2 (b) 3 (c) 4 (d) 5

Q.9 While entering records in a table, we can move to the next field by pressing the ________ key.

(a) Tab (b) Ctrl (c) Enter (d) Shift

Q.10 Which of the following is true about primary key of a table?

(a) Every table must have a primary key
(b) The data values in primary key field cannot be duplicated.
(c) A primary key field cannot be left blank
(d) All of the above

Answers

1. (c) 2. (b) 3. (c) 4. (b) 5. (c)
6. (a) 7. (b) 8. (a) 9. (a) 10. (d)

B. State Whether the Following Statements are True or False

Q.1 The text data can contain special characters.

Q.2 Memo data type can be used to store descriptive data.

Q.3 A Boolean data type can have two or more than two values.

Q.4 We cannot store audio data in LibreOffice Base.

Q.5 The properties of a field change according to the data type selected.

Q.6 Field description may or may not be entered while designing a table.

Q.7 ⏮ is pressed to move to the last record.

Q.8  appears when the record is being edited.

Q.9 A table once created in a database cannot be edited.

Q.10 Sort dialog box can only help to sort data in ascending order.

Answers

1 True 2 True 3 False 4 False 5 True
6 True 7 False 8 True 9 False 10 False

C. Fill in the Blanks

Q.1 A _______ refers to the type of data that will be stored in that particular field.

Q.2 The ________ data is a combination of letters, numbers or special characters.

Q.3 ________ data type can be used to store Aadhar number.

Q.4 The ______ data type used to store digitized images.

Q.5 The shortcut key to save a table is ________.

Q.6 ________ on the Base Interface Window displays information about the type of view of the object in the database.

Q.7 A _______ icon appears before the field name indicating that it is a primary key.

Q.8 The data can be entered in a table only in ________ view.

Q.9 The black pointing arrow just before the field name in a table is called _______.

Q.10 The process of arranging the records in particular order on any field is called _______.

Answers

1 Data Type	2 Text
3 Text	4 Binary
5 Ctrl+S	6 Status bar
7 Key	8 Datasheet
9 Record Pointer	10 Sorting

D. Answer the Following Questions

Q.1 Differentiate between:

(a) Memo and Varchar data type

(b) Number and Decimal data type

(c) Design View and Datasheet view of a table

Ans. (a) Differentiate between Memo and Varchar data type are as follows

Memo	Varchar
Used for storing longer text or large blocks of text, such as paragraphs or long descriptions, without a strict character limit	Used for storing shorter text or string data, typically with a defined maximum length

(b) Differentiate between Number and Decimal data type are as follows

Number	Decimal
Number data type consists of numbers.	Decimal data type consists of numbers with decimal.

(c) Differentiate between Design View and Datasheet View of a table are as follows

Design View	Datasheet View
Used to define the structure of a table, including setting up fields, data types, field sizes, and other properties like primary keys, validation rules, and default values. Design View is where you establish the schema of your table.	Used to enter, view, and edit the actual data in the table. It presents data in a grid format, similar to a spreadsheet, where you can add records, update values, or delete rows.

Q.2 Name the menu items present on the Base User Interface,

Ans. Base User Interface- Title Bar, Menu Bar, Standard toolbar and Status bar.

Q.3 Label the components – Title Bar, Database Pane, Tasks Pane, Status Bar of the LibreOffice Base User Interface.

Ans. Refer to text on page no. 228 (User interface of LibreOffice Base).

Q.4 How can we define a primary key in a table?

Ans. Every table must have a primary key that uniquely identifies a record in the table. To make a particular field as the primary key, place the mouse pointer before the field name, say EventId and right click.

A pop up menu appears. Select the Primary Key option from pop up menu and a key icon appears before the field name indicating that it is a primary key.

Q.5 Write steps to sort the table in descending order of primary key.

Ans. To sort a table in descending order based on the primary key field, follow these steps:

Step 1 Open the database and locate the table you want to sort.

Step 2 Double-click on the table name to open it in Datasheet View (which displays the data in rows and columns).

Step 3 Identify the column with the primary key. This is usually marked with a key icon or labeled as the primary key in the table design.

Step 4 Click on the column header of the primary key field to select it for sorting.

Step 5 In the toolbar or ribbon, look for the Sort options.

Step 6 Select Sort Descending (often represented as a "Z-A" or "9-1" icon).

Step 7 The table will now be sorted in descending order based on the primary key.

Step 8 Verify that the records are organized from the highest to the lowest value of the primary key.

Q.6 What is the use of navigation box with respect to tables in a database?

Ans. The black pointing arrow just before the field name is the record pointer.

To navigate through various records of the table, we use the navigation box present at the bottom of the datasheet window which indicates a current record of the table at any given time.

EXAM PATTERN EXERCISE

Including Competency Based Questions

Multiple Choice Questions

1 **The length of the field value of text data type is ______ characters by default in DBMS.** **CBSE SQP 2022-23**

(a) 10 (b) 25

(c) 20 (d) 50

2 **Identify the mode, where we can modify in the structure of table?** **CBSE SQP 2022-23**

(a) Datasheet view (b) Structure view

(c) Design view (d) All of these

3 **A table is a set of data elements that is organised using a model of vertical __________ and horizontal __________.** **CBSE SQP 2021-22 Term I**

(a) rows, tables (b) columns, rows

(c) rows, columns (d) forms, reports

4 **Rudrakshh wants that the name column of a table must not be left blank. Help him to identify the field property for this purpose.** **CBSE SQP 2020-21**

(a) Length (b) Default

(c) Entry Required (d) Format

5 **__________ can be set for a field if the user doesn't provide any value while entering the values in the table.** **CBSE SQP 2020-21**

(a) Required (b) Default

(c) Primary Key (d) Format

6 **Suraj wants to create a database for his clients. For this purpose, she needs to store the Email IDs of his clients. Which datatype should he use to accomplish this purpose?** **CBSE SQP 2023-24**

(a) Numeric (b) Varchar

(c) Binary (d) Boolean

7 **A table can have only __________ primary key in a database.** **CBSE SQP 2023-24**

(a) 1 (b) 2

(c) 3 (d) Many

8 **Binary data types in a database can be using for storing __________.** **CBSE 2023**

(a) photos, music files, etc. (b) integer values

(c) only image files (d) only video files

9 **Which type of data can be stored using the VARCHAR data type in LibreOffice Base?**

(a) Fixed-length text

(b) Descriptive text with up to 64,000 characters

(c) Variable-length text up to a specified length

(d) Numerical values with decimal places

10 **What is the maximum range for a BIGINT data type in LibreOffice Base?**

(a) -2.3×10^{18} to 2.3×10^{18} (b) -2.14×10^{9} to 2.14×10^{9}

(c) 0 to 255 (d) Unlimited

11 **With reference to LibreOffice Base, which of the following is a valid data type to indicate the monetary values?** **CBSE 2025**

(a) Money (b) Currency (c) Rupee (d) Dollar

12 **In LibreOffice Base, which data type is used to store dates and times together?**

(a) Date (b) Time

(c) Timestamp (d) Numeric

13 **What type of data can be stored using the MEMO data type?**

(a) Fixed-length text

(b) Descriptive text up to 64,000 characters

(c) Numerical values with decimal places

(d) Boolean values

14 **Which data type allows for storage of images and audio in LibreOffice Base?**

(a) Boolean (b) Binary

(c) Date (d) Decimal

15 **What is the purpose of the BOOLEAN data type in LibreOffice Base?**

(a) To store numeric values

(b) To store text data

(c) To store true or false values

(d) To store images

16 **What is the main difference between FLOAT and DOUBLE data types?**

(a) FLOAT is used for fixed-length text, while DOUBLE is for variable-length text

(b) FLOAT has a lower precision compared to DOUBLE

(c) DOUBLE is used for Boolean values, while FLOAT is for images

(d) There is no difference; they are the same

17 **Which of the following data types would be most appropriate for storing a license plate number?**

(a) INTEGER (b) CHAR

(c) FLOAT (d) DATE

18 **What does the NUMERIC data type offer compared to DECIMAL?**

(a) NUMERIC has a fixed range, while DECIMAL does not

(b) NUMERIC allows unlimited precision, similar to DECIMAL

(c) NUMERIC is for text data, whereas DECIMAL is for numeric data
(d) NUMERIC is only used for dates

19 **What is the first step to create a new database in LibreOffice Base?**
(a) Click File → New
(b) Click Start → LibreOffice Base
(c) Click File → Open
(d) Click Start → LibreOffice Writer

20 **Where is the Database Pane located in LibreOffice Base?**
(a) At the top of the window
(b) At the bottom of the window
(c) On the left side of the window
(d) On the right side of the window

21 **Which component of the LibreOffice Base interface displays the name of the database and the application?**
(a) Status Bar (b) Menu Bar
(c) Title Bar (d) Standard Toolbar

22 **To create a table using the wizard in LibreOffice Base, what is the default selection in the Table Wizard window?**
(a) Use an existing table (b) Create a new table
(c) Import data from a file (d) Create a new form

23 **How can you open an existing database in LibreOffice Base?**
(a) Click File → New
(b) Click File → Open and browse for the file
(c) Click File → Save As
(d) Use the keyboard shortcut Ctrl+N

24 **In Design View, which column allows you to specify the data type for each field?**
(a) Field Name (b) Description
(c) Field Type (d) Field Properties

25 **What should you do if you want to delete a record from a table in LibreOffice Base?**
(a) Press the Esc key
(b) Select the record and press the Del key or use the Delete option
(c) Click the Save button
(d) Click the Undo button

26 **Which component of the LibreOffice Base interface shows information about the current view of the object?**
(a) Menu Bar (b) Status Bar
(c) Database Pane (d) Title Bar

27 **To set a primary key in a table using Design View, what is the correct action?**
(a) Right-click on the field and select "Set Primary Key"
(b) Enter a description in the Description column
(c) Click the Save button
(d) Use the Sort Ascending option

28 **Cust_photo field. Suggest a suitable data type from the options given below.** **CBSE 2024**
(a) IMAGE (b) PICTURE
(c) LONGVARBINARY (d) GRAPHIC

29 **By default, all the fields in LibreOffice Base will have .... datatype.** **CBSE 2024**
(a) int (tiny) (b) Boolean
(c) text (varchar) (d) text (char)

30 **If you need to store a detailed product description that exceeds 255 characters, which data type should you use?**
(a) CHAR (b) TEXT
(c) MEMO (d) VARCHAR

31 **You have a field in a database that needs to store a unique identification number for each record. Which data type and attribute should you use to ensure that each record can be uniquely identified?** **Competency Based Que.**
(a) Use INTEGER data type with Primary Key attribute
(b) Use VARCHAR data type with Foreign Key attribute
(c) Use FLOAT data type with Unique constraint
(d) Use DATE data type with Not Null constraint

32 **Which action would you take to view and edit data in a table?**
(a) Double-click on the table icon
(b) Right-click on the table and select "Delete"
(c) Click File → Save As
(d) Use the "Create Table" wizard

33 **The process of arranging data in ascending or descending order is known as ....** **CBSE 2025**
(a) Filtering
(b) Tracking
(c) Purification
(d) Sorting

Answers

1. (d)	2. (c)	3. (b)	4. (c)	5. (b)
6. (b)	7. (a)	8. (a)	9. (c)	10. (a)
11. (b)	12. (c)	13. (b)	14. (b)	15. (c)
16. (b)	17. (b)	18. (a)	19. (a)	20. (c)
21. (c)	22. (b)	23. (b)	24. (c)	25. (b)
26. (b)	27. (a)	28. (c)	29. (c)	30. (c)
31. (a)	32. (a)	33. (d)		

Very Short Answer Type Questions

1 **List Numeric and Alphanumeric Datatypes in LibreOffice Base.** **CBSE SQP 2022-23**

Ans. The Numeric and Alphanumeric Datatypes in LibreOffice Base are as following:

- **Numeric** SMALLINT, INTEGER, BIGINT, FLOAT, DOUBLE, DECIMAL
- **Alphanumeric** CHAR, VARCHAR, MEMO

2 Explain any four data types of DBMS. CBSE 2023

Ans. The four data types of DBMS are as follow:

- **INTEGER** Integer is a data type in DBMS which stores whole numbers within a specific range.
- **VARCHAR** VARCHAR stores variable-length text strings.
- **DATE** DATE data type stores date values in the format of YYYY-MM-DD.
- **BLOB** This data type stores binary data like image or audio files.

3 What does the CHAR data type store in LibreOffice Base?

Ans. The CHAR data type stores fixed-length text, where the length is specified by the user.

4 How can you represent a date and time together in LibreOffice Base?

Ans. You can use the Timestamp data type to represent both date and time together.

5 Which data type would you use to store an employee's photo in LibreOffice Base?

Ans. You would use the Binary data type to store an employee's photo.

6 What is the range of values for the SMALLINT data type?

Ans. The range for the SMALLINT data type is -32,768 to 32,768.

7 How is the REAL data type different from the FLOAT data type?

Ans. The REAL data type provides a wider range and higher precision compared to the FLOAT data type.

8 How can you navigate to the next record in a table using the Navigation Box?

Ans. You can navigate to the next record by clicking the right arrow button in the Navigation Box or by pressing the Tab key.

9 What should you do to enter data into a table in LibreOffice Base?

Ans. To enter data into a table, open the table in Datasheet view, type the data values into the fields, and use the Tab key to move to the next field or record.

10 What is the purpose of the Status Bar in LibreOffice Base?

Ans. The Status Bar displays information about the current view of the object in the database, such as record number or view mode.

11 What is the difference between sorting data in ascending and descending order?

Ans. Sorting in ascending order arranges data from smallest to largest or alphabetically from A to Z, while sorting in descending order arranges data from largest to smallest or alphabetically from Z to A.

Short Answer Type Questions

1 Explain any four data types of DBMS. CBSE 2023

Ans. Refer to text on page no. 226-227 (Data type).

2 Explain the process of sorting data in a table. How can you sort data by a specific field, and what options do you have for sorting?

Ans. Refer to text on page no. 231 (Sorting data in the table).

3 You have a table with the fields: Student_id, Name, Class, and Sec. Answer the following:

(a) How would you set the Student_id field as the primary key?

(b) Describe the process to enter data into this table.

Ans. (a) To set the Student_id field as the primary key, open the table in Design View. Right-click on the Student_id field name and select "Primary Key" from the context menu.

This action will mark the Student_id as the unique identifier for each record.

(b) To enter data into the table, open the table in Datasheet view. Start typing data into the fields of each record.

Use the Tab key to move to the next field or record. Continue entering data until all fields for the record are filled, then the cursor will automatically move to the next record.

4 To delete a record from a table, follow these sub-steps:

(a) What key or option is used to remove the selected record?

(b) What happens after you select the Delete option?

Ans. (a) To remove a selected record, you can press the Del key on your keyboard or choose the "Delete Record" option from the Edit menu or context menu.

(b) After selecting the Delete option, a confirmation box will appear asking if you want to permanently delete the record. Clicking "Yes" will delete the record, while clicking "No" will cancel the action.

PRACTICAL ASSIGNMENT

1 Annual Sports Day is being held in Ruhi's school in which various sports competitions will be conducted. Ruhi has been asked to create a database consisting of various sports activities and its players. She decides to create a database named, 'Sports Day' consisting of a table 'Events' that contains the following fields:

- **Event_Id** to store Event identification no like E001, E002, etc.
- **Event Name** to store name of the event
- **Date** to store date on which the event will be conducted
- **Winner 1 Name** name of the winner
- **Winner 1 Points** points earned by the winner

What should be the data type of the fields of the table Events that has to be created by Ruhi? Which field should be made the primary key?

2 Create a database having the table "CourseTable" with fields Course_id, Course_Name and Credit_score. Perform the following:

- Set Course_id as the primary key.
- Enter 5 records in the table.
- Save the table.
- Sort the data according to credit score.

3 Ananthu wants to create a directory containing data –SerialNo, Name, MobileNumber, Email_id, DateofBirth of his friends.Create a table using LibreOffice Base. Make SerialNo as primary key. Enter minimum 5 records in the table. Sort the table in alphabetical order of name.

4 There are 5 houses in Ruhi's school – Ganga, Yamuna, Satluj, Beas and Narmada. Once student can participate from each house in a particular event. Create a table Participants with following fields.

- Event_Id
- Event Name
- Ganga
- Yamuna
- Satluj
- Beas
- Narmada

Also add minimum five records in the table.

CHAPTER 10

Working with Multiple Tables

Once you have learned to create databases and tables in them, either through the wizard or in design view, you can perform various operations on tables like entering data, editing data, sorting data, and deleting data. In this chapter, we shall talk about all these operations in detail.

Tables are the easiest way to store, organise and present a large amount of information. They are the building blocks of a database. Tables play an important role in storing data. All the data is stored in tabular form. A well designed table helps the users to retrieve the data from a database easily.

In the previous chapter, you learnt the steps of creating table using the Table Wizard and Table Design View. In this chapter, you will learn about the various operations that can be performed on tables to add and manipulate the data.

10.1 Editing and Deleting Tables

Editing a Table

Editing a table includes tasks like adding new fields, removing existing ones, or modifying the properties of any field within the table. To edit a table, follow the given steps:

Step 1 Open the Database User Interface window.

Step 2 Select the Table object in Database Pane. A list of tables appears in the Table Area.

Step 3 Right click on the table name and select Edit option. The design window of the table will get displayed.

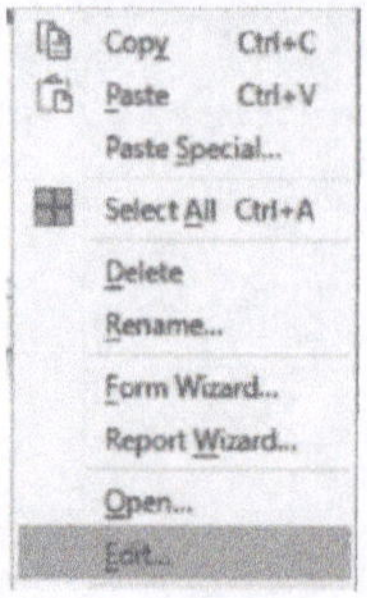

Note *The changes so made will not affect the previous records entered in the table.*

Renaming a Table

To rename a table, follow the given steps:

Step 1 Right-click on the table in the Table Area.

Step 2 Click on the Rename option. The Rename to dialog box appears.

Step 3 Enter a new name to the table.

Step 4 Click on the OK button. The table will be renamed.

Deleting a Table

To delete a table, follow the given steps:

Step 1 Right-click on the table in the Table Area.

Step 2 Click on the Delete option. A confirmation box appears.

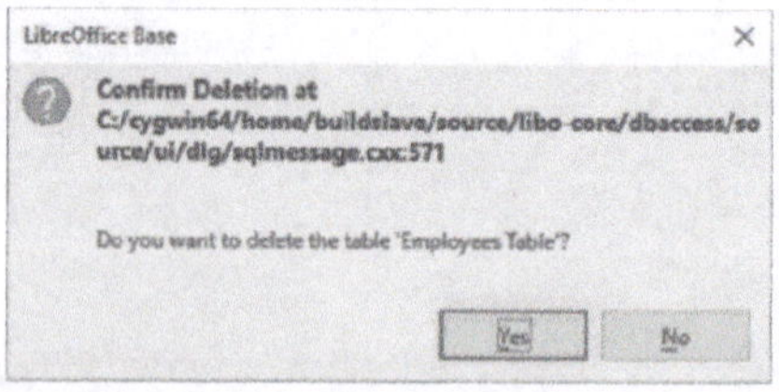

Step 3 Click on Yes to delete the table. The selected table will get deleted.

10.2 Relationship between Tables

When working with multiple tables, it's essential to ensure that data redundancy and inconsistency are avoided. A record for a specific entity should not be duplicated, and there should not be differing values for the same entity across the database.

This is achieved by establishing relationships between tables. The key requirement for creating such relationships is the presence of a common field(s) between the tables.

Let us consider an example by taking two tables:

Table 1 : Students_Personal_Details

Admission _No	Name	Father Name	Mother Name	Contact Detail
7001	Ramaya Ranjan	Mohan Ranjan	Priyanka Ranjan	9877777770
7002	Shiksha Swamy	Yogesh Swamy	Neeta Swamy	9567890000
7003	Sudipta Saha	Rahul Saha	Shalini Saha	9742234677
7004	Yamini Yadav	Deep Yadav	Preeti Yadav	9421234455
7005	Udipta Udhas	Orang Udhas	Anshu Udhas	9123445565
7006	Saurav Sharma	Yashpal Sharma	Shobha Sharma	9233455566

Table 2 : Students_Grade

Roll_No	Admission_No	Class/Sec	Grade
23	7001	X/A	A
24	7002	X/A	B
25	7003	X/A	A
26	7004	X/A	B
27	7005	X/A	C
28	7006	X/A	D

In the Students_Personal_Details table, Admission_No serves as the primary key. In the Students_Grade table, Roll_No is the primary key, while Admission_No acts as a foreign key.

Each record in the Students_Grade table contains an Admission_No value that corresponds to a matching record in the Students_Personal_Details table. It's crucial that the data types of the common field (Admission_No) in both tables are the same; otherwise, LibreOffice Base will display an error and prevent the relationship from being established.

Once the relationship between the tables is set, the DBMS ensures data integrity. This means that a record in the Students_Personal_Details table must exist before the corresponding Admission_No can be entered in the Students_Grade table.

The Admission_No in the Students_Personal_Details table is considered the master record, while the corresponding record in the Students_Grade table is viewed as the transaction record.

Hence, Students_Personal_Details is known as the master table, and Students_Grade is referred to as the transaction table.

Try These 10.1

1. **What does establishing relationships between tables help prevent in a database?**
   (a) Data redundancy and inconsistency
   (b) Data entry errors
   (c) Slow database performance
   (d) Unauthorized access
2. **What happens when you press the Esc key while editing a record in a table?**
   (a) The changes are saved
   (b) The table is deleted
   (c) The changes are canceled and the original data is restored
   (d) The record is permanently deleted
3. **When deleting a record, a confirmation box will appear, and you need to click on ______ to confirm the deletion or ______ to cancel it.**
4. **What is the purpose of setting up relationships between tables in a database?**

10.3 Types of Relationship

The relationship between two tables in a database depends on the number of records in the transaction table that correspond to records in the master table. There are three primary types of relationships that can be established between two tables in a relational database:

1. One-to-One 2. One-to-Many 3. Many-to-Many

One-to-One Relationship

In a one-to-one relationship, each record in the master table corresponds to exactly one record in the transaction table.

For example, the Admission_No in the master table (Students_Personal_Details) will have a unique corresponding record with the same Admission_No in the transaction table (Students_Grade). This is because no two students share the same admission number.

One-to-Many Relationship

A one-to-many relationship is a common type of relationship in databases, where a single record in the master table is associated with multiple records in the related transaction table.

For example, one author can write multiple books, or one customer can place multiple orders, one teacher teaches many students in a class. This illustrates a one-to-many relationship between an author and their books or between a customer and their orders.

Many-to-Many Relationship

In a many-to-many relationship, multiple records in one table correspond to multiple records in another table. This type of relationship is used when entries in both tables can be associated with multiple entries in the other table.

For example, in a school setting, a teacher may have multiple roles such as a class teacher, activity coordinator, or exam supervisor, and each of these roles could involve multiple students. Similarly, a student might participate in several different activities or classes overseen by different teachers. Therefore, a many-to-many relationship exists between teachers and their roles, as well as between students and the activities they participate in.

Note *Junction table is an intermediary table used in many-to-many relationship containing foreign keys from both related tables.*

Try These 10.2

1 **In one-to-many relationship, which table is typically considered the "master table"?**
   (a) The table containing multiple records
   (b) The table containing a single record
   (c) The table with the foreign key
   (d) The table with the primary key

2 **Which table in a many-to-many relationship example between books and customers contains the foreign keys linking books and customers?**
   (a) Books_Details (b) Customers_Details
   (c) Purchases_Details (d) None of the above

3 **In a one-to-many relationship, the table with multiple related records is called the ________ table, while the table with a single record is called the ________ table.**

4 **In the many-to-many relationship example between books and customers, the table that links customers with the books they have purchased is called ________.**

5 **In many-to-many relationship between books and customers, how can each book be related to multiple customers?**

10.4 Advantages of Relating Tables in a Database

Relating tables in a database offers several benefits, including:

- **Reduces Data Redundancy** Establishing relationships between tables helps minimize the duplication of data across the database.
- **Maintains Referential Integrity** Relationships help ensure that changes or deletions in one table are consistently reflected across related tables, preventing discrepancies. This concept, known as referential integrity, will be explored further in this chapter.
- **Prevents Invalid Data Entry** By setting up relationships, you can restrict the entry of incorrect data in fields that are linked to other tables.
- **Ensures Consistent Updates** Updates made in the master table are automatically propagated to related transaction tables, maintaining consistency throughout the database.

Creating Relationships between Tables

To create relationship between two tables, let us take examples as:

Table 1 : Students

Student_id	Name	Class	Sec
[illegible]	Aashima	10	A
A1	Aayavir	10	A
A2	Angshuman	10	B
A5	Armaan	10	B
A3	Amika	10	C
A6	Arpita	10	C

Table 2 : Students Academic

ID	Student_id	Total marks	Grade
0	A1	345	C
1	A2	489	A
2	A3	499	A
3	A4	250	E
4	A5	300	D
5	A6	400	C

Note *Student_id is the primary key of Students table and foreign key of Students Academic table.*

To create relationship between these two tables, follow the given steps:

Step 1 Click on Tools → Relationships option. The Add Tables window appears.

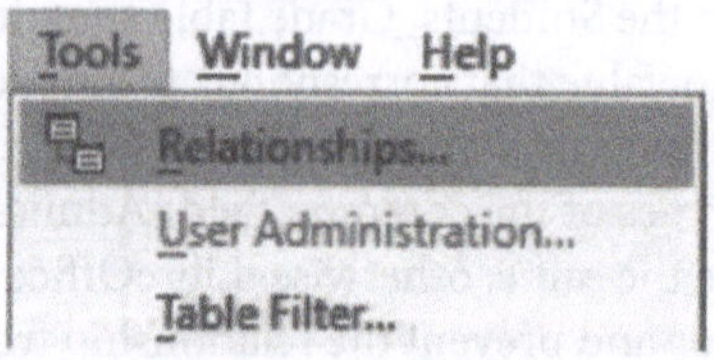

Step 2 Click on the table to be added and click on Add button.

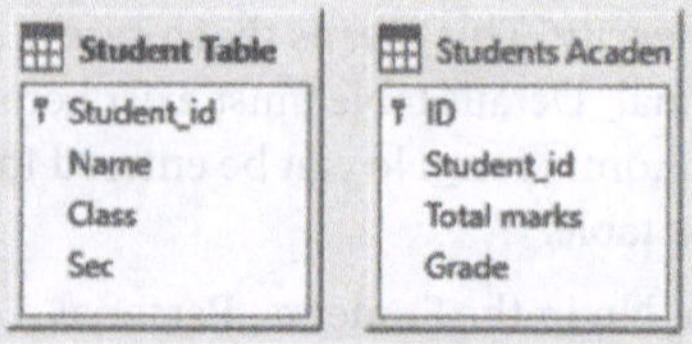

Step 3 The two selected tables appear in the Relationship window.To close the Add Tables window, click on the Close button.

Step 4 To create relationship between these two tables, just drag the common field(Student_id) from the

Students table and drop it in the Students Academic table.

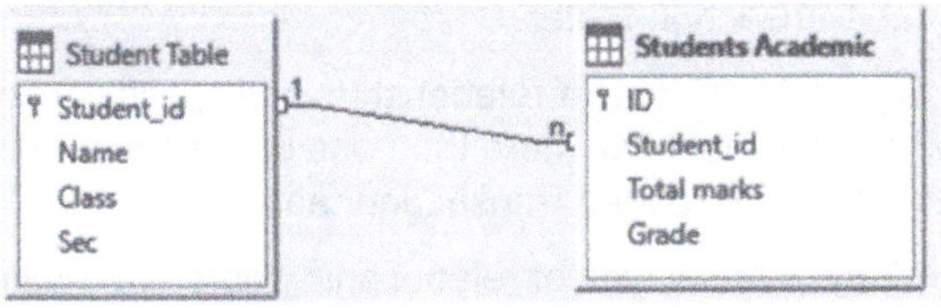

The line is labeled as '1' on the primary key side and as 'n' on the foreign key side. Hence the Student_id from Students table as primary key will have unique values and is called **referenced field.** On the other hand, in the Students Academic table, the values of Student_id might be repeated.

Here it is known as **referencing field**. It shows that the Student_id of the Students table is referenced field and Student_id of the Students Academic table is referencing field. This type of relationship where one value of a table is associated with multiple values in another table is a One-to-Many relationship.

In this relationship Students is the master table. So the master record with a particular Student_id has to be added in Students table first. Only then the corresponding record can be added in the Students Academic table. Also, only one record with a specific Student_id will exist in the master table but multiple values of Student_id might exist in the transaction table, thereby forming a One-to-Many relationship.

10.5 Referential Integrity

Referential integrity is a concept in database management that ensures the consistency and accuracy of relationships between tables. The principle of referential integrity ensures that all foreign key values in a database must match a primary key in the related table.

For example, if an employee record with EmployeeID 101 is removed from the master table (Employee_Details) in an HR database, there should be no record with EmployeeID 101 in the related transaction table (Employee_Projects). Similarly, in a library management system, if a book category with CategoryID B005 is deleted from the master table (BookCategories), there should be no record with CategoryID B005 in the transaction table (Books).

In the library database example, only CategoryIDs present in the BookCategories table should be allowed in the Books table. Once relationships between tables are established, the Database Management System (DBMS) will ensure that only valid records are maintained.

LibreOffice Base offers the following four options to maintain referential integrity:

- **No Action** This default option prevents updates or deletions in the master table if there are related records in the transaction table.
- **Update Cascade** This option allows updates or deletions in the master table, automatically applying the same changes to related records in the transaction table.
- **Set NULL** This option sets related fields to NULL if the master record is updated or deleted.
- **Set Default** This option assigns a default value to related fields if the master record is deleted or updated.

To set the relationship properties, follow the given steps:

Step 1 Double click on the relation line joining the two tables, Students and Students Academic. A Relations dialog box will open.

Step 2 By default the radio button with No action option will be selected.

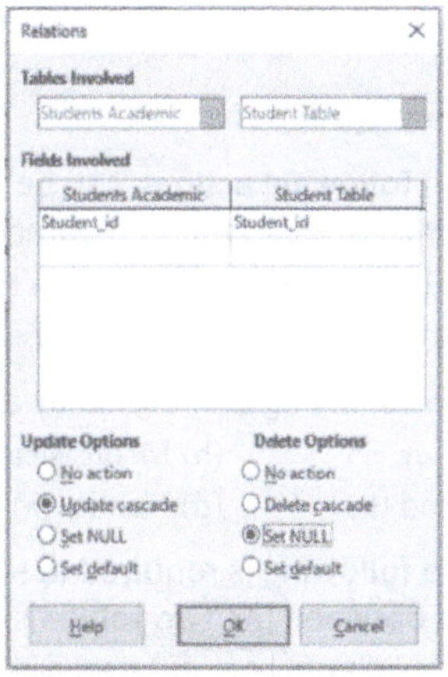

Step 3 Choose any of the desired option and click on OK to set the referential integrity between the two tables.

Try These 10.3

1 **Which field in the relationship between the Students and Students Academic tables is known as the referencing field?**
   (a) Student_id in the Students table
   (b) Student_id in the Students Academic table
   (c) Student_Name in the Students table
   (d) Student_Grade in the Students Academic table

2 **To establish a relationship between the Students table and the Students Academic table, the field ________ from the Students table is used as a primary key, and the same field is used as a ________ key in the Students Academic table.**

3 **When creating relationships in a database, the line between two tables in the Relationship window is labeled as '1' on the ________ key side and as 'n' on the ________ key side.**

4 What is the purpose of maintaining referential integrity in a database?

5 In the context of the Students and Students Academic tables, what must happen before adding a record to the Students Academic table?

Summary

Relations are set up between the tables to control data redundancy and inconsistency.

The most important prerequisite for setting a relationship between the two tables is that there must be a common field(s) between the two tables.

In One-to-One type of relationship, one specific record of a master table has one and only one corresponding record in the transaction table.

In One-to-Many type of relationship, one specific record of the master table has more than one corresponding records in the related transaction table.

In Many-to-Many type of relationship, there are multiple records in the master table that correspond to multiple records in the transaction table.

According to the principle of referential integrity, no unmatched foreign key values should exist in the database.

NCERT FOLDER

Complete Explanations of all NCERT's Questions

A. Multiple Choice Questions

Q.1 Which of the following actions can be performed once the tables are created in a database?

(a) Add a field in a table (b) Rename a table
(c) Delete a table (d) All of these

Q.2 Which of the following is checked by a DBMS?

(a) Redundancy (b) Inconsistency
(c) Both (a) and (b) (d) Neither (a) nor (b)

Q.3 Which of the following is required to set a relationship between the two tables?

(a) Both the tables must be in different databases
(b) Both the tables must have a common field
(c) Both the tables must have the same name
(d) Both tables must be stored in documents folder only.

Q.4 If a record is added in a master table, which of the following is NOT true for transaction table

(a) The record in the master table is called the master record
(b) The corresponding record in transaction table can only be entered once.
(c) The record in the transaction table is called the transaction record.
(d) It is possible to add a record in the master table

Q.5 Which type of relationship exists between a student and the subjects studied by him/her?

(a) One-to-one
(b) One-to-many
(c) Many-to-many
(d) All of the above

Q.6 Consider the following tables. Which type of relationship can be established between the two tables?

Table 1: Item	Table 2: Item_Category
Item_Code	Category_Code
Item_Name	Cat_Name
Price	Item_Code
Qty	Cat_Disc
Category_Code	

(a) One-to-one (b) One-to-many
(c) Many-to-many (d) None of these

Q.7 Which of the following menus contains the Relationship option?

(a) Edit (b) File (c) Tools (d) View

Q.8 The list of tables to be added is displayed in the ________ dialog box in the Relationship Screen.

(a) Add Tables (b) Add Databases
(c) Both (a) and (b) (d) Neither (a) nor (b)

Q.9 In the relationship design screen, the relationship between the two tables is done using ________ operation.

(a) Click (b) Double Click
(c) Drag and Drop (d) Right click

Q.10 Which of the following is NOT an option that can be used to maintain referential integrity in a database?

(a) No Action (b) Set NULL (c) Set Default (d) Set Value

Answers

1. (d)	2. (c)	3. (b)	4. (b)	5. (b)
6. (b)	7. (c)	8. (a)	9. (c)	10. (d)

B. State Whether the Following Statements are True or False

Q.1 Redundancy is preferred in a database.

Q.2 In a table, a record for a particular entity should not be repeated.

Q.3 A single field should always have only one data value.

Q.4 If a table is edited, the records already entered in it are deleted.

Q.5 The record in master table should be entered before the corresponding record is entered in the transaction table.

Q.6 In one-to-many relationship, one specific record of the master table has more than one corresponding records in the related transaction table.

Q.7 The Relationship option is present in the Widows menu.

Q.8 In a database, the referential integrity is maintained by the user.

Q.9 A relationship is always set between the tables based on a common field.

Q.10 If the master record is deleted, the transaction records will always be deleted.

Answers

1. False	2. True	3. True	4. False	5. True
6. True	7. False	8. False	9. True	10. False

C. Fill in the Blanks

Q.1 A table to be edited is displayed in ________ view.

Q.2 The most important prerequisite for setting a relationship between the two tables is that there must be a ________ between them.

Q.3 In ________ relationship, one specific record of a master table has one and only one corresponding record in the transaction table.

Q.4 ________is one of the most common types of relationship between the tables in a database.

Q.5 A record being entered in a ________ table must always exist in a ________ table.

Q.6 The principle of ________helps prevent missing data by keeping deleted data from getting out of synch.

Q.7 Creating ________ between tables restricts the user from entering invalid data in the referenced fields.

Q.8 Data integrity is maintained by ________.

Q.9 A relationship between customers and products is an example of ________ relationship.

Q.10 The ________ window is used to set relationships between the tables.

Answers

1. Design	2. Common field
3. One-to-one	4. One-to-many
5. Transaction, master	6. Referential Integrity
7. Relationship	8. DBMS
9. Many-to-many	10. Relationships

D. Answer the Following Questions

Q.1 Give any two advantages of relating a table in a database.

Ans. Two advantages of relating tables in a database are

- A relationship can help prevent data redundancy.
- It helps prevent missing data by keeping deleted data from getting out of synch. This is called referential integrity.

Q.2 How is redundancy and inconsistency controlled in a database?

Ans. While working with multiple tables, you need to check the redundancy and inconsistency of data. The record for a particular entity should neither be repeated nor different data values should appear for a single entity in the database. This is done by setting relationship between the tables of a database. The most important prerequisite for setting a relationship is that there must be a common field(s) between the two tables to create a relationship.

Q.3 Define referential integrity. Who maintains referential integrity in a database?

Ans. Referential Integrity helps prevent missing data by keeping deleted data from getting out of synch. According to the principle of referential integrity, no unmatched foreign key values should exist in the database. The database management system (DBMS) maintains referential integrity.

Q.4 Differentiate between one-to-one relationship and one-to-many relationship. Give suitable example to explain your answer.

Ans. A **one-to-one relationship** in a database means that each record in one table is related to only one record in another table. For example, a **Person** table and a **Passport** table, where each person has only one passport, follow a one-to-one relationship. In contrast, a **one-to-many relationship** allows one record in the primary table to be linked to multiple records in another table. For example, a **Customer** table and an **Orders** table represent a one-to-many relationship since one customer can place multiple orders. This type of relationship is commonly used to efficiently manage related data while maintaining data integrity.

Q.5 Explain many-to-many relationship with an example.

Ans. Refer to text on page no. 239-240 (Many-to-many relationship).

EXAM PATTERN EXERCISE

Including Competency Based Questions

Multiple Choice Questions

1 What does referential integrity in a database ensure? CBSE SQP 2024-25

(a) All primary keys are unique across the database.
(b) All records in a table must have a value in every column.
(c) Every foreign key value must match a primary key in the referenced table or be null.
(d) Data can be freely deleted from any table without constraints.

2 There are ________ types of relationships in a table of a database. CBSE SQP 2023-24

(a) One (b) 3
(c) 4 (d) Many

3 In LibreOffice Base, the relationship applied on the tables can be removed with the help of .... option. CBSE 2024

(a) Clear (b) Remove
(c) Drop (d) Delete

4 What is the primary purpose of establishing relationships between tables in a database?

(a) To increase data redundancy
(b) To avoid data inconsistencies and redundancy
(c) To allow multiple primary keys
(d) To decrease data integrity

5 Which of the following is NOT a type of relationship between two tables in a database?

(a) One-to-One (b) One-to-Many
(c) Many-to-Many (d) Many-to-One

6 What type of key ensures that each record in a table is unique?

(a) Foreign Key (b) Primary Key
(c) Composite Key (d) Secondary Key

7 Which option in referential integrity settings allows automatic propagation of updates or deletions to related records?

(a) No Action (b) Update Cascade
(c) Set NULL (d) Set Default

8 Which action would you take to delete a record from a table using a keyboard?

(a) Press Enter
(b) Press Delete key
(c) Press Escape key
(d) Press Insert key

9 In the context of databases, what does the term "referential integrity" ensure?

(a) That records are unique within a table
(b) That data types of fields match
(c) That foreign key values must match a primary key in the related table
(d) That tables are not related

10 Which of the following is NOT a valid referential integrity option in LibreOffice Base?

(a) Set Default (b) Update Cascade
(c) No Action (d) Remove

11 What does a one-to-many relationship imply about the number of records in the related tables?

(a) Each record in the master table corresponds to one record in the transaction table.
(b) Each record in the transaction table corresponds to one record in the master table.
(c) Each record in the master table corresponds to multiple records in the transaction table.
(d) Each record in the transaction table corresponds to multiple records in the master table.

12 In the database example given, which field in the Students_Grade table serves as the foreign key?

(a) Roll_No (b) Admission_No
(c) Class/Sec (d) Grade

13 When you drag a field from one table to another in a relationship window, which type of relationship is established if the field values might be repeated?

(a) One-to-One (b) Many-to-Many
(c) One-to-Many (d) Many-to-One

14 What should you do if you want to update records in a master table and have those changes reflected in related tables?

(a) Set Default (b) Update Cascade
(c) Set NULL (d) No Action

15 What happens if you delete a master record in a table with a "Set NULL" referential integrity option?

(a) Related records are deleted
(b) Related fields are set to NULL
(c) No action is taken
(d) Related fields are updated with default values

16 Which of the following actions can be performed directly in the datasheet view of a table?

(a) Adding new fields (b) Deleting fields
(c) Inserting and editing records
(d) Renaming a table

17 **If you have a table of Customers and a table of Orders, and you need to link them such that each order is associated with a specific customer, which type of relationship would you set up?**

(a) One-to-One (b) One-to-Many
(c) Many-to-Many (d) None

18 **In a university database, if a student can enroll in multiple courses and each course can have multiple students, what type of relationship exists between students and courses?**

(a) One-to-One (b) One-to-Many
(c) Many-to-One (d) Many-to-Many

Answers

1. (c)	2. (b)	3. (b)	4. (b)	5. (d)
6. (b)	7. (b)	8. (b)	9. (c)	10. (d)
11. (c)	12. (a)	13. (c)	14. (b)	15. (b)
16. (c)	17. (a)	18. (d)		

Very Short Answer Type questions

1 **Name the relationship in which one column of the primary key table is associated with all the columns of the associated table and vice-versa.** CBSE SQP 2021-22 Term I

Ans. Many-to-Many relationship

2 **Give any two benefits of creating relationships between tables in a database.** CBSE 2024

Ans. The two benefits of creating relationships between tables in a database are as follow:

- Its ensure the data consistency and prevents errors by enforcing data relationships and rules.
- It minimize data duplication by storing related data in separate tables which reduces storage space and maintenance efforts.

3 **How does a one-to-many relationship function between two tables?**

Ans. In a one-to-many relationship, one record in the master table can be associated with multiple records in the transaction table.

Each record in the transaction table refers back to a single record in the master table.

4 **What are the important prerequisites for setting a relationship between two tables in LibreOffice Base? Mention any two.** CBSE 2025

Ans. Prerequisites for setting relationships in LibreOffice base include:

(i) Identifying common fields in both tables.

(ii) Ensuring both tables are correctly structured with primary and foreign keys.

5 **What is the difference between sorting data in ascending and descending order?**

Ans. Sorting data in ascending order arranges records from smallest to largest (e.g., A to Z or 1 to 10), while descending order arranges records from largest to smallest (e.g., Z to A or 10 to 1).

6 **How can you delete a record from a table using the user interface in LibreOffice Base?**

Ans. To delete a record, select the record, press the Delete key, or use the Edit menu and select the Delete Record option. Confirm the deletion in the confirmation box.

7 **What is a many-to-many relationship, and how is it typically implemented?**

Ans. A many-to-many relationship occurs when multiple records in one table relate to multiple records in another table. It is typically implemented using a junction table that holds foreign keys referencing both tables.

8 **Why is it necessary to set relationships between tables?**

Ans. Setting relationships between tables helps reduce data redundancy, maintain referential integrity, prevent invalid data entry, and ensure consistent updates across related tables.

9 **What actions can be performed in the design window of a table?**

Ans. In the design window, you can add new fields, modify existing fields, set field properties, and define primary and foreign keys.

Short Answer Type Questions

1 **Explain the process of creating a one-to-many relationship between two tables in a database. Include steps for setting up the relationship and the role of primary and foreign keys.**

Ans. To create a one-to-many relationship, follow these steps:

- Identify the master table and the transaction table. The master table contains the primary key, which will be referenced by the transaction table.
- Open the database interface and navigate to the Relationships view.
- Add the master table and the transaction table to the Relationships window.
- Drag the primary key field from the master table and drop it onto the foreign key field in the transaction table.
- Define the relationship and set referential integrity options as needed.
- The primary key in the master table uniquely identifies each record, while the foreign key in the transaction table references these records, allowing multiple related entries.

2 Discuss the advantages of using referential integrity in a database. How does it contribute to data accuracy and consistency?

Ans. The key advantages of using referential integrity in the database are as follow:

- **Better Decision Making** Referential integrity contributes to better decision-making based on reliable information because it ensures data accuracy and consistency.
- **Data Security** It restricts modifications of data that could potentially violate the defined relationships, protecting the integrity of the database.

It contributes to data accuracy and consistency by enforcing relationships between tables, preventing data errors, and ensuring data updates are propagated correctly.

3 Describe the steps involved in editing a table's structure in LibreOffice Base. How do these changes affect existing records?

Ans. To edit a table's structure:

- Open the Database User Interface and select the Table object.
- Right-click on the table name and select the Edit option to open the design window.
- Make changes such as adding or removing fields or modifying field properties.
- Save the changes. Existing records will remain unchanged, but new records must confirm to the updated table structure.

Adding columns, empty fields to existing records. Removing columns deletes existing data. Modifying column properties can affect data display and storage. Setting primary key can impact relationships with other tables and data integrity.

4 (a) Give any two advantages of relating two tables in a database. **CBSE 2025**

(b) Explain many-to-many relationship between the tables in a database.

Ans. (a) Two advantages of relating two tables in a database are

1. It reduces data redundancy by linking tables based on shared attributes.
2. It enhances data integrity and accuracy by ensuring data consistency across tables.

(b) A many-to-many relationship in a database occurs when multiple records in one table relate to multiple records in another table. For example, a student can enroll in multiple courses, and each course can have multiple students enrolled. This relationship requires a junction table to link the two tables.

5 You are designing a database for a library. You have a table for Books and a table for Authors. Each book is written by one author, but each author can write multiple books. Explain the type of relationship and how you would implement it.

Ans. The relationship between Books and Authors is a one-to-many relationship. Each book (in the Books table) is associated with a single author, but each author (in the Authors table) can write multiple books. To implement this, the Authors table will have a primary key (Author_ID), and the Books table will include a foreign key (Author_ID) that references the primary key in the Authors table.

6 In a school database, you have a table for Students and a table for Extracurricular Activities. Students can participate in multiple activities, and each activity can involve multiple students. Describe how to set up this many-to-many relationship.

Ans. To set up a many-to-many relationship, create a junction table, such as Student_Activities, with foreign keys referencing both the Students table and the Extracurricular Activities table.

The Student_Activities table will contain records linking student IDs to activity IDs, allowing each student to be associated with multiple activities and each activity to involve multiple students.

7 A company database includes a table for Employees and a table for Projects. Each project can have multiple employees working on it, and each employee can work on multiple projects. How would you model this relationship?

Ans. This is a many-to-many relationship. To model this, create a junction table, such as Employee_Projects, that contains foreign keys referencing both the Employees table and the Projects table. Each record in the Employee_Projects table will link an employee to a project, allowing for multiple employees to work on multiple projects.

8 Explain the term "Referential Integrity". Why is it important in a database? **CBSE SQP 2023-24**

Ans. Referential integrity is used to maintain the accuracy and consistency of data in a relationship. In Base, data can be linked between two or more tables with the help of primary key and foreign key constrains.

Referential integrity is important in DBMS as:

- It prevents the entry of duplicate data.
- It prevents one table from pointing to a nonexistent field in another table.
- It prevents the deletion of a record that contains a value referred to by a foreign key in another table.
- It prevents the addition of a record to a table that contains a foreign key unless key unless there is primary key in the linked table.

PRACTICAL ASSIGNMENT

1. Create a one-to-many relationship between two tables: Customers and Orders. CustomerID in the Customers table should be the primary key, and CustomerID in the Orders table should be a foreign key.
2. Name the type of relationship for the following:
   - Citizen and his Driving License
   - Customer and Product
   - Student and Course
   - Team and Match
   - Player and Country
   - Employee and Project
3. Form a table in Sports Day database in which one-to-one relationship can be established. Write steps to create such relation in LibreOffice Base.
4. Prakasan lives in Happy Home Society. He wants to create a database so as to store and manage the maintenance dues received from flat owners of the society. Create the following tables for his database.

Table: Residents Details	**Table: Maintenance Dues**
FlatNo	Receipt_Id
OwnerName	FlatNo
ContactNo	Date
FlatCategory	Amount

   Relate the two tables and thereafter enter minimum five records in both the tables. Which type of relationship did you create? In which table did you enter the data first?

5. Uzair manages a boys hostel in an engineering college. He wants to manage the records of the people staying in his hostel by creating a database with the following tables and also set a relationship between the tables.

   Table : Student_Details

   - Student_Id
   - Name
   - DOB
   - Course
   - FatherName
   - ContactNo_student
   - ContactNo_ guardian
   - RoomNo

   Table: Room_Details

   - RoomNo
   - Floor (data value can be first, second or third)
   - Category (data value can be AC / Non- AC)
   - StudentId
   - DOO (Date of occupancy)
   - MonthlyRent

CHAPTER 11

Queries in Base

Queries provide a powerful way to retrieve specific data from database tables based on defined criteria. This chapter will guide you through the process of creating queries in Base, allowing you to extract valuable information from your data.

A database is designed to store data in a structured way, allowing for easy and accurate retrieval. To locate and retrieve specific records, users interact with a Database Management System (DBMS) by submitting queries. These queries define the criteria for the data being requested, such as the fields to display or the values that filter the records from one or more tables.

Essentially, a query is like a question posed to the database. Based on the query's criteria, the DBMS searches through the tables and retrieves the relevant records, presenting the results in the specified format. As the volume of data grows, manually finding information becomes increasingly difficult.

11.1 Queries

Queries are a crucial feature of any DBMS, allowing users to retrieve and display data from one or more tables in a database. By providing specific search criteria, users can access the exact information they need.

In LibreOffice Base, you can create and save queries as objects within the database, enabling you to run them multiple times as required. Through a query, you can specify which fields to display and set conditions for filtering records. Data can be retrieved from a single table or multiple tables, and the results are presented in a tabular format with field names as columns and records as rows.

For example, in an Employee database, if we want to display the names and departments of employees who have been with the company for more than 5 years, we would provide the following details to the database:

Table name: Employee

- **Fields** Name, Department
- **Criteria** Years of service greater than 5

In this chapter, we will learn how to create, save, and run queries whenever needed.

11.2 Creating a Query

A query can be created in three ways. In this chapter, we will learn the first two methods to create a query:

(i) Using a Wizard (ii) In Design View
(iii) In SQL View

Using a Wizard

Consider the Sports Day database have two tables – Students and Students Academic. Let us create a query that will display the names, total marks of the students having grades A. The desired data has to be retrieved from both the table. To create a query using a wizard, follow the below steps

Step 1 Open the database.

Step 2 In the Database Design window, click on Queries button present in the Database Pane on the left.

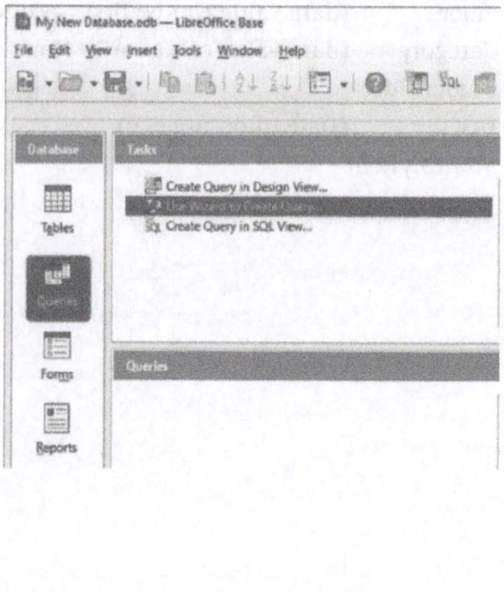

Step 3 In the Tasks Area, click on Use Wizard to Create Query... option. The Query Wizard will start. It contains the Steps Pane on the left and the Query Details Area on the right.

Step 4 The first step of the wizard is to select fields from the respective tables.

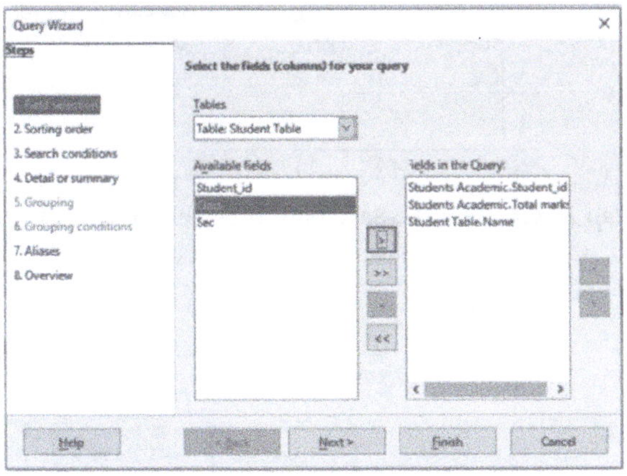

Step 5 Clicking on the Next button will display the screen to select the sorting order. The result of the query can be displayed in ascending or descending order of any particular field of the table. Since we do not want to set in a particular order, so we click on Next button.

Step 6 The next step is to set the search conditions; this is the step where actually the query is set up or the conditions can be given to the database. You can specify up to three search conditions and choose whether to match any one or all of them. Once the conditions are set, click the "Next" button to proceed.

Step 7 Click on the Next button if you do want to summarize or write the details of the query.

Step 8 The next step focuses on assigning alias names to column headers for better readability. By default, field names are used as column headers, but you can choose more descriptive alias names. Once you've completed these steps, click the "Next" button to continue.

Step 9 The last step of the Query wizard displays the entire overview of the query. All the steps performed till now are shown in a summarised manner.

It includes the following:

- **Name of the Query** By default, the name of the query is Query_Students by default. If desired, type the new name in the text box.
- **The action to be performed after the wizard finishes** By default Display Query option will be selected. Click and select the Modify Query radio button if the query has to be edited in the Design view.
- **Complete detail of the query** This section contains a summary about the query that has been created.

Step 10 Click on Finish button. The record will be displayed on the screen.

Try These 11.1

1 **Which of the following is not a way to create a query in LibreOffice Base?**
   (a) Using a Wizard (b) In Design View
   (c) In SQL View (d) In Spreadsheet Mode

2 **In LibreOffice Base, the query results are presented in a _______ format with field names as columns and records as rows.**

3 **When creating a query using the wizard, the final step involves viewing the __________, which provides a summary of the query and the action to be performed.**

4 **What is the purpose of a query in a database?**

5 **What are the basic steps involved in creating a query using the Query Wizard in LibreOffice Base?**

Using Design View

Another way to create a query is using the Design view. This is a more flexible method to create a query from either single or a multiple tables of a database. Let us take an example of two tables:

Employee_Details table

Employee_id	Employee Name	Salary	Address
E01	Ramesh	12000	Noida
E02	Suresh	14000	Delhi
E03	Sukanya	15000	Delhi
E04	Shamli	13000	Noida
E05	Rinku	10000	Ghaziabad
E06	Paresh	11000	Ghaziabad

Department_Employee table

Department_id	Department_name	Employee_id
D01	Security	E01
D02	Sewing	E02
D03	Repairing	E03
D04	Maintenance	E04
D05	Testing	E05
D06	Hardware	E06

To create a query in Design View, follow the given steps:

Step 1 Click Queries icon on the Objects Pane in the Database Window.

Step 2 Click Create Query in Design View icon in the Tasks Pane. The Query Design Window appears. In the middle of the window the Add Table or Query dialog box is displayed.

Step 3 Click on the Employees_Details table and click on Add button.

Step 4 Click on the Department_Employee table and click on Add button. Click on Close button to close the Add Tables window.

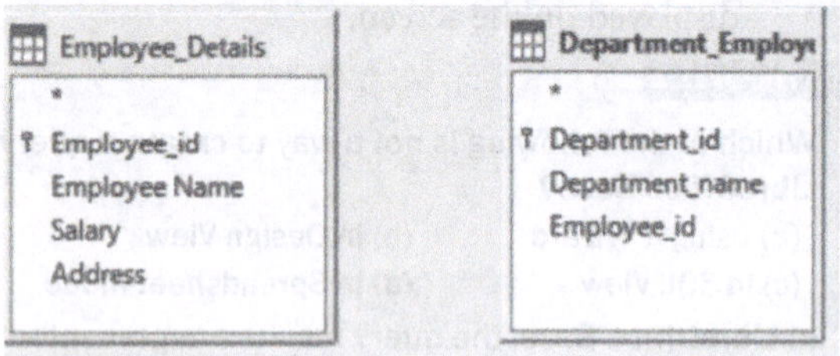

Step 5 Create relationship between the two tables by dragging the primary key of Employee_Details table to the foreign key of Department_Employee table.

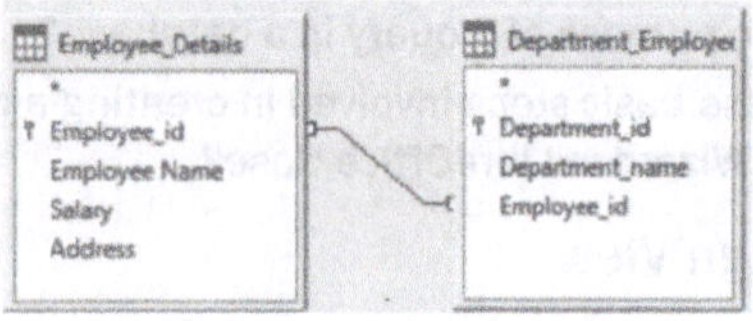

Step 6 This step involves selecting the fields and criteria for displaying data in the Query Design window. The field name and the table name are displayed in the lower half of the window.

By default, the Visible Check Box is selected for all fields, meaning they will be visible when the query runs. If you want to hide a field's data, you can deselect the corresponding check box.

Field	Employee_id	Salary	Department_name	
Alias	ID of Employee	His/her Salary	His/Her Department nam	
Table	Employee_Details	Employee_Details	Department_Employee	
Sort				
Visible	☑	☑	☑	☐
Function				
Criterion		> 10000		

Step 7 In the grid, there is a row titled Alias. As mentioned before, it can be used to display meaningful names in the output.

Step 8 By default, the data that is displayed as a result of the query is not sorted. To sort the records in either ascending or descending order of a particular field, the Sort row is given in the grid.

Step 9 Once the query is designed, click Run Query button on the toolbar or press F5 key. The query result will be displayed in the Tables Pane area.

ID of Employee	His/her Salary	His/Her Department name
E01	12000	Security
E02	14000	Sewing
E03	15000	Repairing
E04	13000	Maintenance
E06	11000	Hardware

Record 1 of 5

Step 10 Click on the Save button on the toolbar to save the query. The Save As dialog box appears.

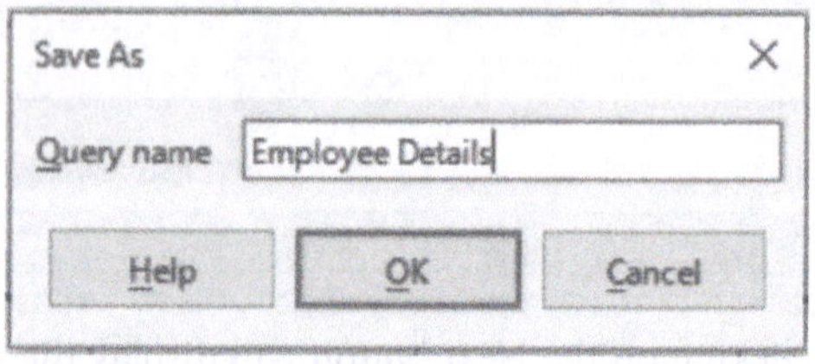

Step 11 Enter a name to the query and click on OK button. The name of the query will be seen in the Objects area in the Database window.

Note *To run the query again and see the results of the query, double click on the query name. The results of the query will be displayed in a separate window. To close the Query window, click on Close button on the top right corner of the window.*

Editing a Query

To edit a query, follow the given steps:

Step 1 Click on the Queries icon of the query that has to be edited. The list of queries that have been created will be displayed in the Objects Area.

Step 2 Right-click on the query to be edited and click on Edit option. The Query Design window will be displayed.

Note *We can use the Criterion row to apply multiple conditions as well. Also note that we can apply all relational operators like <, >, <=, >=, != and = for all conditions that can be given in Criterion row.*

11.3 Working with Numerical Data

Up to this point, we have been retrieving data from tables in our queries. However, we can also use various mathematical functions to calculate values such as count, sum, minimum, maximum, and average. Let's create a query that displays the average points for each event category. To perform query using numeric data, follow the given steps:

Step 1 In the Database Window, click Create Query in Design View button to open the Query Design Window.

Or Open an existing query by right-clicking → Edit option.

Step 2 Click on the Function and select the required function.

Field	Employee_id	Salary	Department_name	Employee Name
Alias	ID of Employee	His/her Salary	His/Her Department nam	Employee Name
Table	Employee_Detail	Employee_Detail	Department_Employee	Employee_Detail
Sort				
Visible	☑	☑	☑	☑
Function		Maximum		
Criterion		>= 12000		

Step 3 Press F5 key to view the output.

Try These 11.2

1 **Which step in creating a query in Design View involves establishing a relationship between two tables?**
(a) Step 3 Add tables
(b) Step 5 Create relationship
(c) Step 8 Sort records
(d) Step 10 Save the query

2 **What is the purpose of the "Alias" row in the Design grid of a query?**
(a) To sort the data
(b) To set a search criterion
(c) To create relationships between tables
(d) To display meaningful names in the output

3 **To sort the records in either ascending or descending order, the _______ row is used in the Design grid.**

4 **In the Design grid, the _________ check box determines whether a particular field's data will be displayed in the query results.**

5 **How do you run a query in Design View after creating it?**

Summary

A query is used to retrieve and display data from one or more tables in a database.

A query can be created in three ways, in this chapter we learned only first two: Using Wizard, In Design View, In SQL view.

We can also use various mathematical functions to calculate values such as count, sum, minimum, maximum and average.

The result of the query is displayed in tabular form with field names in columns and the records in rows.

NCERT FOLDER

Complete Explanations of all NCERT's Questions

A. Multiple Choice Questions

Q.1 Which of the following is refer to asking questions from the database?
(a) Report (b) Table
(c) Query (d) Database

Q.2 Which of the following are the ways to design a query?
(a) Wizard (b) Design View
(c) SQL (d) All of these

Q.3 Which is a flexible way to create a query?
(a) Wizard (b) Design View
(c) Both (a) and (b) (d) Neither (a) nor (b)

Q.4 Into how many parts is the query design window divided?
(a) One (b) Two
(c) Three (d) Four

Q.5 Which of the following is NOT true about queries?
(a) It can be created using multiple tables
(b) Multiple queries can be created in a database
(c) A query can run multiple times
(d) A query once created cannot be edited

Q.6 Which of the following is the shortcut key to run the query?
(a) F3 (b) F4 (c) F5 (d) F6

Q.7 Which of the following functions can be performed on numerical data while designing a query?
(a) Sum (b) Minimum
(c) Maximum (d) All of these

Q.8 In a Query Design wizard, which of the following buttons is clicked to move a field from 'Available fields' list box to 'Fields in the query' list box? CBSE SQP 2024-25
(a) > (b) < 9 (c) ∨ (d) ∧

Q.9 Which of the following relational operators can be applied to set the criterion while designing a query in LibreOffice Base?

(a) > (b) =
(c) != (d) All of these

Q.10 Which of the following dialog box is present when the Query Design window is opened for the first time to design a query?

(a) Add Table (b) Add Query
(c) Add Table or Query (d) None of these

Q.11 Which of the following step is not performed if there is no numerical data to be worked upon in a query?

(a) Selection of fields (b) Giving Aliases
(c) Summarizing (d) Selection of tables

Answers

1. (c)	2. (d)	3. (b)	4. (b)	5. (d)
6. (c)	7. (d)	8. (a)	9. (d)	10. (c)
11. (c)				

B. State Whether the Following Statements are True or False

Q.1 You can run a query only once.

Q.2 A query cannot be created from multiple tables

Q.3 The shortcut key to run a query is F5.

Q.4 LibreOffice Base provides us with two ways to create a query.

Q.5 A query with numerical data cannot be saved.

Q.6 By default the query result is not sorted.

Q.7 A query can be used to display the average value of a numerical field.

Q.8 While designing a query, the criterion can be set on only one field.

Q.9 Alias is an alternative name for a field in a query.

Q.10 In query Design window, the visible check box is selected by default.

Q.11 A query once created using a wizard can only be edited in the Design view.

Answers

1. False	2. False	3. True	4. False	5. False
6. True	7. True	8. False	9. True	10. True
11. True				

C. Fill in the Blanks

Q.1 A _____ is a sort of question asked from a database.

Q.2 The result of the query is displayed in ________ form with field names in columns

Q.3 A query can be created in ________ways.

Q.4 The Query Design window is divided into ______ sections.

Q.5 The shortcut key to run the query is _______.

Q.6 The conditions to filter the records are set in the ______ row.

Q.7 When a table is selected in a Query wizard, the corresponding fields are displayed in the______ list box.

Q.8 The result of the query can be displayed in ______ or ______ order of any particular field of the table.

Q.9 At the most _______ search conditions can be given in the query wizard.

Q.10 The last step of the Query wizard displays the entire _______ of the query.

Q.11 The _______ view is a more flexible method to create a query.

Q.12 To edit any query, right click on the _______ icon of the query that has to be edited.

Q.13 In the ______ row of the Query Design grid, we can type the column heading that will be displayed instead of field name when we run the query.

Answers

1. Query	2. Report	3. Three
4. Two	5. F5	6. Criterion
7. Available fields	8. Ascending, Descending	
9. Three	10. Overview	
11. Design	12. Saved query name	
13. Alias		

D. Answer the Following Questions

Q.1 Define a query? What is the need of creating a query in a database?

Ans. A query is an SQL command used to retrieve, modify, or manage data within a database. It serves as a means for users to interact with the database and obtain the information they need. The need of a query includes:

- Retrieving Data
- Modifying Data
- Filtering Data
- Aggregating or Analyzing Data
- Ensuring Data Integrity or Consistency

Q.2 Rearrange the steps given below so as to create a query using a wizard. Give Alias, Select the field, Set the criterion, Set the sorting order, and Give table name.

Ans. Select the field, Give Alias, Set the criterion, Give table name, Set the sorting order.

Q.3 What all information is seen in the overview (last step) of the Query Wizard?

Ans. The overview (final step) of the Query Wizard displays the following information:

(i) The name assigned to the query

(ii) Whether the query is being created by displaying or modifying an existing query

(iii) A summary, including selected fields, sorting order (ASC or DESC), search conditions (if any), groups, and group conditions.

Q.4 What is the use of Alias row in the Design grid of the Query Design window?

Ans. Alias row in the Design grid of the Query Design window can be used to display meaningful names in the output.

Q.5 Name any four mathematical functions that can be applied to numerical data in a query.

Ans. Mathematical functions to find the count, sum, minimum, maximum or average of data values.

Q.6 Name the three ways of creating a query in Libre Office Base?

Ans. A query can be created in three ways.

(i) Using a Wizard

(ii) In Design View

(iii) In SQL view

EXAM PATTERN EXERCISE

Including Competency Based Questions

Multiple Choice Questions

1 Which of the following dialog boxes appears when the Query Design window is opened for the first time to design a query? CBSE SQP 2024-25

(a) Add Table (b) Add Query
(c) Add Query or Report (d) Add Table or Query

2 _________ means that the query uses criteria you provide to hide some data and display only required data. CBSE SQP 2022-23

(a) Filtering (b) Sorting
(c) Report (d) Forms

3 In database _________ help us to retrieve the filtered data based upon some conditions. CBSE SQP 2020-21

(a) Forms (b) Reports
(c) Queries (d) Table

4 Which of the following is used to interact with a Database Management System?

(a) Tables (b) Queries
(c) Forms (d) Reports

5 In LibreOffice Base, how are queries stored?

(a) As tables (b) As database objects
(c) As reports (d) As relationships

6 In a query, what is the grid called where you add fields and criteria in Design View?

(a) Query Wizard (b) SQL Pane
(c) Query Design Grid (d) Field Selector

7 Which of the following can be retrieved using a query?

(a) All records from a table (b) Specific records from a table
(c) Data from multiple tables (d) All of these

8 Data can be retrieved and displayed from one or more tables in a DBMS using a .... CBSE 2025

(a) Referential integrity (b) Domain
(c) Query (d) Field

9 To combine data from multiple tables into one query, you would use:

(a) Queries tab (b) Tools menu
(c) Query wizard (d) Design view

10 To select all fields, form a table named "Grades" in a query. You would use the expression:

(a) All.Grades (b) Grades.All
(c) *Grades (d) Grades.*

11 Function that calculate a single value from a group of values, such as SUM or AVERAGE, are called:

(a) Row (b) Aggregate
(c) Final (d) Summary

12 In the summary query, data is grouped and summarized based on _________.

(a) primary key (b) sort-field
(c) group-field (d) foreign key

13 To filter a query to show only records where the "Score" field is greater than 85, you would use the:

(a) Field row (b) Function row
(c) Criterion row (d) Alias row

Answers

1. (d)	2. (a)	3. (c)	4. (b)	5. (b)
6. (c)	7. (d)	8. (c)	9. (c)	10. (d)
11. (b)	12. (c)	13. (c)		

Very Short Answer Type Questions

1 What is a database query?

Ans. A database query is a request for data or information from a database. It can involve retrieving data from one or more tables and can specify criteria, such as filtering conditions or fields to be displayed.

2 What is the purpose of the 'Criterion' row in Design View when creating a query?

Ans. The 'Criterion' row is used to filter records based on specific conditions. You can apply operators such as =, >, or LIKE to retrieve records that meet the given criteria.

3 What is the function of the 'Alias' in a query?

Ans. An 'Alias' is a temporary name given to a column or field in the query result. It helps in renaming fields for better readability or display purposes without changing the actual field name in the table.

4 What is meant by sorting data in a query?

Ans. Sorting data in a query refers to arranging records in a specified order, either ascending or descending, based on one or more fields.

5 What are the two ways of creating queries in Base?

Ans. In Base queries can be created:

(i) Through Query Wizard

(ii) Through Query Design View

6 What are the advantages of queries?

Ans. The advantages of queries are as follow:

- Efficient data extraction
- Efficient data filtering and sorting
- In-depth data analysis
- Enhanced data security

Short Answer Type Questions

1 Explain the process of creating a query using a wizard in LibreOffice Base, step by step.

Ans. To create a query using a wizard in LibreOffice Base, follow these steps:

- Open the database and click on the 'Queries' button in the Database Pane.
- In the Tasks Area, click 'Use Wizard to Create Query…'. The Query Wizard opens.
- Select fields from the respective tables that you want to display in the query result.
- Click 'Next' to choose the sorting order (ascending/descending) for any field.
- Set the filtering criteria in the next step by specifying conditions for the records to be displayed.
- Choose whether or not to summarize data in the query output.
- Provide alias names for the fields if desired, to make the result more readable.
- Review the query summary in the final step, name the query, and choose whether to display or modify it in Design View.
- Click 'Finish' to run the query and display the results.

2 What are the main differences between creating a query using Design View and Query Wizard in a DBMS?

Ans. Differences between Design View and Query Wizard

Design View	Query Wizard
Design view offers greater flexibility and control over the query's structure.	Query Wizard is a simpler, step-by-step approach for creating basic queries.
Design view is more complex which requires a deeper understanding of SQL and database structure.	This suits for users having limited technical knowledge.
It allows for complex queries with multiple joins, subqueries, and advanced filtering.	Query wizard is less flexible compared to design view, especially for complex queries.

3 Explain the process of creating and running a query in Design View, including the steps for filtering data, sorting records, and saving the query.

Ans. Creating a query in Design View provides flexibility to retrieve data from one or more tables, apply conditions, and format the results. Below is a step-by-step guide on how to create and run a query using Design View:

Step 1 **Open Design View** Start by opening the database and accessing the Query Design window.

Step 2 **Add Tables** Select the tables you want to include in the query.

Step 3 **Define Relationships** Establish connections between related tables using primary and foreign keys.

Step 4 **Select Fields** Choose the specific fields you want to display in the query results.

Step 5 **Apply Filters** Use the criteria row to filter records based on specific conditions.

Step 6 **Sort Records (Optional)** Organize your query results by arranging records in ascending or descending order based on a specific field.

Step 7 **Run the Query** Execute the query to view the filtered and sorted results.

Step 8 **Save the Query** Save the query for future use, allowing you to quickly re-run it without having to rebuild it from scratch.

PRACTICAL ASSIGNMENT

1. Prakasan lives in Happy Home Society. He has created the following tables in his database so as to store and manage the maintenance dues received from flat owners of the society.

Table: Residents Details	**Table: Maintenance Dues**
FlatNo	Receipt_Id
OwnerName	FlatNo
ContactNo	Date
FlatCategory	Amount

Create a query to display the following information

FlatNo	Owner	ReceiptNumber	Date	Amount

(Please note the change in column headings)

2. Uzair manages a boys hostel in an engineering college. To manage the records of the people saying in his hostel, he created a database with the following related tables.

Table: Students_Details

Student_Id
Name
DOB
Course
FatherName
ContactNo_student
ContactNo_ guardian
RoomNo

Table: Room Details

RoomNo	
Floor	(data value can be first, second or third)
Category	(data value can be AC / Non- AC)
Student_Id	
DOO	(Date of occupancy)
MonthlyRent	

Create a query to display the following tabular format

RoomNo	StudentName	Category	MonthlyRent

Create a query that displays total monthly rent collected for each category.

CHAPTER 12

Forms and Reports

Tables in databases aren't user-friendly. LibreOffice Base offers Forms for easy data entry and Reports for clear data presentation. Both forms and reports are considered database objects and can be created and managed within the LibreOffice Base environment.

Tables in a database are used to store data in an organized way. To do this, we need to input data into these tables. While data can be entered directly through the datasheet view, as discussed in previous chapters, this row-and-column format is not always user-friendly. For users who are not well-versed in computers, it is important to develop an easy-to-use data entry screen.

Additionally, during data entry, there's a risk that the user may accidentally or intentionally modify the data in the table. To address these issues, LibreOffice Base provides the Form feature, specifically designed for data entry.

Similarly, when data is retrieved from one or more tables in a database through queries, it is displayed in datasheet view. However, the Report feature in LibreOffice Base offers a more user-friendly, organized, and formatted way to present this data.

Both forms and reports are considered database objects and can be found in the Database Pane of the LibreOffice Base user interface. This chapter will explore how to create forms and reports using LibreOffice Base.

12.1 Forms

A form is a database object that provides a user-friendly interface for data entry and viewing, displaying information in an attractive and easy-to-read format. It serves as the front-end for entering and modifying data in a database, presenting the data in a customized layout rather than a basic row-and-column format.

Forms primarily consist of field controls, which are organized in a user-friendly manner. Each field control includes a label and a field value text box.

The label is a piece of text that indicates the type of data to be entered, while the field value text box is linked to the corresponding field in the database table.

You can include all or selected fields from the table on the form. In addition to field controls, forms can also feature additional text such as titles, headings, names, graphics (e.g., logos), list boxes, and radio buttons.

There are two ways to create a form:

- Using a Wizard
- Using the Design View

Using a Wizard

This is the simplest way to create a form. To create a form using wizard, follow the given steps:

Step 1 Open a new or an existing database.

Step 2 Click on the Forms icon on the Database pane.

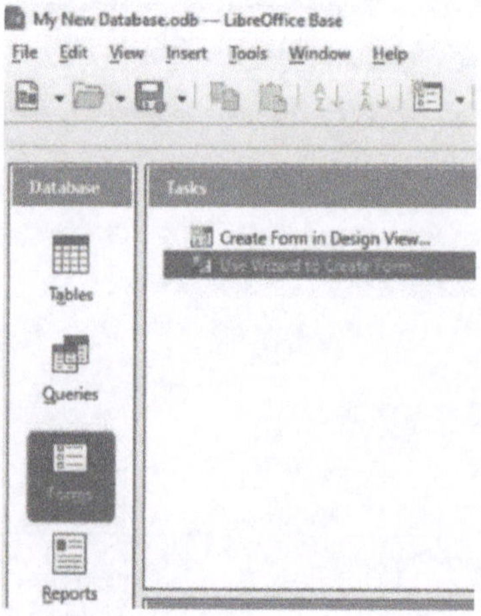

Step 3 Click on the Use Wizard to Create Form option. The Form Wizard appears.

Step 4 Select the tables or queries for which the form has to be created.

Step 5 Select all the fields listed in the Available fields list box. As we require all the fields to appear in the form, shift all the fields from Available fields list box to Fields in the form list box using button. All the fields are shifted to fields in the form list box.

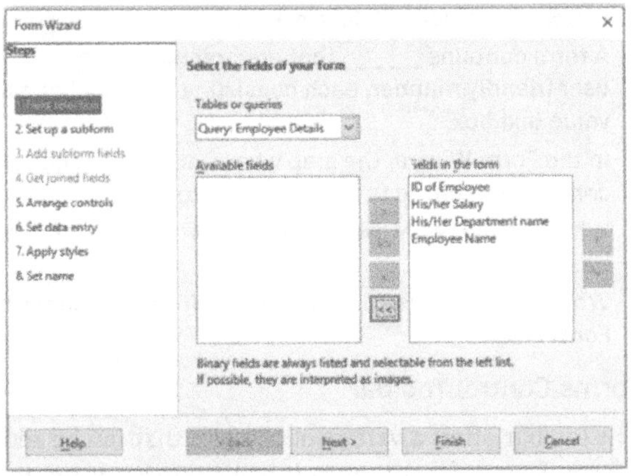

Step 6 Click on Next button.

Step 7 The second step consists of setting up a subform, i.e. a form within a form.

Check the checkbox "Add Subform" to add the subform.

Step 8 Since we do not want to set up any subform, click the Next button to proceed further.

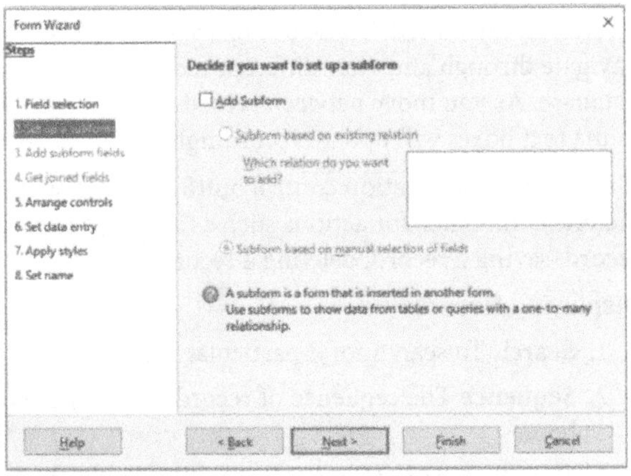

Step 9 Click Next button.

Step 10 The wizard skips the next two steps that relate to the subform and moves on to Step 5.

This step arrange controls i.e. to set up the design of the form. By default, all controls will be left aligned. Click on Right Align radio button to align the controls from the right side of the form.

A field control consists of two parts – label and the field value text box. So in this step, we arrange the label and field value text boxes as we want them to be visible on the screen.

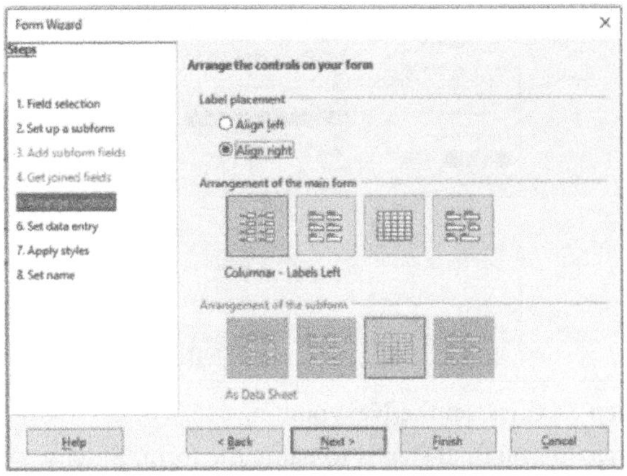

Four layouts are given in this step of the wizard to choose from:

- Columnar display with Labels on the left of the field value
- Columnar display with Labels on top of the field value
- Display as datasheet
- Block display with labels on top

Here, we have selected Columnar Display with labels on the left arrangement.

Step 11 Click on the Next button.

Step 12 Here, the wizard asks whether the form will be used for displaying data, entering data or both. As we go with the default settings, so we click on the Next button.

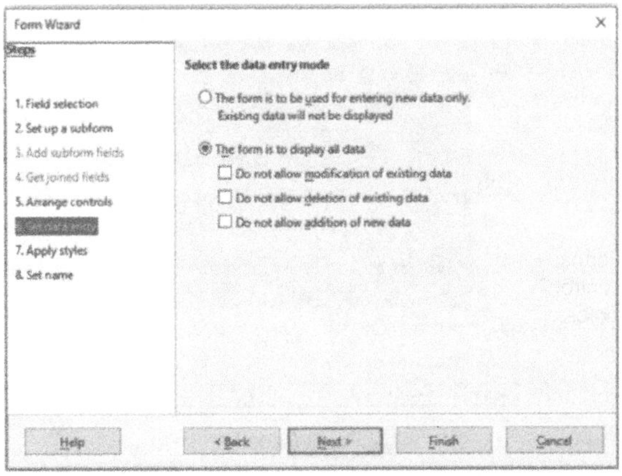

Step 13 The next step is to apply styles to the form being created. We can select the desired background colour and border type of the field value text boxes.

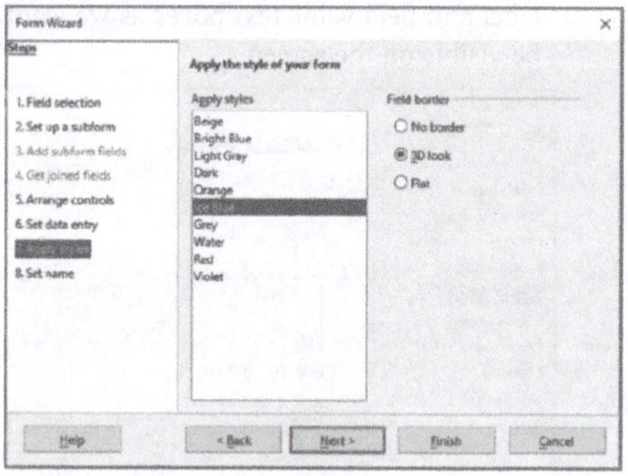

Step 14 Click on the Next button.

Step 15 The final step is to name the form. Enter a different name to the form.

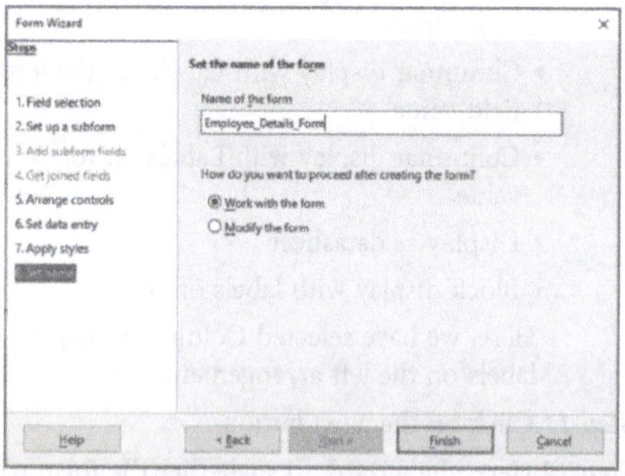

Step 16 Click on the Finish button. The form with the first record will be displayed on the screen in a separate window.

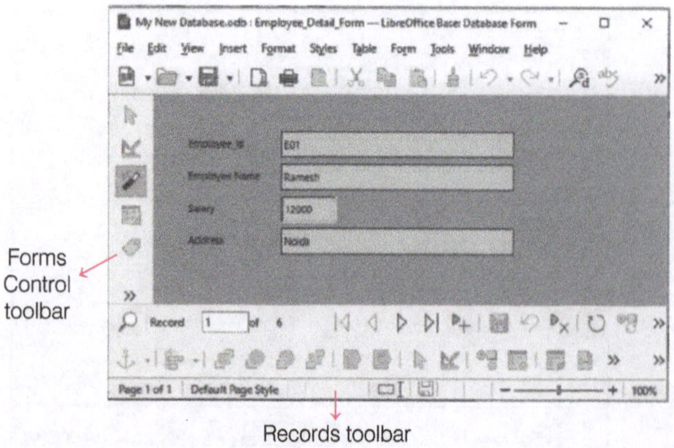

Try These 12.1

1. What is the main purpose of a form in a database?
   (a) To store data
   (b) To present data in a customized layout
   (c) To retrieve data from multiple tables
   (d) To edit queries
2. Which of the following is NOT a form layout option in the Form Wizard?
   (a) Columnar display with labels on the left
   (b) Display as datasheet
   (c) Block display with labels on the left
   (d) Block display with labels on top
3. A form contains ______ that are organized in a user-friendly manner, each consisting of a label and a field value text box.
4. In the Form Wizard, the step where you can align the controls is referred to as the _____ step.
5. What are the two ways to create a form in LibreOffice Base?
6. What is the purpose of the "Add Subform" checkbox in the Form Wizard?

Forms Control Toolbar

The toolbar offers a variety of controls that can be added to a form. Some of these controls will be covered later in the chapter.

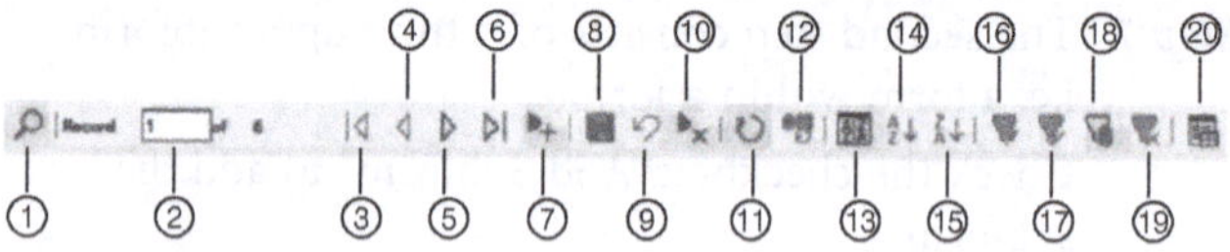

Records Toolbar

The Records toolbar includes navigation control buttons located on the far left. These buttons allow users to navigate through and view different records in the database. As you move between records, the record number in the text boxes will update accordingly.

It displays the navigation control buttons, which also include commands for actions such as adding a new record, saving a record, deleting a record, and more.

Displaying Records

1. **Search** To search for a particular record
2. **Sequence** The sequence of records are displayed here.
3. **First Record button** Click it to display the 1st record.
4. **Previous button** Click it to display the last record.
5. **Next buttons** Click it to display the next record.

6. **Last Record button** Click it to display the last record.
7. **New Record button** Click it to enter a new record.
8. **Save Record** After entering a new record, click this button to save the record.
9. **Undo : Data Entry** Click it to undo the entry of new data.
10. **Delete Record button** Click it to delete the record.
11. **Refresh button** Click it to load the changes done to the form.
12. **Sort button** Click it to sort the records according to ascending or descending order.

Modifying a Form

Modifying a form is possible at any time after its creation. You can make changes such as adjusting the background color, altering the font size and text color, or repositioning various controls within the form.

Changing the background color

To change the background color, follow the given steps:

Step 1 Open LibreOffice Base User Interface and click on Forms icon in the Database Pane. The name of the saved form will be displayed in the Objects Area.

Step 2 Right-click on the form name and select Edit...option. A separate Form Design View will open.

Step 3 To change the background color of the form, right-click on the form and select Page Style... option. The Page Style : Default Page Style dialog box will appear.

Step 4 Click on the Area tab and choose the desired color from the palette.

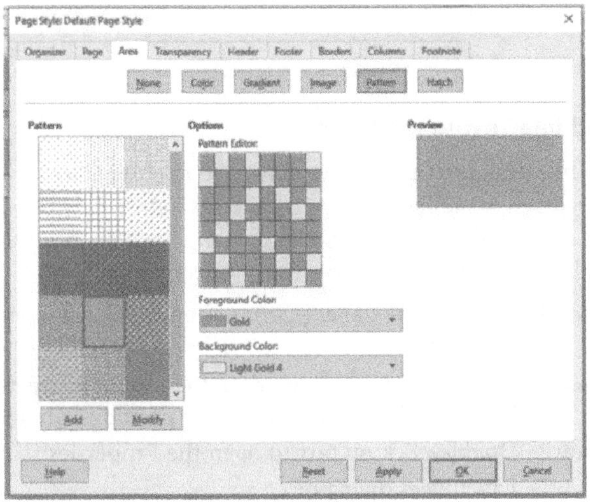

Step 5 Change the required setting and click on Apply and then OK button. The background of the form changes accordingly.

Editing the labels

To edit the labels, either by changing the text or by changing the formatting effects, follow the given steps:

Step 1 Place the mouse pointer over the label to change it.

Step 2 Press the keyboard shortcut key Ctrl+Click to select the label. The position boxes will appear around the label.

Step 3 Right click on the selected label and select Control Properties... option. The Properties: Label Field dialog box will appear.

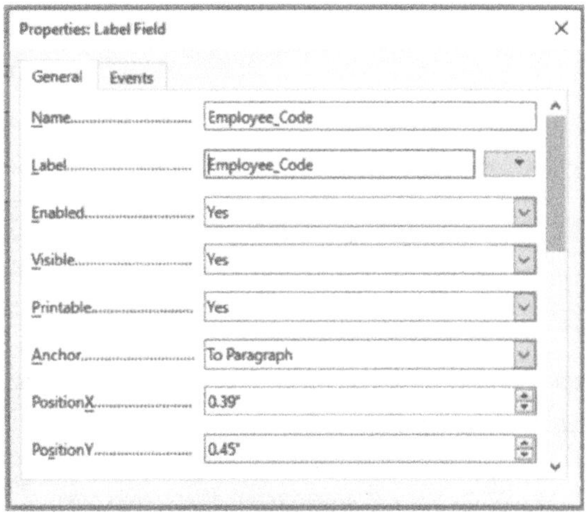

Step 4 Enter the label to be displayed.

Note *Similarly, we can change other properties of the selected label like width, height, alignment, font style and font size in the Properties dialog box.*

Moving a Control

You can move a control to a different location within the form. To do this, click on the control you want to move. Both the label and the field value text box will be selected, and position handles will appear around the control.

If you want to move only one of these elements, hold the Ctrl key while clicking on the specific control. Then, click and drag the control to the desired location.

Changing the size of the textbox control

To resize the textbox control, hold the Ctrl key while clicking on the textbox. This will select it, displaying position handles around the control. Hover the mouse pointer over any of these handles, and it will change into a double-sided arrow. You can then click and drag to adjust the textbox to the desired size.

Adding a Tooltip

A tooltip is a brief text message that appears when the mouse pointer hovers over a specific control.

To enter a tooltip, follow the given steps:

Step 1 Press the Ctrl button and click on the control to be which tooltip is to be added.

Step 2 Right-click and select Control Properties... option. The Properties: Text Box dialog box will be displayed.

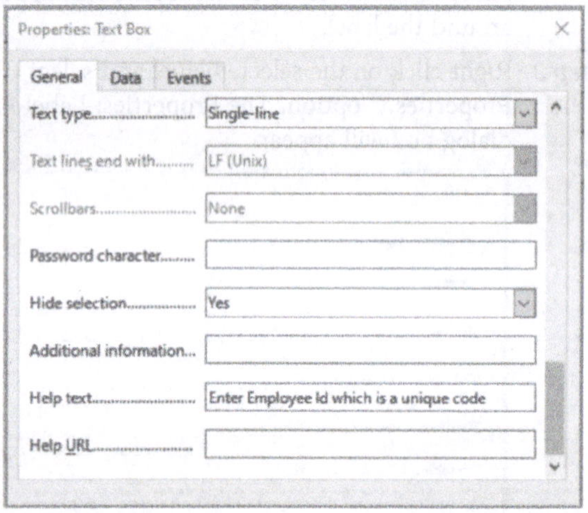

Step 3 Scroll down till Help Text property appears.

Step 4 Type the required tooltip.

Step 5 Close the dialog box.

12.2 Forms Control Toolbar

The forms control toolbar contains various tools to add or edit controls on the form. Let us learn to use few of these tools

Adding a Calendar for the Date Field

While filling up a form on a computer, mostly a calendar is displayed. This is because it is easy to choose a date rather than typing it. To add the calendar to the date field in the form, follow the given steps:

Step 1 Place the mouse pointer over the Date text box and press Ctrl+Click to select it.

Step 2 Right click and select Control Properties.... option.

Step 3 In the Properties: Date Field dialog box, scroll down for Date Format property. By default, Standard (short) format will be displayed.

Step 4 Click to open the list box and select Standard (long) format.

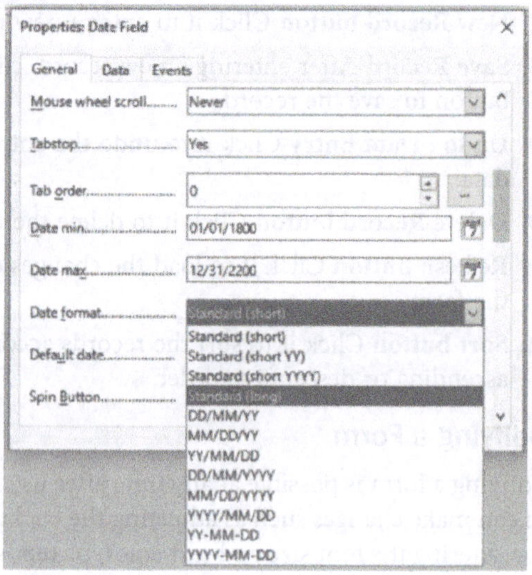

Step 5 Scroll down further till you find the drop-down property. By default its value will be No. Select Yes. The control properties is set.

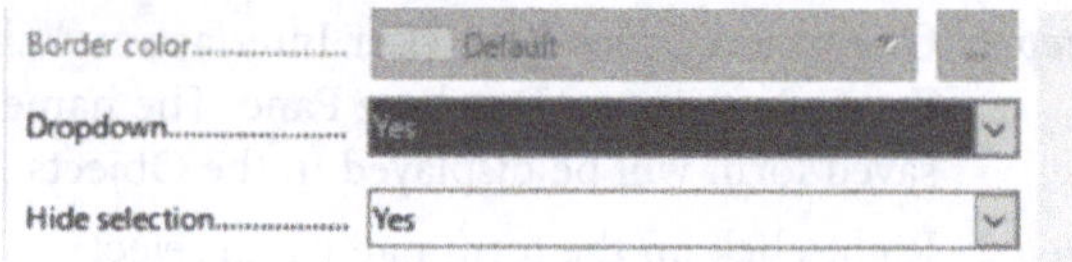

Step 6 Close the dialog box. The selected date control text box on the form changes to a list box with an arrow being displayed in the extreme right.

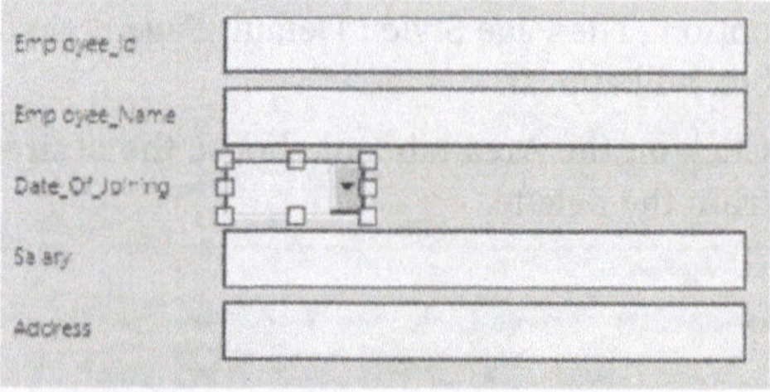

Adding Text to the Form

While designing a form, we may need to enter titles, headings or subheadings. It is called as Labels. It is possible to create Labels in the form while designing. To insert the title text in the form, follow the given steps:

Step 1 Click on the Label ( ) tool on the Form Controls tool box.

Step 2 On the form, click and drag the mouse to create a label field box. It will also have position handlers.

Step 3 Double-click on box to open the Properties: Label Field dialog box.

Step 4 Type the title as "Data Entry Form" in the Label property.

Step 5 Set the Font property by clicking the Font button in front of the Font property. The Character dialog box will be displayed, where you can set the font type, style and size. Choose the desired font style and size and click on OK button.

Step 6 Close the Properties: Label Field dialog box.

The title with the selected formatting effects will be displayed on the form.

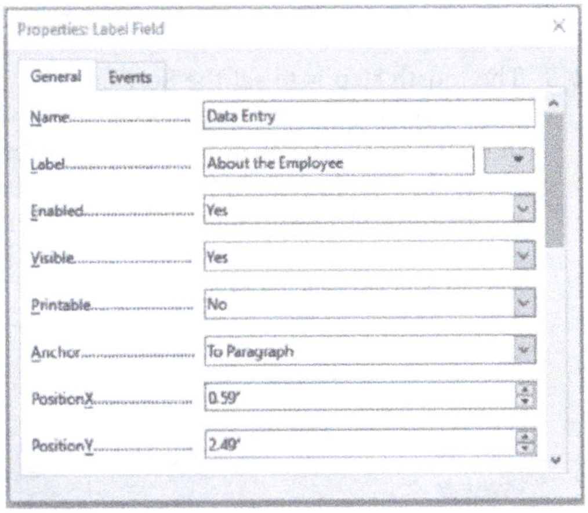

After applying and editing various controls, the final form for entering data.

Adding a new record using a form

After you have finished designing the form, you can display or insert records using this form. For this purpose, you have to shift from Design View to Form View by clicking on Design Mode( ) button on the Forms Controls toolbar. The Form View window appears with the first record displayed in the respective text boxes.

To add a new record into the table using this form, click on New Record button on the Records toolbar.

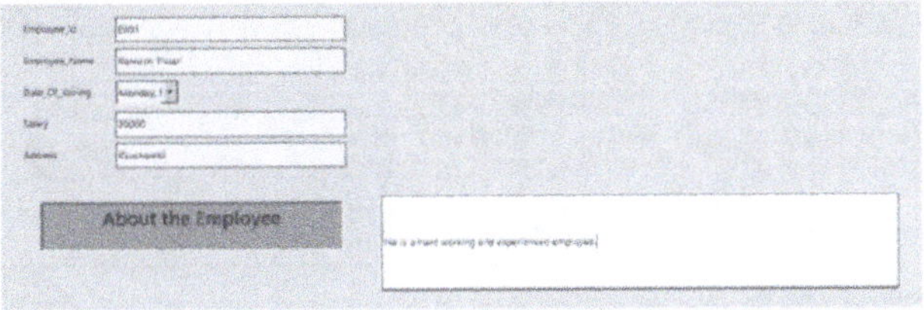

A blank form with the cursor blinking in the first text box. Click on the Save Record button to save the record.

Note *To toggle between Design view and Form view press Design Mode button on the Forms Controls toolbar. When we create a form in Design View, all the controls are placed on the form using various tools given in the Forms Control toolbar.*

Try These 12.2

1 **What is the function of the "New Record" button in the Records Toolbar?**
 (a) To delete a record (b) To save a record
 (c) To display the last record (d) To enter a new record

2 **Which property is used to add a tooltip to a control in a form?**
 (a) Font (b) Help Text (c) Label (d) Date Format

3 **The _______ toolbar includes navigation control buttons that help users move between records in the form.**

4 **The _______ button in the Records toolbar is used to undo the entry of new data.**

5 **What happens when you click the "First Record" button in the Records Toolbar?**

6 **How do you resize a textbox control in a form?**

12.3 Reports

A report is a valuable feature of a database management system. While query results are typically displayed in a basic row-and-column format, reports allow us to present the retrieved data in a more visually appealing and customized way. Reports can be generated based on a table, a query, or both. However, when a report needs to pull data from multiple tables, it's recommended to first create a query and then use that query to generate the report.

To create a report, follow the given steps:

Step 1 In the LibreOffice Base User Interface, click on the Reports icon in the Database Pane.

Step 2 From the Tasks Pane, click Use Wizard to Create Report... option.

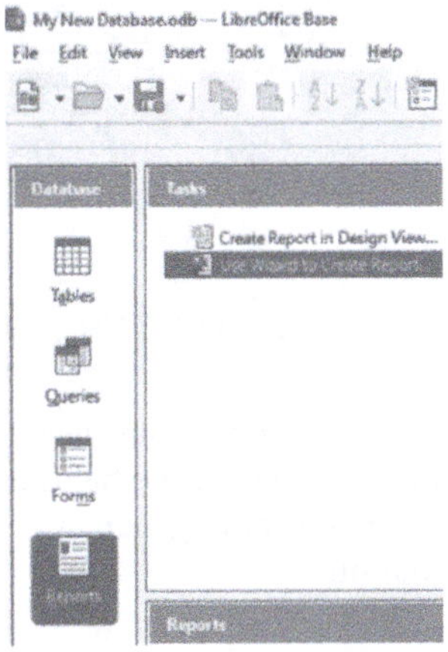

Step 3 The Report Wizard along with two other windows will be displayed. One of the window is Report Builder window and other is Report Wizard.

Step 4 The first step of wizard is to select the table and the corresponding fields that we want to display in our report. Select the required table.

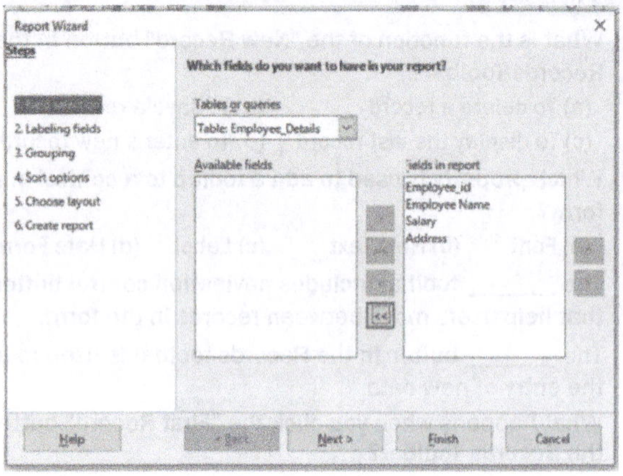

Step 5 All the fields of the Employee_Details table will be listed in the Available fields list box.

Click >> button to shift all the fields to Fields in report list box.

Step 6 Click on the Next button. The next step is to label the fields. By default, the column headers will be displayed as labels or column headers for the field values.

As fields names are generally shortened, to change to more self-explanatory names, type the new names in the respective text boxes.

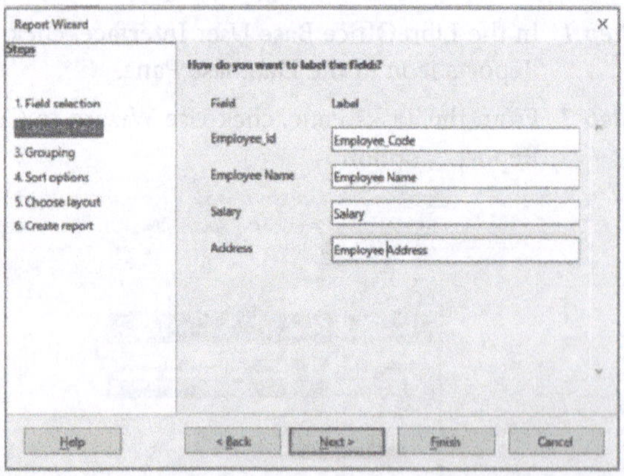

Step 7 Click on the Next button. The next step is to group the data based on any of the fields in the report. Since we do not want to group as of now, click on the Next button.

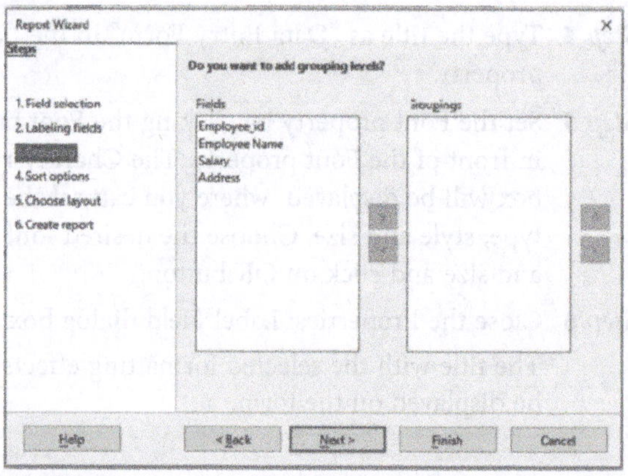

Step 8 The fourth step is to set the Sort options. If the data to be displayed in the report has to be sorted in either ascending or descending order of a particular field, specify the field and sorting order in this step. The radio button for Ascending is already selected. Select Descending radio button to display the records in descending order.

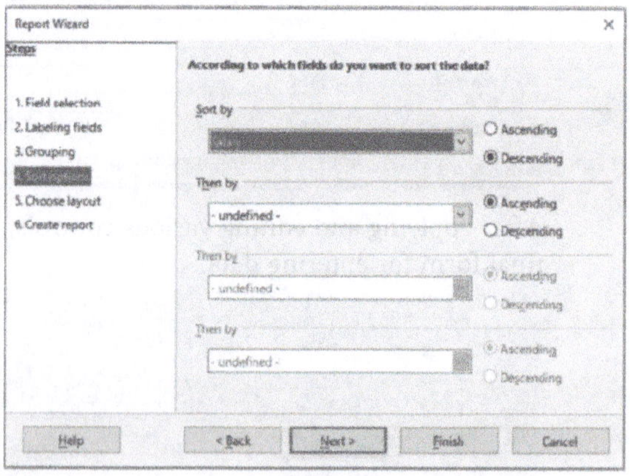

Step 9 Click on the Next button to move on to the next step in which the layout of the report will be selected.

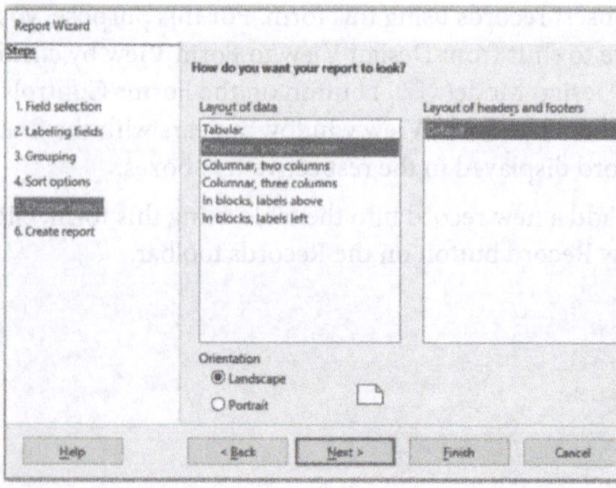

Step 10 A layout is the manner in which the labels, field values and titles will be displayed in the report. Out of various Layout options given, choose the desired layout, say Tabular and also the layout of headers and footers (Default). You may also choose the orientation option Landscape or Portrait in this step.

Step 11 Click on the Next button to move on to the next step in which the layout of the report will be selected.

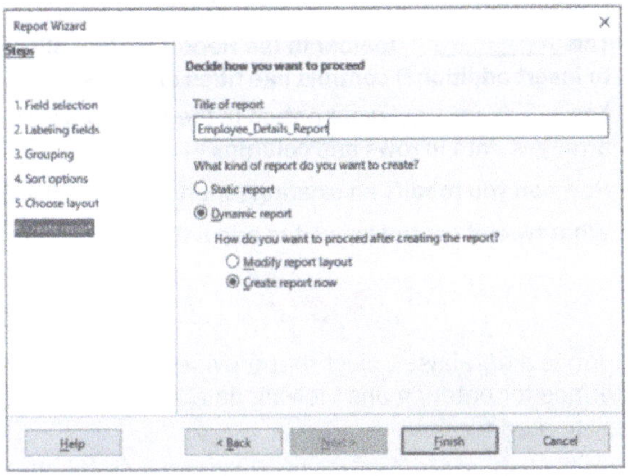

Step 12 Click on Finish button to display the report.

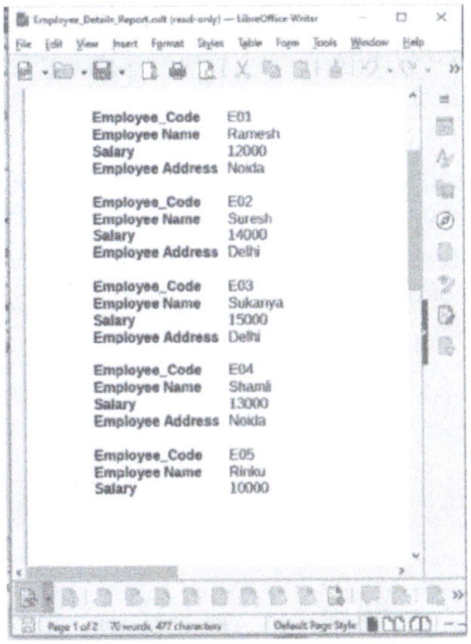

Inserting Other Controls in the Report

We can enhance the presentation of the report by adding additional elements such as titles, author name, date of report generation, and other controls.

To do so, follow the given steps:

Step 1 Right-click on the Report name on the LibreOffice User Interface.

Step 2 Click on Edit... option. The Report Builder window will open. In this window, various controls can be inserted using the Report Controls toolbar.

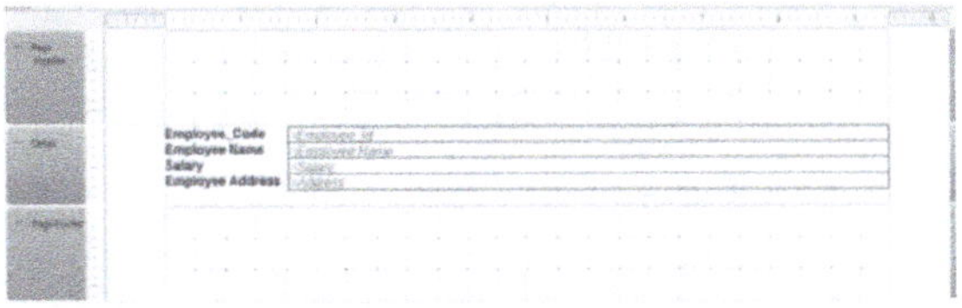

Inserting Titles and Headings

To insert the title of the report, follow the given steps:

Step 1 Click on the Label tool( ) available on the Report Controls toolbar.

Step 2 Bring the mouse pointer on the report. Click and drag to insert the label textbox.

Step 3 Double click on it to open the Properties dialog box. Type the title text that you want to display in the Label property textbox.

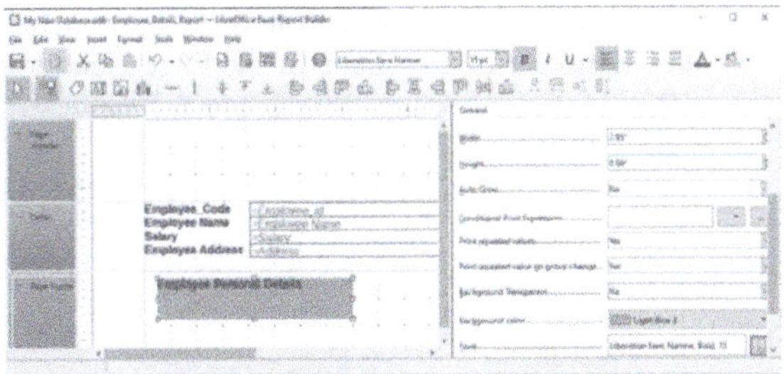

Step 4 Close the Properties dialog box. Double-click on the name of the report in the Reports of Database Pane. The report will be displayed with the formatted effects.

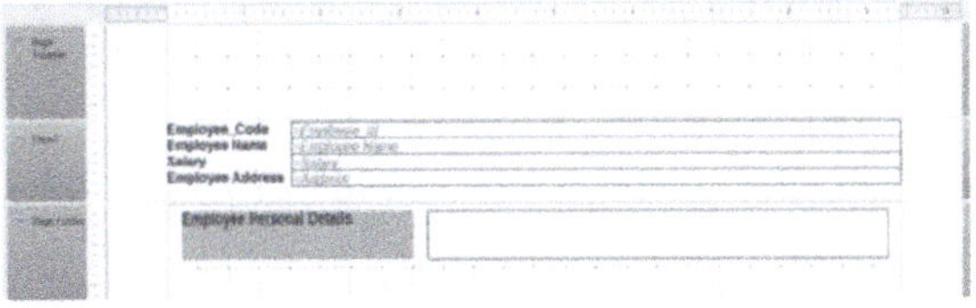

12.4 Inserting Date and Time

To insert the date on which the report is generated, follow the given steps

Step 1 Click in the Page Header area to make it active.

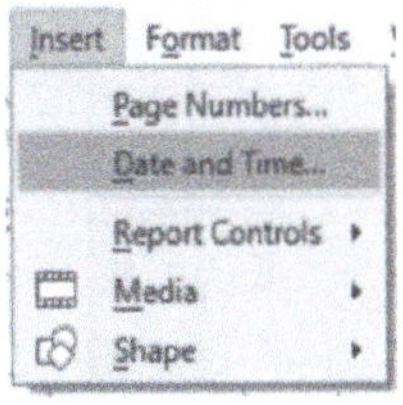

Step 2 Click Insert > Date and Time... option. The Date and Time dialog box will be displayed.

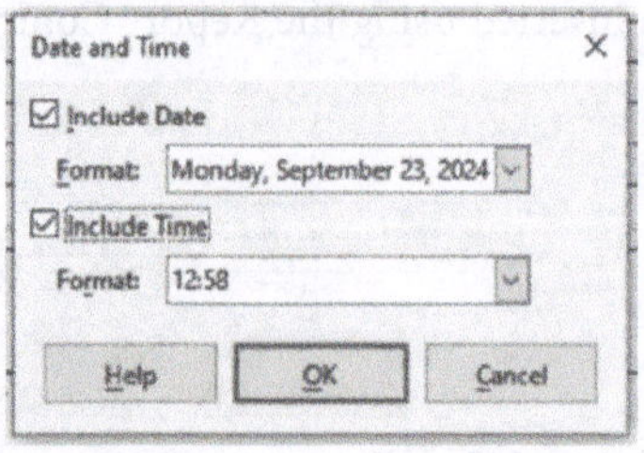

Step 3 Select the desired format for date and time format and click on OK button.

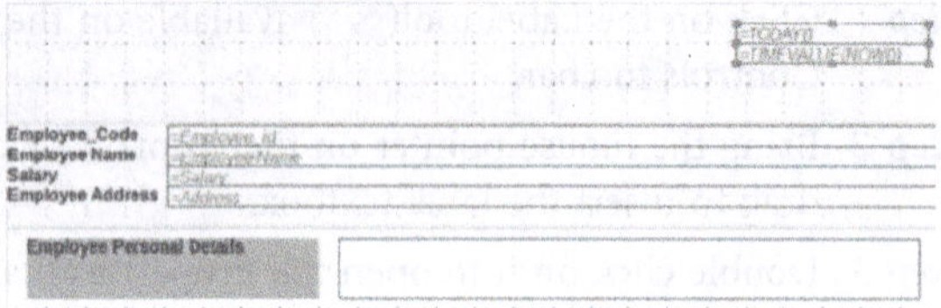

The date will be inserted on the top left corner of the Page Header area. You may click and drag it to reposition it in any place in the Page Header area. The final report looks like as given below:

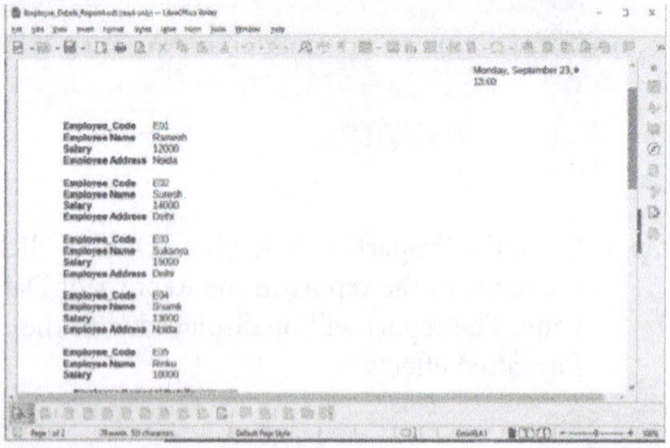

Try These 12.3

1. **What is the purpose of using a query before generating a report that involves multiple tables?**
   (a) To reduce the file size
   (b) To speed up data entry
   (c) To organize and retrieve data efficiently
   (d) To improve layout design
2. **Which step in the report wizard allows you to sort the data?**
   (a) Step 3 (b) Step 4
   (c) Step 6 (d) Step 8
3. **The ____________ toolbar in the Report Builder allows you to insert additional controls like titles or labels.**
4. **The ____________ layout option in the report wizard arranges data in rows and columns.**
5. **How can you modify an existing report in LibreOffice Base?**
6. **What type of control is used to add a title in a report?**

Summary

A form is a database object that provides a user-friendly interface for entering and viewing data in an appealing and easy-to-read format.

Each field control includes a label and a corresponding text box for entering data.

There are two methods to create a form: by using a wizard or through Design View.

The form control toolbar offers various tools for adding and editing controls within the form.

A report is used to present retrieved data in a visually attractive and customizable format.

Reports can be created based on a table, a query, or a combination of both.

NCERT FOLDER

Complete Explanations of all NCERT's Questions

A. Multiple Choice Questions

Q.1 Which of the following toolbars contains the Label tool?
(a) Standard Toolbar (b) Forms Controls Toolbar
(c) Records toolbar (d) Formatting toolbar

Q.2 The Record toolbar has the buttons to move to the
(a) first record (b) second record
(c) last record (d) all records

Q.3 Which of the following is not true about forms?
(a) It is the front end for data entry
(b) It can contain only text fields
(c) Graphics can be inserted on the form
(d) It can contain only fixed number of records

Q.4 Which of the following keys is pressed to select only textbox on the form?
(a) Alt (b) Shift (c) Ctrl (d) Tab

Q.5 Which of the following properties in the Properties: Label Field text box is used to insert a tool-tip on the form?
(a) Tool Text (b) Help Text
(c) Tool Tip (d) Help Tip

Q.6 Which of the following objects of LibreOffice Base is used to display data retrieved from one or more tables in a presentable manner?
(a) Query (b) Form
(c) Report (d) Panel

Q.7 Which of the following values of Date Format property is selected to view a calendar on the form?
(a) Standard (short) (b) Standard (long)
(c) Default (d) Standard (Medium)

Q.8 Which of the following commands on the Forms Control toolbar is used to toggle between Design View and Form view?
(a) Design Mode (b) Toggle Mode
(c) View Mode (d) Print mode

Q.9 Using which of the following objects in a database, can a report be generated?
(a) Tables (b) Queries
(c) Both (a) and (b) (d) Neither (a) nor (b)

Q.10 Which of the following components open along with the Report Wizard?
(a) Report Builder (b) Add Fields dialog box
(c) Both (a) and (b) (d) Neither (a) nor (b)

Answers

1. (b)	2. (d)	3. (b)	4. (c)	5. (b)
6. (c)	7. (b)	8. (a)	9. (c)	10. (c)

B. State Whether the Following Statements are True or False

Q.1 Report is an object of a database but form is not.

Q.2 We can choose the layout of the form.

Q.3 We have to add all fields of the table on the form.

Q.4 There are two ways in which a form can be created.

Q.5 A report is generated in a separate window.

Q.6 Once a control is added on to the form, it cannot be repositioned.

Q.7 The Record toolbar has the button to add a new record.

Q.8 We can create a report only using a table.

Q.9 By default, the records in a report are sorted in descending order.

Q.10 We can group data based on a particular field in a report.

Q.11 A report can have data only in row and column format.

Q.12 We can insert both date and time of generation of report.

Q.13 A report once created cannot be edited.

Answers

1. False	2. True	3. False	4. True	5. True
6. False	7. True	8. False	9. False	10. True
11. False		12. True		13. False

C. Fill in the Blanks

Q.1 A form can be used for ________ and ________.

Q.2 Each field control consists of a ________and________

Q.3 A ________ is a piece of text that specifies the data that should be entered in the field value text box.

Q.4 By default the border of the field text value is displayed in________.

Q.5 A ________ is a small piece of text that is displayed when the mouse pointer is placed on a particular control on the form.

Q.6 The default orientation option for a report is ______.

Q.7 A ________ is the manner in which the labels, field values, titles etc. will be displayed in the report.

Q.8 The option to insert date and time in the report is present in ________ menu.

Q.9 A Report Wizard contains ________ steps.

Q.10 A ________ type of report changes automatically as the field values in the base table or query change.

Answers

1. Enter, view data
2. Label, field value
3. Label
4. 3D
5. Tool Tip
6. Landscape
7. Layout
8. Insert
9. Six
10. Dynamic

D. Answer the Following Questions

Q.1 Give one difference between a form and a report.

Ans. A form is an object of the database that has a user friendly interface where data can be entered and seen in an attractive and easy-to-read format.

A report is another useful feature of a database management system. We have seen that the records that have been extracted using a query are displayed in a simple row and column format.

Q.2 What is a field control with respect to forms?

Ans. A form contains field controls arranged in a presentable and user friendly manner. In addition to field controls, it may contain some additional text like titles, headings and names, graphics like logos, list boxes and radio buttons.

Q.3 Which tool on the Forms Record toolbar is used to insert text on the form?

Ans. Text Field

Q.4 Name the two ways to create a form in Libre Office Base.

Ans. There are two ways to create a form:

- Using a wizard
- Using the Design View

Q.5 What is the difference between a static and a dynamic report?

Ans. Static report means as the field values in the base table or query change, the report will not change automatically.

Dynamic report means as the field values in the base table or query change, the report will also change automatically.

Q.6 Write the function of Forms Controls toolbar and Records toolbar.

Ans. Forms control toolbar contains various tools to add or edit controls on the form.

The Records toolbar contains the navigation control buttons in the extreme left. With the help of these buttons, we can traverse and view the records in the file.

EXAM PATTERN EXERCISE

Including Competency Based Questions

Multiple Choice Questions

1 Which of the following is not true about forms? CBSE SQP 2024-25

(a) It is the front end for data entry
(b) It can contain text fields
(c) Graphics can be inserted on the form
(d) It can accept only fixed number of records

2 A ________ is an interface in a user specified layout that lets users to view, enter, and change data directly in database objects such as tables. CBSE 2023

(a) frame (b) form
(c) relation (d) report

3 It enables users to view, enter, and change data directly in database objects. CBSE SQP 2023-24

(a) Report (b) Query
(c) Form (d) Database

4 What is the primary purpose of using forms in LibreOffice Base?

(a) To generate reports
(b) To create databases
(c) For user-friendly data entry
(d) To store data only

5 While designing a form, it is suggested to get the date input by adding the .... to the date field to prevent entering invalid dates. CBSE 2025

(a) Calendar (b) Text input
(c) Timer (d) Number input

6 What feature allows users to navigate through records in a form?

(a) Form Controls Toolbar (b) Records Toolbar
(c) Report Wizard (d) Query Builder

7 What is the purpose of the tooltip in a form?
(a) To display the form title
(b) To show brief information when hovering over a control
(c) To provide navigation controls
(d) To store data entries

8 Which of the following controls can be added to a form?
(a) Buttons (b) Checkboxes
(c) Labels (d) All of these

9 To modify a form, which view do you need to switch to?
(a) Report View (b) Form View
(c) Design View (d) Datasheet View

10 Which control allows the user to select a date from a calendar in a form?
(a) Textbox (b) Dropdown
(c) Date Field (d) Checkbox

11 What happens when you click the "New Record" button in the Records Toolbar?
(a) It displays the last record
(b) It adds a new blank record
(c) It deletes the current record
(d) It saves the current record

12 Which property must be set to add a tooltip to a control?
(a) Help Text (b) Tooltip
(c) Description (d) Note

13 How do you change the background color of a form?
(a) Right-click on the form and select Page Style
(b) Use the Format menu
(c) Modify the properties in the Records Toolbar
(d) Change settings in the Report Wizard

14 What is the function of the "Save Record" button?
(a) To create a new form
(b) To save the current data entry
(c) To undo the last action
(d) To refresh the displayed data

15 While designing a form, titles, headings or sub-headings may be added using .... tool available on the Form Controls tool box. CBSE 2025
(a) Textbox (b) Label (c) Title (d) Heading

16 In which section of a report can you insert the date and time?
(a) Page Header (b) Detail Section
(c) Page Footer (d) Title Section

17 When creating a report, what should you do if you want to pull data from multiple tables?
(a) Create a new report for each table
(b) Use a query to combine the data first
(c) Use the Report Wizard directly
(d) Manually copy data into the report

18 What does the "Refresh" button do in the Records Toolbar?
(a) Loads the changes made to the form
(b) Deletes the current record
(c) Saves the current record
(d) Navigates to the first record

19 What is the main difference between a form and a report in LibreOffice Base?
(a) Forms are for data entry, while reports are for data presentation
(b) Reports cannot be printed, while forms can
(c) Forms are read-only, while reports are editable
(d) There is no difference

20 How can you access the Form Wizard in LibreOffice Base?
(a) By clicking on the Reports icon
(b) By clicking on the Form icon
(c) By right-clicking on a table
(d) By opening the Query Builder

21 What does clicking the "Undo: Data Entry" button do?
(a) Saves the current record
(b) Deletes the last record
(c) Cancels the current data entry
(d) Refreshes the form

22 If you want to add a radio button for a selection in your form, which control would you use?
(a) Checkbox (b) Button
(c) Radio Button (d) List Box

23 When designing a form, you realize you need to add a field for selecting a category. What control should you choose?
(a) Textbox (b) Dropdown (c) Label (d) Button

Answers

1. (d)	2. (b)	3. (c)	4. (c)	5. (a)
6. (b)	7. (b)	8. (d)	9. (c)	10. (c)
11. (b)	12. (a)	13. (a)	14. (b)	15. (b)
16. (a)	17. (b)	18. (a)	19. (a)	20. (b)
21. (c)	22. (c)	23. (b)		

Very Short Answer Type Questions

1 Define Reports of a database. CBSE SQP 2021-22 Term I

Ans. A report presents structured data extracted and analyzed from a database. They present information in a clear, structured, and easy-to-understand format.

2 In context of LibreOffice Base, explain the concept and significance of the following: CBSE 2024
(a) Forms (b) Reports

Ans. (a) Forms are user-friendly interfaces that allow users to easily enter, edit, and view data in a database.
(b) Reports are formatted presentations of data extracted from a database. They present information in a clear, structured, and easy-to-understand format.

3 What is a form in LibreOffice Base?

Ans. A form is a user-friendly database object that allows for easy data entry and viewing in a customized layout.

4 List two ways to create a form in LibreOffice Base.

Ans. Using a wizard and using Design View.

5 What does the Records Toolbar do?

Ans. It provides navigation and control buttons to manage records, including adding, saving, and deleting records.

6 Explain the purpose of the tooltip in a form.

Ans. A tooltip provides brief information about a control when the mouse pointer hovers over it.

7 What is the significance of the "New Record" button?

Ans. It allows users to add a new blank record to the database.

8 Describe how to insert a title into a form.

Ans. Use the Label tool to create a label field and then enter the title text in the Properties dialog box.

9 What is the default setting for the alignment of controls in a form?

Ans. The default setting is left alignment.

10 How can you modify the background color of a form?

Ans. Right-click on the form, select Page Style, and then choose the desired color from the palette Area tab.

11 What does the "Sort" button do in the Records Toolbar?

Ans. It allows users to sort records in ascending or descending order based on a specified field.

12 How can you change the size of a textbox control in a form?

Ans. Hold the Ctrl key, click on the textbox, and drag the position handles to resize it.

Short Answer Type Questions

1 Explain the steps to create a form using the wizard in LibreOffice Base.

Ans. To create a form using the wizard, follow these steps:

- Open a new or existing database and click on the Form icon.
- Select "Use Wizard to Create Form."
- Choose the tables or queries for the form.
- Select the fields to include.
- Decide on subforms if needed (optional).
- Arrange the controls (e.g., alignment and layout).
- Specify whether the form is for data entry, display, or both.
- Apply styles and name the form.
- Click "Finish" to create the form.

2 Discuss the different layout options available in the form wizard and their uses.

Ans. The form wizard offers several layout options:

- Columnar display with labels on the left: Ideal for clear, organized data entry.
- Columnar display with labels on top: Useful for forms that need more vertical space.
- Display as datasheet: Allows users to see multiple records at once, resembling a table.
- Block display with labels on top: Provides a structured layout that emphasizes each data entry section.

3 Describe the process of modifying an existing form in LibreOffice Base.

Ans. To modify an existing form:

- Open the LibreOffice Base User Interface and click on the Forms icon.
- Right-click on the form name and select "Edit."
- In the Form Design View, you can change the background color, edit labels, move controls, resize text boxes, and add tooltips.
- After making changes, save the form to apply the modifications.

4 A health clinic is developing a patient management system to streamline patient intake, appointments, and medical records. They need to implement forms for various purposes, including new patient registration, appointment scheduling, and updating medical histories. CBSE SQP 2024-25

(a) What is the use of form in DBMS?

(b) What are the different ways to create forms in DBMS?

(c) Where can we find various tools to add or edit controls on the form?

(d) What is the use of the Records Toolbar in a form?

Ans. (a) A form is an object of the database that has a user-friendly interface where data can be entered and seen in an attractive and easy-to-read format. For any database, it is the front end for data entry and data modification

(b) There are two ways to create a form:

- Using a wizard
- Using the Design View

(c) Forms Control Toolbar

(d) The Records toolbar contains the navigation control buttons in the extreme left. With the help of these buttons, we can traverse and view the records in the file

PRACTICAL ASSIGNMENT

1. Prakasan lives in Happy Home Society. He has created the following tables in his database so as to store and manage the maintenance dues received from flat owners of the society.

   Table 1: Residents Details

   Receipt_Id

   FlatNo

   Date

   Amount

   Table 2: Maintenance Dues

   FlatNo

   OwnerName

   ContactNo

   FlatCategory

   In the previous chapter, Prakasan had created a query to display the following information

FlatNo	Owner	ReceiptNumber	Date	Amount

   (Please note the change in column headings)

   Create a form for data entry of Residents Details and Maintenance Dues tables. Also create a report based on the query created above.

2. Uzair manages a boys hostel in an engineering college. To manage the records of the people saying in his hostel, he created a database with the following related tables.

   Table 1 : Student_Details

   Student_Id

   Name

   DOB

   Course

   FatherName

   ContactNo_student

   ContactNo_ guardian

   RoomNo

   Table 2: Room Details

   RoomNo

   Floor (data value can be first, second or third)

   Category (data value can be AC / Non- AC)

   StudentId

   DOO (Date of occupancy)

   MonthlyRent

   Create a query to display the following tabular format

RoomNo	StudentName	Category	Monthly	Rent

   Create a query that displays the total monthly rent collected for each category.

   Create a form for data entry of both the tables.

   Generate a report that displays information retrieved from both the queries in a presentable manner.

SELF ASSESSMENT

Multiple Choice Questions

1. Which of the following is NOT an advantage of using a Database Management System (DBMS)?
   (a) Data Sharing (b) Data Redundancy
   (c) Increased Efficiency (d) Enhanced Validity
2. In the Relational Database Model, what is the term for a field or combination of fields that uniquely identifies each row in a table?
   (a) Foreign Key (b) Primary Key
   (c) Attribute (d) Record
3. What data type should be used to store a student's ID in LibreOffice Base?
   (a) VARCHAR (b) INTEGER
   (c) DATE (d) BOOLEAN
4. Which of the following components displays the name of the database in LibreOffice Base?
   (a) Status Bar (b) Title Bar
   (c) Standard Toolbar (d) Database Pane
5. Which type of relationship exists between the Teachers_Info and Class_Info tables where one teacher can teach multiple classes?
   (a) One-to-One (b) One-to-Many (c) Many-to-Many (d) None of these
6. What is the purpose of a query in a Database Management System (DBMS)?
   (a) To insert new records into the database
   (b) To modify the structure of the database
   (c) To retrieve and display specific data based on criteria
   (d) To delete a table from the database
7. Which SQL statement is used to create a new table in a database?
   (a) INSERT INTO (b) CREATE TABLE (c) ALTER TABLE (d) DROP TABLE
8. In the Query Wizard of LibreOffice Base, what is the function of an alias?
   (a) To sort the results in ascending order
   (b) To summarize the query results
   (c) To assign a user-friendly name to a column in the output
   (d) To delete records based on a condition
9. What is the primary purpose of a form in a database?
   (a) To store data in a table
   (b) To present data in a report
   (c) To provide a user-friendly interface for data entry
   (d) To perform calculations in a database
10. Which of the following controls can be added to a form in LibreOffice Base?
    (a) Text boxes (b) Radio buttons
    (c) List boxes (d) All of these

Very Short Answer Type Questions

11. What is the main difference between data and information?
12. What is the function of the Database Pane in LibreOffice Base?
13. What is the purpose of setting up relationships between tables in a database?
14. What are the three methods of creating a query in LibreOffice Base?
15. What is the purpose of adding a tooltip to a control in a form?

Short Answer Type Questions

16. Explain the advantages of using a Database Management System (DBMS) and provide examples of how it improves efficiency and accuracy in data management.

17. Describe the process of creating a table using the Table Wizard in LibreOffice Base.

18. Explain the concept of a many-to-many relationship in a database with an example.

19. Explain the steps to create a query using the Query Wizard in LibreOffice Base and how to filter records based on a condition.

20. Explain the steps involved in creating a form using the wizard in LibreOffice Base.

21. You are managing a company's employee database and need to ensure that employee ages are always greater than 18. How would you enforce this requirement in the database using DBMS?

22. Consider the following table: Employee

Emp_id	Name	Salary	Designation
E01	Kajal	78000	Manager
E02	Rahul	50000	Sales Executive
E03	Tarun	55000	Clerk

(a) You are tasked with designing a new employee database for your company. Based on the given table structure, identify the fields that would be necessary to store key information about each employee.

(b) As a database administrator, you need to ensure each employee has a unique identifier. Which field in the table would you choose as the primary key, and why?

(c) During a review of the employee database, you realize there could be another field apart from the primary key that can uniquely identify a record. Identify the field and justify why it could serve as an alternate key.

(d) You are integrating the employee table with another table that stores department details. Explain how you would use the primary key from the employee table and a foreign key in the department table to establish a relationship between the two tables. Illustrate with an example.

23. Consider the following table: Product

Product_id	Product_Name	Price	Category
P001	Laptop	50000	Electronics
P002	Sofa	15000	Furniture
P003	Mobile	30000	Electronics

(a) You are tasked with designing a new product database for your company. Based on the given table structure, identify the fields that would be necessary to store key information about each product.

(b) As a database administrator, you need to ensure each product has a unique identifier. Which field in the table would you choose as the primary key, and why?

(c) During a review of the product database, you realize there could be another field apart from the primary key that can uniquely identify a record. Identify the field and justify why it could serve as an alternate key.

(d) You are integrating the product table with another table that stores supplier details. Explain how you would use the primary key from the product table and a foreign key in the supplier table to establish a relationship between the two tables. Illustrate with an example.

Answers

1. (b) **2.** (b) **3.** (a) **4.** (d) **5.** (b) **6.** (c) **7.** (b) **8.** (c) **9.** (c) **10.** (d)

Unit 4

Maintain Healthy, Safe and Secure Working Environment

This unit highlights the importance of safe working practices in the IT industry. It highlights the potential health risks associated with extended computer use and provides guidelines for maintaining a healthy work environment. The unit also covers electrical safety, emergency procedures, and general workplace safety measures to ensure a safe and productive work environment.

Chapter 13 Health, Safety and Security at Workplace

- Introduction to Health, Safety and Security at Workplace
- Policies and Procedures for Health, Safety and Security
- Reasons for Implementing Health, Safety and Security Programs or Policies in the Workplace
- Hazards
- Hazard Control

Chapter 14 Workplace Quality Measures

- Air and Water Quality Monitoring Process
- Guidelines for Clean Air and Clean Water
- Importance of Cleanliness at the Workplace
- Office Ergonomics
- Computer Health and Safety Tips
- Health and Safety Requirements for Computer Workplaces
- Cautions while Working on the Computer

Chapter 15 Prevent Accidents and Emergencies

- Accident and Emergencies
- Types of Accidents
- Handling Accidents
- Types of Emergencies
- Fire Hazards in the Workplace
- First Aid for Electrical Emergencies

Health, Safety and Security at Workplace

CHAPTER 13

A safe and healthy workplace is essential for both employees and employers. It not only enhances productivity and job satisfaction but also reduces accidents, injuries, and illnesses. By prioritizing health, safety, and security, organizations can create a positive work environment where everyone can thrive. In this chapter, we will explore the importance of workplace safety, common hazards, preventive measures, and the role of individuals in maintaining a secure work environment.

13.1 Introduction to Health, Safety and Security at Workplace

Every workplace accident, illness, or conflict carries a cost for both the organization and the affected employees and their families. It is our duty to ensure a safe work environment, which in turn enhances productivity and the overall atmosphere. Employees must take responsibility for their own health and safety instead of relying solely on the "safety officer" or management.

Health

An employee's health refers to their physical, mental, and social well-being. Every organization must ensure a healthy and safe working environment for its employees. Maintaining good employee health prevents the spread of diseases within the organization.

Cleanliness in the workplace is essential, and spaces should be tidied each morning before work begins. A clean environment boosts morale. Proper air conditioning is necessary for clean, cool air, along with filtered water and a cafeteria that serves fresh, high-quality food. Additionally, the company must maintain clean and well-equipped washrooms for employee use.

Safety

The workplace environment must be free from hazards and risks. A hazard is anything that can cause harm, while a risk is the likelihood of that harm occurring. Companies should establish clear safety guidelines that are strictly followed. Employees should regularly practice safety procedures to ensure preparedness.

Security

Employees should feel secure within the company premises. Security means protection from potential harm. Every organization should have a dedicated security department responsible for personal safety, computer system safety, electrical safety, transport safety, and equipment safety. Effective security measures help reduce liabilities, insurance costs, and compensation claims, ultimately increasing business revenue.

13.2 Policies and Procedures for Health, Safety and Security

The Department of Information Technology (DoIT) has developed a policy to ensure a healthy and safe work environment for all employees.

Definition

A health, safety, and security policy is a formal written statement by an employer, expressing the company's commitment to protecting the health, safety, and security of its employees and the public. It represents management's promise to ensure the well-being of its workforce. Such a policy outlines the organization's goals and objectives for maintaining a safe working environment and ensures the protection of workers.

Government regulations specify minimum requirements for health, safety, and security programs, which every employer must comply with. Beyond this, companies should establish their own health, safety, and security committees to identify workplace hazards and specify control measures in their programs.

13.3 Reasons for Implementing Health, Safety, and Security Programs or Policies in the Workplace

Several reasons highlight the importance of having a safety policy, including:

- It clearly demonstrates the company's commitment to the health and safety of its employees.
- It shows that business performance and safety performance can work together harmoniously.
- It emphasizes that the company is not solely focused on profits but is also mindful of the well-being of all its stakeholders.
- The responsibility of every employee in maintaining workplace health, safety, and security is clearly outlined.
- The company can comply with the Government of India's national Occupational Health and Safety (OH&S) policies.
- The policy helps prevent employee injuries and illnesses.

A typical OH&S policy for an IT company may include the following clauses:

- Allocate sufficient resources to ensure continuous improvement in OH&S performance.
- Comply with relevant OH&S legal requirements and aim for leadership beyond mere compliance.
- Establish appropriate OH&S objectives and targets, conducting periodic reviews to assess performance.
- Implement measures and processes to prevent occupational accidents, injuries, illnesses, and near-misses, with ongoing efforts to enhance these processes.
- Promote OH&S awareness and build competencies at all levels to effectively manage individual OH&S responsibilities.

Try These 13.1

1. **What is a primary responsibility of employees regarding workplace safety?**
   (a) Relying solely on the safety officer
   (b) Ensuring their own health and safety
   (c) Ignoring safety guidelines
   (d) Delegating safety concerns to management
2. **Which department in an organization is typically responsible for overseeing various aspects of security?**
   (a) Human Resources
   (b) Marketing
   (c) Security Department
   (d) Finance Department
3. **A health, safety, and security policy is a formal written statement by an employer that demonstrates the company's commitment to health, safety and _________ of its employees and the public.**
4. **Companies should establish their own health, safety, and security committees to identify workplace __________ and specify control measures in their programs.**
5. **What should every organization have to ensure compliance with health, safety, and security regulations?**
6. **Why is maintaining cleanliness in the workplace important for employee morale?**

13.4 Hazards

A hazard is any source of potential damage, harm or adverse health effects of the people at workplace. Hazard is a potential source of harm to the health of the worker or employee. But, the exact meaning of the word hazard can be confusing as often it is combined with the term risk.

Types of Hazards in Workplace

There are many types of hazards that can occur in workplace as follows

Physical Hazards

Physical hazards refer to risks stemming from the physical work environment, such as floors, facilities, walls, and ceilings. They can also include working with machinery or electrical equipment. Specific work processes or assignments may also present physical hazards. While physical hazards exist across all industries, they tend to be unique to each sector and work setting.

Some common physical hazards that can occur in workplace are as follows:

- **Slips, trips and falls** One of the common accidents in workplace is slipping on wet floor or you likely encountered slippery tiled surfaces.
- **Muscle strains** Another common type of accidents is strained muscles. This situation can occur with the person who lifts heavy weights at workplace.
- **Being hit by falling objects** At the workplace, it may happen some objects may fall on you from shelves or out of the cupboard, causing some nasty injuries.Providing adequate storage cages and reminding employees of how to store items safely can go a long way to reducing this risk.
- **Repetitive Strain Injury (RSI)** RSI is another problem that's become increasingly common place at work over the years, though even now some employers don't seem to take it entirely seriously.

- **Crashes and collisions** Accidents resulting in crash or impact injuries are also quite frequent at work. Whether they involve cars, lorries or even smaller vehicles such as forklift trucks, they can have seriously nasty consequences.

Electrical Hazards

Workers can face electrocution or electric shocks due to several reasons, primarily from direct contact with live wires or indirect contact through conductors. While not all electrical accidents are fatal, they can result in severe, life-threatening, or permanent injuries.

Common causes of electrical accidents include exposed or worn-out wiring, overloaded outlets, ungrounded or faulty equipment, and improper use of electrical devices. Employees should be trained in basic electrical safety and instructed to keep water and food away from electrical equipment. Routine inspections by electrical technicians and engineers are essential to identify and address damaged or broken wires.

Fire Hazards

All workplaces must adhere to housekeeping standards to ensure fire safety. Failure to follow these standards can result in fires, causing damage to critical equipment, stock, and buildings, and potentially leading to employee injuries. To prevent fires, it is crucial to implement safety precautions throughout the workplace. The organization should have first response and emergency mitigation systems in place. Employees must be familiar with all emergency exits, fire escape routes, and the locations of fire extinguishers and alarms within the office building.

Health Hazards

Health encompasses the overall physical well-being of workers, including visible aspects like skin, eyes, and ears, as well as less visible elements such as the respiratory, cardiovascular, and nervous systems.

Most workplaces have hazards that can affect various parts of the body. For instance, excessive noise from machinery can impair hearing, while exposure to intense light or toxic fumes can harm the eyes and respiratory system. Long-term exposure to hazardous conditions can lead to serious health issues, such as lung damage from harmful chemicals.

- **Inhaling toxic fumes** While most of us don't work with hazardous chemicals, those of us who do may be at risk of skin or eye reactions as well as potentially more serious injuries when exposed to them without protection.
- **Exposure to loud noise** You might think that industrial deafness is a thing of the past and went out with all those old heavy industries, but that's not the case – not least because many industrial workers continue to be exposed to loud noises while at work.

Potential Sources of Hazards in an Organization

Bright light sources behind your display screen can create contrast issues, making it hard to clearly see your work. To avoid this, consider the following solutions:

- Install blinds or drapes on windows to block out bright light. Adjust the blinds and furniture placement to let light into the room, but not directly into your line of sight.
- Opt for indirect or shielded lighting when possible, and avoid intense or uneven lighting in your field of vision. Make sure lamps have glare shields or shades to direct light away from your eyes.
- Reposition your workstation so that bright light from windows hits the computer screen at a right angle.
- High contrast between light and dark areas on the screen, work surface, and surrounding environment can lead to eye strain and headaches. To reduce this, use well-distributed, diffuse lighting.

Hazards from Using Computers

Using computers can lead to hazards such as poor posture or prolonged sitting, which may cause discomfort and strain. Repeated movements can result in muscle fatigue, and glare from the screen can be harmful to the eyes. To reduce these risks, it's beneficial to stretch regularly or perform simple yoga exercises while seated.

Handling Office Equipment

Improper use of office equipment can lead to injuries, such as cuts from sharp-edged tools. To prevent such accidents, staff should receive proper training on handling equipment. Additionally, the administration should provide a comprehensive manual outlining the correct procedures for using office equipment.

- **Cuts and lacerations** All sorts of office implements can end up leaving their user nursing a painful cut. From power saws to paper trimmers, it's easy to do yourself a mischief at work. The most common causes of these lacerations include poor training, inadequate safety procedures and failing to wear the proper protection.
- **Walking into objects** It's probably safe to say we've all done this at some point. Maybe you're chatting absent-mindedly or maybe you're feeling a little under the weather, when you suddenly find yourself on the

sharp end of a door, table, wall or cabinet. Needless to say, these injuries can sting a bit.

Stress at Work

In organizations, several factors can contribute to workplace stress. Extended working hours and conflicts with colleagues are common stressors. To manage stress, seek effective conflict resolution strategies and engage in relaxing hobbies to counterbalance the effects of long work hours.

Working Environment

Potential hazards in the workplace may involve inadequate ventilation, improperly adjusted chairs and tables, uncomfortable furniture, poor lighting, staff unfamiliar with emergency procedures, or inadequate housekeeping. Additionally, physical or emotional intimidation, such as bullying or group hostility, can be a concern. It is important for staff to be informed about the organization's policies to address and mitigate these hazards related to the working environment.

13.5 Hazard Control

Once hazards have been identified and prioritized, it is essential to implement appropriate control measures. These measures should adhere to a hierarchy of controls, with a strong focus on eliminating hazards at their source whenever feasible:

- **Eliminate the Hazard** Take all possible steps to completely remove the hazard, such as substituting or modifying the process to avoid the risk.
- **Isolate the Hazard** If elimination is not practical, isolate the hazard by implementing engineering controls, such as noise insulation.
- **Minimize the Risk** If neither elimination nor isolation is possible, reduce the risk of injury. Apply effective control measures, such as installing proper exhaust ventilation, providing and maintaining personal protective equipment, and monitoring exposure for at-risk workers.

Safety Guidelines Checklist

- Keep all cleaning chemicals stored in tightly sealed containers within designated cupboards.
- Dispose of garbage daily.
- Ensure that all areas are well-lit.
- Avoid wearing loose clothing or jewellery while operating machines.
- Do not distract individuals working near fires, machinery, tools, or equipment.
- Use protective gear, such as goggles, safety glasses, masks, gloves, and hair nets, where necessary.
- Turn OFF all machines before leaving the workplace.
- Do not tamper with electrical controls or switches.
- Only operate machines or equipment after receiving proper training and authorization from your supervisor.
- Fix any torn wires or damaged plugs before using electrical equipment.
- Avoid using equipment that emits smoke, sparks, or appears unsafe.
- Ensure all food is covered with a lid, plastic wrap, or aluminium foil.
- Refrain from smoking in designated 'No Smoking' areas.
- Report any unsafe conditions or actions to your supervisor.

Try These 13.2

1. **What type of hazard is most likely to be caused by exposed or worn-out wiring?**
   (a) Physical Hazard (b) Electrical Hazard
   (c) Fire Hazard (d) Health Hazard
2. **Which of the following is a common cause of repetitive strain injuries (RSI) in the workplace?**
   (a) Exposure to toxic fumes
   (b) Using computers with poor posture
   (c) Handling sharp-edged equipment
   (d) Inadequate lighting
3. **Workers may experience __________ from exposure to intense light or toxic fumes, affecting their eyes and respiratory system.**
4. **To avoid ________, employees should be familiar with emergency exits, fire escape routes, and locations of fire extinguishers and alarms.**
5. **What is a common preventative measure for avoiding electrical hazards at work?**
6. **Name a health hazard associated with prolonged exposure to loud noise in the workplace.**

Summary

An employee's health refers to their physical, mental, and social well-being.

A hazard is anything that can cause harm, while a risk is the likelihood of that harm occurring.

Security means protection from potential harm.

A health, safety, and security policy is a formal written statement by an employer, expressing the company's commitment to protecting the health, safety, and security of its employees and the public.

A hazard is any source of potential damage, harm or adverse health effects of the people at workplace.

NCERT FOLDER

Complete Explanations of all NCERT's Questions

A. Multiple Choice Questions

Q.1 Workplace safety is essential in organisation ______.
(a) to avoid the accident and injury
(b) to increase the productivity
(b) to improve the work environment
(d) All of the above

Q.2 Which of the following is not mandatory to keep the good health of an employee?
(a) Cleanliness (b) Food court
(c) Clean and fresh air (d) Personal Cleanliness

Q.3 The security department is not responsible for ______.
(a) personal safety
(b) computer system and equipment safety
(c) electrical safety
(d) personal belongings

Q.4 The proper security procedures will increase ______.
(a) liabilities
(b) insurance
(c) business revenue
(d) operational charges of the company

Q.5 Which kind of hazards can occur in IT industry?
(a) Biological (b) Chemical
(c) Physical (d) Ergonomic

Q.6 Which of the following can cause hazards while using computers?
(a) Poor sitting postures or excessive duration of sitting in one position
(b) Lifting heavy object
(c) Mishandling of tools and equipment
(d) Improper handling of office equipment

Q.7 Which of the following statements is likely to result in an injury to the operator?
(a) Selecting the right tool for the job
(b) Wearing safety goggles or glasses
(c) Using a tool with loose handles
(d) Keeping cutting tools sharp

Q.8 What are the potential cause of hazards at workplace?
(a) Poor ventilation (b) Poor lighting
(c) Poor housekeeping (d) All of these

Answers

1. (d) 2. (b) 3. (d) 4. (c) 5. (d)
6. (a) 7. (c) 8. (d)

B. Fill in the Blanks

Q.1 Health of an employee is the state of the physical, ______ and ______ well being.

Q.2 The work places must be cleaned in the ______ before the people start working.

Q.3 A proper ______ provide clean and cool air at the workplace.

Q.4 A fresh food cafeteria helps to maintain the ______ of the employee.

Q.5 The work environment of the organisation must be ______ and free from ______ and ______.

Q.6 The proper security procedures will increase the ______ and will reduce the ______ of the company.

Q.7 Injuries and illness of the employees is prevented through national policy on ______.

Q.8 Physical hazards occurs due to ______.

Q.9 Electrical hazards mostly caused due to coming in direct contact with ______, or indirect contact through a ______.

Q.10 Hazards while using computers occurs due to ______ or excessive duration of sitting in ______.

Answers

1. Mental, Social
2. Morning
3. Ventilation system
4. Health
5. Safe, Hazard and Risk
6. Business revenue, operational charges
7. Occupational Health and safety
8. Physical work environment
9. Live wires, conductor
10. Poor sitting postures, one position

C. State Whether the Following Statements are True or False

Q.1 The employer and employees are responsible for workplace safety.

Q.2 Any injury at work should be reported to the supervisor immediately.

Q.3 No matter how big or small the injury; the injured person should receive medical attention.

Q.4 While working with machines and equipment, employees must follow the safety guidelines set by the company.

Q.5 Bright light sources behind the display screen can create contrast problems.

Q.6 Exposure to bright lights and toxic fumes and vapour could damage the mouth and ears.

Q.7 The use of personal protective clothing and equipment can control the hazards at workplace.

Q.8 Do not throw rubbish daily.

Q.9 Proper handling of office equipment can result in injuries.

Q.10 Stress at workplace can cause hazard in today's organization.

Answers

1. True	2. True	3. True	4. True
5. True	6. False	7. True	8. False
9. False		10. True	

D. Short Answer Type Questions

Q.1 Briefly explain the concept of health, safety and security at workplace.

Ans. **Health** Health of an employee is the state of the physical, mental and social well being. Every organisation must provide healthy and safety working environment for their employees at the workplace.

Safety The work environment of the organisation must be safe. It must be free from hazards and risk. A hazard is the something that can cause harm to the people.

Security Every employee working in an organisation must feel that they are secured in the company campus. Security is a kind of freedom from any potential harm.

Q.2 State the most important reasons for health, safety and security programs in workplace

Ans. There are several reasons that can be specified for safety policy as given below.

- It clearly indicates the company's commitment for their employee's health and safety.
- It shows the performance of the business and the safety performance are compatible with each other.
- It clearly state that the company is not only doing the business for profits but it is taking care of all its stake holders.

Q.3 List out the various workplace safety hazards.

Ans. Safety Hazard at workplace:

Physical, Electrical, Fire Hazard.

Q.4 List out the potential sources of hazards in an organization.

Ans. Potential sources of hazards in an organization include:

- **Using computers** Eye strain, repetitive strain injuries, and poor posture.
- **Handling office equipment** Risks from improper use or maintenance, like paper cuts, electrical hazards, or accidents with heavy equipment.
- **Stress at work** Mental health challenges, fatigue, and decreased productivity.

Q.5 List some of the IT workplace hazards.

Ans. IT workplace hazard: Computer heating, battery bursting, mishandling of computer items.

Q.6 What are examples of potential hazards?

Ans. Examples of potential hazards in an organization include:

- **Ergonomic hazards** Poor posture, repetitive strain from using computers or office equipment.
- **Physical hazards** Risks associated with electrical equipment, slips, trips, and falls.
- **Psychosocial hazards** Stress due to work pressure, poor work-life balance, or workplace conflicts.
- **Chemical hazards** Exposure to cleaning agents or office supplies with harmful chemicals.

Q.7 What are the workplace safety rules?

Ans. Workplace safety rules are:

- Provide adequate resources to ensure continual improvement in its OH&S performance.
- Comply with relevant OH&S legal and other requirements applicable to the organisation and drive for 'beyond compliance' leadership.
- Set appropriate OH&S objectives & targets and conduct periodic performance reviews against these targets.

Q.8 List out different safety guidelines?

Ans. Safety guidelines checklist are

1. Store all cleaning chemicals in tightly closed containers in separate cupboards.
2. Throw garbage daily.
3. Make sure all areas have proper lighting.
4. Do not wear loose clothing or jewellery when working with machines.
5. Never distract the attention of people who are working near a fire or with some machinery, tools or equipment.

EXAM PATTERN EXERCISE

Including Competency Based Questions

Multiple Choice Questions

1 For an organisation, the proper security procedures will reduce _________. CBSE SQP 2024-25

(a) liabilities
(b) insurance
(c) business revenue
(d) operational charges of the company

2 High expectations from self can leave one with chronic anxiety and stress, thus leading to stress. CBSE SQP 2021-22 Term I

(a) Physical
(b) Emotional
(c) Mental
(d) Financial

3 .... is a state of physical, mental and social well-being. CBSE 2025

(a) Richness (b) Popularity
(c) Health (d) Activity

4 The .... has prepared the policy to provide employees with a healthy and safe work environment. CBSE 2025

(a) GoIT (b) DoIT
(c) ToIT (d) SoIT

5 RSI stands for CBSE 2025

(a) Recurring Syndrome Injury
(b) Repetition Symptom Injury
(c) Recessive Stress Injury
(d) Repetitive Strain Injury

6 What is a common cause of electrical accidents in the workplace?

(a) Overloaded outlets
(b) Slippery floors
(c) Loud machinery
(d) Poor posture

7 Which first aid action is recommended for treating a minor burn?

(a) Apply ice directly to the burn
(b) Run cool water over the burn for up to 15 minutes
(c) Use an adhesive bandage immediately
(d) Apply heat to the burn

8 What should be used to cover a large wound if an adhesive bandage is not sufficient?

(a) A clean gauze pad or roller bandage
(b) An ice pack
(c) A heating pad
(d) A cotton ball

9 What action should be taken if a machine emits smoke?

(a) Continue using it until the end of the shift
(b) Report the issue and avoid using it
(c) Clean the machine immediately
(d) Attempt to fix it yourself

10 What is one of the main reasons for implementing a health, safety, and security policy in the workplace?

(a) To increase company profits
(b) To demonstrate the company's commitment to employee well-being
(c) To reduce employee work hours
(d) To increase the number of company meetings

11 Which of the following is a physical hazard commonly encountered in the workplace?

(a) Exposure to loud noise (b) Exposure to toxic fumes
(c) Slips, trips, and falls (d) Stress

12 How should employees manage stress in the workplace?

(a) Ignore it and keep working
(b) Seek effective conflict resolution strategies and engage in relaxing hobbies
(c) Avoid taking breaks
(d) Increase work hours

13 Which one of the following is a wrong safety guideline? CBSE 2025

(a) Store all cleaning chemicals in tightly closed containers in separate cupboards.
(b) Never distract the attention of people who are working near a fire or with some machinery, tools or equipment.
(c) Wear loose clothing or jewellery while working with machines.
(d) Make sure all areas have proper lighting.

14 What is the recommended action for someone experiencing a heat stroke?

(a) Keep them in a warm location
(b) Remove excess layers of clothing and cool their body down
(c) Give them a hot drink
(d) Have them rest in a hot location

15 What should be done with cleaning chemicals to ensure safety?

(a) Store them in open containers
(b) Keep them in tightly sealed containers within designated cupboards
(c) Place them near food
(d) Store them in any available space

16 **Why is it important for employees to be familiar with emergency exits and fire escape routes?**

(a) To comply with insurance requirements
(b) To avoid any possible conflicts with colleagues
(c) To ensure safety during emergencies and reduce panic
(d) To increase productivity

17 **You are tasked with improving safety in a factory where employees handle heavy machinery. According to the hierarchy of controls, which measure should you implement first to manage the risk of injury from the machinery?**

(a) Provide personal protective equipment (PPE) to all employees handling the machinery.
(b) Install noise barriers around the machinery.
(c) Substitute the machinery with safer equipment if possible.
(d) Conduct regular safety training for all employees.

18 **A fire breaks out in an office building. What is the most appropriate immediate action to take before the fire brigade arrives?**

(a) Attempt to extinguish the fire using available equipment.
(b) Ensure that all employees are evacuated and accounted for.
(c) Collect all valuable items and secure them.
(d) Call all employees to gather and discuss the situation.

Answers

1. (a)	2. (c)	3. (c)	4. (b)	5. (d)
6. (a)	7. (b)	8. (a)	9. (b)	10. (b)
11. (c)	12. (b)	13. (c)	14. (b)	15. (b)
16. (c)	17. (c)	18. (b)		

Very Short Answer Type Questions

1 **What is the first step in the hierarchy of controls for managing hazards?**

Ans. The first step is to eliminate the hazard.

2 **Name two common physical hazards that can occur in the workplace.**

Ans. Slips, trips, and falls; muscle strains.

3 **What should be done immediately if someone is suspected to have a third-degree burn?**

Ans. Call for an ambulance and seek professional medical care.

4 **List two safety measures that should be taken when operating machines.**

Ans. Wear appropriate protective gear and only operate machines after receiving proper training.

5 **In a workplace where employees are exposed to hazardous chemicals, what is a key preventive measure to protect their health?**

Ans. Provide appropriate personal protective equipment such as safety goggles and gloves.

Short Answer Type Questions

1 **Explain the hierarchy of controls for managing workplace hazards.**

Ans. The hierarchy of controls is a system used to manage workplace hazards in a prioritized manner to ensure maximum safety. It includes:

- **Eliminate the Hazard** The most effective method involves completely removing the hazard. For example, if a factory has a machine that creates harmful fumes, replacing it with a machine that does not produce fumes would eliminate the hazard.
- **Isolate the Hazard** If elimination is not feasible, isolating the hazard involves using engineering controls to separate the hazard from workers. For instance, installing noise barriers around loud machinery to protect employees from excessive noise.
- **Minimize the Risk** When elimination and isolation are not possible, risk minimization involves reducing the potential for injury. This can include providing Personal Protective Equipment (PPE) such as gloves and masks, and implementing proper training on safe practices.

2 **Discuss the importance of having a health, safety, and security policy in a workplace. How does such a policy benefit both employees and the organization?**

Ans. A health, safety, and security policy is crucial for creating a safe work environment. It benefits employees by clearly outlining the organization's commitment to their well-being, reducing the risk of accidents and injuries. This policy helps employees understand their responsibilities and the measures in place to protect them.

For the organization, such a policy demonstrates a commitment to compliance with legal requirements, helps in reducing liabilities, and enhances overall productivity by minimizing disruptions caused by accidents. Additionally, it fosters a positive work environment and can improve employee morale and retention.

3 **Describe the key elements that should be included in an organization's safety guidelines checklist.**

Ans. A comprehensive safety guidelines checklist should include:

- **Proper Storage** Keep cleaning chemicals in tightly sealed containers to prevent accidental spills and exposures.
- **Housekeeping** Dispose of garbage daily and ensure all areas are well-lit to prevent accidents.
- **Protective Gear** Use appropriate protective equipment like goggles, masks, and gloves to safeguard against potential hazards.

- **Machine Operation** Ensure that all machines are turned OFF before leaving the workplace and that employees receive proper training before operating equipment.
- **Electrical Safety** Fix damaged wires or plugs and avoid using equipment that emits smoke or sparks.

4 Imagine you are a safety officer overseeing electrical maintenance work at a manufacturing plant. To spread the awareness among your team you have to conduct training on safety measures.
List out electrical rescue techniques which you will discuss with them. **CBSE SQP 2024-25**

Ans. The electrical rescue techniques are:

Approaching the Accident

- Avoid rushing into the accident scene.
- Immediately call emergency services (108).
- Approach the accident site with caution.

Examining the Scene

- Visually check if the victims are in contact with energized conductors.
- Be aware that metal surfaces or objects near the victim might be energized.
- Do not touch the victim or any conductive surfaces while they are energized.
- If possible, switch off the electrical circuits.

Hazards and Solutions

- Watch for hazards such as heated surfaces or fire.
- If you cannot turn OFF the power source, exercise extreme caution.
- Keep your hands and feet dry.
- Wear protective gear, including gloves and shoes, and stand on a clean, dry surface.
- Use non-conductive materials to remove the victim from the conductor.

High Voltage Rescue

- Rescuing victims in high voltage situations requires special training.
- Wear appropriate protective equipment, including gloves and shoes.

Applying First Aid

- Administer CPR if necessary.
- If the victim is breathing and has a heartbeat, provide first aid for injuries and treat for shock.
- Ensure the victim receives medical care promptly.
- Provide the attending physician with detailed information to facilitate accurate diagnosis and treatment.

PRACTICAL ASSIGNMENT

1. Conduct a walkthrough of your school to identify potential hazards such as slips, trips, and falls, or electrical hazards. Write in your notebook, each identified hazard and propose control measures based on the hierarchy of controls. For instance, if you find exposed wiring, recommend immediate repair (eliminate the hazard) and ensure proper insulation (isolate the hazard).
2. Develop a basic first aid kit for your home, including items such as adhesive bandages, gauze pads, and antiseptic wipes. Create a first aid procedure guide that includes steps for treating minor burns and handling heat stroke. Ensure that all employees are trained on how to use the kit and follow the procedures outlined in the guide.

Workplace Quality Measures

CHAPTER 14

Organizations today understand the importance of a healthy and sustainable work environment. A clean and safe workplace enhances employee morale and productivity while benefiting environmental health. This chapter examines workplace quality, with a focus on air and water standards, discussing their significance, associated pollution risks, and strategies for monitoring and mitigation.

Maintaining high air quality is crucial for enhancing employee productivity in any organization. Clean, unpolluted air is a fundamental requirement for a healthy working environment. Many IT companies use centralized air conditioning systems to regulate workplace temperature and ensure a comfortable atmosphere.

Water pollution is another significant issue encountered by numerous organizations. Human activities often contribute to the contamination of water sources, which can lead to various health problems. Therefore, it is essential for organizations to implement measures to prevent both air and water pollution.

14.1 Air and Water Quality Monitoring Process

Air and water pollution can be assessed using various methods, including physical, chemical, and biological analyses. To conduct these analyses, samples are collected from the organization's surroundings.

Air and water samples are tested through physical, chemical, and biological procedures. Temperature and sample composition can be measured easily.

For instance, the concentration of different gases such as oxygen, nitrogen, and carbon dioxide in the air can be determined. The pH level of water is assessed through chemical analysis. Additionally, the impact of air and water on local flora and fauna is evaluated, and microbial indicators are used to monitor ecosystem health.

14.2 Guidelines for Clean Air and Clean Water

Organizations should follow specific guidelines to maintain clean air and water. Key points include:

1. Air pollution is often caused by the release of dust, solid particles, and gases into the atmosphere. To minimize pollution, avoid generating dust, solid particles, and gases.
2. The extensive use of vehicles on campus can contribute to air pollution. Organizations should limit the number of vehicles and consider implementing a no-vehicle day each week.
3. Ozone, which can contribute to air pollution and smog, should be minimized. The organization should take measures to keep ozone levels low.
4. Human activities often lead to water pollution, including sewage and wastewater discharge. Ensure that waste does not contaminate surrounding water sources.
5. Avoid excessive use of fertilizers and pesticides, as these can lead to groundwater contamination.

14.3 Importance of Cleanliness at the Workplace

Maintaining a clean workplace is essential for safety and efficiency. Poor handling and storage practices can lead to damage and hazards. A clean work environment not only makes tasks easier but also contributes to a more pleasant atmosphere. All employees should contribute to keeping common areas clean as needed.

- All work areas must be kept tidy. Each employee is responsible for the cleanliness of their own workspace, including tools and equipment.
- Spills and breakages should be addressed immediately to prevent accidents.
- Ensure that spaces around machines and equipment remain clear to allow for free movement.
- Floors should be kept clean and unobstructed to prevent slipping and collisions.
- Lighting fixtures should be regularly checked to ensure clear visibility. Any faulty lights should be reported to the administration so that building maintenance or facilities management can address the issue.

14.4 Office Ergonomics

Ergonomics is the science of designing and arranging work environments to make them safe and easy to use. Applying ergonomic principles can reduce the risk of accidents and injuries, and enhance performance and productivity. In an office setting, repetitive tasks, even those that seem harmless, can lead to injuries.

These injuries can be painful and require lengthy and difficult rehabilitation. Emphasizing office ergonomics helps in identifying early warning signs of potential issues.

Early Warning Signs	Potential Cause	Precautionary Measure
Sore lower back	No lumbar support	Use back rest of chair, put small pillow or lumbar support on backrest of chair
Burning in the upper back	No upper back support from chair	Put document holder or prop up so you can see without leaning forward
Stiff neck	Working with head turned to side tilting head forward holding telephone between the ear and shoulder	Move or raise monitor to centre of desk check if headset is available
Sore shoulders	Reaching forward for long periods or reaching forward frequently	Move closer to the keyboard, bring mouse down to level of keyboard or 1" higher
Arching wrists	Working with wrists extended too much repetition	Add a wrist rest to the front of keyboard and mouse pad rest thumbs on front edge of keyboard so wrists can't drop.
Dry eyes	Forget to blink	Rest eyes periodically and do simple eye exercises
Eye strain and sore eyes	Glares from overhead lights or windows eye glasses not correct need vision check	Re-orient your desk and computer so light is not directly behind or in front of you.

Try These 14.1

1. **Which of the following is a key method for assessing air and water pollution?**
   (a) Physical, chemical, and biological analyses
   (b) Only visual inspection
   (c) Using air fresheners and water filters
   (d) Conducting employee surveys
2. **What is one of the guidelines for maintaining clean air in the workplace?**
   (a) Increase the number of vehicles on campus
   (b) Minimize the release of dust, solid particles, and gases
   (c) Use more fertilizers and pesticides
   (d) Increase ozone levels
3. **To prevent water pollution, organizations should ensure that waste does not ________ surrounding water sources.**
4. **In an office setting, poor handling and storage practices can lead to damage and ________.**
5. **What should you do if you experience sore shoulders from reaching forward frequently?**
6. **Why is it important to maintain cleanliness in the workplace?**

14.5 Computer Health and Safety Tips

The increased use of computers has led to various health and safety concerns, including vision problems, musculoskeletal issues, and body aches. Many of these issues are preventable and can be resolved with simple adjustments.

Musculoskeletal Problems

These issues affect different parts of the body, such as the neck, back, chest, arms, shoulders, and feet, often due to poor posture or an ergonomically incorrect chair.

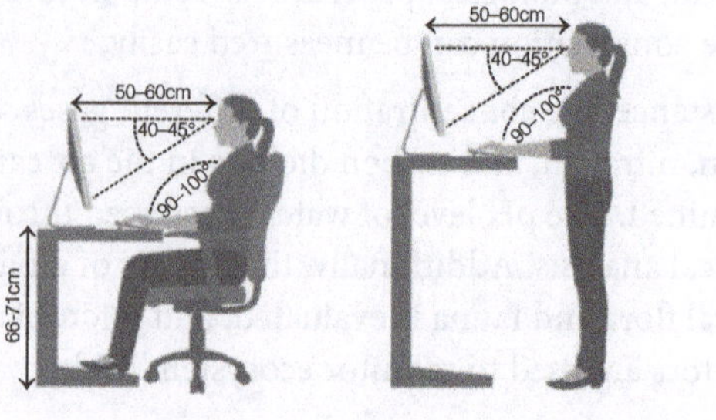

To prevent these problems:

- Position your computer so that the top of the monitor is at eye level.
- Keep your neck aligned with the monitor, avoiding the need to turn your head.
- Maintain a distance of at least an arm's length, or 20 to 30 inches, between you and the monitor.
- Ensure your back is fully supported by the backrest of your chair.
- Adjust the armrests so your elbows are at a 100–110 degree angle.
- Tilt the keyboard slightly away from you if you are sitting upright.
- While typing, keep your hands slightly lower than your elbows, with your fingers pointing downward.
- Avoid excessive wrist movement, both sideways and up and down.
- Use a palm rest only when not typing, and avoid resting your wrists while typing to prevent strain.
- Take regular breaks to stretch your muscles, improve circulation, and rest your eyes.

Occupational Overuse Syndrome

Occupational overuse syndrome, also known as repetitive strain injury (RSI), refers to a range of conditions characterized by discomfort or persistent pain in muscles, tendons, and other soft tissues, with or without visible physical symptoms. This syndrome is typically caused or worsened by work-related factors, including repetitive movements, sustained or awkward postures, and forceful actions. Psychosocial factors, such as workplace stress, can also contribute to the development of occupational overuse syndrome.

Repetitive muscle use can lead to pain in areas such as the neck, shoulders, wrists, or fingers. A common condition related to repetitive computer use is carpal tunnel syndrome, which causes pain, numbness, and tingling in the hand and arm. To prevent these issues, maintain proper posture while typing. Your fingers should be above the 'home position' (asdf and jkl; keys) on the keyboard, with your elbows close to your sides. Avoid gripping the mouse too tightly and ensure that both the keyboard and mouse are at the same level. Additionally, using an ergonomic keyboard and mouse can help reduce the risk of wrist-related conditions.

Strain in Legs and Feet

Sitting for prolonged periods can cause strain in the legs. To alleviate this, adjust your desk chair so that your feet rest flat on the floor and your lower legs are vertical. Using a footrest can provide additional support. Ensure you have enough space to shift your position and stretch your legs periodically.

Eye Strain

The brightness, glare, and flickering of a computer screen can lead to eye strain and visual fatigue. Continuous focus on the screen can cause dry eyes due to infrequent blinking. Computer Vision Syndrome is a condition caused by poor lighting and glare, leading to blurry vision, burning or watering eyes, headaches, and sometimes shoulder and neck pain. Follow the below points to reduce the risk of visual problems:

- Adjust the computer screen's brightness to reduce strain.
- Position the screen to avoid glare from lights or windows.
- Maintain a proper viewing distance from the screen and remember to blink regularly.
- Wear anti-glare glasses when working on the computer.
- Keep the screen clean and use a desk lamp to improve visibility.
- Ensure screen colors are comfortable to view, and text is sharp and legible.
- Take regular breaks from the screen; look away into the distance for a few moments to relax your eyes. Focus on something 30 meters away for 30 seconds every 30 minutes.
- Position your monitor 18 to 24 inches away from your face and adjust it to minimize glare from sunlight.

Try These 14.2

1. **What is one recommended adjustment to reduce musculoskeletal problems while using a computer?**
   (a) Position the monitor at a height lower than eye level
   (b) Keep your hands higher than your elbows while typing
   (c) Ensure your back is fully supported by the chair's backrest
   (d) Use a palm rest while typing
2. **Which of the following is not a suggested method to alleviate eye strain from computer use?**
   (a) Adjust the brightness of the computer screen
   (b) Take regular breaks and look at something 30 meters away
   (c) Position the monitor at a distance of 10 inches from your face
   (d) Wear anti-glare glasses while working on the computer
3. **To reduce the risk of occupational overuse syndrome, ensure that both the keyboard and mouse are at the same ______.**

4 When experiencing strain in the legs from prolonged sitting, it is recommended to adjust your desk chair so that your feet rest _______ on the floor.

5 What is a common condition associated with repetitive computer use that causes pain, numbness, and tingling in the hand and arm?

6 How often should you take breaks from the computer screen to prevent eye strain?

Headaches

Headaches can result from muscle tension or neck pain, as well as eye strain or vision problems.

Regular eye exams can help address vision issues. Maintain a straight posture while working and take breaks to relieve neck strain.

Obesity

Extended computer use can lead to a lack of physical activity, contributing to obesity, particularly in children who spend long periods on electronic devices. To combat this, take breaks to incorporate physical exercise into your routine.

Stress Disorders

Extended use of computers can impact behavior and emotions, leading to increased stress and poor health. Prolonged stress can result in reduced attention span, lack of concentration, dizziness, and burnout. To manage stress, prioritize your health and explore treatment options. Consider practices such as yoga, natural remedies, or prescribed medications to alleviate stress and prevent related health issues.

Injuries from Laptop Use

The increasing reliance on laptops can lead to various strains and pains. Laptops are designed for short-term use, but many people prefer them over desktops due to their convenience.

The proximity of the screen and keyboard on a laptop creates a challenge: positioning the screen at the right height for your back and neck often results in having to lift your arms and shoulders uncomfortably, and *vice-versa*. To mitigate these issues, consider using a desktop setup that is ergonomically correct for extended periods of work.

Sleeping Problems

The artificial light emitted by computer screens can interfere with your brain's production of melatonin, a substance that regulates sleep patterns. To address this issue, avoid using computers right before bedtime.

14.6 Health and Safety Requirements for Computer Workplaces

For computers—including desktops, laptops, tablets, smartphones, television screens, and video monitors—the following health and safety requirements should be met:

Display Screen (Monitor)

- Use modern LED monitors that are large enough to ensure legibility, with adequate spacing between characters and lines.
- The screen should display a stable image with no flickering or instability.
- Ensure the screen is free from reflective glare and reflections that could cause discomfort.

Keyboard

- The keyboard should be adjustable in tilt and separate from the screen to allow for a comfortable working position and to prevent fatigue in the arms or hands.
- There should be enough space in front of the keyboard to support the user's hands and arms.
- The keyboard should have a matte surface to avoid glare and the symbols on the keys should be clearly contrasted and legible from the working position.

Work Surface

- The work desk should be spacious, have a low-reflectance surface, and allow for flexible arrangement of the screen, keyboard, documents, and other equipment.
- The document holder should be stable and adjustable to minimize uncomfortable head and eye movements.

Work Chair

The work chair should be stable and allow easy movement to help users find a comfortable position. It must be height-adjustable, and users should ensure their feet rest flat on the floor or use a footrest if needed.

Space Requirements

The workstation should offer enough space for users to adjust their position and vary their movements comfortably. There should be sufficient desk space to accommodate all necessary equipment.

Lighting

The workstation should have adequate lighting with appropriate contrast between the screen and the surrounding environment. Measures should be taken to prevent glare and reflections on the screen or other equipment.

Reflections and Glare

The design of workstations should minimize direct glare and distracting reflections caused by sources of light such as windows, transparent or translucent walls, and brightly colored fixtures or walls. Windows should be equipped with adjustable coverings to control the amount of daylight entering the workstation.

Noise and Heat

Equipment should not produce distracting noise. If noise is unavoidable, noise-cancelling earphones may help mitigate the disruption. Additionally, equipment should not generate excessive heat that could cause discomfort to users.

14.7 Cautions while Working on the Computer

Ensuring safety while working on a computer is crucial. Static electricity, which can be generated by walking on a carpet, may damage computer components. To protect your system, use a surge protector when plugging it in.

A battery backup system is highly recommended to safeguard against power outages, as it provides a consistent voltage supply. Remove rings, watches, and necklaces while working on the computer. These items are often made of conductive metals that can transmit static electricity and potentially harm computer components.

Always unplug all power sources and cables before working on your computer. Working on a plugged-in system can damage hardware, and modern processors can overheat within 7 seconds if the heat sink is not properly attached.

Watch Out for Cords and Wires

Loose cords and wires can present hazards, including electrical risks. If a cord or wire crosses a pathway, mark it with hazard tape to alert others to potential dangers.

Avoid water when working with electrical equipment. Never touch or attempt to repair electrical components or circuits with wet hands, as moisture increases electrical conductivity and heightens the risk of electrical shock.

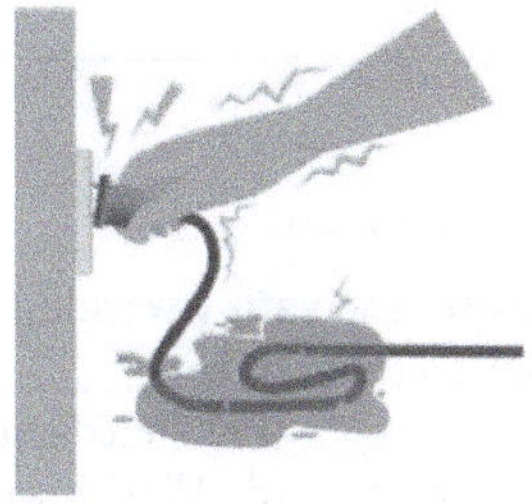

Try These 14.3

1. **Which of the following is a recommended measure to reduce stress disorders caused by extended computer use?**
   (a) Increase screen brightness
   (b) Prioritize health and explore treatment options such as yoga
   (c) Increase the amount of time spent on computers
   (d) Avoid using ergonomic furniture
2. **What is a potential consequence of using laptops for extended periods without proper ergonomics?**
   (a) Improved posture and reduced neck strain
   (b) Enhanced visibility and screen resolution
   (c) Various strains and pains due to poor positioning of screen and keyboard
   (d) Increased overall physical fitness
3. **To prevent headaches and neck pain while working on a computer, maintain a _______ posture and take regular breaks.**
4. **To mitigate issues related to prolonged computer use, consider using a _______ setup that is ergonomically correct for extended periods of work.**
5. **What common condition associated with extended computer use can cause pain, numbness, and tingling in the hand and arm?**
6. **What should be done to address the interference of artificial light from computer screens with sleep patterns?**

NCERT FOLDER

Complete Explanations of all NCERT's Questions

A. Multiple Choice Questions

Q.1 To provide healthy and safety working environment, every organisation must have ________.

(a) Cleanliness (b) Filtered water

(c) Clean wash-room (d) All of these

Q.2 Air pollution is mostly caused by production of the ________ in the surrounding air.

(a) dust (b) mixture of solid particles

(c) gases (d) All of these

Q.3 Repetitive use of muscle may feel pain in your ________

(a) neck (b) shoulder

(c) wrist or fingers (d) All of these

Q.4 The security department organisation is not responsible for ________.

(a) other safety (b) IT department responsible

(c) electrical safety (d) transport safety

Q.5 For an organisation, the proper security procedures will reduce ________.

(a) liabilities

(b) insurance

(c) business revenue

(d) operational charges of the company

Q.6 Do not wear ________ when working with machines.

(a) jewellery (b) safety glasses

(c) masks (d) gloves

Q.7 Sore lower back is caused due to ________.

(a) reaching forward frequently

(b) no lumbar support

(c) no upper back support from chair

(d) reaching forward for long periods

Q.8 What should you do with the problem of dry eyes?

(a) Forget to blink

(b) Rest eyes periodically and do simple eye exercises

(c) Do exercise

(d) Blink the eyes

Q.9 If light is coming directly behind or in front of you then you may suffer from ________.

(a) eye strain

(b) sore eyes

(c) dry eyes

(d) eye strain and sore eyes

Answers

1. (b)	2. (d)	3. (d)	4. (d)	5. (d)
6. (a)	7. (b)	8. (b)	9. (d)	

B. Fill in the Blanks

Q.1 Air and water pollution can be analysed by using – physical, ________ and ________ analysis.

Q.2 The PH value of the water can be measured through ________ analysis.

Q.3 The ________ indicators are used to monitor the health of the ecosystem.

Q.4 Ergonomics is the science concerned with ________ and arranging things.

Q.5 Working with wrists extended too much repetition can cause ________.

Q.6 The repetition of a seemingly ________ task over a period of time can cause an injury.

Q.7 If a cord or wire will cross a pathway safety it should be mark it with ________.

Q.8 Loose cords and wires can cause ________.

Q.9 Glare and ________ on the screen should be prevented.

Q.10 The keyboard should have a matte surface to avoid ________ glare.

Answers

1. Chemical, biological	2. Chemical
3. Microbial	4. Designing
5. Arching wrists	6. Innocuous
7. Hazard tape	8. Electrical hazards
9. Reflections	10. Reflective

C. State Whether the Following Statements are True or False

Q.1 The work environment of the organization must be free from hazards and risk.

Q.2 Practice a no vehicle day in every week to avoid air pollution.

Q.3 Applying ergonomics can improve performance and productivity.

Q.4 **Wear rings, watches and necklaces while working on the computer.**

Q.5 **Never touch or try repairing any electrical equipment or circuits with wet hands.**

Q.6 **Unplug all power sources and cables from computer while working on computer.**

Q.7 **Occupational overuse syndrome, also known as repetition strain injury.**

Q.8 **The work chair must be stable and allow the user to move easily.**

Q.9 **Artificial lighting from computer screens can cause sleeping problems.**

Q.10 **The keyboard and mouse should not be kept at the same level.**

Answers

1. True	2. True
3. True	4. False
5. True	6. False
7. True	8. True
9. True	10. False

D. Short Answer Type Questions

Q.1 **What causes the water pollution?**

Ans. The main water pollutants include bacteria, viruses, parasites, fertilisers, pesticides, pharmaceutical products, nitrates, phosphates, plastics, faecal waste and even radioactive substances.

Q.2 **What is occupational overuse syndrome?**

Ans. Occupational Overuse Syndrome, is a condition of the muscles in the wrist, forearm, arm and neck that is caused by their overuse (or misuse) at work.

Q.3 **What are musculoskeletal problems?**

Ans. Musculoskeletal Disorders (MSDs) are injuries or pain in the human musculoskeletal system, which includes the joints, ligaments, muscles, nerves, tendons, and structures that support limbs, neck, and back.

Q.4 **What cautions to be taken while working on the computer?**

Ans. It is important to rest the eyes while working on the computer. Regularly look at more distant objects, e.g. use thinking time to look out of the window, and take frequent breaks from computer work. Visit the optician for regular eye check-ups and make sure you tell them if you are a frequent computer user.

Q.5 **Why there is no right way to use a laptop?**

Ans. Using a laptop is a tradeoff between poor neck/head posture and poor hand/wrist posture. Occasional users will have less risk of problems than full-time users. Because the neck/head position is determined by the actions of large muscles, you are better off sacrificing neck posture rather than wrist posture.

Q.6 **What causes eye strain and how to avoid it?**

Ans. Eye strain is a common condition caused by intense use of your eyes, such as by reading, using digital devices or driving long distances. Other names for eye strain are eye fatigue and asthenopia. Eye strain can cause discomfort, but it's usually not a serious condition.

Q.7 **What type of display screen is suitable to work on computer?**

Ans. The best display type for a monitor largely depends on your needs, but IPS (In-Plane Switching) panels are generally the top choice for work.

IPS displays offer superior color accuracy and consistency, wide viewing angles, and better overall image quality compared to TN (Twisted Nematic) panels.

Q.8 **What type of keyboard is suitable to work on computer?**

Ans. The QWERTY keyboard layout is comfortable, familiar and time-tested, ideal for everyday typing needs.

EXAM PATTERN EXERCISE

Including Competency Based Questions

Multiple Choice Questions

1 What is a key method for assessing air and water pollution?

(a) Physical analysis (b) Digital analysis
(c) Visual inspection (d) Audio measurement

2 Which type of hazard is caused by exposure to bacteria and viruses?

(a) Chemical Hazards (b) Biological Hazards
(c) Ergonomic Hazards (d) Physical Hazards

3 To minimize air pollution, organizations should:

(a) Increase the number of vehicles on campus
(b) Use more fertilizers
(c) Avoid generating dust and gases
(d) Discharge more wastewater

4 What should be done if a spill occurs in the workplace?

(a) Ignore it until it dries
(b) Report it immediately
(c) Clean it up at the end of the day
(d) Ask a colleague to handle it

5 Which type of hazard involves physical environmental factors like extreme temperatures?

(a) Psychosocial Hazards (b) Safety Hazards
(c) Physical Hazards (d) Ergonomic Hazards

6 What is one precaution to manage eye strain from computer use?

(a) Adjust the screen's brightness
(b) Increase screen size
(c) Reduce screen resolution
(d) Work in complete darkness

7 .... is the science that deals with designing and arranging the things at workplace so that people can use them easily and safely. CBSE 2025

(a) Health science (b) Ergonomics
(c) Fixture science (d) Work economics

8 For proper ergonomics, the top of the monitor should be at:

(a) Eye level (b) Waist level
(c) Below desk level (d) Shoulder level

9 What is a recommended method to reduce musculoskeletal problems while typing?

(a) Keep wrists elevated
(b) Use a palm rest while typing
(c) Tilt the keyboard slightly away
(d) Sit far from the keyboard

10 How can organizations reduce water pollution from fertilizers and pesticides?

(a) Use more fertilizers
(b) Increase pesticide application
(c) Avoid excessive use of fertilizers and pesticides
(d) Discharge more wastewater

11 Which type of hazard results from workplace stress and violence?

(a) Safety Hazards
(b) Ergonomic Hazards
(c) Psychosocial Hazards
(d) Chemical Hazards

12 What is the effect of poor ergonomics on the workplace?

(a) Increased productivity
(b) Enhanced safety
(c) Risk of injuries and discomfort
(d) Improved health

13 Which practice helps to prevent strain in legs and feet while sitting?

(a) Use a footrest (b) Stand all the time
(c) Sit with legs crossed (d) Keep feet elevated

14 How often should breaks be taken to reduce eye strain from computer use?

(a) Every 5 minutes (b) Every 30 minutes
(c) Every hour (d) Every 2 hours

15 What is the recommended distance between your face and the computer monitor?

(a) 10 to 12 inches (b) 15 to 18 inches
(c) 18 to 24 inches (d) 30 to 36 inches

16 Which type of hazard involves the release of dust and gases into the atmosphere?

(a) Biological Hazards (b) Chemical Hazards
(c) General Hazards (d) Ergonomic Hazards

17 What is one of the general evacuation procedures in case of a workplace emergency?

(a) Have trained first aiders on all floors
(b) Avoid reporting injuries
(c) Disregard first aid boxes
(d) Use unsafe exits

18 What should be used to protect computer components from static electricity?

(a) A surge protector
(b) A cleaning cloth
(c) A battery backup system
(d) A dust cover

19 **Which measure can help reduce noise and heat from equipment in the workplace?**
(a) Use noise-cancelling earphones
(b) Increase equipment usage
(c) Keep equipment turned off
(d) Reduce screen brightness

20 **To prevent injuries from laptop use, what is recommended?**
(a) Use a laptop for extended periods
(b) Position the screen and keyboard at ergonomic heights
(c) Keep the laptop at knee level
(d) Avoid using a desktop setup

Answers

1. (a)	2. (b)	3. (c)	4. (b)	5. (c)
6. (a)	7. (b)	8. (a)	9. (b)	10. (c)
11. (c)	12. (c)	13. (a)	14. (b)	15. (c)
16. (b)	17. (a)	18. (a)	19. (c)	20. (b)

Very Short Answer Type Questions

1 **What is a common consequence of poor workstation setup?**
Ans. Strain or injury from repetitive movements

2 **Name one precaution to prevent musculoskeletal problems from computer use.**
Ans. Position the monitor at eye level

3 **What should be done immediately if a spill occurs in the workplace?**
Ans. Address it immediately to prevent accidents

4 **How can organizations limit vehicle-related air pollution?**
Ans. Implement a no-vehicle day each week

5 **What is a recommended practice to reduce eye strain from computer screens?**
Ans. Adjust the screen's brightness

6 **What type of hazard involves repetitive movements leading to discomfort?**
Ans. Ergonomic Hazards

7 **Why is it important to take regular breaks from the computer?**
Ans. To reduce muscle strain and eye fatigue

8 **How can improper lighting affect your work?**
Ans. It can lead to eye strain and reduced visibility

9 **What is one way to reduce stress-related disorders in the workplace?**
Ans. Provide stress consultation services and relaxation spaces

10 **Why should a battery backup system be used for computers?**
Ans. To safeguard against power outages and provide consistent voltage supply.

11. **For a computer workplace, give any two health and safety requirements while using a keyboard.** CBSE 2025
Ans. Health and safety requirements when using a keyboard include:
(i) Maintaining a neutral wrist position.
(ii) Taking regular breaks to reduce strain and prevent repetitive stress injuries.

12. **Excessive use of computers might have a bad impact on your vision. Give any two eye-related problems that might arise due to long hours spent on a computer.** CBSE 2025
Ans. Two eye - related problems from excessive computer use are
(i) Eye strain (Computer vision syndrome).
(ii) Dry eyes due to reduce blinking while storing at screens.

Short Answer Type Questions

1 **Discuss the importance of maintaining high air and water quality in the workplace and how it impacts employee productivity and health.**
Ans. High air and water quality are crucial for maintaining a healthy work environment. Clean air prevents respiratory issues, enhances overall well-being, and can increase productivity by reducing sick days. Clean water prevents waterborne diseases and maintains proper hydration and health. Organizations can improve air quality by minimizing pollutants and maintaining ventilation systems. Water quality can be improved by managing waste and avoiding pollutants. Both factors contribute to a more efficient and safe work environment.

2 **Explain the different types of hazards in the workplace and provide examples for each.**
Ans. Hazards in the workplace can be classified as follows:
- **Biological Hazards** Exposure to bacteria, viruses, and insects (e.g., diseases contracted in labs).
- **Chemical Hazards** Exposure to harmful substances (e.g., skin irritation from chemicals).
- **Ergonomic Hazards** Resulting from poor workstation setup or repetitive movements (e.g., strain from poor posture).
- **Physical Hazards** Environmental factors like extreme temperatures or radiation (e.g., burns from hot surfaces).
- **Psychosocial Hazards** Workplace stress or violence (e.g., anxiety from bullying).
- **Safety Hazards** Unsafe conditions leading to injury (e.g., slips and falls).

3 Describe the ergonomic principles that should be applied to a computer workstation to prevent musculoskeletal issues.

Ans. Ergonomic principles for a computer workstation include:

- **Monitor Position** The top of the monitor should be at eye level to prevent neck strain.
- **Chair Adjustment** The chair should support the back and allow feet to rest flat on the floor.
- **Keyboard and Mouse Placement** The keyboard should be at a height that allows elbows to remain close to the body, and the mouse should be at the same level as the keyboard.
- **Posture** Maintain a straight back, avoid excessive wrist movement, and use a palm rest only when not typing.
- **Breaks** Take regular breaks to stretch and rest eyes to prevent fatigue and strain.

4 What are the best practices for managing and preventing computer-related health issues in the workplace?

Ans. Best practices include:

- **Ergonomic Setup** Ensure workstations are set up to support good posture and reduce strain.
- **Screen Adjustments** Position screens to minimize glare and maintain proper distance.
- **Regular Breaks** Encourage employees to take breaks to reduce eye strain and muscle fatigue.
- **Training** Provide training on ergonomics and safe computer use.
- **Health Monitoring** Implement regular health checks and provide resources for managing stress and fatigue.

5 How can organizations effectively manage and prevent workplace hazards, including both physical and psychosocial risks?

Ans. Organizations can manage and prevent workplace hazards by:

- **Conducting Risk Assessments** Regularly assess and identify potential hazards.
- **Implementing Safety Measures** Install safety equipment, ensure proper training, and maintain a clean and organized workspace.
- **Promoting Safe Practices** Educate employees about safe practices and emergency procedures.
- **Addressing Psychosocial Risks** Provide support for stress management and create a positive work environment.
- **Regular Inspections** Conduct routine inspections to ensure compliance with safety standards and identify areas for improvement.

6 Imagine you are responsible for setting up a new office. What steps would you take to ensure that the office environment promotes both good air and water quality?

Ans. To ensure good air and water quality:

- **Air Quality** Install air purifiers, use low-emission materials, and ensure proper ventilation. Monitor air quality regularly.
- **Water Quality** Ensure proper waste management to avoid contamination, install water filters, and monitor water quality.

7 During an audit, you find that several workstations are not ergonomically set up. How would you approach correcting these issues?

Ans. To correct ergonomic issues:

- **Assessment** Evaluate each workstation and identify specific problems.
- **Adjustments** Make necessary adjustments to chairs, desks, monitors, and keyboards to meet ergonomic standards.
- **Training** Provide training on proper workstation setup and posture.
- **Follow-Up** Regularly check for compliance and address any ongoing issues.

8 You are tasked with designing a new training program for employees on health and safety practices related to computer use. What key topics should be included in this program?

Ans. Key topics should include:

- **Ergonomic Principles** Proper workstation setup, posture, and equipment use.
- **Eye Care** Techniques for reducing eye strain and maintaining visual health.
- **Musculoskeletal Health** Prevention of repetitive strain injuries and the importance of regular breaks.
- **Stress Management** Identifying and managing workplace stress.
- **Emergency Procedures** Responding to accidents and hazards, and using first aid equipment.

9 If an employee reports discomfort from sitting for long periods, what steps should you take to help alleviate their discomfort?

Ans. To alleviate discomfort from prolonged sitting:

- **Adjust Chair** Ensure the chair is properly adjusted for height and support.
- **Footrest** Provide a footrest if needed.
- **Encourage Movement** Remind the employee to take regular breaks to stand, stretch, and move around.
- **Evaluate Ergonomics** Assess the workstation setup and make any necessary adjustments to support a more comfortable seating position.

CHAPTER 15

Prevent Accidents and Emergencies

In today's fast-paced world, accidents and emergencies can occur unexpectedly, disrupting daily routines and potentially causing significant harm. Whether it's a minor workplace injury or a major natural disaster, being prepared is crucial. This chapter delves into the importance of accident prevention and emergency preparedness. We will explore common workplace hazards, emergency response procedures, and essential safety measures. By understanding these concepts and implementing effective strategies, individuals and organizations can significantly reduce the risk of accidents and minimize their impact.

In any organization, even minor accidents or unforeseen events can escalate into emergencies if not addressed promptly. Emergencies may be caused by natural disasters such as floods, hurricanes, or earthquakes, while man-made crises could include fires, toxic gas leaks, chemical spills, illnesses, explosions, or civil unrest.

These incidents have the potential to disrupt or halt operations, cause physical harm, or lead to environmental damage. Although emergencies can occur unexpectedly, anywhere and at any time, the most effective way to safeguard both yourself and the organization is by creating a comprehensive emergency action plan to guide employees during such situations. This chapter outlines common workplace hazards, prevention strategies, safety measures, and tips for maintaining a safe work environment.

15.1 Accidents and Emergencies

An accident is an unexpected, unintentional, or unforeseen event that leads to injury or harm to individuals and damage to property. In other words, an accident at workplace is a physical or mental injury following an incident or exposure. If you accidentally get injured in the workplace, the injury is not necessarily caused by your work. For example: You are getting up from a chair and suddenly got a strain in your neck.

How we examine an accident at work

Before we can assess if you have had an accident at work, we need the following:

- Your employer's signature that the incident or exposure occurred as well as any additional information
- Information about your employer's insurance company
- A medical certificate describing the injury you have sustained due to the incident or exposure

An emergency is a critical or urgent situation requiring immediate attention and action. For instance, a customer experiencing a heart attack or a sudden fire outbreak in your organization demands prompt response.

Every organization has established procedures and practices for managing and reporting accidents, as well as handling emergencies. While many of these procedures are standard across industries, some may be customized to suit the specific nature of a business. For instance, the protocol for addressing slip-and-fall accidents tends to be similar across industries. It's essential to familiarize yourself with both the general procedures and those unique to your organization.

Here are key guidelines for identifying and reporting accidents or emergencies:

Notice and Correctly Identify Accidents and Emergencies

You should be able to distinguish between accidents and emergencies in your organization. The organization's policies and guidelines will help you determine what constitutes each. It's important to be familiar with these incidents and know the appropriate steps for handling each type.

Get help promptly and in the most suitable way

Follow the designated procedure for managing accidents and emergencies. Act promptly according to the provided guidelines, ensuring that assistance is given as outlined in company policy. It's essential not to deviate from these guidelines, even with good intentions. Only trained and certified professionals are authorized to make decisions beyond the organization's policies when necessary.

Follow company policies and procedures for preventing further injury while waiting for help to arrive

If someone is injured, do not rely on impulse or instinct. Stay calm and follow your organization's protocols for handling injuries. Ensure that you act according to the procedures outlined in company policies.

Act within the limits of your responsibility and authority when accidents and emergencies arise

Offer assistance within the scope of your responsibilities. Administer medical help only if you are certified to do so. Otherwise, wait for professional responders to arrive and take over.

Promptly follow instructions given by senior staff and the emergency services

Provide necessary support as specified in your role's guidelines, and carefully follow the directions of senior staff who are trained to manage such situations. Assist them in handling accidents and emergencies under their supervision.

Try These 15.1

1. **What is the primary distinction between an accident and an emergency in a workplace context?**
   (a) An accident occurs suddenly, while an emergency is planned
   (b) An accident causes injury, while an emergency requires immediate action
   (c) An accident requires immediate action, while an emergency is less urgent
   (d) An accident is always caused by faulty equipment, while an emergency is caused by human error
2. **Who is authorized to make decisions beyond the organization's policies during an accident or emergency?**
   (a) Any employee with good intentions
   (b) Trained and certified professionals
   (c) Immediate supervisor
   (d) Security personnel
3. **An accident is an unexpected, unintentional, or unforeseen event that leads to _____ or _____ to individuals and damage to property.**
4. **In case of an accident or emergency, always act within your ______ and responsibilities.**
5. **What should you do if someone is injured at the workplace, but you're not certified to provide medical help?**
6. **What is the first step you should take when reporting an accident at work?**

15.2 Types of Accidents

Below are some of the most common types of accidents that occur in organizations, along with suggestions for minimizing their risk:

Trip and Fall

One of the most frequent workplace accidents involves employees or customers tripping over loose or misplaced materials. This can happen when wires are carelessly left on the floor, goods are left scattered across aisles, or there are uneven thresholds or raised flooring. Such accidents can result in anything from minor bruises to more serious injuries, such as fractures or sprains.

Slip and Fall

Slips often happen when the floor is wet or has been recently mopped, or when liquids have spilled without being cleaned up immediately. This type of accident is usually caused by negligence, and it can also occur if there are broken or uneven surfaces, such as loose or cracked floor tiles. To avoid these incidents, it's essential to put up warning signs like "Wet Floor" or "Caution: Slippery Surface" when the floor is wet.

Injuries caused due to Escalators or Elevators (or lifts)

Although less common, accidents involving escalators and elevators can lead to significant injuries. These are particularly dangerous for children, the elderly, and women. Injuries can occur from falls on moving escalators, as well as from unexpected, jerky movements in elevators that may cause people to lose their balance.

In addition, people can trip over the thresholds of elevators or become trapped inside them, leading to panic and distress. Regular checks and maintenance of escalators and elevators are essential for their safe operation. If you notice any malfunctioning equipment, report it immediately to the appropriate department or authority for timely repairs.

Accidents due to Falling of Goods

Workplace injuries can also result from goods or equipment falling from shelves or wall-mounted storage. This typically happens when items are not securely stored or are piled improperly, leading to them falling unexpectedly and injuring workers or customers. Regular inspections should be conducted to confirm that all storage areas are organized and stable.

Accidents due to Moving Objects

In many workplaces, moving objects such as trolleys, carts, or machinery can create hazards, especially if they are not operated carefully or are left in walkways. These moving objects can strike employees or customers, causing bruises, cuts, or even more severe injuries.

Additionally, poorly stored props, lighting fixtures, or equipment can pose a risk if they are not secured properly. For example, nails sticking out of props or improperly attached lighting fixtures could cause cuts or electric shocks Regular inspections of fixtures and equipment should also be carried out to ensure that they are secure and safe to use.

Try These 15.2

1 **Which of the following is a common cause of trip and fall accidents in the workplace?**
   (a) Wet floors
   (b) Loose or misplaced materials
   (c) Moving objects
   (d) Malfunctioning elevators

2 **What should be done when the floor is wet to minimize slip and fall accidents?**
   (a) Use a broom to sweep the floor
   (b) Put up warning signs like "Wet Floor"
   (c) Avoid cleaning the floor
   (d) Leave the floor as it is

3 **Accidents involving ________ can lead to injuries such as fractures or sprains, especially when materials are left scattered across aisles.**

4 **To avoid accidents caused by ________ in elevators, regular checks and maintenance should be performed.**

5 **What should be done to avoid accidents due to moving objects?**

6 **What is a common cause of injuries due to falling goods in the workplace?**

15.3 Handling Accidents

To prevent accidents in your organization, identify potential hazards and work to eliminate them. If a colleague is injured due to an accident, follow these steps:

Attend to the Injured Person Immediately

Assess the severity of the injury and ensure the injured person receives first aid or medical attention as quickly as possible.

Inform Your Supervisor

Report the accident, including the likely cause and details of the injury.

Assist Your Supervisor

Help investigate the actual cause of the accident and assist in implementing measures to prevent similar incidents in the future.

15.4 Types of Emergencies

A workplace emergency is an unforeseen situation that threatens your employees, customers, or the public; disrupts or shuts down the workplace operations; or causes physical or environmental damage.

Emergencies may be natural or manmade and include the following:

- Floods,
- Hurricanes,
- Tornadoes,
- Fires,
- Toxic gas releases,
- Chemical spills,
- Radiological accidents,
- Explosions,
- Civil disturbances, and
- Workplace violence resulting in bodily harm and trauma.

Here are some general emergency handling procedures that you can follow:

First Aid

First aid kits should be easily accessible to all employees and stocked with essential items to address common injuries such as cuts, burns, headaches, and muscle cramps.

Electrical Safety

Employees should be trained on electrical safety practices, like keeping food and liquids away from electrical equipment. Routine inspections of wiring should be conducted by electrical staff and engineers to identify and address any damaged or broken wires.

Maintain a list of emergency contact numbers, including police, fire brigade, security, and ambulance services. Regularly check that emergency equipment, such as fire extinguishers and alarm systems, are functional.

Ensure that emergency exits are unobstructed and that keys are easily accessible. Never place objects near emergency doors or windows.

Evacuation

It's essential for employees to know who the designated coordinator is to make decisions during emergencies.

The coordinator should be responsible for managing the evacuation process.

General Evacuation Procedures

Every organization has specific evacuation procedures outlined in its policies, and it's essential to familiarize yourself with these guidelines and follow them during an emergency evacuation. In addition to company-specific policies, here are some general steps to follow:

- Evacuate the premises immediately and head toward the nearest emergency exit.
- Assist customers in finding and using emergency exits.
- Help individuals with disabilities move towards the emergency exit if possible.
- Carry only your essential hand-held belongings as you evacuate, but do not return for additional items until the area is declared safe.
- Avoid using escalators or elevators to prevent overcrowding or being trapped in case of a power outage. Use the stairs instead.
- Proceed to the designated emergency assembly area and report any missing colleagues to the appropriate person immediately.

Try These 15.3

1. **What should you do immediately after an injury occurs at the workplace?**
   (a) Inform your supervisor
   (b) Attend to the injured person
   (c) Check for potential hazards
   (d) Leave the area
2. **What should be ensured before evacuating during an emergency?**
   (a) You are the last to leave
   (b) Emergency exits are clear and accessible
   (c) Use the elevators for quick exit
   (d) Carry heavy equipment with you
3. **To assist in handling an accident, you should immediately inform your ________ about the cause of the accident and the injury.**
4. **In an emergency evacuation, you should never use ________ to avoid the risk of overcrowding or getting trapped.**
5. **What should be included in a first aid kit to handle common problems?**
6. **What is the importance of knowing evacuation procedures in an organization?**

15.5 Fire Hazards in the Workplace

The first step in ensuring fire safety is identifying potential fire hazards. In most workplaces, there are three key types of hazards to assess: electrical hazards, combustible materials, and flammable substances.

Electrical hazards, such as damaged extension cords, obstructed electrical panels, space heaters, and overloaded circuits, are common causes of fires. Electrical incidents like arc flashes can also spark fires. It's crucial to regularly maintain power cords and other electrical equipment.

Fires can also result from improper storage of flammable materials or combustible dust, both of which pose serious risks. Dust explosions are another potential fire hazard that should be addressed. Proper handling and storage of these materials are essential for workplace safety.

Fire Prevention Measures

- All employees should be familiar with the location of fire extinguishers and how to use them correctly.
- Fire extinguishers and First Aid Stations must be clearly marked with visible signs.
- Ensure exits, fire extinguishers, electrical switches, and panels are never obstructed.
- Avoid placing materials in front of doors that could hinder their operation in the event of a fire.
- Do not use flammable materials near electrical panels, switches, forklifts, or any electrical equipment.
- Ensure all equipment is properly grounded where necessary.
- Fire extinguishers should be inspected regularly.
- Report any defects in electrical systems, fire prevention equipment, or material handling tools to your supervisor.
- Flammable materials should never be stored around exit doorways.

Identification of Materials and Ignition Sources

Materials are categorized based on their fire risks and are classified as follows:

- **Class A Materials** These include items like wood, cloth, and paper. They do not ignite spontaneously but will continue to burn once exposed to a heat source.
- **Class B Materials** This category includes liquids, greases, and gases that ignite when exposed to ignition sources.

- **Class C Materials** These are electrical materials and equipment. They can quickly cause fires and pose a significant risk of arc flash.
- **Class D Materials** These are highly volatile substances that can ignite rapidly, such as magnesium, potassium, and sodium.

Examples of Ignition Sources

- **Open Flames** Sources like gas ovens, lighters used in smoking areas, and welding torches.
- **Sparks** Generated by wood or metal saws and other equipment.
- **Heat Sources** Includes combustion engines, space heaters, ovens, and machines that generate heat during operation.
- **Chemical Ignition** Occurs with chemicals that ignite at standard working temperatures.

Fire Extinguisher

A fire extinguisher is a safety device designed to put out fires. It is a cylindrical container under pressure, filled with an agent that can be released to extinguish flames.

Types of Fire extinguishers

Choose the appropriate type of fire extinguisher for each class of fire:

Fire Class	Water	CO_2	Dry Chemical Powder	Carbon Dioxide	Mechanical Foam	ABC Dry Powder
Class A	Suitable	Not Suitable	Not Suitable	Suitable	Suitable	Suitable
Class B	Not Suitable	Suitable	Suitable	Suitable	Suitable	Suitable
Class C	Not Suitable	Suitable	Suitable	Not Suitable	Suitable	Suitable
Class D	Not Suitable	Suitable	Not Suitable	Not Suitable	Suitable	Suitable

Try These 15.4

1 **Which class of fire is a water and foam fire extinguisher designed to extinguish?**
(a) Class A (b) Class B
(c) Class C (d) Class D

2 **What is the primary function of a carbon dioxide fire extinguisher in putting out a fire?**
(a) Creating a barrier between oxygen and fuel
(b) Removing the heat element
(c) Taking away the oxygen element and cooling the fire
(d) Interrupting the chemical reaction of the fire

3 **Class B materials include liquids, greases, and gases that ignite when exposed to __________.**

4 **What is the function of a fire extinguisher?**

5 **Which fire extinguisher is effective on Class D fires in commercial kitchens?**

15.6 First Aid for Electrical Emergencies

Electrical accidents often lead to numerous injuries, but many lives can be saved and damage minimized with prompt and correct rescue techniques. These accidents can happen anywhere and at any time, making timely response and treatment crucial. In the event of an electrical accident, muscle cramping may prevent the victim from moving or releasing the electrical source. Therefore, it is essential to have an emergency response plan in place for routine electrical maintenance or work.

Electrical Rescue Techniques

Approaching the Accident

- Avoid rushing into the situation.
- Immediately call emergency services at 108.
- Approach the scene with caution.

Examining the Scene

- Visually assess whether the victims are in contact with live conductors.
- Check if any metal surfaces or objects near the victim are energized.
- Avoid touching the victim or any conductive surfaces while they are still energized.
- If possible, turn off the electrical circuits.

Hazards and Solutions

- Stay alert for potential hazards, such as heated surfaces or fires.
- If you cannot turn off the power source, exercise extreme caution.
- Ensure your hands and feet are dry.
- Wear protective equipment, including gloves and shoes, and stand on a clean, dry surface.
- Use non-conductive materials to safely remove the victim from the electrical source.

High Voltage Rescue

- Rescuing individuals from high-voltage situations requires specialized training.
- Always wear protective equipment, including gloves and shoes.

First Aid

- A victim may need Cardio-Pulmonary Resuscitation (CPR). Follow the CPR steps as demonstrated.

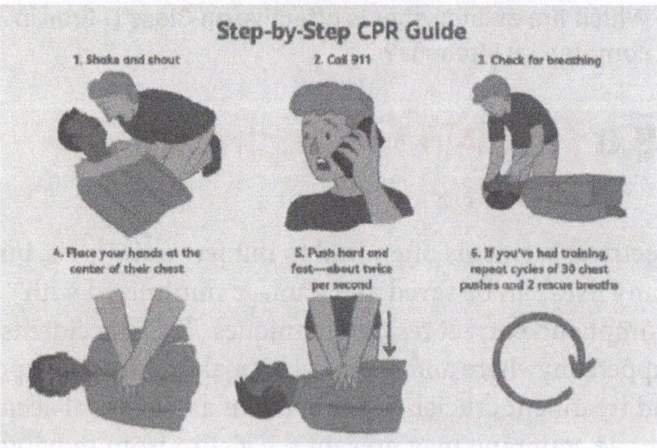

- If the victim is breathing and has a pulse, provide first aid for any injuries and address any signs of shock.
- Ensure the victim receives medical attention as quickly as possible.
- The attending physician should be given detailed information to aid in accurate diagnosis and treatment.

Summary

An accident at workplace is a physical or mental injury following an incident or exposure.

A workplace emergency is an unforeseen situation that threatens your employees, customers, or the public; disrupts or shuts down the workplace operations; or causes physical or environmental damage.

An evacuation plan covers designated actions employers and employees must take to ensure employee safety from fire and other emergencies.

ACTIVITY Time

ACTIVITY 1

Demonstrate the operation of a fire extinguisher.

Step 1 Identify the safety pin of the fire extinguisher, present in its handle.

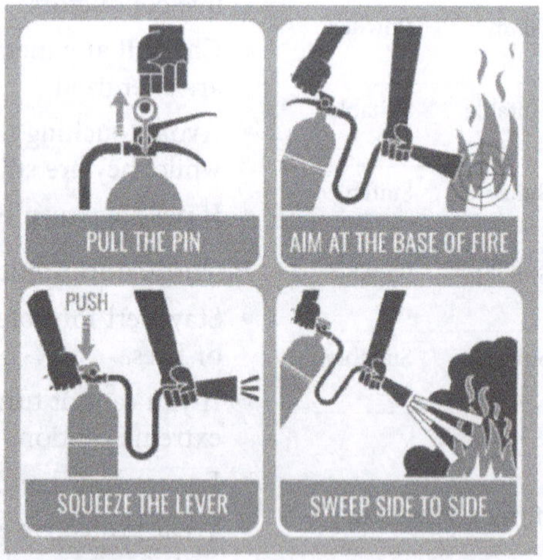

Step 2 Break the seal and pull the safety pin from the handle.

Step 3 Use the fire extinguisher by squeezing the lever.

Step 4 Sweep it from side to side.

NCERT FOLDER

Complete Explanations of all NCERT's Questions

A. Multiple Choice Questions

Q.1 What are the steps necessary for operating a fire extinguisher?

(a) Identify the safety pin of the fire extinguisher which is generally present in its handle
(b) Break the seal and pull the safety pin from the handle
(c) Use the fire extinguisher by squeezing the lever
(d) All of the above

Q.2 Which of the following is an examples of ignition sources of open flames?

(a) Gas ovens (b) Lighters in smoking areas
(c) Welding torches (d) All of these

Q.3 In fire classification, all liquid, grease, and gas material comes under ________.

(a) Class A material (b) Class B material
(c) Class C material (d) Class D material

Q.4 In fire classification, material magnesium, potassium, and sodium comes under ________.

(a) Class A material (b) Class B material
(c) Class C material (d) Class D material

Q.5 In fire classification, material wood, cloth, and paper comes under ________.

(a) Class A material (b) Class B material
(c) Class C material (d) Class D material

Q.6 In fire classification, electrical material and equipment comes under ________.

(a) Class A material (b) Class B material
(c) Class C material (d) Class D material

Q.7 When do we use a fire extinguisher?

(a) In case of flood (b) In case of electric shock
(c) In case of fire (d) In case of burn injury

Q.8 What is the primary fire emergency telephone number is?

(a) 011 (b) 101 (c) 108 (d) 111

Q.9 Which of the following contains everything you need to know about evacuating your facility safely?

(a) Evacuation Diagram (b) Emergency Action Plan
(c) Employee Directory (d) Both (a) and (b)

Q.10 The best course of action to take during a medical emergency is to ________.

(a) Begin first aid immediately
(b) Activate the emergency plan for reporting injuries
(c) Notify the person's family about the situation
(d) Both (a) and (b)

Answers

1. (d)	2. (d)	3. (b)	4. (d)	5. (a)
6. (c)	7. (c)	8. (b)	9. (d)	10. (d)

B. Fill in the Blanks

Q.1 Emergency is a serious or crisis situation that needs________attention and ________.

Q.2 A ________ sign will warn people to walk carefully on freshly mopped floors.

Q.3 ________ signs can prevent accidents on a staircase with a sharp bent or warn against a loose floor tile.

Q.4 The ________ should be responsible to handle evacuation process.

Q.5 Workplace fires are commonly caused by improper storage of ________ material or ________ dust.

Q.6 There should always be an ________ plan for scheduled electrical maintenance or work.

Q.7 If the victim is breathing and has a heartbeat, give ________ for injuries and treat for shock.

Q.8 A fire extinguisher is a ________ containing an agent which can be discharged to extinguish a fire.

Answers

1. Immediate, action
2. Wet floor
3. Watch your steps
4. Coordinator
5. Flammable, combustible
6. Emergency response
7. First aid
8. Cylindrical pressure vessel

C. State Whether the Following Statements are True or False

Q.1 The organization's policies and guidelines is the best guide to handle emergency.

Q.2 If someone is injured, act as per your impulse or gut feeling.

Q.3 Keep water and food items away from electrical equipment.

Q.4 Always switch off the electrical circuits.

Q.5 Always wear protective equipment, such as gloves and shoes.

Q.6 A fire extinguisher is a protection device used to extinguish fires.

Q.7 Flammable materials can be placed around an door exit.

Q.8 You can determine possible evacuation routes from floor plan diagrams posted in your facility.

Answers

1. True 2. False 3. True 4. False
5. False 6. True 7. False 8. True

D. Short Answer Questions

Q.1 What is a workplace emergency?

Ans. Workplace Emergency is a serious or crisis situation that needs immediate attention and action. For example, a customer having a heart attack or sudden outbreak of fire in your organisation needs immediate attention.

Q.2 How do you protect yourself, your employees, and your business?

Ans. Limit access to sensitive company data to only those with a need to know. Make sure your employees utilize and take their allotted vacation/PTO time each year. Not only is it healthy for your employee, but it will likely expose any fraudulent activities should they exist in your business.

Q.3 What is an emergency action plan?

Ans. An Emergency Action Plan (EAP) is a written document that outlines how to respond to various types of emergencies. It's a key part of an organization's safety procedures and can help reduce injuries, property damage, and ensure visitor safety.

Q.4 What should your emergency action plan include?

Ans. An emergency action plan should include details on how to respond to a major incident, such as an active shooter, fire, or natural disaster.

It should outline how employees should behave, where to report emergencies, and how to evacuate safely. The plan should also include information on safety areas, security and law enforcement, local hospitals, and how to notify others.

Q.5 How do you develop an evacuation policy and procedures?

Ans. Steps you can take to develop an evacuation policy and procedures:

(a) **Evaluate the emergency** Consider how fires break out and their leading causes.

(b) **Determine exit routes** Mark clear exit routes that are free of furniture and other objects.

(c) **Identify safe areas** Choose an assembly point outside the building where people can gather after evacuating. Make sure the area is clearly marked with signage.

(d) **Develop evacuation procedures** Include things like closing doors behind you to contain smoke or fire, and staying low to the ground if there's smoke.

Q.6 How do you establish evacuation routes and exits?

Ans. Exit routes should be:

(a) Clearly marked and well lit.

(b) Wide enough to accommodate the number of evacuating personnel.

(c) Unobstructed and clear of debris at all times.

(d) Unlikely to expose evacuating personnel to additional hazards.

Q.7 What are the various types of fire extinguisher and their extinguishing material?

Ans. There are many types of fire extinguishers, including water, foam, dry powder, carbon dioxide (CO_2), and wet chemical.

Q.8 What are the steps for operating a fire extinguisher in case of a fire emergency?

Ans.
- Identify the safety pin of the fire extinguisher, present in its handle.
- Break the seal and pull the safety pin from the handle.
- Use the fire extinguisher by squeezing the lever.
- Sweep it from side to side.

Q.9 Compare the different type of fire extinguisher.

Ans. Different types of fire extinguishers:

(i) Water (ii) Foam
(iii) Dry powder (iv) CO_2
(v) Wet chemical

	Water	Foam	Dry Powder	CO_2	Wet chemical
Fire Class	A	A & B	A, B & C	B & C	A

Q.10 List the different class of fire.

Ans. Classes of Fire: Class-A, Class-B, Class C, Class D.

Q.11 List out electrical rescue techniques.

Ans. Electrical rescue techniques are
- Approaching the accident
- Examining the scene
- Hazards and solutions

Q.12 What is the first aid for electrical emergencies?

Ans. First aid for electrical emergencies can include- Turning off the power, checking the sign of life, covering burns, keeping the victim warm and providing reassurance and staying with the victim.

REVIEW EXERCISE

Including Competency Based Questions

Multiple Choice Questions

1 Which of the following is not an example of ignition sources of open flames? CBSE SQP 2024-25

(a) Gas ovens (b) Lighters in smoking areas
(c) Welding torches (d) space heaters

2 ______ is the process of emptying a place in case of an emergency, disaster. CBSE SQP 2020-21, CBSE 2023

(a) Accident (b) Evacuation
(c) Hazards (d) Exiting

3 Which action contributes to a healthy and safe working environment? CBSE SQP 2024-25

(a) Keeping emergency exits clear
(b) Leaving cables loose on the floor
(c) Ignoring safety warnings
(d) Using unapproved software

4 What is the primary focus of an emergency action plan?

(a) To conduct regular fire drills
(b) To guide employees during emergencies
(c) To reduce workplace accidents
(d) To ensure daily productivity

5 Which of the following is considered a Class A fire material?

(a) Flammable liquids (b) Electrical equipment
(c) Wood and paper (d) Gases

6 What should be your first action if you notice a fire in the workplace?

(a) Call the fire department
(b) Attempt to put it out, regardless of size
(c) Evacuate immediately
(d) Inform the nearest supervisor

7 Which of the following is not a common accident in the workplace?

(a) Slips and falls (b) Strained muscles
(c) Fights at work (d) Remote teleworking injuries

8 In case of a fire, why should you avoid using the lift?

(a) It is too slow during emergencies
(b) You may become trapped if there is a power outage
(c) It's difficult to exit quickly
(d) Fire extinguishers are not available inside lifts

9 Which one of the following is a class B ignition material? CBSE 2025

(a) Paper (b) Gas
(c) Electrical equipment (d) Potassium

10 Which of the following is a proper first aid procedure for electrical emergencies?

(a) Immediately touching the victim to pull them away from the source
(b) Turning off the electrical circuit if possible
(c) Pouring water on the victim to cool them down
(d) Leaving the area to avoid personal injury

11 What should be done after an evacuation during an emergency?

(a) Re-enter the building to gather belongings
(b) Gather at the designated emergency assembly area
(c) Wait outside until the fire department arrives
(d) Call the police

12 What are the two most common hazards leading to fire in the workplace?

(a) Electrical hazards and flammable substances
(b) Poor lighting and wet floors
(c) Loud noise and machinery malfunctions
(d) Faulty furniture and poor training

13 What type of extinguisher should be used for electrical fires?

(a) Water and foam (b) Carbon dioxide
(c) Wet chemical (d) Class A extinguisher

14 Which of the following materials is categorized under Class D?

(a) Magnesium and sodium (b) Paper and wood
(c) Electrical equipment (d) Gases and liquids

15 What is the most appropriate action if you notice a malfunctioning escalator in your organization?

(a) Use it carefully (b) Ignore it and move on
(c) Report it immediately (d) Repair it yourself

16 You notice a small fire starting in a wastebasket due to a discarded matchstick in your home. What should you do first?

(a) Evacuate immediately
(b) Use a fire extinguisher or water to put out the fire if safe to do so
(c) Call the fire department before taking any action
(d) Cover the wastebasket with a cloth to smoother the fire

17 During an evacuation drill, you observe some employees using the elevator to exit the building. What is the correct course of action?

(a) Wait for them to evacuate and then remind them about the policy
(b) Inform them immediately to use the stairs instead of the elevator

(c) Ignore it, as they may have a valid reason for using the elevator
(d) Use the elevator yourself to speed up evacuation

18 While working in a factory, you observe that a colleague is frequently lifting heavy items incorrectly, using their back rather than their legs. What is the best way to handle the situation?
(a) Report the issue to a supervisor
(b) Offer to assist in lifting the heavy items for them
(c) Provide them with tips on proper lifting techniques and recommend ergonomic training
(d) Ignore the issue unless they hurt themselves

19 You find that one of the fire extinguishers in your society premises has expired. What should be your next step?
(a) Continue to use it until the next safety inspection
(b) Immediately report it to the safety officer or society authority and arrange for a replacement
(c) Remove it from its location to prevent misuse
(d) Ignore it if there are other working extinguishers in the building

20 You notice water has spilled on the floor near a workstation in the office. What should you do to prevent accidents?
(a) Warn people around the area and continue with your tasks
(b) Leave the spill and assume someone else will clean it
(c) Clean the spill yourself or report it immediately and place a warning sign until it's cleaned
(d) Put a chair over the spill to block people from walking through it

Answers

1. (d)	2. (b)	3. (a)	4. (b)	5. (c)
6. (c)	7. (d)	8. (b)	9. (b)	10. (b)
11. (b)	12. (a)	13. (b)	14. (a)	15. (c)
16. (b)	17. (b)	18. (c)	19. (b)	20. (c)

Very Short Answer Type Questions

1 List and explain two common safety hazards in a workplace. CBSE SQP 2024-25

Ans. Common Safety Hazards in the Workplace

- **Slips, Trips, and Falls** These hazards can occur due to wet floors, loose rugs, poor lighting, or obstructed walkways. They can lead to injuries such as sprains, fractures, and even serious head injuries.
- **Ergonomic Hazards** These arise from improper workstation setup, repetitive motions, or poor posture. They can cause musculoskeletal disorders, including back pain, carpal tunnel syndrome, and joint issues.

2 Mention any two basic fire safety rules to be followed in any organisation. CBSE 2024

Ans. Basic fire safety rules to be followed in an organization

- **Keep Exits Unblocked** Ensure that all exits, hallways, and stairways are free from obstructions, allowing for a clear and safe evacuation during an emergency.
- **Use Fire Extinguishers Properly** Employees should be trained to use fire extinguishers safely and effectively, following the PASS technique (Pull, Aim, Squeeze, Sweep) if it's safe to do so.

3 What is the main difference between an accident and an emergency?

Ans. An accident is an unexpected, unintentional event causing injury or harm, while an emergency is a critical, urgent situation requiring immediate action.

4 Why is it essential to have a comprehensive emergency action plan?

Ans. To guide employees during unforeseen incidents, ensuring their safety and minimizing disruption or damage.

5 How can employers help prevent repetitive strain injuries (RSI) in the workplace?

Ans. By providing training on proper posture and ergonomics, especially for those working on computers or lifting heavy items.

6 What should you do if someone gets injured in the workplace?

Ans. Provide immediate assistance, notify your supervisor, and assist in investigating the cause of the accident.

7 What is the role of fire extinguishers in the workplace?

Ans. Fire extinguishers help control small fires before they escalate, ensuring the safety of employees and property.

8 Why is it important to have regular maintenance of escalators and elevators?

Ans. To prevent malfunctions that could lead to accidents, injuries, or panic.

9 What are the three key fire hazard types in most workplaces?

Ans. Electrical hazards, combustible materials, and flammable substances.

10 What are some common causes of slips, trips, and falls in the workplace?

Ans. Wet floors, slippery surfaces, and falls from heights, such as scaffolding or stairs.

11 Why is electrical rescue training important?

Ans. It equips workers to safely rescue someone in contact with live electricity without putting themselves at risk.

Short Answer Type Questions

1 Explain the importance of distinguishing between accidents and emergencies in the workplace and the role of company policies in addressing both.

Ans. Accidents and emergencies are distinct events requiring different responses. Accidents may involve injuries that don't always require immediate evacuation, while emergencies demand urgent action to prevent further harm. Company policies play a vital role in providing clear guidelines for employees to recognize and respond to these events. By distinguishing between them, employees can act appropriately, ensuring safety, preventing escalation, and reducing risks. Company policies ensure consistency in handling such incidents and help guide employees through proper channels of reporting and response.

2 Imagine that you have been signed a contract of handling fire safety and emergency in a company. You need to spread awareness on fire safety and emergency handling to the employees. **CBSE 2025**

Answer the following questions:

(a) Give any two fire prevention measures at the workplace.

(b) Give any two basic emergency handling procedures at the workplace.

Ans. (a) Two fire prevention measures at the workplace include

1. Regular maintenance and inspection of electrical wiring and equipment to avoid potential electrical fires.
2. Storing flammable materials properly and ensuring they are away from heat sources.

(b) Two basic emergency handling procedures at the workplace include:

1. Evacuating the building immediately upon hearing a fire alarm or if there's a fire threat.
2. Calling emergency services (such as the fire department) and providing them with accurate information about the situation.

3 Describe the key components of first aid for electrical emergencies and why swift action is crucial.

Ans. First aid for electrical emergencies includes safely disconnecting the power source, approaching the scene cautiously, using non-conductive materials to move the victim, and performing CPR if needed.

Swift action is crucial because electrical injuries can cause severe damage, including cardiac arrest, respiratory failure, and burns. Without immediate intervention, the victim's chances of survival diminish rapidly. Providing prompt medical attention can help mitigate long-term damage and increase the likelihood of a full recovery.

4 Explain the types of fire extinguishers and when each type should be used in the workplace.

Ans. There are several types of fire extinguishers:

- Water and foam extinguishers are for Class A fires (wood, paper)
- Carbon Dioxide extinguishers are for Class B and C fires (liquids, gases, electrical)
- Dry Chemical extinguishers are for Class A, B, and C fires
- Wet Chemical extinguishers are for Class K fires (cooking oils and fats).
- Using the correct extinguisher is crucial to avoid making the fire worse or causing additional hazards, such as using water on electrical fires, which can result in shock or further ignition.

5 How can regular risk assessments and training reduce workplace accidents and emergencies?

Ans. Regular risk assessments identify potential hazards in the workplace, allowing employers to take proactive steps to mitigate these risks.

By addressing issues like improper storage, faulty equipment, or unsafe practices, the likelihood of accidents and emergencies is reduced. Training ensures employees are aware of these risks and know how to avoid them.

It also prepares them to respond appropriately during emergencies, minimizing harm and ensuring a safer work environment. Regular assessments and training create a culture of safety that prioritizes prevention over reaction.

PRACTICAL ASSIGNMENT

1. Identify and name the steps mentioned in the following figures.

2. Conduct a comprehensive fire safety audit of your school to identify potential hazards, assess current fire safety measures, and propose improvements. Write a report summarizing your findings, identifying areas of improvement, and providing specific recommendations for enhancing fire safety. Be sure to include:
   - A list of identified hazards
   - Condition of fire safety equipment
   - Review of the evacuation plan
   - Suggestions for future fire safety training

SELF ASSESSMENT

Multiple Choice Questions

1 What is the primary purpose of workplace safety policies?

(a) To increase profits
(b) To prevent workplace accidents and injuries
(c) To reduce employee working hours
(d) To improve customer satisfaction

2 Which of the following is a common physical hazard in the workplace?

(a) Loud noise
(b) Inadequate lighting
(c) Being hit by falling objects
(d) All of these

3 What is the recommended first aid treatment for a minor burn?

(a) Apply ice directly to the burn
(b) Run cool water over the area for up to 15 minutes
(c) Cover it with a hot compress
(d) Leave it uncovered to air out

4 What is the primary purpose of a workplace emergency action plan?

(a) To report employee grievances
(b) To guide employees during emergencies
(c) To prevent workplace disputes
(d) To promote employee attendance

5 Which of the following types of fire extinguishers should not be used on electrical fires?

(a) Dry Chemical (b) Carbon Dioxide (c) Water and Foam (d) Wet Chemical

6 What should you do first if you witness an electrical accident?

(a) Immediately approach and assist the victim
(b) Call emergency services at 108
(c) Turn off the electricity before helping
(d) Check for nearby hazards

7 What is a common cause of air pollution in IT companies using centralized air conditioning systems?

(a) Excessive use of pesticides
(b) Release of dust and solid particles
(c) Lack of proper water filtration
(d) Improper waste disposal

8 Which ergonomic measure can help reduce wrist strain while typing?

(a) Positioning the monitor at eye level
(b) Adding a wrist rest to the keyboard
(c) Keeping the mouse lower than the keyboard
(d) Using a document holder

9 Which of the following is an example of a physical hazard?

(a) Poor lighting causing eye strain
(b) Chemical exposure leading to skin irritation
(c) Lifting heavy objects improperly
(d) Workplace bullying causing stress

10 How can organizations minimize ozone pollution?

(a) Avoid using fertilizers near water sources
(b) Reduce vehicle use on campus
(c) Prevent discharge of wastewater into the environment
(d) Limit human activities that affect groundwater

11 An employee working with a computer for long hours reports discomfort and eye strain. What is the best immediate recommendation? **Competency Based Que.**

(a) Increase their working hours
(b) Provide them with more paperwork
(c) Encourage stretching exercises and adjust screen brightness
(d) Advise them to ignore the discomfort

12 If an electrical technician discovers worn-out wires during an inspection, what is the most appropriate course of action? **Competency Based Que.**

(a) Continue using the wires until they fail
(b) Immediately report the issue and replace the wires
(c) Ignore the problem as long as the equipment is working
(d) Tape the wires and leave them for later

13 If a colleague is injured by a falling object at work, what is your immediate responsibility? **Competency Based Que.**

(a) Investigate the cause of the accident yourself
(b) Provide first aid only if trained, then notify your supervisor
(c) Call the insurance company immediately
(d) Report the incident to the media

14 During an emergency evacuation, what should you avoid doing? **Competency Based Que.**

(a) Use the stairs to exit the building
(b) Carry essential personal belongings
(c) Use the elevator for a faster exit
(d) Assist colleagues in evacuating

15 If an employee reports headaches and eye strain from using the computer, what immediate action should be taken? **Competency Based Que.**

(a) Recommend taking more frequent breaks
(b) Move the employee to a new workstation
(c) Check the room's lighting and glare sources
(d) Provide anti-glare glasses immediately

Very Short Answer Type Questions

16 Explain why security measures are crucial for a company beyond just physical protection.

17 What are some common risks posed by prolonged use of computers, and how can they be mitigated?

18 What steps should you take if you witness a fire in your workplace?

19 Why is it important to perform regular maintenance on electrical systems in the workplace?

20 What are some strategies to prevent eye strain when working on a computer for extended periods?

Short Answer Type Questions

21 Explain the importance of maintaining workplace health and cleanliness, and how it can impact employee morale and productivity.

22 Describe the different types of workplace hazards, particularly focusing on physical and electrical hazards, and how they can be mitigated.

23 What are the critical steps an organization should take to develop an effective emergency action plan to address workplace accidents and emergencies?

24 What are the main types of workplace accidents, and what preventative measures can organizations implement to reduce their occurrence?

25 What are the key types of workplace hazards, and how can organizations effectively identify and manage these risks to promote a safe work environment?

Answers

1. (b)	**2.** (d)	**3.** (b)	**4.** (b)	**5.** (c)	**6.** (d)	**7.** (b)	**8.** (b)	**9.** (c)	**10.** (b)
11. (c)	**12.** (b)	**13.** (b)	**14.** (c)	**15.** (a)					

Practical Work

Advanced Documentation

Objective To create a new style.

Materials Required A computer system equipped with a word processing application like LibreOffice.

Assignment 1 Format a document and save the done formatting with the new style named "New Style Format".

Procedure

Step 1 Open the document.

Step 2 Apply the desired formatting to the elements, such as paragraphs, frames, spacing, etc.

Step 3 From the toolbar at the top, select the appropriate style category (e.g., paragraph style).

Step 4 Highlight the formatted content that you want to save as a style.

Step 5 Navigate to the Styles panel, click on the **New Style from Selection** icon, and choose **New Style** from the menu. This will open the **Create Style** dialog box.

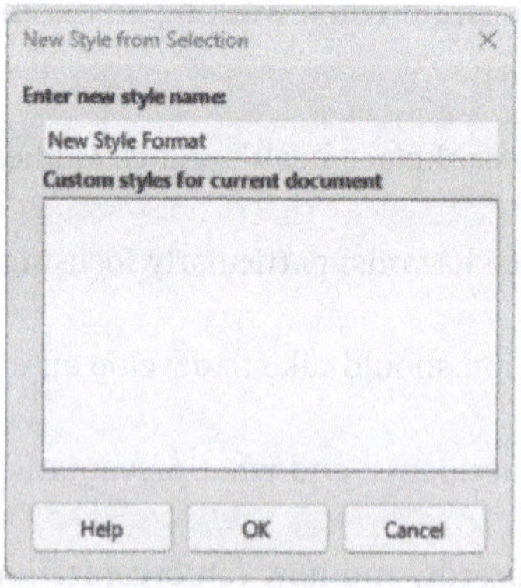

Step 6 Type a name for the new style. The list shows the names of existing custom styles of the selected type, if any. Click on OK to save the new style.

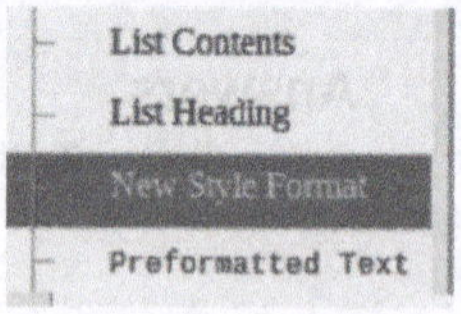

Viva-voce

1. What is the first step in saving a formatted document with a new name?

Ans. The first step is to open the document.

2. Why do you need to highlight the formatted content before saving it as a style?

Ans. Highlighting ensures that the selected formatting is applied to the new style.

3. What happens when you click on the 'New Style from Selection' icon?

Ans. It allows you to create a new style based on the selected formatting.

4. Why is it important to give a name to the new style?

Ans. Naming helps in identifying and reusing the style easily in the document.

5. What is the final step in saving the new style?

Ans. Click OK to save the new style after naming it.

Objective To Insert and image and then crop and rotate it.

Assignment 2 Insert a picture into a document. Now, using the features of the word processor:

(i) Crop this image and insert only right half of the image onto the document.

(ii) Rotate the cropped image.

Procedure (i)

Step 1 Open the Writer document.

Step 2 Insert the picture of landscape in the document using Insert → Image from menu bar.

Step 3 Right-click on the image. Click on Crop from context menu.

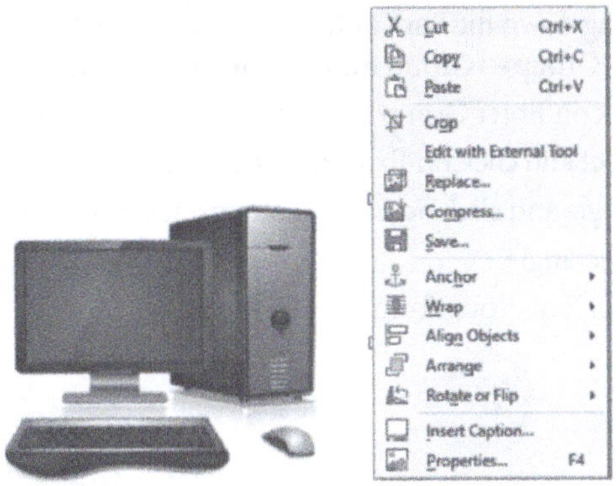

Step 4 Cropping handles appear at the corners and mid-points of the sides of the image. Drag a handle to cut off part of the image.

Step 5 The image gets cropped. Click outside the image to turn off cropping mode.

Procedure (ii)

Step 1 Right-click on the image.

Step 2 Click on the Rotate or Flip → Rotate option. The Rotate handles appear on the corners of the image.

Step 3 Rotate the image accordingly.

Viva-voce

1. How can you insert an image into a Writer document?

Ans. Go to Insert → Image from the menu bar and select the desired image.

2. How do you access the cropping option for an image?

Ans. Right-click on the image and select Crop from the context menu.

3. What happens when you drag the cropping handles on an image?

Ans. Dragging the handles removes unwanted portions of the image.

4. How do you enable rotation handles for an image?

Ans. Right-click on the image and choose Rotate or Flip → Rotate.

5. What is the final step after rotating an image?

Ans. Adjust the rotation as needed and click outside the image to finalize the changes.

Objective To insert different drawing objects and group them as one unit to edit.

Assignment 3 Open a Writer window. Insert a diamond shape, a smiley face and a star shape on the document. Include the three drawings into a single group. Next, reduce the size of the diamond shape and increase the size of the smiley face and keep the third figure unchanged.

Procedure

Step 1 Open the Writer window.

Step 2 Click on Insert tab→ Shape option.

Step 3 Choose your shapes (here, diamond, a smiley face and a star shape).

Step 4 Choose the three shapes by holding down the Shift button. With the objects selected, hover the mouse pointer over one of the objects and choose Format→ Group→Group from the menu bar. The group comprising the three objects is formed.

Step 5 Right-click on the smiley and click on Enter Group from context menu. Reduce the size of the diamond shape.

Step 6 Right-click on some drawing object and click on Exit group from context menu.

Step 7 Right-click on the rounded rectangle and click on Enter group from context menu.

Step 8 Increase the size of the rounded rectangle.

Step 9 Right-click on a figure and click on Exit group from context menu.

Before changes After changes

Viva-voce

1. How do you insert shapes in a Writer document?

Ans. Click on Insert→ Shape and select the desired shape.

2. How can multiple shapes be selected at once?

Ans. Hold down the Shift key and click on each shape.

3. Which option is used to group multiple shapes together?

Ans. Use Format→ Group→ Group from the menu bar.

4. How can you modify a shape inside a grouped object?

Ans. Right-click on the shape and select Enter Group to edit it.

5. What should you do after editing a grouped object?

Ans. Right-click on any shape and select Exit Group to finish editing.

Objective To apply a predefined template onto a document.

Assignment 4 If there is a template with some predefined style, how will you apply it to a newly opened document? Write the steps required to do so. A sample document is given as:

Internet..An Introduction

The vast worldwide network that helps us to keep in instant touch with our friends and relatives by communicating online, near or far, enables us to get the latest news, do research, shop online, do banking from anywhere in the world, and many such activities is called the **Internet**. In short, the **Internet** helps us stay connected with the world and do a lot of activities at our ease. There are millions of computers connected to the internet at any given point of time.
In fact Internet is itself a collection of local, regional, national and international networks. Though these networks are owned by private or public organisations but the internet is not owned by anyone. Knowledge of the internet is one of the key requirements in any field in today's world.

Procedure

Step 1 Open a new document.

Step 2 Navigate to **File→ New→ Templates.** In the **Templates** dialog box, double-click the desired template. A new document will open with the template's predefined styles, text, or graphics.

Step 3 Remove any unnecessary text or graphics from the newly created document.

Step 4 Open the existing document that needs to be formatted (it will open in a separate window).

Step 5 Select the entire content of the document by using **Edit→ Select All** or pressing **Ctrl + A.**

Step 6 Copy the selected content using **Edit→ Copy** or by pressing **Ctrl + C.**

Step 7 Switch to the blank document created in Step 2 and paste the copied content using **Edit→ Paste** or **Ctrl + V.**

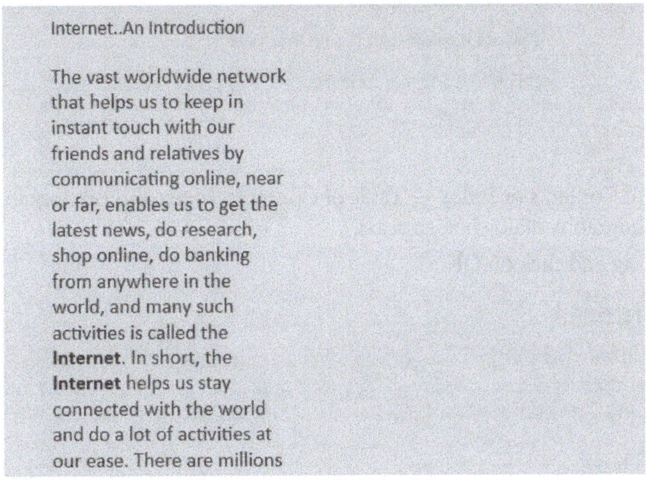
Internet..An Introduction

The vast worldwide network that helps us to keep in instant touch with our friends and relatives by communicating online, near or far, enables us to get the latest news, do research, shop online, do banking from anywhere in the world, and many such activities is called the **Internet**. In short, the **Internet** helps us stay connected with the world and do a lot of activities at our ease. There are millions

Here, the template used is CV.

Step 8 Close the old file without saving. Use File→ Save As to save this new file with the name of the file from which content was taken. When asked, confirm you wish to overwrite the old file. Or, you may prefer to save the new file under a new name and preserve the old file under its original name.

Viva-voce

1. What is the first step to apply a predefined template to a document?

Ans. The first step is to open a new document.

2. How do you select a predefined template in a new document?

Ans. Go to File→ New→ Templates, then double-click the desired template.

3. Why do you need to remove unnecessary text or graphics after applying a template?

Ans. To ensure that only the relevant content remains in the document.

4. What shortcut can you use to select all content in an existing document?

Ans. Press Ctrl + A or use Edit→ Select All.

5. What should you do after pasting content into the new template-based document?

Ans. Update the table of contents (if applicable) and save the document with the appropriate name.

Objective To create a Table of Contents of a document

Assignment 5 Create a Table of Contents(ToC) of the sample given below:

Introduction to Global Warming

Causes of Global Warming

Greenhouse Gas Emissions

Deforestation

Industrial Activities

Effects of Global Warming

Rising Temperatures

Melting Glaciers and Rising Sea Levels

Impact on Weather Patterns

Procedure

Step 1 Click on Insert→ Table of Contents or Index→ Table of Contents, Index and Bibliography option. The Table of Contents, Index and Bibliography dialog box appears.

Step 2 Change the required setting and click on OK.

Table of Contents

Introduction to Global Warming..2
Causes of Global Warming..4
  Greenhouse Gas Emissions..4
  Deforestation..4
  Industrial Activities..4
Effects of Global Warming..5
  Rising Temperatures..5
  Melting Glaciers and Rising Sea Levels..5
  Impact on Weather Patterns..5

Viva-voce

1. What is the purpose of a Table of Contents in LibreOffice Writer?

Ans. It provides a structured overview of document sections with clickable links for easy navigation.

2. How do you insert a Table of Contents in LibreOffice Writer?

Ans. Go to **Insert→ Table of Contents and Index→ Table of Contents, Index or Bibliography** and configure settings.

3. How can you update a Table of Contents after making changes to the document?

Ans. Right-click on the Table of Contents and select **Update Index.**

4. What heading styles are used to generate a Table of Contents automatically?

Ans. Heading styles like **Heading 1, Heading 2, and Heading 3** are used.

5. Can you customize the appearance of a Table of Contents in LibreOffice Writer?

Ans. Yes, you can modify font, numbering, and indentation under the **Entries and Styles** tab in the settings.

Advanced Spreadsheets

Objective To calculate the subtotal.

Materials Required A computer system equipped with a spreadsheet application like LibreOffice.

Assignment 1 You have the following data in a table.

	A	B	C	D	E
1	INTERSCHOOL CHESS CARNIVAL				
2	SCHOOL NAME	Student Name	Class	Category	Result
3	*Bal Bharati Public School*	*Adhimaan*		*7 Under 13*	*1st*
4	*DPS*	*Surabhi*		*3 Under 9*	*1st*
5	*DAV School*	*Dakshit*		*8 Under 13*	*2nd*
6	*Modern School*	*Preeti*		*10 Under 17*	*3rd*
7	*Bal Bharati Public School*	*Shaurya*		*7 Under 13*	*2nd*
8	*Bal Bharati Public School*	*Raghav*		*7 Under 13*	*3rd*
9	*Bal Bharati Public School*	*Prisha*		*10 Under 17*	*1st*
10	*DPS*	*Damanjit*		*10 Under 17*	*3rd*

From the above table, find out the result school wise result. Apply Autofilter and then use the SUBTOTAL feature of a spreadsheet application.

Procedure

Step 1 Open a spreadsheet.

Step 2 Tabulate the information as given in question.

Step 3 With the active cell inside some data in the spreadsheet, click on Data → AutoFilter.

	A	B	C	D	E
1	INTERSCHOOL CHESS CARNIVAL				
2	SCHOOL NAME	Student Name	Class	Category	Result
3	*Bal Bharati Public School*	*Adhimaan*		*7 Under 13*	*1st*
4	*Bal Bharati Public School*	*Shaurya*		*7 Under 13*	*2nd*
5	*Bal Bharati Public School*	*Raghav*		*7 Under 13*	*3rd*
6	*Bal Bharati Public School*	*Prisha*		*10 Under 17*	*1st*

Step 4 Select a particular school for the display of result.

Step 5 Select the cells.

Step 6 Click on Data → SUBTOTAL. The Subtotal dialog box appears.

Step 7 Enter the required information into the two input boxes.

Step 8 Click on OK to return the summed values of points.

Step 9 Choose the category as School name and click on Count function.

	A	B	C	D	E
1	INTERSCHOOL CHESS CARNIVAL				
2	SCHOOL NAME	Student Name	Class	Category	Result
3	*Bal Bharati Public School*	*Adhimaan*		*7 Under 13*	*1st*
4	*Bal Bharati Public School*	*Shaurya*		*7 Under 13*	*2nd*
5	*Bal Bharati Public School*	*Raghav*		*7 Under 13*	*3rd*
6	*Bal Bharati Public School*	*Prisha*		*10 Under 17*	*1st*
7		*0*			*4*
8	*DAV School*	*Dakshit*		*8 Under 13*	*2nd*
9		*0*			*1*
10	*DPS*	*Surabhi*		*3 Under 9*	*1st*
11	*DPS*	*Damanjit*		*10 Under 17*	*3rd*
12		*0*			*2*
13	*Modern School*	*Preeti*		*10 Under 17*	*3rd*
14		*0*			*1*
15		*0*			*8*

Step 10 Click on OK.

Viva-voce

1. How do you enable filtering in a spreadsheet?

Ans. Click on Data → AutoFilter to enable filtering options.

2. What is the purpose of the Subtotal function in a spreadsheet?

Ans. It helps calculate sums, averages, and counts for selected data groups.

3. Which dialog box appears when you use the Subtotal function?

Ans. The Subtotal dialog box appears for input selection.

4. How can you count the number of occurrences of a specific category, like a school name?

Ans. Select the category and use the Count function in the Subtotal dialog box.

5. What is the final step after entering values in the Subtotal dialog box?

Ans. Click on OK to compute and display the required results.

Objective To use Goal Seek Feature to get the desired Simple Interest.

Assignment 2 Create a simple case of evaluation of rate of interest given by a bank based on, principal, time (in number of years) and Interest calculated. Assume that the interest is simple interest.

D3 =(A3*B3*C3)/100

	A	B	C	D	E
1	Simple Interest Calculation				
2	Principal	Rate of Interest	Years	Simple Interest Calculated	Amount after Interest
3	50000	5	5	12500	62500
4	100000	10	5	50000	150000
5	5000	5	2	500	5500
6	75000	7	10	52500	127500
7	60000	5	5	15000	75000

Procedure

Step 1 Open a worksheet.

Step 2 Enter values for Principal, Time and Rate of interest.

Step 3 Put the formula in the formula cell, here D3. The formula is Interest = (P * R * T)/100.

Step 4 Choose Tools → Goal Seek. The Goal Seek dialog box opens up.

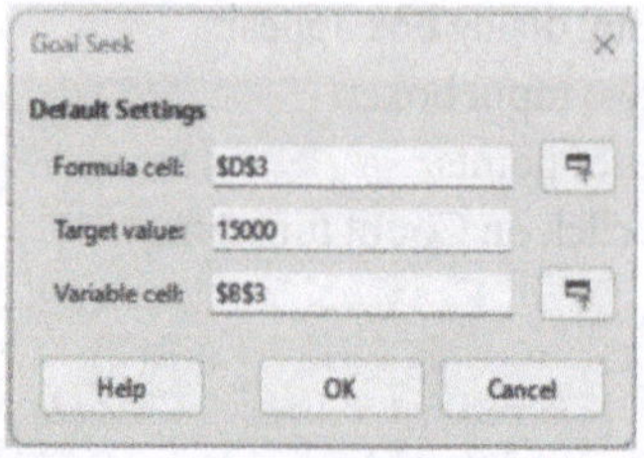

Step 5 In the Goal Seek dialog box, the correct cell is already entered in the Formula cell field.

Step 6 The variable cell is the rate of Interest cell(B3).

Step 7 Click on OK.

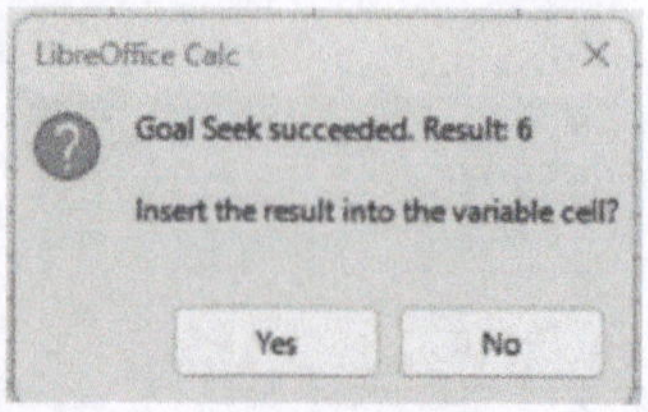

Step 8 The goal seek has succeeded. Click on Yes on the dialog box.

D3 | =(A3*B3*C3)/100

	A	B	C	D	E
1	Simple Interest Calculation				
2	Principal	Rate of Interest	Years	Simple Interest Calculated	Amount after Interest
3	50000	6	5	15000	65000
4	100000	10	5	50000	150000
5	5000	5	2	500	5500
6	75000	7	10	52500	127500
7	60000	5	5	15000	75000

Here, Rate of Interest changed to 6% for the interest 15000(Before it was 12500).

Viva-voce

1. **What is the purpose of the Goal Seek feature in spreadsheets?**

Ans. Goal Seek is used to determine the required input value to achieve a desired result in a formula.

2. **Which menu option is used to access Goal Seek in a spreadsheet?**

Ans. **Tools → Goal Seek.**

3. **What are the three main inputs required in the Goal Seek dialog box?**

Ans. The **Formula Cell**, the **Target Value**, and the **Variable Cell.**

4. **Can Goal Seek be used for multiple changing values at the same time?**

Ans. No, Goal Seek can only change **one variable cell** at a time.

5. **What happens when Goal Seek successfully finds a solution?**

Ans. A confirmation dialog box appears, and the user can choose **Yes** to accept the change.

Objective To refer to values entered in different sheets and add a comment.

Assignment 3 Explain how you can reference a cell from another sheet of the same workbook. Additionally, show how you can add comment to a cell of the spreadsheet.

	A	B	C	D
1	Sheet 1 Values			
2	12	24	45	
3	34	22	13	

H16

	A	B	C	D
1	Sheet 2 Values			
2	67	67	22	
3	12	78	90	
4				
5	Added Values			

Procedure

Step 1 Open a workbook.
Step 2 Fill the worksheet with some data.
Step 3 Enter some other data in the other spreadsheet of the same workbook.
Step 4 Switch to the previous entered spreadsheet.
Step 5 Click on the cell where you want the referenced cell to be copied to.
Step 6 Click the = icon and write the SUM().
Step 7 Switch to the other sheet(to reference the data from).

D5 | =SUM($'Sheet 1'.A2,$'Sheet 1'.B2,$'Sheet 1'.C2,$'Sheet 1'.A3,$'Sheet 1'.B3,$'Sheet 1'.C3,A2,B2,C2,A3,B3,C3)

	A	B	C	D	E	F	G	H	I
1	Sheet 2 Values								
2	67	67	22						
3	12	78	90						
4									
5	Added Values			486					

Step 8 Switch to previous sheet and click on green check mark.

Step 9 Click on Insert → Comment option.

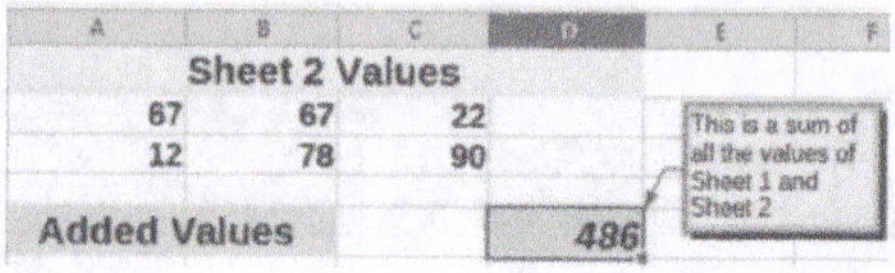

Note *If the comment disappears, you may see the comment by right-clicking on the cell and clicking on Show Comment from context menu.*

Viva-voce

1. **How can you reference data from another spreadsheet in the same workbook?**

Ans. By using formulas like **SUM()** and selecting the required data from the other sheet.

2. **What symbol is used to start a formula in a spreadsheet?**

Ans. The **equals sign (=).**

3. **Which feature is used to add notes or explanations to a cell in a spreadsheet?**

Ans. The **Insert → Comment** option.

4. **How can you make a comment visible if it disappears?**

Ans. By **right-clicking on the cell** and selecting **Show Comment** from the context menu.

5. **What is the purpose of using multiple sheets in a workbook?**

Ans. To **organize related data separately** while allowing references between them.

Objective To consolidate the given values.

Assignment 4 Students have to add up matrices. Answer the following questions:

(i) What feature of a spreadsheet application allows to add up matrices (of the same order) most easily?

(ii) Write the steps required to add up the matrices and copy to some (non-overlapping) location on the spreadsheet.

Procedure

(i) The Consolidate feature of a spreadsheet application can be used to add up matrices.

(ii) Follow these steps to add up the matrices:

Step 1 Open a spreadsheet.

Step 2 Enter the matrices, cell by cell for the three matrices. The matrices here are of 3 rows × 3 columns.

Step 3 Choose Data → Consolidate to open the Consolidate dialog box.

Step 4 Enter the values into the Consolidate dialog box in accordance to your needs.

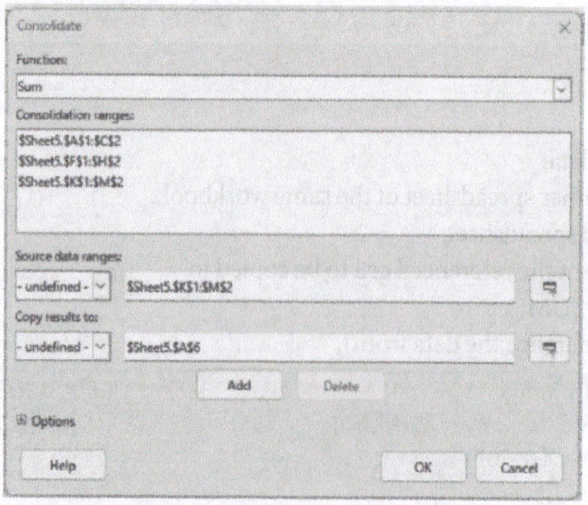

Below is shown the Consolidate dialog box with the matrix ranges filled in.

Step 5 Click on OK. The sum of the three matrices will be copied to cell range as specified.

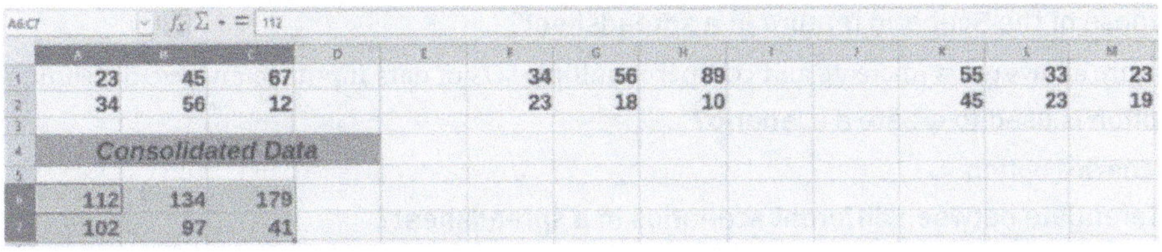

Data after applying Consolidate feature.

Viva-voce

1. What is the purpose of the Consolidate feature in a spreadsheet?

Ans. The Consolidate feature is used to combine and sum data from multiple cell ranges, such as matrices.

2. Which menu option is used to access the Consolidate feature?

Ans. The **Data → Consolidate** option.

3. How do you specify the matrices to be added in the Consolidate dialog box?

Ans. By entering the cell ranges of the matrices in the Consolidate dialog box.

4. What happens after clicking OK in the Consolidate dialog box?

Ans. The sum of the selected matrices is calculated and displayed in the specified cell range.

5. Can the Consolidate feature be used for operations other than addition?

Ans. Yes, it can perform other operations like **average, count, minimum, and maximum**.

Objective To create scenarios.

Assignment 4 This problem will test your knowledge of how to use scenarios in a spreadsheet application.

Create 4 cells to store the following values:Fixed cost, Price per unit, Number of units sold and Total profit.

The Total Profit is stored as cell with formula. The formula is:

Total profit = Number of units sold * Price per unit – Fixed cost

Now, use the Scenarios tool to create one more scenario and show the output for the other scenario as well.

Procedure

Step 1 Open a spreadsheet.

Step 2 Create the values for Cost Price, Selling Price and Number of units sold. Also, create the formula cell for total profit.

Step 3 The three cells with input are selected.

Step 4 The Tools → Scenarios is clicked on. Give the name Case 1 to the inputs. Click on OK in dialog box.

Step 5 With the same three cells selected, click on Tools → Scenarios. This time name the scenario as Case 2.

Step 6 Enter the values for Case 2. The value for total profit would have changed.

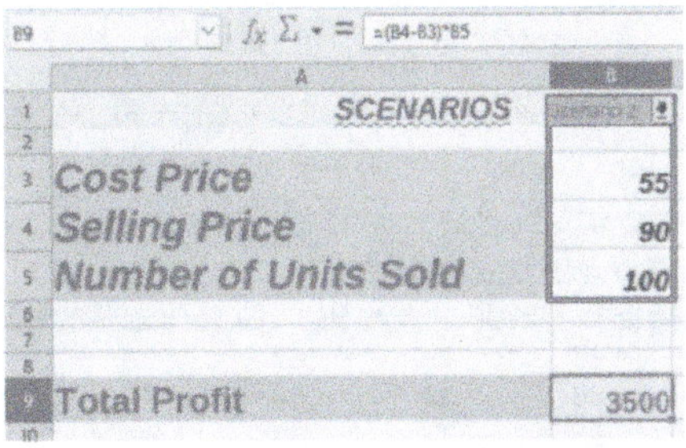

Step 7 Click on the column header for the scenario window. You can see the two scenarios created. You can switch between either for your needs.

Viva-voce

1. What is the purpose of the Scenario feature in a spreadsheet?

Ans. The Scenario feature allows users to create and compare multiple sets of data inputs to analyze different possible outcomes.

2. Which menu option is used to create a scenario?

Ans. The **Tools → Scenarios** option.

3. How do you differentiate between different scenarios in a spreadsheet?

Ans. Each scenario is given a unique name, such as "Case 1" and "Case 2," which allows switching between them.

4. What happens when you switch between scenarios?

Ans. The values in the selected input cells change according to the scenario chosen, updating the total profit accordingly.

5. Why is the Scenario feature useful in financial calculations?

Ans. It helps in comparing different business cases, forecasting profits, and analyzing the impact of changing values on overall results.

Objective To Share the spreadsheet, compare the spreadsheets and merge them

Assignment 5 Perform the following:

(i) Share a spreadsheet

(ii) Change the data of the spreadsheet and save it with another name.

(iii) Compare the two spreadsheets

(iv) Merge the two spreadsheets.

A sample spreadsheet is given below:

	A	B	C	D	E	F
1	Annual Examination Marks					
2	Roll No	English	Hindi	Maths	Science	Social Science
3	1	23	45	67	78	90
4	2	66	34	44	67	78
5	3	55	77	88	90	65
6	4	37	34	45	65	88
7	5	78	66	45	66	90

Procedure (i)

Step 1 Create the spreadsheet with the data and save it with PT1.ods

Step 2 Select and click on **Tools → Share Spreadsheet** from main menu bar. This will open the Share Document dialog window. Put the checkmark on the check box, "Share this spreadsheet with other users".

Step 3 Click on the checkbox and then on OK button. It will display the Confirmation dialog window to activate the sharing mode. Click Yes to continue. Observe that shared is added with the name of the document in the title bar.

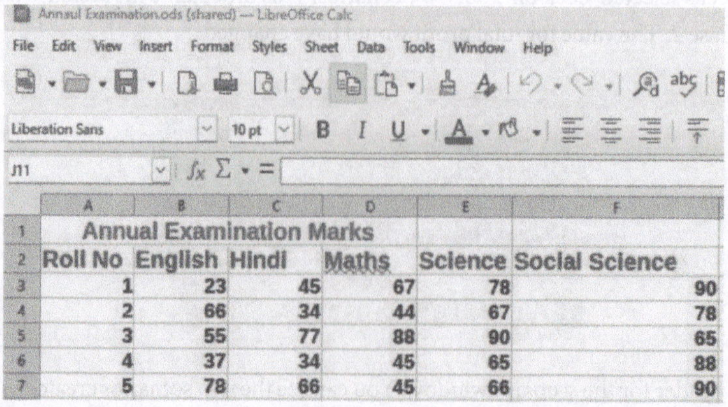

	A	B	C	D	E	F
1	Annual Examination Marks					
2	Roll No	English	Hindi	Maths	Science	Social Science
3	1	23	45	67	78	90
4	2	66	34	44	67	78
5	3	55	77	88	90	65
6	4	37	34	45	65	88
7	5	78	66	45	66	90

Procedure (ii)

Step 4 Total Marks of the students are calculated using =SUM() function and Average is calculated using =AVERAGE() function.

Step 5 The file is saved with another name using File⟶ Save As option. The final spreadsheet is given as:

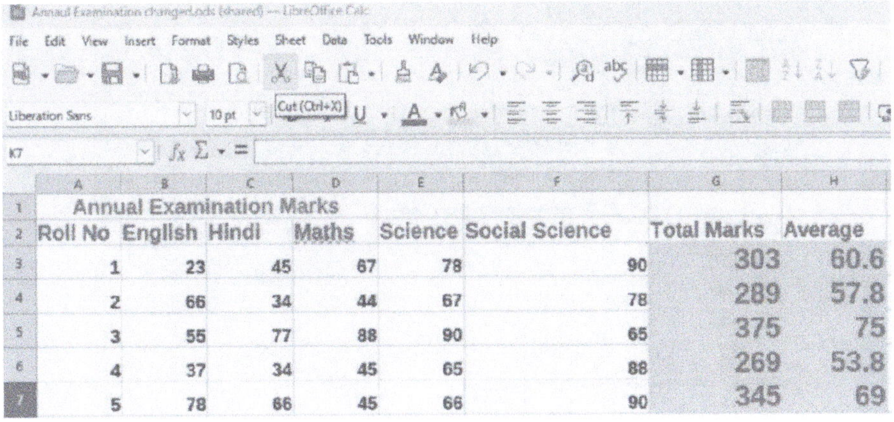

Procedure (iii)

Step 6 To compare the two spreadsheets, click on Edit⟶ Track Changes⟶ Compare Document option. The Compare to Original Document dialog box appears.

Step 7 Click on the required file.

Step 8 Click on Open button. The Manage Changes dialog box appears.

Note *The shared mode is disabled using Tools⟶ Share Spreadsheet option.*

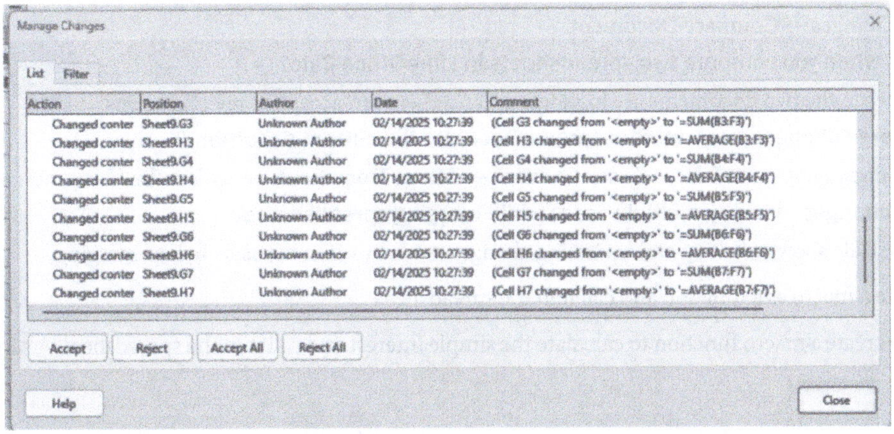

Step 9 Click on required buttons(Accept, Accept All, Reject, Reject All). The changes gets highlighted.

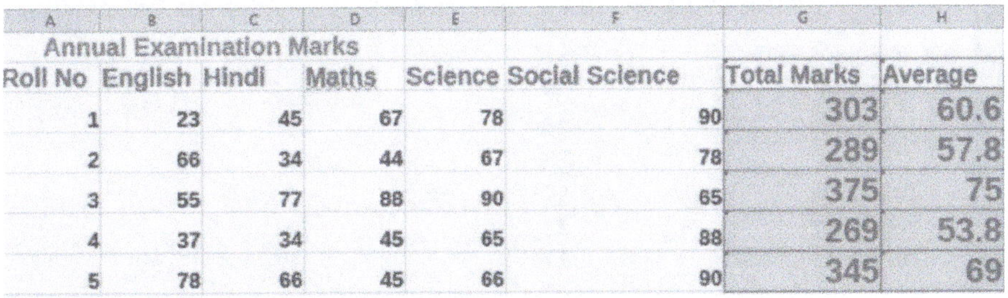

Procedure (iv)

Step 10 Click on Edit → Track Changes → Merge Document option. The Merge with dialog box appears.

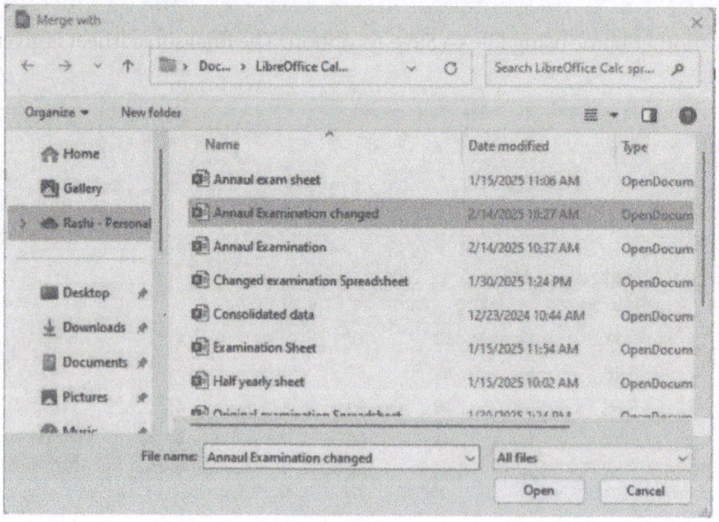

Step 11 Click on the Open button. The Manage Changes dialog box appears.

Viva-voce

1. What is the purpose of comparing and merging documents in LibreOffice Calc?

Ans. It helps identify differences between two versions of a spreadsheet and merge changes.

2. Which menu option is used to compare two spreadsheets in LibreOffice Calc?

Ans. **Edit → Track Changes → Compare Document.**

3. What happens when you compare two spreadsheets in LibreOffice Calc?

Ans. Differences between the two documents are highlighted, and users can accept or reject changes.

4. How do you merge changes from another spreadsheet into the current document?

Ans. Open the main document, go to **Edit → Track Changes → Merge Document**, and select the file to merge.

5. Can you track changes made by multiple users while merging spreadsheets?

Ans. Yes, LibreOffice Calc allows tracking and reviewing changes made by different users before merging.

Objective To create a macro as a function and call it in the spreadsheet.

Assignment 6 To create a macro function to calculate the simple interest and call it in the spreadsheet. A sample data is given below:

	A	B	C	D
1	SIMPLE INTEREST			
2	PRINCIPAL	RATE OF INTEREST	Number of years	Calculated Interest
3	20000	8	10	
4	100000	10	15	
5	350000	5	20	
6	500000	15	5	
7	750000	7.5	7	
8	1000000	10	9	
9	5000000	11	14	
10	7500000	12	8	
11				

Procedure

To create a macro as a function, follow the given steps:

Step 1 Enter data in the spreadsheet.

Step 2 Click on the **Tools menu.**

Step 3 Click on the Macros option.

Step 4 Click on Organize Macros → Basic option. The LibreOffice Basic Macros dialog box appears.

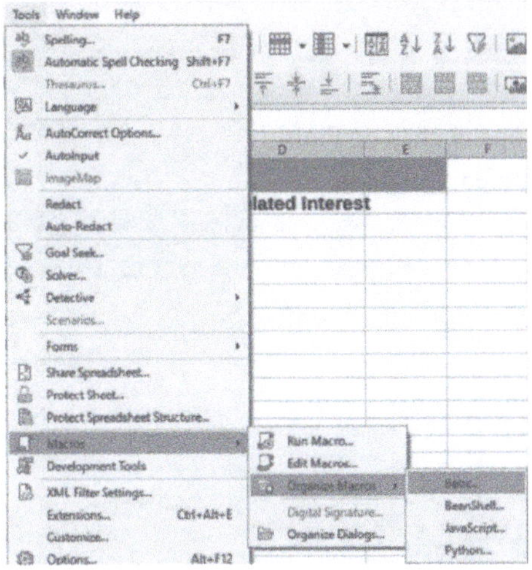

Step 5 Click on Edit button. Write the function as given below:

```
REM  *****  BASIC  *****

Function SimpleInterest(Principal As Double, Rate As Double, Time As Double) As Double
    ' Formula for Simple Interest
    SimpleInterest = (Principal * Rate * Time) / 100
End Function
```

Step 6 Click on the Save( ) button to save the changes done to the macro.

Step 7 Close the window.

To calling the Function as Macro, follow the given steps:

Step 1 Just click on the cell in which result of the function is to be appeared.

Step 2 Call the function as =SIMPLEINTEREST(A3,B3,C3) and press the Enter key.

Step 3 Using Autofill feature, drag the corner handle and find the total amount for all the items.

Viva-voce

1. **What is a macro in LibreOffice?**

Ans. A macro is a recorded sequence of commands and actions used to automate repetitive tasks in LibreOffice.

2. **What is the purpose of creating a macro function in LibreOffice Calc?**

Ans. A macro function automates repetitive calculations, such as computing simple interest, making tasks easier and faster.

3. **Which programming language is used to write macros in LibreOffice Calc?**

Ans. LibreOffice Calc macros are written in **LibreOffice Basic**.

4. **How do you open the LibreOffice Basic Macro Editor?**

Ans. You can open it by navigating to **Tools → Macros → Organize Macros → Basic.**

5. **Which feature in Calc allows users to apply the macro function to multiple rows at once?**

Ans. The **Autofill feature** helps drag the formula to multiple rows for bulk calculations.

Databases

Objective To create a table in a database and sort the records.

Materials Required A computer system equipped with a database application like LibreOffice.

Assignment 1 Create a table named Account Details. The fields of the table should be Account No, Name, Gender and Bank Balance. Enter data into the table using datasheet view. Now sort the data in descending order based on bank balance. Save the table.

Procedure

Step 1 Open a database application.

Step 2 Click on Next from the screen that opens, click on Finish.

Step 3 Save the database with name Assignment Database.

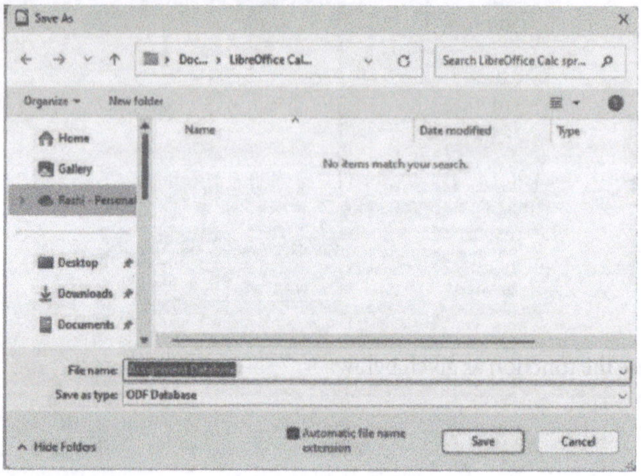

Step 4 The Database window opens. Click on Create Table in Design View.

Step 5 The Design view of table opens. Enter the fields and data types as required by the question. You can see the design view in the below figure.

Field Name	Field Type
Account_No	BigInt [BIGINT]
Account_Name	Text [VARCHAR]
Gender	Text [VARCHAR]
Bank_Balance	Number [NUMERIC]

Step 6 Right-click on Account_No field and click on Primary Key from context menu.

Field Name	Field Type
Account_No	BigInt [BIGINT]
Account_Name	Text [VARCHAR]
Gender	Text [VARCHAR]
Bank_Balance	Number [NUMERIC]

Step 7 Click on Save button from interface. Give the name as "Account Details" to the table.

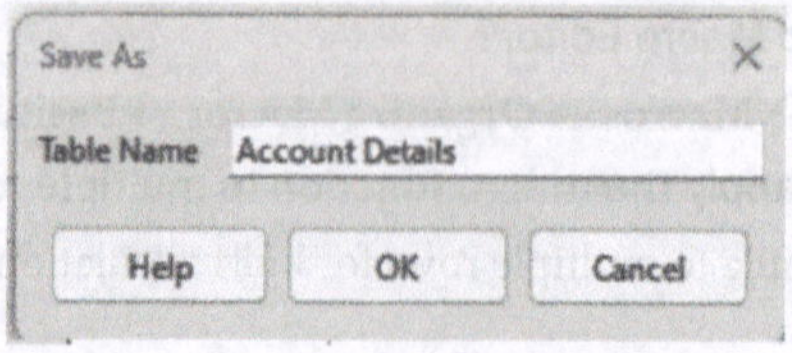

Step 8 Close the design view and open the datasheet view of table.

Step 9 Double-click on the table name. The datasheet view appears. Fill in 5 records in the table with data.

Account_No	Account_Name	Gender	Bank_Balance
1001	Rajesh Das	M	15000
1002	Shantanu Mahagar	M	20000
1003	Srijana Murli	F	100000
1004	Rashmi Dhar	F	15000
1005	Loveleena Gonda	F	40000

Step 10 Click on the Bank_Balance column. Click on Descending Order(Z/A ↓) button. The table gets sorted in ascending order based on Bank balance.

Account_No	Account_Name	Gender	Bank_Balance
1003	Srijana Murli	F	100000
1005	Loveleena Gonda	F	40000
1002	Shantanu Mahagar	M	20000
1004	Rashmi Dhar	F	15000
1001	Rajesh Das	M	15000

Viva-voce

1. **What is the purpose of setting a Primary Key in a table?**

Ans. The Primary Key uniquely identifies each record in the table.

2. **Which view is used to define the structure of a table in a database?**

Ans. The **Design View** is used to define fields and data types.

3. **How can you sort data in a database table?**

Ans. By selecting a column and clicking on the **Ascending** or **Descending Order** button.

4. **What is the function of the Datasheet View in a database?**

Ans. The Datasheet View allows users to enter, edit, and view table records.

5. **How do you save a table in a database?**

Ans. By clicking on the **Save** button and providing a table name.

Objective To create relationship between two tables

Assignment 2 Consider two tables.

Table 1 User Details

Fields User_Id, Name and Email.

	Field Name	Field Type
🔑	User_Id	Text [VARCHAR]
	Name	Text [VARCHAR]
	Email	Text [VARCHAR]

Table 2 Passport Details

Fields User_Id, Passport_Id, Date_Of_Issue and Date_Of_Expiry.

	Field Name	Field Type
	User_Id	Text [VARCHAR]
🔑	Passport_Id	Text [VARCHAR]
	Date_Of_Issue	Date [DATE]
	Date_Of_Expiry	Date [DATE]

Add 5 records in each table. Establish a relationship between the tables by linking the appropriate fields.

Procedure

Step 1 Create a new database, by clicking **File→ New→ Database**, if already open, and then by going through Database Wizard or launch the Base application and go through Database wizard.

Step 2 Create the first table, as asked for in question. Name it as User Details table.

Step 3 Create the second table, as asked for in question. Name it as Passport Details.

The User_Id is the primary key of the 1st table and the foreign key in second table. The Passport_Id is the primary key of the Passport Details table.

Step 4 Enter records in the table as given below:

User_Id	Name	Email
101	Argho	a@gmail.com
102	Ashima	As@gmail.com
103	Armaan	ar@gmail.com
104	Asmita	am@gmail.com
105	Arpit	ap@gmail.com

User_Id	Passport_Id	Date_Of_Issue	Date_Of_Expiry
101	P1	12/30/99	11/30/25
102	P2	03/03/09	03/03/25
103	P3	09/09/99	12/30/99
104	P4	08/08/99	08/08/25
105	P5	04/04/01	04/04/25

Step 5 Check the two tables created in the opening screen of Base. Click on Tools → Relationships. The Relation Design window opens.

Step 6 Click on Add Tables from the window. The Add Tables dialog box appears.

Step 7 Select the 1st table and click on Add button.

Step 8 Select the 2nd table and again click on Add button. The design view of both the tables will appear.

Step 9 Click on Close button to exit the Add Tables dialog box.

Step 10 Drag the User_Id from first table and drop it onto the 2nd table to draw a relationship between the two tables.

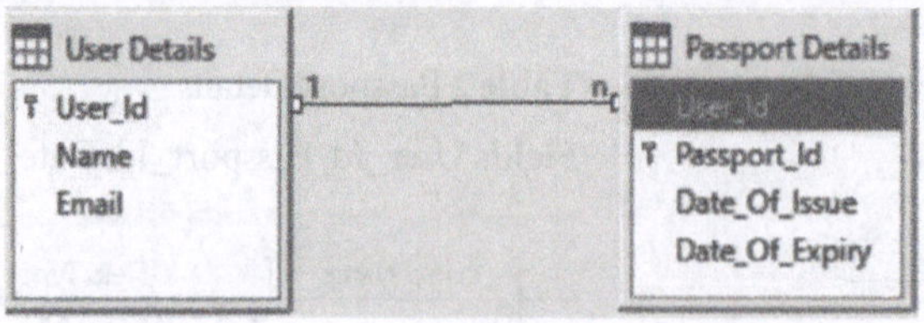

Viva-voce

1. What is a primary key in a database relationship?

Ans. A primary key is a unique identifier for each record in a table.

2. How does a foreign key help in establishing a relationship between tables?

Ans. A foreign key in one table references the primary key of another table to create a relationship.

3. What is the purpose of the Relationships window in LibreOffice Base?

Ans. It is used to visually link tables and define relationships between them.

4. Which type of relationship is formed when a primary key in one table is linked to a unique foreign key in another table?

Ans. A One-to-One (1:1) relationship.

5. How can referential integrity be maintained in a database relationship?

Ans. By ensuring that foreign key values in a related table always match a valid primary key in the referenced table.

Assignment 3 Create a table "Account Details" with the data:

Account_No	Account_Name	Gender	Bank_Balance
1003	Srijana Murli	F	100000
1005	Loveleena Gonda	F	40000
1002	Shantanu Mahagar	M	20000
1004	Rashmi Dhar	F	15000
1001	Rajesh Das	M	15000

(i) Create a query to find out the details of the records having Bank_Balance less than 10000.

(ii) Create a query to find out the details of the records having Bank_Balance between 20000 to 40000.

Procedure

Step 1 Open a database application.

Step 2 Create a table in design view based on question.

Step 3 Save the table with name Account Details.

Step 4 Enter values into the table in datasheet view.

Step 5 Save and close the table.

Step 6 Click on Queries.

Step 7 Click on Create Query in Design View.

Step 8 Click on Add.

Step 9 Choose all the fields in the design grid one by one.

Procedure (i)

Step 10 Place a checkmark in the Visible row for each field.

Step 11 In the Marks in Bank_Balance field, add the criterion "<10000".

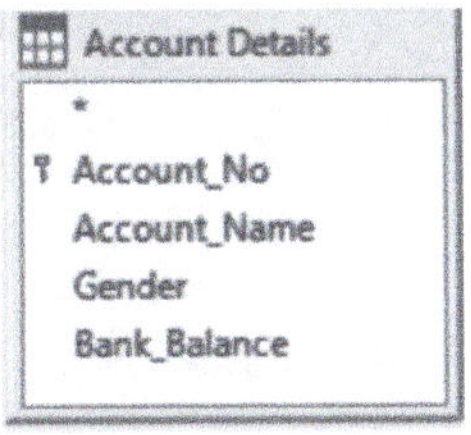

Field	Account_No	Account_Name	Gender	Bank_Balance
Alias	Bank Account Number	Bank Account N	Male/Female/Ot	Balance in accou
Table	Account Details	Account Details	Account Details	Account Details
Sort				
Visible	☑	☑	☑	☑
Function				
Criterion				< 20000

Step 12 Click on Run Query( ) or press F5 key.

	Bank Account Number	Bank Account Name	Male/Female/Other	Balance in account
▶	1001	Rajesh Das	M	15000
	1004	Rashmi Dhar	F	15000
+				

Procedure (ii)

Step 13 Open the query window.

Step 14 Set the criterion in the Bank_Balance as BETWEEN 20000 and 40000.

Step 15 Click on Run Query or press F5 from keyboard.

	Bank Account Number	Bank Account Name	Male/Female/Other	Balance in account
▶	1002	Shantanu Mahagan	M	20000
	1005	Loveleena Gonda	F	40000
+				

Record 1 of 2

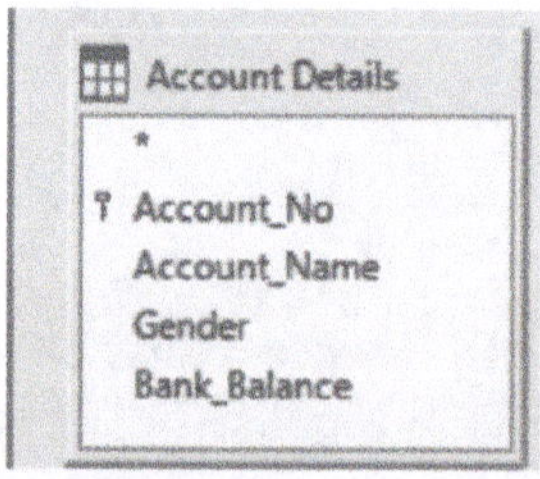

Field	Account_No	Account_Name	Gender	Bank_Balance
Alias	Bank Account Number	Bank Account N	Male/Female/Ot	Balance in account
Table	Account Details	Account Details	Account Details	Account Details
Sort				
Visible	■	■	■	■
Function				
Criterion				BETWEEN 20000 and 40000

Step 16 Save the query using Ctrl+S keys and giving a name to it.

Viva-voce

1. What is the purpose of a query in a database?

Ans. A query is used to retrieve specific data from a table based on given conditions.

2. How do you filter records with a Bank_Balance less than 10,000 in a query?

Ans. Use the condition <10000 in the criteria row of the Bank_Balance field.

3. What SQL keyword is used to filter data within a specific range?

Ans. The BETWEEN keyword is used to filter data within a range.

4. Which key is used to execute a query in LibreOffice Base?

Ans. The F5 key is used to run a query.

5. What is the function of the "Visible" checkbox in the query design grid?

Ans. It determines whether a field's data will be displayed in the query results.

Assignment 4 Create 2 tables namely:

Table 1 Students Personal Details with fields Admission_No, Father_Name, Mother_Name

Table 2 Students Marks with fields Admission_No and Marks.

Create relationship between the two tables.

Write the query such as:

(i) "Marks" is between 200 and 300.

(ii) "Marks" is not between 400 and 500.

(iii) "Marks" is greater than 400.

Procedure

Step 1 Open a database application.

Step 2 Create Table 1 in design view based on question.

	Field Name	Field Type
🔑	Admission_No	BigInt [BIGINT]
	Father_Name	Text [VARCHAR]
	Mother_Name	Text [VARCHAR]

Step 3 Save the table with name Students Personal Details.

Step 4 Enter values into the table in datasheet view.

	Admission_No	Father_Name	Mother_Name
	101	Suresh	Nagma
	102	Ramesh	Rinky
	103	Payal	Deepak
	104	Shubham	Sadhna
	105	Raghav	Aadhya
	106	Sunny	Sujata
	107	Anil	Amna
✎	108	Opesh	Aradhna

Step 5 Save and close the table.

Step 6 Create Table 2 in design view based on question.

	Field Name	Field Type
🔑	Serial_No	Number [NUMERIC]
	Admission_No	BigInt [BIGINT]
	Marks	Number [NUMERIC]

Step 7 Save the table with name Students Marks.

Step 8 Enter values into the table in datasheet view.

Serial_No	Admission_No	Marks
1	101	500
2	102	450
3	103	300
4	104	350
5	105	230
6	106	465
7	107	455
8	108	211

Step 9 Save and close the table.

Step 10 Click on Queries.

Step 11 Click on Create Query in Design View.

Step 12 Add both the tables.

Step 13 Create relationship between the table using the Admission_No field.

Step 14 Choose all the fields in the design grid one by one.

Procedure (i)

Step 15 Place a checkmark in the Visible row for each field.

Step 16 In the Marks field, add the criterion "BETWEEN 200 and 300".

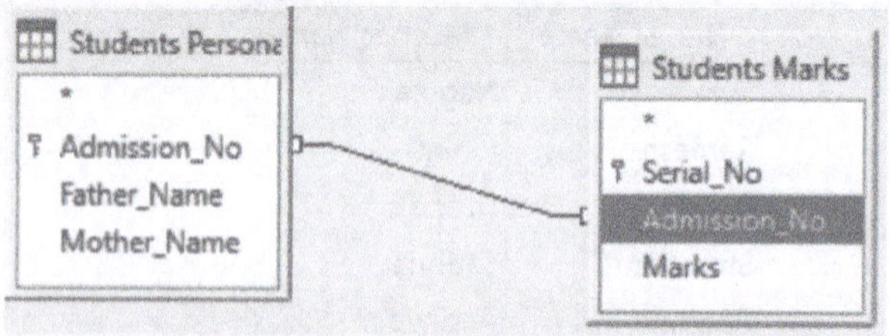

Field	Admission_No	Father_Name	Mother_Name	Marks
Alias				
Table				
Sort				
Visible	✓	✓	✓	✓
Function				
Criterion				Between 200 and 300

Step 17 Click on Run Query or press F5 key.

Admission_No	Father_Name	Mother_Name	Marks
103	Payal	Deepak	300
105	Raghav	Aadhya	230
108	Opesh	Aradhna	211

Procedure (ii)

Step 18 Open the query window.

Step 19 Set the criterion in the Marks in Science as NOT BETWEEN 400 and 500.

Step 20 Click on Run Query or press F5 from keyboard.

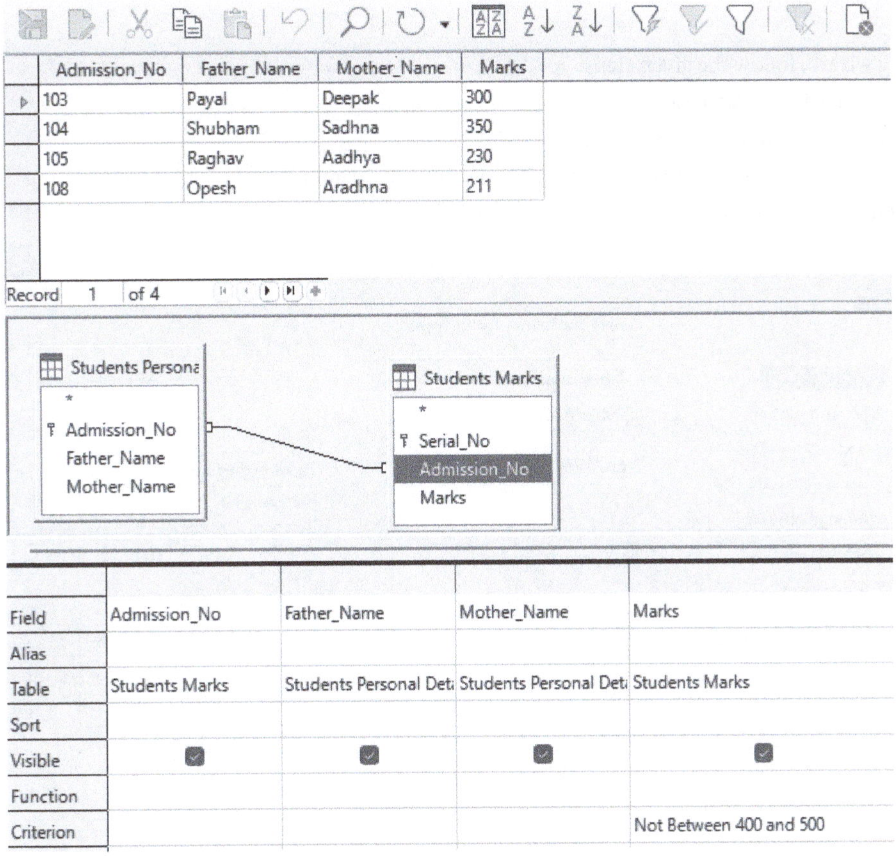

Step 21 Reconfigure the query seen above to set the third condition as " > 400".

Step 22 Run the query or press F5 key.

Viva-voce

1. What is a primary key in a database relationship?

Ans. A primary key is a unique identifier for each record in a table.

2. What type of relationship is created when a foreign key in one table refers to a primary key in another table?

Ans. A one-to-many (1:M) relationship.

3. Which tool in LibreOffice Base is used to establish relationships between tables?

Ans. The Relationships tool under the Tools menu.

4. What is the purpose of the "Join" feature in database relationships?

Ans. It connects tables and allows queries to retrieve related data efficiently.

5. What keyword is used in a query to retrieve records within a specific range of values?

Ans. The BETWEEN keyword.

Assignment 5

(i) Create a form for the table "Account Details" and enter 5 records using it.

(ii) Create a report for the same table.

(iii) Edit the report to add date and time in the report.

Procedure (i)

To create a form using wizard, follow the given steps:

Step 1 Open a new or an existing database.

Step 2 Click on the Form icon on the Database pane.

Step 3 Click on the Use Wizard to Create Form option. The Form Wizard appears.

Step 4 Select the tables or queries for which the form has to be created.

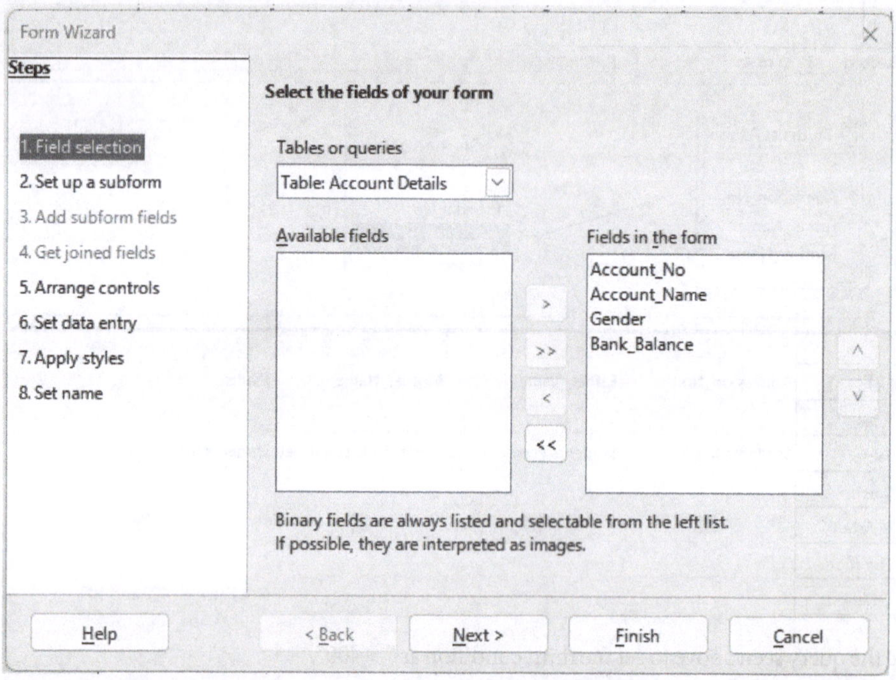

Step 5 Select the fields to be in the form from the Available Fields list box. If the user wants all the fields of the table to be available in the form then click on >> button. All the fields are shifted to Fields in the Form list box.

Step 6 Click on Next button.

Step 7 The second step consists of setting up a subform, i.e. a form within a form. You need to check the "Add Subform" checkbox to add the subform. Since we do not want to set up any subform,

Step 8 Click Next button.

Step 9 Arrange the contents of the form and click on the Next button.

Step 10 Here, the wizard asks whether the form will be used for displaying data, entering data or both. As we go with the default settings, so we click on the Next button.

Step 11 The next step is to apply styles to the form being created. We can select the desired background colour and border type of the field value text boxes.

Step 12 Click on the Next button.

Step 13 The final step is to name the form. Enter a different name to the form. The next step is to apply styles to the form being created.

Step 14 Click on the Finish button. The form with the first record will be displayed on the screen in a separate window.

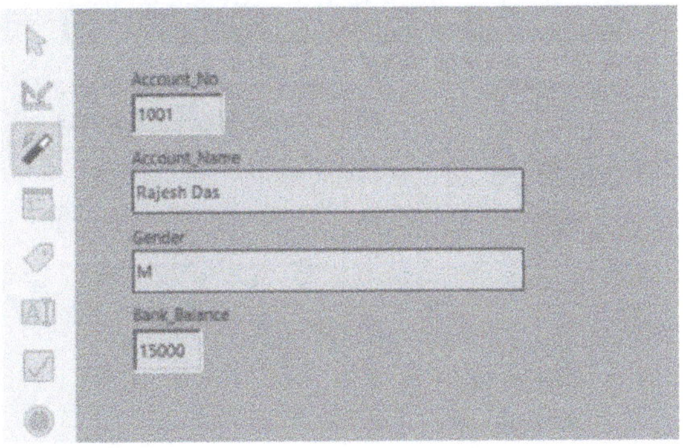

Step 15 Click on the New Record button and enter record in the table.

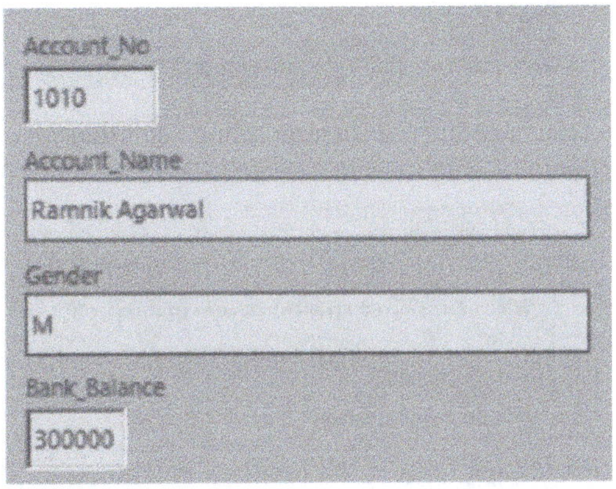

The final records in the table is given below:

Account_No	Account_Name	Gender	Bank_Balance
1010	Ramnik Agarwal	M	300000
1008	Rashi Mondal	F	100000
1003	Srijana Murli	F	100000
1009	Suhana Sharma	F	50000
1005	Loveleena Gonda	F	40000
1007	Rahul Gupta	M	30000
1006	Smriti Gupta	F	20000
1002	Shantanu Mahagar	M	20000
1004	Rashmi Dhar	F	15000
1001	Rajesh Das	M	15000

Procedure (ii)

To create a report, follow the given steps:

Step 1 In the LibreOffice Base User Interface, click on the Reports icon in the Database Pane.

Step 2 From the Tasks Pane, click Use Wizard to Create Report... option.

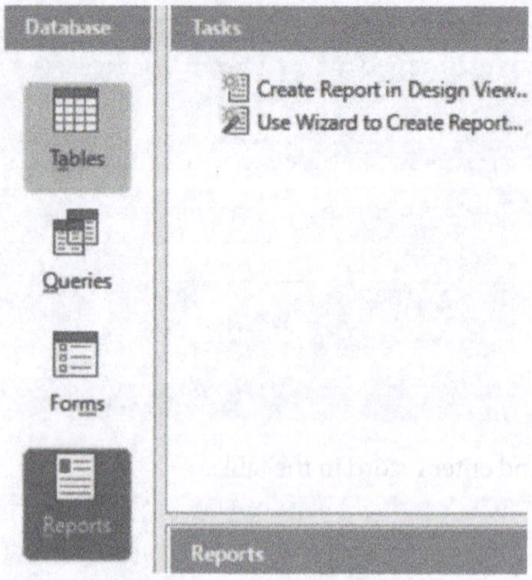

Step 3 The first step of wizard is to select the table and the corresponding fields that we want to display in our report. Select the required table.

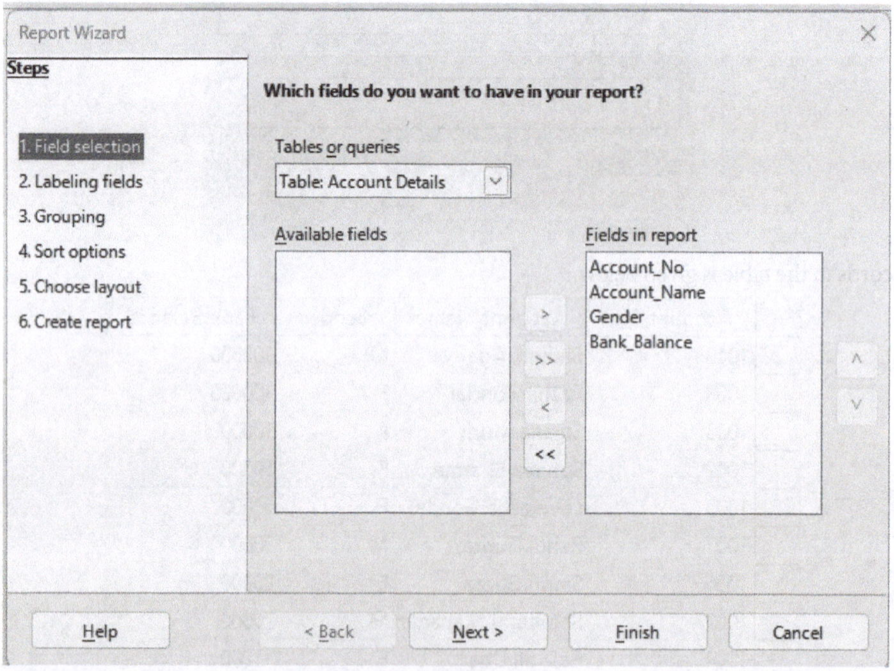

Step 4 All the fields of the Account Details table will be listed in the Available Fields list box.
Click >> button to shift all the fields to Fields in report list box.

Step 5 Click on the Next button. The next step is to label the fields.

Step 6 Click on the Next button. The next step is to group the data based on any of the fields in the report. Since we do not want to group as of now, click on the Next button.

Step 7 The fourth step is to set the Sort options.

Step 8 Click on the Next button to move on to the next step in which the layout of the report will be selected.

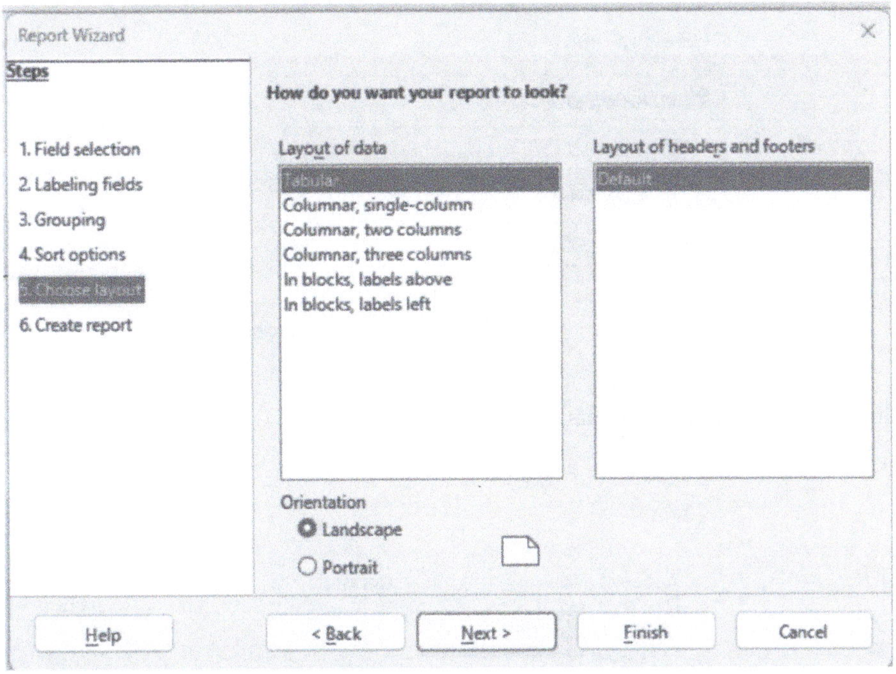

Step 9 Click on the Next button to move on to the next step in which the layout of the report will be selected.

Step 10 Write a name of the report and click on Finish button to display the report.

Account_No	Account_Name	Gender	Bank_Balance
1001	Rajesh Das	M	15000
1002	Shantanu Mahagan	M	20000
1003	Srijana Murli	F	100000
1004	Rashmi Dhar	F	15000
1005	Loveleena Gonda	F	40000
1006	Smriti Gupta	F	20000
1007	Rahul Gupta	M	30000
1008	Rashi Mondal	F	100000
1009	Suhana Sharma	F	50000
1010	Ramnik Agarwal	M	300000

Procedure (iii) To edit the report and add date and time, follow the given steps:

Step 1 Right-click on the report name and click on Edit menu. The Design view of the report appears.

Step 2 Click on Insert→ Date and Time option. The Date and Time dialog box appears.

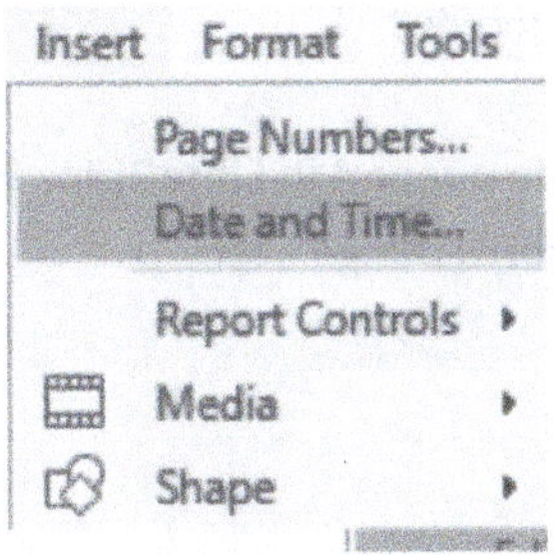

Step 3 Click on the checkbox to include date and time.

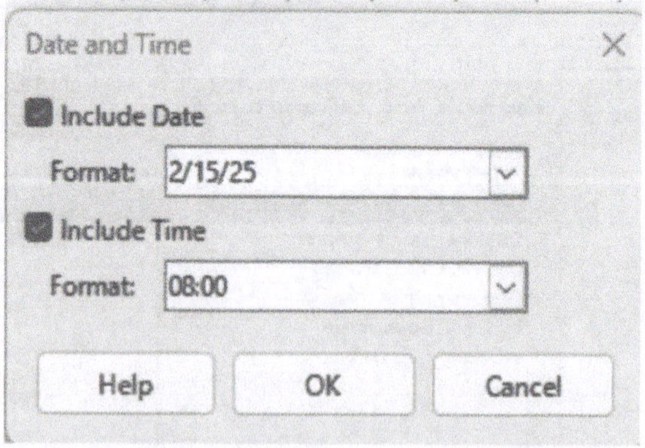

Step 4 Click on OK button. The final report appears.

2/15/25
08:02

Account_No	Account_Name	Gender	Bank_Balance
1001	Rajesh Das	M	15000
1002	Shantanu Mahagan	M	20000
1003	Srijana Murli	F	100000
1004	Rashmi Dhar	F	15000
1005	Loveleena Gonda	F	40000
1006	Smriti Gupta	F	20000
1007	Rahul Gupta	M	30000
1008	Rashi Mondal	F	100000
1009	Suhana Sharma	F	50000
1010	Ramnik Agarwal	M	300000

Step 5 Click on the Execute Report ( ) button to view the final report.

Viva-voce

1. Which tool in LibreOffice Base allows you to create a form step by step?

Ans. The Form Wizard.

2. What is a subform in LibreOffice Base?

Ans. A subform is a form within a form, often used to display related records from another table.

3. How can you add a background color to a form in the Form Wizard?

Ans. By selecting a style in the form customization step.

4. Which feature in a report allows sorting of records?

Ans. The Sort Options step in the Report Wizard.

5. How can you add the current date and time to a report in LibreOffice Base?

Ans. By selecting Insert → Date and Time in the report's Design View.

Sample Question Paper 1 (Unsolved)

Information Technology

Time : 2 hrs	M.M. : 50

General Instructions

1. Please read the instructions carefully.
2. This Question Paper consists of **21 questions** in two sections: Section A & Section B.
3. Section A has Objective type questions whereas Section B contains Subjective type questions.
4. **Out of the given (5 + 16 =) 21 questions, a candidate has to answer (5 + 10 =) 15 questions in the allotted (maximum) time of 2 hours.**
5. All questions of a particular section must be attempted in the correct order.
6. **SECTION A - OBJECTIVE TYPE QUESTIONS (24 MARKS):**
   i. This section has 05 questions.
   ii. Marks allotted are mentioned against each question/part.
   iii. There is no negative marking.
   iv. Do as per the instructions given.
7. **SECTION B – SUBJECTIVE TYPE QUESTIONS (26 MARKS):**
   i. This section has 16 questions.
   ii. A candidate has to do 10 questions.
   iii. Do as per the instructions given.
   iv. Marks allotted are mentioned against each question/part.

Section A : Objective Type Questions

1. Answer any 4 out of the given 6 questions on Employability Skills **(4 × 1 = 4)**

(i) Effective communication is important in the workplace because it
(a) Enhances personal relationships
(b) Improves productivity and efficiency
(c) Reduces conflict and misunderstandings
(d) All of the above

(ii) Which of the following is an example of green building design?
(a) Constructing buildings with no regard for energy efficiency
(b) Using renewable materials for construction
(c) Increasing waste generation during construction
(d) Ignoring water conservation measures

(iii) Stress management infuses a sense of .... and accomplishment.
(a) pressure
(b) control
(c) threat
(d) None of the above

(iv) A .... is a network security device that monitors incoming and outgoing network. It restricts access to unwanted sites.
(a) firewall (b) anti-virus
(c) block sites (d) None of these

(v) .... are the people who are too focused on what others think and they fail to focus on their internal matters.
(a) Seekers (b) Introspectors
(c) Gold diggers (d) Pleasers

(vi) From the following statements, which one is not the positive impact of entrepreneurship on society?
(a) Stimulates Innovation and Efficiency
(b) Creates jobs and Employment Opportunities
(c) Solves the problems of the society
(d) Discourages welfare of the society

2. Answer any 5 out of the given 6 questions **(5 × 1 = 5)**

(i) To avoid inconsistency in formatting and reduce time and effort in formatting a document, we use _______ in Writer.
(a) Styles (b) Templates (c) Macro (d) Clipart

(ii) If you choose styles, and then change the base style then all the .... styles will change as well.

(a) linked (b) edited
(c) copied (d) None of these

(iii) Which tab of writer contains the Hyperlink option?

(a) File (b) Format (c) Insert (d) Tools

(iv) To insert a symbol like © (copyright), you need to click on the...........option of the Insert tab.

(a) Special Character (b) Character
(c) Equation (d) Header

(v) Which option should be used to type H_2O,to get 2 to its proper place?

(a) Bold (b) Superscript
(c) Underline (d) Subscript

(vi) Which of the following is not a style type in Writer?

(a) Frame style (b) Image style
(c) List style (d) Character style

3. Answer any 5 out of the given 6 questions **(5 × 1 = 5)**

(i) Group and Outline in Calc is used to create an outline of the selected data and can group rows and columns together so that one can ___________ to hide it or ______________ it using a single click on it.

(a) Increase, Decrease (b) Expand, Collapse
(c) Increase, Expand (d) Decrease, Collapse

(ii) Which of the following tab is used to run Macro?

(a) Tools (b) Home (c) Insert (d) Review

(iii) If you see #### in place of data in a cell, it means you need to .... the cell width.

(a) increase (b) decrease
(c) Both (a) and (b) (d) None of these

(iv) When a user inserts a new worksheet in spreadsheet software, the new worksheet will be inserted ....

(a) at the end of sheet tab
(b) in the beginning of sheet tab
(c) next to active sheet
(d) None of these

(v) In the given formula, identify the type of reference and the cells that are passed as arguments.
= Average(A5, B5)

(a) Absolute reference; cells are-A5 and B5
(b) Relative reference; cells are-A5 and B5
(c) Relative reference; cells are-A5 to B5
(d) Absolute reference; cells are-A5 to B5

(vi) In order to use data from a worksheet, you need to use its........... name.

(a) alias (b) representative
(c) qualified (d) quantified

4. Answer any 5 out of the given 6 questions **(5 × 1 = 5)**

(i) The extension of Database file of Base is

(a) .mdb (b) .xls
(c) .odb (d) .bdb

(ii) In __________ data type there can be only two values- True or False.

(a) Date (b) Char
(c) Boolean (d) Logical

(iii) Which one of the following is an example of RDBMS ?

(a) MongoDB (b) Windows registry
(c) Publisher (d) Oracle

(iv) A primary key field cannot be null, which also means that it cannot be ....

(a) invalid (b) positive
(c) alphanumeric (d) empty

(v) Information is the processed form of ....

(a) words (b) data
(c) sentence (d) records

(vi) DBMS provides various key fields as

(a) primary key and candidate key
(b) alternate key and foreign key
(c) Both (a) and (b)
(d) None of the above

5. Answer any 5 out of the given 6 questions **(5 × 1 = 5)**

(i) Extensive use of fertilizers and pesticide must be avoided as it can make the ground water __________.

(a) Polluted (b) Safe to use
(c) Safe for drinking (d) Rich in minerals

(ii) Applying this organisation can reduce the potential for accidents, injury to improve performance and productivity.

(a) Ergonomics (b) Rehabilitation
(c) Welfare schemes (d) Right lighting

(iii) ________ bright light, glare and flickering images can cause eye strain and visual fatigue.

(a) LED's (b) Television's
(c) Computer's (d) Car's

(iv) Keep your monitor between __________ inches away from your face.

(a) 18 to 24 (b) 15 to 18
(c) 16 to 18 (d) 24 to 28

(v) ______ lighting from computer screens can trick your brain and suppress its release of melatonin substance that assists your sleeping patterns.
(a) Portable (b) Artificial
(c) Colourful (d) Dim

(vi) The ________ must be stable and allow the user to move easily and find a comfortable position.
(a) work chair (b) work table
(c) sofas (d) tables

Section B : Subjective Type Questions

Answer any 3 out of the given 5 questions on Employability Skills. Answer each question in 20 - 30 words. **(3 × 2 = 6)**

6. Define nature walk as stress management technique.

7. How can individuals contribute to the development of green skills?

8. Explain the use of Antivirus for the protection of the computer system.

9. Describe the role of entrepreneurs.

10. How can active listening improve communication skills?

Answer any 4 out of the given 6 questions in 20-30 words each **(4 × 2 = 8)**

11. Mention the steps to be followed to choose a style for a Word document?

12. Write the steps to freeze the columns.

13. What do you mean by relative cell referencing?

14. Describe various transaction control commands of SQL.

15. Give some examples of ignition sources.

16. Define the following :
(i) Accident in workplace (ii) Hazard

Answer any 3 out of the given 5 questions in 50-80 words each **(3 × 4 = 12)**

17. Tanisha had created a Table of Contents of the project done by her. Tell her the different steps to do the following:
(i) Editing a TOC (ii) Updating a TOC

18. Simran wants to add comments in a spreadsheet application. Tell her the different steps involved in adding and editing comments.

19. Consider the following table ITEMS :

TABLE: ITEMS

Code	IName	Qty	Price	Company	TCode
1001	DIGITAL PAD 121	120	11000	XENITA	T01
1006	LED SCREEN 40	70	38000	SANTORA	T02
1004	CAR GPS SYSTEM	50	2150	GEOKNOW	T01
1003	DIGITAL CAMERA 12X	160	8000	DIGICLICK	T02
1005	PEN DRIVE 32 GB	600	1200	STOREHOME	T03

(a) How many fields and records are there in the table ITEMS?
(b) Write the SQL queries to:
(i) Display the detail of all the items in ascending order of item names (i.e., IName)
(ii) Display IName and Price of all those items, whose price is in the range of 10000 and 22000.
(iii) Display all the information of the items having price less than 10000.

20. Nupur wants to know the differences between the following:
(a) Fields and tuples
(b) Data and information

21. Anil is a software developer working in a corporate office. Anil has been experiencing discomfort and strain in his eyes and neck, and he wants to ensure his workstation setup complies with these norms.

Given the scenario, what are the specific norms Anil should follow to optimize his display screen setup, and how can he adjust his current workstation to meet these standards?

Answers

1. (i) (d), (ii) (b), (iii) (b), (iv) (a), (v) (d), (vi) (d)
2. (i) (b), (ii) (a), (iii) (c), (iv) (a), (v) (d), (vi) (b)
3. (i) (b), (ii) (a), (iii) (a), (iv) (c), (v) (a), (vi) (c)
4. (i) (c), (ii) (c), (iii) (d), (iv) (d), (v) (b), (vi) (c)
5. (i) (a), (ii) (a), (iii) (c), (iv) (a), (v) (b), (vi) (a)

Sample Question Paper 2 (Unsolved)

Information Technology

Time : 2 hrs	M.M. : 50

General Instructions

See Sample Question Paper 1

Section A : Objective Type Questions

1. Answer any 4 out of the given 6 questions on Employability Skills **(4 × 1 = 4)**

(i) Which of the following best describes a "green skill job"?

(a) A job that focuses on recycling materials.
(b) A job that reduces the environmental impact of enterprises and economic sectors.
(c) A job that involves planting trees and conserving forests.
(d) A job that manages waste in urban areas.

(ii) Regular exercise helps pep up your mood and can take your mind off a lot of worry and negativity which are the main feed of stress. Which of the following activity is not considered as exercise?

(a) Walking (b) Jogging
(c) Swimming (d) Talking

(iii) Moving a folder or a file means .... it from its original location and placing it at another location.

(a) Removing (b) Leaving
(c) Pointing (d) None of these

(iv) Society plays a role in boosting entrepreneurship by

(a) creates needs and demands
(b) provides raw materials
(c) creates a need for education
(d) All of the above

(v) What is visual communication dependent on among people?

(a) Signs, symbols, and pictures
(b) Text messages
(c) Posture (d) Body language

(vi) Which of the following is a social benefit of sustainable development?

(a) Increased income inequality
(b) Improved access to education and healthcare
(c) Limited job opportunities
(d) Neglected social infrastructure

2. Answer any 5 out of the given 6 questions **(5 × 1 = 5)**

(i) .... styles are used to format graphics and text frames, including text wrap, borders, backgrounds and columns.

(a) Border (b) Frame (c) Table (d) Text

(ii) ....is a list, usually found on a page before the start of a written work, of its chapter or section titles or brief descriptions with their commencing page numbers.

(a) Preface (b) Table of Contents
(c) Acknowledgements (d) Page title

(iii) To add a new image to the Gallery, you can click on the .... button.

(a) New image (b) Add image
(c) New theme (d) Add theme

(iv) The .... alignment makes sure that none of the edges of text appear ragged.

(a) left (b) right
(c) center (d) justify

(v) .... controls how graphics are stacked upon each other or relative to the text.

(a) Arrangement (b) Alignment
(c) Anchoring (d) Wrapping

(vi) A ....can also be a quick way to take a list of people's mailing addresses and generate labels or envelopes with the address for a different person on each label or envelope.

(a) data source (b) database
(c) mail merge (d) E-mail

3. Answer any 5 out of the given 6 questions **(5 × 1 = 5)**

(i) Neeta is planning to take a car loan to buy a new car. But she is not sure about the payback time, i.e. whether to pay it back in 5 or 6 years considering that her monthly fuel cost will also increase. In such cases, which of the following

features of spreadsheet can she use to get an idea about it?
(a) Consolidation (b) Macros
(c) Templates (d) What-if analysis

(ii) This is a type of hyperlink available in Hyperlink dialog box, which creates a new worksheet.
(a) New document (b) New file
(c) New worksheet (d) New data

(iii) For sorting through macro, the selected cell range must be ....
(a) identical (b) different
(c) Both (a) and (b) (d) formatted

(iv) A worksheet is a
(a) collection of workbooks
(b) processing software
(c) combination of rows and columns
(d) None of the above

(v) .... function takes data from a series of worksheets or workbooks and summaries it into a single worksheet that you can update easily.
(a) Summation (b) Data Consolidation
(c) Data Format (d) Data Chart

(vi) Scenarios are tool test for .... questions.
(a) Auto (b) Goal Seek
(c) What-if (d) Drop Down

4. Answer any 5 out of the given 6 questions

(5 × 1 = 5)

(i) The .... command is used to modify the existing rows in a table.
(a) UPDATE (b) ALTER
(c) INSERT (d) REVIEW

(ii) A...............is a database element that is used to view, enter and edit records in a table.
(a) Form (b) Report
(c) Query (d) None of these

(iii) A .... language is a portion of a DML involving information retrieval only.
(a) DCL (b) Query
(c) TCL (d) None of these

(iv) The processed form of data is known as ....
(a) value (b) information
(c) knowledge (d) None of these

(v) .... determines the range of field values.
(a) Field Name (b) Data Type
(c) Field Size (d) Description

(vi) The candidate key, which is not used as primary key is called .... key.
(a) primary (b) foreign
(c) alternate (d) super

5. Answer any 5 out of the given 6 questions

(5 × 1 = 5)

(i) Which of the following is a fundamental safety rule to follow in the workplace?
(a) Always keep emergency exits locked.
(b) Wear appropriate personal protective equipment (PPE).
(c) Ignore safety signs and signals.
(d) Only report major injuries or accidents.

(ii) What is the most appropriate action to take if you discover a small fire in the workplace?
(a) Ignore the fire and hope it extinguishes itself.
(b) Evacuate the building immediately without warning others.
(c) Use a fire extinguisher to try and put out the fire if it is safe to do so.
(d) Pour water on the fire regardless of the type of fire.

(iii) What is one of the most effective ways to prevent slips, trips, and falls in the workplace?
(a) Use dim lighting to save energy.
(b) Keep walkways clear of obstacles and spills.
(c) Walk quickly to avoid spending too much time in risky areas.
(d) Wear shoes with slippery soles.

(iv) In the event of a workplace emergency, what is the first action you should take?
(a) Finish your current task before responding.
(b) Ignore alarms and continue working.
(c) Follow the emergency evacuation plan immediately.
(d) Call a friend to inform them of the situation.

(v) If an accident occurs and someone is injured, what is the first step you should take?
(a) Move the injured person to a different location.
(b) Leave the injured person and seek help from a supervisor.
(c) Assess the situation and call for medical assistance if needed.
(d) Ignore the injured person and continue working.

(vi) Which of the following practices is essential for maintaining a healthy lifestyle while working?
(a) Skipping meals to save time.
(b) Staying hydrated and taking regular breaks.
(c) Sitting for long hours without stretching.
(d) Avoiding all forms of physical exercise.

Section B : Subjective Type Questions

Answer any 3 out of the given 5 questions on Employability Skills. Answer each question in 20 - 30 words. **(3 × 2 = 6)**

6. What is the role of green skills in mitigating climate change?

7. Explain the term self-motivation.

8. Define multi-processing and multi-user operating system.

9. What do you mean by the term entrepreneur?

10. How can communication skills impact career success?

Answer any 4 out of the given 6 questions in 20-30 words each **(4 × 2 = 8)**

11. Describe the significance of using templates in your documents.

12. State the use of Consolidating Data in a spreadsheet.

13. What is cell reference? Also, write the use a cell reference in one or several formula.

14. Explain the term table used in database.

15. What are the essential steps to take when providing first aid for a minor burn?

16. What are the steps to apply first aid roller bandage to a wound?

Answer any 3 out of the given 5 questions in 50-80 words each **(3 × 4 = 12)**

17. Harmanpreet had inserted an image in a word processor application. Now, she wants to know the use of the following terms. Tell her the correct answer.

(i) Alignment
(ii) Anchoring

18. Samiksha wants to know the use of the following terms. Describe them for her.

(i) Scenario (ii) Goal Seek
(iii) Solver (iv) Subtotal

19. Consider the following

TABLE: APPLICANTS

No.	NAME	FEE	GENDER	C_ID	JOINYEAR
1012	Amandeep	30000	M	A01	2012
1102	Avisha	25000	F	A02	2009
1103	Ekant	30000	M	A02	2011
1049	Arun	30000	M	A03	2009
1025	Amber	40000	M	A02	2011

(i) How many records and fields are there in the table APPLICANTS.

(ii) Write the SQL queries to:

(a) Display NAME, FEE, GENDER, JOINYEAR about the APPLICANTS, who have joined before 2010.

(b) Display the NAMES of all APPLICANTS in ascending order of their JOINYEAR.

(c) Display the details of APPLICANTS of female.

20. Prashant wants to know about Data Manipulation language commands. Solve the following queries for him.

(i) What is DML?

(ii) Explain any three DML commands.

21. At a chemical manufacturing plant, workers handle hazardous substances daily. Recently, an employee suffered chemical burns due to improper handling of corrosive materials. This incident highlighted gaps in safety protocols and the need for enhanced protective measures. What steps should the plant management take to prevent similar incidents in the future?

Answers

1. (i) (b), (ii) (d), (iii) (a), (iv) (d), (v) (a), (vi) (b)
2. (i) (b), (ii) (b), (iii) (b), (iv) (d), (v) (a), (vi) (c)
3. (i) (d), (ii) (c), (iii) (c), (iv) (c), (v) (b), (vi) (c)
4. (i) (a), (ii) (a), (iii) (b), (iv) (b), (v) (c), (vi) (c)
5. (i) (b), (ii) (c), (iii) (b), (iv) (c), (v) (c), (vi) (b)

Sample Question Paper 3 (Unsolved)

Information Technology

Time : 2 hrs	M.M. : 50

General Instructions

See Sample Question Paper 1

Section A : Objective Type Questions

1. Answer any 4 out of the given 6 questions on Employability Skills **(4 × 1 = 4)**

(i) What is a file?

(a) A file is a section of main storage used to store data.
(b) A file is a collection of information that has been given a name and have an extension.
(c) A file is the part of a program that is used to describe what the program should do.
(d) A file can be saved only in CDs.

(ii) In .... , we change from our normal activities to silence.

(a) meditation (b) stress
(c) worries (d) survival

(iii) .... is a common response to danger in all people and animals.

(a) Internal stress (b) Environmental stress
(c) Survival stress (d) Fatigue related stress

(iv) Effective communication involves

(a) Speaking only (b) Listening only
(c) Speaking and listening
(d) Writing and reading

(v) To find a suitable market an entrepreneur performs the functions of

(a) advertisement and publicity
(b) appointment of selling agents
(c) new organisation structure
(d) Both (a) and (b)

(vi) What is the meaning of sustainable development?

(a) Development that focuses on economic growth only.
(b) Development that meets the needs of the present without compromising future generations.
(c) Development that prioritizes social progress over environmental protection.
(d) Development that relies solely on renewable energy sources.

2. Answer any 5 out of the given 6 questions **(5 × 1 = 5)**

(i) .... include fonts, alignment, borders, background, number formats (for example, currency, date, number) and cell protection in document.

(a) Cell style (b) Numbering style
(c) Paragraph style (d) Character style

(ii) When you apply a .... , you apply a group of formatting effects together in one single step.

(a) effect (b) template
(c) style (d) format

(iii) Which shortcut key is used to make the selected text italic?

(a) Ctrl + I (b) Shift + I
(c) F1 + I (d) None of these

(iv) Line or paragraph spacing is measured in terms of lines or points, which is referred as ....

(a) text wrapping (b) PDF
(c) XPS (d) leading

(v) Which tab is used to create Table of Contents in a document?

(a) File tab (b) Format tab
(c) Insert tab (d) Styles tab

(vi) What dialog box opens on choosing File → Templates → Manage Templates in Writer?

(a) The File dialog box
(b) The Manage Templates dialog box
(c) The Templates dialog box
(d) The Record Template dialog box

3. Answer any 5 out of the given 6 questions **(5 × 1 = 5)**

(i) Select .... → Track changes → Record from the menu bar. Thereafter, every change you record on the Calc will have a red border around it.

(a) File (b) Edit (c) Format (d) Layout

(ii) **Calc considers any data that it does not recognise as a number, date, time or formula, as:**
(a) Expression (b) Equation
(c) Text (d) Function

(iii) **In Goal Seek dialog box, the .... we enter the reference of the cell that contains the value to be changed.**
(a) variable cell (b) replacing cell
(c) modifying cell (d) changing cell

(iv) **Rajiv was asked to highlight the cells with green colour where the value entered is either greater than or equals to 120 in the worksheet containing thousands of data entries. Which feature of Calc should he use to get this work done within seconds?**
(a) Conditional formatting (b) Filtering
(c) Sorting (d) Simple formatting

(v) **Which of the following tools will help Swati, if she wants to arrange the height of students in her class in ascending order ?**
(a) Ordering data (b) Sorting data
(c) Presenting data (d) Referring data

(vi) **Rinky wants to know about the Number data type in Calc. Which of the following statement(s) is/are TRUE about it?**
(a) Numbers are generally raw numbers or dates.
(b) Numbers can be started with a dollar sign ($) or with some other currency symbols to display as currency.
(c) By default, number and date data is aligned to the right in Calc.
(d) All of the above

4. Answer any 5 out of the given 6 questions

(5 × 1 = 5)

(i) **When you define a field for a table, in which of the following parameters do access always considered optional?**
(a) Field name (b) Data type
(c) Field size (d) Description

(ii) **A ...... is a language that enables users to access and manipulate data in a database.**
(a) DML (b) DCL (c) TCL (d) DDL

(iii) **Akshat wants to store a huge amount of information about his firm in a database. Which type of table organisation would be most suitable for this purpose?**
(a) Relational
(b) Flat file
(c) Either relational or flat file
(d) Hierarchical

(iv) **................ are the ways to produce the data stored in databases and tables in a printed form.**
(a) Forms (b) Queries
(c) Reports (d) Data

(v) **If the two departments (HR and IT) access the data simultaneously then only one department will see the updates by the other department. DBMS solves this issue. Thus, DBMS helps to avoid.............. which means if a single database is used by multiple users then it also ensures that the same data is present for all the users.**
(a) Data redundancy (b) Data inconsistency
(c) Data piracy (d) Data modification

(vi) **How much space does the DATE / TIME data type hold in Base?**
(a) 2 bytes (b) 4 bytes
(c) 8 bytes (d) 10 bytes

5. Answer any 5 out of the given 6 questions

(5 × 1 = 5)

(i) **What color is typically used for indicating the ground wire in electrical wires?**
(a) Red (b) Black
(c) Green or green with yellow stripe
(d) Blue

(ii) **Which of the following falls in the category of workplace emergency?**
(a) Earthquake (b) Tornadoes
(c) Both (a) and (b) (d) None of these

(iii) **Do not use the elevator in times of fire in the building. Always use.............. for such emergencies.**
(a) office space (b) washroom
(c) staircase (d) None of these

(iv) **Which of the following is considered a physical hazard in the workplace?**
(a) Loud noise (b) Slippery floor
(c) Flickering light (d) Excessive heat

(v) **Which type of fire extinguisher is suitable for Class A fires?**
(a) Water extinguisher (b) CO_2 extinguisher
(c) Foam extinguisher
(d) Dry Powder extinguisher

(vi) **You should conduct regular fire drills in order to**
(a) Eliminate workplace hazards
(b) Prepare for emergencies
(c) Carry out the risk assessment
(d) None of the above

Section B : Subjective Type Questions

Answer any 3 out of the given 5 questions on Employability Skills. Answer each question in 20 - 30 words. (3 × 2 = 6)

6. What is fatigue related stress? Why is it difficult to avoid?
7. In what way does inadequate planning hinder effective communication?
8. What is an operating system?
9. How can individuals acquire green skills?
10. What is the contribution of the entrepreneurs in the execution of Government policies?

Answer any 4 out of the given 6 questions in 20-30 words each (4 × 2 = 8)

11. What do you mean by template?
12. What is the difference between absolute and relative hyperlinks as used in Calc?
13. What is the role of a foreign key in a database management system (DBMS)?
14. What is macro?
15. What are the advantages of having safer and healthy workplace?
16. Explain three conditions following which evacuation is done.

Answer any 3 out of the given 5 questions in 50-80 words each (3 × 4 = 12)

17. Rita is working in spreadsheet. She wants to know about the use of the following terms:
    (a) Quick Sort
    (b) Filtering Data
18. Differentiate between Save and Save As options.
19. Consider the following table PRODUCT

TABLE: PRODUCT

S_NO	P_Name	S_Name	Qty	Cost	City
S1	Biscuit	Priyagold	120	12.00	Delhi
S2	Bread	Britannia	200	25.00	Mumbai
S3	Chocolate	Cadbury	350	40.00	Mumbai
S4	Sauce	Kissan	400	45.00	Chennai

(i) How many fields and records are there in PRODUCT table?

(ii) Write SQL queries for the following:

(a) Display all Products whose Qty is between 100 and 400.

(b) Display S_Name, P_Name, Cost for all the Products whose Qty is less than 300.

(c) Display all the records alphabetically by S_Name.

20. Shubham is learning about DBMS. He wants to know about the following:
    (a) The purpose of DBMS
    (b) Any two uses of DBMS
21. Explain some of the ways to remove workplace hazards.

Answers

1. (i) (b) (ii) (a) (iii) (c) (iv) (c) (v) (d) (vi) (b)
2. (i) (a) (ii) (c) (iii) (a) (iv) (d) (v) (c) (vi) (c)
3. (i) (b) (ii) (c) (iii) (a) (iv) (a) (v) (b) (vi) (d)
4. (i) (d) (ii) (a) (iii) (a) (iv) (c) (v) (b) (vi) (c)
5. (i) (c) (ii) (c) (iii) (c) (iv) (b) (v) (a) (vi) (b)

Latest CBSE Sample Paper
Information Technology

Time : 2 hrs	M.M. : 50

General Instructions

1. Please read the instructions carefully.
2. This Question Paper consists of **21 questions** in two sections: Section A & Section B.
3. Section A has Objective type questions whereas Section B contains Subjective type questions.
4. **Out of the given (5 + 16 =) 21 questions, a candidate has to answer (5 + 10 =) 15 questions in the allotted (maximum) time of 2 hours.**
5. All questions of a particular section must be attempted in the correct order.
6. **SECTION A - OBJECTIVE TYPE QUESTIONS (24 MARKS):**
   i. This section has 05 questions.
   ii. Marks allotted are mentioned against each question/part.
   iii. There is no negative marking.
   iv. Do as per the instructions given.
7. **SECTION B – SUBJECTIVE TYPE QUESTIONS (26 MARKS):**
   i. This section has 16 questions.
   ii. A candidate has to do 10 questions.
   iii. Do as per the instructions given.
   iv. Marks allotted are mentioned against each question/part.

Section A : Objective Type Questions

1. Answer any 4 out of the given 6 questions on Employability Skills **(1 × 4 = 4)**

(i) Rahul moved to Japan from India for work. However, he struggles to adapt because he is not familiar with Japanese customs and etiquette, which affects his interactions with coworkers. This is an example of:

(a) Interpersonal barrier (b) Cultural barrier
(c) Physical barrier (d) Linguistic barrier

(ii) Amina studies diligently to improve her grades because she wants to feel proud of her achievements and also earn a scholarship. What type of motivation is this?

(a) Internal
(b) External
(c) Both internal and external
(d) Not any specific type of motivation

(iii) Rajesh launches a new app, but it fails to attract users and he faces financial losses. He gathers his team to discuss the failure, takes accountability for the oversight, and assures them that he will conduct thorough market research before the next launch. He _______.

(a) takes responsibility for his mistakes
(b) thinks before making a decision
(c) does not give up
(d) is innovative

(iv) Which of the following best describes self-management?

(a) The ability to ignore emotions and focus solely on tasks
(b) The ability to control one's emotions, thoughts, and behavior in various situations
(c) The ability to manage time efficiently without considering feelings
(d) The ability to rely on others for emotional support

(v) A community initiates a tree-planting campaign to restore local forests, aiming to enhance biodiversity, prevent soil erosion, and provide habitats for wildlife. This initiative also includes educating residents about sustainable land use practices to protect their natural environment.

Which SDG can you relate this initiative to?

(a) Clean Water and Sanitation
(b) Life on Land
(c) Affordable and Clean Energy
(d) Climate Action

(vi) How can an anti-virus protect your device?

(a) It can protect it from over-heating
(b) It can increase its performance
(c) It can prevent data from getting corrupt
(d) It can backup data

2. Answer any 5 out of the given 6 questions **(1 × 5 = 5)**

(i) **Which feature in Writer allows you to apply the same style to multiple words scattered throughout the document?**
(a) Format Painter (b) Fill Format option
(c) Style Inspector (d) Font Adjustment Tool

(ii) **Which feature allows you to jump to a different document, spreadsheet, or website from within a document?**
(a) Bookmark (b) Page Break
(c) Hyperlink (d) Format Painter

(iii) **How many levels of headings does LibreOffice Writer support?**
(a) 5 (b) 8 (c) 10 (d) 12

(iv) **Which of the following is NOT true about templates?**
(a) The styles and formatting features can be reused.
(b) Libre Office provides online templates
(c) Templates can have headings, text formats, styles, page numbers, headers and footers
(d) We cannot create our own templates

(v) **Radha is planning a school event and wants to decide how much money to allocate for different activities, like games, food, and decorations. She creates several different budget plans to see how changing the amount for each category affects the total expenses.**

How can Radha efficiently compare the different budget plans for her school event in the same spreadsheet?
(a) By writing down each budget on paper
(b) By using the What-if scenario feature in the spreadsheet to create and analyze different budget options
(c) By asking her friends to guess the costs
(d) By using the Filter function to look at one category at a time

(vi) **What is the main goal of applying ergonomics in an office setting?**
(a) To increase the amount of work done in a shorter time
(b) To design tasks that are more interesting for employees
(c) To ensure easy and safe use of equipment, reducing the risk of injury
(d) To promote social interactions among employees

3. Answer any 5 out of the given 6 questions **(1 × 5 = 5)**

(i) **The code of macro begins with ____ followed by the name of the macro and ends with ____.**
(a) Function, End (b) Sub, End Sub
(c) Sub, End Function (d) Sup, End Sup

(ii) **What is the benefit of inserting an image as a link in a document?**
(a) It reduces the document size by storing only the reference to the image.
(b) It enhances the image quality.
(c) It allows for automatic image editing within the document.
(d) It removes the need for image captions.

(iii) **After incorporating the reviews, Krishna mailed the document to his editor with the Track Changes ON. He made certain changes in the document. Pradeep wants to compare his original document with the reviewed document.**

What is the first step Krishna should take to compare his edited document with the original document?
(a) Open the Manage Changes dialog box.
(b) Select Edit → Track Changes → Compare Documents option.
(c) Save the edited file.
(d) Accept or reject the desired changes.

(iv) **It allows the placement of image in relation to text**
(a) Water mark (b) Trade mark
(c) Copyright (d) Text Wrapping

(v) **What is the primary function of the Subtotal tool in Calc?**
(a) It creates a chart for the data.
(b) It automatically groups data and applies common functions like sum and average.
(c) It highlights cells with conditional formatting.
(d) It removes duplicate data from the spreadsheet.

(vi) **What is one way to mitigate hazards associated with prolonged computer use?**
(a) Increasing screen brightness
(b) Stretching at regular intervals or doing simple yoga
(c) Using a smaller screen
(d) Sitting in a fixed position

4. Answer any 5 out of the given 6 questions **(1 × 5 = 5)**

(i) **A ________ hyperlink stores the location with respect to the current location in LibreOffice Calc.**
(a) Absolute (b) Relative
(c) Mixed (d) Reference

(ii) **______ is a text editor that allows you to create and edit macros.**
(a) IDE (b) Notepad
(c) Open Office Writer (d) MS Word

(iii) **Which of the following best defines "information"?**
(a) Unprocessed raw facts such as names, marks, and addresses.
(b) Organized and processed data that provides meaningful insights.
(c) Audio, video, and graphics stored without any processing.
(d) A collection of unrelated raw facts.

(iv) **What does referential integrity in a database ensure?**
(a) All primary keys are unique across the database.
(b) All records in a table must have a value in every column.
(c) Every foreign key value must match a primary key in the referenced table or be null.
(d) Data can be freely deleted from any table without constraints.

(v) **What should you do with the problem of dry eyes?**
(a) Forget to blink
(b) Rest eyes periodically and do simple eye exercises
(c) Do exercise
(d) Blink the eyes

(vi) **Which of the following data models sets a relation between the two or more tables?**
(a) Relational Data Model
(b) Network Data Model
(c) Hierarchical Data Model
(d) Connection Data Model

5. Answer any 5 out of the given 6 questions **(1 × 5 = 5)**

(i) **Which of the following statements are true about primary key in a database?**
(a) It is a field that can have duplicate values.
(b) It uniquely identifies each record in a table.
(c) It can have null values
(d) It is an optional field in a database table.

(ii) **Which of the following dialog boxes appears when the Query Design window is opened for the first time to design a query?**
(a) Add Table (b) Add Query
(c) Add Query or Report (d) Add Table or Query

(iii) **What feature in OpenOffice Base allows users to present retrieved data in a user-friendly and formatted manner?**
(a) Query (b) Form
(c) Report (d) Data view

(iv) **Which of the following is a recommended way to manage stress at work?**
(a) Engage in aggressive conflicts with colleagues
(b) Work longer hours without breaks
(c) Seek conflict resolution strategies with colleagues
(d) Avoid hobbies that promote relaxation

(v) **Which of the following can lead to musculoskeletal problems while working on a computer?**
(a) Using anti glare screen
(b) Sitting in a wrong posture and using an uncomfortable chair
(c) Using Air Conditioners
(d) Taking frequent breaks

(vi) **In a situation where a small fire breaks out in the office, what should you use to address the emergency?**
(a) A Blanket (b) A Fire Extinguisher
(c) A Towel (d) Baking Soda

Section B : Subjective Type Questions

Answer any 3 out of the given 5 questions on Employability Skills. Answer each question in 20 - 30 words. **(2 × 3 = 6)**

6. **During a team meeting, Sarah is explaining a complex project idea to her colleagues. She speaks too quickly, uses jargon, and doesn't pause for questions.**
As a result, her team seems confused, and the project isn't fully understood.
What can Sarah do to improve her verbal communication skills?

7. **What are the functions of Entrepreneurs?**

8. **List the various ways you can use to protect your data.**

9. **Riya, a Class X student, feels stressed with her exam preparation, extracurricular activities, and family commitments. How can tracking time help her?**

10. **Why has United Nations has made the 17 Sustainable Development Goals?**

Answer any 4 out of the given 6 questions in 20-30 words each **(2 × 4 = 8)**

11. **In OpenOffice Writer, what are the styles? List two OpenOffice Writer style options.**

12. **Differentiate between safety and security of an employee.**

13. **What are the benefits of sharing a spreadsheet?**

14. **Guneet has completed his assessments in four subjects and received the following marks: 75 in**

Math, 68 in Science, 82 in English, and 70 in History. The student needs to achieve an overall aggregate of 75% across all five subjects to meet his academic goals. He still has to take the exam in the fifth subject, which is Geography.

Which Calc tool and menu option he can use to check how many marks he has to score in the 5th subject to get the required percentage?

15. In a database, why is it important to create relationships between the tables?

16. What is Occupational Overuse Syndrome? What are the causes for it?

Answer any 3 out of the given 5 questions in 50-80 words each **(4 × 3 = 12)**

17. A team of writers is collaborating on a report using a word processing software with a Track Changes feature. One writer creates the initial draft, which then needs to be reviewed and edited by the rest of the team.

(a) Why is the Track Changes feature essential for collaborative document editing?

(b) Which menu option can be used to access this feature?

(c) Can reviewers add comments?

(d) Once the changes are made by all the reviewers, who can accept or reject them?

18. A Class X student is participating in a school competition where they need to analyse the performance of different sports teams based on match scores and statistics. The student has collected data over several matches and needs to calculate averages, determine rankings, and generate charts for a presentation.

(a) How are Macros in Calc helpful to him?

(b) How to enable Macro in Calc?

(c) Is solution*word a valid macro name? Justify

(d) Mention any one operation which cannot be recorded by macro.

19. A health clinic is developing a patient management system to streamline patient intake, appointments, and medical records. They need to implement forms for various purposes, including new patient registration, appointment scheduling, and updating medical histories.

(a) What is the use of form in DBMS?

(b) What are the different ways to create forms in DBMS?

(c) Where can we find various tools to add or edit controls on the form?

(d) What is the use of the Records Toolbar in a form?

20. What points should be included in Fire Prevention Plan in the office?

21. Your cousin runs a small bookstore and wants to maintain an inventory of books. He needs to record information such as book titles, authors, ISBNs, publication dates, prices, and stock levels. However, he is not familiar with database management systems. Explain the following concepts to help him understand DBMS:

(a) What is DBMS?

(b) What are the advantages of using DBMS?

(c) Name any two database programs that can be used to create a table and store the data according to his requirements.

(d) Which field can be set as a Primary Key?

Answers

1. (i) (b), (ii) (c), (iii) (a), (iv) (b), (v) (b), (vi) (c)

2. (i) (b), (ii) (c), (iii) (c), (iv) (d), (v) (b), (vi) (c)

3. (i) (b), (ii) (a), (iii) (b), (iv) (d), (v) (b), (vi) (b)

4. (i) (b), (ii) (a), (iii) (b), (iv) (c), (v) (b), (vi) (a)

5. (i) (b), (ii) (d), (iii) (c), (iv) (c), (v) (b), (vi) (b)

6. Think Before You Speak

- Think about your topic.
- Think about the most effective ways to make your listeners understand the topic.
- Write or note down whatever you plan to say.

Concise and Clear

- Speak clearly, loudly and at moderate speed.
- Be sure the information you want to share is to the point.
- Do not repeat the same sentences.

Confidence and Body Language

- Be confident.
- Be friendly
- Maintain eye contact, stand straight and be attentive.

7. Functions of an Entrepreneur are:

1. **Making Decisions** Entrepreneurs make daily choices about what to produce or sell, pricing, and market locations.
2. **Managing the Business** They plan the business's future, arrange for raw materials, hire staff, and ensure plans are followed.

3. **Dividing Income** Entrepreneurs allocate business funds for materials, rent, and salaries.
4. **Taking Risks** They face risks related to fires, theft, and lost items.
5. **Creating New Methods, Ideas, or Products** Entrepreneurs innovate to enhance their business's significance and profitability.

8. To safeguard your data from theft and viruses, consider the following measures:

1. **Use Strong Passwords** Create difficult-to-guess passwords using a mix of lowercase and uppercase letters, numbers, and special characters. This prevents unauthorized access to your computer.
2. **Install Anti-virus and Firewall** These tools monitor incoming and outgoing data, preventing viruses from entering and detecting any that may have already accessed your system.
3. **Encrypt Data** Important information can be encrypted using tools like BitLocker, requiring a decryption password to access the hard disk, thus blocking unauthorized usage.
4. **Secure Sites** Only share credit card or bank information on secure sites, indicated by "https://" and a lock symbol in the browser's address bar.

9. Tracking time helps to:

- Identify time-wasting activities and unproductive habits
- Improve time management for studies and tasks
- Balance academics with extracurriculars and personal time
- Allocate time for relaxation and self-care
- Achieve academic goals more efficiently and reduce stress before exams

10. The 17 SDGs have been made with the aim of taking care of important issues facing businesses, governments and society. Some of these issues are poverty, gender equality, water use, energy, climate change and biodiversity. Countries are now making policies and regulations that will promote sustainable systems needed in all economic sectors to provide a secure, affordable and sustainable economy.

11. A Style is a collection of all formatting information, which you want to save and then apply on the document. Writer provides six Style categories – Page, Paragraph, Character, Frame, List and Table.(Mention any two)

12. **Safety** The work environment of the organisation must be safe. It must be free from hazards and risks. A hazard is something that can cause harm to the people

Security Every employee working in an organisation must feel that they are secured in the company campus. Security is a kind of freedom from any potential harm. Security ensures the safety of the people working in the organisation. This include various security such as personal safety, computer system safety, electrical safety, transport safety and other equipment safety.

13. Refer to Question no. 1 (Short Answer Type) on page 210.

14. Tools →Goal Seek

15. While working with multiple tables, you need to check the redundancy and inconsistency of data. The record for a particular entity should neither be repeated nor different data values should appear for a single entity in the database. This is done by setting relationships between the tables of a database.

16. Refer to text on page no. 285 (Occupational overuse syndrome).

17. Refer to Question no. 1 (Short Answer Type) on page 156.

18. Refer to question no. 3 (Short Answer Type) on page 185.

19. Refer to question no. 4 (Short Answer Type) on page 268.

20.
- All employees must know where the fire extinguishers are located, and how to properly use them.
- Fire extinguishers and First Aid Stations should be clearly marked with signs.
- Never block access to Exits, fire extinguishers, electric switches and panels.
- Do not block or stack material against doors, which would prevent them from operating properly in event of a fire.
- Do not use flammable material near electrical panels, switches, lift trucks or any electrical equipment.
- Make sure all equipment is properly grounded where needed.
- Fire extinguishers must be inspected regularly.
- Report to your supervisor of any defect in electrical, fire prevention or material handling equipment.
- No flammable material are to be placed around an exit door way. (Any 4 points)

21. Refer to question no. 1 (Short Answer Type) on page 224.

CBSE EXAMINATION PAPER 2025

Information Technology

General Instructions

1. Please read the instructions carefully.
2. This Question paper consists of 21 questions in two sections: Section A & Section B.
3. Section A has Objective Type Questions, whereas Section B contains Subjective Type Questions.
4. Out of the given (5 + 16) = 21 questions, a candidate has to answer (5 + 10) =15 questions in the allotted (maximum) time of 2 hours.
5. All questions of a particular section must be attempted in the correct order.
6. **Section A** Objective Type Questions (24 Marks)
   (i) This section has 5 questions.
   (ii) There is no negative marking.
   (iii) Do as per the instructions given.
   (iv) Marks allotted are mentioned against each question/part.
7. **Section B** Subjective Type Questions (26 Marks)
   (i) This section has 16 questions.
   (ii) A candidate has to do 10 questions.
   (iii) Do as per the instructions given.
   (iv) Marks allotted are mentioned against each question/part.

Time : 2 hours Max. Marks : 50

Section A : Objective Type Questions

1. Answer any 4 out of the given 6 questions on Employability Skills **($4 \times 1 = 4$)**

(i) The school is organizing a Career Counselling Workshop. Which of the following will be the most effective method of communication to inform all students of the school?

(a) Face-to-face informal communication
(b) Notice/Poster
(c) Phone call
(d) Meet everyone in person

(ii) Which of the following is the most suitable term for the ability to regulate one's own emotions and help others also to do the same?

(a) Managing emotions
(b) Harnessing emotions
(c) Knowing emotions
(d) Supressing emotions

(iii) Roshni studies in class X and is practising hard with a lot of sample papers to get good marks in her exams. She gets up early in the morning to study and completes her revision work. This is an example of ....

(a) self-awareness (b) self-motivation
(c) influential motivation (d) emotional intelligence

(iv) A .... is a location where a group of files can be stored in the computer.

(a) folder (b) SMPS (c) CMOS (d) UPS

(v) Which of the following is a myth about entrepreneurs?

(a) An entrepreneur should be confident and should be able to take decisions.
(b) Every business idea must be unique or special.
(c) An entrepreneur should keep trying new ideas.
(d) An entrepreneur should be creative and should have different solutions to the problem.

(vi) **Which one of the following is the most important factor for sustainable development and helps us become aware of our role as a responsible citizen?**

(a) Sports (b) Education
(c) Business (d) Illiteracy

2. Answer any 5 out of the given 6 questions **(5×1=5)**

(i) **Ravi has to prepare a project report. He wants to save certain formatting features and then apply them on the project report. He can use the .... feature of OpenOffice Writer.**

(a) Styles (b) Image
(c) Mail Merge (d) Preview

(ii) **During a recent excursion, Roshni has taken some pictures for making a report in Writer. She wants to increase the contrast of the images. Which one of the following image filters should she use in Writer?**

(a) Aging (b) Mosaic
(c) Sharpen (d) Smooth

(iii) **Which one of the following image arrangement options in Writer sends the drawing object behind the text?**

(a) To background (b) To foreground
(c) Behind the text (d) Back one

(iv) **.............. feature of Writer is based on different types of heading styles and is used to give the listing of the contents of the document.**

(a) Table of Heading
(b) Index
(c) Label of Contents
(d) Table of Contents

(v) **............. is the default template for the files being created in Writer.**

(a) Resume template (b) Project Report
(c) Blank document (d) Chapter

(vi) **Shanta is creating a project report in Writer and wants to apply the same style on headings / titles in the entire document as she has done at the beginning of the document. She can use the .... feature of Writer to apply the same format on each line / word, wherever needed.**

(a) Fill Style (b) Fill Format
(c) Apply Feature (d) Apply Character

3. Answer any 5 out of the given 6 questions **(5×1=5)**

(i) **To add your own comments in Calc, select ....→Track changes→Comment.**

(a) File (b) Edit
(c) Insert (d) Data

(ii) **To add a new sheet in the spreadsheet, click on the .... sign located at the left bottom of the spreadsheet.**

(a) * (b) / (c) % (d) +

(iii) **........... is a set of values that can be used within the calculations in the spreadsheet to explore and compare various alternatives depending on changing conditions.**

(a) Sort (b) Filter
(c) What-if Scenarios (d) Comments

(iv) **The recorded macros are actually stored as ....**

(a) a set of instructions in a programming language.
(b) a sequence of data cells
(c) a document
(d) a list of values

(v) **Which creating a hyperlink in Calc, if the complete path along with filename is given then it is an example of ....**

(a) Relative hyperlink (b) Mixed hyperlink
(c) Absolute hyperlink (d) Folder hyperlink

(vi) **This tool in Calc allows you to create a group of cells automatically and apply common functions like sum, average on the grouped data. It is known as .... tool.**

(a) Sum (b) Subtotal
(c) Function (d) Common

4. Answer any 5 out of the given 6 questions **(5×1=5)**

(i) **.............. is the database software that is used to create, manipulate and manage data.**

(a) Ingress (b) Writer
(c) Paint (d) Windows

(ii) **The process of arranging data in ascending or descending order is known as ....**

(a) Filtering (b) Tracking
(c) Purification (d) Sorting

(iii) **With reference to LibreOffice Base, which of the following is a valid data type to indicate the monetary values?**

(a) Money (b) Currency
(c) Rupee (d) Dollar

(iv) **Data can be retrieved and displayed from one or more tables in a DBMS using a ....**

(a) Referential integrity (b) Domain
(c) Query (d) Field

(v) **While designing a form, it is suggested to get the date input by adding the .... to the date field to prevent entering invalid dates.**

(a) Calendar (b) Text input
(c) Timer (d) Number input

(vi) **While designing a form, titles, headings or sub-headings may be added using .... tool available on the Form Controls tool box.**
(a) Textbox (b) Label
(c) Title (d) Heading

5. Answer any 5 out of the given 6 questions **(5 × 1 = 5)**

(i) **............... is a state of physical, mental and social well-being.**
(a) Richness (b) Popularity
(c) Health (d) Activity

(ii) **Which one of the following is a class B ignition material?**
(a) Paper (b) Gas
(c) Electrical equipment (d) Potassium

(iii) **The .... has prepared the policy to provide employees with a healthy and safe work environment.**
(a) GoIT (b) DoIT
(c) ToIT (d) SoIT

(iv) **RSI stands for**
(a) Recurring Syndrome Injury
(b) Repetition Symptom Injury
(c) Recessive Stress Injury
(d) Repetitive Strain Injury

(v) **.............. is the science that deals with designing and arranging the things at workplace so that people can use them easily and safely.**
(a) Health science (b) Ergonomics
(c) Fixture science (d) Work economics

(vi) **Which one of the following is a wrong safety guideline?**
(a) Store all cleaning chemicals in tightly closed containers in separate cupboards.
(b) Never distract the attention of people who are working near a fire or with some machinery, tools or equipment.
(c) Wear loose clothing or jewellery while working with machines.
(d) Make sure all areas have proper lighting.

Section B : Subjective Type Questions

Answer any 3 out of the given 5 questions on Employability Skills. Answer each question in 20 - 30 words. **(3 × 2 = 6)**

6. **Briefly explain the meaning of any 2 C's out of the 7 C's of effective communication.**

7. **What is Stress management?**

8. **Give any four tips to keep the computer in perfect working condition.**

9. **Mention any four main functions of an entrepreneur.**

10. **Explain any two problems related to sustainable development.**

Answer any 4 out of the given 6 questions in 20-30 words each **(4 × 2 = 8)**

11. **Out of various style categories provided by Writer, briefly explain Frame style category in brief.**

12. **What is a Macro? Give any two rules that should be followed while naming a Macro or module in Calc.**

13. **What is the main purpose of Goal Seek in Calc? Give an example to support your answer.**

14. **What are the important prerequisites for setting a relationship between two tables in LibreOffice Base? Mention any two.**

15. **For a computer workplace, give any two health and safety requirements while using a keyboard.**

16. **Excessive use of computers might have a bad impact on your vision. Give any two eye-related problems that might arise due to long hours spent on a computer.**

Answer any 3 out of the given 5 questions in 50-80 words each **(3 × 4 = 12)**

17. (a) **What is the benefit of grouping drawing objects in Writer?**
(b) **Differentiate between text wrapping and image alignment feature in Writer.**

18. **Mr. Amit, Sales Manager of ABC Sales Corporation has created a spreadsheet in LibreOffice Calc that lists Sales for different years in different regions in different worksheets. He wants to summarise and make certain decisions based on it.**

Help him by answering the following questions:

(a) Which tool in Calc can be used to combine the sales data from multiple sheets into a single summary sheet?

(b) Name the Menu Option and Sub-Menu Option that can be used to generate combined summary of all the worksheets.

(c) Name the function that can be used to display total of all sales.

(d) He wants to open a summary document stored at a different location from within the sheet by clicking on a text stored in a cell. How can it be done?

19. Imagine that you have been signed a contract of handling fire safety and emergency in a company. You need to spread awareness on fire safety and emergency handling to the employees.

Answer the following questions:

(a) Give any two fire prevention measures at the workplace.

(b) Give any two basic emergency handling procedures at the workplace.

20. (a) Give any two advantages of relating two tables in a database.

(b) Explain many-to-many relationship between the tables in a database.

21. Consider the following table:

Table: Student

Student_ID	Name	Age	Phone_Number
S001	Amit	15	9876543210
S002	Priya	16	8765432109
S003	Priya	15	7654321098

Answer the following questions:

(a) You are given the task to design the student database for your school in LibreOffice Base. Based on the given table structure, suggest the data type of student_id and age field that would be suitable to store student's-id and age respectively.

(b) As a database administrator, you need to ensure each student has a unique identifier. Which field in the table would you choose as the primary key and why?

(c) Identify the field that can serve as an alternate key. Justify your answer.

(d) How many attributes and records are present in the above shown table?

Answers

1. (i) (b), (ii) (a), (iii) (b), (iv) (a), (v) (b), (vi) (b)

2. (i) (a), (ii) (c), (iii) (a), (iv) (d), (v) (c), (vi) (b)

3. (i) (b), (ii) (d), (iii) (c), (iv) (a), (v) (c), (vi) (b)

4. (i) (a), (ii) (d), (iii) (b), (iv) (c), (v) (a), (vi) (b)

5. (i) (c), (ii) (b), (iii) (b), (iv) (d), (v) (b), (vi) (c)

6. **Clarity** Ensuring the message is simple, clear, and easy to understand.

Conciseness Communicating information in a brief, yet complete, manner without unnecessary details.

7. Stress management is the process of identifying stressors, coping with challenges, and using techniques like relaxation or time management to reduce stress levels.

8. Four tips to keep a computer in perfect working condition:

(i) Regularly update software and security patches.

(ii) Clean hardware components to prevent dust buildup.

(iii) Backup important files frequently.

(iv) Use antivirus software to prevent malware.

9. Four main functions of an entrepreneur are

(i) Identifying business opportunities.

(ii) Organizing resources for production.

(iii) Managing and overseeing operations.

(iv) Taking financial risks and making strategic decisions.

10. Two problems related to sustainable development.

(i) Resource depletion due to overconsumption.

(ii) Environmental pollution from industrial activities.

11. The Frame style category in Writer refers to text and graphic containers, like text boxes or images, which can be positioned, resized, and formatted independently within the document.

12. A Macro is a sequence of commands that automate tasks.

Rules for naming a macro or module in Calc:

(i) Names must start with a letter.

(ii) Avoid using spaces or special characters like underscores.

13. Goal Seek in Calc helps determine the necessary input value to achieve a specific result. For example, it can find the interest rate needed to reach a specific investment goal.

14. Prerequisites for setting relationships in LibreOffice base include:
   (i) Identifying common fields in both tables.
   (ii) Ensuring both tables are correctly structured with primary and foreign keys.

15. Health and safety requirements when using a keyboard include:
   (i) Maintaining a neutral wrist position.
   (ii) Taking regular breaks to reduce strain and prevent repetitive stress injuries.

16. Two eye - related problems from excessive computer use are
   (i) Eye strain (Computer vision syndrome).
   (ii) Dry eyes due to reduce blinking while storing at screens.

17. (a) Grouping drawing objects in Writer allows for easier management, alignment, and positioning of multiple objects as a single unit. This improves the efficiency of layout adjustment and prevents objects from moving independently, ensuring a more organized document.

   (b) Text wrapping in Writer allows text to flow around an image or object, making the layout more dynamic.

   Image alignment, on the other hand simply positions the image in relation to the surrounding text without affecting text flow. Text wrapping directly interacts with text, whereas image alignment affects the position of the image.

18. (a) To combine the sales data from multiple sheets into a single summary sheet, Mr. Amit can use the consolidate tool in Calc.

   (b) The Menu option is Data, and the sub-menu option is consolidate to generate combined summary of all the worksheets.

   (c) The SUM function can be used to display the total of all sales.

   (d) To open a summary document stored at a different location, Mr. Amit can insert a hyperlink in the cell by using Insert → Hyperlink option. He can link the text to the file path of the summary document.

19. (a) Two fire prevention measures at the workplace include:
   1. Regular maintenance and inspection of electrical wiring and equipment to avoide potential electrical fires.
   2. Storing flammable materials properly and ensuring they are away from heat sources.

   (b) Two basic emergency handling procedures at the workplace include:
   1. Evacuating the building immediately upon hearing a fire alarm or if there's a fire threat.
   2. Calling emergency services (such as the fire department) and providing them with accurate information about the situation.

20. (a) Two advantages of relating two tables in a database are
   1. It reduces data redundancy by linking tables based on shared attributes.
   2. It enhances data integrity and accuracy by ensuring data consistency across tables.

   (b) A many-to-many relationship in a database occurs when multiple records in one table relate to multiple records in another table. For example, a student can enroll in multiple courses, and each course can have multiple students enrolled. This relationship requires a junction table to link the two tables.

21. (a) Suggested datatype for Student_ID and Age fields:
   - **Student_ID** The datatype for Student_ID should be Text because student IDs typically consist of alphanumeric characters (e.g., "S001", "S002"). The text datatype in LibreOffice Base allows storing these mixed characters without restriction.
   - **Age** The datatype for Age should be Integer, as age is represented by whole numbers, and Integer is used to store numeric values without decimals.

   (b) Primary key selection

   The Student_ID field should be the primary key since it uniquely identifies each student.

   (c) Alternate key identification

   The phone number field could serve as an alternate key, assuming it's unique to each student. While phone numbers may sometimes repeat, they are generally unique to each individual in a school database, making it a good candidate for this role.

   (d) The table has 4 attributes (Student_ID, Name, Age, Phone Number) and 3 records (Amit, Priya, Priya).